W9-BLD-590

RE-PORT-ING

MITCHELL V. CHARNLEY
University of Minnesota

THIRD EDITION

Holt, Rinehart and Winston
*New York Chicago San Francisco Atlanta Dallas
Montreal Toronto London Sydney*

Library of Congress Cataloging in Publication Data

Charnley, Mitchell V
    Reporting.

    Includes index.
    1. Reporters and reporting. I. Title.
PN4781.C43   1975   070.4   74-34017

ISBN 0-03-089649-5

Copyright © 1959, 1966, 1975 by Holt, Rinehart and Winston
All rights reserved
Printed in the United States of America
  6 7 8 9   059   5 4 3

About This Book

Reporting is craft, and it is art.

And it is a great deal more. It is a principal means of building and maintaining the kind of society a democratic people wants.

As craft, reporting is a practical complex of skills and stratagems growing from thought and experience. It can be described and it can be taught. It can be passed along, by those who have studied and mastered it, to others who have the capacity and the dedicated desire to develop it.

As art, reporting can be nurtured only in fertile soil, though its virtuosity can be heightened. Artistic expression in journalism, as in music, clay, or line and color, blossoms from the guidance of craft through intuitive awareness and personal gift. A journalist whose brain cells and nerve ends are sensitized to the creative possibilities in materials as well as to their latent impact must, to be called an artist, master the craft; art becomes effective as control over craft grows. But the journalist must provide the artistic impulse from within. It cannot be drawn from books, a voice behind a lectern, or even from infinite sweat and toil.

Reporters use their craft in everything they do. News gathering—the fundamental act of reporting—has a thousand skills; its companion, the writing of news, has as many. It is in the writing that reporters apply their talents for evocation of meaning and emotion. Great reporting is a combination of the character, understanding, and insistence with which the craft is exercised and the embellishment and vitality provided by the art.

This book describes some of the natures, uses, and potentialities of the crafts of reporting and proposes precepts and examples in which their artful as well as their artistic possibilities are examined.

The paragraphs above are like those that opened the first two editions of *Reporting*, with one substantial addition: the second paragraph.

That paragraph, one that might now appear in any book about journalism, suggests the principal "new" character of this third edition of *Reporting*. More than in any ten-year period in American history, the world that American journalism serves has changed. Chapter 1 describes this new atmosphere and the new challenges that face the journalist; other portions of the book develop the theme. This third edition could not have been written when the second edition was written; of necessity this edition, far more than its predecessors, aims to accent awareness that we live in a new world and that the responsibilities of journalists are more highly charged with *social* responsibility than any they have known before.

The concepts that have guided the preparation and revisions of *Reporting* are not my exclusive property. Most comparable books follow them. But their statement may guide the reader:

News is news, and reporting is reporting—whatever the subject matter, whatever the medium. The differences between newspaper news, broadcast news, and magazine news are differences of degree, not of kind. The man or woman who develops competence as a newspaper reporter can move confidently into other news-reporting channels.

A reporter must become more than a news technician. As fact assemblers and carriers, reporters are in one sense passive agents; but in what they do with the possibilities open to them they can (and I believe should) become catalysts of social action. They need the sensitivity to perceive and the skills to reflect the news they report against its relevant context—and the understanding to recognize the consequences of what they do.

A "first" book about news communication cannot be a last book. It cannot be all things to all students; it cannot go from all the sublime generalizations to all the occasionally ridiculous particulars. It cannot provide everything a reporter ought to know (no one is more aware than its author that it leaves untouched or lightly touched a dozen important areas). *Reporting* makes a bow, in broad terms, to the special fields of reporting. (Such specifics don't have to be banished from the classroom. But I preach the doctrine that what a reporter can study, practice, and assimilate on the job ought to be left to the job.)

Nobody can be made a reporter in a classroom. Students can be informed about the problems and obligations of reporters; they can be introduced to critical examination of news recognition, processing, and dissemination. They can in the classroom setting be exposed to knowledge and insights that they are unlikely to gain on the job; thus their period of apprenticeship can be eased and shortened. They can develop pride in news work, self-confidence, and (if they're lucky) a sobering view of their own shortcomings. But there's no classroom alchemy that will transform students into pros.

A good teacher is always stronger than a good textbook. And no textbook will serve fully all the demands of a particular teacher or a particular student. *Reporting* suggests many questions and answers some of them. Some of the answers will be different from those supplied by readers (just as some of them have changed from those in the first edition of almost two decades ago).

No two students, no two teachers, will use the book in just the same way.
Its organization is planned to make it flexible. Some teachers or students
may wish to begin with Part Two, "News Gathering: Problems and Processes"; some with Part Three, "News: Writing and Style." As presented,
with Part One outlining the context against which journalists work, the book
follows my conviction that this is where you start. But it is possible to begin at other points, or to begin at more than one place.

Even a reporting textbook can't be a model of objectivity. Though it rests
on a body of fact, its usefulness is in what it says (or chooses not to say)
about its postulates. Reporting takes positions; readers should examine them
watchfully, bring new evidence to bear on them, and let them stand only
when they deserve it.

This third edition of *Reporting* differs from the second in three specific
ways. One is the expanded attention to the environment of today's journalism. The second is a rearrangement of content, a change that has produced
three more chapters but not a broadly different range. Some areas—relations
of reporters with news sources, for example—have been amplified, others
condensed. Third, new illustrations have been introduced, both to bring the
book into the mid-1970s and to enhance what may be called its inductive approach, the use of example to arrive at general rule. Examples that remain
from the earlier editions—there are a number—are those that I can't improve on or in a few cases those that I simply think no reader should miss.
One other point: the Style Sheet, an appendix in the first two editions, is
omitted. The cooperative Associated Press-United Press International Style-
book is now widely used and generally available; for this reason, students
should become familiar with it rather than with other style guides.

The book emphasizes newspaper practice because the newspaper system
is dominant among the systems of news dissemination. Newspapers deal
with more kinds of news and treat news in more detail than other media.
And Americans still know more about newspaper practices than about their
competitors' practices. Journalists go more often from newspapers into other
forms of mass media than the reverse. Knowledge of newspaper practice is,
in my opinion, the model for all news practice.

● ● ●

The writer who knows precisely where to pay his debts, and just how
much they add up to, is a writer I have not met. A book grows from every
experience its begetter has survived (including some that almost killed him);
it is the product of work, learning, and counsel, of brilliance and blunder.
Its germs are often invisible, unremembered.

Some debts, nonetheless, are apparent. My friend of more than fifty years,
Ralph D. Casey, helped get this book started, and his unceasing critical
standards have kept it on track. I'm deeply gratified to realize how much I
owe to some of my earliest reporting students—George Hage, Bud Nelson,

George Moses, and others of their caliber who became journalists with the kind of standards that were models for their colleagues and later for their own journalism students.

Such a book could not be brought together without the scores of unwitting "contributors" who wrote many pages merely by doing their jobs. I hope the score or more of them who are among my onetime students will be aware, when they learn how I've cribbed from them, that their teacher is beholden and knows it.

I am indebted to authors and publishers whose permission to use published material has been freely (no loose usage) given. First should be named the Minneapolis Star and Tribune Company, from whose newspapers I have lifted lavishly—partly because they are at hand, but mainly because they show things that ought to be shown. Permissions have come also from the St. Paul *Pioneer Press* and *Dispatch*, the New York *Times*, the Washington *Post*, the Los Angeles *Times*, and the Associated Press.

All this can be said. But how can one name, or even know, all his creditors? What about the city editors from Walla Walla to Honolulu to Detroit whose brains I picked or the radio and television news editors with whom I worked? How can I trace my debts to teachers, colleagues, and friends who challenged ideas, exposed bad thinking, sometimes demanded the unattainable? How does a teacher assess what he learned from students—students whose questions forced him to understand more of art and craft and social involvement than mere practice ever demanded?

Finally, how do I thank that one of my first Minnesota reporting students who became a writer of distinction . . . a wise and compassionate minister to her society . . . and a lady of the quality of taste that let her marry me?

M.V.C.

Contents

NEWS: ITS ANATOMY AND ENVIRONMENT

CHAPTER ONE

The meaning of "news"

THE ENVIRONMENT

News reporting in America has never served as many people as well as it does today. Yet never in its 300 years has American journalism faced obstructions, criticisms, and suspicion as widespread. Only a few of these problems have their roots in the newsrooms. Among those that come from outside:

- Information that the public has a right to have—must have—is bottled up by cynical, self-seeking, or merely stupid news sources (often in high places).
- Misdirection, double-talk, lies—from Pennsylvania and Madison Avenues to a thousand small-town Main Streets—have become everyday tools to control public attitudes or to shield private concerns (Watergate, of which more later, is a glossy example).
- "Management" of the news, for centuries an acknowledged device of government, big and small business, and every kind of public and private institution seeking public approval or trying to avoid disapproval, has

become a tool even of crime (example: the kidnappers of Patricia Hearst in 1974 virtually dictated what might be reported about the case).
* Misconceptions about the news media and their reliability are studiously fostered. Spokesmen for government twist media behavior in a way that denies the public its implicit constitutional right to full disclosure and discussion.
* Partly because of such assaults, public confidence in the media, never as robust as news performance merits, has been eroded.
* Public alarm at political dishonesty joins with skepticism about business morality to confirm a cynical expectation that few institutions, the news media included, can be trusted.
* The agencies of government themselves contribute to erosion of the American system of news dissemination. One example is the Florida "right-to-reply" law that would make full reporting a physical impossibility; another is the proposal to adopt the first federal libel law in nearly two centuries.

These forces combine with a number of shortcomings in the behavior of the media themselves:
* Failure to look under enough rugs and to use existing procedures to pry loose information improperly "classified" or shielded.
* Failure to reach into what *happened* to find out what *made* it happen and to lead toward sensible speculation about what *will* happen, tomorrow or next century.
* Failure to use the tools and follow the principles of good news journalism so as to produce reporting at the level that professionals know is possible.
* Failure to inform the public of the achievements and the general record of dependability of the press in such a way as to win it the public confidence it deserves.
* Thoughtless acceptance of "pseudo-events" as though they were worth public attention and frequent overplay of them (the Evel Knievel fraud at Snake River Canyon is a prime example).

These conflicting currents flow in an environment of a complexity unimaginable a half-century ago. It is no longer possible for a person, whether newsmaker or news reporter, to go deeply into more than a few areas of knowledge. No mere human can learn everything he would like to know about the dynamics that activate his life or his neighbor's. How many gas station attendants or county politicians or Vassar graduates—or reporters—have enough knowledge to undertake a penetrating analysis of a welfare program, a price-control system, an arms-limitation agreement, or the movement of blue-collar workers to white-collar economics?
The consequence of all this is that we all get to know less and less, relatively, about what surrounds us. Though the news media deliver more news and deliver it faster, only a constantly shrinking share of it all can be passed

along. There's only so much news space or news time available (as a result, all those hourly-on-the-hour radio news programs get to sound like a stuck record).

Under such constraints, can the media really hope to keep people informed about what's going on? Aren't they stymied before they start?

If the answer to the first question were a clear "no" and that to the second a clear "yes," this book would be a rhetorical exercise. But *Reporting* is built on a belief that the goals are approachable, that enough effort will produce a rewarding measure of success. More than that: whatever may be the shortcomings of the news media, their history of persistent improvement will continue. Enough men and women in journalism believe in the importance of the task and give it the dedication it demands so that its difficulty will not become the alibi for second-rate performance.

It would be hard to recognize today's newspaper as the great-grandchild of the journalistic parents of one or two centuries past. Colonial patriot-editor Sam Adams wouldn't know his progeny. We have never had so rich and productive a news service as the world is getting now. Some of the factors that support this belief are:

- Journalists are aware of efforts to close the channels of information and to make things seem what they aren't, and persistently develop counter-tactics.
- As manipulative devices multiply and interlace, newsworkers' sophistication expands to untwine and clarify.
- Popular concern about the news media and the quality of their service, though it is sometimes naïve or selfish, is deep, and it gains character from thoughtful analyses in both specialized and general literature.
- There is an outburst of critical effort from the news world itself, from journalists whose concern at their profession's shortcomings goes beyond rancor to pointed and thoughtful precept. The reporter-written "journalism reviews" are supplemented by a spreading demand that those who write and edit the news be given a voice in policy-making and by the slow growth of "press councils" to serve as watchdogs of news behavior.
- Occasional shots in the arm—Hersh's reporting of My Lai, Bernstein and Woodward's initiation of the Watergate exposé, and Anderson's spotlight on the ITT scandal are stirring examples of reporting at its best.
- Better and better writing, editing, and display of news; a slow recognition by TV of how much it can do in some forms of reporting, together with a return to broadcast documentaries as a tool of news coverage and analysis; awareness that the elementary principles of news accomplishment remain valid; and a tireless belief in the worth and the joy of news achievement.

In short, today's reporters, though they too often fail to pursue promising new leads, nevertheless cover more kinds of news than their predecessors ever did. Though they may never be able to invade every newsworthy enclave, they are better equipped and better educated than were their fathers (and some of their elder brothers); and the trend toward specialized expertise expands their effectiveness.

Perhaps most important, the effort to put news into context, to explain it and make it meaningful, gains ground every year.

Black, white, and gray factors like these underlie the content of this book. The chapters that follow deal with many of them.

THE ANATOMY OF NEWS

News is tomorrow's history done up in today's tidy package. News, said Stanley Walker, noted city editor of the New York *Herald Tribune* in its great days, is the "inexact measure . . . of the ebb and flow of the tides of human aspiration, the ignominy of mankind, the glory of the human race. It is the best record we have of the incredible meanness and the magnificent courage of man." The speed of life in the twentieth century would have been a crawl if the world's masses had not been informed by the news systems about the social-technological-humanistic complex, the mixture of vulgar and noble. News is the fuel that powers the wheels of change and growth.

News, to define it more precisely, is current information made available to a public—information without which people cannot decide what to think or how to act. News is the concise, accurate report of an event—not the event itself. News isn't a Supreme Court decision or a hurricane or a landing on the moon; it's the newsman's record that the decision, the disaster, or the "giant step" took place . . . and that it's important to somebody to know about it.

When news is defined as "report" rather than "event," it means that until knowledge of the event has been passed from one mind to another no news exists. Suppose a car tumbles off an isolated mountain road into a deep ravine: If no one misses car or driver or discovers the wreck, is it news? The murders of a score of migrant workers in California weren't news for years —not until somebody found the graves and reported them. The auto wreck and the murders aren't news, but merely the stuff of which news can be made.

Extension of this definition implies three components of news: an *event* in which some kind of action occurs; a *report* describing the action in under- standable terms; and a *reader* or *listener* (more likely a *group* of them) to whom the report is offered—in print, on the air, by word of mouth . . . by smoke signal, if you like. The report may provoke thought or response in some of the people it reaches, or it may not. Usually it does. Usually an event is made the basis for news because a reporter or his editor decides that it will have dynamic meaning for a group of consumers (and, if you want to be pragmatic, that the report will sell papers or build audiences). A report may be called news, however, whether it arouses a response or not;

all the definition demands is that the report make current information available.

There are scores of channels for delivering news to audiences. The expansion of the variety of news media is a twentieth-century phenomenon. Until the end of World War I there was no serious threat to the newspapers' monopoly of the mass dissemination of news. The year 1920 saw radio getting feebly into the act, and 1923 brought the first of the modern weekly newsmagazines. Before World War II movie theaters offered skimpy newsreels, but they disappeared entirely when television broke out of its cocoon after the war. Proliferation of news media in other parts of the world, though it did not run on the same timetable, followed a similar pattern.

THE MEANING OF "MASS"

The term mass, *widely but often loosely used in such phrases as* mass media *and* mass communication, *deserves sensitive treatment. Its careless application to all news media is sometimes taken to imply that all the media seek the same mass audience. It takes little perception to spotlight this fallacy. In New York City the Times and the Daily News, each with huge circulations, are both mass media. But the Daily News mass differs radically from that of the Times—in education, income, taste, sophistication. In more than one city a single ownership may operate both AM and FM radio stations with the same call letters, but one station may shoot for teen-agers with lots of light music and the other may play only serious music. (Chapters 4 and 6 examine the problems of defining and selecting news for different kinds of audiences; Chapter 6 points out that every audience, no matter how large, is made up of individuals and must be so perceived.)*

Thousands of publications and broadcasters do not seek mass audiences if mass *is taken to mean across-the-board. Trade and technical journals, house and industrial organs, fraternal association magazines, and scores of other specialized periodicals publish material important for their own readers but of no concern at all to millions of others: does a General Motors secretary want to be informed about the retirement of a Chrysler janitor? Such publications and most broadcasting outlets provide little matter beyond the interest areas of their chosen clientele.*

So the particular mass of a given medium may be a relatively limited group.

Nevertheless, the impact of the journalist is potentially enormous. Journalists reach their goals daily, weekly, or at least monthly—a frequency of contact uncommon to any other group of professionals.

The news media have had impact on the life of America and the world that is both easy to see and hard to erase. Americans today know vastly more about the peasant across the globe, thanks chiefly to what the news media have told them, than they did as recently as twenty years ago. And more about the man across the street. If the responsibility of the newsworker is measured by the number of lives his work impinges on, he has never before been so heavily burdened.

Though the responsibilities and the effects of the reporter's work have been expanded by the advent of new media and the technological revolution, the fundamental concepts of news and the techniques of reporting are less changeable. Reporting, the process of gathering information and packaging reports for prescribed audiences, is a formalized process, no matter what the medium. Especially in the fact-gathering phases of the process, the techniques for working with speed, accuracy, and perspective remain relatively uniform (tools sometimes differ), whether the products are to appear in black and white, living color, or sound waves. The manner of presentation, the shape and size of the package, differ from one news channel to another, but the reporting task is a constant. Professional performance in all news fields is based on one set of ethical and social principles and on essentially the same techniques and skills. The conviction that the basic concepts, purposes, and responsibilities of news reporting are common to all media is a keystone of *Reporting*.

Projects

1. Find several examples of reporting that seem to be seeking limited audiences within larger groups (one might be a story in a general-circulation newspaper about a coin collectors' meeting) and several that clearly have wide interest for, and effect on, large groups. How do you evaluate the use of news for limited audiences?

2. Analyze several major stories from newspaper front pages or TV broadcasts with a view to determining—or speculating on—how many of the readers and listeners they reach will be directly affected by them.

Related Reading

David Wise, *The Politics of Lying: Government Deception, Secrecy and Power*, Random House, 1973. — An experienced Washington correspondent reports and comments on deception as an instrument of government and politics. Fascinating reading. Well documented.

CHAPTER TWO

News:
its relation to its world

*The press must be totally free with respect to everything external
to it. But internally it has to control its freedom—to be responsible,
wise, just. . . . The press made my freedom possible. What it
published liberated me.*
ALEXANDER SOLZHENITZYN
Russian Nobel Prize author, in a 1974 interview with Walter Cronkite of CBS

Your city is to hold a referendum to decide whether to build a freeway through a park. As a good citizen, you want to vote wisely. You have questions: Will it speed up traffic? Get rid of that 7 a.m. bottleneck at Seven Corners? Save commuters' time and money? Will it add to your tax bill? Will it turn obsolete as new kinds of transportation develop? Will it help you *personally*—or harm you?

How do you get the information you need to decide whether to vote yes or no?

There are many sources. Word of mouth is one: the men and women at the office, your bowling teammates, friends and acquaintances and neighbors (some of whom tell you "facts" that aren't so). Another source might be a nonpartisan analysis mailed to you by a civic association: paving contractors on the one hand and taxpayers on the other provide frankly biased views. If you really work at it, you can find yourself swamped.

But if you're like most Americans, you rely primarily on the news media —the newspapers, television, radio. From them comes the information a citizen needs to reach conclusions about most of the things he considers important, whether highways, hijackings, or high finance. These channels of communication help him decide whether he wants the Republican candidate or the Democrat to win. From them he learns about tonight's TV schedule, the shift of his bowling night from Tuesdays to Thursdays, and the selection of the pretty young girl down the block as Miss Baton Twirler of the Year. He finds information on the big and the little, the momentous and the trifling —information that helps him to plan not only the routine of his daily life but also its major decisions. It is a principle of American policy that every man has the right to know about matters that concern or interest him.

All through its three centuries, as the American news system has come to put its informative function foremost, it has developed a pragmatic interpretation of the freedom the Constitution promises it. "Freedom of the press" in the constitutional sense does not mean simply, "Government, keep your hands off!" It means, "Keep your hands off so that the media may help the people to preserve the democratic system." Freedom of the press is the means, not the end; the protectorate is the public, not the publisher.

Legal protection against governmental restriction or interference is no bar against other kinds of attempted or actual restrictions—political, economic, social, religious. This book will consider many such restrictions.

The right to free speech was won by a fight in a new nation's earliest days; its evolution into the people's right to know, the positive principle on which the American news concept is based, developed painfully into recognition that without unhampered news gathering and reporting there can be no real democracy.

It is a hard and sober fact that after 200 years both of these elementary rights are under attack.

GROWTH OF THE NEWS IDEA

News grows out of its period and its society's demands. There have been patterns of news as long as there has been articulate life among men—what we call civilization. Before there were newspapers in English, there were newsletters—reports of financial, social, and political currents provided by professional letter writers for friends or subscriber-clients. Business newsletters existed in Europe in the 1600s, along with news pamphlets and broadsides—hastily printed mongers of sensational information. News, to these publications, consisted of reports of public affairs, the activities of government, war, law enforcement, and of chronicles of such common enemies of man as crime, pestilence, and disaster. Some such reports were printed by authority to counteract political, social, or religious dissidence. The activities of individuals were not often reported unless crime, disaster, or the accident of royal birth was involved.

Although current information was eagerly sought by early American newspapers ("current" meant the most recent you could get, even if it came two months late by sailing ship from England), the news served up by the first professional journalists was limited in quantity and in concept.

American colonial publications, under the shadow of England's Star Chamber system of control of printing, were threatened with suppression when they published fact or comment that offended authorities. In 1671 the British governor of Virginia declared that "learning has brought disobedience and heresy and sects into the world; and printing has divulged them and libels against the government." In an authoritarian world dissemination of knowledge was a peril the powerful hoped to avoid. An early victim of this preference was Benjamin Harris, the Boston bookseller who brought out the first American newspaper. *Publick Occurrences*, a three-page leaflet (its fourth page was blank) published by Harris in 1690, was suppressed before a second issue could appear because, in the opinion of the Massachusetts colony governor, it contained "Reflections of a very high nature." The second colonial newspaper, John Campbell's *Boston News-Letter* of 1704, displayed prominently the protective legend, "Published by Authority."

A pioneer newspaper in New York gave rise in 1734 to the famed John Peter Zenger trial, in which it was determined that a jury rather than a governor had the right to decide whether a published statement was libelous. The trial also introduced the then-novel principle that printing the truth was not a criminally libelous act and that, therefore, truth from any source could be published. These historic decisions helped establish the legal rights of a free press.

Political difficulties were not colonial newspapers' only concern. Their technical problems today seem appalling. The lack of swift transportation and communication hobbled the news-gathering process. Primitive mechanical facilities—slow handpresses, scarce paper, type set letter by laborious letter—made for snail-paced production, high costs, and limited distribution. The small-paged weeklies and semiweeklies went mostly to the few citizens who had the money to buy and the education to read, and it was to this elite that the papers directed their news.

News in the colonial period was not what we take it to be today. We say that news has certain inherent characteristics: that it is fair, current, accurate, concise, balanced, objective. All these attributes are implied when we define news briefly as "full and current information made available to an audience" or as "the accurate report of a recent event." (Chapter 3 examines these and other essential qualities.) The early newspapers exhibited only a few of the characteristics that distinguish twentieth-century news reporting from other forms of prose communication. (A news report taken from *Pub-*

WHAT DOES "PRESS" MEAN?

Literally, the term press refers to communication in print. Today, however, it is taken as an umbrella that covers all journalistic, and especially news, activities: the broadcast newsman as well as the newspaper worker, the Time editor or the freelance correspondent. Reporting uses the term in this broad sense.

---

lick Occurrences opens Chapter 12.) Although the colonial press strove for the right to print the news as the editors saw it, it was often less than fair.

News could be, and was, colored to suit the reporter's bias; it was easy to omit entirely the facts unfavorable to the proprietor's views. News was often incomplete, often neither accurate nor current, and certainly not objective. Harris, Campbell, and many of their successors paid lip service to the principle that their prime function was to inform, but news was commonly selected and written so as to lead readers to see events as the editors saw them. Many newspapers were "dedicated" party organs or vehicles for the promotion of causes; the publisher whose prime concern was to spread his hate for George III or to abolish a tax he didn't like felt slight compulsion to push news coverage beyond his own purposes.

As a reader, you could choose the kind of fare you wanted. Both sides in the colonial struggle had their weekly news organs and their publicists, their James Rivingtons on the Loyalist side and their Sam Adamses bleeding for independence. Although the newspapers were propagandists, however, their vitality and their passion strengthened the principle of free expression that laid the groundwork for the "press of information" that was to come. Thomas Jefferson and his colleagues gave stirring expression to the belief that a government of the people must allow free expression and that such a government must exercise no censorship.

When the young nation took form in 1789, there was insistent demand for a governmental guarantee of press freedom. The Jeffersonian principle that a people's government must stand on a full flow of public information led to inclusion of a specific provision (italicized here) in the First Amendment to the Constitution:

> Congress shall make no law respecting an establishment of religion, or prohibiting the free exercise thereof; or *abridging the freedom of speech, or of the press;* or the right of the people peaceably to assemble, and to petition the Government for a redress of grievances.

All fifty states include in their constitutions similar provisions.

In the early days of the new nation freedom from government control resulted in as much license as liberty. Even Jefferson had to qualify his earlier

---

LIBERTY ... LICENSE?

What is license in news treatment? Usually it means news practices that, however legal, are not consistent with the responsibility to provide balance and fairness and to keep within the bounds of good taste. License means indulging in news practices that are offensive to public mores and judgment. If its report is accurate and properly weighted, a news story involving corruption, prostitution, or juvenile indulgence in heroin is not "yellow journalism." It is license, however, to over-emphasize the sensational aspects of such news, to distort it by scare headlines and photos, or to crowd news of significance out of sight. It is license to give readers faulty impressions of relative values. It is license to overdramatize news in order to permit readers to lick their lips over indecency, cruelty, suffering, or human frailty.

---

statements as a response to the scandalmongering, the scurrilous libel, and the falsehoods that emerged in the name of political liberty during the Washington, Adams, and Jefferson presidencies. The obscenities and excesses of this period died of their own poison, but for most of a century the press was more often a political instrument or a special pleader than a straightforward news medium.

The Industrial Revolution that began in England in the mid-eighteenth century soon crossed the Atlantic. By 1830 a higher percentage of Americans were readers—public education was making itself felt. As newpaper advertising revenue began to increase, publishers could depend less on political subsidies and income from the sale of papers. Faster presses and, later, typesetting by machine meant that in an hour thousands of papers, instead of hundreds, could be produced.

In 1833 a canny young printer in New York, Benjamin H. Day, put the changes and improvements to use to produce America's first successful penny paper. Ben Day not only published his New York *Sun* in quantity but also developed a new definition of news. He did not ignore news of public affairs, politics, government, but he cut down the share of space it received. By using unimportant "soft" news, he found a way to build a new and wider newspaper audience. He sent a reporter to New York's police court every day, and each morning the *Sun* gave its readers vignettes of the drunks, the petty thieves, the brawlers who came before the magistrate. The pictures were often sordid and maudlin, but they were human, and they dealt with ordinary people. The new public to whom Day appealed, a public able to buy the *Sun* because it cost only a penny, grew greedy for this new kind of fare.

Though Ben Day introduced the change, James Gordon Bennett, one of the most talented of American journalists, gets major credit for bringing it to maturity. Bennett, a Scottish immigrant with a sardonic face and a cutting wit, brought out the New York *Herald* in 1835, and using the *Sun*'s own formula, soon outstripped his competitor in vitality, in color, in inventiveness . . . and in circulation. When a sensational murder in a New York bordello occurred in 1836, Bennett himself covered the story, giving it column upon daily column of space; to get the news, he developed—some say invented—the news form known as the interview. Bennett not only got all New York talking about the murder (and the *Herald*), he also established that the young blade accused of the crime, seemingly on the verge of conviction, had not committed it.

Bennett had started with Day's belief that the activities of "little" citizens, especially when they violated society's mores, made news. But to this concept he added his passion as a crusader and his virtuosity as a journalist. For thirty years he balanced his shrewd perception of what the growing public wanted to read against his personal view of what it ought to read, and he adhered stoutly to his belief that the public must be fully informed. During the Civil War he made the *Herald* a burr and a goad to President

Lincoln and his aides. It was one of the first papers to hold that the causes it disapproved and the views it abhorred were nevertheless legitimate basis for news. Bennett believed that news should be offered to provide information rather than to support causes or make converts.

TOWARD NEW DEFINITIONS

The penny-press revolution of the nineteenth century broadened the range of news sources and redirected the American press toward some of the lost goals of Campbell and other early editors. News came to include not only government, politics, and such topics as literature and "the science of agriculture," but also, along with the shenanigans of the police courts, the progress of business and industry. Bennett and Day were called everything from heretics to pimps. But eventually they established a news pattern that others had to follow—belief in news for its own sake. When Henry J. Raymond founded the New York *Times* in 1851, one of his aims was to avoid the partisan discolorations of so many contemporary papers.

In the thirty years following the Civil War the American press moved from its political-opinion character toward becoming a channel of information; the purpose of the strong newspapers became to print the facts and let the reader do his own thinking. Samuel Bowles the younger, for many years the editor of the respected Springfield (Massachusetts) *Republican*, said in 1885 that the prime design of his paper was to furnish "the raw material" so that the reader might "compare and weigh and strike a balance for himself."

Fifty years after the *Sun* was founded, a quarter of the daily newpapers in the United States had come to label themselves politically independent, and by the end of the century the frankly political newspaper, presenting news to support its views, had virtually disappeared from the American

---

EDITORIALS VS. NEWS

To a student of news practice the difference between the news columns and the editorial columns is obvious. But laymen often fail to make the distinction. In theory, at least, the editorial page is the place where a newspaper and its editors express their views about the news; in the news columns they report the facts. Reporters and their editors know and largely respect this dichotomy. The layman's problem of discriminating may have been made more difficult in the last half-century by the growth of "news analysis," the kind of treatment of news that couples acknowledged commentary and evaluation with reporting of facts. A radio or TV newscaster is usually not a commentator.

---

scene. A large majority of newspapers today call themselves independent politically (some "independent Democrat" or "independent Republican"). But even when they profess clear political leanings or one-sided social or economic views, they commonly try to report news on all sides of issues (some with more devotion and success than others).

As the press developed a sense of obligation toward its readers, it also developed understanding of its constitutional freedom from government control. This freedom, which the Constitution guarantees only to industries dealing with communications, is necessary because a democratic society cannot function in the dark, but only in the glare of full information and knowledge.

CHALLENGES AND SAFEGUARDS

Whatever intelligence, integrity, and devotion the journalists themselves bring to their work are the chief guarantees that their constitutional freedom will be used responsibly. Only constant vigilance detects governmental failure to respect the intent of the First Amendment. A thousand compulsions move in on the press; if most of them are innocent of intent to subvert, they nevertheless have the capacity for subversion if they go unrecognized.

The change from service of private goals to the ideal of open-minded news presentation did not occur overnight. Horace Greeley's New York *Tribune* of midcentury was the prototype of the personal journalism that advocated primarily its proprietors' or editors' personal views, and this kind of journalism will never completely disappear. There have always been excesses. Yellow journalism in the news wars of William Randolph Hearst and Joseph Pulitzer in New York City threatened to bury news responsibility under an avalanche of sensationalism. In their slambang fight for circulation leadership, Hearst's *Journal* and Pulitzer's usually humane *World* reached circulation figures through feats of sensationalism that Bennett and his competitors had not dreamed of. Both papers made crime, violence, and outrage their staples; their insistence on war with Spain, though it did not have as much to do with starting the shooting as some historians have asserted, yielded vast readership.

The yellow journalism of the 1890s influenced American news judgment for a good fifty years. For more than a quarter-century Hearst newspapers were characterized by emphasis on news of outrage, lust, and disaster and accompanying disdain for personal dignity. The readership scramble among New York's maudlin "picture papers" in the 1920s, glorifying the same kind of news judgment, tempted other papers around the nation into similar intemperance.

Most big cities were host to scandal sheets before World War II. These cynical newspapers pretended interest in routing out local vice and corruption, but their real purpose was to sell papers or, in some cases, to engage in extortion and blackmail. In 1931 the Supreme Court, although it recognized the vicious character of one such weekly paper, held that the First Amendment forbade its suppression. But few such publications have prospered in recent years; they hold small appeal to a public able to see their malice if not always their journalistic faults.

Indeed, yellow journalists have always been a minority, even when they were most visible. Adolph Ochs entered the New York City newspaper scene at the peak of the Hearst-Pulitzer conflict. Ochs, accepting Henry J. Raymond's platform, took over the New York *Times* with a sober promise to present news impartially and fully, "regardless of party, sect, or interest." The *Times* came to gain circulation on a steadily rising curve and won the undefined sobriquet "the world's best newspaper" because of its awesomely complete news coverage. In all parts of the world the newspapers that are most respected—Washington *Post*, Milwaukee *Journal*, New York *Times*, Minneapolis *Tribune*, Manchester *Guardian*, *La Stampa* of Turin, *Le Monde* of Paris, *Frankfurter Zeitung*, *Journal de Genève*—are those that hold to high standards of public service and responsibility. The color of yellow journalism continues to fade.

THE GROWTH OF NEWS RESPONSIBILITY

By the middle of the twentieth century the American press had established a practical definition of news responsibilities based on principles of freedom and the right of the public to information. Such a code can never be fully spelled out, though a number of news organizations have tried (see Appendix C). But its major tenets are not difficult to suggest:

1. The press recognizes a positive obligation to give its audiences the news of significance to their lives as fairly and completely as competent professional practice and judgment permit.
2. The press as a whole holds that it must give people the opportunity to know, understand, and evaluate all facets of important news events, especially those involving such social controversy as that of partisan politics. This responsibility has been sharply underlined in a day when more than 90 percent of American dailies have no local newspaper competition. The very lack of competition obligates papers to try to present *all* news and views, including those that might otherwise have been offered by the opposition.
3. The press must seek to become strong financially, so that it can resist pressures. A firmly based paper can use its strength to support whatever views and attitudes and groups and parties it believes deserve support, and it can reject attempts at pressure that it believes arise from selfish or unwise impulses.
4. The press recognizes as valid the principles underlying laws that make false or malicious defamation a crime.

That these principles are generally accepted does not mean that they are universally observed. It would be myopic not to see that some news that ought to be published is suppressed; that treatment of political news does not always meet the ideal of fairness; that financial strength can be used against the public interest as well as for it; that standards of decency and the dignity of privacy may not get the honor they merit. Selflessness and high wisdom are possessed by few. But newspaper performance more than

WHEN IS A PAPER INDEPENDENT?

That the label "politically independent"—a label self-applied in 1972 by more than half of the 1,750 United States daily newspapers—is not entirely an idle boast was demonstrated by the movement of dailies from Republican to Democratic support in the 1964 (Johnson–Goldwater) Presidential election. From 1932 to 1960 the country's dailies favored Republican candidates (67 percent in 1952, as low as 52 percent in 1932). In 1964 only 35 percent favored Goldwater. But in 1968 some 90 percent of the papers that made decisions advised "vote for Nixon," and in 1972 the Republican preference rose to nearly 95 percent. (The number of papers that couldn't—or didn't—make up their minds rose from less than 10 percent to nearly 20 percent.)

pious editorial protest testifies that such principles are the guides responsible journalists seek to follow.

This chapter has talked principally in terms of the newspaper. This is for convenience only: the principles of freedom from governmental restraints and of responsibility toward news consumers apply in all forms of journalism. Newsmagazines summarize and comment on current affairs in broad terms rather than in the detail of "spot news." But this difference is one of technique, not of fundamental character. Freedom from prior governmental interference along with responsible portrayal of the contemporary scene is tacitly assumed. The newsmagazines have on occasion emphasized one aspect of a news event at the expense of another; they have dwelt unduly on the trivial; they have expressed opinions in the guise of news or analysis (*Time*'s editors, in its early years, were quoted as saying they felt no obligation to make *Time*'s news objective). But they contribute hugely to the knowledge of their millions of readers.

News on the air   Broadcasting presents a different problem. Radio and television are under limited government control. The Federal Communications Commission is directed by the Federal Communications Act to regulate broadcasting "in the public interest, convenience, or necessity," at least in assignment of channels and assurance of orderly traffic. Broadcasters often think that the FCC exceeds the intent of Congress—by expressing approval of one type of program and frowning on another, for example; by establishing the right-of-reply, or the equal-time, principle; even, in rare instances, by withholding or questioning renewal of a station's license because of the nature of its programming. In the early 1940s the FCC examined the control of a city's newspaper and broadcasting properties by one ownership as a threat to full public expression of opinion; by taking no action, it seemed to assess the danger as small. (In 1974 the Justice Department took the same tack, with emphasis on monopoly of a community's advertising as well as of its news flow. Neither the Justice Department nor the FCC had pushed the investigation to a conclusion as this book went to press.)

The FCC changes complexion as its personnel changes and as social and

PUBLIC INTEREST

The term public interest is easy to misunderstand and misuse. In the Communications Act it denotes actions or attitudes that serve the general welfare. But as Everette E. Dennis of the University of Minnesota points out, an action in the public interest and one of public interest are not necessarily the same thing. The Social Security Act, for example, is considered to be in the public interest. The accelerating inflationary trend of the 1970s was of but not in the public interest—that is, it concerned and affected the public but did not serve it.

To complicate all this—here lies the greatest misunderstanding—an act or event that is of interest to the public may be neither the one nor the other. The death wishes of a flamboyant motorcyclist interested the public mightily—millions hung on the news of his propelling himself from an Idaho canyon wall. But the event can hardly be said to have been good for the public or to have affected anything but its adrenal glands.

political values fluctuate. At one time it commanded radio stations not to editorialize; at another it said expression of opinion is a necessary part of good programming. It has insisted that equal time be made available to conflicting points of view. It has established controls on various forms of advertising.

The industry insists on its First Amendment rights, but not all broadcasters accept the public's right to be informed as a primary obligation. Broadcasting is an entertainment business, not fundamentally a news medium, and owners and managers are not commonly news-oriented except insofar as news broadcasting is profitable. Public and FCC pressures led TV in the mid- and late 1960s to strengthen news broadcasting and to move toward notable documentaries (the TV parallel to the interpretive magazine article), and some stations achieved notable records. Though government threats in the Nixon years somewhat dampened network ardor, the impressive possibilities of TV news coverage were shown in 1974, when millions of Americans watched the Senate Watergate investigations and the House impeachment hearings as though they had been on the spot. But news in many radio stations and a smaller percentage of TV stations, in spite of clamorous claims about "up-to-the-minute news" and "our big 24-hour newsroom," has remained a stepchild.

The development of new news media has not altered basic news concepts; but each medium has its own requirements. Each reports events in a manner that suits its peculiar facilities, audiences, and methods of delivery. Within each medium, moreover, individual outlets are as night and day. *Time* could hardly be confused with the sober, conservative *U. S. News & World Report*, and the New York *Post* and the New York *Times* are as dissimilar as a robin and a roadrunner.

New or improved communication processes in the middle third of the twentieth century have extended the reaches of news interest. The new processes have made communications more rapid in words and in pictures;

they have shrunk the world and made its peoples more sophisticated, more interdependent, and more eager for knowledge of each other. In an age when two world wars, a world depression, and an unbelievable realignment of national identities, boundaries, loyalties, and interdependencies have crowded into a half-century, when planes cross the Atlantic between breakfast and lunch and men bounce on the moon, when satellites let the whole world watch the signing of an uneasy peace—in such an age the interests and concerns of men everywhere, in Skykomish, Washington, Dairen, China, and Stein-am-Rhein, Switzerland, are inevitably more expansive (and at the same time more uniform) than they were in a simpler era.

But the obligation of the newsworker is a constant: to provide information.

THE CURRENT SCENE

Although basic news concepts stand unaltered, their expression today has been both enriched and endangered, sometimes both at once. The following paragraphs introduce briefly some principal journalistic problems; several receive attention in later chapters.

Interpretation   One twentieth-century characteristic is the burgeoning emphasis on explanation as a kind of fourth dimension of news. Today a major news story that stands by itself, without relation to its environment or its genesis, without signposts to help the reader find its overlap with other news, is only half a story. You do not find many events that are entirely isolated; reporting that ignores context and relevance is unfinished reporting. News possesses not only length, breadth, and height but also depth, orientation, perspective—not the political or personal perspective of the nineteenth century, but rather a cause-and-effect orientation validated by objectivity.

It is this kind of orientation, for example, to show how a Supreme Court decision about public housing affects a local urban-renewal project; or to explain reportorially (factually rather than through opinion or comment) how the returning Vietnam soldier, unable to find a job or social role, sometimes has become a peacetime casualty and a social enigma. Newsmen refer to this fourth-dimension news treatment as interpretation, analysis, or background. They devote many thoughtful hours to discussion of the need for it. Nearly all of a three-day conference of the International Press Institute in London was devoted to this theme, and few meetings of journalists pass without attention to it.

That it raises at least one quandary is readily apparent—the problem of explaining without pontificating, reporting without editorializing. This and other news problems outlined briefly at this point will receive expanded examination in Chapters 3 and 21.

Access and the right to inform   Newsmen point out acidly that "if you can't get it, you can't report it." If the facts about a newsworthy event remain hidden, there is either no news or the news merely that something is hidden. This is no new problem, but it has grown in recent years. In a number of ways (to be examined in Chapter 9), government agencies as well as private newsmakers have become more and more adroit in the delicate art of cover-up. The use of secret documents is an example—the kind of practice brought to light in the 1971 Pentagon Papers case (in which Daniel Ellsberg laid himself open to criminal action by revealing government papers that penetrated the dark history of the Vietnam adventure). This case is an extreme example, but throughout American government the withholding of public documents, for reasons good or bad, has become common. More threatening than the clumsy political Watergate burglary were the wiretapping that it revealed and the refusals to make available to courts and congressional committees—agents of the public—materials for which there was clear public need. Congressional recognition of the importance of protecting avenues to information appeared both in 1973, when Congress turned down a proposal to prohibit the release of "classified" governmental information, and in 1974, when it overrode President Ford's veto of provisions strengthening the mild "freedom of information act" of eight years earlier. Newsworkers and the public thus gain modest assurance that many public records will be less carelessly or deviously withheld than had been the case for a generation.

Denying reporters access to events they think the public should know about is a related problem. Congressional sessions have been open to everybody for more than a hundred years, but committee hearings are often closed. Attention to making public meetings public has been general only in the last half-century. In part because of pressure by journalists and their professional groups, Congress, legislatures, city councils, and other public bodies have moved toward relaxed policies to govern meetings and the use of public records. (One of the factors that brought about Nixon's downfall was his determination not to open records the public believed it needed.)

Credibility gaps   This handy phrase has been used to describe two kinds of phenomena: popular belief that government does not always tell the truth; and lack of confidence that the news media report fully and accurately. (There is a mistaken tendency to hang a falsehood issued by government or a private news source around the neck of the media that report it.)

The gap in public confidence in governmental agencies, from the White House down, can be traced to solid sources.

Beginning in the Cold War period in the 1950s, a series of what can be described only as lies issued from the White House (those about the U-2 spy plane incident under Eisenhower, the Bay of Pigs disaster under Kennedy, the landing of marines in the Dominican Republic under Johnson, the series of misleading or false reports about Vietnam operations and intentions under Nixon, as well as the incredible Watergate deceits). In many high places the cynical view was that the end justified the means. "National security" was

often the plea offered for these deceptions—sometimes sincerely, but often
without reasonable cause. Reporters and the media, believing it their task

---

WHAT DO YOU BELIEVE?

*A curious contradiction is displayed in the nature of public confidence in two major
American institutions, press and government. The public was "pessimistic and
alienated" in its attitudes toward government, according to public opinion polls in
1973 and 1974; it repeatedly expressed fear that the press was not giving it full information. Nevertheless, it based its opinions about government on reports in newspapers, newsmagazines, and broadcasting. Thus, the public makes decisions on
what the media offer at the same time that it doubts them. (For some years TV has
been the news medium in which Americans place the greatest confidence; the apparent reason, since TV news is the same news that appears in print, is that when
you see it, or see the reporter, you identify more confidently with it.)*

---

to inform, earned credit for opening public eyes to the incidents big and
little that "government spokesmen" had described less than forthrightly,
falsely, or not at all.

Even though the press usually behaves in the public interest in such instances, the effect of accurate reporting can be damaging to the reporter.
The public does not get the information directly from the sources, but rather
through the channels of news—newspapers, radio, television. So "the media
said it," and the hurried news consumer often attaches the error to the news
carrier rather than to the originator. Moreover, the correction never catches
up with the error, so the responsibility may be laid at the wrong door. Add
to this the fact that the news media have all too often earned mistrust
through their own errors or their own failures of judgment (one of the purposes of this book is to identify such errors and failures and to suggest how
they can be attacked). The newspaper reader does not often distinguish between the miracle of daily service performed by most of the press and the
fact that a relatively small part of press performance is shoddy or worse;
being human, therefore, he looks at all performance with a bias that dis-
colors.

Criticism of the press   It is trite to point out that newspapers, proud as well
as jealous of their duty to reveal public wrongdoing and censure antisocial
behavior, shrink when the finger of criticism reverses to point at them. The
charge has less weight today, when newsmen themselves are moving more
and more toward self-examination. Self-criticism comes at two levels—the
kind offered at the publishers' and editors' meetings, by such respected
journalists as Norman Isaacs of the Louisville *Courier-Journal*, Ben Bagdikian of the *Columbia Journalism Review*, and James Reston of the New
York *Times*, as well as scores of other editors and writers (and a few publishers); and the newer kind that comes from the new "critical journals"—
[MORE] of New York, the *Chicago Journalism Review*, and a handful of

others whose often-angry purpose is to spotlight the failings of the publications that employ their writers. These are healthful and helpful criticisms.

THE OMBUDSMAN

Overt self-criticism was instituted about 1970 by several respected newspapers—the St. Petersburg Times, Louisville Courier-Journal, and Washington Post among them. The Courier-Journal's critic was directed to investigate and report on public grievances against his paper. The Post's ombudsman was expected to monitor the paper each day as to its "fairness, balance, and perspective," and to look into complaints from the public. One Post ombudsman, Ben Bagdikian, a severe but perceptive and informed press critic, resigned after short service because he "could not reconcile being an independent critic with belonging to the management team" and because he found that handling complaints did not leave him enough time for independent criticism; he also thought he should be free to criticize management. In St. Petersburg a study showed that the Times staff reacted favorably to its ombudsman's criticisms and suggestions.

The Columbia Journalism Review suggested that a large newspaper should employ two critics, "one to see that management's standards are applied to day-to-day operations, the other to serve as a public critic, setting the paper's performance in the context of major issues."

Hardly defensible is a political attack of the kind employed by Vice-President Agnew in the two years before the 1972 Presidential elections and by other figures who appeared either thin-skinned or fearful of press analysis and even of reporting. The first of the Agnew attacks on the press, characterized by the "effete Eastern snob" label he used to describe media that had displeased the White House, were often uninformed and clearly politically inspired. There is no doubt that they had a disturbing effect on a public already doubtful about some of the news service they received.

Protection of sources   A tradition of news journalism is that a reporter keeps faith with his news sources—that his promise not to reveal identity of a source will withstand any attempt to wring it from him. For nearly 200 years reporters have stood firm on this principle. Before 1970 about twenty states had adopted "shield laws," which gave reporters the privilege of refusing to divulge news sources if they believed that to do so would hamper their news-gathering effectiveness. The 1970s brought a rash of court orders denying this qualified privilege, however, and a number of reporters went to jail under contempt-of-court citations. More serious threats to reporters' operations were posed by the grand juries and congressional committees that resorted to the subpoena to force surrender of information. The Columbia Broadcasting System was ordered to produce in court tapes of material it had gathered in making documentaries but had not used on the air; other reporters were ordered to produce their notes and similar unpublished information. These efforts at legal extraction of news matter were resisted. One of the strong defenses came from the newsworkers themselves, through the Reporters' Committee for Freedom of the Press. In Congress and in a number of state legislatures shield laws to protect reporters' pledges of confidentiality were introduced. Chapter 10 deals further with this problem.

Prior- and postpublication controls   The clearest meaning of the First Amendment is that government, at any level, may not either prevent or compel publication. Laws that make the press liable for damage caused by what it publishes—the laws of libel—penalize those who do such damage, when it does not meet certain measures of permissibility, but they do not prohibit it. There have been few attempts to abort or circumvent the First Amendment. The Sedition Act of 1798, under which a number of editors were jailed for criticizing the government, expired after three years without test of its constitutionality. The so-called Minnesota Gag Law was ruled out by the U. S. Supreme Court in 1930 because it permitted prior censorship. And the court moved in precisely the opposite direction but to the same effect in 1974, when it threw out an ancient and never-enforced Florida law requiring Florida newspapers to give political candidates "free space" to respond to editorial criticisms. The court said firmly that "a command to publish amounts to the same kind of unconstitutional governmental interference as a restraint on publishing." The decision agreed that fairness might be violated by such an interpretation, but it said that "press responsibility cannot be legislated" and that the freedom to criticize, fairly or unfairly, is an imperative social value. (Newspaper executives had held that such a requirement "would put us all out of business"—that to print everybody's response to every charge would leave no space to print the news, and that it would inhibit anything but bland and meaningless editorial comment.)

SECONDARY PURPOSES OF NEWS

As an editor fingers through the day's copy, deciding what to use and what goes into the wastebasket, he has more in mind than providing information. He also would like to attract an audience. To interest or to entertain is to attract, and to capture regular attention is to increase audience and financial strength.

Entertaining his audience was one of Ben Day's goals when he established the *Sun.* He attained his aim by replacing the customary news fare with news of human interest—news of the pangs and pleasures of New York's back streets—and by injection of a light touch into his reporting.

Today entertainment is added to the news by selection of events that are amusing or exciting or tear-laden or by reporting the events, often trivial, so as to emphasize their human-interest nature or by good writing. Much of the most admired journalistic writing grows out of reporting of this type. The medical reportage of Berton Roueché for *The New Yorker* and Ernie Pyle's front-line reporting in World War II are classics of factual entertainment. Truman Capote's *In Cold Blood*, called a nonfiction novel when

---

THE LIGHT TOUCH THAT HURTS

*Ben Day's light touch was not always gentle, as may be seen in this example from
the Sun's police court news:*

> *Catherine McBride was brought in for stealing a frock. Catherine said she
> has just served out six months on Blackwell's Island, and she wouldn't be sent
> back again for the best glass of punch that ever was made. Her husband, when
> she last left the penitentiary, took her to a boarding house in Essex Street, but
> the rascal got mad at her, pulled her hair, pinched her arm, and kicked her out
> of bed. She was determined not to bear such treatment as this, and so got
> drunk and stole the frock out of pure spite. Committed.*

The readiness to ridicule that Ben Day permitted himself is no longer common.

---

it appeared in 1965, was referred to as a new literary form. Nonfiction novel
it may be, but it is not a new form. It represents a kind of dramatized reporting (sometimes colored by the reporter's views, sometimes not) that has had
a distinguished career.

Critics of modern journalism whose zeal exceeds their judgment or their
logic think it craven to seek large audiences. Big audiences give a publisher
or a broadcaster strength because, as has been said earlier, the newspaper
with a big and assured circulation or the radio or TV station with a wide,
dependable clientele, has financial security. Advertisers, who contribute the
bulk of the financial support of the news media, support most heavily the
media whose audiences promise the greatest buying power; and many advertisers, though not all, find the largest audiences the most profitable.
Popular legend to the contrary, an advertiser can seldom dominate or even
influence the newspaper or broadcasting station that has a stable audience;
every newsman knows at first hand a collection of tales of attempted pressures that failed.

No responsible journalist condones, in his own work or in others', distortion, over- or underemphasis, or sensationalizing of news. But every
journalist who respects his profession, his publics, and himself works hard
toward writing all his stories for the largest group to whom it is likely to
have appeal.

News as history   Reporters don't often think of themselves, as they face
their typewriters, as historians. Yet they are just that, for their stories are
often the only permanent records of contemporary lives and events. As a
sentence in Chapter 1 puts it, "News is tomorrow's history . . . " At any future
date, from tomorrow to 2184, the newsman's story may be exhumed; every
newspaper is a potential source for the historian, the sociologist, the political scientist. Most newspapers, it is true, give little daily thought to their
historical function; but the "newspapers of record" such as the New York
Times consider the role of historian one of the valid controls on decisions
about which news, and how much, to print.

Although the uses of news as historical record broaden the news concept, the requirements of history do not change its meaning or add to the responsible newsman's burden. The main purpose of news remains to provide current information, and the primary responsibility of the reporter is to inform a contemporary audience. The reporter who succeeds in meeting today's news demands, however, is inevitably enriching the files of history. When he makes his story accurate and objective and balanced, he has written a form of history that will be informative on a thousand tomorrows, to thousands of different readers, in thousands of different places.

WHO MAKES THE DECISIONS?

"How did that dry stuff about the city council get in the paper?" . . . "Why didn't they broadcast something about my Aunt Emma's golden wedding celebration?"

Those, you'll recognize, are questions asked by newspaper readers and broadcast listeners; you've almost certainly heard them, perhaps asked them yourself. They question the news judgment of the men and women who prepare the news and give it to you, or keep it from you.

Why do newsmen look on a given set of facts in one way while those whom they are trying to serve, the news consumers, often see it differently?

The reason is that a news professional, though he must think of "you" as an individual and write what he writes for the eye or ear of a single person, has to see you at the same time as a member of a group or a multitude. He may know that you, as an individual, would like to see Aunt Emma's party recorded in print; he also knows that there are few in his audience who have ever heard of Aunt Emma. He takes into account that other events, though they may not interest you, are of concern to a great many of your neighbors. And so, since his newsprint space or broadcast time is nonstretchable, he has to make a decision: leave out Aunt Emma so that he can include the city council.

(He is likely, too, to know of factors that you don't. Chapter 1 suggested that sometimes outside forces—from kidnappers trying to protect a ransom drop to real estate men worrying over an investment—may be exerting pressure that he has at least to consider.)

Is this a conflict of interest? Yes, of a kind. Can it be avoided? Not always. The reporter or editor must make decisions of this kind repeatedly. He has to decide to present facts that interest few of his audience but that nevertheless should be made available to all; on the contrary, he may withhold facts of enormous interest because he feels he cannot justify the results their publication would bring.

He may not always make the right decision. He may exclude news matter that ought to be made available, and vice versa. But more times than not—since he is a professional, since he has been through this dilemma thousands of times, since the responsibility to solve it properly is of both professional and practical importance to him—the chances are that his batting average will be a good one.

Projects

1. From three issues of the daily paper you read most often, make a tabulation of all the local, regional, national, and international news. On the basis of what you learn, write a brief report of your opinion of the news balance (or imbalance) the paper maintains.

2. Make a list of three or more of your principal adverse criticisms of your favorite newspaper or newscast. From current issues or broadcasts select an example of each of the characteristics you have listed. Write a defense of your criticism in each instance, and try to show in what more acceptable manner you would like each example treated.

3. Name three or four examples of failures of your daily paper (or a newscast) to report news you think should have been presented, or of the opposite: presentation of news you think inappropriate. Write a brief critique to explain why you think the news judgment in these cases was faulty.

Related Reading

William L. Rivers and Michael J. Nyhan, editors, *Aspen Notebook on Government and the Media*, Praeger, 1973. — Serious and searching discussions, in dialog drawn from the Aspen Workshop on government and the press, about reporter-government relations, press rights and responsibilities, the "right to know," access to and public confidence in the media, and other problems.

Broadcasting and the First Amendment, Center for the Study of Democratic Institutions, 1973; cassettes. — Discussions at the Center by ranking authorities on licensing of broadcasters, the quality of TV news, the National News Council, censorship, and the "right to be unfair."

Jerome A. Barron. *Freedom of the Press for Whom? The Right of Access to the Media*, Indiana University Press, 1973. — Suggestions for opening the media more widely to minority points of view.

CHAPTER THREE

News:
essential elements

You can use raw cotton in making either baby clothes or high explosives. You can use the components of news—facts—for sociological exposition, propaganda, fiction ... or news reporting. The materials from which news stories grow respond to a profusion of pressures. Although the raw stuff of news can, like cotton, be woven into many patterns, a master form has developed through the years, a distinctive profile. A news story is more than the sum of the facts that compose it; it is the sum of the facts plus the form a reporter gives it. Its characteristics distinguish it from all other forms of writing.

Chapter 1 said that modern news is accurate, concise, and current. It is more: it is fair and objective (not always the same thing), and it is clear. Without these qualities a report of an event is not looked on as true to the news model, though it may be high art or incisive scholarship. John Hersey's *Hiroshima* is an incomparable report of a series of occurrences, but it was not news because it was not current when it was published, and it was not selectively concise.

The distinguishing traits of news are so firmly built in that they not only

27

determine the characteristic forms of news practice but also serve as guides to the presentation and evaluation of news. They establish the working principles that condition a professional's approach to news and direct him in his daily functioning.

NEWS IS ACCURATE

Students on many American campuses decided, on learning of the 1972 mining of Haiphong Harbor, to protest what they considered the abhorrent prolongation of a war. Nobody on these campuses saw the laying of the mines; none of the protesters were there; few had firsthand word of what had taken place.

News reports were what provoked their anger.

Thus is the accuracy of news taken for granted. Some readers question this assumption. "I never believe what I read in the papers," they say, or "That announcer always gets it wrong." A university dean I know says he has never seen an entirely accurate news story dealing with an event of which he has personal knowledge. Yet that same dean, like all nonbelievers, not only accepts what the news media offer but also bases his life on the information he receives as news. He knows from experience that when a news story says the Saturday ball game will begin at 1 p.m. instead of 1:30, or that the driver failed to stop at a red light, or that the new state's attorney will be so-and-so (or that mines are being laid in Haiphong Harbor), he can rely on the stated facts. Many are reluctant to admit that news is a guide for their acts and thoughts; many produce evidence that this set of facts or that is in error; but few deny that the vast bulk of news is dependable.

"... VIRTUE IS TO A WOMAN"

Soon after he retired as editor of the New York World, *Joseph Pulitzer had this (among many other things) to say about accuracy:*

"It is not enough to refrain from publishing fake news; it is not enough to avoid the mistakes which arise from the ignorance, the carelessness, the stupidity of one or more of the many men who handle the news. . . . You have got to . . . make everyone connected with the paper—your editors, your reporters, your correspondents, your rewrite men, your proofreaders—believe that accuracy is to a newspaper what virtue is to a woman."

What accuracy means literally is that every element in a news story, every name and date and age and address, every definitive word or expression or sentence, is a precise and unequivocal statement of a verifiable certainty. Not only that: it means also correctness of general impression, correct perspective achieved by the way the details are put together and by the emphases they are given.

If the meaning and the imperative need for accuracy are easy to understand, the quality itself is not easy to attain. A news story with fewer than a dozen specific facts would be hard to find; most stories contain as many as they have verbs, nouns, and phrases. It is hard for even the seasoned reporter, careful as he tries to be, to make absolutely certain of every detail. He must fight the haste of news work; his story may be changed by the copy editor's pencil, by distortions in the printing process, by the nuances of a radio announcer's inflections. Any issue of a newspaper or presentation of a newscast offers literally thousands of opportunities for mistakes. Most errors are minor and not misleading—typographical errors or faulty pronunciation. The chances for error are so vast that the wonder is the accuracy of news as we know it, rather than the mistakes.

WHAT IS A STORY?

Reporters write "stories." The term news story denotes factual record; it connotes no kinship with the short story or any kind of fiction. Sometimes newsworkers, bored by their own jargon, talk about "yarns" or "pieces" or even, with elaborate irony, "items" or "articles." These two terms, unless ironic, suggest unfamiliarity with news work.

Nevertheless, there is that charge that the media "never get things right." This is a model of the human penchant for generalization from little evidence. Most newspaper readers see only the stories that interest them or the news columns dealing with subjects they know something about—small percentages of everything their papers offer. The errors they find, therefore, get disproportionate attention. If the paper spells Smith's name Smyth, if it refers to a yawl as a ketch, if it reports (as one paper did) that President Johnson's body was borne to his grave on a motorcycle ("motorcade," for the record), if it says that a hundred parents attended the PTA meeting when only seventy signed the attendance record, the confidence of the reader who identified the error is eroded. He is likely to draw an inference that is unjustifiably broad rather than to limit his complaint to the specifics he is sure of. It is only when he observes that the paper repeats errors that generalization may be justified.

What are the reporter's safeguards? How can he protect himself, his paper, and his reader against inaccuracy? The best protection is patient vigilance. Make legible notes of every fact (memory's rarely good enough), particularly such specific details as names, ages, dates, times, addresses. Take nothing for granted. Is what sounded like Smith really Smith? Or is it Schmidt, or Smeeth, or even Psmythe? When the secretary said the meeting would be on Friday, August 17, was he sure August 17 will be a Friday? And if August 17 is a Thursday, which day does he intend? Is it correct to call the minister "Dr. Brown"? Perhaps she's not a Dr., but only a Ms. Or does she prefer some other title? If she does, she'll call what you use wrong even if it's right.

Patient vigilance needs as its partners skepticism and a passion for double-checking. Skepticism means that the story clipped from the morning paper as a tip for afternoon treatment must be vouched for by a trustworthy source—it isn't accurate just because it was printed or broadcast. Two outrageous hoaxes gained wide publication in 1973 because of failure to look twice. The *Times of London* swallowed a propaganda story about a brutal massacre in a fictitious African village; papers everywhere printed it until the London *Economist* exposed it. Some American papers reported that enormous quantities of military supplies had been buried at an Air Force base in South Carolina; this falsity was exposed by the Detroit *News*. Columnist James J. Kilpatrick speculated that "the stories were published because editors were subconsciously ready to believe rumors about unpopular institutions—the Portuguese in one case, the military establishment in the other. Facts weren't checked."

These were atypical incidents. Most of the time relentless use of common reference tools is enough—city and other directories, telephone books, dictionaries, encyclopedias, *Who's Who*, government manuals ... or a dogged search for the one man who really knows the answer.

HOW HIGH WAS WRIGHT?

A wire service story opened a nostalgic feature by saying that "Orville Wright made history when he flew to a height of 120 feet in 1903." The fact: Wright covered 120 feet along the ground, never more than 10 feet above it. A two-minute combination of newswriter and encyclopedia would have avoided the error.

A Washington reporter wired his paper that President Eisenhower had "pushed a phony button" in a tree-lighting ceremony. The reporter called the button "phony" because "the secret service would be appalled ... to let ... the President monkey with a switch big enough" to do the job, so a low-current circuit had been substituted. A reader pointed out that a circuit of minuscule amperage, which is what the President used, would be enough to activate the system, even if it wouldn't actually light up the bulbs. Did that make it "phony"?

Vigilance also means awareness that sometimes the man who knows the answer won't, or for any of a number of reasons can't, tell it accurately. It is a plague of reportorial life that information sources are usually less reliable than journalists.

Studies of news accuracy   A number of American newspapers have conducted regular surveys of their own accuracy. They use a technique developed in university schools of journalism: submission of hundreds of newspaper stories to people closely enough concerned with the events to know the facts. The individuals are asked to report on accuracy both of detail and of general impression. Most responses in such stories show extremely high factual accuracy (correct names, times, dates, statistics, and other specifics). In half a dozen academic studies of more than 3,000 stories, the incidence of errors—big and little—was lower than one per story.

The kind of error cited most frequently was "mistake in meaning," which usually meant that the story—from the checker's viewpoint—gave a faulty impression. Any newsman, however, would point out that the news source and the news reporter are likely to see a given set of facts differently. Suppose, for example, that the man who gives a talk on use of marijuana wants primarily to express his belief that marijuana is relatively harmless. But the reporter's judgment is that for his readers the most significant thing the speaker says is that legal penalties for smoking pot should be abolished, and his story carries that emphasis. Who's right—the speaker, who knows what message he hoped to present, or the reporter, who thinks that for the audience concerned a different element was most important? It is the reporter's responsibility to make this kind of decision. Because of his experience, his purpose, and his lack of self-interest, he is more likely to make it objectively than the man who sees the event from an inner perspective.

NEWS IS BALANCED

It is clear that accuracy of fact doesn't always guarantee accuracy of meaning. Accurate facts loosely or unfairly selected or arranged can be as misleading as outright error; from too much emphasis or too little, from inclusion of irrelevant facts or omission of facts that ought to be there, a reader may gain a false impression. A reporter for the journalists' union, The Newspaper Guild, reporting a conference on "The Mass Media in a Liberal Education," chronicled only the remarks made by a Guild representative. His report gave an erroneous view of the conference.

True accuracy, thus, is a product not only of literal fact but also of balance.

Balance may be as difficult to attain as accuracy of fact. As the reader's or listener's representative, a reporter has to try constantly to place each fact or group of facts in proper proportion, to relate it meaningfully to other elements, and to establish its relative importance to the story as a whole. Though a reporter covering a baseball game might be scrupulously accurate in every fact he uses, he would cheat his reader if he tells of the home team's home runs but leaves out the other team's. A report of a campus "riot" (use of the word itself may weight a story falsely) that pictures police swinging clubs but fails to portray protesters' provocations is out of balance. It would be unfair, in reporting a speech at a Rotary meeting, to omit mention of the Good Citizen awards ceremony, especially if the speech were routine and the awards received with cheers.

News is usually thought complete when the reporter has presented a competent summary of all relevant parts of the event. News coverage does not mean reporting every trifling circumstance in painstaking detail; it means selecting and arranging the significant facts in appropriate fashion and quantity. Literal completeness is seldom desirable, but some stories in today's journalism are close to it: play-by-play sports stories, full texts of speeches or court testimony, stories that reconstruct with photographic fidelity such dramatic events as a President's inauguration or his funeral. For the most part completeness in reporting means fair, well-considered summary, rather than second-by-second minutiae.

The reporter is the agent of the news consumer. He goes to the baseball game, gathers facts about next year's city budget, or covers the riot so as to supply information to thousands of laymen who depend on him because they can't be there themselves. His statement of selected particulars should enable his readers or listeners to reconstruct the main lines of the news events and to put them into meaningful perspective.

OUT OF BALANCE

Senator Hugh Scott once wrote to major American news services to urge them to balance the "inflammatory statements of violent extremists" such as Rap Brown with appeals for law and order by moderate black leaders.

Eric Sevareid of CBS once cited the fact that broadcasting has at times forgone coverage of riotous events for fear of drawing undue attention to them. He pointed out that a network check, after CBS was accused of "devoting too much time to black militants," showed that more time had been given to moderates than to militants. But "more time" to one side than to the other does not guarantee balance, nor does it deny the danger of unfairness.

A news story about a legislative hearing on the Equal Rights Amendment, after stating that the hearing was one-sided because opposition was sparse, devoted most of its space to what the proponents said. Off balance? The reporter said that the weight of the story accurately represented the weight of the hearing.

Balance can be lost wholesale or retail. A Texas paper whose editor was personally involved in a campaign to raise money to build a "fountain dedicated to freedom" devoted so much space to the campaign that it slighted other categories of local news. That was impressive and open imbalance. But when a press service said of the Senate Watergate hearings that "the witness will have his chance to counter-attack tomorrow" when in fact he had not been attacked, the off-balance treatment of facts was almost unnoticeable.

One way not to attain balance is to count words, minutes, or lines of print. A Pacific Coast radio station decided to achieve "absolute impartiality" during a presidential campaign by giving each candidate precisely the same amount of news time each day. It quickly discovered that the news events themselves didn't balance—that you couldn't report either fairly or accurately by devoting exactly fifteen lines of typewriting to a major campaign speech on the one hand and a twenty-four-hour stretch of complete silence on the other. A bill introduced in Congress sought to achieve fair news treatment for political candidates by requiring that a candidate who thought himself criticized on radio or TV be given second-for-second time;

the bill died a deserved death. In facts, thoughts, and ideas, mathematics is no guide to equality.

OBJECTIVITY

The principle that news is objective reporting has been called the principal contribution of American journalists to their profession; for almost a century it has been the yardstick of reporting in the United States. It is the essential precept by which newsmen have tried to write news that is fair to the news consumers who cannot be present at events or who do not have access to news sources.

Yet in the last decade it has been subjected to criticism, doubt, and, by some, ridicule.

News is the factual report of an event at the time it occurs. It is not the event as a preconception might expect it to be, or as the reporter might wish it, or as those involved in it might like to present it. It reports the facts without prejudice, precisely as they have developed. Though reporters are not always as dispassionate or as literal as a man from Mars might be, they are expected to report events *as they are.*

Objectivity means that the news comes to the consumer untainted by conscious bias or external influence that could make it appear anything but what it is. Most news media act (or pretend or think they act) on the belief that news presentation is inviolable, without slant or deceiving tint. The reporter is expected to look at events through glasses that are neither rose-colored nor smoked. Only assurance that news is "pure" can give the consumer confidence in the reports on which he bases his opinions.

Back in the years when Day and Bennett were offering their revolutionary penny papers to New York, the journals they were challenging were often not newspapers in the modern sense. These papers did not shrink from printing "facts" that were not facts; their view of the facts was colored by what was favored by publisher, editor, or writer. As Elmer Davis put it, these papers printed " . . . 'what helps our side.' No nonsense of fairly reporting what was said on both sides, of giving the other fellow a break. What they printed was what the editor and his political backers wanted." It was when Day and Bennett came along with a new definition of news, with the purpose of giving the facts and letting readers think what they might, that news presentation began to change.

The American Society of Newspaper Editors recognized the principle in 1923, when one of its guides to ethical behavior stated that partisanship in the news columns must be considered "subversive of a fundamental principle of the profession." In 1943 Paul White, who later won a Peabody Award for his achievements as news director of the Columbia Broadcasting System, expressed his conviction that "the fact that objectivity is an ideal difficult to attain ... does not impair the ideal itself nor excuse the broadcaster from a constant and vigilant effort to attain it."

White's "effort to attain it" is impeded by many sorts of obstacles. One

---

"WE CANNOT BE A LITTLE BIT IMPURE"

These are words of an assistant managing editor of the New York Times, *written just after the convulsions that surrounded the Democratic national convention in Chicago in 1968. He went on: "It is understandable that a reporter, viewing the ... violence of Chicago, will be moved by normal human feeling; it is his job to report what happened without adopting a subjective approach. If he reports skillfully, the reader will be able to decide the truth of what happened. It is neither necessary nor desirable to prefix the loaded word 'brutal' to the strong word 'clubbing' ... a sharp line must be drawn between desirable interpretation and undesirable subjectivity, characterization, or editorializing."*

---

is that reporters, like other humans, can never wholly escape the weight of their own psyches. It is no problem for a reporter to state fairly the straight news that the local Society of Ophthalmologists will hear a speaker on optical pathology next Thursday; this simple news puts no strain on reportorial blood pressure. But suppose that on Thursday the speaker branches off into a tirade on welfare payments to employed mothers, and that the reporter holds diametrically opposed opinions. His problem of keeping his own leanings out of the story may be something else again. If he is alert to the problem and faithful to his responsibility, he has a good chance of coming up with an impartial story. But if he doesn't recognize his prejudices, or if wittingly or unwittingly he lets himself serve them, objectivity goes out the window.

And if he starts with a disbelief in objectivity itself, he's sunk. The brilliant young Texas journalist Molly Ivins says wittily, "Objectivity is getting the facts straight and letting the truth go hang." The aphorism itself falls down because its very pungency misses the point. Objectivity is getting *all* of the facts straight and letting each reader find his own truth in them.

Most American newsmen accept the challenge of objectivity; most of the news presented to the American public is reported with a high standard of impartiality. But it would be foolish to deny that lapses occur. A middle-size midwestern daily's publisher fired a reporter who wrote a story that made the publisher's Rotary Club "look bad," even though he admitted the story was fair and accurate; the executive then rewrote the story so that it was neither fair nor accurate. A radio station's news editor said he could never send one of his reporters on a story involving Catholics because the reporter was a pope-hater and couldn't forget it. The Chicago *Tribune* under publisher Robert R. McCormick persistently reported news of British-American relations as though George III were still sending redcoats to Boston, and its pro-Republican bias (which let it report in 1948 that Dewey had defeated Truman for the presidency, a longed-for conclusion to which the *Tribune* jumped before the returns were in) made it notorious for coloring much of its Washington reporting. Sophisticated readers of William Randolph Hearst's newspapers, before his death, knew that anything they printed about the use of animals in medical experimentation was conditioned

---

CAN POLITICAL REPORTING BE OBJECTIVE?

In the national election campaign of 1952, Democrats complained that many newspapers favoring Eisenhower did not give Stevenson a fair share of attention; in 1960 Nixon growled that he had been flagrantly shortchanged; in 1972, said McGovern, the press "painted a negative picture" of him. (Winners rarely call the press names.) Well-documented studies have shown that charges like these arise in every campaign and have more passion than substance. "Republican" papers, in the effort to treat opposing candidates fairly, have often given more space and bigger headlines to the Democrat than to his opponent.

Some candidates are newsmakers, some aren't. In 1972 McGovern conducted a frenzied campaign, and it was voluminously covered; McGovern sometimes made news he regretted, but its fair coverage was not a reasonable accusation against the press. On the other side, Nixon was said to have "campaigned in his bedroom"; he rarely appeared in public, played it cool. The result, no news . . .

Walter Lippmann, commenting on complaint that the news media played only "the sensational side" of Senator Joe McCarthy's red-baiting, said that "McCarthy's charges of treason, subversion, espionage, corruption, perversion, are news which cannot be suppressed or ignored. . . . But with what are the news editors to balance the news of the McCarthy charges? Not, I take it, with news of inspirational talks to the Girl Scouts. . . . Had President Eisenhower . . . refused to cooperate with this gross perversion of the congressional power to investigate, that would have been news that the news editors would have been only too pleased to publish. . . . They would treat it as very big news indeed if it were reliably reported that a President had raised a standard to which the wise and the honest can repair. . . ." Instead, as Lippmann reported, Eisenhower was silent. And silence rarely makes news.

---

by "the old man's" vitriolic hatred of vivisection. Examples like these are well known, but they are not the rule. And that objectivity or prejudice in news is closely linked with personal attitudes is suggested by the fact that, with the deaths of Hearst, McCormick, and archconservative Norman Chandler of the Los Angeles *Times,* news practices of their papers underwent radical upgradings.

Another challenge in the quest for objectivity is the fact that the reporting of facts sometimes fails to depict the totality of a news situation. Objective reporting may assume that the consumer, using his own resources and with no outside help, can apply proper perspective to whatever facts a story gives him—that he can separate the genuine from the phony, the pure from the poisoned, the complete from the fragmentary, the trustworthy and benevolent from the dishonorable and malicious. Even in the nineteenth-century era of political and personal journalism, it was a rare news consumer who could do it for himself; the modern world is so complex that no man can grasp or evaluate it all. No matter how much news he is given, the everyday citizen often cannot untangle the aggregate of facts. The very mass of news may so overwhelm him that he escapes to the comics, the Super Bowl, or the current TV serial about private eyes.

HOW TO BE NONOBJECTIVE

A wire service story out of Lisbon reports a trial of three Portuguese feminists charged with writing a pornographic book. The story includes this sentence: "The three authors are all mothers of young children." This sentence adds the reporter's insinuation that a young child's mother ought to know better.

A story about a paroled convict's insistence that he did not commit murder includes this unattributed clause: "He still wants the truth to emerge about his innocence." Thus the reporter accepts as fact the man's unsupported statement.

A story about discipline in schools carries this passage: "He said things are better than they were 20 years ago. That may be good or it may be bad. But it does make one wonder about all the supposed changes that educators have talked about and journalists have written about in recent years." Thus the reporter, who has not been established as an expert, tells you what he thinks.

When objectivity collides with complexity, it is the reporter's obligation to help the consumer see the facts in perspective—often by providing background or tangential information. It is a fallacy to think that objective reporting discharges fully the newsman's responsibility. Listen again to the perceptive and dedicated Elmer Davis:

> This striving for objectivity was in its beginning a good thing; but it went a little too far. From holding that newspapers ought to present both sides it went on to the position that it was all right to present only one side if nobody happened to be talking on the other; and it was not the business of the newspaper to tell the reader if that one argument happened to be a phony.

> This . . . reached its peak, I think . . . in the administration of Calvin Coolidge, when it was the opinion of a great many American citizens that things are what they seem. In those days, if the Hon. John P. Hoozis was important enough to be interviewed, you might see half or two-thirds of a column embodying his views on some topic or other, with no indication that what he said was a lie from the beginning to end—even if the editor who printed the story happened to know it—and no indication that the Hon. John P. Hoozis might have a powerful personal interest, financial or otherwise, in getting the view over to the public. He had said it; and if it was important enough to be news, it would not have been objective not to print it.[1]

[1] Elmer Davis, *The Press in Perspective,* Louisiana State University Press, 1963, pp. 60–61.

Davis's colorful rhetoric points out that objective reporting, admirable in itself, is not enough in itself. It is admirable to report a speech by a political leader accurately and completely; it is by no means so admirable to report it without mentioning that another leader has previously denied or disproved some of its "facts," or views acknowledged facts differently. A news story should contain, in addition to the clear facts, whatever related information may be necessary to broaden the consumer's perspective. Though objective reporting is the "report of an event as it occurred," a good newsman must frequently report pertinent background information as well as literally observable facts. Unless balanced and complete information is presented in appropriate context, objectivity may only add to the consumer's confusion. It is also true that objectivity is not attained, as one might infer from Davis's last sentence above, by withholding publication of the dishonest claim or the deceitful speech. The newsman's obligation is to print it so that the reader may know that somebody did it, that an event took place, that a candidate lied. The obligation is discharged only by printing it *with* (or closely followed by) whatever clarification is needed.

"OBJECTIVITY IS BULLSHIT"

Renowned reporter David Halberstam delivered this inelegant opinion in answer to a question from a group of journalists in 1973. Halberstam went on to say that competent reporting is "realistic, analytic, and fairminded." If reporting is all of these things, and informed as well, it can hardly fail to be objective in the broad meaning of the term, for it must therefore put what it says into understandable and illuminating context.

Calculated departure from objectivity is a practice of hundreds of news and topical media. The "alternative newspapers" of the 1970s often misrepresent the totality of an event because they talk about only what their readers (or their editors) are interested in. The *Village Voice* of New York, once the voice of the Greenwich Village left, turned into a paper whose point of view dictated its news selection. It gave three columns to the Liebling III counterconvention session (1974) on women's place in journalism (should you use Ms. or not?) but a brushoff to the rest of a meaty program (the counterconvention was a New York meeting of hundreds of rebellious journalists, most of them under thirty-five, who hoped to provide a counterweight to the "Establishment views" expressed at meetings of their publishers and editors). The *Voice* pictured the event falsely not by *how* it was covered but by *what*.

America's journalists were once almost alone in their devotion to objectivity. This is no longer true. In Western Europe today newspapers and broadcasting, often sponsored by special interests or even by government, put a premium on news presentation that is accurate, reliable, complete. The newspapers of the Western world, and those of parts of the Eastern, are adopting American patterns.

The reporter as advocate   The validity of seeking objectivity in news has come under sober, and sometimes angry, question since World War II. Had you listened to after-hours bar talk among newsmen, you might have heard remarks like this: "Objectivity is passé ... dishonest ... unreal. Nobody is objective—everybody has attitudes. Reporting that doesn't show what the reporter thinks is gutless and deceitful. 'Objective' reporting is desensitized, dehumanized, vacuous."

Such comments, usually from relatively young men and women, express the conviction that honest news exposition demands the reporter's response to the facts along with the facts themselves. Reporting, it says, must reflect the reporter as well as the event. A major newspaper recently asked its news staff to express opinions of what has come to be called "personalized," "humanized," "point-of-view," or "the new" journalism. Among the comments of those clearly favoring it:

> We need it to ... help the people relate to the paper by identifying the writer.

> I am female, white, under 30, and well-educated. With the best will in the world I can't perceive the world the way a 45-year-old black man with eighth-grade education would.

And some who favor it with qualifications:

> [I favor] personalizing by experienced hands under reasonable supervision by good editors.

> There are situations in which a reliable, knowledgeable, perceptive reporter should be allowed to fill the interstices between unassailable facts and quotations with his impressions, provided that it is clear they are impressions.

A respected "liberal" journalist and critic, Nat Hentoff of the *Village Voice*, asks the question: "If to be neutral all the time is the only way for a reporter to assure his 'credibility,' has this desensitized way of reporting outrageous events contributed to the deep detachment—or cynicism, if you will —of much of the citizenry?" Hentoff offers an implied "yes" in an article in *Civil Liberties* (1972); but he also qualifies his meaning by distinguishing between reporting facts and commenting on them.

And a *New Republic* critic, John Seelye, says in reviewing a book by Tom Wolfe, one of "the new journalism's" high priests:

> On its plus side, the New Journalism is basically satire—tough, witty, unmerciful to all manner of pretense, immediate, jazzy, alive and terribly readable. On the negative side it is cold, hard, often piously smug, blind to any but urban values (including pastoral sentimentality), phonily "honest," and willing to sacrifice a fact for the Larger Truth.

The qualifications in these comments bring them close to the traditional view of objective reporting held by most experienced hands: It remains an ideal that can be approached even though it can never be fully attained.

ADVERSARY JOURNALISM

Much has been made in recent years of the notion that the press and government are inherently at war. This seems to have grown out of the implicit suggestion in the First Amendment that the government might actively seek to interfere with press performance, and therefore must be enjoined—an idea that has been given support by the naked attempts by the Army, the White House, and other federal agencies, in the 1960s and 1970s, to do so. There is the added fact that the press is the most vigorous and audible critic of government. But to assert that these facts add up inescapably to attempts by either to control the other is unsupportable. The press's function vis-à-vis government is not to fight it but rather to make it possible for people to form judgments about it. A Department of Defense public affairs officer in 1973, Jerry Friedheim, said that "the press is not a partner of the people with both arrayed against government, but rather a bridge between the two. The press has a stake in order; as Eric Sevareid put it, 'We can't defend liberty if we don't have it.' "

If at times the press has a battle to get information, or if at times it trumpets its belief that what government is doing is misconceived, it is not fighting against government but rather for the clientele.

Without objectivity there can be no fair reporting. Objectivity is a tool of impartial treatment; it is a method of reporting, a reportorial attitude, that is fair to both facts and their recipients. Fairness means a great deal more than lack of bias; it means coverage that includes all principal facts, emphasis on what is truly salient, selection of news topics that serve the broad needs of the identified audience, vigilant search to learn for sure what the needs are. None of these would be possible without the objective orientation that starts the whole process going.

This should not be taken to mean that there is anything wrong about advocacy. Tom Paine was an advocate; so were John Milton, Lincoln Steffens, and Walter Lippmann. They held views, and they made abundant use of fact to support and argue in favor of their positions. But when they were writing with the purpose of persuading—when they were advocating—their reporting became secondary. They were not painting scenes in order to let readers come to uninfluenced opinions, but rather to lead readers to see the scenes from the advocate's point of view. Advocacy is a high calling and an honorable one. It should not be called what it isn't.

NEWS IS RECENT

The word *news* itself signalizes the importance of the instant—what is new. It has always been thus. Julius Caesar's Rome invented a form of daily reporting, the *Acta Diurna*, posted in public places in the pre-Christian Forum; though the news in those posterlike news sheets was not always today's or yesterday's, it was the latest available. The invention of printing 500 years ago gave the word *news* a new meaning. The first daily journal in England, the *Daily Courant*, emphasized currency in both of its title words.

Stress on the time context of a story is today taken for granted; news consumers never question it. The world moves fast, and its citizens know that they must run, not walk, to keep up with it. Events are transitory, and what seems true today may not seem true tomorrow. Because news consumers want fresh information, most news stories report events of "today" or, at the most distant, "last night" or "yesterday." News media are carefully specific about time factors to show that their reports—more than merely "recent"—are no less than the last word.

The media have grown expert in handling news fast so as to preserve this last-second quality. A prime stimulus to speed is media competition. The reader demands the current and the new, and every newsman works to give the good or the bad tidings ahead of his rivals. Every news office in America is organized so that it can gather, write, edit, and publish the news swiftly.

The printed media have permanently lost the race for speed. There is no present way that newspapers can gather, write, edit, print, and distribute news as rapidly as broadcasting delivers it. As the newspapers' competitive position has changed, their staffs ask themselves questions they would have done well to ponder before: How valid is speed as a factor in news selection? Is it *always* an important element? Does a man reading the paper really care whether the Legislature's report on public housing reaches him two hours after it is released, rather than two days? If reporters and editors had those two days instead of two hours in which to prepare the news, would they not be likely to turn out more carefully edited, more thorough, and more useful stories?

The torture of accuracy in the name of speed showed up dramatically when, on a winter evening in 1973, a jet airplane slammed into an Alameda, California, apartment house. A TV report within an hour said that 200 people had been killed. The news the next morning changed it to "200 lived in the building; nobody knows how many got out." That evening: "Forty or fifty may have died." Next morning: "Eight bodies found, fourteen missing." And so on until, on the third evening, the report was that eight bodies "and a portion of a ninth" had been found.

Every newsman knows from experience that estimates of deaths in the heat of disaster are exaggerated. It's fair to ask: What would be lost by reporting the major lines of such an event but leaving details for the time when information is dependable?

And how much are the news media the victims of their own passion to get it first? Would news consumers demand frantic speed if the newsmen had not trained them to expect it?

Carl Lindstrom, near the end of his distinguished career as editor of the Hartford *Times,* told an audience of newsmen:

> The newsroom clock is the master of us all. We are slaves to its hurrying hands. There's always the deadline; there's never time to do the job as well

as we would like to do it. . . . We are rushing through the ripe fields grabbing handfuls of golden grain and leaving the big harvest to the gleaners. The rich aftermath goes to the weekly and monthly periodicals of journalism.

Newspapers accept the fact that they can't do it as fast as radio and television. The newspaper extra has almost disappeared (did anybody see an extra reporting the Ford pardon of Nixon in 1974?). Voices like Carl Lindstrom's call for more penetrating and more thorough news treatment by newspaper and broadcaster alike. The quality of news is more to be prized than surface glitter.

NEWS IS CONCISE AND CLEAR

News reporting exists to serve, and to serve best it has developed conventions of form and manner. News presentation, at its optimum, must be digestible fast. That means rhetoric that is concise, clear, and simple. Its effectiveness dwindles as it becomes diffuse, disorganized, ambiguous. Reportorial writing should be terse, direct, and coherent; it should be well-paced, and above all it should be so lucid that it never needs a double take.

It is true that news style is often "bad." A common term for slipshod writing is *journalese*. Prose characterized by trite phrases, loose diction, and banality is stigmatized as "journalistic." But it is frequently said of one of the century's most powerful short stories, Ernest Hemingway's "The Killers," that its dynamic movement grows from its "journalistic style," its spare, intense, racing rhetoric. Journalese is always bad; journalistic style can be, and often is, very good indeed.

Good journalistic style, like that of any kind of writing, is not easy to acquire or to maintain. A newsworker who uses yesterday's clichés instead of fresh and explicit terms, one who writes "convince" when he means "persuade," "cinema star" for "movie actor," or "criminal assault" for "rape" wins no prizes. Nor does the lazy reporter who thinks, "Let the copyreader fix it—that's what he's paid for."

Effective newswriting, though painstakingly precise, gives the effect of fluid ease; it has natural color without flamboyance or rhetorical overkill. It is brief, pointed, faithful, revealing. These are qualities that any writer should seek.

Finally, newswriting is terse for good reasons. One is that tight writing, without side trips or gratuitous decoration, is easy reading. One is that a story that doesn't waste a reader's or listener's time is likely to hold him: the story that bores him loses him. And one is that no newspaper's columns, no broadcasting station's precious seconds, can accommodate all the news that is available; if you report every play in every inning of a baseball game, you have to leave the new coach at Whatsis College entirely unmentioned. Tell the first story in its essentials and you have room for the other.

Projects

1. Select a long news story on a local event—a new shopping center, a veto by the mayor, plans for a St. Patrick's Day celebration. Check every specific fact in it: addresses, dates, times, dollars, everything you find checkable. Use every source you can think of, from city and telephone directories to the men and women named in the story. Then compute a "batting average" for the story—the percentage statement of its accuracy.

2. Select a newspaper report of a local speech, one whose speaker you can reach. Take the story to him and ask his comment on the story, whether he finds it accurate in meaning and fact. If he thinks it in error, find out why.

3. Examine all the stories in one issue of a newspaper (or a news broadcast, though you'll need a tape recorder) and see whether you can discern instances of reportorial opinion or bias. Write a commentary on your findings.

4. Edit a long newspaper story to see whether you can "tighten it up"—eliminate unneeded words, phrases, or paragraphs to make it move faster.

Related Reading

Thomas Griffin, *How True: A Skeptic's Guide to Believing the News*, Atlantic-Little, Brown, 1974. — Well-written and well-supported opinion—mostly favorable to the press—on such topics as news bias, newsman's ethics, and how journalists work.

CHAPTER FOUR

News:
selection, evaluation,
emphasis

Not everything that happens becomes news. Most things most people do and say during a day go unchronicled and unremembered. Most men and women pass through weeks, months, and years without taking part in events that are newsworthy. They live their daily lives, they work and eat and sleep and play, without experiences that must be reported. Sometimes they venture into the periphery of news events: they go to baseball games, watch parades, vote in elections. But they are secondary, not primary, participants.

Once in a while their personal adventures get into the papers. Suppose that the city hall elevator, which has operated without mishap for twenty-seven years, is equipped one morning with brand-new safety doors. That day the safety doors crush the operator's fingers. Neither the elevator nor the operator ever broke into print before; but now the city hall reporter writes a brief story that earns front-page space. Somebody has decided that a minor event should not be tossed into limbo, that it merits a place in the daily record. It becomes news.

How is the decision made? Who or what turns an event into news? What makes some events "better" than others? How are stories selected?

To answer these questions, this chapter will examine the theory and the practices that guide professional newsmen's selection and evaluation of news. Whoever they are, whatever their background, news experts are not demigods with celestial intuition. Like most humans, they work and make their decisions in an environment studded with guideposts.

News stories do not develop in a vacuum. On the contrary, they are integral with their era and their society. Social customs, history, geography, economics, and other conditioners affect the meaning of an event and determine its value as the stuff of news. The conditioning factors are so well known to newsworkers that two (or twenty, or two hundred) newsmen, given the same group of events from which to select, would make substantially the same decisions. The decisions would vary in some details because of differing audience requirements and explicit medium limitations—some events that earn newspaper space, for example, are not reported on the air—but in the important respects their selections would coincide. (Such standardization imposes the danger of a news diet that is too uniform and too unimaginative. More of this later—see "News in Ruts," page 59.)

NEWS DEFINED

A few of many definitions of news:

"News is anything timely that interests a number of persons, and the best news is that which has the greatest interest for the greatest number."—Willard Grosvenor Bleyer

"News is what a well-trained editor decides to put in his paper."—Gerald W. Johnson

"News is usually stimulating information from which the ordinary human being derives satisfaction or stimulation."—Chilton R. Bush

"... to many newspapermen no news is bad news, good news is dull news, and bad news makes marvelous copy."—Leo Rosten

This book's definition: "News is the timely report of facts or opinion that hold interest or importance, or both, for a considerable number of people."

Let it be said quickly that no precise or codified rules exist. The newsman does not have a list labeled "Components of News" pasted over his desk; IBM has not yet developed a computer that determines which stories ought to be published and which rejected. Nevertheless, even a beginner in newswork, with years of newspaper reading and broadcast listening, has a fairly good idea of what makes news, and the news veteran has his rules of thumb ready for almost automatic application.

Any professional can describe the requirements of "good" news—news that is worth carrying to an audience. Some of the requisites are sharp and obvious, some so subtle that their description is difficult. Although different professionals define news differently, however, they usually agree on two main requirements—significance and interest.

As the reporters collect facts and write stories, as the editors evaluate the

stacks of copy that cross their desks, there are two questions that continually cross their subconscious minds: "Is this something that will affect our
particular audience?" and "Will it *grab* them?" Reporters or deskmen are
rarely aware they are using so precise a significance-interest analysis, but
they go through the process perhaps a thousand times a day. They do it at
top speed, for news practice gives little time—the more's the pity—to stop
and think it over.

How do they make their rapid-fire decisions? They start with those two
underlying questions. Newsworkers know that if a story is to attract and
hold audience attention, it must affect a considerable number of people,
or appeal to their interests or emotions, or both. To be either significant or
interesting, a news story must relate to a particular audience, whether national or limited by geographical, cultural, economic, or other factors. A
report about the development of a new fertilizer means more in an agricultural area of Iowa than in a shoe-manufacturing town in Massachusetts;
and it is a "better" story today, in an age of food shortages and tired soil,
than it would have been in 1880.

The significance and appeal of any story must be evaluated in terms of a
specific audience. Although no audience is fully homogeneous—every group
larger than a table of bridge has individuals with widely differing characteristics and needs—the newsman hopes to select news that will satisfy as
many interests as possible.

RESPONSIBILITY FOR NEWS
DECISIONS

No responsibility in any news medium is as heavy as that of the editor who
makes its news decisions. His judgments govern whether a newspaper or
a newscast serves its clientele well or badly. If he looks down on his audience, if he bases decisions on expediency and audience figures, if he grows
mentally fat and lets news stereotypes make his judgments, or if he fails to
keep abreast of the impulses and yearnings and life currents of his time,
he cannot fulfill his public's expectations. If, on the other hand, his attitudes and decisions grow out of experience and sound background, out of
broad sympathy and a recognition of society's dependence on the quality
of its information, he is likely to earn his colleagues' approval and his community's respect.

What are the lines of responsibility for news decisions?

The organization chart of a newspaper is usually headed by a publisher,
that of a broadcasting station by a general manager. This functionary is
likely to be the owner or to represent ownership, and in the American economic system the buck stops there—his decisions are final. But in large-
scale operations—metropolitan newspapers, large-market broadcasting—the
news-decision buck rarely reaches him. In a typical large newspaper the
head of the news operation is the managing editor; his colonels, majors,

and captains are the news editor, other desk editors, and subdepartment heads (no two patterns are just alike). Major news decisions in big newspaper offices are often made at daily "news conferences," where the principal editors examine the day's prospective news and decide how it is to be treated and emphasized. (The wire services term the daily schedule of upcoming stories the "news budget.") Lesser decisions are made by the city editor and his assistants, often following the recommendations of the men and women who actually gather the news, the reporters. Decisions on wire news are made by the news conference and the wire, news, and telegraph editors, as well as by the head of the copydesk, where news copy is polished and headlines are written.

Smaller newspapers and broadcast news operations follow the same general lines of organization. More details about these patterns of operation appear in Chapters 7, 8, 9, and 10.

Reporters also are constantly making news decisions—decisions whether to spend time on this story or that. Their judgments are likely to take the form of recommendations to the city desk, where they are subject to review (in practice, they are usually honored).

What qualifies a newsworker to make decisions? Ideally, he[1] should be gifted with intelligence, perception, and social purpose, as well as such personality traits as a skeptical curiosity, imagination, sympathy, and energy. He usually has had specialized news training and education; he should start building on-the-job news experience before he graduates from algebra if he can, and keep adding to it unceasingly. There are other roads: William Randolph Hearst was given the opportunity to put his remarkable journalistic talents to work by his father's millions; Edward R. Murrow came to radio and world renown from a background in education and public affairs; I know two excellent newspaper reporters who had their first journalism lessons on state prison journals. But for the most part those who decide which events have the makings of news are well grounded in news experience. The responsibility for news decisions is one that calls day after day for what is colloquially called know-how. And it also calls for what sometimes seem superhuman qualities of understanding, tolerance, forthrightness, and courage. That mere mortals perform consistently in the public interest is a continuing marvel of twentieth-century journalism.

DECISIONS ABOUT SIGNIFICANCE

"Is it of consequence to a good share of my audience?" is a primary question an editor asks himself as he looks at an event. During the years of the Vietnam slaughter, war news had ready meaning for almost everybody; it

---

[1] The masculine pronoun to mean two sexes is a space- and time-saver as well as a rhetorical convention. Most things males can do females can do at least as well. One that both can avoid is unproductive wordplay.

affected everything from the price of pork to styles in shoes and movies. Not all war news has the same value; in the 1970s an editor had to ask himself, "How much space do we give border fighting between Israelis and the Palestinian guerrillas?" The news media reported it as part of the day's events because any such international flareup may have dynamite underneath. But they gave more attention to the war in Vietnam, a war that cut intimately into American lives. Many people had some kind of contact with servicemen and -women; the national pocketbook was pinched; passions were aroused in Washington and in Bangor, Flagstaff, and Des Moines; the national future was clouded.

The relevance of location to news significance shows clearly in evaluation of election news. The election of a senator in Arizona is obviously big news to Arizonans, and Arizona media cover it abundantly. In Pennsylvania the same news has no local significance, but the election of a senator anywhere can affect John Doe in Pennsylvania, and the media in Pennsylvania give it space. Those same media may find neither national nor local significance in the election of a mayor just across the state line in Youngstown, Ohio; they may not report even his name. But the Youngstown paper gives the story banner lines, and those in Cleveland, Columbus, and Cincinnati report it in some detail.

Geographical factors show themselves in other ways. Suppose the Department of the Interior decides to open previously closed areas of a Minnesota national forest to big-game hunters. Newsmen in Indiana, which boasts neither a national forest nor a wild animal larger than a buck deer, pay little attention. Newsmen in Oregon, with forestlands and game similar to those in Minnesota, give the event space because it might happen to their own forests. Media in Minnesota not only give the news prominence but make it the peg for "local angle" stories—stories that show graphically the impact of the action on Minnesota hunters, the Minnesota resort industry, and the conservation of wildlife in the state.

The geographical factor is a variant among media and areas and from one decade to the next. Radio stations of different powers have different ranges and, therefore, quite different audience areas—areas measured in states for a fifty-kilowatt clear-channel station, in counties for a 250-watter. The speedup in transportation has widened the newspaper's area: air freight and fast trucks make it possible to "lay down" a morning paper at 7 a.m. on doorsteps hundreds of miles from the point of publication. As the audience widens, dominant characteristics and interests change, and the news selected must reflect the changes.

The numbers game   The significance of news may be determined by the size of the audience segment on whose lives an event makes direct contact. Every man in Youngstown is somehow affected by the election of a new mayor, and the event is reported locally in detail. But the election of a chairman of the crewel-and-macramé section of the Women's Library Club gets only four lines in the paper and no air time because few local residents besides the new chairman's husband (and her sisters and her cousins and her aunts) would find the event of interest.

The size of the community affects news selection. Newspapers and broadcasters in large cities give small notice to the ordinary affairs of the private citizen, or even to such organized or semipublic activities as the sewing group's choice of a new chairman. In some small towns, however, the weekly paper and the local radio station report cases of chickenpox, shopping trips to the nearby city, and the town druggist's plan to build a third bedroom over his garage. A good many barbs have been aimed at the small-community newspapers that report blessed events in the barnyard and write that "Grocer Sam Bilker has painted his front," but the barbs ignore the relative significance of the small event in the small world.

"Big names"   The run-of-the-mill affairs of the ordinary citizen—butcher, baker, candlestick-maker—do not make news, but the slightest variation in the routine of the Dignitary or the Celebrity must be reported. Nobody notices when most of us have colds, but sniffles along the Potomac or aboard the Onassis yacht are heard around the world. A globe-circling vacation by a textile manufacturer from Birmingham, Alabama, is worth only a note in a local society column, but a modest weekend of a British princess or an American cabinet officer is enveloped by newsmen, and the details are reported in hour-by-hour stories from Ketchikan to Khartoum. What in one case is a private affair becomes in the other a matter of concern to millions.

HOW MUCH DETAIL?

The clinical detail with which illnesses at famous addresses are reported has drawn critical fire. Nobody denied, when President Eisenhower suffered heart and intestinal ailments, that the news had importance, but the intimacy with which the President's troubles were described was thought by many to be in bad taste. Bad taste, too, was a charge against the drawn-out and repetitive series of reports about former President Truman's final illness and about the breast surgery performed on President Ford's wife.

Breadth of impact   Relatively unimportant events sometimes achieve a spurious importance by virtue of the wide interest they attract. The Super Bowl each January can hardly be said to have lasting effect on more than a few hundred Americans, but no yearly event gets more attention. Newsmen argue that the World Series, for a full October week holding fifty million Americans glued to their TV sets, and thus for a brief period altering the pace and texture of national life, acquires an importance that has nothing to do with its intrinsic content.

The relativity of news   All of this indicates that the significance of a given news story is relative. An event is important primarily because of the extent of its influence on the lives of those who learn of it. Some news is important for everybody, everywhere. But much news is important only in limited context; the conditioning factors are the radius of an event's influence, its power to attract attention and stimulate response, and its relation to a community's size and composition.

Hard and soft news News that is significant for relatively large numbers of people is often called hard news. This is the news of government activity, of politics, of international relations, of education, of religion, of legislatures, courts, and most public and private civic activities—sober news. And, to most audiences, dull news. This kind of news is not always easy to understand, and often makes difficult reading. Hard news draws smaller audiences, though it is commonly of greater moment than soft news—human-interest stories, news of crime and lust and comedy—that attracts people more readily. This anomaly is the challenge and the despair of every newsworker. Graphs are not needed to demonstrate that most news consumers would rather hear about the latest nose bloodied by a top movie player in a Las Vegas casino, remote as the event may be, than about the recent devaluation of the dollar. Though devaluation may mean that they'll eat less U. S. choice beef next year, it's more fun to learn what Frankie did to Dean (or vice versa).

"INTERESTING" NEWS

Reporters have a traditional after-hours game, speculation about the event that would make the "biggest" news story. Their inventions range from the solemn to the absurd, the irreverent to the catastrophic. During World War I the death of the Kaiser was a favorite "event," and in World War II this became the deaths of Hitler and Mussolini (fantasy that became spectacular fact and drew enormous headlines). Some suggest the Second Coming; some the discovery of a cure for cancer; some the first giant step by a man on Mars. Each of these events would be of high importance, but each would also have a powerful popular interest; each would not only shake the world but also make brisk talk over every breakfast table, every lunch pail, every cocktail glass.

FOUR SURE-FIRE ELEMENTS

A sardonic example of what might make the "best" news grew from a reporter's statement, at an after-hours reportorial seminar, that what readers want is news of sex, royalty, the deity, and mystery. Get them all together, said this man, and you have the biggest of all news. His example: "My God," said the Duchess, "I'm pregnant! Who done it?"

An event of high interest may, it is clear, be of little genuine significance. Just as some important events leave the public apathetic, so some vastly interesting occurrences are important only to their participants. As the news-men's game suggests, however, importance and interest often come in the same package. When this happens, journalists beam. They have news that not only gives the audience something solid but that also will be listened to, read, remembered.

To select news high in interest, the reporter or editor must know what impels attention to news and what leads to preference for one kind of news fare over another. One generalization can safely be offered about all audiences: They give closest attention to news when they can reasonably expect to "get something out of it." They give eye and ear to news when it promises to fulfill some need or desire, whether it is recognized or below the horizon of their awareness.

What kinds of news will an average family—parents and two high school children—want to get when they pick up the evening paper or turn on the six o'clock TV news? They will be offered three broad groups of news materials:

1. "Important" news that will somehow affect their lives and futures. They want to know the size of the paving assessment to be added to local taxes next year. They are concerned about the *coup d'état* in the Middle East—didn't somebody say it might start another war? They wonder whether the new school building will be ready for the coming fall. The degree of attention they give to the subjects varies from one individual to another. Each will respond according to the extent a given topic seems related to his own life.

2. As average Americans, they spend a major share of their time with news that entertains them. They chuckle over the zookeeper locked in a cage by a monkey. Some of them want the sports news, some the human-interest feature about a dangerous canoe trip. They attend closely to stories that arouse their sympathy, that make them angry, that thrill or surprise or amuse. They may all spend time on news of movie personalities, of the latest bank holdup, or the promise of a sunny day.

3. In varying degrees they give time to non-news material that will help them to "better themselves" (there's more of this in the paper than on TV). They study columns on buying more economically, bidding better bridge, getting along with the neighbors, building better bird feeders. As they read about the effects of smoking on their lungs, they congratulate themselves . . . or wonder whether they shouldn't try again to drop the habit.

When they have taken what they want from the columns of the paper, they are through with it; they let it fall with a casual "nothing else here."

Responses to hard and soft news   Experienced editors and reporters know the relative values in the two broad groupings of news, hard and soft. They base their news selection on an understanding of the impulses that lead the news consumer to react faster, and often more vigorously, to human-interest news than to informative, significant news.

News of dollar devaluation is important—the news consumer grants that. Why, then, is it difficult for most readers to settle down for a nice relaxed ten minutes with a story about federal money manipulation? The devaluation story tells about appropriations and expenditures, it names figures in millions and billions, it lists congressional committees, it reports senatorial approval or indignation. But all these facts, for the average reader, might have come from Tierra del Fuego instead of Capitol Hill. Devaluation isn't a topic to which he can relate personal experience. He has no way of putting himself in the place of a congressman who has to vote on the matter. He possesses no picture of the legislative labyrinth through which financial proposals must work their way; sums in billions of dollars might as well be in light-years or feather beds. There may be nothing in the story to show him how the new dollar will affect his take-home pay, his plan to start building a new house in the spring, or his hope that he and the wife and kids may be able to swing a couple of weeks at that nice fishing lake. He finds no points of contact between his own life and the complex facts the story relates.

The puzzled man glances briefly at the story, mutters something about a lower income next year, and turns to the story in the next column. This one is about a local high school girl who yesterday beat all the experts in the week's contest for the biggest panfish taken from the county's lakes. He reads this story with close attention; he smiles at the three-column photograph showing the bikini-clad girl holding her fish up for the judge to weigh. Perhaps he calls out to his wife to say that next week he'd better get in on this—he could use one of those outboard motors they're handing out as prizes.

STRAIGHT NEWS

Newsmen use the terms straight news and features. Straight news is news that is presented "straight," in the conventional straight-forward news story form, for informative purpose. The term feature has many meanings (see Chapter 18). It defines news whose prime purpose is to entertain or supplement rather than to inform. Straight news may be either hard or soft; the term applies to the form of presentation, not to the story's content.

Why has this story captured him? Because he can relate it to himself. It's a local story; he might fish in the lake it mentions, and he could easily enter the contest. He may not know the girl or her family, but her address may mean something to him. And the image of the teen-age girl is a specific image, not something off on another planet, like the devalued dollar. Moreover, the story includes competition, which is always interesting—a contest, a winner, some losers. There's a touch of comedy in the fact that a seventeen-year-old girl came out ahead of older, more experienced, better-equipped men. And the bathing suit picture, though it is discreet enough, piques his interest (and that of his wife—readership studies show higher interest in "cheesecake" pictures among women than among men).

The fish contest story is loaded with elements that hold audience atten-tion, that help readers to identify with the tale it tells; it is a story about humans, not about abstruse concepts. As news people put it, it is strong in human interest.

HUMAN-INTEREST NEWS

A story strong in human interest is one that has emotional impact through eye or ear. It makes you say "For gosh sakes," "What a shame!" "Wish I'd been there," "Sure glad I wasn't." Hard news often has human-interest ele-ments—the shooting of President Kennedy was close to the satirical ex-ample on page 49. But the "pure" human-interest story does not require the element significance. It establishes emotional contact quickly, and it pro-vides an emotional rather than an intellectual experience. When a story horrifies a reader or makes him laugh, saddens or angers him, appeals to his self-interest, he becomes a vicarious participant. Such a story, with a grip on his emotions, requires less concentration and effort than hard news demands.

Several of the components of news described in Chapter 3 may be of little importance in human-interest news. If a story makes its readers laugh, they don't notice that it's a week old. If its writer shows clearly that he's moved by the pathos he's developing, his subjectivity may be forgiven.

Human-interest news is published or broadcast, obviously, to entertain. It is rare that a newspaper goes to press without a seasoning of this kind of content—news of the child who falls into a well, the athlete crippled by an accident, a gangland murder, a student who breaks out of jail to take his final exam, a starlet who marries a prince. Everybody knows that such stories are easy to digest even though they are seldom enriching.

HUMAN INTEREST ON THE AIR

Radio newscasts carry a lower proportion of human-interest news than do either TV or the printed press. Radio often has less elbow room, with its many three-minute newscasts. Television has been charged with devoting too much time to murders, spectacular fires, and pretty faces; but TV human-interest news in recent years is likely to be news of conflict and personality rather than of cheesecake and petty disaster. It remains a fact of TV news life, nevertheless, that it is easier to present good pictures of a high school girl who won a fishing contest than of a proposal to devalue the dollar.

Adventure and conflict   Since most humans respond to adventure and contest, newsmen give a degree of priority to news of war, athletics, ex-ploration. The extent of newspaper sports pages and the domination of Saturday and Sunday afternoons by televised sports measure the media's awareness of the pulling power of athletic rivalries and of the hero worship accorded the man who can run faster, punch harder, or throw straighter than anybody else. News of crime and violence, news of conflict, is moving news; critics insist that too much of it is given the public. (Reliable studies show that from 2 to 10 percent of newspaper space goes to crime news.) Editors point out that failure to report crime and violence would be failure to report the world as it is. They are aware of the obligation to keep its use in balance; a study in the 1960s showed that Indiana newspapers' use of the crime news provided them by wire services was in almost exact proportion to their use of the other types of news they received. You don't need readership studies to know that audiences like to read crime news; and some newspapers and radio stations (few television stations) overplay it. The decline of newspaper competition, however, has meant that the newspaper that plasters this kind of customer bait throughout its pages is about as hard to find as a Model T Ford.

A question asked at the Liebling III convention (see page 37)—"Is the press being held for ransom?"—underlined a burgeoning problem in crime reporting and news evaluation: the "publicity crime," as *The New Yorker* called it. The case in point was the Patricia Hearst kidnapping—a crime in which, as *The New Yorker* (June 3, 1974) said, "an extremist group virtually without power commits, or threatens to commit, spectacular but senseless outrages in order to gain visibility and a small amount of leverage." The dilemma of how kidnappings should be covered is a journalist's headache: Do you report all the news you can get as fast as you can get it, regardless of consequence? Or do you go along with law officers' requests to keep the facts hidden either for the safety of the victim or the recovery of the ransom? The news media have answered this question both ways, and it is by no means clear that silence always serves best. Most media are inclined to hold back, as long as the cover holds firm; but the cases in which wide news coverage has contributed to happy outcomes are frequent.

The "publicity crime," however, presents added puzzles. "If publicity crimes are propaganda," *The New Yorker* goes on, "they are also real events. ... The question that the newsmen face is whether someone who commits murder to get on television should have his wish granted." One suggestion is that the best way to handle such news is to report it, but in a low key —let the world know it happened, but don't spotlight it. No solution that satisfies everybody has been found.

Nor has any computer puzzled out the moral and social enigma of the role of crime news as a breeder of crime. Knowledge of any kind of social behavior, whether "good" or "bad," is unquestionably a stimulant to imitation. Airplane hijacking became epidemic in the early 1970s in part because its illusory profits (as well as its spectacular excitement) were made so widely known. The spate of kidnappings a year or so later enjoyed the same nourishment. But social psychologists believe that notoriety is more likely to affect the form of criminal misbehavior than to act as its seed.

And journalists point out properly that deviant activities cannot be corrected or controlled if they are not known. The arguments for suppression of crime news because it is a repugnant model are self-defeating.

Blair Justice of the Houston *Post* found by querying journalists that the emphasis given crime news is often repulsive to the reporters and editors who provide it. "They have less taste for blood and guts than they get credit for," he concluded. But they believe the public has a right to ugly news that helps to describe their society.

Proximity Being close to a news event gives it added interest for the consumer, and often added importance. A man can relate more readily to an auto smashup, a union picket line, or a campaign speech if he can picture its scene, place it among people he knows, or imagine himself as spectator or participant.

Proximity may mean more than physical distance. The man reading about the girl who won the fishing contest has heightened interest if he recognizes the winner as that kid who used to sell his wife Girl Scout cookies. The football fan who has been at the game is likely to be a more interested reader of the next day's story than the man who didn't attend. The father of the tailback who went ninety yards for a touchdown is a searching reader.

Humor Every editor wants his customers to chuckle now and then; the leaven that humor and irony provide is in high demand. It is also in short supply. News that is genuinely comic is hard to find; the humorous story can rarely be planned in advance. It is usually unforeseen, and it has to be caught on the wing—the story of a fire delivered to the fire station (see page 306) or the one about the thugs who cracked a safe and made off with $500,000 in stage money. A few papers are blessed with reporters who can turn out humorous features several times a week; but every "funny" writer produces his share of duds. The "brights," brief comic stories with which some newscasters like to conclude their programs, are often pretty dull. High level for humorous stories is hard to maintain not only because writing them requires special talent but also because the makings of them are scarce.

Pathos-bathos In the heyday of yellow journalism many city newspapers employed "sob sisters" (often cigar-chewing males) who supplied daily tear-jerkers; their excesses and their cynical insincerity brought news of human distress under suspicion. Although the sob sister is no longer a staff fixture, the news media are alive to the human-interest appeal of the story about the babies orphaned by a tornado or the courageous invalid who died just before treatment reached him; they use such stories as they come along. Any staff member is expected to be able to write effective stories about suffering and sorrow. Today's mode is one of restraint and moderation; the fine art of understatement has kept many writers on the safe side of bathos.

The "sex-angle"   Since the Victorian era it has been respectable to acknowledge that men and women respond actively to the sex stimulus. The
news media did not wait for the decline of Victorian prissiness to recognize
the sales value of the love nest; beginning with Ben Day, sex crimes and
unconventional boy-girl relationships were played and overplayed. Emphasis on love triangles, divorce among notables, and adultery came to a peak
in the 1920s, during the circulation wars among New York tabloids. Since
then, most media have held such news within bounds. Occasional stories,
such as the infamous trial of Charlie Chaplin on Mann Act charges in 1943
or the call-girl "scandals" in London more recently, have gone overboard,
with an intemperance that repelled thoughtful newsworkers and readers
alike.

Changing times   The changing mores governing sex relations and the open-
ness with which they are discussed and pictured appear to justify two forecasts: News and views of sexual activities, as well as portrayal of nudity,
will decline in audience-pulling power, and their journalistic use will become
dependent on genuine news value rather than on their declining power to
shock or titillate. Most American news media in 1972 used the tragic picture
of a naked little Vietnamese girl running toward the camera to escape the
fire that had burned her clothes off her. Television, which once gauged its
subject matter for a "living-room audience," one with first-graders and
grandparents, now goes into bedrooms and almost under the covers. The
editor of the *Atlantic* stated it as the policy of his thoughtful and traditionally conservative magazine that it would use whatever language was appropriate to its subject matter.
  Signs of this trend abound. Where people once blushed or smirked when
they used the euphemism "four-letter word," they now use the word itself.
In the 1930s Ernest Hemingway larded *For Whom the Bell Tolls* with the
clumsy substitution of *obscenity* for such words, or sometimes of *obscenity
obscenity obscenity* when he wanted to be really emphatic. Norman Mailer,
in his novel of World War II *The Naked and the Dead,* invented thinly veiled
substitutes, as did *Esquire* some years later in its sniggering report of movie
stars' love making at Puerto Vallarta. Today writers and editors use the
words that mean what they want to say—conventional words when appropriate, or four-letter colloquialisms when they clearly fit the case.

The odd and the unusual   Critics have deplored the emphasis in news handling on the extraordinary—the freak accident, the two-headed calf, the man
who mislaid an elephant. That the atypical proves a useful and often valid
basis for news selection is evident: A wedding at the First Presbyterian
Church is not page-1 news, but if the bridegroom shows up on a stretcher it
is interesting and possibly important. Only the vital-statistics column reports the birth of a single child, but triplets get a paragraph, quadruplets call

for annual birthday stories, and quintuplets remain news all their belea-guered lives. The news media are eager to present the odd and the unusual because readers give quick attention to departure from routine, and because news of it brings color into the gray sameness of the day's fare. News high on the oddity scale doesn't have to be important. Few lives are affected when a Missouri family names all five of its sons Joe. But the odd facts get broadcast and print attention everywhere, and maybe even a spot on late-night TV.

Critics say that emphasis on the unusual leads to a glorification of the unique, the strange, or the atypical. The comment has merit. Yet if the media excluded all news of "abnormal" events (and who is to decide what is normal?), they would be implying that every current in their communities runs flat and placid—no misbehavior, no accidents, no ruptures of the local calm, no change from yesterday. Critics who ask that news of odd or unpleasant activity be suppressed because it is not representative seem to accept a worse kind of misrepresentation: That there is no abnormal or anti-social behavior they want to know about. Just as society must in self-pro-tection pay attention to the asocial minority who rob, slug, or defraud, so must the news media report such activities. You can't treat a sore thumb if you don't know that it's sore.

"Good" news   A letter to the editor that comes in a thousand versions but always says the same thing goes on like this: "Why do you give us only the news of the bad things that happen? We'd like to hear about husbands who help with the dishes as well as those who beat up their families." A retired Southern California wire service man wrote a weekly column of "good news" and sold it to nearly 200 newspapers a few years ago. Interest in it dwindled, however, and papers discontinued it (largely, its author thinks, because it was becoming repetitious: "The differences in good news were only in datelines and names, not in 'news plots' "). The *Saturday Review* had failed with a similar column some years before, for some of the same reasons.

A selection of stories composed entirely of rays of sunshine, whatever their glow, fails to picture the world as it is. The *Saturday Review* is quick to report that some plays, books, and movies are bad. Balance is the word for competent news selection.

James Reston put it differently: "It is not the earthquakes but the tides of history to which more attention should go," he told a Columbia University audience. "It is the slow, quiet changes of the family, the scientific labora-tory, and the computer that are changing the fabric of the world, and it is reporting these changes that leaves too much to be desired."

Reston did not advocate silence about the "earthquakes." The spot news, about violence or anything else, must be reported, he said. "But we should give as much space to the quiet news, the underlying news of change...."

Self-interest   A psychological truth that journalists translate into copy is the fact that a man is interested in events that affect his well-being. Self-interest will lead him to read a Washington story about a social security plan rather than one about a foreign-aid program; the first promises to benefit him directly, the second indirectly or not at all. He willingly spends time on news of advances in his own profession or business; he wants to know about medical developments that augur better health for him and his family; he reads attentively about better housing, better clothing, better foods, better personal appearance.

JOURNALIST AS PSYCHOLOGIST

Every newsman is a practicing psychologist; he depends in some measure on his sensitivity to human responses and reactions. Part of any reporter's assignment is a grasp of the fundamentals of applied psychology. College training and wide reading will supply knowledge, but knowledge becomes understanding only when it is combined with relevant experience.

Names   One way to give a reader a sense of personal association with the news is to salt it with names. Thus the shopworn but valid axiom that "names make news." Small-community papers publish many columns of "personals" where specific names provide direct contacts for hundreds of readers.

Almost as interesting as what the reader knows by personal experience is what he knows because he has seen or heard it in the news—the name that has prominence, notoriety, or perhaps only a familiar ring. The trifling event involving the well-known citizen gets play in the news because the reader draws on an established attitude toward the familiar name; it has a personal meaning, even though no real contact is involved.

The small event built around the big name—a sore throat in the White House—may have importance as well as personal interest.

THE TIME ELEMENT

The time of a news event—when it occurred, when it will occur—is an essential component of any news story. Time is a vital element in the selection and evaluation of news . (Time element and speed are not the same thing: The former is a statement of the time of events; the latter is the relation of time of publication to the time the news became available.)

For instance, a story tells that the mayor announced at the Council meeting *yesterday* that he will name a new commissioner of taxation *Tuesday.* There are two time elements already—*yesterday* and *Tuesday.* There could be more, for the story could go on to say that the new commissioner will take office on *July 1.*

Yesterday in this example is the basic time element because it tells when the event happened and shows that it could not have been reported earlier. But the story would not be complete without the added time orientations. The reader would be unable to *place* the mayor's announcement or the developments that are to follow if all the times were not stated. "Readers often like to identify themselves with news stories," says a New York editor; "thus they are interested not only in the place but also in the time the event occurred. 'Where was I when that boy was pulled to safety off the ledge at One Fifth Avenue?' they ask."

Two qualities related to the time element—timeliness and seasonableness —may give news materials validity even when they have no currency.

Timeliness   A story is timely if it is appropriate to the audience at the time it is printed or broadcast. The difference between current news and timely news shows up in the treatment of material in a newspaper celebrating its city's hundredth birthday. On the peak day of the celebration, the paper publishes a special edition. In the news section the reader finds the details of the celebration—where the parade will pass, what the speaker said at last night's rally, what the governor said in his congratulatory message. All this is fresh news about current events, with a clear time element. In a second section the paper prints historical articles, stories of the city's founding and its pioneers, as well as speculation about its future, the changes that the next quarter-century will bring. None of this information is recent; it is not news in the usual sense of the word. Yet its strong timeliness, its appropriateness to the time at which it is published, gives it special meaning.

TIME COPY

Not everything that a news medium presents is news. In addition to current and timely material, there is usually matter that has no relation at all to current affairs. Examples are entertainment features, comic strips and cartoons, and columns of household, family, and medical advice and comment. Newsmen use the all-inclusive term "feature" to blanket in all such material (see Chapter 18).

Much of such material is what is called time copy, which could be published in a month as appropriately as today. Time copy (timeless might be a better adjective) is not pegged to a day, date, or season. It is something the editor keeps under his desk blotter to pull out on the day the news slows up—the local history tale, the feature telling where the Gregorian calendar came from, the story recounting all the attempts to climb Mt. Everest or swim the Channel.

Seasonableness   Timeliness that is tied to a particular period of the year or a season is seasonableness, timeliness of a special kind. Seasonable stories may be appropriate to natural seasons such as spring, the winter-storm period, harvest time, or to holiday periods: Christmas, the Fourth of July, Halloween, Easter. A news story about the increase of toy production in the United States piques readers' interests if it is published during the Christmas season; in July it would lack seasonableness (except for toy manufacturers or importers, whose key season comes in summer). An article on the protection of tulip bulbs during the winter is seasonable only if it appears in the fall. A story about a well-known accident to a cherry tree gets space on February 22, but it's out of place at other times.

Much that is worth reporting because of timeliness or seasonableness is not properly news since it has no current or recent time element. Historical articles are not news, nor are those about the origin of April Fool's Day, cherry trees, or witches on broomsticks. On the other hand, genuine news may be enhanced if it is also seasonable. A story in early February about a newly unearthed set of Abraham Lincoln letters, important at any time of year, gains interest because it appears close to February 12.

NEWS IN RUTS

Older American newsmen remember the bleak day that the upside-down stomach became news. When physicians discovered in a little girl a congenital disarrangement of some of her abdominal plumbing, they decided to take her to a distant hospital for corrective surgery. A reporter coined the phrase "upside-down stomach." Since the child and her family did not resist the spotlight, the story was a permissible news enterprise. It attracted national interest, the wire services loved it, and the upside-down stomach became table talk from California to Eastport, Maine.

Suddenly upside-down stomachs appeared everywhere. If one upside-down stomach was news, editors seemed to believe, a lot of them were bigger news. The wire services dutifully reported each new case. Newsmen allowed themselves to become both perpetrators and victims of a news stereotype. They finally tired of it, but not before a good many of their customers had lost interest. Finally, one commendably curious reporter revealed that medical men were snickering because neither the upside-down stomach nor the corrective surgery was uncommon.

The newswriters and editors had been misled by their adherence to a defensible principle governing news emphasis: Give the audience what interests it. Here was a subject rich in human interest. It had oddity, it had pathos, it had suspense. It was soft news, easy to grasp. What too many newsmen forgot, however, was that the story gained in banality each time it was retold. In its first telling it had originality, warmth, immediate reward. But as newsmen belabored it—"If it was good yesterday, isn't it good today?"—it moved quickly from fresh to stale.

The upside-down stomach case is an exaggerated example of a common problem. Let a reporter with more enterprise, more imagination, or more luck than his fellows develop a news angle that others have missed, and they are likely to fall in line and work it to an anguished death. When a Philadelphia newspaper reported that a bobbed-haired bandit had taken part in a gang robbery, bobbed-hair bandits popped up on every street corner. The number of flying saucers reported a few years back would have obscured the sun.

It is not hard to define the causes of news fads. For one thing, it's easier to follow a well-marked news trail than to blaze a new one. For another, audiences build up interest rapidly in odd news. A third cause is that merely reporting an odd event may lead to its replication. Harassed college authorities as well as many readers and listeners recall the panty raids of the recent past. They might never have become a popular enterprise had not a newswriter used the term *panty raid* for a bit of campus hijinks that was neither new nor imaginative. But the term and the stunt caught hold, first in the news media and then among sophomores who had to do what the other boys were doing. Before the epidemic ended, there had been some eighty forays differing in little but geography, all duly reported from Waco to Winnipeg. Reporting them was a legitimate obligation; an epidemic of mass assaults on women's dormitories deserves notice as much as an epidemic of measles. But newsmen ought to keep in mind, when they follow a news fad, that they may trace a circle that ends in reader ennui as well as their own.

Anybody can name examples of this kind of news circle: flagpole sitting; streaking (a fad that was brief both because everybody was amused rather than outraged and because the weather changed); marathon dances; goldfish, phonograph record, and straw hat eating; telephone booth stuffing. There are less frivolous manifestations, too, including efforts to control or prevent the sale of comic books or "obscene" publications, or to take up residence in college presidents' offices. These incite public interest, and when duly reported, suggest repetition.

Stereotypes also develop from lazy diction. Not all newsmen consider every coed "pretty" and every divorcee "glamorous," but they use the term *star* with thoughtless abandon (a star is one of two kinds—any actor, of either sex, who has ever been in Hollywood, or any man who has ever worn an athletic uniform). *Turncoat*, after the Korean war, for a time lost its validity as a generic term when it became the only name by which you could refer to American soldiers who had "gone Communist." Auto race drivers are "crack," police roundups "dragnets," soldiers of a month's experience "veterans," and professional football players "brawny." Happily, "kiddie" went out when Shirley Temple grew up.

Among hackneyed news stereotypes is the one that any story about a lost dog or a child under three (especially if he is taking a bare-bottomed stroll) should get top billing. News and pictures of cats that set off fire alarms and canaries that chirp "Dixie" have become stale, even to people who love cats and canaries.

Of more concern are the stereotypes of routine reporting. Two Washington reporters turned up the Watergate story because they were not satisfied with asking the usual questions in the usual places and getting the usual answers; they saw a place to dig and dug, which was more than scores of

CRITICS ... AND CRITICS

Americans dismayed at the shortcomings of the press found a critic to their liking in A. J. Liebling, whose jibes at the laziness and superficiality of reporting fueled his "Wayward Press" columns in The New Yorker and the books that grew out of them. Many of his criticisms had merit, but a Liebling reader must watch for his free-swinging generalizations and his lapses into ridicule that is merely witty. (The Liebling III convention was named for him.)

More balanced press criticism has come from Ben Bagdikian (now of the Columbia Journalism Review), William L. Rivers of Stanford University, and Douglass Cater, director of the Aspen Program on Communications and Society.

reporters with equal opportunities did. It's easy to report the surface of today's school board story if you merely see how yesterday's was handled. Political events, baseball games, and commencements have familiar patterns, but no two are identical, and reports of them shouldn't make them all seem hatched from the same eggs. The revealing reporter is the one who finds the elements that make today's happening *different* from all the others rather than those that make it the same.

**SENSATIONAL NEWS—
SENSATIONALIZED NEWS**

When U Thant was Secretary-General of the United Nations, he told a meeting of the American Newspaper Publishers Association that "sensationalism, unfortunately, is a characteristic of the modern world." He made the statement in the context of a discussion of "sensational" news stories about the UN and its activities. His comments were kinder than many criticisms of the press—criticisms whose theme is that "the press always overemphasizes." The theme goes on to say that the news media, to sell papers or draw audiences, seize on events of high interest, overdramatizing and often distorting them. Newspapers and broadcasters are often but not always guilty of these charges. The preponderance of news published and broadcast is, for the preponderance of the audience, pretty dull stuff. And the social climate suggested by U Thant must be taken into account.

Much news is sensational—it charges a man's emotional batteries, it gives off sparks. This nation has rarely experienced an event more sensational than the shooting of President Kennedy. Some news reports of it were longer, and gorier, and more repetitive than they needed to be. Yet it was truly the major topic of the day; the nation was eager for details; newsmen would have been delinquent had their reports not made it as spectacular as it was.

When they overdid it, they were sensationalizing. But the sin is not in reporting the sensational event; the sin is in building it bigger than life. It is wrong to use the word *riot* when a rumble between two teen gangs is quickly dissipated. It is sensationalizing to write that a driver crashed his car into an abutment when he gave it a mild sideswipe.

HOW CAREFUL IS CAREFUL ENOUGH?

In the period in the 1960s when "racial incidents"—usually street fights between blacks and whites—were frightening America, a number of broadcasters and newspapers agreed to delay publishing news of such events, or to understate them, so as to avoid public terror or widespread participation. Thus they tried to achieve the opposite of sensationalizing what were undeniably sensational events. They succeeded in some cases, failed in others.

This question, however, should be asked: Suppose withholding news of the seriousness of a street fight at Main and Center streets permits citizens to venture into the war zone? And suppose later the citizens say of the news medium, "It can't be trusted. It failed to warn me"? Can it safely be said that understatement is more tolerable than overstatement?

"Sensationalizing" news events is one of the primary faults of news media throughout the world. But no newspaper or news broadcast is likely to be free of sensational news, no matter how carefully it is handled. As U Thant said, we live in a sensational world.

Projects

1. Get five daily newspapers from five different states (buy them at a newsstand or use them in a library), all published on the same day. Record and contrast the types of news they emphasize, noting especially what they do with nonlocal news.

2. Make the same kind of comparison-contrast of news in your local evening paper and that offered by three local afternoon or evening radio or TV newscasts.

3. From the information you gained in Project 1, write a commentary on the relative weight given by the papers to local and nonlocal news. Render your own judgment on the news editors' selections and emphases.

4. Make a list of all the stereotypes you find in one issue of a newspaper—stereotypes of diction and of news selection.

CHAPTER FIVE

The news channels

"NOSE FOR NEWS"?

The salty city editor of the New York *World* in its brilliant days, Charles Chapin, once said that the kind of reporter he wanted was "the one who knows in advance where hell is going to break loose and is on hand to cover it." Chapin meant that a good reporter can often anticipate the events the public needs to know about. Laymen are likely to assume that he meant Hollywood-type reporters with built-in antennae that quiver when a 747 is about to crash or a football coach is about to fire a halfback. The legend suggests that reporters cover events, whether through luck or sixth sense— the "nose for news"—by being on hand as the news is being made.

Happy coincidences do occur. A spectacular news broadcast in TV's early days was NBC's report of a big Chicago fire. But it was not intuition that had led NBC executives, years earlier, to put their studios high up in a building that looked straight down into the heart of the fire. It was not extra-sensory perception that told a Tacoma newspaperman to drive onto the bridge spanning an arm of Puget Sound on a certain November afternoon—

he was simply following his daily homeward route. The long bridge always trembled in a high wind; that day it waved like a ribbon. The man abandoned his car and crawled along the span to shore . . . in time to call his paper before the bridge plunged into the Sound. He was on hand to cover hell when it broke loose, but he gets no credit for prescient news vision.

News breaks like these can't be planned; if the media depended on foreseeing them, the public would indeed be ill informed. It is true that the media anticipate newsworthy events, but the anticipation grows from carefully organized planning rather than intuition. Many events cast shadows ahead, and many others worth reporting take place within well-defined news orbits or are such that the facts about them are available at identified and manned centers of news. Every news medium—newspaper, broadcasting, magazine, wire service—depends on following a scrupulous routine. Thorough coverage of news centers provides advance information about most events that ought to be reported. News coverage, in other words, is 95 percent organized and 5 percent luck. The reporter gets the story because he plans to be on hand or to ask the right questions in the right places.

PLAN VS. LUCK

Of seventy-six general news stories in one issue of a metropolitan morning paper (excluding sports, business, society, and other specialized news), only five had no relation to advance knowledge or preparation for covering them. The rest, seventy-one, appear to have come through regular, organized news channels.

Much reporting occurs *after* the event—after the crime has been revealed, the polls closed, the Supreme Court decision reached.

**DIFFERENT PURPOSES, DIFFERENT
CHANNELS**

Channels for the delivery of news differ according to who the desired audiences are, where they are, and what their interests are. The geographical factor described in the preceding chapter is an obvious influence. A man in Yuma is interested in a great many news events that do not concern the man in Youngstown or Yakima, and each local paper reflects its own community. But some news carriers—chiefly the newsmagazines, the wire services, and the broadcasting networks, but also "national" newspapers like the *Wall Street Journal*, the New York *Times*, and the *Christian Science Monitor*—reach broader audiences with more than provincial interests. The small-community daily carries news of nonlocal matters, but its primary job is local. The typical small-town weekly and a few small-town radio stations ignore nonlocal news and hammer hard at covering events they can reach out and touch.

Though newspapers are not often designed to serve narrow interests, some do: The Chicago *Defender* covers only news of concern to Chicago's black citizens, *Women's Wear Daily* primarily news of the garment trade, the *Guild Reporter* little beyond the activities of The Newspaper Guild.

UNDERGROUND TO ALTERNATIVE

The 1960s were a time of youth rebellion against the Establishment—the time of "speed" and marijuana, horror at slaughter in Vietnam, candor in sexual activity, blaring rock music. Youth's anger and resentment spawned the "underground press," which expressed the frustration of the counterculture, a passionate abhorrence of bonds that seemed intolerable and of what seemed lack of principle in the seats of power. For its first years the counterculture's press—underground because it was often edited or printed secretly, though it usually sought wide visibility—flailed at the mores it despised, flaunted obscene language, and gave hotblooded though often poorly reasoned comfort to underdogs.

Interest in Vietnam tailed off. Rock riots lost their muddy glitter. The war against pot quieted. And calling names got to be less fun as the names themselves palled. But the core of resentment at social and political immorality remained. As some of the newborn newspapers folded, lacking money or editorial ardor, others changed direction to become effective agents of social complaint and political expression. They became the "alternative press," the call to reform of things as they are.

Nobody knows how many such newspapers continued into the 1970s. Some lived a moth's one-night life, others became useful social instruments. A paper in Ann Arbor, Michigan, was given much of the credit for replacement of the local prison sentence for marijuana possession by a five-dollar fine. In Los Angeles the Free Press, with a circulation of some 90,000, discovered that all candidates in a mayoralty election wanted space in its columns.

The alternative press rarely resembles what it calls "the straight press" in manner, form, or substance. It is a press of advocacy, usually with a limited group of interests and a conviction that objectivity is a fetter on effective journalism. Speculation is that, like the underground press in France following World War II, some of it will disappear, some will continue as a press of more or less radical criticism, and some will merge into the dominant journalistic patterns of the day.

Advertising content is an index to the differences among media. TV advertising is heavily national—promoting commodities or causes accessible from Atlantic to Pacific. Before TV bloomed in 1952, radio advertising was largely national; in face of TV competition, however, it became more and more a medium for the local furniture store and the neighborhood supermarket. Though news publications rarely concentrate on news for one sex, they are willing to dedicate important sections to what are considered one-gender concerns. The advertising content of magazines clearly shows narrowed interests: You wouldn't find a compressed-air stapler advertised in *The New Yorker*, men's hats in *Ms.*, or a Cadillac in the *Boot and Shoe Recorder*.

Another form of classification is that of intellectual, artistic, or sociopolitical interest (again better seen in magazines than in newspapers): *Har-*

per's selects its contents for an educated elite, the *New York Review of Books* for people who read books and like to read *about* them, and the *Progressive* for men and women with a liberal sociopolitical point of view.

NEWS-GATHERING ORGANIZATION

In the typical daily newspaper organization the managing editor is the executive charged with supervision of news coverage—the captain of the news team. It is his responsibility to make sure that the paper presents a fair and complete picture of the major news, local and distant, of importance or interest to his readers. The detail work, of which he does little himself, is delegated to subeditors and their staffs.

CHANGING PATTERN

Though the table of newspaper organization is representative of most communications media—print and broadcast, American and foreign, newspaper and magazine —variations emerge, especially in recent years. Majority stockholders in the Milwaukee Journal are staff members of the paper, a fact that is given credit by some critics for the enlightened news and editorial policies of the Journal. In a few newspapers—the Burlington (Iowa) Hawk Eye is one—the publisher gives his staff a "yes" or "no" on a candidate for the managing editorship before he is hired. The staff of what is often called France's best paper, Le Monde, owns and controls the paper. The International Federation of Journalists in 1972 adopted a resolution asking for "regular consultation with employees about editorial operations." A number of magazines in the United States are literally owned and run by their staffs; Ms., the principal "women's liberation" periodical, extends democracy in the editorial rooms to the point that each editor does his or her own typing. Many underground and alternative papers are strictly the creatures of their owner-employees.

The managing editor is usually in the third echelon of the newspaper's chain of command (a chart of typical newspaper organization appears on page 68). At the top is the publisher, the paper's owner or ownership's representative. On the next level are the executive editor or editor-in-chief and the principal business executive. The editor is responsible for the entire editorial operation of the paper ("editorial" means everything that isn't advertising); the managing editor ordinarily reports to him. The business manager is charged with the management and financing of the enterprise. His immediate subordinates are the heads of circulation, advertising sales, promotion, production, and other departments concerned with business, mechanical, and distribution operations. This is not the only pattern of newspaper organization, but it is typical of most and similar to all.

The newsroom   On most papers, the managing editor's largest and most important staff group is under the direction of the city editor, who directs news coverage of the paper's city or local community. He may be responsible for covering an entire city and its suburbs, or a small town and several outlying communities, or a section of a city. However the zone is defined, it is the city editor's mission to see that his staff finds and brings in its news each day. And it is what his staff provides that gives the paper a personality different from that of any other news medium.

According to fiction and popular misconception, a newsroom (or city room) is a madhouse, and its city editor is profane, harried, and always in a lather. Sometimes he (and in some cases she) is all of these. But more frequently he is a soft-spoken, self-controlled news professional who gets results by careful management and thorough planning rather than by shriek and shout. Chapin of the *World,* who was both colorful and eccentric, was a master of organization.

The city editor bases his planning on the fact that most news information centers around specific hubs. News of city government is to be found at city hall and other municipal offices. County news is gathered at the county building; crime news comes from police headquarters, from sheriffs, the FBI, the courts; business and financial news from banks, the chamber of commerce, trade associations, labor unions, and individual businesses; news of social welfare from service agencies and certain governmental offices. Sports news, transportation news, school and education news, church news, health and science news, suburban news must all be collected through appropriate centers.

To each such news center the city editor assigns a "beat" or "run" reporter. Sometimes several reporters are on a large beat with many news sources; sometimes one reporter has several limited beats. No two beats are exactly alike. Covering the waterfront is a difficult and important beat assignment in New York, Houston, Seattle, and Honolulu, but it's an old song title in Butte, Phoenix, Indianapolis, and Calgary. The reporter needs to become familiar with every corner of his beat in order to gather all its publishable news each day. Chapter 7 provides a view of methods and challenges of beat reporting.

In addition to his beat reporters, whose work schedules remain about the same from week to week, the city editor has at his disposal a number of "general assignment" reporters to whom he makes spot assignments Many such assignments arise from nonbeat sources; sometimes a beat reporter tips the city editor to a story he hasn't time to cover so that a general-assignment reporter can take it on. As a guide in such assignments, the city editor keeps a comprehensive "futures book," so that he can anticipate news events. Other newsworkers under the city editor's direction are his staff of photographers (reporting by picture is a brilliant adjunct to words in twentieth-century news practice); one or more rewrite men, whose principal job is to write stories telephoned in to the office by "legmen," the outside or beat reporters; secretaries; copy aides or messengers, who were called copy boys before Women's Lib; and others.

In some newspaper organizations other departments are supervised by the

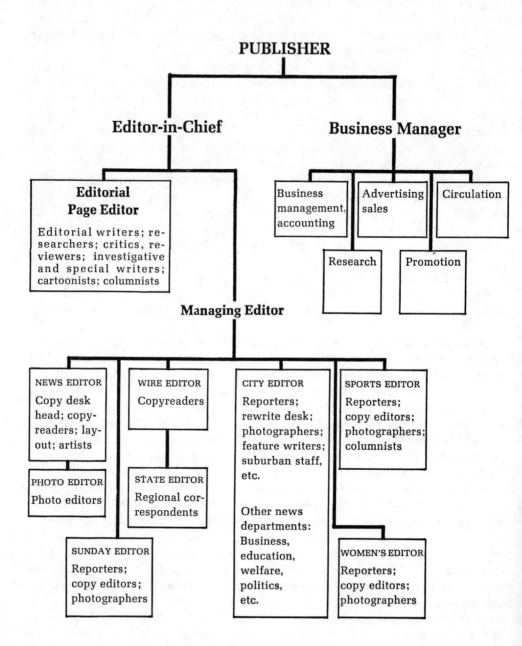

PUBLISHER

Editor-in-Chief

Business Manager

Editorial Page Editor

Editorial writers; researchers; critics, reviewers; investigative and special writers; cartoonists; columnists

Business management, accounting

Advertising sales

Circulation

Research

Promotion

Managing Editor

NEWS EDITOR

Copy desk head; copyreaders; layout; artists

WIRE EDITOR

Copyreaders

CITY EDITOR

Reporters; rewrite desk; photographers; feature writers; suburban staff, etc.

Other news departments: Business, education, welfare, politics, etc.

SPORTS EDITOR

Reporters; copy editors; photographers; columnists

PHOTO EDITOR

Photo editors

STATE EDITOR

Regional correspondents

SUNDAY EDITOR

Reporters; copy editors; photographers

WOMEN'S EDITOR

Reporters; copy editors; photographers

city desk: Important among them are the sports department and the women's or "society" department (a trend toward this department's consolidation under the city desk denies the questionable belief that news for women usually differs from that for men). On most papers, however, the sports department is jealously independent. Such departments follow procedures similar to that of the city operation; each has its director, its beat and general reporters, its photographers, and sometimes its own copy desk.

News from "outside"   A second major division of the news operation brings in news from more distant points. Most large newspapers have a wire or telegraph desk, directed by a telegraph editor. This desk receives from the Teletypes and edits news from one or more of the news or wire services, Associated Press and United Press International (large news operations also subscribe to the British agency Reuters and others). No "general" daily newspaper can fulfill its functions without some such service. A major metropolitan daily or a broadcasting network may receive news also from the Canadian Press, the Chicago Tribune–New York Daily News Syndicate, the Los Angeles Times–Washington Post and the New York Times services, and other nonlocal or syndicated sources.

Many papers have a system of correspondents within their circulation areas. Everybody knows of the country correspondents of the small-town weekly—usually women—whose chore is to mail in "personals" and other news of events big and little in their own neighborhoods. Dailies often have state desks that direct strings of correspondents. Larger papers maintain reporters at the state capital and some in Washington, in neighboring states, in foreign countries. Simple or elaborate, county-wide or world-wide, systems like these must be directed, and the copy that pours through them must be edited. Every newspaper must have an editor charged with these reponsibilities.

The Teletypesetter and the computer, technological developments of mid-century, have modified the traditional wire-editing operations of hundreds of American dailies. Electric telegraph devices and punched tapes operate typesetting machines, often at great distances, without human intervention. Other developments such as "cold type," which is an adaptation of the photographic offset process, are replacing hot metal. But all such changes affect editing and mechanical procedures more than they do basic news gathering.

The chart on page 68 shows the typical staff organization of a metropolitan newspaper. With obvious changes, it also represents broadcasting news operations. Radio and television news organizations, like those of newspapers, range from the far-reaching and complex to the one-man operation. Producers, directors, announcers, and electronic equipment replace composition and printing presses, but news gathering, evaluation, and editing are basically analogous.

Other editorial functions   If newspapers contained only news, the city, wire, news, and copy desks would suffice to provide most editorial content. But newspapers not only inform but also offer views, opinions, and entertainment. For these functions there are separate departments.

The views-and-opinion section of the paper comprises the editorial page, sometimes a facing ("op-ed") page, and allied sections. An editorial page editor, whatever his title, is responsible for these sections. He is usually aided by editorial writers, researchers, columnists, and investigative and feature reporters; many papers' charts of organization assign critics and reviewers to his direction. He is responsible to the executive editor and may have no operational relationship to the news department; a newspaper cannot be fully effective, however, unless its news and editorial-page departments work in tandem. The editorial page may borrow reporters for special assignments, and the city desk may use editorial writers for interpretive or investigative features.

Entertainment and service material in newspapers is of many kinds. Much of it is in the form of news features, prepared by the city staff or furnished by outside services. Much is syndicated material that can be printed with little local editing or modification. Comic strips are in this category; so are many health and home-service columns, serial features, and Broadway and Hollywood gossip columns. The editing of this material is sometimes assigned to the copy desk, sometimes to separate specialists.

Papers with Sunday editions have separate Sunday departments. Much of the content of the Sunday paper, however (half of which is ordinarily printed by midweek before the date of issue), is turned out by the regular staff or comes from nonstaff sources.

THE BROADCASTING NEWSROOM

Radio news   A radio newsroom that offers serious news coverage is in most ways a small version of the city room of the newspaper against which it competes. But there are significant differences both in practice and intent, and wide variations among radio newsrooms themselves.

The prime function of the newspaper is news; for most radio and TV news reporting is secondary. News gets a small portion of the day's broadcasting schedule even on the stations that take news responsibilities seriously, spend money to support news operations, and work hard at competing with print. (A study reported in *Center Reports*, published by the Center for the Study of Democratic Institutions, says that commercial stations "give about twenty percent of prime evening time to public affairs programs. Public or noncommercial stations try to give thirty percent of prime time to such programs.") Traditionally the newspaper publisher takes interest and pride in the editorial effectiveness of his paper; few radio stations are directed by men reared in the news tradition, and few hold that "news comes first."

News is for most broadcasters only one profitable form of audience magnet.

The amount of news broadcast in a day by the typical radio station comes to only a fraction of what a daily newspaper presents. Radio must tell its news stories in fewer words, and so it must communicate fewer details. A fifteen-minute sponsored newscast contains about 1,800 words and twenty-five stories; one issue of a metropolitan paper may contain more than 100,000 words and hundreds of stories. Radio puts the same story on the air half a dozen or more times a day; the few all-news stations repeat more often.

The average newspaper takes pains to cover the news of its area. Whether it's small-town or metropolitan, the task that demands more staff time than any other is detailed coverage of its own precincts. In contrast, most radio stations make small effort to serve local or regional news needs; many "rip and read" the wire service news that comes from national or regional wire service headquarters. Some small stations emulate the country weekly and broadcast news of local activity only, but few cover local news as thoroughly as their printed competition, and many develop no local news at all.

Size of station and of home community do not always determine the quality of a station's news efforts. Some big-city stations have no newsrooms and no qualified news personnel; on the other hand, some 500-watt

---

WHERE DO YOU GET YOUR NEWS?

When news took to the air, in the 1930s, the broadcasters had a fight on their hands: a fight against the newspaper system, against the fact that when people thought of news, they turned to newspapers. For a quarter of a century, in quantity and usually in prestige, broadcasters remained second choice. But in 1963, when respondents to a reputable annual head count were asked, "Where do you get most of your news?" a majority said that they favored TV over newspapers.* The margin had grown to about six to five by 1972. Perhaps more significant is that in 1961 TV overtook newspapers as the more credible medium; the 1972 preference score was more than two to one for TV. These attitudes were reported at every educational and economic level. In an important sense television has become America's dominant news medium (radio is a poor third on all counts).

But statistics are notoriously tricky, and both newspapers and broadcasters have indulged in occasional statistical shenanigans. Barebone figures are difficult to interpret. Though TV was the "preferred" news carrier through the early 1970s, the same period showed a hundred million adult Americans professing "exposure" every day to a newspaper, ninety million to TV, and eighty million to radio. In 1974 about a fifth of Americans, especially those in the upper economic and cultural levels, spent more time daily with radio than with TV; few gave as much as forty-five minutes to newspapers. But the time spent with newspapers was mostly on news; that with TV was more likely to be on "The Price Is Right" or "All in the Family."

More information and better interpretation are needed.

* Most of these figures come from surveys conducted by the Roper research organization. Because the surveys were commissioned by the Television Information Office, they have been accused of bias. The accusations are almost certainly unjustified.

stations in small communities maintain aggressive and adequately manned news departments. A few have developed strong staffs for news editing and interpretation and for vigorous local investigative reporting.

"COMMUNICATION IS ALL ONE JOB"

The quotation is from Louis M. Lyons, who for years conducted the Nieman "enrichment program" for professional journalists at Harvard University. Lyons wrote in the December, 1964, Atlantic Monthly that whether a journalist "reports for print or over the air, in newspaper, magazine, or topical book, or as an aid to public men in presenting public programs, [he] is gathering and evaluating information, writing, eliting on public affairs. The educational need is the same: To understand the issues in the great areas where a knowledge of history, government, economics, supplies the background to give meaning to the reports."

A radio station's news director is its managing editor, responsible for running the department, making assignments, and establishing policy and news patterns. An increasing number of newsrooms maintain beat reporters who work in competition with newspaper reporters. A well-financed station may boast a vigorous local news department with a dozen or more news employees: newswriters, editors, reporters, and "air men." Air men (or women) may be either the reporters themselves or announcers who specialize in news. In a small radio station the newsman is likely to be jack of every trade: He gathers local news, writes it for broadcast, selects and edits national and foreign news from the wire, fits the pieces together for each succeeding air edition, and then goes to the microphone. He sometimes also serves as disc jockey and control console operator.

THE COUNTERFEITS

Self-respecting newsmen decry the phony newscasting that mars some station schedules. They scorn the irresponsible boasts of twenty-four-hour newsrooms" that present the news from "Mr. News himself"—all without news professionals, news-gathering or newswriting activities, or balanced or complete news programs. Such stations make no effort to give listeners an honest basis for understanding the news. Professional news performance is never the product of ignorance and inexperience, and news offerings at such a level tend to reduce consumer confidence in all news media.

Many stations employ specialists—sports specialists, women's program directors, agriculture editors. In stations that identify themselves with specific regions the news department may get news from correspondents in surrounding communities.

Most radio stations buy at least one wire service. The Associated Press and United Press International furnish twenty-four-hour Teletype service for broadcasters, with news written and programmed for radio and TV. Many stations supplement news broadcasts with network news; a few rely entirely on news from the networks (thus ignoring local news). The major networks maintain elaborate and expert news organizations, with reporters and commentators in news centers around the world and correspondents for assignment to special events. Well-financed broadcasters may have more news channels feeding their microphones than the newspapers offer—wire services *plus* network news services. The press rarely has access to news the broadcasters develop, though it is becoming common to read in the newspapers that "such-and-such a network reported" or to hear on the air that a statement "comes from such-and-such a newspaper."

Radio has developed its own distinctive news procedures. Because speed is more important and lengthy detail less important to broadcasters than to the printed press, telephone news gathering is a staple in air reporting. Radio deadlines are more frequent than a newspaper's, and the telephone is faster than legs or wheels. Radio uses it heavily for local news gathering; a competent inside man can call a city's principal centers several times a day and collect all the news a station can use.

The radio newsman uses the tape recorder more than his newspaper rival (a cassette recorder is easier to carry than a portable typewriter, and more flexible). The tape recorder can be used for anything from a colorful sentence or a thirty-second interview to a full-length speech—and in the voice and emphases of a speaker.

Television news   Television news, after a shaky start, has become a full-blooded sibling to radio news. Some TV stations have no radio connection, but the two kinds of news often come from the same newsrooms and from the hands and voices of the same newsmen and announcers. The number of stories used in a fifteen-minute TV newscast is about the same as that in a radio show of the same length; excellent pictures may tempt a TV news editor to stretch a story beyond its merit, but poor visuals may have the opposite effect. TV news has less total space than radio because it programs fewer shows a day.

TV news has far outstripped radio in use of money and manpower. The anatomy of the television newsroom is vastly more complex than radio's; TV needs cameras, darkrooms, editing equipment, production crews, even stage sets. It has all the news-handling facilities of radio—wire services, reporters, writers, editors, announcers—in addition to expensive photography equipment, mobile crews, picture services, elaborate studios, and many more technicians.

News practices in TV vary as widely from station to station as they do in radio. Some radio-TV stations have staffs of dozens of newsworkers, but one TV newsroom got started by adding a Polaroid camera to its radio newsroom (it didn't stay that uncomplicated very long).

The need for pictures compels the TV newsroom to send crews to the scenes of news events. A radio or a newspaper reporter could, if necessary, cover a fire or a parade by telephone, without leaving his desk. TV pictures have to be made where the news is being made. For this reason television has developed wide-ranging mobile units that sometimes give telecast news better local coverage than radio achieves—a fact that has led TV news to emphasize freeway accidents and burning buildings beyond their news value.

An unsolved problem for TV news is access for camera and sound equipment to courtrooms and other scenes of officialdom in action. The American Bar Association holds stubbornly to its position that picture-making in the courtroom is likely to interfere with the processes of justice—a position whose merit appears to decline as picture-making techniques grow less clumsy and obtrusive. Though the Supreme Court has supported the ABA principle, a slow trend forecasts more and more freedom for TV cameras.

This trend is supported by the maturation of TV news techniques and formats. The half-hour news show is no longer a novelty; the development of background and brief documentary news shows has marked recent years. Many TV news shows use the so-called magazine format, with a number of news specialists instead of the single man-on-camera of the 1950s, and attention to in-depth coverage of such current topics as consumer interests, environment protection, and the like.

NEWSMAGAZINES

Newsmagazines like *Time, Newsweek, U. S. News & World Report,* and the *National Observer* (which uses newspaper format), despite their less pressing deadlines and their broader range, maintain news-gathering and editing organizations similar in outline to the patterns described in this chapter. The long list of names on the *Time* masthead shows the far-flung character of the operation as well as the essential similarity to the newsroom plan. Newsmagazines depend heavily on wire and picture services; they have beat reporters in news centers around the world, and large staffs of editors and researchers at headquarters. Since they aim at national and international audiences, they deal in news of wide rather than parochial interest.

The two major Time Inc. magazines, *Time* and *Fortune,* have developed a staff operation that they call "group journalism." Under this system a single news or feature story may be the work of scores of reporters, researchers, writers, and editors; this is one of the reasons that you see few by-lines in *Time.* (The *National Observer* depends heavily on named reporters; *Newsweek* follows a middle course, combining group journalism with the products of by-lined specialists.) An editorial decision at *Time* may call for a report on food resources in Southeast Asia. Reporters are assigned to the area; researchers at home and abroad begin digging into facts; photographers start shooting. Eventually all the information flows into the New York editorial office, where writers and editors, after filtering and refining the copy, produce the final story.

Some specialized newsmagazines follow similar procedures. *Business Week* maintains news bureaus and correspondents in more than fifty American cities; a few correspondents or a good many may contribute to a one-column story. *Time* maintains a large corps of specialists in the subject areas it covers, from foreign affairs to motion pictures.

THE WIRE SERVICES

The news-gathering operation of an international wire service is another version of the city room plan. Although an earthquake in Santiago presents more complex reporting problems than does a cave-in at the old quarry north of town, the operation follows the same basic lines. Like the local news systems, the wire services assign men to the nerve centers of significant news activity, to be on hand when hell, or anything milder that is newsworthy, breaks loose.

A fundamental difference is that the newspaper or local broadcaster is primarily concerned with news for a local area. The wire service, on the other hand, reports news for other localities; the purpose is to bring to subscribers news that develops beyond their limited spheres of operation. The great news services—Associated Press and United Press International in the United States, Reuters in the United Kingdom, Agence France-Presse in France, Tass in the Soviet Union—more often assign their enormous staffs to world, national, and state capitals than to city halls. They put men on America's Cup yacht races, but not on high school games. Their reporters cover news that is likely to be published in many places, news that is of interest in spite of, rather than because of, its point of origin.

The Associated Press, as an example, maintains bureaus and correspondents in every major world capital; it has a Washington news staff of a hundred; it covers every state capital; it has a roving sports staff and a science department to cover medical and scientific developments anywhere. AP carries significant news about Little Rock, Arkansas, not for the Little Rock media but for the papers and broadcasters elsewhere that want Little Rock news of more than local impact.

This does not mean that the AP's news about Little Rock or Chicago is never used by the Little Rock or Chicago members of the AP. Members get, and are free to use, whatever local news their AP bureaus put on their Teletypes; they occasionally ask a local bureau for help in coverage of local events.

Wire service operation   AP and UPI have been providing radio wire service to broadcasters since the 1930s. In addition to news wires, they furnish telephoto services, features, editorial interpretations, and background articles.

Distribution of wire service news is a complicated operation. A story written for the wire service may go to hundreds of audiences, worldwide. A story about a cloudburst in a small Indiana town must be relayed through state and regional bureaus to national headquarters in New York, thence to members or subscribers throughout the nation. Until the 1970s the relays

---

MEMBERS OR CLIENTS?

Newspapers and broadcasting stations receiving news from the AP, the older of the two principal American wire services, are AP members; the AP is a cooperative association rather than a profit-making enterprise. Those getting news from UPI and most other wire services, however, are clients, or subscribers. UPI is a news-selling business controlled by the Scripps-Howard newspaper interests. In the United States exclusive or monopoly contracts for news service are illegal; a paper or a broadcasting station may buy as many wire services as it cares to pay for.

Every member of the AP is a news-gathering agent for every other member. Thus the AP is "protected" in Amarillo, Texas, by its two local members, the morning News and the evening Globe-Times. News developed by these two papers and other AP members automatically becomes AP property for general circulation; each member is obligated to "file" stories of more than local interest so that AP can use them promptly. UPI commonly maintains its own local correspondents, often members of local news staffs, to cover such stories.

---

were "manual," passing through editors' hands at most relay stations. But electronic retransmission, using elaborate computerized control systems, is taking over; by a code system provided by the reporter or the bureau of origin, a story can be directed instantly to the members or clients of the services for whom it may have interest. (Electronic writing and editing is moving into the wire services as it is into newspapers. See Chapter 8.)

Computerized transmission is more advanced in international wire services than in local. Reuters, the British service, started it in 1968, UPI followed in 1970, AP more recently. Under these systems—no two are precisely alike—a newswriter in Moscow, for instance, puts on his copy a three-letter code that directs the story to a client in (say) Sydney, Australia. From any point on an agency network a correspondent can transmit, automatically, to any other point on the network—or to all of them. As the manager of the London UPI bureau explains it, "The responsibility is thus shifted from central editorial desks to the correspondents, not only to produce finished copy ready for use as it leaves their typewriters but also to decide which of the agency customers should get the material."

The stories that reach broadcast newsrooms are usually different from those the newspapers get. For broadcast a story is written for vocal rather than printed delivery. The wire services once wrote newspaper material first, then rewrote it for radio—thus giving newspapers a few minutes' time advantage. But today the time differentials are at a minimum; the first served is usually that with the more pressing deadline.

WORD OF MOUTH

A book like *Reporting* gives only passing attention to one of the principal channels of news transmission—person-to-person communication. The reason is obvious: Such communication, unorganized and unplanned, is a topic one studies as a sociopsychological phenomenon, not as journalism. But some notion of its flexibility as a news distributor was discovered by a team of communications researchers at the University of Minnesota on November 22, 1963.

On that day, at a little before 1 p.m., an assassin murdered President Kennedy in Dallas. Beginning at 5:30 that afternoon, the researchers made 200 telephone calls in Minneapolis and its suburbs to find out by what avenues citizens had first learned of the shooting, and how much they knew of it. A summary of some of the findings provides material for thought:

1. Every respondent had already learned of the shooting. Three-fourths had heard of it by 2 p.m., all by 3:30.
2. Half of the men and almost half of the women had learned the news from another person—direct personal communication. Most of the women were in their homes when they learned it, and most of them got it first from TV. One person reported hearing of it from sixty other individuals.
3. About half of the respondents told somebody else about it. A quarter of the women telephoned others to report it.
4. Most of the respondents heard it from only one news medium—most commonly TV. But those with college degrees had used two or three media by the time the interviews took place.
5. Accuracy of the "knowledge" varied widely. A few knew the name of the man held in jail in Dallas; less than a fifth expressed reservations as to his guilt. A few described him as Communist, pro-Castro, a Russian, or a Cuban.

Dynamic news like this travels fast by word of mouth. That it often changes shape as it travels is an indication of the need for organized, dependable mass-communication systems.

FEEDBACK

In face-to-face communication the process called "feedback" is fundamental. Feedback is the return message given by receiver to sender: "Is that so!" or "What did you say?" or "I can't believe it" or "I better call Joe." In ordinary mass communication there is little feedback. The newspaper reader may write a letter, cancel his subscription, or order a hundred extra copies. Broadcast listeners may call the station, scold or praise the sponsor, or write postcards. But the mass-communication systems make little provision for instant response, and they get little.

This is one of the reasons that some broadcasters and a few newspapers go to costly lengths to stimulate feedback—to ask what their audiences think of what they're getting, and why. More about this in Chapter 6.

Projects

1. From examination of all the stories on a front page of your daily paper, make a list of all the *sources* from which their news information has come. Then make a list of all the *carriers* of information you can identify: local reporters, wire services, others.

2. Ask ten or more strangers how they first learned about some striking current event. Then write a summary and comment on your findings.

3. Keep a week's "diary" of your personal news consumption. Make it as complex as you like. Record the amount of time you spend with different news media and the number of different stories and news subjects to which you gave attention. You might also record varieties of sources and news channels, differences between printed and broadcast information on the same events, many other arrangements of data. Write a commentary on your patterns of news intake.

CHAPTER SIX

News media audiences

Joseph Pulitzer published two of the great "mass newspapers" of his day, the New York *World* and the St. Louis *Post-Dispatch,* newspapers whose circulations were the despair of their competitors. They were successful because they were not edited for Pulitzer. When this brilliant journalist was old and blind, he employed young men to read to him the news that served his personal interests and enthusiasms. News thus distilled to serve the taste of one individual would not have served any other man as well as it served Pulitzer; its news would not have been the same, in quantity or in emphasis, as that chosen by an editor who hoped to communicate with a mass audience.

News media cannot afford to select news to suit the interests or tastes of one person. News is a report to a community, not to a single individual, and editors think in terms of collective audiences that often comprise many thousands of men, women, and children. In a journalistic utopia each publication and each broadcast would attract everybody. Like objectivity, such a goal will never be achieved; unlike objectivity, it would be insane to try to reach it.

Newsmen know that the audience for each medium and for each story is peculiar unto itself. The size and nature of smaller audiences is determined by a welter of technological, geographical, economic, cultural, and social factors; each medium's gross audience takes in smaller audiences with different backgrounds, different needs and desires, impelled by differing influences. Newsmen are, moreover, aware of the paradox that the mass audience must be reached through the eyes and ears of individual men and women. Since no two humans and no two audiences are duplicates, a single news story is not expected to interest everybody (a story seen and remembered by 25 percent of those who get the paper containing it is considered widely read). In practice, therefore, the goal of news practice is to interest as many people as possible as much of the time as possible. Although a great deal of "narrow-interest news"—for groups within groups, for specialists, for minority interests—is offered by newspapers and newsmagazines, and less of it by radio and TV, newsmen always hope to make meaningful contact with the largest number of people they can.

PERSON-TO-PERSON JOURNALISM

When Lee Hills was editor of the Detroit Free Press, he said that "the tremendous success of good Action Line columns shows the need for the kind of person-to-person journalism that helps people to solve their individual problems." He might also have cited personal-advice columns such as that of Ann Landers and other features that respond individually to individual questions.

Such columns justify themselves in editors' eyes, however, not because they are one-to-one journalism but because they are widely read. They can rarely be called news.

AUDIENCE IDENTIFICATION

To realize its full potential, a news carrier must know precisely to whom it is talking. Audiences have well-defined limitations, interests, and characteristics. Many are apparent to casual observation; many are identified or described in standard reference works such as encyclopedias, histories, almanacs, and U. S. census publications. Some can be pinned down only by painstaking research. Geographical proximity is a prime audience-defining factor, since an audience is usually the population within reasonable delivery distance or acceptably clear radio or TV range. Although some media—broadcasting networks, some news and other magazines, a few newspapers—reach beyond state or regional lines, most media have more narrowly limited audiences.

Geographical definition   A common newspaper and broadcasting practice is to provide area maps that show precisely where an audience is concentrated. Newspapers speak of the areas in which they reach a majority of homes as "saturation areas." Radio and TV stations call the locales in which their signals are satisfactorily received by a majority of receiving sets "primary areas." The maps defining these areas are often prepared, so that space and time salesmen can show advertisers the exact coverage they offer. But since they show not only the physical extent of an audience but also where it is light or heavy, they obviously carry messages for editors: Has the newspaper its share of audience in suburban areas? Do listeners in industrial districts tune the station's signal in or out?

When a radio or TV station is established, the potential extent of its primary area is predetermined by sending into the field engineers armed with instruments that register where the signal is strong and where it isn't. A station on the air often follows up by house-to-house surveys to determine how many of the families that *might* tune to it are actually doing so. It may decide to stretch its primary area, in effect, by broadcasting programs that will pull in listeners from its secondary areas, especially if such areas get weak reception of other signals. Or it may decide to direct its appeal to only a part of the primary area—to the urban but not the rural sections, for instance, or to a foreign-language enclave within an urban area.

Audiences are thus limited and differentiated by technical and geographic factors as well as by particular interests. Imagine four radio stations in a big city (most big cities have a score or more): a clear-channel station of 50,000-watts power and a regional of 10,000, both with national network affiliation; an educational station of 5,000 watts; and a "local" of 500. The clear-channel station covers several states; its audience may include residents in millions of acres of wheat and dairy land, a developing oil-well area, a desert or two, half a dozen urban industrial areas, and some resort land. Its listeners are a microcosm of the nation; they represent almost every occupation, taste, and economic and social level. Such a station selects news with a sweeping hand; it cannot afford narrow concentration.

The less powerful stations have smaller, less diversified audiences. The 10,000-watt station may cover a primary area only a quarter the size of that of its powerful competitor, and the 500-watt signal may reach little more than its own county. The educational station's coverage may be nearly as wide geographically as that of its 10,000-watt neighbor, but it purposely limits its audience by ignoring popular entertainment—often with a slight tilt of the nose. Its programs, news included, are selected and treated more soberly than those of other stations. Its listeners, thus, are selected not only by electronic range but also by their cultural and educational levels, which give them more esoteric interests.

All TV stations have nearly the same geographical range, since added power doesn't increase signal range much. "Translators" that pick up and relay a station's signal may extend its area, however. And cable systems, which bring in programs from a dozen or a hundred producing sources, wiring them into homes on a fee or rental basis, rival the networks. Nearly 4,000 cable systems are now operating in the United States; in the early days their prime function was to furnish TV service to communities isolated by distance or terrain from direct TV broadcasts, but their future seems to promise program variety, including specialized news services, far beyond what "free TV" has made possible. The FCC and Congress have spent years seeking a satisfactory regulatory system for the cable outlets.

The circulation range of the newspaper is analogous to the electronic range of direct broadcasting. What are the practical distances to which trucks, airplanes, and trains can deliver a paper in the relatively short period in which its news is fresh? The Chicago *Tribune* maintains one of America's largest circulations—more than three quarters of a million—chiefly because it is delivered at 7 a.m. daily not alone in Cook County but also in neighboring Indiana, Wisconsin, Michigan, Iowa, and Missouri.

Most papers do not attempt such extended coverage. Small papers cannot support wide-ranging truck fleets, and nearby areas within easy delivery range often boast adequate papers. Some papers arbitrarily decide to concentrate coverage on their own communities—suburban papers and rural weeklies are examples. In Chicago, where the *Tribune* is supreme as the regional paper, two other dailies put their prime efforts into metropolitan coverage.

The size and nature of an audience are also limited by a medium's news-gathering facilities. How far can its reporters and correspondents range? Should it, like WMT in Cedar Rapids, Iowa, maintain a staff of stringers to cover its primary area and competitors' areas? Or should it limit itself to sources and events within local telephone reach? Are there reasons for supporting wide-coursing foreign staffs, as do the New York *Times*, the *Christian Science Monitor*, *Time* magazine, and the three networks? Should a newspaper maintain a state desk and a corps of regional correspondents? Are suburban reporters necessary? No two newspapers or broadcasters give precisely the same answers to these questions.

Radio and TV coverage, commonly less ambitious than newspaper coverage, serves more limited fare. It does not seek audiences-within-audiences as vigorously as the newspapers do. It highlights the significant news, but it gives news of crime and passion less baldly than does the press (even though the "living-room character" of broadcast audiences, a factor that sharply restricted broadcasting's range of subject matter until the late 1960s, is now more and more disregarded). Broadcasting is primarily an entertainment medium, and entertainment and advertising almost always take precedence over news.

Every American newspaper, six-page weekly or great daily, offers its own well-defined audience a selection of news that would serve no other audience as well. You don't need to read the Hartford *Courant*, for instance, to speculate that it would not fare well in Sacramento. It is obvious when you examine the San Diego *Union* and the Burbank *Daily Review*, both Copley-owned papers published only 100 miles apart, that they are edited for their communities alone. You find that the *Union* shrills "San Diego" from every page (advertising included): San Diego business, San Diego education, San

Diego shipping, San Diego politics and sports; a feature reviews annual developments at the San Diego naval base, and another reports problems of illegal immigration over the nearby Mexican border.

Newspapers that transcend their geographical limits usually do it by addressing bodies of readers unified by topical rather than regional interests. The *Wall Street Journal* is known as a national newspaper, but this does not mean that the *Journal* would be a newspaper satisfactory to all America, or even to the entire news audience of Tulsa or Tuscaloosa; it means that a small group of readers in Tulsa, another in Tuscaloosa, and others country-wide are enough interested in the *Journal*'s coverage of American financial news to buy the paper. One of the few national newspapers, the *Christian Science Monitor*, has the smallest circulation among Boston-published dailies.

WHY CAN'T TULSA HAVE A "TULSA-NEW YORK TIMES"?

"Why?" asks the New York Times or the Wall Street Journal fan in Tulsa or Tuscaloosa. "Why can't we have a local paper that treats news in the same way? Why can't we have the sweeping news coverage of the Times or the financial news of the Journal?" The reason is that there are not enough special-interest readers in Tulsa to provide a commercially profitable audience. Most Tulsans wouldn't buy a paper like the Times even if it carried a Tulsa dateline. They are more concerned with Oklahoma oil and tornadoes than with thousands of words of United Nations news.

Other identification factors   If every news event and every kind of news offering were of interest to everybody, it would mean that society had settled into psychological and biological monotony; every reader of the Miami *Herald*, every reader of *Variety*, and every listener to NBC would have become his neighbor's carbon copy. Since, happily, the Aldous Huxley Brave New World concept of a brainwashed populace seems unlikely to come about, news will continue to offer different rewards and affect different consumers in different ways. The degree of stimulation offered by any piece of news will vary with the number of consumers it reaches, for no two of them have identical origin, background, education, environment, tastes. Yet a newsman needs to know the broad factors that have contributed to the background and interests of those he serves in order to know how to reach them.

Primary influences on a community are the economic and social conditions in whch it exists. The audience of a newspaper or a broadcasting station in eastern Massachusetts is concerned with shoes and textiles, metal goods, labor-management relations, and anything that affects industrial production. The people of a county in eastern South Dakota find wheat and soybeans, feeder cattle and farm subsidies, more to their liking.

National origins, religious traditions, political attitudes, and other factors in a community's social and cultural environment help to identify audiences. Newspeople in El Paso don't forget that Chicanos are among their clientele; in St. Louis and Milwaukee and New Ulm, Minnesota, they attend to the German ancestry of their audiences. News of the Catholic church, of Catholic activities, appropriately gets more emphasis in Boston than in neighboring New Hampshire. The effect of political attitudes on the character of a community meant that for a hundred years in the Deep South, where the one-party Democratic tradition dominated, few newspapers supported Republican causes or candidates (something that was modified markedly in the days of Kennedy, Goldwater, and Nixon). In some areas of the Deep South, until the "revolution" led by such editors as Hodding Carter in Greenville, Mississippi, and Ralph McGill in Atlanta, few newspapers published news about Blacks and their activities. A news medium in a small town whose chief enterprise is a state university depends heavily on news that would put a Montana rancher to sleep. A newspaper in northern Wisconsin knows that its readers are concerned about the tourist industry, the fishing prospects, and the likelihood of an increase in government appropriations for highways. A Kansas radio station broadcasts immediate and long-range weather forecasts several times a day: its farm audience is listening. The Miami *Herald,* at the northern edge of the Caribbean, carries a regular page headed "Around the Americas" to report news of nations to the south.

Such factors guide news editors in selecting and emphasizing news. Sometimes the guides are self-evident, but sometimes you need documented help. Data on the social composition of an audience come from scores of secondary sources. Census reports help to identify national, industrial-economic, religious, political, cultural, and ethnic backgrounds of American communities.

Such description by external signs is imperative, but it is not enough. It does not explain the inner responses to news or analyze the effects of news on the hearts and minds of the men, women, and children the media reach. For nearly a half-century the polling technique of describing audiences has been an American institution. It began when a Drake University journalism teacher named George Gallup, who was also a trained psychologist, challenged the conventional patterns of news judgments made by newspapers. From his own experience Gallup knew that every newspaper office in the land discarded scores of news stories, hundreds of lines of copy, thousands of words of fact and opinion and human interest every day because editors thought readers "wouldn't be interested."

"You may be right," he said in effect, "but you may be wrong. You don't know. You're just guessing."

Gallup persuaded the editors of a Des Moines paper to play along in an experiment. He picked stories from the paper's discards, and the paper published them ("piffle-hook news," it was called in Des Moines). Then Gallup interviewed the paper's readers. He discovered that a lot of piffle-hook news drew greater reader attention than much news routinely selected. He also discovered that individual reader responses varied at least as much as did group responses to individual stories.

From those experiments Gallup developed the widely used aided-recall method of studying reader responses. In its simplest form the "Gallup method" is a formula for finding out how a public responds to given newspaper material by questioning a cross section of readers. The interviewer and a reader of the current issue of a paper go through it item by item, recording what the reader has seen and what he has read in full or in part. When enough responses have been gathered to constitute a satisfactory sample, they are tabulated and matched with identifying information: How many of those polled are women? Men? Children? Are they in upper, middle, or lower economic levels? Are they well or poorly educated?

The Gallup method and other kinds of audience studies, most of them using variants of the personal interview, have become staples of mass media practice. They have provided information for editors to use not only in editing more effectively, but in picking sources of news as well. They tell how readers respond to the news fare they are given, what they think about public affairs, public mores, popular fads, politics, social welfare, schools, abortion, marijuana, juvenile delinquency, short skirts, Women's Lib.

Audience research means that the media now know more than ever before about the impact and effects of news, and that they can tailor their work with surer hands. They can gather news with minimum waste, and they can select story emphases with assurance.

AUDIENCE RESPONSES

Responses to the stimuli of news differ as widely as the people who make them. Though similar patterns develop—most people are repelled by a picture of the shattered body of a bomb-torn soldier; most register approval at news of an advance in the "war" on cancer—no two react with precisely the same thoughts or actions.

Some responses are anything but subtle or veiled. Let radio broadcast the news that a fire has gone out of control at the corner of Main and Fourth streets, and in minutes police lines are engulfed by spectators rushing to see the fire with their own eyes. Let the newspaper report that the Watch and Ward Society has demanded the closing of a movie it calls "obscene," and the box office is swamped. There is no need for costly research or analysis to show the effects of such news on audiences.

Many newsworkers believe, however, that news can serve its public best when they know exactly how given kinds of news treatment affect given audiences. Researchers have developed a number of techniques for analyzing what news does to people. A regiment of specialized agencies for communication research has grown up since World War II: commercial agencies such as Gallup, Nielsen, Roper, the Pulse; academic or nonprofit agencies at universities, often oriented toward particular social or psychological studies; communications research agencies at the schools of journalism at the Universities of Illinois, Minnesota, Wisconsin, Stanford, Indiana, Syracuse, Texas, and others.

These agencies have investigated the effect of news on political attitudes and voting behavior, on the development of juvenile delinquency, on knowledge of public affairs, on adherence to passing fads, on popular language. They have devised tests to find out which parts of newspapers and newscasts hit audiences hardest and are remembered longest, and what techniques of news presentation yield the greatest comprehension. They have studied typography, rhetoric, and illustration. Most communication researchers would say that studies in these areas have only just begun. A reporter, a newswriter, or an editor can work at his craft better if he knows the products of communication research and something of the possibilities it holds.

Through the years scores of studies have been made of individual papers and their problems, some long-range and others in one-shot surveys. Some papers make such studies themselves; others employ commercial research organizations to do it. Among the findings of one major newspaper in a 1974 survey are these:

- Six out of ten of its readers were between 18 and 50 years old.
- 67 percent of the readers had some high school education; 40 percent had been to college, and 15 percent had college degrees. (All percentages were larger than those in a similar survey 15 years before.)
- 40 percent of the readers considered themselves Democrats, 22 percent Republicans, and 31 percent independent; 17 percent called themselves "liberal," 48 percent "moderate," and 30 percent "conservative."
- 80 percent of readers lived in single-family homes; 33 percent of the families had two cars. 30 percent were union members.
- 94 percent of the families carried health insurance.

Useful data were gathered also on radio and TV attention and on time spent with the newspaper ("regular" readership was reported by 80 percent of respondents).

The newspaper that gathers such information can edit with a sure hand. It knows that a majority of its readers are in the "prime of life," but that it would make a serious mistake to ignore its sizable younger community. It knows how many older readers prefer *Reader's Digest,* how many the *Atlantic.* It knows that a negligible few read *The New Yorker* (a favorite of the paper's editors).

One of the most extensive American analyses of newspaper readership, the Continuing Study of Newspaper Readership—140 dailies constituted the "sample"—led to some "response-facts" that appear basic: that women were more interested than men in news about people; that women are more interested in advertising than in all other content; that editorials drew attention from 24 percent of women and 43 percent of men, percentages higher than those for most categories of general news; and that their readership follows their socioeconomic level (business and professional men read most, unskilled laborers least).

What a newsman does with this ever-growing bulk of data is up to him. One newspaper experimented by making two trial front pages, one of news that scored high in female readership and one of news preferred by males. The results were not "good": in the editors' judgment, any newspaper built only of "popular" news would hardly be a newspaper.

Research by other media   Other media also look in the mirror. Magazines and broadcasting started studying audiences and their products' effectiveness before the newspapers did. Radio and TV news broadcasts, for example, were modified when studies showed what would be the optimum number of stories for a fifteen-minute newscast, what kind of audience is listening where, and at what times. A welter of research agencies serve the industry, both in elaborate listener-viewer nose-counting and in gaining knowledge of audience opinions about individual programs and broadcasting services in general. Congress, the FCC, and the public have looked askance at methods of audience counting and at the use made of audience ratings; abuses that once were rife have come under a degree of control, though they have not entirely disappeared.

Magazines have conducted intensive audience studies for half a century, at the cost of millions of dollars. *Time* has mountains of data about the character and attitudes of its readers, and constantly adds more. *Better Homes & Gardens* uses both its own research and that of commercial agencies to keep abreast of the habits, daydreams, and yearnings of what it calls the middle majority, the vast body of Americans whose families provide BH&G its multimillion circulation. Advertising agencies and advertisers use this kind of research as a weather vane to guide the expenditure of billions of dollars annually.

And with it all no astute newsman, no editor, no wise media executive thinks that all he needs to know can be gained from researchers' notebooks. "You can't edit a magazine by arithmetic," said one of America's most successful editors years ago. George Horace Lorimer, who made the *Saturday Evening Post* a household word, considered reading his mail and making personal visits to readers his best audience viewers. The expense, complexity, magnitude, and impressive productivity of statistical procedures should never blind the eye to the fact that talent, intelligence, and personal editorial contributions build great editorial enterprises.

Nose-counting and numbers should not blind a reporter to his own responsibilities. Audience studies by his employer and by others may be open to him, and he should use them, but his own questions in the right places, his own observations on and off the job, will help him at least as much as surveys. News must always be collected, winnowed, and written to serve an identified audience; the reporter who does it should, ideally, know more about the audience for each story than anybody else.

Projects

1. "Out of your head," list what you believe are the fifteen or twenty principal broad-scale audience interests of the people in the community in which you live —not in deep detail, but in general strokes: political, industrial and financial, educational and cultural, religious, social, ethnic, and so on.

2. Now go to reliable source books or other information compendiums like census reports, encyclopedias, fact books, library reference materials. Check, supplement, or correct your list according to these factual references.

3. Compare your findings in 1 and 2 with the news your newspaper and your broadcasters give you in a week, to see whether any interests are being favored or ignored.

4. Interview ten or more members of one of the subgroups you have identified in 1 or 2, asking their opinions of the effectiveness of local news coverage of their special interests. Summarize and comment on their statements.

Related Reading

News Research for Better Newspapers, 1966. — An American Newspaper Publishers Association research study into many aspects of newspaper audiences, readership, design, and content.

PART TWO

NEWS GATHERING: PROBLEMS AND PROCESSES

CHAPTER SEVEN

Newsroom organization

Successful news gathering grows out of meticulous organization and planning, inspired by imagination, backed by facts, and activated by sweat and purpose. Reporters are not called legmen for nothing: news gathering is hard work.

In newspaper practice news gathering begins at the city desk. Although radio, television, and the newsmagazines do not always use the term, each has a news director who does what a city editor does. A view of the city room operation of a typical medium-sized daily shows in outline how any kind of news-gathering system functions.

Picture an afternoon daily whose presses start printing the "final" edition at 3:30. Make its locale the county seat of an agricultural area, the trading center for a population of 200,000; the area has some light industry, several radio and TV stations, a small college. Make the city editor a man of forty, experienced on three or four papers. Give him a name: Miller.

Miller gets to work at 6:30 each weekday morning—his paper has no Sunday edition. There's no newspaper competition in his town, but at breakfast he always reads the morning paper from a larger city across the state. He has listened to two early-morning newscasts while shaving and driving to the office. Already he has an overview of the major news of the day. Most of the news stories he has heard or read this morning come from outside his immediate coverage area; he knows that his paper's wire service will cover them. But he has picked out two stories for particular attention, "local angles": one about the Washington crop forecasts; the second deals with a new movie actor announced as the surprise lead in a major Hollywood production. He pegs these two for the day's work.

THE CITY DESK

Miller's first task upon arrival at his desk is to glance through the overset, the proof sheets of news set in type for earlier papers but not used. With a black pencil he "kills" a number of stories no longer usable at all; in some stories he changes "today" and "tomorrow" to "yesterday" and "today"; he clips some of the stories and places them beside his typewriter. The edited proofs go into the basket for the composing room.

Miller reads through the copy turned in by reporters after yesterday's paper had gone to press—a couple of speeches delivered last night and some features he had assigned on earlier days or after deadline yesterday. He checks them rapidly, edits here and there; putting one aside for a new lead, he passes the others to the news editor's desk nearby.

Now he makes up today's local coverage schedule—the run or assignment sheet. He uses a big diarylike calendar, with a page for each day, for recording future events. (City editors use many kinds of tickler files—dated manila folders, sheaves of notes and memos, datebooks, card files, desk pads, and calendars.) Today's page notes a dozen events that must be covered—two conventions, a style show, a visit by a senator, a council hearing, other events—as well as such general reminders as "check new bus depot." He clips yesterday's paper for stories that need follow up today. He fishes in his pocket for notes he has written to himself. He comes up with anywhere from five to fifty tips for today's news by the time the reporters and deskmen come in.

A bonus news source is the news consumer. Tips on local events that have escaped the prearranged news nets come into most newsrooms—if not in a flood, at least in appreciable number. Most of them are trivial, and many of them are not of general interest: "I'm having a birthday party for my baby" or "There's a horse loose on Halsted Street." Either tip might yield a story, but the odds are against using staff time to find out. Radio in its early days complained that even its most faithful listeners called tips to the local paper rather than to the broadcaster. But it probably missed little.

Some papers or stations make pitches for audience help. The Kokomo, Indiana, *Tribune* once established a "red alert" telephone number for readers to report crimes in progress; in Indianapolis a similar program led to the capture of nearly a hundred law-breakers. Any such effort is good publicity—it draws favorable attention. This may be as strong a point in its favor as its value in identifying news.

WHAT'S IN A NAME?

Titles may not mean much on small newspaper staffs. "City editor" is an invariable term, but the wire editor's function may be handled by the managing editor, the copyreading by the news editor, and so on. The duties under each title change from paper to paper and from title to title; each news system molds its own pattern. The sums of all functions, however, are about the same on comparable papers, no matter how the jobs are described or the work divided.

Miller's reporting staff consists of three men and a woman. The woman covers education and club news as well as feature assignments; one man doubles as sports and farm-and-business editor; another gets all government offices except those of the city itself; the third, a young photographer-reporter, declares that he does "everything else." Miller covers the city hall beat.

In addition there are a wire editor, a news editor-copyreader, and a copy aide. The managing editor will be in later; one of his jobs is writing editorials (he did a couple yesterday afternoon). The elderly editor—"the Old Man"—who is also the publisher, not very active in recent years, will come in late in the morning, bringing copy for his I-remember-when column for the editorial page.

The city editor's major early-morning task is the assignment sheet (some city editors do it the night before). This may be a long memo posted on the office bulletin board or a series of individual memos to reporters. Miller follows the practice of writing each reporter's instructions on a separate sheet. He keeps a carbon for himself; as the assignments are met, he checks them off. Typical of assignments are those for the young reporter:

```
MEDICAL CONVENTION
     Here's yesterday's clip. Follow up for today. Cover
Osborn cancer speech this a.m.—we'll give it a play. Get
something on the afternoon panel if you can talk in advance
to a couple of participants. Try to get the slate of
nominations for the elections tomorrow. We can use up to a
column, or maybe two shorter pieces.

FIRKINS TRIAL
     Anything on this today? Is it on the calendar? How
jammed is the District Court docket?

SWIMMING POOL
     Doc Nelson told me last night he thinks the pool in City
Park is polluted. See him; also park officials. Try to get
```

Nelson and/or the park superintendent to talk. The super
will probably be mad. See Nelson first.

FEATURE
      There ought to be a good longish piece on the number of
nonmunicipal official and quasiofficial agencies we have in
town—federal, state, county, etc. Include the Grange, the
Am. Legion, Civic League, and so on. Might start on this
after deadline this p.m. No hurry. . . . Some photos would
help.

CONCERT
      Could you take a look in at the band concert tonight? We
don't want a lot, but we ought to have a short piece. Or a
feature if you can dig one up. This is a pet of the Old
Man's, and he can give you some background.

COUNTY OFFICES
      Give them a quick look when you're up at District Court.

Miller makes similar sheets for his other reporters. On the woman's sheet
he writes:

BY ANY OTHER NAME
      Check up on Jay Jensen, the actor picked for that big
film role. If I'm not mistaken, he used to be Ole Hanson
from a farm north of Elden Center. Get before and after
pictures if you can.

To the farm editor:

CROP FORECASTS
      See what the county agent and five or six leading
farmers think of the Washington forecast that came out
yesterday.

   Now Miller has a conference with the wire editor and the news editor;
together they decide what the "play stories," local and wire, are to be. The
news editor, who supervises make-up, wants a front-page picture; Miller
amends the swimming-pool assignment: "Get a shot of a lot of kids in the
pool." A telephone call from the airport announces a flight of Air Force
planes on an unscheduled visit; Miller tells a reporter to get there later
with a camera.
   Then Miller goes out "on the street." First he takes his daily cup of coffee
at the Corner Drug, where he chats with cronies and, as always, picks up

story ideas. After that he moves onto his beat, the city hall—mayor, council-men, other officials, police and fire departments, and the rest.

Back in the office, Miller writes the stories he has picked up; he takes some hasty notes from a pocket and writes his daily column of local anec-dotes. The reporters check in to write their stories. They tell him when they have failed to complete assignments or when they are developing new leads. Miller's pencil cuts through the copy as it comes across his desk—paring, editing, sharpening. Then the copy goes to the copyreader, who writes heads for it, gives it final polish, and sends it on its way.

NO NEWS?

"No news today," a novice sometimes growls. He doesn't mean it literally; the paper will carry as many stories as usual. He means that the news is dull, that the day has not produced stories of interest or importance.

No inhabited community is literally without news. In the modern world the wire services always supply more nonlocal copy than a newspaper or broadcaster can use. The local news may not be exciting, but only a ghost town in the Nevada desert has no news (and even a ghost town provides a color story). When a reporter finds a shortage of local news, he should examine his own enterprise and imagination. The store of publishable news is limited by a misconception of news, not by lack of newsworthy material.

Miller has had a fairly routine day. Some days are more strenuous—the days of big blizzards, elections, the annual harvest festivals. At such times routine may go out the window, and everybody from the Old Man down will be pressed into service. But the daily schedule usually resembles the pattern of this one, with its rhythm of covering focal news points, iden-tifying salient events that must be reported, and seeing to it that staffers are where they ought to be and when.

Deadline and after   The burden of the day's work is finished by noon. Most of the local copy has been written; the beats have been covered; the wire and local news for the day has been selected, edited, and prepared for the press. After a hasty lunch Miller and his staff check last-minute stories; perhaps they make final runs over principal beats. They telephone for late information. By early afternoon the last copy deadline has passed, and the presses roll. The paper is in thousands of homes before the families sit down at dinner.

Before that hour the staff is at work on tomorrow's paper. The young re-porter is beginning his feature on nonmunicipal official agencies; the woman reporter is looking into the history of a farm boy named Ole Hanson. The farm editor starts planning next Friday's market page, which has to have a roundup of food and produce news from half a dozen nearby communities. Miller checks his futures book, entering events that he must be sure to cover next week, next month, next year. He advises a reporter on the con-struction of a new lead to get his story off to a quicker start, and he makes a

SILENT REVOLUTION

For most of the last hundred years news copy has gone to the composing room to be set in type, then to the presses. A few years back many newspapers converted to offset publication—printing from plates made by a photographic process rather than directly from type. But great change is under way.

The change was dramatically emphasized when, in the winter of 1973–1974, a network TV crew visited the Detroit News city room to make a film report on newspaper ethics. They had intended to use as background the News's newly installed computerized newswriting and news-editing processes. After a short time, however, the TV crew moved to another office. Why not the newsroom? "No type-writer clatter," they said. "No paper on the floor. No tension. Not what you expect of a newsroom."

The full news staff was at work, reporters and editors and rewrite specialists, doing what they would have been doing in the "old days." There was one vast difference: instead of typing and editing on copy paper, they were working on some fifty cathode-ray tube terminals (CRTs), which are small TV screens above a type-writer keyboard with too many keys.

The News was a pioneer in the computerized electronic techniques that are changing the face of newspaper production. Some experts say that by 1980 most American dailies will be using variants of the new processes. In simplified terms this is what happens at the News:

A reporter sits at his oversize keyboard, facing his twenty-five-line screen. He strikes a series of keys that identify him and the story in a line of capital letters at the top of the screen; with other keys he indicates the news department for which the story is intended, the date, and so on. He goes on to type the story exactly as he would on a typewriter. If he makes errors, he uses correction keys: he can trans-pose, strike out, or add letters, words, or phrases; he can move paragraphs about at will; he can in fact do everything he could have done with typewriter, pencil, and paper—but much faster, much more surely. When he has made all corrections and typed his "30," he strikes a key that "stores" the story in a huge computer two floors above him. Another key tells the city editor that the story is ready.

Using an identical CRT, the city editor calls the story to his screen, decides what to do with it, and passes it along to the copy desk; on another CRT the deskman edits and heads it. And then, over a telephone circuit, it is moved instantaneously to the News printing plant twenty-three miles north of Detroit, where it goes through photoelectric and other computer and automatic processes that prepare it for the presses.

There are many variants of the new technology. The Davenport, Iowa, Times-Democrat reporters write their stories on twelve-line CRTs, but editing is done on the larger screens. Papers from Miami to Honolulu are moving to new methods of typing, editing, and producing the news. Most of the systems are in early stages.

One thing sure is that hot type—molten metal formed by line-casting machines—will disappear (the News sold its last twenty-five Linotypes in 1974). A second is that new production methods do not change what the reporter does as reporter—gather news and write it. Reporting remains reporting.

list of assignments for the fiftieth-anniversary issue to be put out in six months. Perhaps he runs down the street to talk with a banker who has been stuffy about giving out financial information. He helps plan a picture story on the backyard zoo some kids on the west side have started. He's likely to be hard at it long after all staff typewriters are silent.

OTHER DEPARTMENTS

The city desk is the heart of most news-gathering systems; but it is surrounded by and works closely with other departments (see the chart of newspaper organization on page 68). Among the principal ones are the picture desk, correspondents, and news specialists.

The picture desk   Most photo assignments are made by or through the city editor or the editor of a specialized department, such as sports or education. But pictures are edited and captioned by the picture editors, and picture features are largely planned by them. (Only the larger papers maintain separate photo desks.)

Correspondents   Stories from a newspaper's correspondents, if they come by wire, are usually routed through the wire editor (big papers have cable, foreign, or international desks as well); if they are regional, they may go to a state or regional desk. The smaller newspaper that maintains regional coverage may have a correspondence desk in charge of stringers—correspondents paid by the published column inch.

Specialized coverage   Large or small, any news operation is pretty sure to have news specialists. Giants like the New York *Times* and the Los Angeles *Times* list at least twenty-five specialists, each assigned to one news field only; the Walla Walla *Union-Bulletin,* serving a small city, has nearly as many news specialties but only about ten reporters—many with double or triple assignments. Sports and women's departments are almost universal; other areas that often get special attention are business, agriculture, entertainment, and science.

Projects

1. Read carefully all the front-page stories in one issue of a daily paper and identify all the news sources from which their information came (remember that a wire service, such as AP or UPI, is not a *source* but a *carrier*). Write an analysis of what you have found.

2. From all the local news stories in one day's issue of a daily, develop a list, or assignment sheet, of the events you think the paper should cover the next day. Then check the next day's paper to see how your list and the paper's performance agree.

3. Using all the tips and sources you can muster, write an assignment sheet for the next issue of your school paper.

CHAPTER EIGHT

The reporter at work

*What the best journalists achieve in the everyday run of work
is ... good reporting. It's the heart of the profession. Reporting
means to go out and look into what most people don't know
about, or what they've heard about but don't understand, or what
they see every day but overlook, and then to come back and make
it known. It means telling a story that enlightens. The rest is
whipped cream ...*

JOHN RUSSELL
Professor of history, University of Sussex, Brighton, England, quoted in the
British Broadcasting Corporation's *Listener*

ORGANIZING A BEAT

The news media have developed two kinds of beat organization: subject
matter and geographical.

The first, which asks a reporter to cover news in one subject field or in a
group of related fields, is common to big newspapers, network news operations, and newsmagazines. Most of the familiar beats follow the subject-
matter pattern: police, city hall, education, religion, federal, business, sports,
social services. The pattern calls for reporter-specialists who concentrate
on news of education, health, aviation, entertainment. The sportswriter is
a specialist; so is the political writer. When a newspaper is well heeled
enough to support a corps of specialists and when its coverage area provides enough newsworthy activity to keep them busy, the pattern is the
efficient one.

The beat dictated by geography groups together news centers that can be
conveniently covered by a single pair of legs. This is the more usual beat

HOW A BEAT GROWS

When the writer of this book was a Honolulu Star-Bulletin reporter—his first job after journalism school—the shiny nameplate on his desk labeled him Marine Editor. When the city editor wanted him, he rasped "Waterfront!" The marine editor was assigned to the waterfront beat, covering piers and ship movements, business that had to do with Honolulu's important shipping industry, the harbormaster's office, and portside businesses. But the beat mushroomed. The post office was on the waterfront—why not have Waterfront cover federal news as well? So federal courts, customs offices, Prohibition enforcement, immigration were added to the beat, even though some of the offices were far from the harbor. Next to one of the federal offices was the Hawaii Department of Education, so education was added. Visitors to Honolulu, who disembarked on the waterfront, went to hotels; by osmosis hotels became part of the beat. And so it went.

pattern for the small newspaper. For example, a reporter may be assigned to cover the news in a city's largest industry. This is a good-sized assignment in itself, with the plant's trade union, the demand for better housing for workers, pollution problems, expected expansion, management's response to a city plan to broaden its tax base. "Look," says the city editor, "the plant is way out on the line between Brighton and Wilshire. You might as well cover those suburbs too. And the veterans' hospital is on your way back to town."

COVERING A BEAT

Suppose you follow the all-over-town reporter on a typical day, the day Miller gave him the assignment sheet described in Chapter 7. Before he leaves the office—he arrived about 7—he has morning chores at his desk. Most reporters have office assignments: bringing stories up to date, giving the copyreader or wire editor a hand with overnight features, telephoning to check facts in clippings for rewrite, making appointments for interviews, checking signals with photographers.

The reporter leaves the office before 9. His first stop is the leading hotel—now called motor inn—where the State Medical Association is in session. He rechecks the clipping of the story he wrote yesterday. Then he stops at the reception desk for a moment's chat with the clerk. He runs through the registration cards for story ideas.

"You ought to see the man in 209," the clerk says. "I told him to expect a ring from you. He's a vice-president of Greyhound—I think he's here about the new depot." The reporter congratulates himself on having a desk clerk who knows how to be helpful. A call to Room 209 yields an appointment for 11:30.

On the mezzanine the reporter greets the Chamber of Commerce stenographer acting as receptionist for the medical convention. She helps him find Dr. Osborn, who is to talk on cancer. Osborn makes his task easier by giving him a script of the talk with the assurance that he isn't going to depart one word from it.

The reporter now finds the chairman of the afternoon panel and gets material for a couple of summary paragraphs. He questions the secretary of the association about the slate of new officers, but the secretary tells him that it won't be ready before the voting tomorrow afternoon.

"We'll vote at 2 o'clock," the secretary says. "But I can't give you the results until we adjourn about 3:15."

The reporter explains that he has to have the names earlier if the story is to make tomorrow's paper. May he check with the secretary by telephone when the balloting ends . . . or would the secretary call him? The secretary becomes cooperative; a plan is set up so that the news will reach the paper with ten or fifteen minutes to spare. If the voting is routine as usual, the slate will be accepted without change. The reporter points out that he can write the story ahead of time, if the secretary will let him have the names now, in confidence. She agrees.

One major assignment is wrapped up.

The county courthouse is across the street. In the sheriff's office all is quiet. "The boss?" says the deputy. "Said he'd be back at noon. Nothing doing today. Some farmers out by Penbrook say they're going to picket the dairy—but they've said that before."

Questioning reveals that the sheriff is probably out looking into the threatened picketing; the reporter makes a mental note to check with the farm editor to see who'll do the story.

He goes on to other offices. The county clerk, a cooperative source, hands him a typed list of marriage licenses. The reporter exchanges a few words with the stenographer about the TV show they both saw last night. Quick checks in the auditor's and engineer's offices develop a cluster of minor stories. He sticks his head in the county agent's door, and agrees quickly to the agent's request to "have your farm man be sure to call me about the picketing."

The county clerk tells him that the judge isn't in today. Anything new on the Firkins trial? "Nothing," says the clerk. "Probably put it on the November calendar in a few days." He hands the reporter a printed announcement from the state capital about a schedule of civil service examinations for secretarial and clerical positions. "Just got it in this morning," says the clerk. "And there've already been seven chicks in here about it."

The reporter frowns. "How'd they know?"

"Heard it on the radio."

As the reporter turns to leave, a light strikes him. "I shouldn't think there'd be many people in this town interested in state jobs," he says, a question in his tone.

"Son, you'd be surprised. I'd say offhand there are two-three hundred holding jobs like these in this town right now. And of course a lot of our kids go up to the capital each year. Housing and equal rights . . ."

The reporter leaves, planning the story as he goes. *Have to remember to tell Miller I'm doing it.*

At the Board of Education office the reporter gets the pedigree of the new social studies teacher at the high school. From the sidewalk engineers on the block where they're digging the basement for the new supermarket, he learns that proceedings were halted for half an hour this morning when a daydreaming mother pushed a baby stroller into wet concrete. A few questions develop a paragraph for Miller's local-anecdote column.

Though he's now in a hurry, he decides on a brief detour to the bus station. The local manager is cautious, but he admits that the man at the hotel is here about the new "depot." "He spent all evening poking about the vacant lots up the street."

At 11 the reporter is back at the hotel, listening to Dr. Osborn's talk, following the words on the script. Osborn keeps his promise—he sticks to his text. "Wish I had taken a chance," mutters the reporter. He gets away at 11:30 for his appointment with the Greyhound vice-president.

At first the official is cagey. But the reporter finds that the tip from the bus station manager pays off. When he asks a direct question about the vacant lots, the Greyhound man smiles and produces the whole story. The company is going to put in a new $950,000 station and convert the old one into a garage. "Sure—go ahead and print it."

Elated, the reporter snaps several photos of the Greyhound man, then telephones Miller. This is a bigger story than Miller had expected, and he and the wire editor will want to plan how to play it.

Back in the newsroom: "I haven't touched the airport story yet. Mind if I do it by phone?" He telephones the airport for information. He isn't going to get to the swimming pool piece today, he reports.

He had to skip his usual morning coffee at the Sugar Bowl, but he stops now for a fast lunch and a word of greeting to the garrulous waitress who "knows everything that goes on in town, whether it's true or not"; she always gives him a lead or two. Ordinarily he has a luxurious half-hour for lunch—on the days when he's not covering Rotary or Optimist luncheons—but today he is more pressed than usual. He finishes his hamburger in ten minutes and dashes for the office.

Before he starts writing, he calls the sheriff's office. "No news," says the sheriff. "Just went down the county a piece to check a fool tale about a kidnapping. Nothing to it. . . . Yes, I talked to your man about the dairy picketing." But questioning brings out a story of a frantic mother who had seen disaster in an hour's disappearance of a toddling daughter. She had aroused a score of households before the child was found—asleep in an upstairs bed.

For an hour the reporter writes fast. First the medical convention; then the bus station story. The copy flows out of his typewriter; he has learned to plan his stories as he gathers information, so there's no sitting around waiting for inspiration. When he hands Miller the bus station story, he gets a laconic "Good work!"

Then more phone calls—some of them repeats of the morning's calls. He reaches Dr. Nelson and makes a late-afternoon appointment to talk about the swimming pool; Miller says they'll want the story tomorrow if he can get a good picture or two.

By copy deadline he has hammered out half a dozen stories. By 4, when he leaves the office, he has made progress on two features, the swimming pool and the nonmunicipal offices stories. He thinks this last story pretty dull, but he can see that it will make an informative background feature. And maybe there will be something in the interest in civil service jobs.

DEVELOPING THE BEAT

When a reporter has pursued a beat for six months, he thinks he is "beginning to know it." When he tagged around with his predecessor for two or three days before he took over, he may have thought it a man-killer. How could he ever get to know everybody in the county building? After six months he may say cautiously that he has it under control. Give him another six months and he will have mastered not only the idiosyncrasies of his own assignment but also many of the techniques of successful reporting.

Most reporters never verbalize all the things they have learned. They know what they know about their craft by experience and repetition, but they rarely reduce their knowledge to formula or generalization. This is an unhappy fact, for few learning processes are as productive as telling somebody else precisely how to perform a task. Halfbacks, pastry cooks, artists of all kinds (reporters included, since reporting is both art and craft) are likely to do their work by instinct, impulse, or reflex. Masterly products may be turned out even when the producers can't explain exactly how; but all would become more expert, and better able to extend their skills, if they disciplined themselves into composing careful descriptions of what they do. Continuing growth depends not only on gaining of knowledge but also on giving it.

The notes that follow in this chapter are a compendium of precepts and suggestions about beat reporting from a hundred sources, principally beat reporters themselves. They are presented in the form of a memo from an experienced reporter to a beginner.

KNOW YOUR BEAT—The cardinal rule, underlying all others, is: know your beat.

There are all kinds of ways of knowing a beat. You've barely begun when you capture the obvious indicators—names on doors, the principal activities in the offices, telephone numbers. You can get control of this kind of knowledge in the first few days. But the kinds of knowledge that make you a subsurface reporter instead of a skimmer take time and thought and a lot of pure hard work.

In a major office in the county building you have a principal officer—a county clerk, an auditor, an assessor, a sheriff—and a lot of second- and third-level employees. You have a certain number of routine activities and responsibilities, and you might say that any kid in a high school social studies class could name them. But that's about all the high school kid could do. You have to go deeper. You have to get into the official government manuals to learn the nature of county organization in your state, especially if you crossed state lines to get to this job. No two states (maybe no two counties) have identical practices or laws, and knowing one doesn't mean you know another. They don't call official records or proceedings by the same names from one state to another. . . . You better read up on public administration to see whether the offices you cover depart from standard practice, and then find out why. You'll need time in the library, in your paper's morgue, and other places where there might be useful information.

KNOW YOUR SOURCES—A beat reporter has to get to know "his" people. He has to know not only the county recorder but also the whole office staff; sometimes he has to know the staff better than he knows the recorder. In almost every office there's one member—a steno, a clerk, the receptionist—who not only has an eye on everything that's going on but who loves to gab. From such sources a reporter gets all kinds of news tips, even though he often has to go to the top man or an outside source to corroborate or amplify.

Not everything a source—even a reliable source—tells you is fact. Your gabby receptionists may tell you that "a woman died in the courtroom today—I saw her body carried out." Checking, you find that she fainted and is now at home getting dinner.

Along with knowing your beat, be sure that your beat knows you. A reporter on his first visit to a news source introduces himself so that he'll be remembered. Maybe he writes his name and telephone number down for each news contact—a good way of making a firm initial impression. He gets on informal terms with the staff. Sometimes it's easier to arrive at a friendly relationship with the stenographer than with the boss.

Nevertheless, a reporter has to reply heavily on the top man. This is the man with the last word, the one who can hold back or release information. He usually knows more than you do about the subject you're talking about, and you have to depend a lot on his judgment. A beat reporter doesn't necessarily have to see the boss every time he steps into an office; but he ought to have a regular schedule to see him, perhaps every day or so.

Word from its chief, however, is only one way to <u>finding out</u> <u>what's</u> <u>going</u> <u>on</u> <u>in</u> <u>an</u> <u>office</u>—and not always the best way, in a world in which concealing newsworthy facts, for good reason or bad, has become common. There are other ways. One of the best is chatting with knowledgeable people— sometimes with people who merely think they are knowledgeable. Every bulletin board is a source of tips; sometimes the janitor or the girl at the candy stand notices things that "insiders" think too routine to mention. There's no such thing as being too curious. Get the head man to tell you what he thinks are the really important jobs he and his staff are charged with; then find out what his staff thinks. You may not agree with the evaluations; when you don't, you have to remember that they come from people who probably know things you don't. When you're doubtful or skeptical, dig.

Another thing: you can't cover the county recorder this year without knowing what news his office yielded last year and the year before. <u>Spend</u> <u>some</u> <u>time</u> <u>going</u> <u>through</u> <u>back</u> <u>issues.</u> Often last year's stories give you material without which this year's would be incomplete.

READ THE SIGNPOSTS—You learn quickly to watch for signposts that help you to <u>establish</u> <u>rapport</u> <u>with</u> <u>your</u> <u>news</u> <u>sources.</u> Suppose you see a northern pike mounted on an office wall or a rod and reel in a corner. You don't have to be clairvoyant to figure out that talk about fishing will please the man across the desk (but be sure you don't call the northern a bass). If a secretary has a stack of travel folders about the Virgin Islands on her desk, you've got an opening. You might be surprised to find how many questions about travel in the Caribbean you can ask and what they'll yield in goodwill, in news tips, and in access to information. (Be sure you know where the islands are . . . and which syllable in <u>Caribbean</u> to accent.)

This leads to a warning: don't be a phony. If you're no fisherman, don't pretend. Use the obvious gambit

discreetly. Confession of ignorance, in fact, may be a
door-opener. And don't forget that if the news source wants
something from you, he's likely to start interviewing you
about your collection of New Orleans jazz.

GET UNDER THE SURFACE—Much significant news is under
cover, intentionally or accidentally. Getting it requires
the imagination to ask questions and the patience and drive
to dig out the answers. It's routine to report the motions
passed at city council meetings. But suppose you note that
every vote for six weeks has showed the same eight
councilmen on one side and the same five on the other.
Coincidence? Suppose that instead of the usual two policemen
stationed in a courtroom there are, at a particular trial,
six: why? Suppose that you discover a quiet campaign by a
local industry to buy up all the property in an area south
of town: what's up? Suppose the county clerk tells you that
twice as many marriage licenses—or dog licenses—were
issued last month as in any preceding month. Will you have a
story if you find out the reason? And if there's no reason
discernible, will the fact in itself be worth a paragraph
or so?

DON'T BLOW SMOKE—At least, don't blow it in an office
or a living room where you can't spot ashtrays. Good manners
are a prime tool in any reportorial kit. If you know the
play called The Front Page, or almost any play or movie
about reporters, you may have picked up the notion that
reporters are drunks or boors. The Front Page was a
reasonably accurate portrayal of one kind of Chicago
newspaper life in another era and generation; it has little
but jargon to do with journalists of today. Reporters are
people, and if they behave in a civilized manner, they get
civility in return. Movie reporters have tilted hats glued
to their heads; real reporters, male or female, say "please"
and "thank you" just as frequently as stockbrokers or
schoolteachers. Reporters don't sit down until they're asked to;
they first-name their news sources only when first names
are appropriate (though they know how valuable first-name
relationships can be). They behave with common courtesy,
and they get courtesy in return.
 The New York Times issued a memo to its staff in 1968
that said its publisher had "a strong feeling that the Times
should insist on reasonable standards for the personal
appearance of young men who work for it. . . . their hair

should be cut reasonably short, and they should be clean shaven and neatly attired, with clean, business-style shirts with neckties, where appropriate to the work situation." That was in 1968. Most papers today acknowledge that not all reporters wear neckties. Beards yes—tangles no. Pants suits, yes—halters and cut-off jeans, questionable.

BUT BUILD SMALL FIRES—Being courteous, however, doesn't preclude being aggressive. Sometimes a news source doesn't want to talk: for a good reason, such as that he doesn't know the answers; or a bad one—private gain at public cost, for example, or concealment of somebody's misbehavior. Sometimes it may take weeks of asking the same question, in dozens of places and in many different ways, to break the facts you need into the open. There is an answer to almost every question. If you keep digging long enough and hard enough, you'll usually find a reward.

There's no virtue in not looking for help. Maybe the seasoned business reporter on your paper, who has known the reluctant banker for years, can get him to talk when you can't.

Remember that you are the expert on news. Everybody thinks he can run a newspaper better than the editor, and everybody tells the reporter how to do his job. A news source may say that you "can't" run such-and-such a story— "that's not news"—or that you had better run it or else. The reporter doesn't have to get rough, but sometimes he has to be tough. If the public is entitled to the information he is seeking or has gathered, if he has obtained it through acceptable channels and methods, he and his editors make the decision whether the news event becomes a news story. When a reporter is in doubt, he'll never make a mistake by asking his city editor to share in the judgment.

Reporters increase efficiency and production if they work at getting cooperation from news sources. You will be asked often to hold off publishing a story. Sometimes the request is one you should not and cannot honor; in some cases, however, you serve your readers just as well, and at the same time meet your informant's wish, by doing so.

NEWSMEN KEEP PROMISES—Reporting has responsibilities that have become honored traditions. Every reporter knows that journalists keep their word. They don't loosely break release dates; they don't print information given to them in confidence; they don't reveal the identity of sources they have agreed to cover. But these principles of behavior can be used against you. A news source can gag you by putting you "off the record." If a reporter finds he's been had by this kind of ruse, he may decide he must retract his promise (with due warning to the source).

If you're alert, you can avoid getting your foot in this trap. A Boston editor once said, "I make it a practice to refuse to let people tell me news facts 'off the record.' In almost every case I can get the facts through other channels. Some news sources have said to me, 'Well, I'm going to tell you anyway. Use your own judgment as to whether to print it.'"

RELIABILITY—Responsibility means other things, too. It means that you keep appointments and keep them punctually. It means that you return the stenographer's carbon copies when she lends them to you—in good shape and on time.

You don't have to see every source on your beat every day. Not every source has news every day; some pay off only once in two weeks or a month. Sometimes public officials or business executives are genuinely too busy to allot you time daily. You can usually check on prominent or busy sources through their secretaries. Busy people are often the easiest to deal with; they will give you time gladly for legitimate news, though they'll resent your taking time you don't need. And lots of times—once they trust you—they'll call you in to give you stories.

Be specific. One of the most practical pieces of advice an experienced reporter can give is don't ask general questions. Ask for specific facts. People think more easily and respond more fluently to questions that are concrete rather than abstract. It is easy for a man faced with a vague "Do you have any news today?" to give an equally vague reply: "Guess not." If you ask him, "What do you know?" he'll probably reply "Nothing." But ask him whether he has decided to accept the position with the city planning commission and he'll give you an answer that makes a story.

Most beat reporters find it a good idea to keep their own futures books, something like the one a city editor keeps. You can't trust your memory for every upcoming date and event.

The futures book is also a good place to jot down feature ideas or hunches for pieces you can develop, on or off your beat. Although a beat man's primary assignment is covering the regular news, he's doing no more than 51

percent of the job if he doesn't have an eye open for
features, for stories that may take extra time or digging.
If you watch for such opportunities, you'll soon have more
work than you can handle. If you don't have time to work on
them yourself, tell the city desk so that somebody else
can be assigned to them.

Always keep the desk informed of what you're doing.
Sometimes somebody else is working on the same yarn you've
dreamed up. The city editor is the man who knows. Moreover,
he's the boss. If you have doubts about working on a story
or using information you've gathered, consult him.

GENERAL ASSIGNMENT

Ask a student who hopes to become a reporter what kind of work he hopes
to do and you're likely to get one of three answers: features, his own column, or general assignment. Feature stories get attention in chapters that
follow. Writing a column may be reporting or it may be pure self-expression
(usually it's something in between); many of this book's suggestions relate
to aspects of column writing. And anything you say about reporting applies
to general assignment. The term means availability for particular assignments not covered by beat reporters or specialists. Young reporters consider "general" a plum, for it is usually earned by proven competence. It
departs from the routine of beat reporting, it usually means the more important and tougher stories, and—since it often earns by-lines—it allows
freedom of style and approach.

Since general assignment takes skill and experience for granted, it is
freer from supervision than beat reporting. But a beat reporter uses all the
tools the general assignment man uses, and faces all the problems. What
he does depends on his own energy and imagination rather than on tips from
the desk. He is often more his own man than the "star."

THE TOOLS OF REPORTING

There was a time when a soft black copy pencil and a wad of copy paper
were the total equipment of a reporter. A couple of black pencils and four
or five sheets of copy paper folded into pocket size are convenient and
cheap. But copy paper is soft and perishable, and copy-pencil longhand
can smear into illegibility. Hard pencil or ballpoint on notebook paper is
neater and longer-lived. Notes for news stories don't have to last long, for
most stories are written within hours. In writing a long feature or a magazine article, however, the order and permanence of ink and a notebook or
light file cards are to be preferred.

The typewriter   Every kind of news communication requires skill and ease
with the typewriter. If you can't type thirty-five words a minute without

HOW TO TELL A MOVIE REPORTER

Few reporters imitate Hollywood and wave pencils and note pads at people they want to question. They'd look and feel silly, and they know that they'd be running the risk of freezing news sources into self-conscious silence. Reporters usually carry press cards—badges of identification issued by local police or by city desks— but they don't flaunt them. They produce them to pass through police lines or to prove they're not FBI agents masquerading as journalists. But they don't often pin them to jackets or stick them in hatbands.

eyes glued to fingers, if your copy is splotched with strike-overs or xed-out errors, if you haven't learned to compose on the typewriter and to produce a competent first draft that needs little black pencil, you'd better take a course in typing.

Typing skill becomes more important as CRTs and computerization move into city rooms. With a few hours' instruction, a good typist can master CRT techniques. It took Detroit *News* reporters about two hours each.

The camera   Photographs have been recognized as reliable and sometimes incomparable reporting instruments since Mathew Brady's Civil War pictures introduced a new brand of journalism. Today every journalist except the radio reporter needs to know how to handle a camera. Help-wanted ads in *Editor & Publisher* for beginning reporters commonly ask for camera skills.

The motion picture, the picture magazine, and the TV screen often justify the adage "one picture is worth a thousand words." But the truism shouldn't be stretched too far. It is no more dependable than its companion, "pictures don't lie." A news photo, like a news story, can be transformed by the flow of time and events, and camera reports can be as contrived and deceitful as the falsest words. A photograph without the help of words tells only one side of any story; it cannot report what lies behind the façade.

The tape recorder   Although radio journalists think of the tape recorder as an instrument peculiarly theirs, it is a standard tool today in print reporting. For radio and sometimes for TV it records live interviews and speeches in exact words and accents; it provides the crackle of rifle fire or the blare of the marching band. For the print newsman it assures precise and accurate notes. And a dependable tape machine can be carried in a pocket or a handbag.

It is partly thanks to the recorder that a "new" form of interview—verbatim question-and-answer—has become prominent in newspaper and magazine journalism. Bennett and Greeley used the Q-and-A story more than a hundred years ago without electronics, but they may not have used it as well, for example, as have two such different magazines as *Playboy* and the *Paris Review*.

A problem in using the tape recorder—beyond the transcription time it demands—is that an interviewee sometimes ties his tongue in knots out of stage fright. This problem can be alleviated by the right kind of reportorial diplomacy, as recorders become familiar. It is of more concern that occasionally interviewees refuse to talk onto a tape because they know there's no chance of saying later, if challenged, "I didn't say it."

The telephone   The telephone has been called the enemy of good reporting. A reporter extracts the most from an interview when he is face to face with his interviewee. A fact is a fact, a nonfact is a nonfact, however communicated; but subtleties surrounding statements may not be revealed by telephone. Most newspaper reporters gather news by telephone only when face-to-face interviews are not feasible.

But the long-distance interview has added a dimension to reporting. The telephone-recorded interview (some states require two-party consent), the conference call, two-way radio, and the telephone patch are devices common in news practice. And sometimes a telephone call will bypass an office door when pounding won't get it open.

Newspaper legmen who need to meet deadlines use telephones for speed; rewrite men wear headsets. Some reporters almost never write their stories themselves—police reporters who must never be long away from their beats, for instance, or suburban reporters.

Two patterns for phoning stories in have developed. In each the reporter opens with a summary of the nature, tone, and substance of the story. In the less common method the reporter shapes the story in advance and dictates a virtually complete text, from well-formed lead to organized body. He is in effect dictating to the rewrite man's typewriter; his story should need only minor polish after the receivers are on their hooks.

The other method resembles the casual manner you use to tell a friend about an event. The reporter departs from pure conversation by weeding out facts that don't help the story; he may suggest points of emphasis; but he does not dictate the final form. A reporter using this method might sound something like this:

This is Williams from the police press room. This one's about a drowning this morning. I'll give you his name first: Felix Horsfelt. Felix: F as in Frank, E, L as in Louisiana, I as in independence, X as in X-ray. Horsfelt: H as in Hartford, O for Omaha, S as in Sam, F as in Frank, E, L as in Louisiana, T as in Tennessee. He was 22 years old, according to his driver's license. Lived in Dayton, Ohio. . . . Here's the story: The cops say he was hitch-hiking westward—they found his clothes and a backpack with "Seattle" in big letters on it. Where? Mishpinish River, just south of where I-95 crosses it. Clothes lying on the bank. Squad car saw them as it crossed the bridge. Looks as though he stopped for a dip, and it got to be permanent. No sign of foul play or injury. . . . Yes, just happened—about 10:15. . . . No, I didn't go out. They brought the body to the morgue. . . . No—that's F, like Frank. Not S, like sank. Horsfelt.

Note how the reporter reported the information:

1. He identified himself and the source of his information.
2. He summarized substance and time in three words: "drowning this morning."
3. He pronounced the name and spelled it carefully.
4. He provided identifying information.
5. He summarized the facts briefly and repeated the source of his information.
6. He gave the hour of the event.
7. Answering a question, he reported a final fact.
8. He answered questions and checked a spelling error.

While Williams was talking, the rewrite man was taking fast notes. Williams talked at conversational speed; rewrite did not try to record every word, but rather took down key words and phrases and specific facts. (Most reporters develop their own forms of speedwriting. Few American reporters use shorthand, though it is virtually mandatory in Britain. If the rewriter's telephone is hooked to a recorder, he has it made.)

The technique to ensure accurate spelling isn't the private property of journalists. Most people who use it invent their own lists of letter identifications—many keep a list taped to their desks. Geographical names are favorites because they are easy to identify: A for Alabama. Given names are common: A for Alice.

New methods   Chapter 7 provided a brief introduction to technologies that are transforming writing and editing procedures. The computer is also coming into use in storing and retrieving information. Two Wilmington *News and Journal* reporters, Ralph S. Moyed and Jay T. Harris, in 1971 stored thousands of items of information about criminal drug traffic in a computer so that it could be sorted, combined, and analyzed in seconds. The New York *Times* has developed a system of computer storage of the content of newspapers and magazines. A visiting professor asked the *Times* information bank how many stories had been printed on Supreme Court decisions and how many had appeared on page 1. The computer gave him the answers instantly.

Projects

1. Pick a news center on your campus or in your school—a college or department office, the Union, a religious center, a school sport. Looking on it as your beat, list all the news stories growing from it that a local newspaper might cover within the next two weeks.
2. Get the permission of a beat reporter for a newspaper or broadcasting newsroom in your community to accompany him on his daily rounds. Write a report of your observations. See whether you find story possibilities that he ignores.

3. Get a professional reporter's consent to interrogate one of his principal beat news sources about the coverage of his newsworthy activities. Then discuss the news source's comments with the reporter.

Related Reading

Philip Meyer, *Precision Journalism*, Indiana University Press, 1973. — Application of social science methods to journalism—how you use computers, statistics, surveys, and polls, along with public records and other aids, to improve the quality of reporting.

CHAPTER NINE

Getting the news

No book is big enough to consider all the problems that a reporter encounters in gathering news. No journalist will experience them all in a lifetime. This chapter, rather than attempt to cover their whole range, suggests many but concerns itself particularly with three kinds of challenges: recognizing news; getting to it; and digging it loose.

A hoary newsroom anecdote tells about the novice reporter who was assigned to cover a Kiwanis luncheon talk. Back at the office, he told the city editor, "No story. Speaker had a stroke just as he got up to talk." However old, the tale underlines the truism that you have to recognize news when you meet it. Facts aren't news until they're reported; if your personal radar doesn't glow at contact with a news event, the process never gets started.

PROFILE OF A REPORTER

What goes into the alertness essential to any good reporter? What qualities produce the abilities to diagnose a set of circumstances and translate them into a news report? There are no pat answers, but newsworkers who have puzzled over such questions have come up with suggestions.

Experience   You learn more from baiting a fishhook than from reading about it. You learn how to report by reporting. Self-evident? Next question: How do you get experience?

Most new reporters today base their first job experience on education, usually at the college level. It may or may not be professional education in a journalism school or department; the proportion of beginners who enter reporting by way of journalism education is high, and the demand for their services is heavy, but their route is not the only one. Newspapers and broadcasters often salt their incoming staffs with girls from Radcliffe or boys from Yale or Yankton, equipped with liberal and humane knowledge if not professional training. Most major employers like to hire men and women with small-town or small-media experience (you work harder and write more stories in a day or a year on a small daily than you would in a metropolitan city room, and you explore a wider range of subjects). Many think initial newspaper experience more useful than radio or television work because newspaper reporting offers greater variety and depth. In any case the base is intellectual equipment to understand and make sense of society (or to recognize its nonsense), and as much "amateur" experience as possible. Work on a college paper is a good start, especially if the paper is a good university daily. Summers on community or suburban papers or in small radio stations may be valuable beyond appraisal.

Curiosity   The skeptical, inquisitive, seeking approach leads a reporter to be forever asking, "Why? How? Said who? True or false?" A good reporter never accepts today's event as a replay of yesterday's. He is always trying to find what differentiates it from anything else that ever happened. He demands proof of anything that is not self-evident. He asks to see the broken switch that caused the wreck—it isn't enough merely to be told about it. And he gets more information about an event than his audience needs to know. He can always cut out nonessentials as he writes the story, but he can't invent substance he failed to get.

Imagination   A novelist uses his imagination to build a fantasy of life out of whole cloth. The reporter uses imagination, too, but in a different way. He takes facts that often seem unrelated and puts them into context so that they re-create reality. His imagination and curiosity are demonstrated in the questions he asks. "How will this event affect my reader's family? his job? his community? Who can tell me why it occurred? How much of it will listeners understand? If the answer is 'not much,' how do I treat it to let light into it?"

Reportorial imagination depends on foresight as well as hindsight. One of the principal complaints against news media is that they permit major events to burst on the public without warning. Why did the subjugation of America's blacks come so abruptly into focus? Why were the cancers that led to the riots of Watts, Detroit, Newark, Chicago not reported so that the disease could be treated in advance? Wasn't the generation gap present before the 1960s, or wasn't it at least foreseeable? What are medical scientists doing *now* to prepare for the next influenza epidemic? Should the world have been astonished when Sputnik arrived to change it forever?

Reporting *before* the event means watching political, social, and technological trends and relating them to similar sequences in the past. This kind of reporting is not clairvoyance; it is hardheaded inference that draws on knowledge and imaginative observation. It is the most difficult of the reportorial arts, and the one practiced least successfully.

ARE REPORTERS CYNICS?

Cynic: One who believes that everybody is motivated by self-interest. *Does the "typical" reporter hold to this philosophy?*

A fairly general belief that he does is likely the result of confusing skepticism with cynicism. They are not the same. "Being a cynic is so contemptibly easy," wrote Molly Ivins, an experienced Texas newswoman, in the Houston Journalism Review. *"If you're a cynic, you don't have to invest anything in your work. No effort, no pride, no compassion, no sense of excellence, nothing." She goes on to suggest that it's "the kids who come staggering out of J-schools into city rooms pretending to be characters out of* The Front Page *who assume the cloak of the unbeliever. A good reporter is skeptical: he questions facts and often motives; he wonders how the $500-a-month bookkeeper got that Cadillac. But he doesn't jump to conclusions before he gets his facts."*

Knowledge Recognizing a newsworthy event requires knowledge that fuels curiosity and imagination. Knowledge means months or years of perception in advance of an event: study, research, tireless questions. The man who understands the principles on which computers operate—even if he can't program one himself—knows what to look for when he reports on new information storage-retrieval-delivery system.

"It is impossible in today's society," wrote Wally Allen, managing editor of the Minneapolis *Tribune*, in a memo for his city room bulletin board, "to reduce our guidelines to a simple list of Dos and Don'ts. Thorough, reliable and responsible coverage of racial matters demands deep knowledge and understanding on the parts of the editor and the reporter—something 'rules' can't teach." Though this warning dealt with a sensitive area, race troubles, you could substitute any adjective descriptive of a news field for its "racial."

GETTING TO THE NEWS

Access "Access," most people agree, is something the First Amendment seems to take for granted. Every American has the implied claim to the information he needs to make decisions and guide actions. Government shall not get in his way or in the way of his agent, the journalist.

That news of government is sometimes hard to get is a fact as old as government (the Continental Congress met in secret). It is not surprising that some agencies of the people like to make their own decisions about what to reveal. But the American system says decisions shall be open, not veiled in bureaucratic secrecy; and the news media, with their commitment not only to public service but also to the practical necessity of publishing news that will sell papers or draw audiences, have traditionally opposed governmental roadblocks to information.

In early United States history it was common for national and state legislatures to operate behind closed doors; as news demands increased, however, closed doors began to open. Congressional procedures permit secret meetings, but in practice neither the Senate nor the House has been barred for years. Newsmen of press and broadcasting had freer access to official news by the time of World War II than ever before.

The war produced a new barrier. United States news media observed a wartime self-censorship system under which they voluntarily held back information whose dissemination was classified "of aid or comfort to the enemy." The phrase "national security" became the touchstone. "Withhold anything that would, if revealed, damage the war effort." The 99-percent success of the controls firmly established in the popular mind the principle of the desirability of blacking out anything threatening to national security. It also established in many official quarters an ominous tendency to look on withholding as a way of life; it became all too easy, in peace as in war, to decide that information was "dangerous" and, by labeling it classified or top secret, to bottle it up.

The tense years of the twin bogies communism and nuclear catastrophe, along with a series of little wars that might have become big ones, helped strengthen official desire to close the curtains. The supercautious or the overzealous in government carried "security" far beyond good sense. An information officer of the Department of Defense, after the public found out it had been lied to by the White House in the U-2 spying-on-Russia crisis and the abortive invasion of Cuba, expressed the candid view that "management of news" was a governmental responsibility. This he took to mean that government might withhold news, or present news in what it thought the appropriate light, or even invent "facts," at its own inclination.

So the public was denied information about many kinds of governmental activity, and neither the media nor the public liked it. "A secrecy system, with authority vested in file clerks as well as in top officials, is as likely to be used to mask mismanagement, stupidity, or corruption as to protect national welfare," said critics of the "security" system. "Moreover, harm from occasional unwise release of information is less menacing that not letting people know what government is doing."

The cynical view that "we tell 'em only what we want 'em to know" no doubt provided a base for the "classification" of information and the doc-trine of executive privilege employed one way or another by every U. S. president from Truman on. And it contributed to the bizarre willingness to eavesdrop, steal documents, and cover up that came to light following the infamous Watergate affair.

EFFORTS TO OPEN DOORS

Press and civil liberties agencies have protested (many think not strongly enough) the use of secrecy in areas of public policy. "Freedom of information" or "freedom of the press" efforts have been led by professional societies and by a handful of newpapers, broadcasters, and magazines—but rarely by those who have most to gain, the elected representatives of the public. In 1966 Congress adopted a so-called Freedom of Information Act that somewhat restricted the authority of federal agencies to bottle up information, and in 1974—over a Presidential veto—extended it so as to increase press access to government records.

The strongest implement—wide publicity at any such efforts—has helped to keep some doors open. But the war has not been won.

The system has not been eradicated as this is written; it has in many areas been extended. Governmental offices are not the only ones that have learned that the best way to keep information from the public is to reveal it to nobody; private and nonofficial agencies on which there might be a moral compulsion to act openly but no legal or statutory pressure have learned it too. The newsman is committed to constant crusade to overcome the shrewd devices that conceal information the public ought to have.

Cover-ups at work   You don't have to look far or deep to find manifesta-tions of this problem. Watergate did not invent it—it only popularized a term.

Local officials like city and county clerks, police, judges and other court officers, and sheriffs decide from time to time to close their records to news-men. A county clerk, with more warmth than wisdom, refuses access to marriage license records: "I'm not going to let it out that those kids got married just a month before the baby came," he says. A desk sergeant denies access to records of local arrests: "How do we know they're guilty?" Humane acts these, but often illegal and almost always violation of public policy. Newsmen have stronger arms than mere arguments to open such doors, as some examples show:

- When police refused to give a Connecticut newspaper information about a car theft, a reporter got it from other sources (and incidentally brought about recovery of the car).
- A Wisconsin police chief refused to give out information about allega-tions that his men had been fixing traffic tickets. A judge issued an order for release of the information under a state "release of public records" law.

- An Illinois judge ruled that information officially designated "of public record" could not be denied to local news media.
- A Minnesota school board held private "agenda meetings" at which it made important decisions: hiring and firing, construction contracts, taxation levels. The news director of one of the local TV stations, with strong backing from his management, protested that such secrecy violated state law and procured an injunction forbidding it. He later learned that a "planning meeting" was to be held at a resort a hundred miles away (outside the school district, and at public expense); he arranged with the sheriff that board members would be arrested if they sought to carry out the plan. The meeting was not held. (Both the state Newspaper Association and the Broadcasters Association provided financial and other support to the station; the local newspaper and other local broadcasters declined to assist.)

Courts sometimes establish arbitrary limits on release of information in criminal or highly charged cases to protect the rights of participants. Reporters often accept reasonable restrictions, though no one has arrived at a generally applicable definition of what is "reasonable."

Legislative committees and subgroups of city and county councils sometimes decide to meet behind closed doors. Most governmental bodies hold hearings and take evidence in public, but sometimes they make their decisions privately. The news media, by reporting that public business is being done in secret, often arouse enough public concern to halt it.

Public relations   Every sophisticated news source knows that shrewd PR operatives can conceal information as well as make it public. The goal of a public relations man or woman is to nurture a favorable attitude toward the client—business, social cause, political party, baseball club. It may suit the purpose to "forget" information that would hurt a cause, or to color it rosy. Newsmen are wary of handouts and other controlled information that may give only part of the story or a contrived, slanted view of it. They watch out for what social critic Daniel Boorstin calls "pseudo-events," the kind that provide manufactured news (Henry Ford once spent a million dollars for a widely reported celebration to honor his friend Thomas Alva Edison, only to discover later that the whole thing had been invented to bring attention to the National Electric Light Association).

PR men, however, are often invaluable to reporters—opening doors reporters can't pass on their own or digging out in minutes information they couldn't get in weeks. Competent PR operatives, of whom there are many (PR workers are commonly recruited from newsrooms), have standards on a level with journalism's best. Some stories couldn't be covered at all without the help of an aide who works from the inside.

Releases   News releases can be boon or bane. A release is a prepared news story marked for use at a prescribed time. It is typically prepared by a public relations department, and thus straight from the wellspring—often factual, complete, well-timed. If all releases had these qualities, they would save thousands of hours for reporters. On big tables at the National Press Club in Washington are hundreds of handouts from government agencies, and the legend is that the lazy reporter can do his whole day's work here if his briefcase is big enough.

But journalists know that handouts often tell only one side of the story. The news media that depend widely on them are rarely dependable media.

The proper use of the handout by a reporter is to look on it as a news tip—a suggestion about an event or concept that somebody wants people to know about—that needs searching investigation for signs of self-interested slanting and for completeness and accuracy. Most releases have to be developed by further reporting to make them most useful to particular audiences. The handout from a distant headquarters of a steelworkers' union may carry information of interest to Youngstown, Ohio, steel mill employees, but it usually can be made more meaningful by comments and further facts from local sources.

Release dates provide headaches at times. It is accepted practice to observe the timing shown on a release. But sometimes holding it until next Tuesday evening will make it useless; sometimes the reporter discovers that what it says is already widely known. When the Milwaukee *Journal* was upbraided by the Chrysler Corporation for stories about the new Plymouths to be offered publicly three weeks later, the managing editor replied that the new cars were already on many streets; and he made a further point that most media support:

> We honor release dates on our paper. But we also follow the time-honored
> practice of considering a release date broken for all when it is broken by one.

Most media, like the *Journal,* "honor release dates." But sometimes, like the *Journal,* they demur at requests they think unreasonable. The Chicago *Tribune*'s reporter was barred from a science convention after the *Tribune* ignored an "order" that convention proceedings must not be reported by morning papers, although they had occurred "on *Tribune* time"—during the hours just before the *Tribune* appeared. The *Tribune* called the edict arbitrary, unreasonable, and contrary to usual practice, and sent two additional reporters to make sure that coverage was complete even though they could not attend the meetings.

The Toronto *Globe and Mail* for a time refused to publish any hold-for-release news in the belief that release-setting may constitute news management.

Off the record   The stratagem of keeping information off the record has a proper place in the movement of facts from source to reporter, but it can also be abused. "Background facts" are sometimes dealt out to reporters not for publication but to help them understand, evaluate, and put into perspective the events they cover. Cagey news sources, however, knowing that the ethical principle dominant among journalists impels them to honor promises of confidentiality, have all too often trapped reporters into unwilling silence. The problem is both moral and tactical; individual journalists may avoid it by refusing to listen, and the media may do so by office rules against it.

OFF THE RECORD: USE AND ABUSE

Dwight D. Eisenhower told a group of reporters in New York of the trustworthiness of the war correspondents with whom he had dealt. During his North African preparation for the invasion of Sicily, he said, "I took the reporters into my confidence ... and they never let me down."

But Eisenhower also knew how to prevent reporters from reporting. "Their reports were getting a little too close to the truth" in hinting at the coming invasion, he said. So he laid his plans open to the correspondents, off the record, "to shut their mouths—to stop them from writing. Later, some of them said to me, 'General, don't ever do that again.' They appreciated and respected my trust but they didn't want it repeated."

Norman Cousins, editor of the Saturday Review, *was halfway through a talk to a large audience when a man rose and stalked ostentatiously from the hall. The man was Paul Block, Jr., publisher of the Toledo* Blade *and* Times. *Later Block explained to Cousins: "You were giving a public speech. You suddenly announced that you were about to throw in off-the-record remarks. You were willing to have a mass of people hear what you said, but not to have us report it. Our reporters have been ordered not to accept off-the-record stuff; I thought you were taking advantage of your situation, and I refused to listen."*

Cousins later told Block that his position was "wise and uncontestable," and that Block had acted "in the best interests of newspaper publishing."

Other distortions of off-the-record information—or a variant, not-to-be-attributed information—are common. A news source who is unwilling to take responsibility for the news he is handing out but who wants to "leak" it may tell reporters they may use its substance without revealing where it came from. So the "authoritative spokesman" is born. This leads to the possibility that a reporter can write stories on his own responsibility but avoid saying so; or to the equally unhappy frequency of leaks and trial balloons. A government official, if he is embarrassed by such a leak, can always deny that he said it, knowing that a reporter may be unable to prove he did. On the other hand, a reporter using unattributed information that is nevertheless authentic faces the temptation—not always resisted—of taking credit for having "exclusive" inside sources. Moreover, as a city editor of the

Chicago *Daily News* pointed out to the American Society of Newspaper Editors, "a story can be given a kind of breathless quality if the reporter does not identify its source."

The news conference   Until broadcasting got into the act, the prearranged meeting of a group of reporters with a news source was called a press conference. It was invented early in the twentieth century (Theodore Roosevelt and Woodrow Wilson are both given credit) as a means of economizing a news source's time. A public official, a sports or industrial or political figure, could meet with two, twenty, or two hundred reporters at one time and place and reach enormous audiences. After broadcasting came along, the word "news" replaced "press" (not without print media squirming), and television brought what the president said and how he said it into every living room.

The news conference has been well used and badly used. Along with its virtue as a time-saver, it permits the most inexperienced or inept newsman to profit by the interrogation of the experts (a fact that annoys the experts but undeniably serves the public). It gives scores of reporters access to newsmaking figures, access most could not otherwise attain. It assures the interviewee—politician, corporation president, labor leader—a wide audience, and it permits him to control the flow of information and opinion he issues, to release only as much as he wants to.

But a serious shortcoming lies in this very control. One newspaper editorialized in 1973 that the news conference "is usually staged by someone trying to make a score. And if he has any skill at all, he can manipulate the conference to his own ends—not really answering any questions he doesn't want to answer and phrasing the answers he wants to give in the most acceptable fashion." In 1974 a Washington correspondent writing of one of the infrequent Nixon news conferences made the point more sharply:

> President Nixon's press conference Monday night demonstrated again how difficult it can be to pin down a president—even a troubled one—who does not wish to be pinned down. . . .
>
> On the question of defining an impeachable offense, for example, he did not hesitate to respond in a narrow way that would benefit his own self-interest and self-preservation. . . . He chose to ignore the very large body of opinion that says that the founding fathers intended that a president could be impeached not only for criminal acts but for political transgressions, such as the misuse of office. . . .

The shrewd interviewee can use a news conference to conceal or withhold news. He may gain points merely by the fact of presenting himself before reporters, but he can contrive to produce less information than would a mimeographed release. Moreover, he may be able to bottle up information under the guise of candor: "I'm telling you thus-and-thus for your information—but not for publication."

International news   News sources of foreign governments are often difficult to penetrate. Many nations hold to the principle that the public ought to know only what government chooses to let it know. For three years a United Nations subcommission on freedom of information labored to formulate a code for international exchange of news; it disbanded in despair, nothing accomplished, because so many UN nations refused to support any such exchange. Some were more interested in setting up mandatory control of news.

Problems in broadcasting   Radio and television news, no longer newcomers to journalism, have always faced their own obstacles. One that is now dissipating was the public's tardy acceptance of radio and TV as news media. Today most audience surveys show greater public dependence on broadcast news—especially the kind that has living color—than on printed news. But it was not always thus. It took some twenty years for radio correspondents to persuade the White House and the Capitol to admit broadcast newsmen to the press galleries and the professional organizations. This manifestation, as well as print newsmen's scorn and fear of the electronic media, has largely passed. But the public is still more likely to "call the paper" than the broadcaster when it learns of something it thinks is news.

TV CAN BE MISUSED

One case in which TV was misled to photograph an unplanned but nevertheless staged event is reported on page 129. The case is not unique. Time and again crowds seeking either trouble or entertainment have gone into eruption when they knew the TV cameras had arrived. And TV newsmen have more than once demanded that crowds they were photographing "yell" or "fight" or do almost anything that would make interesting pictures. Such misbehavior on either side of the camera appears to be becoming unfashionable.

More rapid advances have been made in admission of broadcaster equipment to news events. For some twenty years after television appeared, the intrusion of the news camera and sometimes of radio's tape recorder raised hackles. Camera coverage of courtrooms is specifically labeled a threat to fair trial procedures by the unofficial but potent Canon 35 of the American Bar Association. Some judges, though not many, defy the ABA dictum. On the other hand, the prolonged restriction on camera reporting of congressional hearings and such public functions as city council meetings started to break down by the early 1950s—few Americans were not reached by the Edward R. Murrow broadcasts of Senator Joe McCarthy's Army hearings or the 1973 Senate Watergate hearings or the impeachment hearings in 1974.

In any case campaigns by newsmen's organizations of both print and air, together with picture-taking techniques that make cameras less and less intrusive, have dented official reluctance to accommodate live TV. Telecasts of presidential news conferences have been common since John F. Kennedy first permitted them.

Reporter–news source rapport   Good relationships between reporters and their news sources should be weighed on a jeweler's scale. If a source has doubts about a reporter, he's not likely to talk freely; he may refuse to grant an interview or to permit the use of a tape recorder. Lack of rapport may end a story before it starts.

A first tool in establishing easy relationships is the simplest—good manners. A young woman fumbled away an interview that had started well when she slurped her coffee. Phrases like "May I" and "Thank you" may be tired, but they're not tiresome. The day when male journalists slouched, called women "baby," and swigged from the hip went out with the fringed surrey.

It is also important to know what you're talking about. You don't refer to country-and-western music as jazz. You don't ask a county agent about sowing corn. If you're to interview an astronomer about the distant white star he has just discovered, you find out something about what "distant" means in the astral universe, what a white star is, and why it's called white (don't all stars have the same color?). Above all, you don't call him an astrologer.

Read the signs about a news source's wishes and tastes. Note the likes and dislikes in the clothes he wears, the decorations in his office, the books on his reading table. If you can find a can of tennis balls on his desk, you have a conversational gambit. You don't have to like his taste in neckties or politics in order to be courteous, and you don't have to dissemble yours to gain his respect.

In some areas productive relationships face built-in obstacles. In society today, for fairly obvious reasons, many policemen are distrustful or even fearful of reporters or cameramen who are "spying" on them. When a cop loses self-control and starts swinging a riot stick, and a camera catches it, he's not likely to thank the cameraman. A study of police attitudes toward journalists in Bloomington, Indiana, showed that police and reporters were mutually distrustful, the police hostility slightly greater than the reporters'. Angry police chiefs have issued orders that only "authorized spokesmen" may give information to journalists. But the Bloomington study discovered that patrolmen involved in newsworthy events were likely to leak information to the media even when they had been told not to. Such leaks are usually the product of good personal or individual relations between police and reporters.

Rapport with the tycoon, the cop, or the congressman who knows the answers to your questions is essential.

Experienced reporters know that there can be too much rapport. The reporters who went all over the world with Henry Kissinger found him altogether friendly and approachable. Some of them believed this made them less aggressive in questioning, overready to accept as fact whatever Kissinger wanted them to believe. A former Kissinger aide, Roger Morris, reported in the May/June, 1974, *Columbia Journalism Review* that half-truths and even nontruths were accepted and became news. "Good relations" that leave skepticism and hard-nosed reporting behind are a liability.

DIGGING OUT THE NEWS

"Digging out" is too pretentious a term for much of what reporters do. Most news gathering is straightforward and uncomplicated. You are assigned to cover a hockey game, a convention, or a meeting of the city water board. You get background information; you attend the event, observe it, make notes; you ask for further information or seek corroboration; you write your story. Or you conduct an interview (see Chapter 17), check facts or statements that leave you doubtful, and go to the typewriter.

But it isn't always that simple. You may experience access problems or any of a hundred other obstacles. There is no way you can be forewarned of all of them. But some of the more common are described below.

News-gathering methods   If public sources are sometimes reluctant to provide information, private sources may be more so. The law does not say that a businessman, a physician, a church official, or the operator of a bowling alley, a brothel, or a boardinghouse must talk to a reporter about his actions, even when they are clearly of public significance. Every reporter has experienced difficulty in prying knowledge that he thinks ought to be public out of disinclined news sources. A source may prefer silence for defensible reasons: release of information might endanger his business plans, might cost him money, might invade his privacy; or he might not have the authority to release it. He may seal his lips for causes a reporter rejects: embarrassment, the wish to cover bad behavior, sometimes misguided diffidence. In many such cases a reporter, if he believes his audience should not be denied the information, is obligated to find ways to dig for facts.

Sometimes there is no better way than persuasion—convincing the possessor of the facts that he's making a mistake to withhold them. But there are other ways:

• A reporter can almost always find alternate sources. It is rare that newsworthy facts are corked up in only one flask.
• He may publish a story reporting the source's refusal to talk. Often such a story is itself newsworthy—when the man who admits he owns the murder pistol refuses to say whether he used it, his silence says something to the newspaper reader (it may, of course, say the wrong things). This device is strong medicine, and it is a dangerous one; it is so effective a journalistic weapon that it must be used with scrupulous care.

• A young reporter, seeing two businessmen in a tête-à-tête that he believed might concern an important business deal, was turned away when he questioned the men. He reported to his city editor, a man of community standing; the city editor quickly got his questions answered.

Generalization about such devices is difficult—every case needs its own solution. Reportorial imagination, ingenuity, and insistence will open most doors.

News by sleight-of-hand   Fiction about journalism is full of reporters who disguise themselves as gardeners, grease monkeys, or schoolmarms to get the news (Hollywood prefers "crack the case"). Like most fictional creations, they have prototypes in reality. A reporter borrows a white jacket and a tray to get into a senator's hotel room. Or he grows a ragged beard and puts on his oldest jeans before going to a junkie hangout. Can such deceit be defended?

No two cases have just the same values. The two just suggested, both "real," may be as far apart in their merits as they are in their circumstances. The "waiter" gains entry by a deception; does he maintain the disguise after he's in? If he does, can he hope to conduct a successful interview, to ask acceptable questions, to get respectful answers? Is his action moral? Is it a form of theft? Is it a defensible invasion of privacy? Is it mitigated by the fact that the senator belongs to the public? What if the reporter gets information that is genuinely newsworthy, something to which the public is entitled? Does this justify subterfuge? What if the senator intends to release the information a few hours later? Finally, if the senator discovers he has been had, what effect does the trick have on his confidence in journalists in general?

As for the seedy reporter with the junkies: what if he gets information about drug traffic that the police have been unable to get? Does this justify trickery? Is acknowledged public concern an acceptable defense? Most newsworkers and most among their audience would say "yes."

Consider another case, again factual. A defeated political candidate appeared before a small campus group of his party members to speculate about the party's future. Two reporters showed up, one from a city paper and one from the campus daily. They were asked to leave on the ground that the meeting was private, not open. The campus reporter departed, but the other refused to go until he was, in effect, thrown out. He found a way to listen to the meeting ("He put his ear to the keyhole," one observer said).

The campus paper published a two-and-a-half-inch story reporting that the closed meeting had been held and that the politician, in a later telephone interview, had offered such-and-such comment. The city paper used a fourteen-inch story that detailed the meeting, adding that "the press was barred, but one reporter heard a portion of the remarks before he was persuaded to leave." This reporter said later that the meeting, being political, was one the public should hear about. The campus reporter said that he considered the meeting nonpolitical, like study groups common on the campus.

The conflict here is typical; there are difficult problems in many stories. Each has to be evaluated on its own ground. Some news executives make the unequivocal demand that their staffs never seek, take, or accept information without the knowledge and consent of the source; some ask hardheadedly only that the reporter come back with the story. Some journalists, either because they believe that getting the news at all costs is their job or because they think of outwitting news sources as a game, do not hesitate at trickery. Others refuse to countenance it.

PAYOFF

A reporter hid in a closet off a city council meeting to listen in on an executive session discussing a proposed open-meeting ordinance. The reporter was discovered and thrown out; the council then decided to reject the open-meeting proposal.

The news world as a whole takes satisfaction in the fact that the fine old art of picture stealing has become passé. Time was when a beginning reporter on the Hearst Chicago *American* said soberly that he would have been fired in his first difficult weeks if he had not been so adept at getting into homes through basement windows. That this kind of confession—not today a boast—is rare may be explained in part by the lessening of newspaper competition. It is consistent with what one newspaper executive referred to in the 1960s as "the change of the occupation from game to profession." That journalists don't admire sneaky news gathering is a symptom of maturation.

The competition   In Seattle some years ago, where reporters all shared the police press room, the police reporter for paper A discovered that his rival from paper B was lifting his carbons from his desk and basing stories on them. Legally, reporter B was liable to prosecution for theft of physical property, the carbon copies, and for theft of news as property. (The law has held that a medium that gathers a set of facts owns them as long as they have commercial value, which means until they are published. Had Reporter B learned of the events on his own, he could have investigated and reported them without penalty.) But Reporter A met the problem differently. He planted a sensational phony story among his carbons. Paper B put an eight-column banner on the story in its first edition . . . and red-facedly reduced the story through the day until it "denied the rumor." (Reporter A, meanwhile, bore the onus of having caused the circulation of "false news.")

Competition was keen to bloody in the days when every city had two or more newspapers. That was the day of the scoop and the constant fight to outwit rivals. But fewer than forty cities have this kind of newspaper competition today; such rivalry seemed on the way to extinction when radio and television gave it renewed life. Broadcast news competition does not often worry the strong newspaper, but in some one-newspaper cities radio and TV competitors drive paper-and-ink reporters hard.

It has always been true, even when competition has been bitter, that reporters from rival media have developed labor-saving ways of cooperating. In the police station or city hall of a good-sized city, where thorough coverage is more than one beat man can manage, it is a familiar practice to "syndicate." The reporter for the *Graphic* covers the first and second floors, the man from Station WWWW the third and fourth; they protect each other by sharing routine news. Thus each gains fuller coverage than he could alone.

But each reserves the right to his own exclusives, and each has well-guarded private alleys to news information. Each is on the watch to divine what the other is up to when he's out of sight. A common tale is that of the reporter who bottles up a news source—taking him on a tour of the city, out for golf, into the back room of a bar—until it's too late for rivals to get at him profitably.

Some news directors and editors lay down firm rules against syndicating or any kind of cooperation with the competition. Initiative is dulled by it, they say; reporters get lazy and their coverage becomes routine. There is merit in such cautions. But syndication is a firmly rooted practice, in some cases accepted and necessary. When an important news source is willing to talk to one reporter but not to a roomful, a pool arrangement is mandatory. When President Kennedy's body was flown to Washington following his assassination and President Johnson was sworn into office on the plane, one reporter represented all wire services and a second all the other media; no more were permitted on the flight.

ACCURACY

Getting it right   A reporter can depend on the facts he gathers only when he *knows* they are facts. That means first of all a stubborn insistence on seeing them as they are. It means working to attain the unachievable ideal —objectivity—and to distinguish between what they *really* are and what his personal prejudices might make him wish the facts were, or what biased or self-interested witnesses say they are, or what public relations efforts try to make them. And it means lightning-fast observation and mental recording of fast-breaking events. A time-honored classroom device is the staged brawl before a group of reporting students, followed by a "write-the-story" assignment. Students see pistols that weren't there; they mistake the colors of hair, clothes, skin, eyes; they report remarks that weren't made.

The problems of student observers are not entirely those of inexperience. Some fifty journalists—reporters, copy editors, editorial writers, news executives—looked out of windows of the Detroit *News* building one rainy spring morning when they heard gunfire in the street below. The reporter assigned to write the story interviewed everybody who had seen any part of the event and got broad agreement from them that payroll bandits had run from the *News* front entrance toward a waiting car, nearby policemen had shot at them, one policeman had been struck, the bandits got in the car and fled. But no two of the observers' stories checked in all details. There had been four to eight bandits, one to three policemen. Some of the bandits had carried sawed-off shotguns or rifles; or all had carried handguns; or only two had been armed. The policemen had been wearing white raincoats, black raincoats, no raincoats. A wounded bandit had been dragged into the car by his mates; nobody (not even the policeman found dead on the sidewalk) appeared to have been shot. All of this is not to denigrate the journalists' observations, but merely to show the difficulty of observing fast and surely.

How can a reporter hope to approach accuracy? First, he must pay scrupulous attention to detail and impose a self-discipline that most people don't have but that most can develop. Second, he must be a compulsive notetaker—memory is rarely good enough. Third, he must check and double-check, ask questions relentlessly, query when in doubt. One of the Washington *Post* reporters who developed the story of the Watergate burglary and cover-up said, "We never accepted a statement of fact as true until we had at least two witnesses we could trust without vestige of doubt."

SOME SPECIFICS OF ACCURACY

Patience As the quotation above tells you, a prime quality in the search for accuracy is the patience it takes to make sure: dogged persistence in running down the little facts, such as titles, addresses, names, times, dates; patience to go back to notes, to refer to telephone books, directories, almanacs, government manuals, and the like ... to make that extra telephone call, to knock on an extra door.

Slow down Chapter 3 proclaimed the virtues of taking your time; they bear reemphasis. Holding back a story is no sin if delay makes the difference between getting it right and getting it wrong. One broadcast newsroom has a sign on its wall that says, "It's better to get it right than to get it out." A tornado warning has to move fast, but details about the new school tax plan, when you're not sure they're firm, will be just as useful tomorrow, confirmed, as they are today.

Emphasis Select the key facts and subordinate or throw out those you don't need. Get rid of the irrelevant or the distracting. Choose between the meaningful and the merely interesting in order to put the weight where it belongs.

Emphasis may go wrong in obvious ways, such as overplay of secondary aspects of an event at the expense of the primary. But it is also possible to

emphasize falsely in subtle ways. One example: a story reporting a legislative investigation into university faculty moonlighting said that the inquiry
was looking at "faculty members shirking their teaching responsibilities."
Actually the search sought to learn whether, in general, faculty members
were in default; it was not aimed at specific teachers—a delicate but misleading difference.

Get all of the story   A good-natured multiracial crowd gathered to watch
a fire in a Washington, D.C., warehouse. As the spectators jabbered and
joked, the firemen came . . . and then the TV cameras. Some of the crowd,
according to a reporter who saw the entire event, "grabbed a grinning Negro
fireman" and demanded "that he be made fire chief. The fireman laughed,
shook them off, and went about his work. . . . But the camera kept grinding
and the young man played to it and finally an Army jeep drove up and
somebody put in a radio call. In minutes the police were there, brandishing
billy clubs and advancing with swift efficiency toward the crowd." The
police threw some tear gas, and the crowd, with mocking laughter, retreated.
As the reporter commented: "You could tell it any way you liked. Your
headline could have said POLICE ROUT ANGRY MOB. Or you could have
told it like it was—a piece of theater staged for TV. But to get it right, you
had to get there early and see it all. If only a few feet of film were shown,
with what looked like angry shouting Negroes, you sent a message. But it
was a false message."

Add and multiply right   A story says that the sum $653.50 is "1,500 percent
of the original 98-cent price." But 100 percent of 98 cents is 98 cents; 1,500
percent is 15 times 98, or $14.70. The sum $653.50, more than 650 times 98,
is something more than 65,000 percent.

   "Five local citizens, three men and two women, will head the Swarthmore
PTA next year," says a lead. "They are Arthur Morrison, Ted Walpuski, Bob
Gilmore, Henry Stebbins, Jane Quayle, and Mrs. Felix Simons. . . . " Count.

Watch your estimates   The Department of Justice and Washington police
estimated a 1970 Victory Rally in Washington at 15,000 to 20,000 people;
the Washington *Post* counted part of the crowd at 7,500, who "were joined
by 7,500 others." The *Christian Beacon*, whose editor had inspired the rally,
put the number at 200,000 to 250,000.

   Estimating is a hazardous business, even when it's nonhuman—be careful
how many fish you say died in the poisoned stream. There's no easy guide
to the art of estimating, especially when time pressure is often heavy. A
student of estimating ends an article (*Society*, April, 1972) thus: "When in
doubt, discount." A relief worker in Honduras after the 1974 hurricane
answered a reporter's question about the number of deaths: "Pick a number.
Pick any number you want. The bottom figure is 5,000; the government puts
it at 20,000." (The reporter used "5,000 or more.")

Hearsay   "They just found a kid dead in the administration building," a secretary told coworkers. "How do you know?" "Somebody just came in and told me." "Who?" "I don't know him—a guy." "Did he see it?" "No, he got it from his wife." "How did she know?" "Well, this guy says she overheard it at the grocery . . . " The fact: a man had fainted, but recovered and walked away.

Deceit   The outgoing administrative assistant to the mayor says he resigned because he's going into business for himself. The next week it is revealed that he was fired for giving inside information to competitive bidders on the new city auditorium.

CHECK, DOUBLE-CHECK, TRIPLE-CHECK

The New Yorker magazine has been called "the most accurate publication in America." How did it get the reputation? By its rigorous checking of facts. The magazine employs a full-time staff of seven whose sole function is to ferret out mistakes. The statement that "every fact The New Yorker publishes is accurate" is not totally accurate, but it is so close as to be a publishing miracle. Telephones, references, interviews, library research, and long investigative journeys all are regular parts of the checking process. Sometimes an article is held up for weeks to make sure that a date it uses is right.

The owner of the roofing-paper plant tells you that neighbors' complaints about polluted air from his chimneys are hogwash. "Why, we've got laboratory tests to show nothing bad is in that air." You investigate and discover that no laboratory tests have ever been made.

There is more to accurate reporting than this book and all the teachers and city editors since Moses can tell you. It is primarily a matter of the reporter's own self-respect and dedication. Curiosity and imagination, advance preparation and realistic skepticism, patience and the careful second look are all weapons in the arsenal.

THE REPORTER AS NEWSMAKER

When is it appropriate for a reporter to put himself into a story he writes? When may he frankly abandon objectivity and say "I"?

What should he do, for example, when he is at a bathing beach and a swimmer shouts for help? If he yanks off his shoes, plunges in, seizes the swimmer, and tows him to shore, he has become a part of the event. How does he write the story?

This is not a very difficult case. Had another bystander made the rescue, his name and what he said about it all would have been routine. In the case on which this example is based, the reporter wrote a first-person story, reporting not only the event but what he felt and thought about it. A by-line protected his subjectivity. But he could have written it straight, objectively and without showing that he was both writer and rescuer. Either method is acceptable, though it is likely that the first pattern, with its added human interest, would be preferred by most media.

In general, a reporter's participation in an event seems permissible if it is necessary to gain information, if there is no other way to get it, or if he is by chance thrown into the middle of the event. The reporter who crawled from a bridge falling into Puget Sound (Chapter 5) told a more dramatic story in the first person than he could have written in the third.

Projects and Questions

1. Ask ten or twelve friends who have attended a "crowd event" at which you were present to estimate the number of people involved; add your own estimate. Then try to get an estimate, or the exact figure, from an official of the event management. How do you explain the differences?

2. After you have been told about some colorful event by a friend or a family member, do a reporting job on it—go to original sources and trace down the facts. Write an explanation of the differences between the two versions.

3. Write a criticism—pro or con—of the news-gathering method used by the reporter who posed as a waiter to get into a senator's hotel room.

4. Identify, if you can, a print or air news story that seems to you inadequate—lacking in information to tell its story fully. Make a list of the details you think should have been included.

5. Find out from reporters, city officials, or other sources whether local government business—public records, council and commission meetings, and the like—are open to the news media. Write a report and comment on what you discover.

Related Reading

Carl Bernstein and Bob Woodward, *All the President's Men,* Simon & Schuster, 1974. — The two Washington *Post* reporters who broke the Watergate story tell practically all. A fascinating and often revealing account of the reportorial feat that every journalist ought to study.

Sigma Delta Chi Awards, *The Quill,* June, 1974. — Accounts of how more than a dozen journalists won national prizes, mostly for outstanding reporting. Some of the accounts don't say much, but most are worth your time.

CHAPTER TEN

Pressures
in news gathering

News-gathering and news-handling problems that are under the control of the reporter—how he acts to meet particular circumstances—were the subject of Chapter 9. This chapter talks about different kinds of problems—"inside" and "outside" pressures over which he has little control. Some of these pressures involve moral or ethical judgments, or decisions as to the propriety of accepting them.

NEWS IS A BUSINESS

In an ideal world there would be no selfish interest to influence what a news medium publishes or what a reporter finds out. But that isn't the way it is. Forces of a thousand kinds shape and manipulate what people want and the events the news media report. A reporter must comprehend the drives and purposes behind the events he is asked to re-create. He dare not see them through half-open eyes; he must maintain a reasonable skepticism about whether things are really what they seem, about who is behind attempts to manage the news.

It is a basic fact of journalistic life that the news media are profit-making businesses. This does not have to mean that they are purchasable or unaware of social needs, civil justice, and the rights of the fellow on the other side of the tracks. But to remain alive they need the support of the economy in which they live. They are often under pressure for "favorable" treatment, at every level from ownership and management to the editorial page and the newsroom. Such pressures do not influence news policy as much as most people think. The American newspaper is traditionally jealous of its independence, and it is usually strong enough, in twentieth-century newspaper economics, to resist dollar pressures. Broadcasting does not differ much from the printed press in financial stability; but it has never had the devotion to news service as a principal function, and this fact sometimes alters its view.

Internal pressures   A common complaint of "liberals" is that newspapers, broadcasting stations, and the business world that supports them are all run by the same people. It takes money to operate a business, and people with money have kindred interests and values. Publishers, broadcasters, and their advertisers, according to the critics, all belong to the same country clubs. There are wide differences in social and political values among any group of publishers or station owners. But the publishers mostly belong to generally conservative associations like the American Society of Newspaper Editors, and the broadcasters to the National Association of Broadcasters. They like good cars and good living, and they need profits to stay in business. The aggregate of newspaper and broadcasting ownership is not the monolith that angry or aggrieved assailants sometimes make it; but in general it obeys one set of economic and social rules.

SHOULD GOVERNMENT AND REPORTERS BE CHUMS?

"The cozy atmosphere surrounding publishers and their peers—business tycoons and government leaders"—is a threat to free and full reporting, in the opinion of David Halberstam, Pulitzer Prize reporter called "one of the two most influential American journalists." Halberstam says that reporters who get chummy with presidents and cabinet members tend to accept and report official views rather than to seek qualifying information. "Top people just don't tell you anything . . . the people sitting around in the dark corners of the State Department are your real sources."

Nobody believes that ownership never colors news selection. A Southern newspaper owned largely by railroad interests once let its staff know that "derailments aren't news on this paper." Patrick Owens, a labor reporter with editorial management experience, says that "indifference to the situation of working people" and the impulse to use news space for private or institutional benefit are "almost universal in the American press." (His example, the New York *Times*'s promotion of its "Neediest Cases" Christmas benefit each year, is not the best he could have chosen.)

Views of news executives appropriately impose themselves on reportorial news judgment. They are usually "good," for managing and city editors are hired for expertise and good sense. But their biases sometimes get out of hand. In one newsroom reporters used to say, "If you want a by-line, write a piece about a pet. The city editor loves cats."

There are more salutary influences. Hundreds of journalists have bosses like the Midwest radio station manager who told his news staff, "I have no rights in this newsroom. Kick me out if I ever try to tell you how to play a story." The news staff, the men and women at the desks around you, are traditionally more liberal in social and political views—more likely to vote as Democrats than Republicans—than the occupants of the front office.

And there is increasing concern among reporters and editors about "power in the newsroom," a voice in shaping news policies. The rebellious and unprofessional underground press of the 1960s that developed into the 1970s' alternative press was characterized by anger at Establishment conservatism and by moral vigor, logic varying from sober to passionate, and social purpose. Local journalism reviews—critiques by newsroom staffs of their own papers—blossomed in more than a dozen cities after the first influential one, the *Chicago Journalism Review*, appeared in 1968.

Monopoly ownership   The attrition of newspaper competition in American cities—not 5 percent of American daily newspaper cities have more than one newspaper ownership—concerns not only journalists but also any serious believer in the American sociopolitical system. Democracy depends on many voices, on hearing every side of every story. There are a thousand fewer daily newspapers in America today than when William Howard Taft was president, and 2,000 fewer weeklies. The 9,000 broadcasting outlets are only a partial replacement for the lost newspaper voices. Radio is heard everywhere, and TV sets serve more than 95 percent of American homes. But broadcasting, though its news service improves steadily, does not equal the printed press in quantity, variety, or interpretation of news. Radio, which served up dozens of commentators and an impressive array of documentary programs before television arrived, now does little but present news highlights; TV does not often cover news in depth.

Though the decline in newspaper competition furrows the brows of those who fear its implications—"if nobody's threatening you, you stop trying hard"—the danger is lessened by the fact that in dozens of cases monopoly ownership has not withered newspaper quality. William L. Rivers, in *The Mass Media* (Harper & Row, 1964), says that monopoly newspapers are in a minority among those commonly accepted as America's best. But a third of the 19 "best" papers in his lists are in one-ownership cities, and two others are the *Wall Street Journal* and the *Christian Science Monitor,* "national" newspapers. There was never a time when quantity of competition guaranteed excellence; in the big cities there were more "bad" newspapers than "good" in the years when papers were plentiful. Competition has frequently been a degrading influence. New York City had three widely circulated but disreputable papers in the 1920s, during the circulation wars of the newly invented tabloids. In Detroit in the same period, when Hearst journalism entered the scene and brought "sensational" practices with it, the other papers tended to fight it by imitating it.

Monopoly newspapers are almost always strong financially, thus have the means to develop and maintain high standards of news and editorial service. Not all local monopolies take advantage of their position; but on the whole the level of newspaper performance has never been as high in America as in the last third of the twentieth century. An editor of the Louisville Courier-Journal, which is always on lists of the "ten best," said in the 1960s, "Yes, we are that despicable thing, a newspaper monopoly"; but, he pointed out, in Boston when newspaper competition was bitter, the papers ranged from "mediocre to miserable."

The publisher who is strong financially, in short, is the one who can most easily turn dedication into performance, just as he is the one who can most easily abort it. In practice, monopoly papers seek fair presentation of news and multisided comment. There are more papers that are politically independent every four years; this might say that more are dodging the responsibility (and the headaches) that go with political commitment, but it doesn't seem to work that way.

Advertising pressures   A weekly newspaper in Iowa refused to withhold a story about a drunk driving charge against the son of a leading local retail advertiser; the retailer canceled his advertising and persuaded other advertisers to join him. But all of the advertisers were back, full strength, within four weeks. . . . A big New York department store withdrew advertising from the New York *Times* when the *Times* published news the store ownership considered "unfavorable"; this advertising also returned quickly. . . . When the *Wall Street Journal* used stories about General Motors' next season's cars before GM wanted the news to break, GM canceled its $250,000 advertising contract—but renewed it, without concessions from the *Journal*, within a month.

The moral to these examples is that, in a day when few newspapers that exist in any community are financially strong, there is considerable truth in the axiom that "the advertiser needs the newspaper more than the newspaper needs the advertiser." A reporter threatened by an advertiser usually need only inform his editors to make sure the "objectionable" story will be published. Some papers fall over backward to demonstrate their fairness and independence. A major page-1 Sunday story in a Minneapolis paper reported an accidental death in an elevator in the store that was the paper's largest advertiser; another story was given more space than comparable news received to detail sordid divorce charges against a local movie theater advertiser. Of different color but the same cloth was overplay of paternity charges against a member of a paper's executive staff. A paper gave undue space to a charge that one of its circulation employees used "vacation stop orders" as tips for burglaries at vacationers' homes. On the contrary, it barely mentioned the fact that one of its executives had become director of an annual community fund campaign.

This is not to say that advertiser pressure never keeps news out of the paper or gets it in, but rather that most newspapers have the strength to resist if they have the will; and that the will toughens as strength grows. Broadcasters resist less often, largely because news and its integrity have not been the prime concern of broadcasting. The critical journals tell stories of elimination of the word "gas" from a broadcast at the behest of the local public utility and the inclusion of a "puff" for a time-buyer's anniversary celebration.

CENSORSHIP OF ADS?

The Los Angeles Times in the mid-60s adopted a screening practice to keep "lewd advertising" out of entertainment copy it published. "It is not our intention to be either picayunish or prudish ... but we trust that we can find a better standard of values in the area of good taste." The broadcasting networks maintain "continuity acceptance" departments whose charge is elimination of offensive material from proposed broadcasts.

A reporter asked to twist, withhold, or publish news in any manner that he considers unacceptable can always say no, subject to action by his city or managing editor (whom he should inform). He will usually get support.

Commercial names   For many years news media shied from using names of specific businesses or products, especially in local news. Before 1965 the phrase "small foreign-made car" almost had to mean Volkswagen, but after the invasion of other European and Japanese cars the phrase meant nothing. In recent years many newspapers and some broadcasters use commercial names whenever they add to the meaning of the news. The New York *Times* has issued a series of guidelines. Use commercial names, said the *Times*

> if they provide necessary information (the brand name of the poisonous food); if they provide pertinent information (the name of the local firm sponsoring the Soap Box Derby); if their omission is curiosity-arousing (which self-adjusting camera are you writing about?); if to omit them seems niggardly (writing that the greyhound in the picture is identified with "a bus line" is pretty silly).

But, the guidelines went on, you don't have to say "Scotch-taped" if "taped" does the job.

The spread of consumer or ombudsman columns and broadcast programs in which commercial names are often imperative to meaning has made their use common. The TV program that reported that "nineteen percolators, all of one make, were found to be dangerous" reported worse than nothing. A common reader-listener ploy—today a naïve one—is to tell a newspaper or broadcaster that "you won't use this because it will displease an advertiser." Newspapers (broadcasters less frequently) mostly follow the rules described by the New York *Times*.

FAVORS

An ancient and dubious practice among newsmen is that of accepting "considerations" from news sources. It used to be that freebies all the way from movie tickets to junkets to Europe were common and hardly questioned. A radio station news director reported one February that he was "still entertaining with the booze received two Christmases ago." A newsmen's magazine reports the comment of an editor attending an Associated Press Managing Editors convention: "Every corner suite at the Waldorf this week has some company (paper suppliers, news syndicates, travel associations) handing out free drinks." Hundreds of newsmen, from top echelons to bottom, have traveled millions of miles as "guests" of airlines, foreign governments, and wealthy businesses.

Why not? Does acceptance of a fifth of Scotch, a pair of movie tickets, a new dress, or a sports jacket, obligate a journalist to modify treatment of news about the donor?

Many journalists, beneficiaries of the practice or not, deny that freebies affect news handling or news judgment. "I always tell the guy that I'll go along on the fishing trip," one feature writer explains, "but that it won't affect what I write about it." The reporter covering the Rotary meeting does not say to himself—consciously, at least—"That was a good free lunch. I'll make the talk sound good." He looks on the complimentary meal as a routine aid to coverage. "I'll judge the news on its merits," he says.

If freebies have no effect on news treatment, millions of dollars have been poured fruitlessly down the sluice. Madison Square Garden one Christmas gave a number of sportswriters sterling silver dinner services (some refused, most accepted). Sportswriters and broadcasters are favorite targets for this kind of persuasion: their Christmas stockings aren't big enough to hold the bottled goods, TV sets, tickets to Las Vegas, or casting rods that come their way. Theaters have not only furnished free seats for critics but often for anybody else on news staffs willing to accept them. A state legislature once gave costly briefcases and desk sets to reporters ("acceptance of these gifts, bought with public funds, is highly improper," commented one editor in the state). Transocean junkets "to observe foreign politics" are offered and accepted (apparently on the principle that a reporter—if accompanied by wife or guest—can learn all about the Common Market in two-hour visits to two countries). The professional journalism societies have only recently given up elaborate convention entertainment by such hosts as Sears Roebuck, Chrysler, Ford, and Humble Oil. The American Society of Newspaper Editors, the Society of Professional Journalists, and the Radio-TV News Directors Association are among major professional societies that now reject this kind of bounty. The freebie practice is under fire. Individual media —at the moment more print than broadcasting—have adopted codes of practice that outlaw gratuities; the Louisville *Courier-Journal* and *Times,* whose operating procedures seem to have eliminated acceptance of freebies, are "the acknowledged Messrs. Clean of the newspaper industry." Major league baseball clubs used to pay the freight for the sportswriters who covered them; now most newspapers bear the costs. Theater critics sit in seats their employers have paid for, and the sheafs of "comps" for Ringling Brothers Circus passed around every newsroom are now often refused. Some employers stand on a shaky middle ground: "Never take anything too big to hold in one hand." The Chicago *Daily News* and *Sun-Times* went to the extreme one Christmas of intercepting employees' mail and returning gifts that were suspect. The Chicago Newspaper Guild, saying that it approved "the policy of not accepting gratuities," asked in 1970 that the newspapers' executives, to conform to the general policy, reject "educational trips" and other hospitality offered them. A majority of the news staff of the Memphis *Press-Scimitar* pledged in 1971 to "reject all gifts that could be construed as forms—subtle or otherwise—of 'payola,' bribery, or coercion."

Few journalists think their integrity so fragile that it can't withstand a hand-holdable gift now and then. But journalists are human, and they don't always read their subconscious impulses accurately. A reporter who values his independence and the dependability of the news knows that his hands can't be too clean. Each favor accepted shadows not only its recipient but everybody working in journalism. Walter Lippmann told the International Press Institute in London in the mid-1960s that "the powerful are perhaps the chief sources of the news. They are also the dispensers of many kinds of favor, privilege, honor, and esteem. . . . The temptations are many: some are simple, some are refined; often they are yielded to without the consciousness of yielding. Only a constant awareness offers protection."

Checkbook journalism   The reverse of purchase of news favors in wampum, whiskey, or wardrobes is the purchase of the news itself. Is buying news facts proper? The answer is frequently yes. Compensating the holder for information he holds, especially when it is personal or private or the product of his own efforts, is both common and appropriate. Private information is a form of private property; it may be honorably bought and sold.

But if the information has public impact, the complexion of the problem may alter. Exclusivity is the key. When a newspaper or a network sews up a newsworthy figure so that no other medium can get significant information he possesses, the competition—and the public—are justified in feeling shortchanged.

Checkbook journalism has been big business for years. *Life* magazine was a leading buyer of "exclusive rights." The personal stories of forty-seven astronauts were contracted to *Life* through the 1960s, for example. As long ago as 1927 the New York *Times* and the St. Louis *Post-Dispatch* bought all rights to the first-person story of Charles A. Lindbergh, the "Lone Eagle" Atlantic flier. NBC helped finance young East Berliners in an attempt to tunnel under the Berlin Wall, and NBC was the only medium to film the adventure.

Among objections to the practice are these:

- That exclusivity automatically limits the number of media that offer a story, and thus limits the breadth of its audience.
- That news sources who think information they possess has cash value may refuse to divulge it if the price isn't right ("no pay, no story; a low price, part of the story; a fat price, a barn-burner").
- That only the wealthy media—the great dailies, news services, networks, and magazines—can compete; the little fellows are squeezed out.
- That the news holder is in prime position to manage the news, to put out only as much as he wants to, and to color it any way he pleases.

Not all news can be thus packaged and marketed. A spot news story has to be covered on the run, and its facts are usually as readily available to the fifteenth reporter as to the first. You can't bottle up actions of courts and most other governmental bodies, or natural catastrophes, or events open to the public. But you can sign the All-American basketball player to an agreement that he'll talk to nobody else about professionalism or the burning question of whether lady tennis players ought to make matches with gentleman tennis players.

Reporting is healthier when it is not at the mercy of the bankroll.

Conflicts of interest   A cousin of the favors problem is affiliation of journalists with newsmaking groups. There may be no philosophical-ethical problem in today's news journalism on which practitioners are more widely divided. Here are summaries of statements by the pros and cons:

- *Pro:* We want our reporters to be associated with all kinds of public and community service enterprises. How can they keep up not only with spcific news but also with trends in public thinking unless they're closely associated with business, clubs, churches, civic organizations, and the rest of the newsmakers? Can a political reporter report politics if he doesn't know politicians, political management, and political shenanigans first hand?
- Besides, this kind of community activity is good for us as an institution. If our readers and listeners know that we are active in civic affairs, they'll respect us more.
- Moreover, we have no right to say to a man or woman, "You have chosen to be a journalist. Your choice denies you the personal satisfaction, growth, and community contribution you could enjoy if you belonged to some other profession."

- *Con:* The instant we have a reporter affiliated with a newsmaking activity, we are under suspicion. How can news about the school board, or comment on what it does, be trusted if the reporter covering it, or the editorial writer who analyzes it, is a member? How can a reporter be objective about labor-management news if he's a union member (or half-owner of a bicycle shop)? Would you expect a pollution-control official to write without bias about automobile exhausts, sewage disposal, or garbage pickups? Newsmen should sit at a distance and report from the outside.

The pro views appear to be gaining. Reporters and their editors and managers are more commonly taking part in community enterprises. Direct political activity is rare, however. In 1973 The Newspaper Guild's Washington headquarters demanded impeachment of President Nixon, but a number of local Guild chapters issued prompt disclaimers. A number of newspapers and broadcasting stations seek to have it both ways by establishing community relations officers, who, without news responsibilities, can offer public service in the name of their companies without commitment to this party or that, Blacks or whites, inner city or suburbs.

The cynics doubt that Olympian disinterest is possible. But the record holds many tales of reporters who expose the civil rights violations of organizations to which they belong or reveal the illegal duck bags of their own gun clubs.

There is no ready answer. The problem is pragmatic, philosophic, and ethical, not legal or journalistic.

CREDIBILITY OR FREE SPEECH?

Geraldo Rivera, a reporter for WABC-TV, was taken off the air by his station in 1972 because he refused to give up making political speeches while he was off duty. The New York Civil Liberties Union, defending the reporter's position, said that no proof had been offered that his "reporting is less than objective, or that his work on the screen reflects his views as a private citizen. You are merely saying that outside appearances alone compromise his position as a newscaster ... an unconstitutional position." The response from station ownership: "[Journalistic ethics] require that a reporter refrain from actively campaigning. ... We consider adherence to this professional standard essential for our newsmen. Participation in behalf of a cause ... would preclude the kind of independent judgment we expect from our reporters. ... Without credibility a reporter is nothing."

Ranking members of the news staffs of all three networks agreed with management.

WHO OWNS NEWS?

Most news information is everybody's property. An event open to all comers—the laying of a cornerstone, the scene at a city beach on a hot day, a ballyhooed revival meeting—belongs to all insofar as the right to observe and talk or write about it is concerned. Semipublic events such as theater productions and church services, though those who manage them are in a position to deny admission and have the right to do so, are "reportable" by anybody who gets information about them. An event that is in a public street or is observable from a public vantage point may be used as basis for news by anybody who sees or hears of it.

Managers or participants in private events may refuse to give reporters information, just as they may refuse to talk about public events. But information about them is public property if a fact-gatherer (a reporter, a policeman, the woman next door) finds a legal way to get it. (See page 154, "The Right to Privacy.") If a reporter gets such information, he may make his own decision about its use; he may publish it, turn it over to his city editor, or throw it in a trash can. He may decide against using it because he thinks it unnewsworthy, because it contains libel he cannot defend, or because he believes it might cause damage or pain beyond its public value.

Another class of information—that growing out of governmental activities —is almost always public property, open to any citizen who demonstrates reasonable need or use for it. Use of public information (laws, governmental records, court proceedings, and the like) as a basis for news is legally reasonable need. So is the public's right to know. (Out-of-bounds information is that affecting national security and certain types of economic data and trade secrets.) The fact that some public officials try to keep information under cover does not affect the principle; injunctions and other devices may enable the journalist to gain access.

In the early 1970s a legal philosophy considered a threat to freedom of the press became prominent: the definition of information as property subject to laws governing ownership and theft. In 1971 the federal government's initial action to restrain publication of the Pentagon papers was related to this legal base, though disposition of the action was on the constitutional prior-restraint basis. A Washington reporter was arrested by FBI agents in 1973 because he had in his possession papers taken illegally by a group of American Indians from the Bureau of Indian Affairs (he was in fact helping to return the papers to government hands, and a grand jury refused to indict him). The threat to press freedom in such cases is not on the basis of the right to publish without prior censorship, but of the use of property laws to achieve censorship. There is no dependable forecast of the length to which this device may be carried.

Does a reporter own news he collects?   Suppose a reporter is assigned to gather facts for a news story. To whom do these facts belong?

Under the usual legal definitions, a reporter is acting as a paid agent, and disposition of the material collected is ownership's prerogative. Ownership may publish it, or sit on it, or toss it. In law the reporter has no more right to use it for his own purposes than has the hired trainer of a racehorse to enter the horse in a race. The horse trainer must acquire and train his own horse; the reporter has to gather information for personal use on his own time.

In practice this hair is not often split. News information is ordinarily used or thrown away promptly; once published, it is anybody's property. If a reporter wants to make later personal use of it, asking the publisher's blessing is more a courtesy than a rule of practice. Some employers—the New York *Times* is one—restrict staff free-lancing; but doing so is regarded by most reporters as cruel and unusual, and it is generally winked at by both employers and employees.

In short, the product of a reporter's effort is formally the property of the agency that pays for his time and skill, until it is released—to him or to somebody else, gratis or for "valuable consideration." Or until it is published.

THE NEWS COUNCIL

How can the private citizen or the private or pseudo-public organization get a hearing for a complaint against the press? First Amendment immunity means that any law that seeks to compel or inhibit publication of news or to modify a press attitude is a violation of the Constitution. The press, in effect, can do as it likes. How can a mere reader-listener bring it to heel if in his opinion it misbehaves?

In the 1970s a novel critical instrument gained favor in the United States: the news council, a voluntary body of laymen and professionals charged with rendering judgment on allegations of journalistic misfeasance. When such a council was proposed just after World War II by a commission of well-known lawyers, academics, and social critics (but no journalists), the proposal was ridiculed and ignored by an almost unanimous press. A contemporaneous suggestion for a "broadcasting council" (from Senator William Benton, an advertising and broadcasting leader) got nowhere. In Great Britain, however, a Press Council comprised of laymen and journalists has operated for more than a quarter-century, taking evidence on charges against the British newspapers and rendering judgments that either censure or absolve. The Press Council is unofficial and has no power of sanction. Nobody says that it has purged the British press, but the consensus is that it has observably upgraded news performance and press responsibility.

Several small-scale attempts at press councils or boards of informal lay criticism have appeared in America, most of them initiated by newsmen themselves: councils in Bend, Oregon; Littleton, Colorado; and Minnesota—a council dealing only with print media—and one in Rochester, New York, organized by the management of WHBC-TV as a partial answer to criticism of the station by the local minority community. The most elaborate effort took form in 1973, after the Twentieth Century Fund provided two million dollars to support a five-year "experiment," a National News Council composed of nine public members and six journalists. It is charged with investigating complaints about the news and editorial actions of the national news suppliers—two wire services, five national newspapers or their syndicated services, four broadcasting networks (including public TV and radio), and two newsmagazines—and rendering public judgment of fault or merit. Most lay opinions and four out of five media views about its purposes and probable effects are positive, but some media show the same fears that appeared when the first such council was proposed in 1947 (the New York *Times*, for instance, asserted that it will neither cooperate with the council nor listen to its judgments). The distinguished political journalist Douglass Cater stated his analysis in these terms before the Association for Education in Journalism in 1973:

Principal negative arguments (not, in Cater's view, supported by "careful thought and analysis"):
1. Such a council is its own grand jury, prosecutor, and judge.
2. The press is already subject to plentiful criticism.
3. No one person or group should decide for another what is accurate or fair.
4. The plan is "voluntary regulation" (New York *Times*).
5. Focus on national news suppliers means that the smaller and weaker elements of the press—perhaps those needing criticism most—will receive least attention.
6. The media are "interfered with enough by government" (Elmer Lower, ABC news manager).

Principal favorable arguments:
1. Unwillingness to accept outside criticism is arrogant and fearful.
2. Private and lay criticism is to be preferred to government control.
3. The courts do not have the knowledge or background for analysis of press performance that the News Council will provide.
4. News Council judgments will not have the force of law, but only the force of competent and informed analysis.
5. The Council will expose the "real threats" to press performance and public service, rather than those defined by governmental, political, or self-interested exigency.

Supporters of the council plan cite the effectiveness of the Minnesota Council as evidence that it can work. In its first two years this group produced opinions that were generally accepted by both public and media. One action censured more than thirty Minnesota weeklies for publishing, unedited, a publicity release (sometimes as news, sometimes as an editorial) without showing its source. It criticized sharply the activities of newspaper and television reporters whose overly aggressive shadowing of the FBI prevented a ransom drop in a kidnapping case (the newspaper admitted its error); but it rejected complaints against several newspaper editorials and news stories, after hearing the evidence. Its first judgment was an adverse criticism of news behavior of one of its own members.

Will the National News Council provide public access to the press, expose mistakes, and "educate" the public? Will it leave untouched such problems as concentration of financial control and incompetence? Will it become merely an Establishment tool, thanks to its elite composition?

Even if news councils accomplish none of the things they hope for, nobody will be the worse off for the experiments.

LAWS AND THE PRESS

Confidentiality   Respected and generally observed among newsmen's ethical concepts is the principle governing information given them "in confidence."

When a news source tells a reporter, "I'm revealing such-and-such to you for your private information, but not for publication," he can be sure that only once in a thousand times will his confidence be misplaced. A practical reason is that a betrayed news source becomes a news source no longer. But equally impelling is journalists' professional and personal pride in the sanctity of such promises.

The very insistence of newsmen that a confidence is inviolate, however, raises problems. Two troublesome ones: manipulation by crafty news sources to dam up information that ought to become public property; and the "protection" of the identity of informers.

The first problem, familiar under the term "off the record," is discussed on pages 120–121. The second, concealing news sources' identities, is one of the most trying that journalists face. "Sure, go ahead and use it," says the news source. "But don't let on that I told you." This tactic may be used by an informant to escape liability for carelessness with fact or to plant lies, libel, or information keyed by self-interest. It takes no reporter long to realize that the danger is always present and to learn to guard against it. The promise to withhold a source's identity should be given rarely, and never lightly.

But sometimes concealment of a news source is appropriate. When you are sure of the accuracy and reliability of the source, when revealing his identity would put him into an unjustly embarrassing, compromising, or perilous position, and *when you can make the news just as meaningful without his name as with it*, you may think it proper to refer to him as "a broker with local as well as New York connections," "a responsible official of the party," or even "a Skid Row dope-pusher who said he would be rubbed out if he were fingered." But your own confidence in the source's dependability (or clear warning that it is not dependable) is a minimum necessity.

Refusal to reveal sources sent a handful of reporters to jail for contempt

HOW FAR DOES A SECRECY PLEDGE REACH?

Does one reporter's pledge of confidentiality bind others?

Edward Cox, a Nixon son-in-law, decided soon after the President's resignation that the public needed to know more than it was being told. He described the former President's illness in somber detail to a wire service reporter, under a promise his name would not be used. Almost instantly (as Cox perhaps should have expected) another reporter identified him and used his name.

Journalistic practice supports the second reporter. News once published is everybody's property, and it serves to tip further investigation that is not bound by the initial limitation. But the justification for the pledge—protection of intrafamily relationships—continues to exist. In practice and law such facts, freely obtained, are usually not protected. The opinion that the second reporter violated a broadly professional commitment would be laughed out of most newsrooms. But the question is one to ponder.

---

of court—usually in criminal rather than civil cases—between 1900 and 1975; and some paid fines. Courts sometimes held that, though the newsman is personally admirable in his unwillingness to reveal a name, the welfare of society or the right to fair trial may demand that he break his promise. Public welfare in such cases may take precedence over personal or professional codes of behavior. Nevertheless, a number of newsmen have defied court orders and paid fines or served jail sentences (usually short ones).

More than a third of American states have adopted "shield laws," which forbid the charge of contempt of court in protection-of-confidence cases; most such laws make immunity an "absolute privilege," though some let the court demand breaking of confidences if to do so would serve the ends of justice. Disagreement exists as to whether the reporter's fidelity to his promise should be regarded in the same light as that of the clergyman, the physician, the lawyer, the social worker. A defensible principle is that, highly as the reporter's integrity is esteemed, the court is the instrument of society vested with the right to decide whether private or public values carry the greater weight. Some courts have criticized reporters' refusals to name sources but have honored them nevertheless.

Government attack—and support   About the time the Pentagon Papers case broke into view in 1971 (which was about the time that Vice-President Agnew instituted his war against the networks and the "elite Eastern news media"), the desultory efforts of news organizations to extend protection of confidences were given new impetus by a rash of court demands for "secret" information. A new element entered the scene—the issuance of subpoenas by the courts and grand juries for news information gathered but not used. The newspapers and broadcasters resisted vigorously and on the whole successfully, protesting that such action made them "a part of the law-enforcement system"; a 1972 Gallup Poll revealed that nearly three-fifths of the citizenry supported the protection of news sources. The Supreme Court denied support to the principle.

Newsmen and the news media are not in agreement on the subject. The case of journalists who believe the privilege must be protected was well expressed by Senator Alan Cranston of California, one of the sponsors of some twenty-eight shield laws presented to Congress in 1972:

> When public or private power is abused, it is often abused secretly. And as a police department often must depend on a tip to solve a crime, so investigative reporters often must depend on a knowledgeable inside informant to discover abuses of power.

He quoted a Harvard law professor in support of "absolute" protection:

> It is impossible to write a qualified newsman's privilege. Any qualification creates loopholes which will destroy the privilege.

But some journalists see it differently. Some believe nothing more than the First Amendment is needed. This comment comes from the Raleigh (North Carolina) *News and Observer:*

> The threat to freedom of the press is not nearly so great as the power of the press. And the basis for the press's power could be compromised by giving reporters special legal rights and protection. [Such protection] could make its freedom and power seem special privilege.

A seasoned investigative reporter, Robert W. Greene of *Newsday* (Long Island), adds another peril:

> Shield laws give government the power to define what a newsman is. This is a substantive danger, for it gives government a foot in the door.

In other words, if definition of who is protected by a shield law is established by legislation, government agencies can also decide who is *not* protected, and even whether a reporter or editor may make his own decisions. Perhaps this is a distant danger, but it is not an unthinkable one.

Libel   Libel, says the dictionary, is "any written, printed, or pictorial statement that damages a person by defaming his character or exposing him to ridicule." To that definition add the word "broadcast" before "statement." Before radio, defamation by spoken word was slander—derogatory statement by use of the vocal cords. Since a man's shout doesn't go as far as a printed page can be circulated, it was generally held that slander—though similar in many ways to libel—wasn't likely to be as damaging; therefore the penalties to which it might lead the way were less severe. Since radio, and later TV, range as widely as print, however, defamation by broadcasting is looked on as libel.

But note that defamation by itself may not be actionable—that is, the kind of act for which the individual defamed may get damages through court action. The defamation must also be untrue; and if it deals with a public man or matter, it must be what is called malicious—that is, uttered with intent to injure, or without good reason to think it is true. Examples will show this difference:

- A published or broadcast news story says that a citizen was seen breaking a window in a home not his own, climbing inside, and later emerging with a well-packed burlap bag. The factual statement is true: the citizen was so observed, and the paper can prove it. The defamation therefore is not actionable.
- The same story is published or broadcast, but it is false. The citizen is therefore falsely derogated, and his suit for damages would be likely to succeed.

Now inject malice, or lack of it:

- In the second case the citizen may be able to show that the newspaper or broadcaster put forth the allegation knowing that it was false; or that, knowing it or not, he had made statements to the effect that he was "going to get" the private citizen. Courts would usually take proof of these facts to indicate "actual malice," intent to injure, and might award both general and punitive damages—the latter considered punishment of the libelor, the former compensation to the libelee.

Take another case: a newspaper opposes a candidate for election to the city council. It publishes an editorial (editorials can be as libelous as news stories) saying that the candidate has not always paid state income taxes. The candidate sues for damages, calling the publication both false and malicious. Under the so-called "New York *Times* decision" of 1964, he could not recover damages if the newspaper could prove that it honestly believed the statement to be accurate. This decision has established the broadest kind of freedom for reporting public affairs; it has been castigated and feared as an open door to irresponsible reporting and commentary. In recent years the Supreme Court seems to be moving away from the New York *Times* decision. A reporter should read his law books.

A number of rules of thumb are available to help the reporter who is not a lawyer to judge the usual run of libel problems:

1. Truth of a statement is in most cases a full defense against libel actions. In rare cases absence of malice must also be shown.
2. "Privilege" that attaches to governmental and judicial proceedings is usually a full defense. "Privilege" is the right to make accurate reports of court and other public or governmental proceedings and all the charges

and testimony that are a part of them, no matter how defamatory, if the *reports* rather than the statements are entirely accurate. Inaccuracies may destroy the privilege and may be looked on as indications of malice.

3. The laws of "fair comment and criticism" permit journalists and others to express honest opinions or judgments of all kinds of "public" actions, from those of governmental and judicial personnel to the performances of actors, public speakers and musicians, and athletes. Such comment or criticism must be based on the actions under discussion, and it must be reasonable and fair. You can call a man a disreputably bad tennis player if he participates in an open tournament (whether others agree with you or not), as long as there is no showing of malice in your attitude. But you cannot say of him that "a man who beats his wife every morning ought to swing a tennis racket better" unless you can prove that that's the way he conditions himself.

4. You may write of him anything he has given you consent to say (but you better have the consent in writing).

5. The so-called "right of reply" permits you to respond to an attack in kind—to attack back. Your response may be vigorous, but it can't be false or malicious.

6. Many states have retraction-and-apology laws under whose provisions you may reduce liability for actionable statements.

Many more libel suits are threatened or introduced into court than come to trial or to decision by judge or jury. This is because libel suits are expensive, and both the suers and the sued often prefer to settle out of court.

Finally, some libel actions are efforts at vindication more than attempts to gain compensation in dollars. President Theodore Roosevelt once sued for, and was awarded, six cents.

Somebody once said, "Write correct; don't write mean; and you've got 'em cornered"—oversimplification that will take you a long way.

Copyright   The copyright laws are designed to protect "the products of a man's mind." They say that you cannot make more than limited verbatim quotation of a copyrighted news story; its style and literal mode of presentation belong to its writer until it is published or otherwise presented to the public, but after that only if it has gone through the federal process of copyright. You may sell or give away the copyright; if you retain it, you can control its exact reproduction or most other use for gain for two successive twenty-eight-year periods.

But its content is something else. The substance of a news story, the facts it presents, becomes anybody's property—goes into the public domain—when it is publicly released. This means that although you can't reprint your competitor's copyrighted news story, you can use the materials it presents for your own purposes—a rewrite, tip for your own further reporting, background information.

Reporters face few copyright problems; newspapers and broadcasts are not always copyrighted. The intricacies of copyright law are far more involved than this brief résumé indicates; anybody who has a question should go to his company's lawyer or to the library. But he won't have to do it often.

Congress has been fumbling for years with the copyright problem, and there seems some prospect that renovation and improvement of the laws that date back to 1909 may be in the offing.

Projects

1. Note in a dozen issues of your local daily the number of news-story references *by name* to advertisers, trademarked products, or other commercial activities; do the same for a dozen radio and TV news broadcasts. Interview at least one news executive about his medium's policy in such usage. Then write a report of your conclusions.

2. By reference to newspaper files of December, 1971, to February, 1972, refresh your memory of the attempt by Clifford Irving to foist a fraudulent biography of Howard Hughes on *Life* magazine and the McGraw-Hill publishing house. Do you consider *Life's* attempted purchase of exclusive rights to this manuscript, thus shutting out other periodicals from publishing it, a violation of ethical practice?

3. Write a statement of your views, based on adequate reading of appropriate materials, about (a) the publication of the Pentagon Papers by the New York *Times* and the Washington *Post*, or (b) the propriety of a journalist's refusal to tell a court the source of information he has published about a blackmail ring.

CHAPTER ELEVEN

The reporter
as professional

American journalists and a large part of their clientele look on reporters as professionals. A reporter is expected to be more than an artisan; the work of newsmen and newswomen is directed by defined and socially approved characteristics:

- Its principles and practices can be handed from one worker to another, by formal or empirical education.
- It operates with a recorded and expanding body of knowledge.
- It has its base in the culture and mores of its time.
- Its practitioners are motivated by concern for human welfare.
- It is guided by concepts of ethical conduct.
- It exhibits a critical awareness of its own shortcomings.

Acceptance of these principles as the base for responsible news work is implied throughout this book. They apply to all journalists, the brass in the front offices as well as the men and women on the action front. The reporter's charge is to behave so as to serve both the big and the little interests of his community. He takes account of broad social concerns as well as more limited community prerogatives.

Many of the specifics of achieving this dual goal have been described (Chapter 10, dealing with shielding news sources, resisting pressures, and other concerns that have clear ethical overtones, may be reexamined in this light). But reporters recognize that individual as well as communal values concern them. A reporter who merits the term *professional* respects individual dignity and the private and personal rights of citizens; in some situations he regards them as overriding.

And he observes and guards his own dignity. He can serve only if he earns the confidence of those he hopes to serve—confidence that follows from, rather than precedes, what he thinks of himself.

This chapter deals with a few of the specific situations in which, reporters believe, the personal lives of news figures deserve protection. Some of these have been examined earlier (for example, the right not to be libeled and the right to property value in literary or intellectual productions), primarily as problems that affect news-gathering practices. But there are other times when reporters believe they must consider the sensitivities, the attitudes, and the dignity of those about whom they write—times when privacy and other intangible factors carry more weight than the community need for information. Shielding those who make the news in certain circumstances may be as professional as revealing things about them.

NAMES AND IDENTIFICATION

The problems in the use of names get serious attention at newsroom policy conferences. Reporting is usually not considered complete if participants in events are not identified. Yet the news media are in consensus that some circumstances call for concealing identities. A conspicuous example is in reporting juvenile misbehavior.

For years most news media have agreed that leaving teen-agers nameless when they get into trouble may be a service to them and to society. The boy or girl under eighteen who is caught shoplifting, runs the argument, is not an habitual evildoer. Rehabilitation is of more concern than punishment; since 1899, when Cook County in Illinois established the first American juvenile court, courts and newspapers have moved toward the belief that "the important thing is not what can be done *to* the child but what can be done *for* him." In reporting "atrocious" crime—killing, rape, sadism—or spectacular or repulsive public offenses, it is agreed, names often must be used. When a fifteen-year-told takes a rifle, walks into the family living room, and shoots his mother, most news media think his identity is a piece of knowledge the public ought to have. But if he heaves a rock through a school window, and it's a first offense, few papers or broadcasters would name him.

This approach is not universal. In Helena, Montana, in the early 1950s Judge Lester Loble made public the names of all juveniles who came before him on felony charges, and by speech and widely published writing claimed that he decreased crime in his district. But Helena police statistics did not bear out his assertion; and nearby Great Falls, under a "Loble Law," had one of America's highest crime rates. J. Edgar Hoover believed in publishing names, too. But after a six-month trial in Webster City, Iowa, of nonpublication of *any* news of juvenile vandalism, with radio and newspaper cooperating, police reported that vandalism had dropped more than 30 percent.

A writer in *Quill* said that "the sad truth is that no one really knows the answer." No one has figured out how many youngsters have been rehabilitated because they were unnamed. Nevertheless, American media in general believe in giving misbehavers under eighteen the benefit of anonymity.

Names in sex crime   Journalists are on surer ground in withholding names of women who have been raped and of children who have been sexually mistreated. The justification, however, is quite different: protection of victims from embarrassment or humiliation. Few dispute this practice.

Names in personal news   Some newspapers and most broadcasters do not use news of routine divorce, custody cases, and the like. This is both to avoid spotlighting what are essentially private matters and to get rid of repetitive news that is usually of little general interest. In Detroit some years ago, after a fruitless contest between two papers to make divorce news juicier and juicier, the papers agreed—to everybody's benefit—to forget the whole thing. Names are necessary when they are important or widely known and sometimes spectacular details demand publication. Lack of newspaper competition in a city reduces the temptation to overplay such news.

Names in the family   News media, print and air, are sometimes justly accused of protecting their own—staff members, officers, relatives, sometimes social or business associates. Lack of competition, it is often feared, may induce newspapers to cover up news that ought to be published; but in many cases monopoly papers fall over backward to prove they can't be influenced. A publisher of a newspaper in the Southwest once complained to his news editor, "Do you have to report every parking ticket I get just to show we're fair?"

Identification in the third world   Identification of members of minority groups by racial, religious, or national labels is not the general pattern today. The usual news policy is to describe a figure in the news by such a word as *Black, Chinese, Indian, Jewish,* or *Italian* only if the news can't be understood without the tag.

This enlightened policy is less widely accepted in areas with heavy minority populations; but even in the South the habitual identification of Blacks by race is less and less common. (As is the use of "no Black news except bad Black news" that was once followed by some papers.)

The difficulty cannot be washed away by blanket rules. In New York City, with teeming Puerto Rican, Black, and other minorities—most at low economic levels—it may be both good reporting and fair reporting to say that the muggers in Central Park were white. In Decorah, Iowa, description of the man suspected of a dozen purse-snatchings as a Black may aid in his arrest.

First names   Newspapers and news broadcasters occasionally have to refer to people in the news by their first names. When the news figure is a child, or when he's habitually called by given name or nickname, his last name may sound stuffy. In a personality story about the City Hall janitor whom everybody in town has known for fifty years as Chris, it would be pompous and confusing to call him Mr. Sutherland. Few—including himself—would object to reference to the Great Crooner as Bing. Circumstances, custom, and the nature of the news often justify familiarity.

But what about the examples that follow?

> Police arrested Mrs. Janet Stringster yesterday on a charge of shoplifting. Janet declared . . .
> The Rev. Billy Graham won't be speaking at City Park tonight. Billy has found that a conflict of engagements . . .
> Photographers took pictures of Mrs. Aristotle Onassis on a Manhattan shopping trip yesterday. They snapped Jackie entering Lord & Taylor's . . .
> College kids don't like former Sen. Eugene McCarthy as well as they used to. When Gene spoke yesterday to students at . . .

What are the objections to these usages?

- They violate accepted social custom.
- They are subtly disrespectful, especially when they are applied to men and women involved in petty law violations.

A generalization: Use first names only when everybody would; be chary of them when the news is disparaging.

Names in "injurious" news   Names have to be used in most news that casts their owners in unfavorable light. But a problem arises—one suggested in a "cardinal, unbreakable" instruction given to reporters and copyreaders on the New York *Times:*

> If a person is mentioned derogatorily in a news story, he should be given immediate chance to respond. If he can't be reached, the story should be held over if possible. If it's something that ought to have instant publication, the story should say the person was not reachable, and efforts to get to him should continue until he can be heard from.

(This rule does not always apply to such news on the public record as court news, indictments by grand juries, and the like. Formal charges of illegality have built into them opportunity for defense.)

THE RIGHT TO PRIVACY

"The right to be let alone" has been recognized for a century as a fundamental principle of American life. "A man's home is his castle"; his personal acts are his and nobody else's business, and within certain limits he may reasonably expect to live as free from outside observation and interference as he wishes. But is privacy a right or a privilege? The Constitution does not mention it, though the first eight and the Fourteenth amendments are considered by lawyers to support the principle tangentially. In recent years there has been massive development of devices that intrude on privacy:

ARE LAWS NEEDED?

Protection-of-privacy laws have been proposed in Congress and in several states to halt or curtail government digging into personal affairs, but comprehensive legal safeguards do not exist. A Department of Health, Education, and Welfare study reports that "laws of personal record-keeping . . . do not add up to a consistent body of law." A major newspaper in 1973 reported that a small-town Kansas police chief was running police record-checks on newcomers to his town for the benefit of landlords and employers, apparently without violating any law.

hidden camera eyes observing private or non-newsworthy activity, development of a national data bank with detailed information on millions of Americans, records in credit bureaus about habits good and bad of local citizens, security checks by public and private agencies. More records with more facts about more Americans exist—often without the consent or the knowledge of those concerned—than ever in history. (Congress is working, as this is written, on bills to curtail wire tapping, control government collection and distribution of personal information about individual citizens, and guarantee to a citizen the right to examine whatever files have been gathered about him. The abuses of Watergate are given credit for the new concern about personal privacy.)

The journalistic aspects of invasion of privacy, though they must be looked on as part of a broader American problem, have particular characteristics of which every gatherer of news has to be aware. The question does not often arise in reporting acts of government or events planned to draw audiences. It does come up in reporting events and activities that have no public character and that take place beyond the public spectrum. Some examples illustrate where charges of invasion are likely to develop:

1. A senator elopes with his secretary. He would like to keep it secret, but reporters learn of it, get details, and publish stories. Though marriage is a personal affair, the stories would not be considered invasions of privacy

because the private behavior of a public figure is of legitimate concern to his constituents.

But suppose a photographer follows a couple on their canoe-and-camping wedding trip and gets photos of them swimming without clothes in what they think is an unobserved haven?

2. A magazine published a picture of a man and his wife in mild embrace with a caption that suggested they represented a case of "love at first sight." The caption was in error, and a court agreed that they had cause for an action for violation of privacy.

3. A Birmingham newspaper published a picture showing a boy being comforted by a woman after he had been hit by a car, Nearly two years later, a magazine published the same picture with a suggestion that the child had been hurt because of his carelessness—an untrue suggestion. The court awarded the child $5,000 for invasion of privacy.

4. The family of a World War II veteran charged invasion of privacy in a factual news story about the veteran's pre-war indictment for theft. The court said they had no case.

Some general principles:

- Wiretapping and bugging are generally looked on as invasions of privacy unless they have legal authorization.
- Photos of individuals or their testimonials may not be used in most states in advertisements without written consent.
- Public figures, either in government or in the industries and activities in which they seek public attention, are generally judged to have given up privacy in their *public* activities, but not in their private life.
- Those involved in news events have no protection of privacy insofar as the events or their extensions and consequences are concerned.

What it comes down to, for the reporter and his paper or broadcasting station, is that there is little protection of privacy, in news coverage, except in the decision whether an event or a personal act is of significance or justifiable interest to a news audience. The problem is often ethical rather than legal. It would entrance TV viewers to see that a group of local bankers play poker every Thursday night while sitting fully clothed in tubs of ice water. It would be legally permissible to publish the fact if it's true. But what about the bankers' private right to enjoy themselves outlandishly outside the public spotlight?

GOOD TASTE

One reason that reporters don't always observe an individual's right to privacy is that privacy and the right of the public to information may be at odds. Another difficult decision for reporters is that between good and bad taste. What might be called good taste is journalistic behavior that observes the sensitivities of the community, of readers, and—sometimes most delicate of all—of the news figures about whom reporters write. When the feelings of readers or of the figures in the news conflict with the mandate to report what ought to be reported, the decision may be easy: the mandate wins. But in scores of news situations each day there are ways the community will accept and ways that offend. A morning newspaper used a column and a half to catalog the horrid beating that had killed a handsome young call girl; it described her mangled body, quoted a policeman who mused that "she was a good whore," and reported her meticulous book-keeping. The competing afternoon paper used a third of a column, omitting such details; it gave the news, and offended nobody.

Matters of taste are ill-defined because yesterday's vulgarism is today's routine usage. Four-letter words that were taboo in the 1960s became usable —in print, on radio and television, in living rooms—in the 1970s. The U. S. Supreme Court geed and hawed as it tried to define *obscenity*. Times change, customs change, and what hurts or offends loses its barbs among the new proprieties.

PROFANITY, OBSCENITY

Memo on a newspaper city room bulletin board:

> *This paper does not use profanities and obscenities except in direct quotations. Determining factors are the person quoted, the circumstances, and the importance of the quotation. If an obscene or vulgar word is necessary to accurate meaning of a significant comment on a significant subject, we print it. . . . It will usually occur in a spot news story in which it is spoken in public. . . . In some cases, exact words are necessary . . . to reflect a person's philosophy or personality. The test is whether the words are essential to the purpose.*

News that is offensive   Some readers will recall the time when a British government almost fell because of sensationalized news about its war minis-ter and a notorious London party girl. The young woman was sexy, the man was upper class, and the story was ballooned by the fireworks journalism of London Sunday newspapers. American media followed suit; for ten days American readers licked their lips over a "sex scandal" across the Atlantic. At length interest flagged, as fresh particulars gave out. The Chicago *Tribune*, a bit righteously, announced that it would stop printing the "sordid and de-praved" testimony because "we cannot feel that our readers would be im-proved by acquaintance with it." A reader of another paper wrote to its letter column that "no one would have felt any loss if we had been spared the details of the mess."

Frank modern journalism does not often resort to this kind of sensation-alizing. (One leading radio station, when a first-magnitude American movie star was charged with a Mann Act violation, used two-sentence stories on the case—one when the charge was brought, one when the man was acquitted.) The candor in American movies, the new attitudes toward marriage and man-woman relationships, the relaxations in family patterns and life-styles—however you view them—make such news pretty dull stuff.

Offense by camera   Photographs sometimes are prime offenders against the dignity of their subjects. Some cases:

* A mother is caught by a camera as she stands shattered at learning that the blanket on the pavement covers her child.
* A wounded policeman grimaces in anguish as he is lifted onto a stretcher.
* A young couple, unable to find housing in the city where the man has taken a job, spends its nights in the city bus station. With their permission, they are photographed asleep on a bench, their baby in the mother's arms. This may be human interest, but it makes the couple the object of community pity and perhaps scorn. What if the reporter, instead of calling for a photographer, had pointed out some of the dignified ways to meet their emergency?

These are familiar pictures. They are moving, and they may have the beauty of tragedy. They tell stories powerfully; they have high popular interest. But grief and pain are deeply personal emotions that rarely belong to the public. When is it defensible to make capital out of human suffering?

There are defensible cases. A noted Vietnam war photograph showed a naked little girl running toward the camera, her face a spasm of pain; her clothes had been burned off in a bombing raid. It is not often true, the adage to the contrary, that a picture is worth a thousand words. This one was.

EXPLOITING THE ANGLE

Every well-built news story has an angle—a focus that gives the story its theme. As you approach a story, you hope for an angle that hasn't been used a hundred times—if you're lucky, a unique one. Often the search is fruitless. Football games, burning buildings, and civic improvement association meetings follow consistent patterns. Though each offers an appropriate point of emphasis, the story about it may sound distressingly like the one you wrote yesterday.

So reporters are led into excesses—development of minor or misleading themes. In sports stories for afternoon papers, when the morning paper or last night's broadcasts have taken the cream, reporters tend to put emphasis on what the winning (or losing) pitcher said and neglect to tell about the game: "I wasn't thinking of a no-hitter when that guy walloped my ninth-inning two-out slider into the gap. All I was thinking about was winning for my team." (This kind of angle, a bromide of current sportswriting, has

the added quality of incredibility. Does any baseball player talk like that?)
Off-the-track, if not off-beat, emphases crop up in any kind of reporting:

- What did the housewife who was sent to the workhouse for shoplifting wear to jail? A stole.
- What did the reporter do with the personality report he had bought clandestinely from a "psychological counseling service"? He "put it in the basement storeroom, behind the dill pickles, and went to bed."
- What happened when a dreary derelict pleaded guilty for the ninety-second time to the charge of public drunkenness? "Wilcox was sent to the city lockup to sober up for appearance No. 93."

Ridicule is not a tool of responsible news work. Art Buchwald, Russell Baker, and writers of their skill and standing use it, under by-lines and rarely about any public figures. But satirical writing like the following story, which is cruel in its lack of respect for private dignity, is not to be tolerated:

> NEW YORK, N.Y.—Those three rude hotel detectives who burst in on Angelo del Carlino and his pretty wife Leonora on their wedding night bruised them $10,000 worth. This was disclosed in a sealed jury verdict opened Monday by Judge Nathan Edwards.
>
> Injuries to Angelo, owner of a beauty shop, were physical, he testified during trial last week. Leonora had the marriage annulled two years after that humiliating night. She said her wounds were spiritual.
>
> She had so wanted a beautiful evening, she said, but it wasn't beautiful because of "those awful men."
>
> Jurors scorned defense testimony that the trio burst in on the Del Carlinos because they had been creating a disturbance.

TRIAL BY NEWSPAPER

This term, as most people know, refers to news of alleged misbehavior without due caution to show that it has not been proven. Chapter 10, in the section on libel, touches on this problem. It is the practice of reporting damaging news in such a way that a reader or listener, who is in a hurry anyway, might look on allegation or circumstantial evidence as flat statement of guilt. In an extreme case a Chicago police official was quoted, accurately, as saying "we have caught the murderer" after a man he suspected of having perpetrated a series of killings had been arrested. John Ehrlichman, in 1974, pleaded unsuccessfully that he could not get a fair trial in Washington, D.C., because he had already been tried by excessive news attention. An Ohio doctor, found guilty of his wife's murder in a case that became a national circus of sensational news, was eventually freed by the U. S. Supreme Court on the plea that his trial was conducted in an atmosphere of prejudgment and unfairness. Charges of this kind of prejudice are not always successful or always soundly based, but the newsworker who is not on guard against prejudicial treatment cannot be trusted with crime news of political or social conflict.

Overplay of sensational news is not the only peril. Carelessness with loaded words may be just as harmful. Note this example:

> The bank president *admitted* that he owns a block of stock in the bankrupt company. He *denied* that he voted it to protect his personal interests

Suppose the banker had neither admitted nor denied, but rather had merely described his stock ownership and voting. The loaded words suggest something quite different.

In another case the term *welfare-fraud* became the customary press tag by which to refer to a particular grand jury investigation. Since the grand jury had not yet reported, details of the charges were not known. Welfare fraud has come over the years, however, to refer to chiseling by welfare recipients, and this was common audience assumption. When the grand jury report was released, the welfare fraud turned out to be manipulation of welfare funds by a group of county agency employees, to their own—not the clients'—benefit.

Even the leeway provided by the courts in certain kinds of libel can be misused. The New York *Times* decision of 1964 (see Chapter 10), which many lawyers and jurists think "virtually eliminated the law of libel in the public sector," gives reporters a freedom that must be used with utmost caution. Bernstein and Woodward, reporting on their Watergate efforts in *All the President's Men*, tell of having named three White House officials, on the basis of White House sources they believed, as parties in the Watergate cover-up. Later, after publication, they learned the information was incorrect. They corrected it in print; but three damaged men, as public officials, had no basis for libel action.

The safeguards against journalistic misbehavior of this kind are such simple ones as triple checking, slow movement, and a respect for all three entities involved: the human subjects of the news, the human clientele, and reportorial integrity itself. Without precautions like these, reporting may deserve most of the savage epithets sometimes aimed at it.

Members of the York, Pennsylvania, Newspaper Guild pointed up the opposite danger to trial by newspaper, however, when in 1974 they protested a decision by four regional newspapers and seven radio and television stations to withhold news of a murder trial at the request of a judge. The judge made the request to avoid "prejudicing" jurors in related trials. One of the newspaper managing editors responded to the protest: "I was ashamed of myself the minute I walked out of the judge's chambers." The news was withheld, but since hundreds of spectators attended the trial, the result was only to keep accurate information from those who couldn't get in.

There are external formulas for professional behavior. Fifty years ago the prestigious American Society of Newspaper Editors adopted a set of Canons of Practice. They were noble in principle and concept, but they have been framed and hung on editors' walls rather than injecting themselves into journalists' bloodstreams. A basketful of codes to guide journalists' practice have been formulated by newspaper and broadcast editors and reporters (the most recent is summarized in Appendix C).

No code can alchemize a reporter, beginning or old-timer, into a professionalism by its tenets and truisms. But it represents the thinking of men and women who have lived its principles, who believe of their own experience that journalism is a mode of life with a ceiling as high as Everest. They are a promise to their followers—a promise of service, growth, and infinite reward.

NEWS: WRITING AND STYLE

:. A very *Tragical Accident* happened at W4-ter-Town, the beginning of this Month, an Old man, that was of somewhat a Silent and Morose Temper, but one that had long Enjoyed the reputation of a *Sober* and a *Pious Man*, having newly buried his Wife, The Devil took advantage of the Melancholy which he thereupon fell into, his Wives discretion and industry had long been the support of his Family, and he seemed hurried with an impertinent fear that he should now come to want before he dyed, though he had very careful friends to look after him who kept a strict eye upon him, least he should do himself any harm. But one evening escaping from them into the Cow-house, they there quickly followed him, found him *hanging by a Rope*, which they had used to tye their *Calves* withal, he was dead with his feet near touching the Ground.

CHAPTER TWELVE

News story form and organization

NEWS FORMS YESTERDAY

The story reproduced on the opposite page appeared in the first American newspaper, *Publick Occurrences*, in 1690. Had a like event been reported in a local newspaper two hundred years later, it would have looked something like this (specifics added):

Arthur B. Snow, 92, 2189 Coldspring Road, Watertown, was found hanged in his cowbarn yesterday by friends who said he had been despondent since the March 29 death of his wife Maria following an illness that had kept her bedridden for several months. Mr. Snow was dead when found.

Since he became a widower, Mr. Snow had become more silent and morose than was his wont, his friends say, and they had attempted to watch his movements carefully. He escaped their attention night before last, however, and apparently used a calf tie-rope as the means of ending his life.

There are no known survivors, although some say that an older brother of the deceased passed through Watertown some twenty years ago on the way to claim a homestead in Dakota Territory.

Mr. and Mrs. Snow had been residents of Water-town since 1852, when they moved to this community from southern New York State. Mr. Snow was well known in the vicinity as a careful and scrupulous carpenter. In recent years, however, he had been unable to work because of a back injury, and friends said that his wife had been the family's principal support. Mrs. Snow tended the Snows' fine herd of Jersey cattle which provided many local families with milk.

The contrasts in the stories need no underlining. The unhurried tone of the 1690 story suited the needs and moods of its unhurried age; the failure to identify the "old man" was discreet in a small, tightly knit community where everybody knew of the event anyway; the rigidly moralistic comment of the writer would have been echoed by his readers.

The later story is one that demanded more reporting, more fact-gathering. It approaches the modern news form; though it is long-winded and presents facts or near-facts most readers could get along without, it has a lead, a time element, and all the principal facts except real assurance as to the *why*, which is only implied. But it is not a truly modern news story. It is only a step toward the news story form of the latter twentieth century. We shall talk more about the form and this particular example later in this chapter.

To understand why changes in form have occurred, think again of the way news practice constantly adjusts itself to new audience needs and new technologies.

Chapter 2 outlined the social and technological developments that have altered American journalism and the public's use of the news media. Necessity plus invention turned leisurely artisanship into mass production. And the new concept of news said that you publish facts about events because they are current facts, not because you approve or disapprove of them. You have to tell a reader more, and do it succinctly; you have to help him select rapidly among the mass of news offerings at his fingertips, and make it possible for him to absorb rapidly what he chooses.

MODERN NEWS FORM

The news forms that evolved through the late nineteenth century were not always the outcome of self-conscious contrivance; no newspaper Archimedes leaped from his bath shouting, "I have invented the modern news story." It was the interplay of experience and necessity that brought the newspaper into the 1900s with a news form designed to help the reader read and comprehend fast. The principal implements of the design were the *headline* and the *lead-summary* news story form.

The headline is the newspaper device (sometimes orally borrowed by broadcasting) for describing with brief emphasis the salient content a story is to present. It is the newspaper's showcase and often its table of contents. It helps a reader to decide at a glance whether a story is for him. (The delicate and abused techniques of headline writing, and the confining shortcomings of the pattern, are not within the range of this book.)

The lead summary news story form opens with a quick statement of an event's principal facts, its central import. Then it adds secondary or supporting facts, arranged in order of decreasing importance. This story form has been given various labels; the most apt is *inverted pyramid*. Principal facts at the top, least important at the bottom, it rests on its upside-down apex.

The rationale lies in the expectation that, when a reader's eye catches a headline, his judgment tells him quickly whether he wants to know more. If he decides to go on, he reads the lead, and the selective process continues. Perhaps, after reading a few paragraphs presenting the more important details, he has had enough; the form provides easy "breaks"— places where he can leave the story. If his interest persists, he continues, either to a new break or to the end. The design shows clearly in this wire service story:

BIRMINGHAM, Ala.—An intoxicated surgeon started shooting at police Friday while holding his infant granddaughter in his arms. A policeman braved the fire until the doctor put the baby down, then shot him dead.

The lead paragraph summarizes the major facts. It uses two sentences rather than the one more common in leads, and gains clarity and force by doing so.

First break

The slain surgeon was Dr. Arthur A. Arthur, 59. Coroner Joe Hilginson called his death "justifiable homicide."

Summary of two important elaborating facts.

Second break

Police said Arthur, for many years a prominent surgeon but lately less active, was paroled recently from a hospital for narcotic addicts.

Summary of additional background facts.

Third break

Yesterday police were called to the family home. There Patrolmen B. L. Buchanan and C. D. Guy found Arthur holding his granddaughter, 11-month-old Helen Jane Smithson. Arthur started cursing them, the patrolmen said, and Guy went for help.

Before he returned, the doctor whipped out a pistol and fired three shots at Buchanan. The officer backed away rather than fire while Arthur held the baby.

Arthur then put the baby down and followed Buchanan downstairs, where he cornered him and announced, "We'll shoot it out here."

Buchanan drew his service revolver and fired five shots. Two struck Arthur, who was dead on arrival at a hospital.

The last four paragraphs reconstruct the event chronologically for a reader who continues beyond break three. But those who stop sooner already have the essential facts.

If you contrast this story with the second version of the *Publick Occurrences* story, you will see further refinement in the form of the lead— greater condensation, avoidance of nonessential detail. Chapter 13, Straight-News Leads: Form, Design, Content, goes more deeply into these subjects.

The two stories below show again the typical design of inverted-pyramid structure:

The mid-August heat wave will continue today with local temperatures expected to climb to 95.	*A quick summary of major facts—and a quick answer to "How hot?"*
	First break
The only relief in the state will be felt in the northwest portion, as a low-pressure area moves eastward.	*Supporting facts summarized in two closely related paragraphs.*
Highs today in the state will be from 80 to 85 in the northwest and 90 to 95 in the south and east.	
	Second break
The weatherman promised a little relief tonight with a predicted low of 70 in the city. A few showers are expected.	*These two paragraphs might have preceded the two above. A concession to nonlocal readers?*
Yesterday's high in the city was 96 at 4 p.m. At 6:30 p.m. the relative humidity was 41 percent.	
	Third break
[A final paragraph reports highest temperatures in neighboring states.]	*The most expendable facts are in the last paragraph.*
A local man and his wife were killed in a home fire today.	*A quick, laconic summary.*
	First break
Found dead by firefighters in a burned-out house at 417 16th Ave. S. shortly after 1 a.m were John Doe, in his 60s, and his wife, Mary, 58.	*Important facts to expand the summary lead.*
	Second break
David L. Jamieson of the arson squad said he was told by neighbors Mrs. Doe was in the habit of throwing extra fuel into the oil heater. Under such circumstances, he said, sudden ignition of the extra oil would blow open the heater	*"Background or explanatory facts, elaborating on major facts.*

<table>
<tr><td>

door and flame and smoke would puff out.

Doe's charred body was found under a pile of debris. Mrs. Doe was declared by the medical examiner's office to have died of smoke inhalation.

Neighbors said Doe was retired.
City Hall records indicate that the house and the one next door at 415 16th Ave. S. were built in 1867.

</td><td>

Third break

Further elaboration.

Fourth break

Expendable facts. Should they have been omitted?

</td></tr>
</table>

These examples show, among other things, that there is no ironclad formula for news story construction. Chapter 18 will describe an alternative form, the suspended-interest pattern. Even within a form, a writer may depart from pattern, juggling sub-elements as he goes. Two competent reporters arranging the same set of news facts may assess them differently, even when both are following a standard pattern.

SOME PYRAMIDS ARE NOT INVERTED

The inverted pyramid (or order of decreasing importance) story form helps both the copyreader who edits it and the printer who puts it into the page form. A copyreader, pressed for time, knows that he can cut final paragraphs with least damage to a story's meaning. A makeup man who has a seven-inch inverted-pyramid story to squeeze into a five-inch space can drop the last paragraph or so and retain major content. But sometimes the practice trips up careless printers. If the story isn't inverted-pyramid—if it's a suspended-interest story with the kick at the end—he's likely to come up with something like this:

> WASHINGTON — Curiosity got the better of an Army secretary this week, and she sneaked a look at the contents of three neatly-tied paper bags on her boss's closet shelf. The sign on them said "Trash. For official use only."

That's all there was. The printer dropped the punch line, and nobody will ever know the point of the story.

It can happen in sober news, too. A Washington UPI story in a morning paper said that the New England states would get an extra day of grace for income tax payment in a certain April. That's where the story stopped. In the afternoon paper the same story appeared—with a final paragraph that told why.

VARIATIONS IN STORY FORM

A complaint about the American newspaper is that it is overstandardized, dull in its confinement to upside-down pyramids, and repetitious—that it ignores time-sequence logic. News stories in foreign papers, say the complainers, aren't imprisoned in a single mold. A news story in a Dublin paper about a political convention begins with half a column of names, and gets around on page 2 to what happened. One in *Giornale d'Italia* of Rome opens, "Innocence has triumphed against every machination of men and affairs," goes into a homily about home, mother, and the good life, and finally tells you that a young man has been acquitted of a murder charge. The London *Daily Express*, reporting the arrest of a young Briton in Moscow on a criminal charge, gives prime attention to how much friends like him and his wife, who is "24 and pretty."

Some foreign reporting that departs from American patterns is often extremely effective. British, French, and Italian reporting of American politics, though it is usually interpretive rather than "straight," is often of a high order. In these and other countries, following studies of American patterns and usages, newspapers are coming more and more to find merit in the more direct form of reporting of the American press.

If patterns across the Atlantic show readiness to change, so do those at home. Traditions die hard, but the prediction of a United Press International editor, Roger Tartarian, in the mid-1960s, is borne out by the journalism of the 1970s: "The inverted-pyramid style . . . will remain a useful tool," he said, "but the narrative news story is more fun for the journalist," and will be one of print journalism's responses to radio and TV. The *National Observer* has made distinguished use of stories long and short that depart from the routine patterns; so have the newsmagazines.

The departures cannot be sharply classified; indeed, if they could be, they would soon lose their freshness and vitality. Wide use of the narrative or chronological story is a characteristic of the *National Observer's* manner. This can hardly be called new, however; the form was old long before the summary lead was invented. What is new is wide application of novel patterns to news situations that for half a century were thought to demand "straight" handling.

That the *Observer* is weekly is doubtless one cause of its interest in new forms. In a weekly the importance of immediacy is low, and other emphases and reader attractions must be found. But an additional impulse in American journalism is the need to reach particular audiences with the right implements (the monotonous business-news pages with their stock-market tables are anything but attractive or exciting, but they do their job).

Newswriters who successfully break the shackles of news story convention do it by viewing both material and audience needs with imagination. They don't select pattern or form first and then apply it to a set of facts, but rather perceive that given material can be brought to life through a

DESCRIPTION, EXPLANATION, EVALUATION = DEE

The Wall Street Journal, *one of America's best-written newspapers, talks of its DEE story form. The acronym stands for description, explanation, and evaluation, the three parts of long "trend" stories, which report general movements among men and institutions—a new direction in farming or industry, a change in national patterns of higher education, the rise of new preferences among sports fans. Such stories follow their leads, either straight or feature, with the three types of exposition. The third, evaluation, has to come either from outside expertise, by interview or research, or from subjective treatment by the writer himself.*

custom-made contrivance of story or manner. The story following this paragraph, an example of unorthodox structure, opens with an anecdote and continues in an almost episodic manner. A less imaginative story might have led with what appear to be the most important facts (that an experiment in school integration began Tuesday with great success) and followed with materials in the last six paragraphs to pull the significant facts together. Instead, the writer gave the story flavor and "humanization" by relating it to individuals, and at the same time made it attractive enough that most readers would stay with it to the end.

"I'm the only brown child in my room," Joetta Harris told her mother on the way home from Groveland Park School in St. Paul Tuesday.

Mrs. Robert Harris' heart sank.

But it was all right, Joetta said. She had made lots of "best friends."

She did object to the pupil who sat behind her, however.

"Why?" asked Mrs. Harris, fearful again.

"He's a boy," said the 6-year-old scornfully.

The Negro mother laughed.

"Well, boys are people, too," she explained.

Joetta was one of 75 children from St. Paul's predominantly Negro Selby-Dale area who transferred to five predominantly white elementary schools yesterday.

The children rode in a private school bus. Nearly all paid at least part of the $35 fee. The rest was made up from more than $5,000 in contributions, said Mrs. Harry Swanton, 1175 Davern St., spokesman for Parents for Integrated Education, the sponsoring organization.

Joetta and her sister, Pam, 9, were among 15 Negroes who transferred to Groveland. Normally they would have gone to Maxfield School, which was more than 91 per cent Negro last year.

The Harrises, who live at 795 Central Av., decided last spring to transfer their girls.

Harris is one of four Negro firemen at the St. Paul Fire Department. He was brought up in an integrated neighborhood in the North End of St. Paul. He had seen Negroes from the ghetto to fail when they were thrown in with whites on jobs.

"I think they should have this relationship with white kids early," Harris said Tuesday.

But, having decided, the Harrises were faced with a problem—how to explain their decision to Pam without spoiling the naturalness of the interracial contact.

Pam solved the problem when she came home from camp with her best friend and asked:

"Maggie's going to a different school this fall. Why can't I?"

Harris rejects the idea advanced by some Negroes that private busing is inadequate, saying, "It's a beginning, at least."

On the other hand, he doesn't accept as valid the objection of many whites that interracial dating may become a problem.

"I don't care what color their dates are so long as they come to the house to meet my daughters," he said.

There were no problems at any of the five schools yesterday, according to Robert Indehar, school social worker assigned to advise on the transfer project. Besides the 15 Negro students at Groveland there were 15 at Edgecombe, 27 at Highland, 3 at Horace Mann and 15 at Mattocks, he said.

The greatest fear of the sponsors was that the Negro transfers would be alone and, in effect, segregated at noon when the neighborhood white children went home to lunch.

To avoid that, principals took advantage of a long-standing policy to urge parents of children living more than three quarters of a mile from the school to send lunch with their children.

The open enrollment policy that made yesterday's transfers possible is also a long-standing school board policy. Some Negroes say its only previous racial application was by whites to escape ghetto schools that became predominantly Negro.

Its use as a means to end de facto school segregation was urged last October by the Committee on Racial Imbalance in St. Paul Schools. But the school board could not afford to bus the students.

The idea of a privately sponsored bus originated with Mrs. Swanton, a former school board member, and a group of her white friends. Together with Negro parents like the Harrises, they formed Parents for Integrated Education.[1]

A brilliant example of imaginative structure is the Linda Fitzpatrick story on pages 355–360. J. Anthony Lukas's account of the two sides of a tragic young life, of what a girl was and what her intimates believed her to be, is not easily forgotten. The influence of human-interest material on story form receives attention in Chapter 18.

News form on the air   Broadcast news stories show both similarities to and differences from news written for the eye. These two brief stories are representative:

The U.S. dollar hit the highest mark it's been at in two months today on money markets in Europe. Dealers say it's because of improvement in the U.S. balance of payments. Some dealers say President Nixon's Watergate speech apparently had little effect on the market. The price of gold . . . It also rose, to ninety-six dollars an ounce in London. That's two dollars higher than yesterday morning.

– 0 –

Border inspectors between California and Mexico aren't watching for dope smugglers so much these days as illegal traffic in black market beef. They say sixty-three hundred vehicles a day are crossing the border with beef. But officials say the meat is not always the best. One border inspector says one woman carried in thirty pounds of ground meat . . . and there were bits of lung and other parts that would not be used for dog food here in the States.

Among the characteristics of these stories you find:

- A softened or modified inverted pyramid form
- Short leads—often "soft" leads that introduce the listener easily to details that are to follow
- Short, straightforward sentences of simple construction

[1] Copyright © 1964 by the St. Paul *Dispatch-Pioneer Press*. Reprinted by permission.

• Diction marked by familiar words, colloquialisms, contractions, and sentence fragments

The three stories that follow show both typical radio news structure and the manner of covering a fast-breaking spot news story. The first is a bulletin that interrupted a nonnews program. It shows signs of haste; its opening is abrupt rather than soft, and the nature of the event doesn't come through until the second sentence:

NEWS SOUND

WE INTERRUPT THIS PROGRAM FOR A BULLETIN FROM THE WCCO
RADIO NEWS BUREAU. . . .
        All available ambulances and doctors have been summoned
to the village of Maple Plain on Highway 12 about twenty-
five miles west of Minneapolis. There is a report of an
explosion and fire at the Molded Plastics Company there.
Rescue workers at the scene of the blast have put out a call
for asbestos suits to withstand the heat of the fire.
Sightseers are warned to stay away from the area where rescue
work is now under way.
        Stay tuned for more details as soon as they become
available.

That story was broadcast at 9:55 a.m. Seventeen minutes later it was followed by a second story that was closer to normal radio news copy than the bulletin:

        Here are more details on the explosion at the plastics
plant in Maple Plain.
        It is now known that at least two persons were injured
in the blast at the Molded Plastics Products Company about
an hour ago. Both were workers in the plant, which manufactures
plastic toys. One was identified as Mrs. Alice Sohns
(SOWNS). The other was a workman whose name is not
immediately available. Both have been taken by ambulance to
the hospital in nearby Watertown, Minnesota.
        According to an eyewitness, Gust Giese, an oven for
heating the plastics material exploded when it was lighted.
Giese said the force of the blast shattered one wall of the
plant and blew off a portion of the roof. The plant is
located on Highway 12 in Maple Plain, about twenty-five
miles west of Minneapolis.
        Fire which followed the explosion has now been brought
under control. A WCCO Radio newsman is on his way to Maple

Plain, and we'll have his complete report in the noon news. Roadblocks have been established to seal off the area from sightseers.

The story was wrapped up two hours later by the on-the-spot broadcast promised earlier:

This community of Maple Plain, about twenty-five miles west of Minneapolis, was rocked by an explosion this morning when gas ignited at a plastic toy manufacturing plant. Three workers were injured in the blast and the fire which followed at the Molded Products Company. Those injured in the explosion were Mrs. Alice Sohns of Mound, Rose Nagel of Watertown, and Allen Sullivan of Maple Plain.

None of the injured is in serious condition this noon, though Mrs. Sohns is still under treatment at the hospital in Watertown. All three were working in the plant near the plastics heating oven when the gas was ignited. The plant owner says that highly volatile fumes develop when the oven is lighted, and he believes the blast was touched off in that ignition period.

The Maple Plain assistant fire chief, Helmar Anderson, said the damages would amount to several thousand dollars. A cinder block wall was broken and a portion of the roof was destroyed. Fire followed the blast, but the flames were brought under control within thirty minutes. The plant, which employs about fifty persons, will be out of production for several weeks.

Note the care with which first and second stories warned sightseers to stay away. This is a caution not always observed when news breaks fast. Police and firemen often complain of broadcast-drawn crowds that get in their way.

Television news style is that of radio, except that it is often written to the picture. This means two things: that story structure can't always follow a conventional plan, since order and emphasis depend on what the cameras have caught and how the films are put together; and that some of the detail, since it's on the screen, can be left out of the script.

UNITY IN THE NEWS STORY

The guide to effective news story structure and organization is the principle of essential unity.

Briefly, unity in a news story is attained when the story is built around one central idea or one set of facts. A unified story attempts to tell only one story. Its details are selected for their relevance to the central core, the major import; tangential or unrelated material is ruthlessly discarded.

News story unity can be attained in many ways. Look again at the story of the surgeon (page 165): every paragraph but the third relates directly to the principal event, and the exception provides relevant background. Note that the four closing paragraphs tell the story chronologically, in the order in which its details occurred. The chronological pattern, moving from beginning to end in simple time sequence, is one prime method of keeping a story unified—if you stick with such a sequence and keep out extraneous events, unity is assured. Although the form is used more often in human-interest stories than in straight news, variations of chronological narrative (like that in the shooting story) are common, and often effective. When a newswriter faces a mass of facts—names, addresses, times, and the like—against an action background, he may decide that the narrative pattern will deliver most meaning to readers. But if he decides on some other pattern, he is pretty sure to move only into confusion if he fails to pick out a central theme and relate all details to it. The poor quality of the story that follows is in large part the result of the reporter's failure to decide what one element his story will center on:

An early-morning 90-mile-an-hour chase that had all the ingredients of a movie thriller today resulted in the capture of a suspected young auto thief, minor injuries to two local policemen and the wrecking of a police squad car.

The summary lead confuses by including too many elements. The "movie thriller" phrase promises something that the story does not deliver.

First break

Figuring in the chase were at least half a dozen squad cars, directed by Sgt. Paul Ridley, dispatcher, who carried on a two-way conversation first with the squad car before it was wrecked and then with another that continued the chase.

Secondary detail, some too trivial to deserve second-paragraph position. The multi-idea sentence diffuses attention, and you never learn how the squad car was wrecked.

Held at the Public Safety building is David Satoiw, 19, of Milgrim's Landing, who police say admits stealing the fleeing car Thursday night.

Important detail. (But how do you steal a fleeing car?)

Patrolman Gerald Hangge, 29, of 1248 Farr Street, suffered knee cuts. Patrolman Leonard Marsch, 23, of 427 Fulton Street, is nursing a forehead cut and bruises on his leg and hand. Both were treated at City Hospital.

Is this secondary detail properly placed in the story? Does "both" refer to bruises, patrolmen, or "leg and hand"?

Within 11 minutes after the play-by-play account of the chase was broadcast to the chasing squad cars, the suspect was captured.

Confusing language ("account of the chase" broadcast to "chasing squad cars") and confusing position in the story.

After the first squad car had been put out of the chase, the police dispatcher carried on his two-way signals with Squad Car 303, with Patrolman Lawrence Swanson at the wheel and Patrolman Joseph Carchedi at the car telephone.

Chronological sequence is not clear; identification of Car 303 is not clear.

Although the radio part of the chase did not enter into the picture until 6:44 a.m., the chase actually started several minutes before.

Again the time sequence is not clear. Why name the precise hour?

[The story now goes into nearly a column of confusing detail about the origin of the chase, its route (six streets are mentioned), and the accumulation of squad cars. It closes with a minute-by-minute record of the squad cars' radio reports.]

Three factors help to destroy this story's unity. The phrase "ingredients of a movie thriller," gratuitously thrown into the lead, introduces an idea that is left dangling, without later reference. The early emphasis on two-way radio suggests that the radio conversations are important to understanding the event, but the story's closing paragraphs (not quoted here) show that they are not. Finally, the disorderly mass of detail—route of the chase, nature of minor wounds, post of a patrolman "at the car telephone," the loose "at least half a dozen squad cars"—confuses more than it contributes.

One more story to illustrate the scattergun effect of failure to build a story around a clearly defined theme:

A 15-year-old Indian was shot in the face and killed early Saturday when he did not surrender a double-barreled shotgun he was aiming at three Redlake Chippewa Reservation policemen.

This lead might do if it didn't contain excess detail ("shot in the face," "double-barreled," "he was aiming") not adequately explained later.

First break

The shooting by the Bureau of Indian Affairs policeman sparked trouble yesterday in Redlake. After a

"Sparked trouble" early in the story suggests further development later; you have to guess that "demonstra-

suspected case of arson, bureau officials banned distribution of gasoline in the village and barred outsiders.

tors" in the last paragraph relates to it. The relation of arson and the gasoline ban to what follows is unclear.

No good break

Richard Leonard, criminal investigator for the bureau, said yesterday the shooting occurred after two policemen "were pinned down for a couple of minutes" by gunfire from the roadside.

Relationships of these facts to those that precede remain cloudy.

Possible break

Police responded to the officers' call for aid and began searching for those who had shot at them.

Expendable detail?

The victim, Brian Des Jardait, was seen running from the scene, and was surrounded by the three officers after being chased, Leonard said.

Since the lead emphasis is on the killing, some of this detail should come earlier in the story.

"Our men told him to drop his weapon," Leonard said. "And when he didn't surrender his weapon he was shot."

Final break

Authorities jailed a number of demonstrators following the shooting.

Detail that may be important but that is not tied to the rest of the story.

Contrast these two stories with one by the New York *Times'* James (Scotty) Reston, written when he was a Washington reporter. The story loses no part of its charm from the fact that the name of its chief figure dates it:

WASHINGTON—The usually solemn Secretary of State Dulles was in a mood of relaxed good humor at his news conference Tuesday.

The opening paragraph establishes the story's unifying theme, the "relaxed good humor" of the news conference. The theme is supported in the second paragraph by introduction of topics not usual subjects of a State Department news conference (note that it's "news," not "press").

He expounded to the reporters the glories of being fingerprinted, disclosed that he is the first pistol-packin' Secretary of State since Cordell Hull, and announced he is going off on his first two-week vacation since taking over the State Department almost three years ago.

First break

This last point may have explained his sense of well-being, but the real reason probably is that his foreign policy ideas are back in ascendancy in Washington. [Nine paragraphs now develop the subtheme just introduced. Then back to the original theme:] As for the lighter portions of the conference, it went like this:

A carefully designed transitional paragraph to move from the story's structural theme to a more sober subject.

Dulles said he himself gets fingerprinted a couple of times a year. Why? asked a correspondent.

Return to the opening theme holds the story together and satisfies the reader's curiosity.

Because, said the secretary, he has to be fingerprinted in order to get his pass to the State Department building. And also, he added with a rather sheepish grin, in order to get a permit to keep his pistol. This drew considerable interest.

Fortunately, said the secretary, he hasn't had to use his gun at all. Apparently aware that he had dashed the hopes of the whodunit fans in the news corps, Dulles explained that his revolver is one he was given in 1917 when he made his first trip to Central America. He has kept it ever since.[2]

Reston has tied the news elements in a not-very-productive news conference into a unified package by a contrived but skillful and convincing use of a major theme.

Everything in the following story belongs where it has been placed. That some of its writing is pedestrian does not destroy its unity.

Radio pickups were broadcast Friday for 26-year-old Leslie Douglas Ashley after persons in Wharton and Houston reported they saw a man resembling him during the afternoon.

All of the leads turned out to be false, however, in the search for the one-time female impersonator, indicted on a charge of mur-

A long-winded two-paragraph lead that delays reporting the major fact—that no arrest was made—until the second paragraph. There are at least five major ideas in this lead.

[2] Copyright © 1955 by The New York Times Company. Reprinted by permission.

der, who escaped from a San Antonio state mental hospital early last month.

First break

Wharton County Sheriff H. R. Flournoy said that about 12:30 p.m. a woman in a Wharton dress shop called to say a man who looked like Ashley and a blonde woman were shopping for women's clothes and fled all of a sudden when they saw they were being stared at.

This is the first of three instances offered to support the lead idea. The three are offered chronologically rather than in order of decreasing importance, since they are all of about the same weight.

A check proved that the man was definitely not Ashley, Flournoy said, after the Department of Public Safety had broadcast a statewide pickup.

Second break

Four hours later, a television station porter in a company car thought he saw Ashley getting into a small light-colored compact car outside a store in the 700 block of Travis.

The porter told police that when the man spotted his car, which was marked with the station's call letters, he jumped back into his own auto and drove away with two others, a man and a woman.

Second instance.

Third break

Sometime later, a woman who works at a cleaning plant in the 2700 block of Montrose thought she spotted Ashley driving around in a light-colored car, and called police.

Four police cars, two Harris County Sheriff's Department units and about 40 newsmen flocked to the scene, but quickly dispersed after it was learned that the man in the car was not the one they sought.

Third instance.

Fourth break

Ashley is under indictment for the gun-torch slaying of Fred A. Tones, a Houston real estate man, in 1961.

Convicted and sentenced

to die in the electric chair, he was granted a new trial. Before he could be tried again, he was found insane and committed to the hospital at San Antonio.

His attorney, Lloyd M. Lunsford, was out of town, but an associate of Lunsford said Ashford has not yet communicated with his lawyer.

Summary of earlier facts of the case, presented for those who are not familiar with it.

From such examples you can draw some generalizations about the attainment of unity.

Adherence to theme   A news story is unified when its central theme or idea states the reporter's selection of major facts (usually the lead presents the theme) and the supporting facts develop it. In straight news writing the first step after decision on theme is the selection of supporting material. This is a further decision-making process, since whatever doesn't contribute toward understanding, or distracts attention from the theme, must be rejected. The second step is putting the theme into focus in a summary (the lead).

Unity of structure or mood   A writer may contrive unity by structure or mood. In the Reston story about Dulles a mood of relaxed good humor is established and then supported. In the Linda Fitzpatrick story (page 355), which has other kinds of unity as well, the framework of the story—the counterpoint of the parallel narrative paths—holds the two tales together as it underlines their contrast.

Structural or rhetorical devices like these are the tools of masters, and should rarely be attempted by workers who are still using blunt instruments. They are found more often in editorial or feature writing than in straight news. But even in routine news a reporter can usually frame a unifying theme to tie separate-but-similar facts or events together: "Seven drownings occurred in three state boating accidents yesterday." Radio, with its need for saying things fast, uses the device repeatedly: "Foreign trouble spots are quiet today for the first time in a month."

AXIOMS

Better that the news consumer see the forest than every separate tree.
Better that he grasp the outlines and meanings of a news event than be confused by too much detail.

Dilutions of unity   Even when details are logically related to the theme, essential unity may be diluted or concealed by their careless use, especially in the lead. In the auto-chase story the lead confuses the reader by introducing elements not later developed and by a clutter of facts that don't seem even secondary. Details like these detract from the central impression of a story unless they are shown to be essential. Often such nonessentials—the route of the chase, the policemen's two-way radio chatter—are better presented in sidebars.

SIDEBARS

A sidebar is a secondary story that develops minor facts or related angles of a news event covered in a principal story. If unity is to be maintained in the main story, minor facts must often be left out. This is constantly true in events involving many participants and many activities—a national convention, a catastrophe, a Wimbledon tournament. The sidebar is a device to flesh out and add color or supplementary meaning to the principal event.

Sidebars often deal with human-interest angles of straight-faced news. When the carnival comes to town, the local paper carries a routine report of attendance, hours of special events, and so on. Sidebars report seven heat prostrations the first day; more visitors to the city than at any time since three astronauts dedicated the new airport; the fat lady missing because she's honeymooning with the mayor of the last town the show visited. Most such angles could be separate paragraphs or sections of the main story. But separate treatment gains visibility and keeps clutter out of the main story.

An example: On a day when a principal front-page story dealt with anniversary observances of the atomic bombing of Hiroshima, sidebars reported a propaganda broadcast from Peking, some comments from the chaplain who counseled the crew of the plane that dropped the bomb, the refusal of the plane's pilot to talk about it, and the wreath placed at the Unknown Soldier's tomb at Arlington by a Hiroshima survivor. Another example: Accompanying its story about V-E Day anniversary celebrations in Bonn and East Berlin, Le Figaro of Paris used a paragraph about West German annoyance with Soviet "bad taste" in staging a giant cocktail party in Bonn the same day.

A story usually loses unity when a minor fact, even a sensational one, is selected for lead emphasis. Unity requires that the major facts as well as the central theme be established in the lead. Overemphasized minor facts are likely to frustrate any attempt to organize a balanced or unified inverted-pyramid story. You'll see this problem in a speech report in which the speaker's throwaway is made the lead. Asides sometimes are loaded with reader interest and sometimes with genuine news value. But when a reporter emphasizes a speaker's accidental tumble from the platform, he may bury the fact that the speaker had something important to say. A reader might assume, with justification, that the tumble from the stage would become of importance in the story.

This kind of distortion, fairly common in the work of novice reporters, is sometimes seen in the craft of experienced hands. Both ought to know better.

Leads that include too many facts, or too few, usually make unity hard to attain. If the lead promises story development that doesn't come, or if it fails to forecast what is to come, it has dissipated the structural strength of the story. Both of these faults may appear in one lead, as in the following example:

A special alarm fire which sent a pall of smoke over the Whitby district Wednesday night caused damage estimated at $80,000 to the A. B. Filpott Co., 693 Edgeland Rd.	*The lead suggests that both the special alarm and the smoke cloud will get attention later. But it never comes.*
Firemen fought the stubborn blaze without masks or other precautionary measures until the arrival of firm officials who warned the buildings contained chemicals which could easily form poisonous gases. Although the fire was almost out, Chief William Wentworth ordered his men from the area until they had donned masks. A number of the firemen who had been exposed to the fumes were administered oxygen at the scene.	*A clumsy sentence introduces a new element, the danger of poison gas, which provides the basis for most of the rest of the story. It should have had lead position.*
The Filpott firm manufactures neon and other illuminated tubing for electric signs.	*Background that could be omitted.*

The following story avoids the error. Its third paragraph, after a two-paragraph lead, establishes that the story will deal with more than the lead subject. (Only the opening paragraphs of the story are presented here.)

Rejection of a civil rights ordinance ended a six-hour City Council meeting last night.	*The story's major topic is introduced first; the reader is then warned that a second topic will appear. Fourteen following paragraphs develop the civil rights ordinance topic; the remainder deals with identification cards. If paragraph three were omitted or placed after development of the civil rights topic, the reader might well ask, "How did this subject get in?"*
The Council voted 9 to 4 to table the proposal whose purpose was to make racial and religious discrimination illegal in employment in any business in the city.	
The Council also turned down a proposal that all schoolchildren must carry identification cards.	

Unity in the long feature   The longer the story, the greater the possibility that it will wander. Many long features (the Joetta Harris story, page 169, is an example) open with specific cases or anecdotes that serve as attention-getting illustrations or examples of the subject matter to follow. Such openings are strong because their focus is both narrow and human; they seize a reader's attention more readily than a general summary lead is likely to. But they need to be tied to the major topic by a summary or transitional paragraph, to prepare the reader for what is coming. One series of stories about the plight of the elderly poor depended heavily on case material. In one story a moving word-picture of the plight of Mr. and Mrs. "N" went along for a dozen paragraphs; the story then moved abruptly to general information about the city's housing problems and policies, and the Ns were forgotten—to the reader's puzzlement and justified annoyance. In the same series another case example is described in four poignant paragraphs; the fifth paragraph links the case to the broader problem that gets the rest of the story's space.

Transitions In a story as carefully constructed as the one just described or as the City Council story on page 180, the transitions are easy for both writer and reader. Transitional devices like these demanded in essay and theme writing but are uncommon in newswriting. It is on the *sense of transition*, rather than on mechanical device, that the newswriter depends. Such a sense derives from the very unity of the story—from the selection of a dominant theme and the flags near a story's opening to say that secondary topics will be coming along. To say it again: the unified pattern demands that distracting irrelevancies and even a good many pertinent but minor details must be ruthlessly rejected.

This does not mean that straightforward rhetorical transition never appears in newswriting. Longer stories, particularly those not constructed in the standard news form, often have to acknowledge directly that a change of topic, or a different aspect of the old topic, is coming up.

REVIEWING THE BACKGROUND

Not everybody gets to the news every day. This leads to the journalistic necessity of briefing audiences on what happened earlier—yesterday's, last week's, or last year's events out of which today's news has grown. The running story, which has new developments daily, must devote a few lines to retelling the background.

There is no best way to manage such review (some newsrooms call it tieback). It may be placed early in a story, soon after the lead; it may come at the end. Feature and sometimes other stories may put it into a precede, a short passage placed ahead of the lead. In any case it ought to be tightly written, using only the salient facts.

Occasionally the flavor of a story betrays a writer into overdoing it. Americans were retold ad nauseam the 1972 story of Clifford Irving's attempt to counterfeit a biography of Howard Hughes. Many columns of space

were wasted in repeating widely known details of the Symbionese Liberation Army's kidnapping of Patricia Hearst, usually tagging her a newspaper
heiress (which she wasn't).

Even overdone, the tie-back provides a service. There are always readers
or listeners who scratch their heads and say, "Who dat?"

GETTING STARTED

Only a newswriting novice permits himself the luxury, when he comes with
a batch of notes to his keyboard, of sitting and thinking it over. The mark
of the pro is the readiness with which he begins writing. He gets at it fast
because he has used the time between fact-gathering and desk to plan what
he is going to write. Usually he has decided what to put in the lead and
how to write the opening paragraphs; often he has mentally outlined the
whole story.

The experienced reporter can follow this businesslike procedure because
he has learned a good many rules for lead writing—likely more rules than
he knows he knows. Some of the guides for lead writing are outlined in the
next chapter.

Among the questions a reporter has asked and answered are these: What
is the dominant theme of this set of facts? What are the major facts that
portray and illuminate the theme? What major impression should the reader
or listener carry away? What are the focuses for emphasis? What is most
significant? What is most interesting? Are they the same? What should I
leave out?

The significance-interest conflict may be a prime problem. Often this conflict takes care of itself—what's important is also interesting. But sometimes
the trivial will grab an audience when the important is dull as dirt. The fact
that a senator dedicating a public building discovers, when he rises to speak,
that he has forgotten his suspenders, and publicly pays the penalty, is not
likely to rank in importance with what he has to say; but it's more entertaining. The reporter has an embarrassment of choices. He could emphasize
the senator's absent-mindedness and his red face; he could build around
the event into a unified package; he could ignore the misadventure entirely.
Any choice is hard to defend as the best. Although the press is often lam-
basted for emphasizing popular interest rather than public significance, it
does seem that today's news media more than ever before cover the news in
true perspective.

An example of the significance-versus-interest choice: a fire and theft
in a building across the street from the sheriff's office and a fire station.
Significance lies in the crime itself; interest in the criminal's thumbing their
noses at authority. Which element should the reporter stress? Or should he
stress both? Answer the questions for yourself before learning how one reporter solved them.

Brazen thieves got by with burglary and arson within eye-view of the county sheriff's office and a stone's throw from fire department headquarters at 1 a.m. today.

The lead combines both elements, significance and human interest.

First break

The thieves broke into the Weston Engraving Co. on the third floor at 415 S. Fourth Street. From its window you can look down into the sheriff's office on the ground floor of the courthouse across the street.

The human-interest element.

However, the sheriff's office was unoccupied. During night hours, the sheriff's radio tower is the nerve center of patrol activities.

Honest reporting makes the lead emphasis a phony.

Second break

Firemen were first on the scene, summoned by an ADT alarm that was set off by a sprinkler, which in turn was set off by a fire set by the burglars.

Now the story leaves its theme—the thieves' brassiness—and goes to detail.

Investigators found evidence they had started three fires—one in a trash container, one under a desk with papers pulled out of drawers, and a third among papers in an open area between the safe and a desk.

Detectives who were called in said the burglars probably became disgruntled when they were unable to open the safe. The dial had been knocked off but no entry made.

Fire damage was almost negligible, with sprinklers checking the blazes and firemen finishing the job. However, water damage was heavy in the engraving firm and in the second floor office.

Third break

The firemen's cleanup job lasted an hour and 45 minutes.

Why include this detail?

Analysis of this story shows what happens when a reporter overplays a minor fact in order to grasp at audience interest. The facts do not justify the phrase "got by" in the lead; the reporter toiled to justify it, but ended with a confused and unsatisfying story. Perhaps he would have fared better had he opened his lead thus: "Brazen burglars failed in attempted theft and arson ... "

The Reston story (page 175) approached the significance-interest conflict differently. Reston seems to have decided that the news conference was not of much significance but that its human interest was intriguing enough to provide a point of departure. He therefore built his story around this element, establishing the "relaxed good humor" mood in the lead and relating most of the story to it.

There exists no blanket rule to help a newswriter make such decisions. He approaches each new story with whatever judgment and experience he can produce, and each time comes to new conclusions about organization and emphasis. There is no problem in understanding the rationale for the inverted pyramid form that dominates American news presentation. The difficulties lie not in the design but in the decisions—what facts go where, what can be defended as order of decreasing importance. The design is suggested by the lead but not often fully outlined by it.

To repeat: A reporter can help himself and his audience if, before he starts writing, he decides on:

1. The story's theme—its central substance, its unifying element
2. How the facts can be grouped so that first things come first, and secondary groups of facts can be arranged to conform to theme and to order of declining importance

In newswriting as in politics, unity and strength are partners.

Projects

1. Reread the auto-chase story and the comments on it. Rewrite it insofar as you can with the facts it presents, so that it has a one-idea lead and more unified treatment.

2. Rewrite the Joetta Harris story with a conventional summary lead and any other changes this treatment makes necessary.

3. Pick three or more stories from current newspapers that seem to you to depart from the conventions of straight news story structure. Rewrite them to bring them into the standard pattern. Comment on the validity of your changes.

4. Select half a dozen local stories from a newspaper or a news broadcast and rewrite them for use by a wire service delivering them to distant communities. Note and defend the changes you have made in lead, structure, and content. If you have written them in the first instance as newspaper stories, do it again for broadcast.

5. Rewrite the *Publick Occurrences* story on page 162 in modern form.

CHAPTER THIRTEEN

Straight-news leads: form, design, content

On June 9, 1864, readers of the New York *Times* had to labor through four columns of agate type (fourteen lines to a column inch) before they learned that President Lincoln had been renominated. On June 19, 1896, the *Times* opened its story of the Republican convention thus:

> William McKinley of Ohio was nominated as the candidate of the Republican party for President, and Garret A. Hobart was named for Vice President.

The modern news lead had arrived.

Effective news story organization and unified story structure point to two basic guides for writing leads:

1. An effective lead, especially when facts for a story are clearly significant, opens with a brief, sharp statement of the story's essential facts, the

theme around which the story is to be unified. (The suspended-interest lead, which departs from this pattern, is discussed elsewhere.)

2. The lead limits itself to the central idea or concept that introduces the theme and major content of the story. A one-idea lead usually says more to a reader than one that makes him divide his attention. And it's a rare reader or listener who can take in several ideas at a gulp.

Today's newswriting emphasizes brevity; the standard or straight news lead, to draw from an earlier sentence, is a quick roundup of the major facts of the story. Whether it consists of a one-sentence paragraph, as do nine-tenths of today's leads, or of two or more sentences or paragraphs, competent newswriters try to keep it as short as content permits.

COMPONENTS OF THE LEAD

When news story form jelled at the end of the nineteenth century, the dominant characteristic of the straight-news lead was its painstaking and painful comprehensiveness. The Associated Press, under the careful Melville E. Stone, was in large part responsible for developing the stereotype that every good lead must answer the questions who, what, where, when, why, and how. A lead with all these components—the "five Ws"—is customarily called the AP lead because for so long the AP and Stone insisted on it. The five Ws plus the H made a lead complete, but often they also made it long, heavy, and confusing; it is sometimes called the clothesline lead because everything hangs on it.

An example of the AP lead shows both its virtues and its shortcomings:

> Two men, Joseph E. Hastings, 24, 1119 Woodbine Boulevard, Centerdale, and Dominic Tucci, age unknown, of Elmira, New York, were killed at 4:30 a.m. today at Fourth Street and Skystone Avenue when a tire on Hastings' small foreign car blew and caused the car to overturn, pinning its two occupants beneath it, both with broken backs.

This lead supplies answers to:

- *What?*   Two men killed in an accident
- *Who?*   Hastings and Tucci, carefully identified
- *When?*   4:30 a.m. today
- *Where?*   Fourth Street and Skystone Avenue
- *Why?*   Tire blew out
- *How?*   Pinned beneath car, backs broken

It's all there—the entire event summarized. It has fifty-six words, enough to fill thirteen lines of type; seventeen or eighteen specific facts, none sharply emphasized; an air of ponderous confusion. Reading it to the end, can you remember its earlier facts?

The AP lead remained the model for American newspapers until the years surrounding World War II. A number of influences at that time combined to turn most newswriters against it. Radio was one of the principal causes. For the first time the newspaper had a serious rival in the presentation of daily news—the upstart child of Marconi, De Forest, and Sarnoff. Radio news was unfettered by tradition. Radio practice quickly revealed that the long-winded lead (which announcers in the early 1930s often stole by reading direct from newspapers) neither held nor adequately informed a listening audience. A reader's eye can retrace a complicated lead if it has to. But the ear may lose the story entirely if it misses a key word. Radio newswriters realized that their news must have simplicity of structure, content, language, and sequence of facts. Abandoning the AP lead, they developed their own distinctive rhetorical form. A radio story about the automobile accident might open thus:

Another pair of auto deaths today—two men killed in an accident in downtown Centerdale.

The radio lead has seven facts and fifteen words; it makes no pretense of giving all the answers; it is made up of two sentence fragments. But it gives the essential facts and it introduces the story more clearly to the ear than would a longer version. It is readily understandable, and it alerts the listener to taking in added details as they come along.

Radio's claims were undeniable. They started newspaper writers to wondering whether the simplified lead might not have something for them. Readers were devoting fewer minutes a day to newspapers as news competition grew stiffer and more demands were made on their time—not only by radio and, after the war, by television, but also by increased leisure, more money for play, more opportunities for diversion. The newspapers concluded that they too could make news stories more readily comprehensible, easier to take, faster to read.

The Associated Press and the United Press hired readability experts to analyze their prose style and suggest improvements. Individual newspapers put analysts and researchers to work seeking new approaches to easy legibility. In 1954 the managing editor of the New York *Times* posted a memo in his city room: "We feel it is no longer necessary, and perhaps it never was, to wrap up in one sentence or paragraph all the traditional five Ws."

The effects of all this interest in simpler writing, though they didn't come overnight, are unmistakable. A dozen years after its expert made his report on its style, the Associated Press announced that the ease-of-reading level of its copy had reached the desired level. And with all this came the virtual death of the clothesline lead. An up-to-date version of the accident story lead might run like this:

> Two men were killed early today in downtown Centerdale when their car overturned.

If you contrast the three leads, you'll note that the second newspaper lead is closer to radio's than it is to the first.

The "modern" newspaper lead above is shorter than most newspaper leads; it is even two words shorter than the radio lead which, in good broadcast style, repeats a major fact, the *what*. Incidentally, the newspaper lead would be a good one for radio.

The move to a simpler lead pattern does not make the task of the news-

---

LEAD LENGTHS

The lead paragraphs of all the front-page stories of two 1924 metropolitan papers (picked at random) averaged 53.2 words. Those of a 1955 paper averaged 26.4; of a 1965 paper 25.9; of a 1974 paper 25.1. With one exception, the 1924 leads were longer than the longest of thirty to fifty years later. The 1924 exception—shortest of any among those compared—was a fourteen-word paragraph under a famous byline: Elmer Davis.

---

writer easier. He can no longer routinely follow the ready-made formula. From the five Ws and the H he has to choose what most truly catches the flavor and meaning of a news event. He has to compose a lead in half as many words as his grandfathers used. In many newsrooms there are firm rules. One paper says that "no lead graph may exceed thirty-five words" (*graph* or *graf* is newsroom shorthand). Others limit leads to three lines of typewriter copy.

Today's news lead formula, then, is both more and less demanding than the old one. It does not follow the old formula, but it requires constant reference to it. From among its six elements a reporter must choose those that define the essential meaning of an event. Which elements, he asks himself, must be included in the lead? Which can I put later in the story? Can any be omitted entirely?

The clothesline lead uses all six elements. The modern version of the same story offers the what and the when, suggests the who, where, and how, and omits the why. Since the modern lead does not tell everything at once, some elements must be presented later. Although time and place (when and where) can usually be given in a phrase, and who in a few words, what, how, and why cannot be so easily compressed. When these elements appear in the lead, they are usually given in sharply summarized form as promise of later elaboration.

For quite different reasons the what and the when are almost invariably included in all news leads. They deserve first attention.

What   Since the primary purpose of news is to communicate what has happened or what is about to happen, the what is the element that appears in straight news leads more often than any other. A lead today cannot include all the relevant facts or suggest all the highlights, but it must tell what the story is about—what the main facts are—so that the reader can decide whether he wants to spend the time on it, and to give him a point of reference it he gets into it. (The suspended-interest story uses a different technique to emphasize the what.)

Once a reporter has established the theme of a story, writing the what into the lead imposes no very difficult problem. Look at the news columns, especially those on the front page, of any newspaper, or listen carefully to any newcast. You will discover many examples of effective what leads, most of them simply constructed. A brief summary of an event or definition of its principal meaning usually suffices.

A pitfall peculiar to writing the what into a lead may trap a writer in his zeal for brevity. A reporter who has been covering a field of news or a long-lasting sequence of events month after month runs the danger of assuming that every reader knows as much about the topic as he does. Note how the writers of the following examples have failed to provide enough information to enable every reader to identify the what:

The Council decided yesterday not to make the projected improvements in three areas of the city.	*What council? What improvements were projected, and by whom? What areas? And were improvements projected in more than three areas?*
The long-range capital expenditures committee Tuesday appointed 10 task forces to make sure its $196 million program doesn't stall before it gets started.	*Does the committee represent a city, a state, a corporation, a chamber of commerce? What kind of program?*

Leads that omit essential facts may be permissible if the news circumstances are so widely known that nobody will scratch his head. It would have been appropriate, for example, to write in 1974:

The President resigned today.

Where would you find a reader or listener who would not have known that it was *the* President? But it is unsafe to rely on this kind of public knowledge in any but the most important or the most spectacular of news events.

When   The time element is firmly and properly established as a major factor in news, and workmanlike straight-news leads rarely omit it. Leads that neglect explicit references to when usually do so only if the time element is implicitly present. In the high-speed twentieth century it is often necessary to place an event in time in order to convey its full meaning. A reason of less specific gravity is that today's audiences have been conditioned to think that only "hot" news is worth much of their time.

The basic when element of any news story is the time the news becomes available. This means that, in one sense, every news story is in past tense: a reporter must have found out, at a given point in time, what he was going to write about before he began to write. An event had occurred, or a given batch of information had become available.

These examples show typical uses of the time element:

Twenty groups demanding "liberation for women" met in the Mayflower Hotel last night.	*A simple time element— the meeting was last night.*

Centerdale does not have enough policemen, Mayor Wilcox said today.	*"Today," when the mayor made the statement, is the time element (though the lack of policemen may be old stuff).*

The time element does not alter the essential meaning of either of these stories. Both the meeting and the statement could stand alone without "last night" or "today." But a reader finds the meeting story more satisfying and possibly more meaningful if he knows that the event occurred last night; he can relate it to what he was doing last night, or wonder whether that's where his friend Nancy was going when he saw her on the street. And he can react to the immediacy of the lack of policemen; perhaps "today" tells him that the mayor is thinking of the recent rash of grocery store holdups.

In the following example the time element is implied:

The Centerdale Yacht Club's Electra is leading in the Chicago-to-Mackinac race.	*The present tense makes the time clear; the race is under way, the time is now.*

The implicit time element is common in radio and TV news, whose stress on news currency is so strong.

The lead that follows, from a Midwestern daily, shows how misleading the lack of time element can make a story:

Four German students who spent six months at the local university studying American educational techniques reported that controls imposed on American students are "shocking."	*The lead makes the complaint sound like a current event. As the story lengthens you find that it occurred two years ago, and had been reported at the time.*

Perhaps the omission was inadvertent. But to informed readers it opened the reporter, his paper, and the wire service that carried the story to suspicion of concealment. At best, it presented the facts out of context.

An "old" event, however, may acquire legitimate current interest. Twenty years after Franklin D. Roosevelt's death the news media used a story about an event that had not been known by news media during his lifetime. The Associated Press reported, "President Roosevelt opposed the return of Indochina to France at the end of World War II, according to historical papers published Monday." A 1944 act became news in 1965 because it became public in 1965; the *Monday* defines the time element. Facts about the private lives of the pharaohs are reported 4,000 years after their occurrence because penetration of pyramid tombs brings old information to new light: "Archeologists learned *yesterday* that the rulers of ancient Egypt ... "

There may be two or more whens in a story. Those just cited are examples. Many future-tense stories have past-time elements as well, and it's usually the past that gives such a story its newsiness. For example:

> Centerdale will hold its Fall Festival Sept. 19 to 24 next year, according to a committee announcement today.

Note that this story could subordinate the *today* further:

> Centerdale will hold its Fall Festival next year on Sept. 19 to 24.
> This decision was announced today by ...

This lead treatment spotlights the story's main fact, its what.

Should the time element become the opening phrase in a lead?

Look at the news columns of any well-edited newspaper and you'll find an answer: "rarely." Seldom is the when a story's most meaningful element. And since a tenet of lead-writing is stress on its strongest element— more about this principle soon—the time element seldom opens the newspaper lead. (It is more common in broadcast news leads, again because of radio and TV emphasis on currency.)

On occasion, however, the when is the focus of a story, and then it deserves prominence:

> April 15 has replaced March 15 as the date on which income tax returns are due.

> Jan. 29, for the third year in a row, was winter's coldest day.

Who   Though it's safe to say that the *when* ought to be in every lead and that the *what* is rarely absent, the *who* is frequently the opening element. This is true sometimes even when the *who* carries less weight than other elements. The reasons are manifest, and what may be the commonest is also the poorest—that the *who* lead is the easiest to write. It's not much tax on a writer to open a lead with the name of a person or a group.

A better reason may be that the *who* is the human element in a story, and that often it introduces the characteristic *prominence*.

When, for example, the President of the United States appears in news material, chances are nine in ten that his name will open the story. The name has audience magnetism; it suggests at least something about the nature of the news; it seems to many a news reader to concern him personally in one way or another.

Clearly, the pattern may depart from the logic of structure or emphasis. Sometimes *what* the President says or does provides a better lead opener than his name. Which of the following leads do you prefer?

> President Nixon said last night he will resign today.
>
> President Nixon plans to resign this noon.
>
> The nation was told last night by its President that he plans to resign today.
>
> Resignation of President Nixon will be a fact at noon today.
>
> For the first time in history, a United States President will resign his office.
>
> The President resigns!
>
> Gerald Ford will be sworn in as President of the United States today.
> This will follow . . .

When the *who* is neither prominent nor of value to lend distinction to a story, it should rarely open the lead. But special *who* characteristics may justify a *who* opening, even in a case in which specific identification is not given:

> An 11-year-old boy, scolded for practicing the wrong music lesson, smashed his violin and tried to hang himself today.

> A blind man was today made chairman of Nyack's new commission to rid the city of "smutty" movies.

Some leads may contain no who element:

> Eighteen trucks, nine buses, and more than sixty passenger cars piled up in smog and smoke on the New Jersey Turnpike yesterday.

> The city's heliport will be located only two blocks from the City Hall.

> Rain this month has already exceeded Centerdale's average for an entire year.

> The desperately-needed polio vaccine arrived this morning at the City Health Department.

When to put prime emphasis on the who, when to subordinate it, when to delay its appearance, and when to omit it are matters for editorial judgment and common sense. Experience and the best interests of the news consumer are the guides.

Where   Somewhat the same points may be made about treatment of the where. Proximity, or its absence, is one of the factors influencing audience response, and a statement about it may be essential to understanding or to interest. The location of an event, when it is not explicitly stated, should always be suggested or implied. In wire stories the dateline usually serves.

The place element, like the time element, rarely opens a lead. But it should get first position in some stories:

> Miami has been chosen over Los Angeles as the site of this year's national Republican convention.

> A billiard table in a saloon became an emergency operating table this morning.

How   The how does not share priority with what, when, and where in leads. Note that most of the leads used in this chapter do not tell you how the what occurred. How cannot always be briefly summarized, and since the modern lead does not try to tell everything at once, how is often left for development later in the story. You will also see that how is sometimes implicit rather than spelled out: when a lead says "Congress declared war," it is not necessary to add "by taking a vote on a resolution." A story about a panic in a burning nightclub describes the course of events and in so doing suggests the causes of fear and hysterical behavior. But not in the lead.

Why Much the same may be said about the why. Only a few of the examples show causes of the events or actions described. One that does is the lead about the boy violin player; another is that about the capital expenditures committee. Most don't; the nightclub fire story's lead might suggest why the fire started or why the panic occurred (probably not both), but it would have to do so in tight phrases.

The imperative need to inject more why and how into today's reporting is urgently recognized in America, sometimes more fully by critics of the press than by journalists themselves. One fact that critics may not see but that journalists recognize is that digging out the why-how elements often requires much more than hurried on-the-spot reporting. Often it takes more than one story to bring to full light the underlying causal relations.

Later chapters explore these problems from other angles—one of them the search for the why through expert opinion rather than by factual reporting.

WRITING THE LEAD

Two rules of thumb for writing leads:

1. Open a lead with a capsule expression of the story's strongest element.
2. Follow the one-idea-to-a-sentence principle as far as materials and effective rhetoric permit.

The strongest element You can put the first rule differently: get the best facts of the story into the lead's first word or phrase.

What are "best" facts? They are the facts that most sharply express the heart of the story; those to which everything in the story relates; those whose brief summary states the story's dominant theme. Here are examples:

> A jack-o'-lantern crisis is looming in Arizona. Not enough pumpkins.
>
> Two hundred Tampico residents died when hurricane Ione hit yesterday.
>
> Homes for 175 families are to be built here next year.

> Repavement of Centerdale's main streets will be debated at . . .

In these leads the openings summarize key facts—the phrases use three, five, four, and five words, respectively (one group includes the verb—a bonus value). In each case most rearrangements would not summarize so succinctly:

> Dryness and the curly-top virus have all but wiped out the pumpkin crop in Central Arizona.

> A hurricane that hit Tampico caused . . .

> Home construction here next year will . . .

> A debate on whether Centerdale's main streets . . .

These rephrasings, it may be argued, are almost as strong as the originals. But each one takes longer to get the central facts into focus. The key is to choose a statement of facts (there are usually several ways to phrase it) that does most to make the story meaningful—that not only starts to tell the story but that is likely to arouse interest.

IN ENGLAND, TOO

The Manchester Guardian, one of Britain's best newspapers, says in its 1969 style sheet: "In news stories, would writers and subeditors please put the point at the beginning? . . . Opening sentences are always important, both to capture the reader and to inform him."

In some cases the "eternal conflict" may be resolved in favor of interest rather than significance:

> A quarrel over a recipe for chili sauce upset a Latin American government today.

> Dollar bills showered out of a clear sky on a Centerdale home this morning.

And sometimes the newswriter takes advantage of the element of prominence:

> Queen Elizabeth will attend the races at Epsom Downs today.

> Jack Benny, admitted by free complimentary ticket, will open the State Fair Spectacular tonight.

In any case the opening phrase can be, and usually should be, the guide to unification of a story. If the right key facts have been selected for it, building the rest of the story around it becomes simple.

Misleading emphasis   Failure to open a lead with the key facts may send readers off in wrong directions.

> Eighteen advertising cases were resolved by the advertising division of the local Better Business Bureau during August, according to its monthly activity report released yesterday.
>
> Nine cases were dismissed after advertisers furnished proof of claims their ads had made or offered other satisfactory explanations....

Most readers and most news editors would think the fact that 50 percent of charges were thrown out more meaningful than the bland statistical statement that opens the lead.

The *Progressive* magazine complained in 1974 about an Associated Press lead that said:

> Government outlays for support of farm commodities are expected to run close to a record seven billion dollars in this fiscal year.

But the story later showed that the *cost* to government, because of sales and repaid loans, would be only one-tenth of seven billion.

> Fire broke out at the Prince River Lumber Co., Winston, Wednesday and Winston police said the lumber company was almost a total loss.

The significant fact is not that fire broke out, but that the loss was heavy.

A story about a tornado's hitting a trailer camp opened with four paragraphs about a sad little boy who lost his toys. Four paragraphs down the story gets around to reporting death and desperate destruction caused by the twister. The opening is an attention-getter, but it doesn't key the story.

Another story with the same fault—this from the *Christian Science Monitor*—uses three paragraphs to report what everybody already knows: the traditional American vacation period has been two weeks. In the fourth graph comes the lead—a survey shows longer vacations are "a growing trend."

One idea to a sentence   The one-idea-to-a-sentence principle is parallel to what has been said about the modern lead in contrast to the antiques of another era. A reader, and even more a listener, can rarely digest a smother of facts piled one on top of another; good sentences ask him only to take in a single major concept between each set of periods. The problem is compounded when the long sentence is a lead, for the consumer isn't prepared —he can't see the facts coming, he hasn't been given knowledge of their nature or direction.

Here are two examples of overlong leads, with rewrites that compress them:

Original	*Rewrite*
The first three concerts in the 1973–1974 Imperial Orchestra season were cancelled Friday as negotiations between the Imperial Orchestral Association, governing board of the orchestra, and the orchestra musicians, members of Local 129, American Federation of Musicians, bogged down after almost eight months. [44 words]	The first three concerts in the 1973–1974 Imperial Orchestra season were cancelled Friday after negotiations between the musicians' union and the orchestra's governing board broke down. [27 words]
Sixty-eight hijacked passengers were released from an Amman, Jordan, hotel and flown to Nicosia, Cyprus, Friday, and 23 passengers held aboard a British Overseas Airways Corp. (BOAC) jetliner—one of the three planes with 300 people captured and taken to the Jordanian desert—were transferred to Amman. [48 words]	Sixty-eight passengers from hijacked planes were released from Amman, Jordan, Friday, and 23 more of the 300 aboard the three planes in the desert were transferred to Amman. [29 words]

Examine the two rewrites to see whether, in your judgment, essential elements have been omitted or nonessentials included. A useful exercise would be to try your own rewrites ... and, for good measure, briefer versions of the leads below:

> Work on a comprehensive airline lease agreement basic in the underwriting and financing plans for Fort Lauderdale–Hollywood International Airport's new, larger passenger terminal facility now due for construction over the next 24 months has "made real progress," Lee Wagener, Broward County airport director, said today. [46 words]

> The testimony concerning the firing of former Police Lt. G. Peter Grande was wrapped up last night with the defense calling as its only witness Grande himself, who denied the charges leveled against him and further claimed there was a conspiracy to get him ousted from the department. [47 words]

The omission of a useless fact from the lead below tightens and strengthens it:

> Wyn Sargent, a sociologist who married a New Guinea tribal chief, *said she was ill Saturday and* refused to discuss her life among the stone-age natives.

STRONG LEADS

You might say that the first rule of thumb on page 194 says it all: open a lead with a story's main point.

But specifics support the generalization. One is that strong leads usually open with the subjects of simple declarative sentences—nouns or noun phrases. Another is that the verb or verb phrase should not be long delayed. You'll find examples in the leads discussed on pages 194–196 and these:

A jack-o'-lantern crisis is looming in Arizona.	*Three opening words state the subject; the verb follows.*

Two hundred Tampico residents died when hurricane Ione hit yesterday.	*Here the verb—the fifth word—is part of the subject.*
Homes for 175 families are to be built here next year.	*Four-word major subject; verb and time phrase amplify it.*
Repavement of Centerdale's main streets will be debated ...	*Five words say what the story's about (the verb doesn't add much).*

Any reporter could invent scores of other word arrangements for these leads, and most could find other emphases among the facts from which the stories develop. You can often argue that Joe's lead is stronger than Marian's, or weaker; and even when there is no argument as to appropriate emphasis, the definition of strong rhetoric is a matter of critical judgment. Once an emphasis is chosen, however, the number of vigorous alternatives may be limited.

Names   You don't have to look long at a newspaper, or listen to radio long, to find support in practice for the journalistic bromide that "names make news." A count of leads of major general news stories in three newspapers showed forty-three opening with names, forty-one with title, group, or association openings, and thirty-two "other."

Not every name opener is the right one. Prominence of a name makes it an attention-getter, but its use to get the story going may be mistaken. When a tornado strikes a prairie town, for example, and a senator who happens to be driving through is among the 100 dead, should his name get lead emphasis? Don't answer too quickly—circumstances alter cases. Look at some possibilities:

Sen. John Doe lost his life in a tornado here yesterday.
A senator and 100 others were killed by a tornado ...
One hundred deaths were counted here after yesterday's tornado.
A tornado that killed 100 persons, including a United States senator, ...

A dozen other patterns, or a hundred, could be developed. But note some of the characteristics of these four:

* Use of the name to open the story slows up arrival at what most would say is the major fact: 100 deaths.

- One opens "Sen. John Doe," another "A senator." Which is better?
- One leaves the senator out entirely. Right or wrong?
- Would you criticize the term "were counted"?

A name is a good lead opener, in brief, when the name itself is clearly dominant among the facts of the story (what, for example, if the senator in the tornado had been a leading candidate for the presidency?), or when the attention it gains for the other facts of the event is great enough to overbalance the fact that it is *not* dominant. (A punctilious newswriter would say that the second "reason" is irresponsible, and his position would be easy to defend.)

Quotations Quoted opening words or phrases—sometimes even clauses—within quotation marks attract attention and often add meaning:

"Fog" from a broken steam line caused two auto collisions...	*The quotation marks around "fog" say quickly to the reader, "It wasn't really fog."*
"Crime always pays," an ex-convict told an audience...	*The quoted sentence is not only interesting, but presumably an adequate summary of the talk.*
"The Merchant of Venice" will be presented by home talent...	*A play title, say most style sheets, must appear in quotation marks.*
"The three musketeers" of the West Side were arrested last night...	*A reporter's device for identifying quickly a group that has broken into news under the catchy nickname.*

In the "musketeers" lead the reporter might be merely reaching for effect. If the facts that preceded today's story, or those that follow the lead, don't justify the metaphor, the reader feels cheated.

A caution about quotation leads: a long quotation as an opener is almost always to be avoided. The principal reason is that the reader doesn't know who is doing the speaking, or why. Moreover, it's a lucky reporter who comes upon a long quotation, by a speaker or an interviewee, that gives him a sharp summary of his story's facts. Speakers are rarely that obliging.

A short quote that strikes a sharp note may be excellent, however, if it also summarizes or characterizes the story's theme. "Crime always pays" is such a lead; so are such examples as "Win for Wilson!" on a high school pep rally story; "What Washington needs is a good five-cent lie detector"; and "No man ever dominated me!"

Question leads

> Can the police close down a movie they call obscene?
>
> Will the rains ever stop?
>
> Is polio really licked?
>
> "Who won the turkey?" is the question everybody was asking . . .

Such question leads meet the criteria suggested at the beginning of this chapter. Each states the principal topic of its story quickly, simply, and with a suggestion that an answer may be forthcoming. But the suggestion raises a problem: if the reader is not to be left dangling by the question, the newswriter must take him off the hook soon. Police can (or can't) close what they think are dirty movies, says a court; the weather bureau promises a week more of rain; five local doctors think polio will never again be a major threat; five citizens held winning tickets at the turkey raffle.

Another trap the question lead sets for the unwary reporter is that it may not get the answer he expects. Suppose he writes, "Would you like a free trip to Tahiti?" Some readers would glow and read the story; some might answer, "Hell, no!"; and some conceivably might say, "What's Tahiti?"

Short leads   What is sometimes called the "cartridge lead"—because it packs power in a small parcel—is often just right for "big" or familiar news. If you can assume safely that your audience already has the background information to know what you are writing about, you can write leads thus:

> The President is dead.
>
> The new mayor—Richard Roe.
>
> Rain today ended the drought.
>
> Rain!

Even without much background a reader can provide the necessary context for such leads.

Cartridge leads don't appear often, largely because they demand particular circumstances. They should be used carefully; they are defused by overuse.

"You" in leads   Should you use "you" in leads?

The answer, as to any question about lead effectiveness, is "Yes, if you gain emphasis and interest without prejudice to clarity." The tendency in newswriting is toward informality and ease. If a newswriter thinks he can help his consumer to identify with the story, to apply it to himself, use of "you" may be a plus.

The "you" in lead or body usually suggests news that can be treated informally. It ought to appear chiefly in stories in which readers can picture their own participation. The weather lead suggested on page 201 affords an example: "Did you think the rain would never stop?" or "You may have given up on the sun" or "You can plan a picnic this weekend." But such informal flavor would be unsuitable for some kinds of news.

Longer leads   Some stories are so fact-laden that brief leads will not do. Newswriters have learned to meet this problem by modifying the usual pattern. Some leads may go to two or more sentences or two or more paragraphs. Analysis of the following examples suggests news situations in which longer leads may be justified:

The most controversial welfare program of them all —aid to dependent children—was the topic of a hearing at the capitol yesterday.

The result: controversy.

Hampton will have two new fire stations next year. This was decided last night at the fifth stormy Council session in 72 hours.

Is utterance of a four-letter word to the police a form of expression protected by the U. S. Constitution?

Or is it an obscenity outside the safeguards of the First Amendment?

The State Supreme Court heard arguments on that issue Thursday in the case of . . .

School enrollments will drop 20 percent within 10 years.

There will soon be a surplus of teachers.

The city's 10-year school building program must be cut back.

These warnings came today from the Board of Education.

Two players who "didn't have a chance" will meet today for the state tennis championship.

One had played in every such tournament for nine years without reaching the quarter finals.

The other, though he has played the game for 30 years, had never before entered a tournament.

Their names: . . .

LEADS FOR BROADCAST NEWS

As suggested earlier, radio and TV leads vary from those in print in two important particulars: they are more leisurely, and they are less detailed. The man getting his news by ear must be eased into the story gently. He is accustomed to the looseness and generalities of casual conversation rather than the quick plunge and the concentrated facts of most printed leads. His friends don't say to him, "Hampton will have two new fire stations next year," nor do they talk in the pattern of the three paragraphs of the school enrollment lead above. They are more likely to say, "They're going to put a new fire station downtown," or "There's trouble ahead for the school board." Radio and television take their cues from such conversational informalities.

Many of this chapter's observations about printed leads hold also for writers for the air. If the first sentence merely opens up the summary of the story, the second ought to complete it:

```
Well, the President is back at the White House. He came
there this morning from an economics conference at Camp
David with half his Cabinet.

In the Middle East, however, hope for peace is higher.
Representatives of both sides met on neutral ground . . .
```

Name leads, cartridge leads, and "you" leads are common in radio-TV newswriting. One lead that is taboo on the air is the quotation. The listener can't hear quotation marks—he thinks he's listening to the news announcer until he's told otherwise.

LEADS AND STORY ORGANIZATION

This chapter suggests the basic principle that a summary lead is the guideline for organization of a news story. It says to its consumer that he can expect development of the points it makes as the story progresses; often it helps a writer to decide on the order of materials in the body of the story.

Carelessness in relating lead to story may produce either of two errors (in rare cases, both in the same lead): inclusion in the lead material that doesn't show up in the story, or putting into the story major material that the lead hasn't forecast.

An example of the first fault is the police-chase lead on page 173. Here the reader has been led to expect facts that the story fails to develop. A fact important enough to get lead space is clearly important enough to become a part of the story.

The opposite shortcoming appears in this lead:

> A controversial plan to construct lanes exclusively for buses on two downdown streets was presented to the Transit Commission Wednesday.

The story then devotes half a column to details of the plan and the controversy. So far so good. But it goes on, without warning, into five paragraphs about a proposed city car pool plan. Reader A complains that the car-pool proposal doesn't belong in the story. Reader B, who couldn't care less about bus lanes but yearns for a car pool, failed to get that far in the story. There's an easy way to serve both readers as well as to provide sound story construction: insert after the lead paragraph a second short one saying that the commission also gave attention to the car pool plan.

This device, too often overlooked, is one that meets the problem of unifying a story based on a mass of miscellaneous material. It often is not enough to say that "the Transit Commission discussed two city traffic problems Wednesday"—such a lead is unspecific and uninteresting. Use of a secondary lead is often an easy solution (look again at the multiple-paragraph leads on page 202).

SOME LEAD "DON'TS"

One of the hallmarks of the novice writer is straining for devices that are "different." When such devices add life and variety to any kind of writing, they are gems; when they overreach, watch out. Substitutions for such simple, apt words as "said," "senator," "coach," and "investigation" succeed usually only in distracting and confusing a reader with words that don't say what the writer means. More about word-yearning in the chapter on style.

This is the place to add that the same impulse, sometimes abetted by laziness, may cause inexperienced or careless newswriters to mangle leads. There seems little other explanation for weak, wandering, or badly aimed leads that occasionally find their way into print or onto the air. There are more ways to miswrite leads than can be counted or named. But some of the common traps can be defined.

Preposition leads A lead that often stumbles before it gets started is the one that opens with a prepositional phrase. Look at samples:

> At a meeting of the Kenworth Keglers last night, a six-team bowling tournament was ...
>
> For the first time in ten years, members of the Kenworth Keglers will ...
>
> With a burst of enthusiasm, the Kenworth Keglers decided last night to ...
>
> In an unprecedented decision, the Kenworth Keglers voted last night to ...

Not one of these leads really tells you anything about either the Kenworth Keglers or what they did that made news. It wouldn't be far wrong to call the "at a meeting" lead the worst of all leads: (1) it says nothing newsy;

(2) it could be used on a dozen stories in almost any issue of any paper (it *is* used again and again by novice newswriters); and (3) it is a "label." The others, though not so stereotyped, waste words, space, and time without advancing knowledge of what happened. If an "unprecedented decision" is what made an event newsworthy, why not open the lead with it?

Participle leads   What has been said about preposition leads applies to most participial-phrase lead openers. These examples show why:

> Meeting at the Downtown Brauhaus, the local Rotary Club . . .
>
> Faced with certain defeat, rebels in the Atlas Mountains . . .
>
> Cheering as it took the final vote, the Senate yesterday . . .
>
> Bringing its membership near the 500 mark, the Alliance . . .

Leads like these delay getting at the news. They wander.

Sometimes, it is true, one can argue for a participial opener. A participle is a verb form, and verbs are action words. The present participle *cheering* above has color, and conceivably might presage an important part of the story's facts.

The gerund—which looks like a present participle—is something else. It is a verb form that has a noun use, and it sometimes gets a lead off to a good start:

> Cheering that interrupted his sermon took the Rev. Joseph Klinger by surprise . . .

Dependent-clause leads   Opening a lead with a clause used like a noun, especially when it is introduced by *that*, seems stilted:

> That all schools should long ago have been integrated was the conclusion of a Student Forum meeting . . .
>
> That America is drifting far from fundamental spiritual values was the contention . . .

Recasting such sentences to let them open with strong words or phrases (school integration, America's spiritual values) is often preferable. Grammarians moan at a common journalistic sidestep:

> Schools should long ago have been integrated, a Student Forum concluded...
>
> America is drifting far from fundamental spiritual values, speakers at the Ladies Aid Assembly contended...

This usage may be frowned on, but it has the virtues of directness and of opening the lead with a strong word or phrase.

Weak "folo" leads   Often the most businesslike lead for a short "prelim" (a brief announcement of an upcoming event) is one that sounds almost like a poster, one that gives principal facts fast and stops:

> Mayor Henry Oakes will speak on air pollution before the Kiwanis Club at Oakgrove Hotel this evening.
>
> Air pollution will be Mayor Henry Oakes' topic before the Kiwanis Club's annual meeting tonight.

But such a lead, repeated with only tense changes in the "folo" story the next day, would probably be the worst a tired reporter could devise. Most folo leads ought to throw emphasis on something not available for the prelim. What the mayor said, or even the fact that somebody threw a hard roll at him, is pretty sure to be a more meaningful and attractive lead than regurgitation of yesterday's story.

Upside-down leads   There are leads that end where they should have begun. Here is a long-winded example:

> Even without formally receiving the Broward County court order demanding it provide more rehabilitative services for dependent children, the Florida Department of Health and Rehabilitative Services in Tallahassee *today began a study of needs and available financing.*

You read twenty-eight words before you get to the when, the action verb, and the what. Such leads usually are characterized by long identifications and titles, sometimes complicated by modifiers, to start them off. Note that in the following examples you read from seventeen to thirty-four words without finding out what the stories are about:

> A 25-year-old law-school student confirmed Thursday night that he and some others who survived a plane crash and 70 days in the Andes mountains had ... WHAT?

> Dr. Norman Borlaug, an American agricultural scientist who by developing new high-yield types of wheat and corn may have done more than any other individual to fight starvation among the world's growing populations,... WHAT?

> An appeal board of the Atomic Energy Commission (AEC) recommended Wednesday that more information be given opponents of ... WHAT?

> The U.S. Food and Drug Administration (FDA) announced Wednesday night that it will advise doctors to curb drastically... WHAT?

The heart of each of these stories is not the who but the what—what somebody did or said. It shouldn't be relegated to the backyard. Stand such leads on their heads and you'll strengthen them. (The what in the first example was "eaten the flesh of dead companions to stay alive." Try inverting the sentence.)

Credit-line leads   Though many leads need credit lines, many don't. If the credit line ("so-and-so said yesterday") comes at the start of the lead, it's likely to blunt the story's point. If it comes at the end, it sometimes makes the lead heavy. The following credit-line openers throw the emphasis where it doesn't belong:

> Police Chief Ralph Johnson said today that local crime has decreased 13 percent under last year's.

An ex-GI testified today in the trial of soldiers and civilians charged with fraud in management of army food shipments to Vietnam.

President Nixon pledged in Washington today that he would insist on full investigation of the alleged Watergate "cover-up."

These leads close unnecessarily with credit lines:

The city has taken delivery of six new police squad cars, Police Sgt. Elmer Brysted said today.

Halfback Otto Fink, who won a game for Franklin High Saturday, broke his leg in the last play of the game, Team Physician Arthur Wilson said today.

All but one of the hundreds of forest and range fires that had ravaged half a dozen Western states for 11 days were under control Saturday, Gov. Cecil Andrus of Idaho reported today.

In these leads the story can be told—assuming that the reporter is sure his facts are accurate—without the credit line. Tagging it on at the end only slows up the reader. In most cases, however, the attribution ought to appear later in the story.

"The" leads   To some copydesk pundits the lead that opens with an article —*a, an,* or *the*—is anathema. They'll stand a lead on its head to avoid an A opener. Simple articles, however, are often less ostentatious than an artificial contrivance. Usually the reader doesn't see them, and the listener certainly doesn't hear them. Some newswriters self-consciously avoid *the* simply by omitting it (see the first revision below, and note its clumsiness). Writers who like to do it should note that radio writers, seeking conversational prose, wouldn't think of forgoing it when it is natural to use it. Some instances:

Original lead

The Stadium will be enlarged next year by the erection of 2,000 bleacher seats.

Revisions

Stadium will be enlarged ...

Enlargement of the Stadium ...

	Two thousand bleacher seats... Erection of 2,000 bleacher seats...
A ton of dynamite exploded at Old Fort Quarry this morning.	Explosion of a ton of dynamite occurred... Two thousand pounds of dynamite... Dynamite amounting to... Old Fort Quarry was the scene of...

Revision of such leads may improve them, but rarely because *the* or *a* has been put someplace else.

LEADS THAT LEAD

Many examples of leads in this chapter show what *not* to do. Here is a small collection of the other kind—leads that do their jobs quickly and directly:

A Senate committee investigating hunger in America found migrant squalor and a furious Florida governor waiting for them here today.

Prof. George King, a principal in a controversy earlier this year involving black activist Mahmoud El-Kati, will be reinstated as chairman of the Afro-American Studies Department.

The Biafran war effort is being waged with test tubes and slide rules as well as from behind the barrel of a gun.

Mr. and Mrs. James Baer had their first five children Friday night—three girls and two boys.

Vice-President Spiro Agnew was balked yesterday in his attempt to get Congress rather than the courts to investigate allegations of corruption against him. [from the London *Daily Telegraph*]

"It's all over. The President has directed everybody to tell the truth."

That is how Jeb Magruder, deputy director of President Nixon's reelection campaign, told a friend April 17 that their Watergate cover had blown.

A "no-fault" divorce bill, designed to ease the agony of divorce proceedings for the 10,000 Minnesota couples who terminate their marriages each year, appears headed for passage in the State Senate.

Sensitivity training sessions probably hurt as many people as they help —especially if the leaders are incompetent—several psychologists said Thursday.

No gasoline shortage exists, either nationally or in Southeast United States, executives of the petroleum industry told the News yesterday.

Reserve Mining Co. yesterday revealed the strategy it plans to head off government efforts to force it to stop dumping taconite wastes into Lake Superior.

The county tax assessor's office will stay open Saturday and Sunday for last-minute homestead exemption filings.

Broward County is headed for a population of slightly under three million, housed in 775,000 dwelling units, according to a study made on behalf of the Area Planning Board.

The following two-paragraph lead is a violation of the lead-writing rule that the first paragraph must be explicit summary; yet it is a good lead on

a long story in which the time element is minor and the purpose of the
story exposition of a series of related facts rather than report of an event:

> The world is a disorderly
> place today. There is war
> in the Middle East, energy
> is in short supply, peoples
> in many nations are starv-
> ing—the list of the world's
> problems   seems   much
> longer than the list of prac-
> tical solutions. But there are
> those who believe that the
> list of solutions can be
> made as long as the list of
> problems   and   that   the
> world can be put back in
> order.
>   This is not a utopian be-
> lief, according to three
> members of the Center for
> International Affairs, but a
> goal that can be realisti-
> cally pursued through de-
> velopment and application
> of knowledge.
>   *[The story continues to
> quote the "three members"
> to explain the generalities
> of the two lead graphs.]*

By a somewhat roundabout but entirely clear route these two paragraphs
let the reader know what to expect.

When may a reporter depart from pattern? There are two conditions that
justify variations:

1. When he is so fully the master of basic newswriting, so entirely aware of
   the logic of the pattern, that in departing from it he still observes such
   essentials as unity, clarity, and concision. This usually means that it is
   the old hand, the reporter who has written thousands of leads, who is
   either qualified or permitted to do it. Novices often try, but they generally
   come to sorry results (the lead above, however, was written by a new reporter on a college daily. Was she lucky, or a genius?).
2. When haste in making the story's point isn't necessary; when making its
   point too fast would puzzle more than enlighten; or when the story molds
   readily into suspense or narrative form.

The Miami *Herald* lead below introduces a ready-made human-interest
event. The writer has trod dangerously close to sob-story ground; but unusual lead structure, lots of detail, and restraint in writing keep him from
going too far:

Most of them never knew Meredith (Skip) Runck, but he was a cop killed in the line of duty, and that was enough.

So on Tuesday his fellow police officers came here from across the state, and even from Atlanta, Ga., for final tribute.

Runck, 32, who was to celebrate his first wedding anniversary this week, answered a routine domestic complaint Friday afternoon. An ex-boyfriend was giving his ex-girlfriend's mother an unusually hard time. When Runck tried to arrest the man, the man wrestled away Runck's holstered .357 magnum and shot Runck four times.

Monroe Holmes, a Riviera Beach man, was arrested and charged with first degree murder shortly after the shooting.

So his brother policemen came Tuesday, almost 400 of them, to give Runck his last goodbye. They came in cars and on motorcycles. They came from Gadsden County in the Panhandle. They came from Miami and Fort Lauderdale and Deerfield Beach and Stuart. In all, 40 or more departments were represented.

They wore their dress uniforms. They had braided ropes on their shoulders, ascots or ties around their necks, and freshly shined shoes. Their uniforms were neat and clean. And they were reverent....

Projects

1. Select from a daily paper six news stories each of which emphasizes a different lead element (who, where, why, when, what, how). Rewrite each lead to throw the emphasis on a different element. Then write a criticism, showing judgment as to whether your rewrites are to be preferred.

2. Cover a speech or meeting for which you have read a prelim in a paper. Write as many leads for the folo story as you can—all varying from the lead on the prelim.

3. Follow the suggestion on page 198 to rewrite the two long leads. Or find leads in any paper you read that you think could be shortened to advantage, and work them over.

4. Study all the name leads you find in the general news pages of your daily paper, and write a commentary on what you think to be their effectiveness or how they could be improved.

5. Find six or more examples of leads that depart from the simple straightforward manner—cartridge leads, question leads, quote leads—and rewrite them in the five-W-and-H manner. Compare them to the originals and write commentaries on variations in effectiveness.

CHAPTER FOURTEEN

Style in news stories

There is no such thing as good style or bad style.
The question is,
Does it accomplish its intention?
CHRISTOPHER MORLEY
Essayist, critic, novelist, editor

Morley was talking about "literary" writing, and the main issue is whether or not a piece of writing does its job. The question is not Is it graceful? or Is it moving? or Is it colorful, or exciting, or learned? but rather, Has the author combined his words and phrases and sentences to carry facts and ideas and emotional impulses economically, directly, and understandably to the specific audience he has selected?

To put it differently: Morley meant that there is no such thing as an absolute criterion by which to evaluate all kinds of style. Nobody would hold that *Who's Who* or a telephone directory has literary style. But each has simplicity, directness, concision, and lack of ornament; each accomplishes its mission in a way you'd find hard to improve.

What Morley said applies in spades to journalistic writing. The style of a sample of repertorial writing may be effective, or it may be ineffective. And what is effective in one area of journalism may be deficient in another. What does its work well on the sports page would look silly and perhaps offensive in reporting church news. What is "good" for the *Christian Science Monitor* may not do at all for the New York *Daily News*.

MANY WAYS TO SKIN A CAT

Traditional handbooks on grammar and usage employ a carefully systematized style, straight-faced and straitlaced, businesslike, clearly suitable for their function. But a greatly admired and respected book, Fowler's Dictionary of Modern English Usage, offers wit and now and then caustic jabs, along with its precepts of rhetoric, grammar, and diction. Another, the recently revised Strunk and White, Elements of Style, is anything but formal, pedantic, or starchy. Both would grace any writer's desk.

Nevertheless, the guides to effective journalistic style have more similarities than differences, and the similarities are fundamental. In most examples of effective news story style, as in those called by other names—literary, expository, narrative, technical, pedagogic—there is a common core of essentials. The familiar qualities are constant: simplicity, directness, economy, color, pace, precision. You evolve overall guides to word choice and complexity of thought and structure according to the audience's characteristics, then write as simply as your skill, time, knowledge, and patience allow.

Self-respecting journalists are profoundly weary of a pair of common fallacies: the assumption that simple writing is also simplistic (the prose of John Milton, Charles Lamb, F. Scott Fitzgerald, and James Reston is one but not the other), and the mindless generalization that because some journalistic writing is shoddy all journalistic writing is shoddy. These conclusions come from ignorance and mental laziness. That simplicity in writing is to be desired will be denied only by those who think that polysyllables spell elegance and that fancy rhetoric indicates a high IQ.

The second fallacy, though you'd be hard put to construct a syllogism from its premises, has more meat on its bones. A high proportion of writing in newspapers, on the air, and in advertising accomplishes its intention as well as any writing anywhere. But too much of it is characterized by imprecision, curbstone diction, sloppy grammar, and lazy acceptance of yesterday's clichés. How much of this may arise from the haste of journalism, how much from incompetence, and how much from lack of appreciation of human dignity it is hard to say. All such influences contribute.

Certainly, a great deal of newswriting leaves much to be asked, and nobody realizes this more painfully than the newsworkers who take their craft seriously. They are their own severest critics. A number of agencies of the press have employed readability experts to help them improve the writing of their staffs. Scores of local and national awards—in individual newsrooms, in Newspaper Guild contests, through the Society of Professional Journalists (Sigma Delta Chi), the wire services, and many other sponsorships—attest to the professionals' wish to do their work better. A comparison of the press of recent years with that before 1900 shows that today's level of writing is surer, sharper, and clearer than most of its ancestors.

College journalists are sometimes told by "composition" teachers who ought to know better that "journalism will ruin your writing." This book has already suggested that some of the influences in newsrooms must be resisted. But other influences will help: the demand for tight writing, for accuracy, for telling clarity and vividness ... not to mention the competition with the man or woman at the next desk. You can gain facility in the newsroom more surely than almost anywhere else; whether you get it at the expense of quality depends on your personal artistic integrity.

Newsroom workers aware of the Hemingways, Reasoners, Herseys, and hundreds of others who have turned initial reporting experience to profit and critical acclaim, rather than disaster, are appropriately piqued at the counsel that "it will kill you as a writer." They know that it will kill no writer but the one whose laziness or lack of purpose means that he is not going anyplace anyway.

STYLE "FOR EVERYBODY"

A conditioning factor in journalistic writing is its character as mass communication. A news story or a magazine article is not written in the hope that it will reach literally all 220 million of us. But it is designed to reach a significant share of a defined audience. Some journalism frankly seeks audiences of millions: for example, news stories broadcast by the networks, national advertising, and the kind of magazine fare that *Reader's Digest* publishes. None is designed for one set of eyes or ears, and not much for select groups.

This fact puts double emphasis on simplicity, clarity, and directness. The broader the audience, the more necessary the use of vocabulary and rhetorical patterns that rate "easy" on the readability scales.

Yet when they try to follow these precepts, incompetent or slovenly craftsmen produce the vulgarity and oversimplification that critics of journalism deride. Such writing contributes to the cult of the lowest common denominator, the descent to banality as a way of journalistic life.

But the search for simplicity need not lead to the shallow or the crass, to lack of precision, or to cheapness or counterfeit. Journalistic writing that has meaning for the largest audience is likely to be that with the surest diction, the most artful as well as the most artistic design, the most subtle and discriminating selection of fact and detail.

The writer of this sort of journalistic prose approaches his daily task with respect for his audience and an informed desire to serve it. One of the emptiest of clichés is that the average American is fourteen (or twelve, or ten) years old. Whatever validity such loose talk may have is complex and involved; it is not the simple, flat aphorism its proponent would have you think. Just as exceptionable is H. L. Mencken's caustic observation that you never go wrong by underestimating popular intelligence. Even if these were dependable guides to audience evaluation, they would not justify "writing down" or condescension as the means to the end.

Moreover, they would not make writing easy. There is common among young hopefuls dreaming of careers as writers the notion that they'll "start with stories for children because that's easiest." They are hallucinating: writing simply and with crystal clarity is hard work.

GUIDES TO GOOD
JOURNALISTIC STYLE

Just as there are pitfalls to bypass in newswriting (some of them pinpointed in Chapter 15), so there are signposts that point in the right direction. Some of the guides to effective newswriting are as follows:

1. Thorough reporting
2. Orderly structure
3. Precise diction and grammar
4. Economy
5. Vitality, color, imagination

Know your story's facts   No one has discovered a substitute for thorough reporting. A writer needs a full grasp of all facts relevant to the story he wants to tell. Without it, he cannot locate the center of his material—he cannot decide on the theme of his story, its essential summary. He can neither define nor move toward the flavor the finished story should offer. He does not abandon objectivity when he plans what effects he wants his

---

OBSCURITY DEFINED

"Obscurity is not at all the same thing as unintelligibility," wrote John Ciardi, poet and essayist. "Obscurity is what happens when a writer undertakes a theme and method for which the reader is not sufficiently prepared. Unintelligibility is what happens when a writer undertakes a theme for which he himself is not sufficiently prepared."

---

story to produce on the consumer's mental and emotional states. It is basic to the concept of objectivity that he make up his mind what the facts ought to say ("ought" not moralistically, but realistically and accurately). Without full mastery of his subject, no writer is ready to make this decision.

For these reasons, among others, Know your story is the newswriter's first commandment.

Make and follow a story plan   Without organization, no piece of writing can be fully successful.

Your story plan is the blueprint that gives form, direction, and logic to what you write. It starts the story at a point that defines its substance and nature, then lets your reader follow it in orderly fashion. It brings him and you to the same destination. And it aids you in selecting what to include and what to leave out.

Few newswriters beyond the novice stage put their plans down on paper (though sometimes doing so would help). Usually a reporter depends on a clear mental image of what he wants to do.

Words, single and together   Words are symbols we have agreed on to represent simple meanings. In the rich but sometimes confusing English language one such symbol may have a number of meanings. But it has only one meaning at any one time.

Sentences are combinations of a number of words whose juxtaposition brings meanings together to form a more complex meaning.

Grammar is a system of rules for putting the words and sentences together in a pattern that is both orderly and familiar. The rules of grammar are the traffic rules of Communication Avenue. They grow from centuries of experience, from agreement by a people that they help in building words into phrases and phrases into digestible sentences. Ignoring or fracturing them is a good deal like making your own rules for driving a car in traffic. Suppose you turn left against traffic at Broadway and 42nd Street. You may get by with it, but it is more likely that you will snarl the purposes and tempers of a swarm of other drivers, and possibly end up with a bashed fender to boot. You have failed to achieve your objective, or worse. The analogy is easy to complete.

Rhetoric is the art of prose—the manner in which words, sentences, and grammar are put to work to accomplish a desired effect. You can use words correctly in grammatical sentences but achieve only clumsy or confusing rhetoric:

Such nonsense never was written. Such nonsense was never written. Never was such nonsense written.	*Three sentences, all with the same words, all grammatical—but with contrasting rhetoric, contrasting meaning.*
... we may expect by the year 2000 three-quarters of the people of this nation will have significant hearing impairments.	*Does the date apply to the expectation or the impairments?*

The rules of grammar are not inviolable. Like traffic laws, they change as the needs of people change; they bend and give way before stresses of social and intellectual climate. There are times when the effect a writer seeks can be gained only by breaking them.

But, in general, good English, English that observes the rules, is the clearest and most forceful English. It gives the eye or the ear what it is accustomed to. It offers no unnecessary challenge; it doesn't stop the consumer with the uneasy suspicion that something is wrong. Ordinarily it lays down the easiest, the most economical, the surest path to understanding.

The same comment applies to use of words. A self-respecting craftsman wields his tools with pride and tender regard. He wants them sharp and strong and delicate, and he knows that each time he misuses them, each time someone lets slip *flaunt* for flout, *literally* for *figuratively*, *nominal* for *small*, a word is degraded. The sloppy writer asks, "If everybody knows that I mean *small* when I say *nominal*, why not use it?" The answer: what if you really mean *nominal*? Does everybody think that you mean *minimal with regard to real value*? Five cents is a small sum, but it's a nominal price for a stick of gum only when you mean it's the price named. One million dollars would be the nominal price for a rowboat if that's what you were asked to pay for it, but it's hardly a small price.

"LIKES SHORT SENTENCES"

Basil L. Walters, the American newspaper editor known widely and affectionately as "Stuffy" (perhaps because he wasn't), preached the short-sentence-short-paragraph doctrine to his newswriters. Sometimes reporters and copydesks complained that he went too far. One newspaper subjected him to this gentle spoof:

Stuffy Walters dropped by Charlotte the other week.
Visiting.
Nice fellow.
One of the boys.
One of the really great boys.
Big.
Almost a legend.
Maybe strictly a legend.
Who's to say?
Stuffy grew to size as a managing editor.
It's a title.
Means "boss."
Nowadays it's called "executive editor."
New age.
Same meaning.
Stuffy does most of his bossing around the Chicago Daily News.
Nice, nonetheless.
A little peculiar, maybe.
Likes short sentences.
Terse.
Gets 'em.
We're glad he came by.
Glad.
Honestly.

Tight writing A quip attributed to a corporation executive is that "I didn't have time to write a short letter." It has become a cliché, a witty observation that has been exhausted by overuse. But the truth it expresses is as hale as when it was new. The leanness, the economy, the conciseness characteristic of good journalistic writing are not easily come by. It takes time, thought, and a savage willingness to pare beloved rhetoric to its marrow.

This too is something this book says more than once. Tight writing means:

say it briefly; say it fully and clearly; drop excess fat; cut adornment that hides rather than amplifies; speak your piece and stop.

Copy editors believe that there never has been a piece of writing that could not be shaved to advantage. Experienced writers find surgery on their products painful, but they don't often deny, when time has let judgment temper pain, that they have profited by the operation.

The key to successful paring is not in wholesale elimination of paragraphs or sections of a manuscript; if the early stages of selection and organization of material have been properly managed, there would be no major segment available for outright discard. Successful cutting lies in deleting a phrase here and a sentence there. The true professional guides his pencil by knowing the audience and the effect he seeks. He sacrifices his verbal jewels when doing so informs the consumer more surely, more quickly.

One aid to this process is usually missing in news communication: the advantage of "letting it cool." It is easier to identify words and phrases you don't need when the writing is a day or a week old than when it is still smoking. The newswriter's product rarely gets time to cool. It depends on fast, sure editing judgment.

Give it life   Much of the advice you'll get about effective writing, in this chapter or anyplace else, has to do with bringing it to life. You guard against the perils of haste, you avoid bromides, you are jealous of diction, you slice out verbosity . . . you use all the writer's arts in the purpose of gaining color, movement, and vigor.

You add to these generalities a horde of specific guides. You remember the counsel of your composition teacher to use active verbs instead of passive: "The jury indicted Smith" rather than "Smith was indicted by the jury." You keep in mind that verbs and verbal words are strong because they connote action; that concrete nouns (*touchdown* instead of *score*, *bananas and oranges* instead of *fruit*) represent specific and instantly identifiable concepts; that you can kill a noun by overdressing it with adjectives (especially if the adjective is *good* when you could say *pious, sterling, safe, skillful, gracious*—whatever is precisely your meaning). You pay attention to the advice of John Ciardi: "Never send an adjective on a noun's errand."

You learn other ways of injecting color and life into your copy. You become aware, in spite of Ciardi's advice, that adjectives and adverbs that "move" are life-giving. You underscore such suggestions as these:

- Don't choose a term simply because it's different or even because it's interesting. Your question must be: Is it *right*?
- Search for the simple word, the commonly used word, rather than the erudite, the fancy, the esoteric.
- Replace phrases with words, clauses with phrases. Keep most sentences short, simple, and direct.
- Look for illuminating figures of speech, but don't let your reach get too long. Don't write that the football "soared like a gull in the autumn sky"

unless for some reason it really seemed to do so. Remember that footballs aren't very good soarers.

The words of professional reporters, those whose experience has made many of the practices offered in this chapter almost reflex, are always worth examining with critical eye. Examples both good and bad are given in this book, but no journalist will ever find enough to warrant giving up the search. Pick your own clinical samples.

Look first at the two stories below. The first is a historic story that won for its writer, George Weller of the Chicago *Daily News*, a Pulitzer Prize during World War II. Time has faded none of its artistry.

"They are giving him ether now" was what they said back in the aft torpedo rooms.

"He's gone under and they're getting ready to cut him open," the crew whispered, sitting on their pipe bunks cramped between torpedoes.

One man went forward and put his arm quietly around the shoulders of another man who was handling the bow diving planes. "Keep her steady, Jake," he said. "They've just made the first cut. They're feeling around for it now."

"They" were a little group of anxious-faced men with their arms thrust into reversed white pajama coats. Gauze bandages hid all their expressions except the tensity in their eyes.

"It" was an acute appendix inside Dean Rector, of Chautauqua, Kan. The stabbing pains had become unendurable the day before, which was Rector's first birthday at sea. He was 19.

The big depth gauge that looks like a factory clock and stands beside the "Christmas tree" of red and green gauges regulating the flooding chambers showed where they were. They were below the surface. And above them—and below them, too—were enemy waters crossed and re-

crossed by whirring propellers of Japanese destroyers, transports, and submarines.

The nearest naval surgeon competent to operate on the young seaman was thousands of miles and many days away. There was just one way to prevent the appendix from bursting and that was for the crew to operate upon their shipmate themselves.

And that's what they did: they operated upon him. It was probably one of the largest operations in number of participants that ever occurred.

"He says he's ready to take the chance," the gobs whispered from bulkhead to bulkhead.

"That guy's regular"—the word traveled from bow planes to propeller and back again.

They kept her steady.

The chief surgeon was a 23-year-old pharmacist's mate wearing a blue blouse with white-taped collar and a squashy white duck cap. His name was Wheeler B. Lipes.

[*The story tells of Lipes' inadequate training; the grim courage with which he and his patient approached the operation; the tension aboard the sub as substitutes for anesthetic, antiseptics, and surgical instruments were improvised. At*

length, the climactic point:]

It took Lipes in his flap-finger rubber gloves nearly 20 minutes to find the appendix.

"I have tried one side of the caecum," he whispered after the first minutes. "Now I'm trying the other."

Whispered bulletins seeped back into the engine room and crew's quarters.

"The doc has tried one side of something and now is trying the other."

After more search, Lipes finally whispered, "I think I've got it. It's curled way up behind the blind gut."

Lipes was using the classic McBurney's incision. Now was the time when his shipmate's life was completely in his hands.

"Two more spoons." [bent metal spoons had become surgical retractors] They passed the word to Lt. Ward.

"Two spoons at 14:45 hours," wrote Skipper Ferrall on his notepad.

"More flashlights and another battle lantern," demanded Lipes.

The patient's face, lathered with white petrolatum, began to grimace.

"Give him more ether," ordered the doc.

Hoskins looked doubtfully at the original five pounds of ether, now sunken to hardly three quarters of one can. But once again the tea-strainer was soaked in ether. The fumes mounted, thickening the wardroom air and making the operating staff giddy.

"Want those blowers speeded up?" the captain asked the doc.

The blowers began to whir louder.

Suddenly came the moment when the doc reached out his hand, pointing toward the needle threaded with 20-day chromic catgut.

One by one the sponges came out. One by one the tablespoons bent into right angles were withdrawn and returned to the galley. At the end it was the skipper who nudged Lipes and pointed to the tally of bent tablespoons. One was missing. Lipes reached into the incision for the last time and withdrew the wishbone spoon and closed the incision.

They even had the tool ready to cut off the thread. It was a pair of fingernail scissors, well scalded in water and torpedo juice.

At that moment the last can of ether went dry....

[The story then reports the operation's success and Rector's return to duty; it tells the reader finally that on a submarine shelf in a bottle "swayed the first appendix ever known to have been removed below enemy waters."]

It takes no Pulitzer Prize jury to see why this kind of newswriting remains compelling more than a generation after the event. The excerpts—less than half the entire story—are a primer of the qualities that turn what could be a two-paragraph story into memorable prose. You will note the classic simplicity and directness of sentence structure and the telling selection of detail —not every detail, but only enough trenchant specifics to turn words into reality. A reader gains the sense of seeing the "flap-finger rubber gloves," smelling the ether, hearing and feeling gobs' whispers and propellers' throb. The dialog is gob language; you can count the formal medical terms on one hand. "Two spoons at 14:45 hours," wrote the skipper. "The doc has tried one side of something," whispers a seaman.

The story attests to the validity of a precept from Theodore Bernstein of the New York *Times*: "One way to give a sense of immediacy in reporting . . . is to inject quotations—if possible, dialog—into a story."

The following story has been selected not only for low-key emotive writing but also for its artful structure. It is in a sense "old news," but old news that could not be told so powerfully as it occurred. The writer was George Moses, an Associated Press correspondent in the Minneapolis bureau. Moses had been a reporter in Bismarck, North Dakota, and knew the storm-swept plains he wrote about. The event covered some four days, and he decided that it could be brought fully to reader perception only by a mop-up story —one that brought widely scattered events into a single focus.

Spring is an elusive visitor to the northern Great Plains. It drops in briefly after the cold of January and February to set the snow melting and to remind the hardy plainsmen winter won't last forever.

Then it usually gives way to another blast or two of icy air before it returns to stay.

March this year opened with such a promise. The sun squeezed water out of a sparse snow cover on the Dakota prairies. Cattle dozed in its warmth. Children brought out jump ropes and bikes.

But the harbinger was brief. By Wednesday, the second day of the month, gray clouds began to cover the sun. The Weather Bureau predicted snow ending by Thursday. Shortly before noon Wednesday the weathermen took another look, predicted heavy snow and strong wind farther east in the Dakotas. They still said it would end Thursday.

One who heard that snow warning was a hardy

rancher named Otto Mettler, who lives 16 miles northeast of McLaughlin, S.D., near the North Dakota border.

Mettler, his wife, and their son, Lyle, 7, had been visiting a daughter in nearby Lemmon, on her birthday. As a light snow began, the Mettlers started home. In McLaughlin they stopped for gas, and Mettler bought 50 cents worth of candy bars.

Across the North Dakota line, in Mandan, three basketball coaches from the Indian reservation town of Fort Yates were watching a basketball tournament. Their team was to play the next day.

Harlan Wash, Allen Mitzenberger and James Barret eyed the thickening snow and the rising wind, decided to drive the 60 miles home to Fort Yates anyway. In their car were three sweet rolls.

Southeast of Mandan, across the Missouri River, lies the little town of Strasburg, N.D. Fading road signs label it the home town of Lawrence Welk. A cousin, Eugene Welk, farms east of town. His 6-year-old daughter, Carleen, splashed around the muddy farmyard in her new overshoes. As usual, she was following her two bigger brothers as they did chores.

Many miles across the prairie to the northeast, at the Raymond Diede farm near another tiny town called Woodworth, a hint of spring had been in the air, too. The Diedes' daughter, 13-year-old Betty, was a seventh-grader in the Woodworth school.

Suddenly there was the snow, and the wind.

The weathermen had been watching an odd combination of low pressure cells. One developed in Nevada and a second in northern Colorado. Deepening, they moved slowly northeast on a collision course. They met that day over the northern plains, linking up with a third low already on the scene.

The snow thickened. The wind rose. Quickly it was hard to see more than a few feet in the white, or to breathe in it. Drifts formed on highways and stopped travel dead over all but northwestern North Dakota and southeastern South Dakota.

The Weather Bureau on Wednesday afternoon added to its prediction a word it doesn't use lightly: Blizzard.

You can usually get an argument at any corner cafe in the north country on when a snowstorm becomes a blizzard. To the weathermen, this yardstick is simple: winds of more than 45 miles an hour, great density of snow, and temperatures of 10 or lower.

Though temperatures first were in the teens—probably sparing lives—there was no argument about the storm that swept over the Dakotas from the southwest that day. It packed winds clocked unofficially in some places at more than 100 miles an hour. It laid down a blanket of snow ranging up to three feet.

Despite its howling, blinding fury, it lumbered northeastward across the Dakotas and northern Minnesota with punishing leisure. Before it blew itself out four days later, the great blizzard of 1966 took 18 lives, stopped outdoor life almost dead in hundreds of towns, and killed unsheltered livestock in numbers that are still being totaled.

Homeward bound, the Mettlers and their boy fought mounting drifts and blinding snow until a tire chain broke. Their car went into a ditch. The Mettler's didn't know it, but they were two miles from their ranch.

Wise to prairie winters, the three put on heavy clothes from the trunk and began a lonely vigil that was to last three dark nights and two snow-white days.

"I kept saying, 'We can't leave the car,' " Mettler said later.

To keep his family from suffocating as the drifts closed over them Mettler would roll down a back window and shovel until he could crawl through enough to widen the hole to the top of the drift. Then he'd crawl back into the car.

Often, in the frightening hours, Mrs. Mettler and Lyle sang the Sunday school hymn, "Jesus Loves Me."

Lyle ate the last of the candy bars Friday evening.

Saturday morning the Mettlers stirred under the feather comforter they shared. The snow and wind had stopped after 60 hours. They fought their way free of the car and walked the two miles home across crusted drifts.

Some 40 miles to the northeast, the three young coaches from Fort Yates were stalled south of Mandan.

Without heavy clothing, they ripped out the back cushion of the car. There, in the back seat, they burned everything burnable—including some wooden fence posts near the road.

"We kept thinking with every sunrise or sunset it would break," said Barret. "Everybody was saying his own prayers. It got pretty quiet in that car."

The men shared the three sweet rolls, grabbed fistfuls of snow for water.

At 2:30 a.m. Saturday a rescue party from Mandan, led by a rotary snowplow, found them. All three were hospitalized for treatment of smoke-irritated eyes from the fire that kept them alive.

Thursday afternoon the blizzard eased momentarily at Strasburg. At the Welk farm, Carleen's two brothers, Allen, 13, and Duane, 11, went to the chicken coop 60 feet from the house, then to the barn another 20 feet away.

Carleen started out with them. When the boys got to the barn, they stopped, frightened. The little girl was no longer with them.

Welk and the two boys looked for her in the wind and snow until dark. Welk tried it again Friday. Search parties couldn't reach the farm.

The storm dying, Welk went out again Saturday, battling 12-foot drifts. A quarter of a mile from home he found Carleen's body. It was in a sitting position, upright in the snow. Her new overshoes were still on her feet, a stocking cap over her brown hair.

At the Diede farm Friday morning, the winds were screaming, the snow still falling. There'd been no school since the storm broke. Betty slipped out of the farmhouse to close a banging door on a chicken coop 100 feet away. Then Betty went to a barn close

by, where a nephew had taken refuge.

The girl started back for the house. She was not seen alive again.

Mrs. Diede, realizing Betty was missing, headed in a frenzy for the chicken coop, then the barn. The boy in the barn pointed in the direction Betty had disappeared—away from the house.

Mrs. Diede followed. She soon realized she too was lost in the blinding whiteness.

The woman remembered the lashing wind was from the north, and that home was in that direction. She kept the wind in her face, and dropped on hands and knees so she could breathe and move. She crawled perhaps 300 feet that way, until her home loomed up in the snow.

Rescue crews from Woodworth could not break through to the farm until the next morning, when the storm slackened. With visibility still bad, they roped themselves together in teams of six.

One group found Betty's body at 11:15 a.m. half a mile from home. It was lying near a railroad track.

"She was a very pretty girl," said her family's minister of the brown-haired seventh grader, "quiet and well-mannered."

In the larger Dakota cities in the blizzard's path, traffic signals blinked foolishly for days, directing vehicles that were stuck in drifts. In some, office workers were marooned for

days, even though home might be just a few blocks away. Emergency workers caught at home risked their lives to report for duty.

And in at least one Bismarck residential area, the first shortage that started neighbors bucking drifts to lend or borrow was in cigarettes.

The blizzard of 1888 is a legendary one on the northern plains. It raced out of Canada on Jan. 12, left at least 112 persons dead, and wiped out cattle herds wholesale.

On Nov. 11, 1940, a sudden blizzard struck Minnesota. The Armistice Day blizzard left 49 dead.

And almost 25 years ago to the day, on March 15, 1941, a blizzard pounced on the Red River Valley of North Dakota and Minnesota, trapping unwarned travelers wholesale in their cars. The loss of life in that one is put at from 76 to 90.

Better forecasting and the speed and spread of modern radio may have helped keep the 1966 death toll relatively low. But in terms of ferocity of the storm itself, the blizzard of 1966 may well rank as the worst in recorded Weather Bureau history. The weathermen are still checking their records.

Winds have been higher, and snows have been deeper. But it is doubtful that any other winter storm in history has circled on itself twice, as this one did, or hit so big an area with so much for so long.[1]

"How did the writer get all the detail?" you ask. Moses explains: "I had a stack of stories both from newspapers in the area and from the AP files. Stories of this kind are often loaded with specifics, and every detail I used

[1] Copyright © 1966 by the Associated Press. Reprinted by permission.

—such as the three sweet rolls in the coaches' car, or the 'stocking cap over her brown hair'—came from this kind of source. One detail I added—the traffic signals blinking at nothing. That seemed legitimate." The three paragraphs about earlier blizzards were drawn from the reference materials such as any news office keeps on hand.

This story is testimony to the effectiveness of understatement, of letting facts carry the message. It uses adjectives sparingly, and only when their validity is apparent. And it depends heavily on simple, short declarative sentences.

Both of these stories are made from dramatic stuff. A compelling story emerges easily from a stirring event if the temptation to overwrite, to adorn, to try to improve on material that doesn't need improving can be downed. One of the marks of the able writer is that he knows how to say no to purple prose.

For a story from more ordinary clay, look again at the Reston dispatch on page 175. The Washington correspondent often must deal with pretty drab material—a congressional debate on the balance of payments, though it may be important, is rarely calculated to make blood run either hot or cold, and this very fact may test his ability to bring routine or complex events to life. Reston would never be called a flashy writer, but by skillful selection of detail, a glint of humor, and direct and simple language he has given the Dulles story movement and sheen.

It is hard to find fault with the following story. The event is charged with pathos, and its writer might have let it become maudlin. But emotions remained under control, with the result that the story evokes the same response in the reader that it must have aroused in the reporter. Note how the almost matter-of-fact description of what happened builds to its climax —the more moving because it is starkly unadorned.

The young doctor leaned back in the chair and smiled. "I'd give the patient another few weeks," he said. "A month or so at the most."

The doctor himself is the patient.

So Dr. Napoleão Leaureano, 36-year-old Brazilian physician, is going home to die. His plane was to leave this morning.

"A man ought to die at home," he said. "We have a fine new home. We've been making payments three years . . ."

He looked at his pretty 25-year-old wife, Marcina, and she said, "Oh, yes, it's lovely. Very lovely."

It has seas of flowers spilling over the wide yards that border on a shady street, and a patio and small pond in back. It's summer in Brazil, and the flowers will be blooming now. Their daughter, little 4-year-old Maria, will be there too.

"We're in a hurry to get back," the doctor said. "So much to do, and so . . . well, so much to do."

About a year ago Dr. Leaureano, a surgeon, completed a specialty course in cancer in preparation for setting up a diagnosis and treatment center in his home town, João Pessoa, Brazil. Shortly thereafter,

he discovered he had the virtually unstoppable lymph cancer (lymph sarcoma) that spreads relentlessly through the body tissue.

Hundreds of his patients and friends, many of whom he had cared for without charge, scraped together a fund to send him to Memorial Hospital here, a major cancer research center.

But the hospital specialists here found it was too late to help.

"Yes, it's a little hard at first to reconcile yourself to it," he said. "But then your perspective begins to change, and you're ready for it. You see things more clearly, more sharply."

And what, a reporter asked through an interpreter, do you see?

"Well, you see how very important work is, especially work that you want to finish. You cherish friendships more than ever. You recognize that affection, good will, and love are the main things..."

He glanced over at his wife, who now sat silently in a corner of the room. He added: "And family, the ones who are close."

He got up and walked stiffly across the room, and put his hand on his wife's shoulder. She stared down at the floor.

The reporter said to the interpreter: "Would you ask her how she feels to have such a courageous husband?"

"She's very proud," the interpreter said. "But I'm not going to ask her, because she's going to cry."[2]

Stories don't have to be long or profound to be attractively written. The one below might have gone unpublished if its writer had not added tongue-in-cheek imagination to its structure:

Local authorities have just solved this city's youngest crime wave.

Beginning: Seven boys, 6 to 13, form a club.

Purpose: Shop-lifting.

Initiation fee: Any stolen article—the bigger the better.

Dues: 50 cents a week, or 40 if stolen from parents.

Insignia: Shoulder patch for outstanding achievement (heist of more than $5).

First meeting: Several weeks ago.

Suspension of operations: Yesterday, at a sporting goods store.

Next meeting: Probate court.

The following routine police story—a squad-car chase and capture of two teen-agers who refused to stop even under gunfire—was turned into something out of the ordinary by its closing paragraphs:

One of the young men, held for investigation, gave this account to a representative of the paper:

"We were gassing at an oil station and bragging about the car's power and speed. We thought we'd give the station boys a thrill, so we burned rubber going out and were spotted by these squad rod boys.

"Our borrowed rod is a 31 Ford full house, Merc head, double stacks, dual carbs, grooved cams, channel job—good for a hundred mph, I guess.

"They tailed us for a few blocks at 70 or 75 mph and then other prowl rods began to close in and they

[2] Copyright © 1963 by the Associated Press. Reprinted by permission.

started pouring 38 specials our way. They nicked one of our rubbers and we said quits—this is for the chaplain.

"Now if you print this in the paper, don't be hard on us hot-rod crocks. We're just a bunch of fun-loving boys."

A newspaper photographer who is a sports car enthusiast translated:

"It is a 1931 model A Ford with completely 'souped-up' engine, made as 'hot' as possible.

"The 'double stacks' are two exhaust pipes. The car has twin carburetors ('dual carbs'), the camshaft has been altered to keep valves open longer, and the floorboards have been cut down to make the car lower ('channel job')."

And finally, the shortest story on record, helped out by wordwide knowledge that England's queen had been pregnant for what seemed a very long time:

LONDON, England—Not yet.

Sports stories, though they are based on color, conflict, human interest, and excitement, don't often live up to their possibilities. Here is one written by a syndicate reporter, however, that turns what might be flat—an offbeat baseball training camp scene—into a reader's delight. It concerns the legendary black pitcher, Satchel Paige, who went from Negro leagues to the big leagues after he was forty. Its charm lies in the simple directness of its description, the color of its diction, and the reality of its dialog:

TUCSON, Ariz. (NANA) —"I hear you got control," said Oscar Melillo, skeptically.

"Man, you didn't hear no lie," Satchel Paige replied.

"How many strikes do you think you can throw out of, say, 10 pitches?" Melillo asked.

Satch considered this carefully.

"Maybe not over eight or nine," he said. "I ain't throwed since October. Gimme another week an' I'll throw 10 out of 10, all of 'em curves."

"A Coke says you can't throw eight," said Melillo.

Satch grinned. "Man, you got yourself a wager."

Jim Hegan placed a shinguard on the outfield grass

to serve as a plate, and Paige recoiled at the implied insult.

"I c'n throw a thousand outa a thousand over that big old thing," he said. "Put a baseball cap down there. That's all the plate old Satch needs."

An audience had gathered, including Dick Roznek, the Indians' wild young left-hander. Roznek's eyes popped.

"Is he kidding?" he asked.

Paige withered him with a look.

"Sonny boy, you c'n get yourself a Coke, free for nothin', if you think I'm kiddin'."

He went into an elaborate windup and threw his first pitch, a sidearm fast ball that crossed the bottom of

the cap-plate, waist high.

"Strike!" said Hegan.

"I gotta give you that one," Melillo conceded.

"Man," scoffed Satch, "you gettin' generous in your old age."

"Look who's talking about old age," Bob Lemon snorted, and Satch turned on this newest heckler.

"You talk like you pitch," he said. "Loud but not smart. What you know about anybody's age?"

"All I know," said Lemon, "is there was a colored man on that barnstorming team of yours out on the coast last winter. He told me he was 47 years old, and I heard you call him 'son.'"

Satch wound up and buzzed another fast ball across the cap. A plumb bob hung from the straight line of its course would have touched the cap's red button.

"Two!" said Hegan.

"Two," Melillo agreed.

Five strikes Satch pitched before he missed the cap's edge by a hair. He cut the narrow strike zone with two more, then missed again.

It was seven strikes, two balls, with one pitch to go.

"You're in trouble," said Melillo. "You're in bad trouble. Because you want to know why? Because the other ball club just sent in a pinch hitter. A midget. He's only this big." And Melillo dropped to his knees. "To make it worse, he hits from a crouch. You only got about six inches between his shoulders and his knees."

"Shucks," said Satch.

He tied his long body into a tortured knot and as he unwound his whip-like arm came down. It halted suddenly in the familiar pattern of Paige's famous hesitation pitch. Then it resumed its motion and the ball left Satch's hand and whizzed across the cap.

"Strike!" said Hegan.

"I guess I used too big a midget," said Melillo.

"Gee," said Roznek, "I wish I had a million dollars so I could buy some of that."

WRITING BY FORMULA

For a number of years in the 1950s American "communication scientists" explored the possibility of evaluating the quality of writing English by formula. Rudolph Flesch developed what he called ease-of-reading scales, a mathematical description of a sample of writing by the number of words in its sentences, the number of polysyllabic words, the complexity of its sentences, and other such characteristics. Other researchers developed similar formulas, and the two major American news services as well as individual news media experimented with application of these programs. Newswriting profited from the critical attention centered on it, but perhaps as much because of the focus as of the formulas. Formulas don't teach writing, although they describe some of its characteristics. In effect they say in a new way what writing teachers have always said: write simply, use familiar words, don't overload or overcomplicate your sentences. You no longer hear much of the formulas.

During a discussion of Flesch and his colleagues at a newspaper editors' convention, the question was asked: Can you apply measuring devices of this kind under newsroom conditions? The answer is that you can't. But their principles are the familiar tools of newswriters. More about this in Chapter 15.

CAN NEWS STYLE BE PERSONAL?

Asking whether a reporter can develop his own newswriting style is something like asking whether two paintings of the Washington Monument by two artists will be identical. Similar in content, yes; identical, no. The conventions of newswriting—form, diction, editing rules—tend to reduce individual difference. If the event covered is routine, two or ten or a hundred newswriters may produce similar but not identical stories. The more the event itself departs from the run-of-the-mill, and the more the imagination and perceptiveness of the reporter are challenged, the more will the stories bear the stamp of author individuality.

Style is often defined as personality—the peculiar imprint that a writer's attitudes, personal skill, curiosity, preparation, and purposes make on his mode of expression. A fascinating area of psychological research deals with the disclosure of a person's psyche through his writing: how much can you discern about a novelist, an essayist, a poet—or a newswriter—by applying psychoanalytical methods to his writing? Not much, say some students; a great deal, say others. But none deny that what he writes depends greatly on what he is.

Expression of personality in newswriting, were it to become an end in itself, might constitute a declaration of war on the purpose of news. A newswriter may not, as a responsible professional, make self-expression a primary goal; he or she must ask constantly how much personality may be allowed to show through. No answer can be an absolute, but as long as imagination is governed by firm tenets of objectivity and responsibility, the effectiveness of newswriting will be directly commensurate with the individuality given it.

Personal style   How do you achieve a personal style?

There is no rule of thumb.

Start with the fundamentals just explained. Do the best job of fact gathering you can. Make certain you know your audience. Select from the facts you *could* use the ones you *must* use. Decide on a story form consistent with the theme.

What you do next will measure how much individuality, how much of your own style, the story will have. Write it in whatever way you think will make it most effective. Choose rhetorical forms and specific words because they seem the sharpest you can find to get the effect you want. Inject color where it's needed, and leave it out where it isn't. Stop when your story is told.

Inevitably your finished work will have *a* style. It may, as Christopher Morley would say, accomplish its purpose or it may not. It may move or it may stand still. It may sing or it may stutter. Moving and singing may be appropriate for one story, standing and stuttering for another. The degree to which you as a unique individual contribute imagination, an eye for distinctive detail, a nicety of rhetoric and word will govern whether it is routine or a product that is indubitably your own.

Style and manner   These terms are often taken to connote the same thing. But a distinction between them clarifies the approach to writing taken in this book. *Style* applies both to the broad characteristics or effect of a sample of writing and to personal particularities. *Manner* means the attitude of a news medium or a group of media to an audience.

For example, the characteristic manner of the writing in the weekly or small-town newspaper is intimate, personal, often folksy. The weekly is typically the servant of a closely knit community, and its literary flavor reflects the fact. Community newspapers today do not carry this manner to the familiar extremes of two or three generations ago, for their audiences more nearly resemble city folk than they used to; their interests, education, and social habits no longer make them a different breed. As the isolation of the small community has declined, the intimacy of community intradependence has waned; home-town informality has lessened. Nevertheless, the manner of the weekly is more leisurely and casual than that of the daily.

Broadcasting has developed a distinctive news manner, one marked by conversational patterns and a studied simplicity. Radio newswriters learned early that what was good for the eye was often unintelligible to the ear. The ear is not accustomed to the formalities of written language, but rather to the casualness, colloquialisms, and ease of face-to-face communication. Radio news copy, therefore—and television copy as well, since its goal is the ear even though it goes along with visual messages—has acquired a manner of its own. The effect of this phenomenon on newspaper style has already been described.

Purple prose   *The New Yorker* popularized the term purple prose to describe overwriting whose creator substituted verbal acrobatics or florid sentimentality for directness and simplicity. The sob sisters of the late nineteenth century reveled in it; so, apparently, did their readers. One such writer—for the Detroit *News,* a paper that should have known better—produced this story:

None lives who can quite understand it.

It isn't just death. Death can be kind as well as terrible. It's the taking of little children, cruelly, suddenly, almost as if some unknown power were striking in utter callousness. The crushing of the bud seems so needless, the heartbreak that follows so bitter.

Little Melissa was 5. That is a tender age, the age that retains the fragile loveliness of babyhood and adds to it the wonderment of a mind and personality developing. To her the world was a bright and shining adventure, its winding ways safeguarded by love. It had been so since the very dawn of her existence.

[*The writer pauses to tell of the "must nots" Melissa had learned, among them* the "must not cross the street without looking." *Then he continues:*]

But this dreadful thing of Wednesday morning. There had been no violation of "must not." In the early springlike morning with its hint of bright days to come, with its bits of deep blue sky breaking gloriously through the clouds, she had gone for a walk, her little four-footed companion racing ahead and barking his delight at being Melissa's own particular property.

She had stopped, just as her parents had told her, at the corner. She had looked up and down. Far away was a car but her swift, flashing little legs could carry her to safety long before—— The car, a ton and more of metal and glass, rushing through the day, its fenders flashing in the sun, rushing on and on, its driver hurrying, hurrying...

Our whole lives seem to be hurrying these mad days of this mad century. Hurrying for what? What is the aim, the goal, the end?

But how was Melissa to know?...Her world was a world of love and tenderness and safety. Not a place where cruel things rush down on little girls, screaming protests to clutching brakes, roaring the power that rises within them.

It was all so sudden. It had been a day of dappling sunshine and the promise of brighter days to come.... And then it was a gray day, a dour and dull and tragic day, with a little figure in the dust, a voice that was still and a frightened little dog standing there with puzzled eyes....

This writer committed a writer's cardinal sin: he fell in love with his own words. He killed genuine pathos with gush, he lost truth in maudlin generalities. You can hardly avoid the question: Did he invent the loose details? He couldn't let the event tell its own story—he added the saccharine comment that is always an invitation to doubt. The reader can be pardoned if he asks, Is this reporter really reporting? Is he honest? Is the story half invention?

This approach is likely to lead all but the most disciplined writer into such stereotypes or, worse, callow affectations as "dawn of her existence," "fragile loveliness of babyhood," "hint of bright days to come," even the "little four-footed companion" that—inevitably in this kind of writing—ends up with "puzzled eyes."

A different kind of overwriting appears in the following excerpt from a wire story—the result of a reporter's strained attempt to find a novel approach:

> Alors, mon enfant, shed a tear this mercredi for the French liner Flandre, très chic, très proud. What a day to weep for la patrie.
>
> She ended ze maiden voyage here—mon Dieu—at the end of ze towline, 24 hours late. On official welcoming luncheon—ze paté, ze vin, ze works—she had to be called off.
>
> And now, nom de chien, her bar run dry, her beer fini, her liqueur all but.
>
> The 20,500-ton vessel left Le Havre July 23. Quel splendeur, so bright ze sun, so proud ze tricolor...

Fresh ways of writing stories are greatly to be desired. But cuteness palls, and so defeats its purpose.

Projects

1. Try your hand at one or more rewrites of the "youngest crime wave" story. What effect would converting it to a straight news story, with a standard summary lead, have on its effectiveness?

2. *Reader's Digest* is the most widely circulated general magazine in the world. Read an issue carefully, then write your analysis of its style characteristics. Does it seem to you to have a "style for everybody"? Why? Why not?

3. Select from a newspaper or a magazine a story you consider well written and one you think poor. Analyze the style characteristics of each; write a new version of the poor one to improve it.

Related Reading

David L. Grey, *The Writing Process*, Wadsworth, 1972. — Subtitled "A Behavioral Approach to Communicating Information and Ideas," this small book looks at writing as a systematic process, one to be understood and honed by analytic examination.

William Strunk, Jr., and E. B. White, *The Elements of Style*, Macmillan, 1972 (2nd ed.). — Thousands of writers and teachers of writing call this 78-page handbook "the best manual on writing ever produced."

Theodore E. Bernstein, *The Careful Writer*, Atheneum, 1968, and *Miss Thistlebottom's Hobgoblins*, Farrar, Straus, 1971. — These two books by the talented producer of the New York *Times* "bulletin of second guessing" pinpointing the grammatical and rhetorical sins of *Times* editors and reporters, would grace any journalist's bookshelf. The latter illustrates Bernstein's growing permissiveness toward today's usages.

CHAPTER FIFTEEN

Journalese and all that

*The official language of the United States is now cant ... The
condition of the real language is critical.*

JEAN STAFFORD
Saturday Review, December 4, 1973

The message is familiar. For generations writers, editors, and the lovers of
language that says what it means have writhed at the abuse some of it gets.
Jean Stafford, novelist, essayist, Pulitzer Prize winner, lays much of the responsibility for dulling the sharpness of words on mass communicators—
newspapers, broadcasting, advertising, the lecture platform. All of these
agents have played their part, but hanging all the onus on them is oversimplification. Distinguished professors with Ph.D.s have been heard to say "he
don't," to mix up singular nouns and plural pronouns, and to give specious
authority to gutter language by using it without the lift of an eyebrow.
Presidents may mangle grammar when they get too far from their speech-
writers. The idols of the multitude, quarterbacks with good arms and movie
starlets with good legs, often talk what would be gibberish if it were on
paper.

So the professional communicators are not alone. But their responsibility
is heavy—especially of those of the print media—because they can be held
to account. What they produce is on record, and what is on record is there
for all to copy.

One of the weaknesses of the critics' case is the implication that everything the journalists produce is bad. Journalistic writing is almost always clear, even if it isn't distinguished. It follows the rules of simplicity, brevity, directness. Yet it is all too often routine, or banal, or marred by a wide range of avoidable faults.

What are the barriers to good journalistic writing? What are the impulses, pressures, or letdowns that turn journalistic writing into journalese? What are the traps that snare reporters who know better into writing prose that is pedestrian, or muddled, or worse?

Here are six of the principal enemies of the journalist:

1. Writing under pressure
2. Carelessness
3. Failure to observe available guides
4. Following the leader
5. Mangling meaning
6. Overwriting

WRITING UNDER PRESSURE

You were reminded in Chapter 3 that time pressure—the news tradition of getting there fustest with the mostest, whether it's bestest or not—is an enemy of excellence in reporting. Of writing, too. The writer with a deadline driving his typewriter fingers has no time for polishing, for niceties of word choice, for the luxury of careful pruning that may save poor writing from futility or turn good writing into excellent. A Nieman Fellow wrote in *Nieman Reports* that modern news is "history in a hurry." The haste characteristic of news handling today inevitably tends to constrict the quality of writing. Experience reduces the casualties of haste—the more a newswriter has sweated under deadlines, the more relaxed his nerves and his fingers. Many an old-timer in a newsroom boasts that pressure stimulates his writing sharpness. "Best piece I ever did," you'll hear such a man say, "was the one when they were holding the first page for me to wrap up some hi-jinks at city hall."

But what he can't say with assurance is how much stronger the story might have been had there been time for pencil-polishing, for cutting a line here and changing one there. It is an article of faith that any piece of copy—journalistic, literary, imaginative, or factual—could be improved by sound second judgment.

Chapter 3 pointed out that the emphasis on speed in newspaper produc-

---

TIME ISN'T ALWAYS ENOUGH

Professor Theordore Morrison, the revered Harvard writing teacher, always told his students that polish and deftness by themselves are not enough. "Any purely literary skill that makes one piece of emptiness more adroit than another is too unimportant to bother about."

tion seems due for decline, thanks to the preeminent speed of broadcasting. But deadlines are here to stay; they occur in the weekly newspaper shop with one press time every seven days just as relentlessly as in the big-city newsroom with seven in one day—in magazines, too, and in news broadcasting more often than anywhere else. And it is all too easy to let today's carelessness, in the name of emergency, bloom into tomorrow's habit.

There is, that is to say, no quick cure for the disservices of overly hasty journalistic footwork. There is no avoiding the newsroom clock. The newsman must live and prosper with it, develop skill in advance planning, learn to make pressure a lubricant and not a fetter.

PRESSURE CAN PRODUCE

Jack Lait wrote his brilliant story about the shooting of hoodlum John Dillinger with INS editors begging for copy. George Hicks of ABC delivered one of the greatest of war broadcasts—the story of D-Day on Normandy beaches—with shells and planes screeching overhead. Will Irwin's "The City That Was" was written while the fires were crimson in earthquake-ridden San Francisco. Russell Jones wrote Pulitzer Prize stories from Budapest with revolution outside his door and twenty-four-hour-a-day UP deadlines pressing on him constantly.

CARELESSNESS

A second cousin of haste that can water down newswriting style is laziness. It is the bane of the writer who can't give patience or pains to the job, who is geared to the energy-saving shortcut. It is the tool of the I-don't-care type, the reporter who never finds time, the writer for whom it's easier to borrow another's imagination than to brush the dust off his own. Its stultified product is called by many names, all coming to about the same thing: cliché, bromide, stereotype, triteness, banality, hackneyed writing.

It is easy to see how the cliché grows. Chapter 4 recited the overwork of the term *turncoat* at the end of the Korean War. Newswriters everywhere found it easier to pick up this handy epithet than to look for fresh language. The term had vigor and quick meaning when it was first used; and once it was established it carried easy recognition. But repetition made it tiresome and flat—a cliché.

In the dim past a sportswriter described a touchdown with a gold-mining term: "Samuels plunged the last yard to pay dirt." Strong picture language, that first time, and sportswriters recognized its worth, for they quickly came to repeat it *ad nauseam* (in one newsroom the weekly football pool was based not on scores but on the number of times *pay dirt* showed up in a local sportswriter's copy).

Newsmen as well as their critics have for years railed at dependence on clichés. City and copy editors denounce it, reporters compose satires on it, and humorist Frank Sullivan turned it to advantage in a wryly amusing form of literary criticism (Sullivan's spoofs about Mr. Arbuthnot, the "certified public cliché expert," used to be a recurring pleasure in *The New Yorker*.) In its continuing war on lazy writing the Associated Press Managing Editors Association one year listed among sportswriting's "ten most disliked clichés" *mentor* (usually *cagy* or *genial*), *inked his pact, circuit clout, clobber, gridder, cager.* (Author's note: Where were *cinder luminary, mat behemoth,* and *veteran hurler?*)

The threadbare term is a threat to effectiveness in writing because, after it has become threadbare, its original gloss has faded. If its use doesn't grow strictly from laziness, it derives from lack of imagination, or boredom, or the thoughtless assumption that because Ring Lardner drew laughs from "tenderhooks" it will draw laughs forever.

A powerful stimulant of news cliché use is the constricting form of the American newspaper headline. Imprisoned between column rules less than two inches apart, a one-column headline has to be written in short words, and the result is headlinese, a language in which verbs become nouns, nouns become verbs, sentences become fragments, and the four-letter word (with some exceptions) is king. From headlinese come such usages as *probe* (verb meaning "explore") for *investigation, nab* (slang) for *capture* or *arrest,* and *gut* ("remove the insides of") for *destroy by fire.* These words and their brethren, imprecise as well as trite, often work their degrading way into news prose, thence into the vernacular. Few of them enrich communication.

This does not say that you should avoid *gut* if that is what you mean. If the fire burned out the insides of the building, the building was indeed gutted and you should say so. But if the fire damaged the basement or burned through the west wall, say that and say it precisely.

New York *Times* writer James (Scotty) Reston scolded both Republicans and Democrats for their bromidic patter after one national election. The Democratic candidates had talked about "freedom and progress," "powerful selfish interest," and "the belief of the Democratic party in the people"; the Republicans depended on the need for a "rudder to our ship of state" and "a firm hand on the tiller." He found the Democratic party "coming apart at the seams" and the United States facing not only "a rendezvous with destiny" but also "the crossroads of its history."

An ironic advantage of this kind of language, you will note, is that it doesn't make any difference what campaign or what candidate uses it. It is all-purpose and interchangeable. The journal of the National Conference of Editorial Writers once published an acid "utility editorial" with options to suit the writer's persuasions: "We must all (get behind, oppose) this (promising, threatening) development in the (ever, never) changing rhythm of time, in order that the (Republicans, Democrats) may (wax more powerful, be sent about their business)." And the New York *Times'* "Winners & Sinners" approached the problem even more caustically: "Fill in the following blanks with exactly two words: 'Telephone switchboards through the district lit up like ——— ———.' "

CAN CLICHÉS BE ELIMINATED?

The AP managing editors' study committee says no. Many are permissible "once in a while in the right places," the AP says. And it chooses a cliché to add that "there are no hard and fast rules—what we need is common sense."

What does a reporter do when a news source speaks in hackneyed English? A story that quotes such a source can't be fully accurate unless it reports precisely what the source said. But reporting is one thing; using stereotypes as a means of reporting is another.

The right word   Precision, saying exactly what you mean, is a hallmark of good writing. The English language is one of man's most delicate tools. Used with care and self-respect, it can inform and illuminate; it lends itself to economy, directness, and readily digestible meaning. It is also of such toughness that it withstands and survives the constant manhandling it gets. Sloppy writers are content to choose words that are loosely in the neighborhood of what they mean or of what the facts are. Unwilling to search for the unequivocal expression, they are more corruptive than the aficionados of the cliché.

One of their subgroups comprises those who believe that "the copydesk will catch it." Prominent in this group are the novices (sometimes with talent) who believe that good writing derives from inspiration and that you get inspiration most handily when you live in Tahiti or Majorca or, in a pinch, in Greenwich Village, Carmel, or Aspen. These are the ones who scorn the effort to write correctly and truly on the ground that "they hire copyreaders to watch your grammar." These are the ones who have slim chance of becoming writers. A writer who deserves the name has too much respect for the sensitivity and delicacy of his tools to leave it to somebody else to use them properly or to hone them for him.

He knows, moreover, that he will never find writing easy. Sharp-edged writing cannot be anything but hard, painstaking work.

A hazard faced by those who are dependents on the copydesk, though they often choose to ignore it, is that no copydesk is infallible. Sometimes the men and women on the rim get lazy, too.

FAILURE TO OBSERVE THE GUIDES

Usage   The terms *use* and *usage*, applied to language, need not say the same thing. *Use*, the broader, means employment of linguistic tools without reference to quality. *Usage* means customary use; it is proper to say that a particular use of a word is good or bad usage. You could be pardoned for calling the concept of usage snobbish, for it depends on whether the right people—writers, editors, the careful and precise, the teacher who watches his language (not all do)—follow a particular use. One handbook of English defines usage in terms of "customary environments, social limitations, and special effects of various expressions."

The difference between good use and good usage may be seen in the term *split end*, which can refer either to football or to what happens to hair when you don't douse it with Bilkins' Nonpareil Shampoo. In both cases your use of the term would be appropriate; the matter of usage does not enter, because no good or bad choice is involved.

You face another problem in the use of four-letter words that are described as "four-letter words." One guide is social acceptability. Such words as *crap*, *shit*, and others were once confined to alleys and the books you had to smuggle into your bedroom; today they are on many lips. This is not a question of accepted meaning, but rather of taste. Would anybody be offended? Is the "anybody" of enough consequence to earn deference?

A guide more persuasive to the writer who respects his language was given by Norman Cousins shortly after he resumed the editorship of *Saturday Review/World*:

> The trouble with four-letter words and foul language is not so much that they are offensive as that they are weak precisely at the points where they are supposed to be strong. Through incessant, indiscriminate use, they lose their starch and produce a flabbiness . . . .

Another way to put it is this: What do you mean when you say a speech was "nothing but crap"? Was it vulgar? Nonsensical? Filthy? Obscene? Erroneous? Uncouth? Discourteous? Illogical? You *might* mean any of these qualities—but who can be sure?

It is the obligation of the reporter to know customary usages—through wide reading, careful listening in the right places, and intimacy with a dictionary and an up-to-date style manual—and to observe how they change. Unless he suits usage to his day and his chosen audience, he runs the risk of writing foolishly, opaquely, or offensively.

The term *usage* has been stretched to include correctness of diction. Thus you may get, under "usage," inventories like these:

wrong: The President's message *inferred* he would ask for more money.
right: The President's message *implied* . . .

wrong: He was *convinced to* change his views.
right: He was *persuaded to* change his views.
right: He was *convinced that* he should change . . .

wrong: She *flaunted* convention by wearing a bikini to the coronation.
right: She *flouted* convention . . . (A fascinating compound of the error is *flounted*)

wrong: The governor delivered a *full-length message* . . .
right: (probably) The governor delivered a *long message* . . . (Any unabridged message, long or short, is full-length)

DICTIONARIES, MANUALS

A writer's bookshelf ought to have a carefully chosen selection of aids to good usage:

Dictionary. *Webster's Unabridged (third edition) is complete and generally available, but it is not discriminating; it lists almost everything and presents no usage judgments. Many newsrooms and publishing houses rely on the college edition of the Random House desk dictionary. I find most useful the American Heritage Dictionary, which provides comments on usage by a panel of about a hundred novelists, essayists, poets, journalists, sports and science writers, public officials, and professors.*

Handbook on grammar, composition, and style. *It is commonly said that the little Strunk and White* Elements of Style *(1972 edition) is "best"—a judgment with which I cannot argue.*

Wordbook. *There are a number of manuals on word meanings, synonyms, antonyms, and the like. Roget's Thesaurus is best known, but in my judgment Rodale's Synonym Finder is much easier to use and more helpful. There are a number of dictionaries of synonyms and studies of word meanings and development.*

Neologisms   New words—newly invented words—are among the richnesses of language. Thanks to many of them, communication becomes easier and richer. *Radar* is an invented term, made of *ra*(dio) *d*(etecting) *a*(nd) *r*(anging), for an electronic process. *Nylon* was supplied by the textile and chemical industries so that we wouldn't have to labor with "synthetic fabrics produced from high-strength, resilient materials, the long-chain molecule of which contains the recurring amide group CONH." *Hippie*, which means many things to many people—it has been defined a dozen ways—came along to describe a new social phenomenon. Thousands of such words have entered the American and the English languages in this century, as thousands of new technological and social forces have entered people's lives. And English has adopted thousands of foreign words like *chauffeur, spaghetti, wiener*. . . . All belong in the language, as long as they define aptly entities for which English has no term as good.

But twisting old words into new meanings or forms usually cheapens the language. Bastard usages (*finalize, muchly, hosted, authored*) have been contrived to express meanings for which other excellent choices exist. They clutter language and dilute it (one American Heritage definition of *neologism* is "a meaningless word or phrase coined or used by a psychotic"). Perfectly good words have been given secondary meanings—sometimes to avoid words about which people are squeamish (*sex* for *copulation, coitus,* or intercourse, *gay* for *homosexual)* and sometimes in the false hope of elegance (*presently* for *now, lady* for *woman).* Some words invented to express concepts that are sidestepped in most spoken communication (*biffy* or *john* for *toilet)* have come into general use. Such words go through probationary periods, during which they may be listed in dictionaries as slang or colloquialisms. The careful writer, using them, remains just that: careful.

A recent atrocity is the distortion of the all-purpose word *that,* which has a legitimate adverbial use. ("Is it *that* complicated?"), into a nonspecific adverb of emphasis: "I'm not all *that* sick" or "The concert wasn't *that* good" to mean "not very sick" or "so-so." Usage may confer legitimacy on this bastard usage, but if it does, the language will be the poorer.

GUIDES TO USAGE

These pages offer a puny sampling of the abuses to which American English is submitted every hour. Fuller catalogs are available in T. E. Bernstein's books and those of Roy H. Copperud (the most recent is Modern American Usage: A Consensus). *Erudite writers swear by the witty and reliable* Dictionary of Modern English Usage *by H. W. Fowler, revised in 1965 by Sir Ernest Gowers.*

FOLLOWING THE LEADER

Fads   Language, like most things tied to contemporary life, has its fads. They are not to be ignored, but they are to be indulged with judgment. The Ten Best-Dressed Women, whose annual nomination is a familiar promotion of the clothing industry, are selected partly because they are prominent and partly because they usually do make good use of contemporary resources and design. Whatever else you may say of their distinctiveness, you rarely find them guilty of overdressing or of blindly following fads merely because they are current; and they scorn last year's fads. By the time the accordion-pleated handkerchief, the bell-bottom slacks, and the four-inch heel are seen on every Main Street, they have long been discarded on Fifth Avenue.

The writer who hopes to dress his materials most effectively must keep his language up to date. But he uses neologisms or the day's slang only when they give his prose the precise sheen or clarity he wants.

More specifically, he sidesteps artificial mannerisms—for instance, Timestyle. Though *Time* for fifty years found tricky diction a useful trademark, its inversions ("Said Richardson, 'I resign' ") and tortured inventions ("cinemactress") were little accepted in spoken language. They drew attention to themselves for the wrong reasons: their attraction was their glitter, and glitter may obscure substance.

Unless you're working for *Time* (which in any case has in recent years toned down its copy), avoid them. Avoid other contrived language patterns. Leave Art Buchwald's style, and Erma Bombeck's, to Buchwald and Bombeck, who use them better than anybody else can. Self-conscious prose reveals its own pretense.

In short, don't be trapped into using vogue terms merely because the writer at the next desk uses them. Though some of them may earn their keep, they lose their market value when everybody puts them to work. To follow this advice at the time this paragraph is written, you would be sparing in use of *polarize, gut issues, low key, get it all together, simplistic, dialog, point in time, communicate.* Last year it would have been *charisma, confrontation, far-out, thrust, clout, input, viable.* Next year—who knows?

Mistakes of this kind can hardly arise from any cause but laziness or insensitivity (which is a fad word). The cure is self-respect plus a dictionary.

Journalese and headlinese   You have been told before that these ailments are interrelated. Many journalistic misusages grow from the word-twisting common in headlines. But a lot of other language called journalese is simply the endless repetition of yesterday's expressions. In some news situations language *must* be repeated—in one state you might be sued for libel if, instead of writing that a man was "charged with breaking and entering a private dwelling in the nighttime with intent to steal," you said that the charge was burglarizing (the long phrase is an example of legal language). But repetition is often failure to find what is distinctive in a news event and to dig out precise words to characterize it. Among the tired phrases (some clearly nonsensical) that are called journalese are these:

> Details were not immediately available.
> Memorials to Windermere Hospital are preferred.
> ... who wished to remain anonymous.
> He died of an apparent heart attack.
> Smith, injured in yesterday's game, is still critical.
> According to a reliable authority, ...
> He has a possible leg fracture.
> Jones admitted that he drinks coffee. ("admitted" suggests guilt)
> Today marks the anniversary of ... (usually meaning that the "anniversary marks today")
> Newcombe literally blasted Smith off the court. (meaning "figuratively")
> An estimated 200 were present. (better: "It is estimated that..." or "a crowd estimated at 200...")

Any follower of the news can expand this list of tired or mistaken usages.

Grammar   Some years ago an Eastern college professor complained to a well-edited magazine, *The Reporter,* that it seemed "not to have heard of certain principles accepted by all competent students of linguistic science." The first, he said, is that a living language is ever-changing, that usage is the ultimate determinant of correctness, and that grammarians record but do not legislate. The second he described as levels of usage: formal written English; the informal spoken English of educated people (colloquial English); and the spoken English of nonprofessional people (called, with no implied disparagement, vulgate). Language, he concluded, is like dress; the question is one of manners and not of morals—what is appropriate and not what is legal.

Grammar, that is to say, changes. Yesterday's error may become today's vulgate and tomorrow's accepted usage. To catalog good and bad grammar is not a function of this book, but note here a few more of the common gaffes in journalistic writing:

- The dangling modifier: *Now 200 years old, she* was dressed in a costume handed down from her great-great-grandmother. . . . *Riding a bicycle, the crowd* cheered the high-wire performer.
- Verb-noun and verb-pronoun disagreement: The *effect* of these laws *are* more crime. . . . The *company* granted wage increases to *their* employees.
- Who and whom: He called up *100* National Guardsmen, *whom* he thought could handle the crowd. . . . He called up the National Guard, *who* he commanded.
- Sequence of tenses: The figure *is* an increase over last year and *was* the 16th consecutive annual growth. . . . He *said* that the figure *was* an increase over last year.
- Nonparallel parallels: They marched *silently* and *orderly* for six blocks (adverb and adjective) . . . The firm could *expand* its West Side plant *more economically* than *a new installation could be built* (clauses with different structures) . . . They want only *their fair share* and *for their people to be recognized* (differently constructed verb complements).

Suspended sentences   Suspended sentences, by definition, are those that leave a reader wondering what it is he has just read. A cunning writer can achieve them in a number of ways. One is trying to cram too much down the reader's gullet in one swallow. Here are two that pack a dozen specifics together (the slashes show idea divisions):

> Several thousand persons / are reported / to have been massacred / during a week / of indiscriminate / and seemingly aimless killings / by antigovernment forces / in the tiny east African country Burundi / where an attempt / at a coup d'etat / was launched / against the régime / of President Michel Micombero / at the end of last month.

> The Tigers / beat / Allison High /   4-11 / and 5-3, / and four reasons why / Coach Brooks / was feeling a little better / about the season opener / this weekend / against Central and Franklin / are pitchers Ken Smitt and Dennis Parker, / plus / Frank Dorman / and Joe Guicciardi.

The second example compounds its sins by suggesting one opener against two teams and by befogging the number of pitchers it is talking about.

Cutting such rhetoric into two or more sentences is often a fog-dispeller. The second key from the lower right on the typewriter not only closes sentences; it also lets the reader stop to regroup his thoughts.

Another device for clouding meaning is misplacement of modifiers. The clarifications attached to the following examples may be superfluous:

> Judge Conroy recessed the hearing, but *upon returning to the courtroom* Consczyk again refused to be quiet. (Who returned— the judge or Consczyk?)

> Those were the *first runs* scored off *Seaton in his third outing* this spring. (First runs *this spring,* or *in the third outing?*)

> The league title belonged to the Tigers Tuesday night *after surviving* the "longest 13 seconds in history." (The title did the surviving?)

Some writers mistakenly omit the conjunction *that* in order to tighten a sentence. *That* is often dropped in spoken English—"he says (that) he'll be there"—but its omission in writing may be confusing or clumsy. Note this sentence in the story on page 180:

> Firemen fought the stubborn blaze without masks or other precautionary measures until the arrival of firm officials who warned the buildings contained chemicals which could easily form poisonous gases. (To write "warned *that* the buildings . . ." would eliminate possibility of a momentary misunderstanding; confusion is worse than the extra word)

A more objectionable *that* omission:

> Jenkins said the red light at the crossing was not working, *but that* it would be repaired at once. (The *but that* phrase demands a *that* after said)

MANGLING MEANING

Write what you mean   Be sure you have said precisely what you mean to say—not something vaguely in the vicinity. Note the following examples of error:

> The President's popularity fell *13 percent, from 55 to 42.* (A drop from 55 to 42 is a difference of 13 percentage points; but it's a decrease of 24 percent, since 42 is 76 percent of 55)

> The policeman put his foot on Fay's stomach as Fay lay *prone* on the deck. (*Prone* means "face downward")

> The critic gave *fulsome* praise to the play. (*Fulsome* means "insincere," not "abundant")

> The police department *revealed* that 64 *less* accidents were reported last month *over* the same period a year ago. (*Revealed* should be *said* unless the

department is telling a secret; *less* should be *fewer;* *over* should be *under* or *than in)*

The Concorde flew the 3,000 miles in 2½ hours—*1,500* miles an hour. (Simple division makes it 1,200 miles an hour)

Word warping   Writers need to guard against letting the word-warping habit get control of their typewriter fingers. American journalism in the last century has often passed the sloppiness of spoken language into print and, even more often, onto the air. Spoken language can be more simpleton than simple; it can twist words to express clumsily concepts already well and honorably represented. It makes nouns and adjectives into verbs (*defense* the passing attack, *firm* the agreement, *author* the book); verbs into nouns (two *wins* and three losses, a *sift* of the nominations); adverbs into adjectives (*hopefully* and *thankfully* to modify a pronoun usually unexpressed—"hopefully he will come" to mean "it is hoped he will come").

Just as common is the curse of giving good words meanings they don't have: *ethnic* to mean *foreign, a minority* to mean *a member of a minority group, ecology* to mean *environment* or *protection of nature, burgeon* to mean *expand widely.* And two favorites of people who don't care what they say: *aggravate* to mean *irritate,* and *nauseous* to mean *nauseated* (as in "I am nauseous," in cases like this a fairly accurate statement).

EXPLANATIONS THAT DON'T EXPLAIN

Newswriting should never force a double take. It must be clear the first time through. Your reader may ask, "How far is that?" if you write, "That's as far as from Montgomery to Birmingham." The reverse may be as bad: "That's about 100 miles." You'd do better to say both, especially for broadcast news.

The opposite sin is overexplanation. Take this sentence: "Close to 40 percent (39.6 percent) of the black children in America and about 10 percent (10.5 percent) of the whites are growing up in dire poverty." Unless painful accuracy is required, leave out the precise figures. Grade schoolers know that 39.6 is about 40. The unneeded explanation, in fact, may make a reader say, "What's he trying to prove?" A double take is a distraction from the mainstream.

Gobbledygook and jargon   Jargon is the specialized language of a distinct activity: sports, business, science, religion. It is a necessary tool in its proper place. A sportswriter covering a golf tournament assumes that his audience will know what he means when he writes *eagle, bogey, lie, one up,* and *explode from the trap.* But the White House reporter covering the vacation of a golfing President has to be more careful in use of such terms in copy that is likely to end up on page one.

And the newsman writing a medical story, a piece on the new discount rate ordered by the Federal Reserve, or a description of animal research at an agricultural college must be equally cautious. Casual readers, usually lay readers in most fields but their own, will be floored by language that is kindergarten talk to specialists.

Jargon works its way into the vernacular, however. Government offices in Washington developed a type of prose that, as a *Fortune* editorial complained, made a "perpetually ratcheting sound composed largely of such terms as *setup* and *offbase* and *cutback*." *Fortune* pointed to such terms as *processing, task force, operator, directive, know-how, programming,* and *level,* and wondered whether "any victory is to be achieved . . . over verbal ugliness." Many such terms have come into colloquial use, and not always to enriching effect; often they are weak substitutes for existing terms.

The necessity to simplify technical material for use in the mass media is one of the journalist's most difficult problems. The expert, the technician who understands a particular jargon is reluctant to have it adulterated so as to make sense to the multitude. The heart surgeon wants the grocery clerk to know about new cardiovascular surgical procedures, but he usually thinks they can be described only in heart surgeons' terms, a language the grocery clerk can't understand. The reporter's problems may be first to persuade the surgeon to accept lay language, second to get his help in telling the story simply and accurately. Reporters often find experts unwilling to cooperate. Their problem then becomes whether to flout the experts' wishes, to write stories that only experts can understand, or to forget the whole thing.

Gobbledygook is jargon turned pretentious—the foggy, diffuse prose so often favored by bureaucrats. We have had it for centuries (writers of legal documents, for instance, have until recently made gobbledygook a tribal rite). From the first "whereas" in a formal resolution down through the mazes of military orders to today's directives, pompous, humorless or unperceptive writers have substituted verbosity for concision and pedantry for clarity. One example is enough:

> To all employees of this commission: Any employe who might be engaged in occasional outside activities and whose services are actuated by the experience or knowledge gained during the course of his or her employment by the commission or because of information available to him or her, the contents of which is directly or indirectly connected with said employment and by reason of such experience, knowledge or availability of information receives benefit which such employe would not enjoy if he were not gainfully employed by the commission.
>
> It is therefore ordered that no employe of this commission shall engage in any business activity as a private citizen which may or might in any way directly or indirectly involve any matter coming under the jurisdiction of this commission, or the outcome of which might be affected or influenced by the result of any action or duty performed by this commission.
>
> This order shall not be construed as taking away from any employe the right to work on his own time when such work is not contrary to the foregoing directive.

What this appears to mean is this:

> Employes of this commission are forbidden to engage in private business in which their commission employment might yield them profit, or which might be affected by commission decisions or actions. They may engage in other activities, however, on their own time.

The commission statement, 178 words; the revision, 38.

The newswriter's concern is first to understand gobbledygook and then to paraphrase it accurately and smoothly.

OVERWRITING

Overwriting is laying it on thick, seeking the fancy or the theatrical in place of the simple and direct. It may be spawned by inexperience, incompetence, or lack of discrimination or humor. It is purple prose, pretentious and precious, and is often long-winded. It is usually very, very earnest. It is rarely as forceful as a thorough purge would make it.

Happily, you don't find much overwriting in today's newswriting. Twentieth-century prose shies clear of the self-conscious sentimentality that colored much late-Victorian writing, and the purpose and form of news demand straightforward manner and style. Most reporters scorn fancy writing, and the workers at most city desks and copy desks run harsh pencils through unneeded decoration.

But every newswriter comes now and again onto a news event with honest emotive values. He or she knows that the reader's imagination, sensitively stimulated by selection of detail and insinuation of mood, is a valuable adjunct to a newswriter's equipment; and experience teaches that it can be aroused more responsively by the delicate nudge than by the free-swinging bludgeon. The hint is likely to hit harder than the haymaker; the hint, sneaking into the reader's subconscious, is nourished there by whatever creative talents the writer has fed it. A reader may not be able to dodge a haymaker, but he puts up the defense of skepticism to soften it.

The old-fashioned sob story (see the example on page 228) was typically marked by overwriting. Sob story overwriting belittles the reader and shows lack of journalistic competence; it is dishonest in intent and usually inaccurate in result. It is often overnice, the kind Bernstein of the *Times* calls "writing with the little finger well out." Bernstein points to the phrase "the Texan took things easily." The idiom, which is good English, is *took things easy*. In the same basket is writing that somebody "felt badly" or that Ms. Jones "works as a charlady." A current example is the clumsy *more importantly* when *more important* is the intended meaning: "More importantly, the governor signed twenty-two bills." The intent is that the achievement was important; what the adverbial form says is that the governor acted importantly, whatever that means.

Nice-Nellyism is a writing sin by no means limited to the journalists. For years the critics have jeered, with no apparent effect, at such pomposities as mortician, bootician, beautician, realtor, display engineer (window dresser), and custodial engineer (janitor).

Newswriting has become more honest and accurate in dealing with sexual acts than it was a generation ago. The word *prostitute* is no longer taboo, nor is *rape* (which used to be either criminal *assault* or *statutory* crime). But *nude* remains less revealing than *naked*, and *disrobe* more genteel than *undress*. (Reporters' gabfests take acid pleasure in the unwritten news story that said, "The lady ran disrobed down the street shouting, 'I have been criminally assaulted.' ")

Another form of reaching for effect appears in the two stories that included these paragraphs:

It was a pretty bad cuttin'.... It was on account of Ben's gal friend's double wooin' and there's some that says they can't blame Ben much—cause of it happenin' twice, and all.

McGinty had this comment: "Begorra an' it's shure Oi am thot no girrul av moine wud dhrink loik thot."

The first overworks an attempt to establish mood and manner; the second exaggerates what its writer thinks is Irish dialect. Either mood or dialect can be suggested by a few sure strokes. Attempt at precise reproduction usually stops the reader in his tracks.

Projects

1. From sports broadcasts and sports pages, make a list of at least twenty-five clichés you hear or read. Break the list down into old-timers and current fad words. File them away mentally for nonuse.

2. Select a story you think is overwritten and rewrite it to eliminate its errors of sentimentality, ornate diction, phony elegance, or self-conscious style. (If you can't find one, use the story on page 228, supplying such facts as full name, address, parents' names, or others you would use.)

3. Examine a newspaper story about a current business or economic development, then contrast it with a story on the same subject in *Business Week, Forbes, Wall Street Journal,* or some other specialized publication. A useful extension of this project would be to contrast treatments of such a subject in four or five publications, since no two seek precisely the same audiences. Other publications you might use are *Newsweek, Time, U. S. News & World Report, National Observer, Fortune,* and a variety of newspapers.

From such contrasts you can draw all kinds of useful conclusions about style in relation to audiences.

4. Analyze any, or all, of the examples of improper usage or grammar under the subheads Journalese and Headlinese and Grammar in this chapter, and rewrite them into acceptable form.

TYPES OF REPORTING

CHAPTER SIXTEEN

Speeches and meetings

People are always talking, and much of what they say makes news.

It makes news when they say it before public audiences, in speeches or meetings or on the air; or when reporters have asked them to talk, in interviews; or when they talk before legislative sessions or committee hearings; or when they communicate at news conferences or through prepared releases. Sometimes what they say in private becomes news when it reaches reporters at second hand (though hearsay news, like hearsay testimony in court, is suspect and must be authenticated).

More than half of all news stories are directly or indirectly derived from spoken or attributed words. Some stories do not originate in oral sources: reports of a hockey game, for example, or of the vote of a house of Congress, or of an airplane hijacking. This kind of report, since it is what news—built of flat, unqualified facts—does not always require supporting authority. You can safely write, "107 passengers were on the plane." But even this kind of news often shows its source—somebody who saw the mugging or a spokesman for a committee. It is often amplified by spoken words. A congressman may explain why he voted no, an airlines official may comment on failure of security measures. And it often reaches the reporter by word of mouth, even though he does not credit the source. Note these examples:

> Hampshire Federated Casualty Society has approved an 18 percent dividend for ordinary policies. Policy owners will get $750,000 on top of the $3.85 million previously estimated for the year.

> The 11th annual North Shore Clambake will take place Saturday at Spring Beach.
> Guests from Indigo Inlet will join the North Shore clammers. About 200 will be present.

> MERIDA, Yucatan—If you're looting any 1,000-year-old Mayan temple sites in Mexico or Central America, look out for the shepherd or the bird hunter.
> Police in Mexico and Honduras have added them to the hazards for illegal excavators who annually sell riches in early American art—at bargain prices—to museums and private collectors.

None of these stories reveals directly that its writer has interviewed anybody—there are no credits to a specific source. But it is obvious in each that some kind of source had been consulted: an official of the insurance company, the club, or the state police—perhaps even a publicity release. Many reporters and editors argue that sources must always be shown. But some news can stand on its own.

This chapter concerns the reporting of speeches and meetings; Chapter 17 is concerned with interviews. Both kinds of reporting rely on the spoken word as the primary source.

SPEECH STORIES

Civilized man has always liked to listen to speeches. From Cicero to William Jennings Bryan, from Savonarola to Hitler to Billy Graham, skilled orators have drawn audiences to public places to listen and to cheer or jeer.

In the twentieth century, with its network of communications to let you read what speakers said, the spoken word remains vital. Civic clubs, stadium dedications, schools, churches, crownings of homecoming queens all offer speeches—scores and hundreds a day. The news media cover them for good reasons:

- As group events they concern definable interests within the community that merit some notice if not always full report.
- Usually a speech is arranged because it illuminates a topic of current concern, one in which specific groups of citizens have an interest.
- The speaker may have something to contribute to the general knowledge.
- The speaker himself may be newsworthy, so that his words deserve public notice even if what they say is piffle.

On the last two scores journalists can grow caustic. Many speeches are banal; many would be better unheard and unrecorded. But it may be as important to let the public know that a speaker has said nothing, or that he has played a familiar tune, as to report real contribution to knowledge or understanding. Reporters sometimes label speech reporting the dullest part of their work; many would scoff at the statistic that only 7 percent of news space goes to speeches. (Because speech stories often run long, sometimes to full texts, they may take more—especially for broadcasters, when a President preempts time.)

However onerous the chore, covering speeches is an elementary reportorial skill. Some of the skills are shown in the following case history of a speech assignment (fiction only in its identifying "facts.").

A woman reporter is told on Tuesday that on Friday she is to cover a talk before the State Chambers of Commerce Association convention by Dr. Wilfred Guntzlin, industrial psychologist. Guntzlin's subject is "Freud Couldn't Sell Machinery." "Sounds silly," says the city editor, "but it might make a good yarn. Write a piece that even I can understand." The reporter casts back into undergraduate psychology to recall what she learned about Freud. A dimmed memory, she finds. Hypnotism . . . the Oedipus complex . . . sex as a life force. Selling machinery? She needs updating.

She calls the Chamber of Commerce secretary and learns about the kind of talk Guntzlin has been asked to give. Then to the public library, where she finds a popular book on Freudian concepts and a nontechnical work on psychology in business. She digs hard into the Freud book, skims the other; she comes up with what she thinks is an elementary understanding of the Freudian approach and some questions about its relation to business.

She calls a psychologist at the local college, who refers her to a psychiatrist. "I used to know Bill Guntzlin in med school," says this source. "He'll make sense. But watch out for overemphasis on free association. Bill out-Freuds Freud on that."

The reporter now needs to know more about Guntzlin himself. Who's Who gives her biographical data: Guntzlin has written two books with titles that sound like his speech topic. Married, with two sons, he belongs to a yacht club, two golf clubs, a handul of professional societies.

All of this, with what the psychiatrist has told her, gives her a decent background for the assignment.

She tries one more step: an interview with Guntzlin. And she'd like a copy of the talk. She learns by telephone that Guntzlin won't be available before the meeting. He will grant an interview later. And she can pick up an advance copy of the talk at the Chamber.

HOW MANY NOTES?

Some reporters adhere to the plenty-of-notes school of reporting. Others prefer reminder notes, jotted phrases to recall points of emphasis, witticisms, colorful illustrations, structural outline; they depend on memory for the fill-in. Reporters debate this problem over postdeadline coffee:

"You get so involved taking notes that you hear about half of what a speaker says," insists one reporter. "You can't see the forest for the trees."

"Not so," replies another. "You learn to follow a talk as you write. The speaker's major points give you subheads, and you get enough so that you don't have to ask yourself later, 'What did he mean here?' You don't take every word—just key phrases, points he hits hard or states well. And you've got to have notes on specific facts—names, statistics, dates, and such. Memory isn't good enough."

Much may be said for the school of thoroughness. A fundamental of good reporting: gather more material than you're going to use.

The reporter runs through the advance copy of the talk and marks what seem to be significant passages. As she settles herself for the talk, she has the script open before her. She underlines points Guntzlin emphasizes, scribbles reminders in margins when he leaves the text, strikes out passages he omits. She notes bursts of applause or other incidents.

(An advance script is not always a duplicate of what comes over the lectern. On ceremonial occasions a talk is likely to follow script literally; when the Secretary of State makes a foreign-policy pronouncement, the words he utters must be precisely those he and his advisers have put together. But often speakers throw the book out the window.)

Our reporter finds that Guntzlin sticks to his text. But she would like to clarify a couple of points. First she telephones a summary to a rewrite man for the final afternoon edition. Then she meets the speaker with her questions. His painstaking attention gives her confidence; she does not have to fear that he is a crowd-pleaser or a mere showman. She is now ready to write her main story.

She is primed as she faces her typewriter because she has reviewed her materials and decided on both lead emphasis and story structure. What have been her guides?

She starts with the assumption that underlies all reporting: the reporter is the personal representative of every member of an absent audience. Her obligation is to write a story that will let each reader (particularly those interested in psychology or business) take from it whatever he would have

TRAP FOR THE UNWARY

Secondary incidents sometimes overshadow the talk itself. If the speaker stalks from the lectern in anger at a question, or if part of his audience walks out in protest, the secondary fact may get major billing. If he keeps his hearers in stitches, the hilarity may become the lead.

But such treatment may be a misleading dilution of the talk's central substance. In a police board meeting the board president suggested that the police chief arrest two visiting baseball players for larceny because their consecutive home runs the night before had robbed the local club of an easy victory. The reporter wrote a "bright" that made the paper's front page; the serious business of the meeting was buried inside. Is this fair reporting, either to the meeting or the public?

gained had he been present. This means objective reporting—a reporter reports, he doesn't comment; it means scrupulous accuracy and balanced summary, scrupulous inclusion and rejection. And it means decision as to what parallel events are to be reported, and with what emphasis. The reporter's thinking, on her way to her typewriter, might go something like this:

> A serious talk—a sober and attentive audience. A number of points of concern to all kinds of business. I'll make the lead on the three kinds of sales tactics Guntzlin said businesses can use .... The Freud angle? He didn't give that more than a nod. Just a trick to furnish a good title. I'll ignore it. There wasn't much incidental color, except that he had such a tight hold on his audience. He made them laugh a couple of times—maybe an example or so ... Should I mention that he's a matinee idol type? How he towered over the lectern?

Now she is ready to start writing. But first a report to the city desk:

```
     I can do three-quarters of a column on Guntzlin. And
I've got stuff for an interview story, on how he thinks
business psychology ought to be taught in high schools.
Maybe we could follow that with a piece on what the high
schools think of the idea.
```

Speech story form American news media have developed a functional pattern for the speech story, one that permits both extensive direct quotation and summary of parts of a talk that do not demand protracted detail. The pattern belongs to the straight-news form: summary lead followed by development of significant detail, usually in order of decreasing importance. Specifically, it involves:

1. A lead of one or more paragraphs, usually in indirect (paraphrased) discourse

2. Passages in direct quotation for the major points or those that justify elaboration; these passages alternate with:
3. Passages in indirect discourse, usually summaries of parts of the talk
4. Circumstantial detail: time, place, pedigree of the speaker, sponsorship, other related matter
5. Secondary incidents (these might go into sidebars)

Different treatments of a speech   In mid-August, 1973, after the Watergate blowup, President Nixon broke silence to define his position vis-à-vis break-ins, cover-up, and White House involvement in the puzzling sequence of events. The speech was covered by wire services, broadcast networks, newsmagazines, and hundreds of individual correspondents. The most widely used stories were those provided by the Associated Press and the United Press International; examination of the wire service stories and a number of others shows both the differences in individual treatment and an overriding fidelity to the customary speech-story pattern.

The reporters agreed on a number of central points in the speech (several published sidebars listing them):

1. Nixon said he had no advance knowledge of break-ins or cover-up.
2. He said he ordered prompt investigations.
3. He admitted an earlier error regarding the date on which he had learned of the Ellsberg break-in.
4. He did not authorize clemency for Watergate defendants.
5. He planned to oppose release of White House tapes.
6. He deplored "illegal political acts."
7. He asked that the courts be asked to settle the questions.
8. He told the country it should concentrate on promoting its peace and prosperity.

The Nixon address made other points, but the news stories analyzed here agreed that these were principal. All but one reported all eight; each included additional points, but not always the same ones. The large newspapers printed full texts of the speech and of the accompanying statement the President issued (most carried separate stories on the statement). Smaller newspapers usually carried two stories, one each for speech and statement, or one story covering both; few printed full texts. The networks and their radio and TV affiliates typically broadcast the entire talk, covered it again in thousands of news programs, and summarized but did not present in full the statement. Thus American citizens were given vast opportunity to know much of what the President said.

Were they all given the same view of it?

The answer is the familiar yes and no: yes in the broad, no in specifics. Note the differences in lead emphases (the figures in brackets refer to the list of central points):

A United Press International twenty-inch story was published in the Still-water (Minnesota) *Gazette:*

> WASHINGTON (UPI)—President Nixon said Wednesday night it is the "simple truth" that he is innocent of guilt in the Watergate affair. [1] He suggested Senate investigators help solve the country's problems instead of trying to put the blame for the scandal on him.
>
> Nixon asked the public to join him in demanding that the Senate end its hearings on Watergate and turn the matter "over to the courts where the questions of guilt or innocence belong." [7]

The Associated Press story was given seventeen inches in the Rochester (Minnesota) *Post-Bulletin* and fifteen inches in the St. Paul *Dispatch:*

> WASHINGTON (AP)—Proclaiming he was not involved in the Watergate scandal, [1] President Nixon has appealed to the nation to let the courts decide the guilt or innocence of individuals involved. [7] "The time has come to turn Watergate over to the courts where the questions of guilt or innocence belong," Nixon said. "The time has come for the rest of us to get on with the urgent business of the nation." [8]

The Washington *Post* ran a thirty-eight-inch story "from news dispatches":

> President Nixon firmly denied last night he was involved in any way in the Watergate scandal [1] but acknowledged that some of his over-zealous subordinates took part in attempts to cover it up and in other election-year abuses in 1972.

The Chicago *Tribune* had a twenty-five-inch story by a *Tribune* correspondent:

> WASHINGTON, Aug. 15 —President Nixon tonight emphatically repeated his denial of any knowledge of the Watergate break-in or subsequent coverup [1] and promised he will try to assure that one result of the scandal will be a "new level of political decency and integrity in America." [6]

The Minneapolis *Tribune* published a thirty-four-inch story by its correspondent:

> President Nixon, trying to put Watergate behind him and restore public confidence in his administration, told the country Wednesday night it is time to refocus on the greater issues of peace and prosperity. [8]
>
> In one of the most important performances of his long political career, Mr. Nixon in a 30-minute nationally televised speech restated his own innocence in the events surrounding the June 1972 break-in at Democratic national headquarters. [1]

Network radio and TV broadcast a five-and-one-half-minute story by a network correspondent:

President Nixon has just finished his long-promised response to suggestions that he was implicated in the Watergate scandals. As expected, he denied that he was involved. [1] He asked the nation to forget Watergate and "get on with its urgent business." [8]

A tally of the leads shows consensus that Nixon's denial of guilt was a dominant theme of the speech—all six leads quoted here used it, and all except one opened with it:

Nixon denial: **6**
Prompt investigation: **0**
Earlier error: **0**
No clemency: **0**
Release of tapes: **1**
Political cleanup: **1**
Court decision: **2**
Get back to work: **3**

WHAT DOES THE PUBLIC GET?

No two of the stories under examination here were identical; so no recipient of one received precisely the impression received by another. This is one of the puzzles of news reporting. All stories on an event seek to give their audiences the same information, and they do it in much the same way. But each story is filtered through an individual set of eyes. For reader or listener, the best solution to this dilemma is to read or listen to a variety of stories.

The problem is complicated by the fact that each paper makes its individual decision as to how much space and what kind of prominence a story is to receive. The twenty-one-paragraph Associated Press story printed on the next page appeared in the Rochester (Minnesota) Post-Bulletin. The story in the neighboring St. Paul Dispatch, drawn from the same AP copy, used the first seven paragraphs, interposed two related paragraphs from another AP story, used paragraphs eight and nine of the original story, and discarded the remaining twelve.

What you conclude is that different reporters, even when all are experienced and responsible, see an event in different ways. This is the reason that variety of news media is so necessary in a democracy.

Here are additional observations on the six stories:

- All follow the organizational plan described in Chapter 12: lead; condensed summaries of secondary elements; detailed attention to these elements in order of decreasing importance.
- All depend heavily on verbatim report. Paraphrase of the words of a President is a liberty reporters rarely take. Most speech stories offer a higher percentage of indirect quotation than do this group.
- All stories (except the broadcast story) alternate direct and indirect quotation, often in one paragraph.
- No story opens with a direct quotation; all rely on summary of a principal point. Five of the six make "President Nixon" their opening words.
- Only one lead permits itself reportorial comment (that in the Minneapolis *Tribune*). This story might be called interpretive rather than straight reporting.

Taking one of the stories apart helps to visualize typical treatment of a speech story. This one is the AP dispatch as it appeared in the Rochester, Minnesota, daily.

WASHINGTON (AP)— Proclaiming anew he was not involved in the Watergate scandal, President Nixon has appealed to the nation to let the courts decide the guilt or innocence of individuals involved.

Lead paragraph introduces two principal points: Nixon's statement of innocence (summary point 1) and his plea to let the courts decide (7).

"The time has come to turn Watergate over to the courts where the questions of guilt or innocence belong," Nixon said. "The time has come for the rest of us to get on with the urgent business of the nation."

Lead continues: more on point 7, introduction of back-to-work theme (8).

Nixon accepted full responsibility for the actions of his aides "because the abuses occurred during my administration and in the campaign for my re-election." He also defended his decision not to turn over presidential tape recordings to the special Watergate prosecutor or the Senate committee.

Extension of lead summary: introduction of Nixon's acceptance of full responsibility (an element not included in the list of central points) and of his refusal to surrender the tape recordings (5).

But he said the Senate Watergate committee had failed to disclose "the slightest evidence . . . that I had any knowledge of the planning for the Watergate break-in."

Return to the major lead topic.

First break

Nixon's nationwide television and radio speech and accompanying statement defended his efforts to learn the truth about Watergate —the facts of which the President said he did not learn until March 21 this year.

Housekeeping information (the speech was broadcast); then further development of major topic.

He concluded with a plea to "not stay so mired in Watergate that we fail to respond to the challenges of surpassing importance to America and the world."

Development of another point introduced earlier.

Second break

Nixon's long-awaited statement did not offer rebuttal to Watergate questions. "It has not been my intention

Explanatory comment by the reporter, followed by support for the comment.

to attempt any such comprehensive and detailed response," Nixon explained.

Nixon reaffirmed the stand his lawyers have taken in federal court—that by releasing tape recordings made of his telephone "the confidentiality of the office of the President would always be suspect.

"That is why I shall continue to oppose efforts which would set a precedent that would cripple all future presidents by inhibiting conversations between them and those they look to for advice," he said.

Nixon deplored the abuses in the 1972 campaign, but said a few overzealous people should not be permitted to "tar the reputation of the millions of dedicated Americans who fought hard but clean for the candidates of their choice in 1972."

He pledged to do all he could to ensure one of the results of Watergate "is a new level of political decency and integrity in America."

Nixon said from the time of the break-in "I pressed repeatedly to know the facts and particularly whether there was any involvement by anyone at the White House."

He said he depended on Justice Department and FBI investigations and assigned White House counsel John W. Dean III to monitor those investigations.

But through the summer of 1972, Nixon said, he was told no White House members were involved.

"I trusted the agencies conducting the investigations," Nixon said. "I did not believe the newspaper

Third break

Return to the tape-recording element. (Note the clumsy structure of the second half of the sentence.)

Development of other points in the speech.

This story "jerks"—it moves rapidly from one point to another, sometimes retreating on itself. The reason is that the speech itself was episodic, a collection of loosely related statements rather than a carefully composed unity. Thus the story may be a fair representation of the speech and at the same time something less than a work of journalistic art.

Note the awkward omission of "that" in the passage's last sentence. This fault occurs several times later.

Fourth break

Introduction and development of a new point (2), the Nixon efforts to investigate the affair.

Though the remainder of the story deals largely with the investigations, it is closely related to the major lead topic, Nixon's assertion of innocence.

accounts that suggested a coverup. I was convinced that there was no coverup, because I was convinced that no one had anything to cover up."

Nixon only obliquely referred to former acting FBI Director L. Patrick Gray III's assertion that he told the President on July 6 last year that "people on your staff are trying to mortally wound you by using the CIA and the FBI ..." to cover up the probe.

Nixon said his own investigation was prompted because "I learned of some of the activities upon which charges of coverup are now based."

He said he was told of fundraising for the Watergate defendants, but not that the money was to buy silence. Nixon added that he was told a member of his staff had talked to one of the defendants about clemency "but not that offers of clemency had been made."

And he said he learned about blackmail attempts by E. Howard Hunt, demanding $120,000 "as the price of not talking about other activities, unrelated to Watergate, in which he had engaged."

The President said the allegations were in general terms and not supported by details or evidence.

The statement conflicts with Dean's testimony, who said he was specific and told Nixon in March that the demands might reach $1 million. Dean said the President said that should be no problem.[1]

Fifth break

Sixth break

Development of a final point.

Seventh break

A concluding paragraph of background information supplied by the reporter.

[1] Copyright © 1973 by the Associated Press. Reprinted by permission.

The treatment of this story corresponds in general lines to the speech-story outline on pages 253–254. It has a lead of three or perhaps four paragraphs. It alternates direct and indirect discourse, seeking to develop briefly the principal points made at the beginning. It varies from usual practice in its repeated use of sentences combining indirect and direct quotation—this because of the necessity of identifying exact words taken from the advance script.

The story has relatively little housekeeping information—time, place, setting—because the speech was not given in a public place but was broadcast from the White House. In a similar analysis of another presidential speech, one made by President Johnson before a university audience, the physical information, including audience reaction, assumed greater importance. The Johnson speech was reported by virtually all reporters in more orderly and uniform fashion because it made fewer individual points.

QUOTATIONS AND QUOTATION MARKS

Verbatim?   The literal meaning of quotation marks is that the words between a pair of them appear exactly as the source gave them—verbatim. In a presidential speech, by common consent, they mean just that.

Whether this rule always must be followed closely is a topic of newsroom argument:

"You have no right to use quotes unless they mean what a literate reader expects them to mean—that they enclose the words precisely as spoken or written," says one side of the argument. "If you put into quotes anything but verbatim quotation, you are deceitful, and you forfeit reader confidence."

"But," says the other side, "the important thing is to give the reader the right impression, and to do it without wasting space. As long as your paraphrase gives the reader accurate meaning and flavor, you have license to depart from strict wording. You can often help a speaker to say what he means better than he says it—a favor both to him and to the reader. And you can keep your stories from getting too long."

Many reporters practice the second principle, but they should always remember that it's hazardous. Some publications fear it enough to advocate the British demand for stenographic accuracy and fidelity in speech reporting, even though the grammatical form the British use is often that of indirect quotation. *Editor & Publisher* commented that a story written thus "contains a lot of the verbiage, by-passes, and repetitious figures of speech with which most of us adorn our spoken words, but no man on earth can impugn its accuracy. The question is, will anybody except the hero of the speech read it?"

Another problem is that verbatim quotation, though it may be literally accurate, may give a false impression. Suppose the speaker is windy and

---

PARAPHRASING

The chairman of a Senate committee used these words in commenting on the testimony of a witness:

"... This witness in my opinion has shown utter contempt for this committee, for the Congress of the United States, and for his government.

"Whether that contempt is actionable I am not at the moment prepared to say. But this committee will give consideration to the question of whether it is actionable.

"If it is found to be, I have no doubt what the judgment and action of the committee will be...."

A news story paraphrased these three sentences thus:

"This witness has in my opinion been contemptuous of this committee, the Senate, and his government," the chairman declared. "Whether this contempt is actionable I can't say, but, if it is, I have an idea that this committee will do something about it."

The paraphrase appears to give accurately the sense of the original words. But it substitutes conversational language for the senator's pompous rhetoric.

Does the reporter misrepresent the senator or deceive the reader?

---

wordy, but able to lard his remarks with effective throwaways and gestures: will the cloud of words let the light through? Suppose he mumbles, or mangles his grammar, or likes to show erudition by using foreign phrases: will precise reporting give as accurate an impression as a careful paraphrase that lets him say what he apparently hoped to say? A politician once told a reporter, "You sure didn't use the words I used, but you said what I meant better than I could."

On the other hand, the defensive back quoted in the following passage might well have had an opposite response: "That's what I said all right, but you made me look like a fool."

> "I think the secondary is closer with each other than probably any other place on the team," he said. "We have to talk to each other. We all know that if we don't and we make a mistake it's going to be us standing there looking embarrassed because the other team will have scored."

Charity may have values that literal reporting lacks, but it's not often a mark of professional newswriting.

Unfortunately, verbatim reporting cannot take account of gestures, inflections, or interruptions, which can only be described or suggested. This is only one of the reasons why some of the audience, including other reporters, may carry away quite different impressions from those one reporter receives. Even the oldest pro may make errors in judgment or judgments with which others disagree.

When not to use quotes   One guide to punctuation says that quotation marks may be used for "words used in an unusual sense; or for coined words for which the author offers apology." True. But if the usage is so out of the ordinary that you have to employ the crutches of quotation marks to say to the reader, "I really know better," or—worse—to call attention to your inventiveness, you'd do better to rewrite. Sportswriters who use quotes around conventional sports terms—"hash marks," "dunked," "sleeper"— show both their own self-doubt and their scorn for their audiences. If you write that "she had a 'gypsy' air" or "he is a religious 'freak,'" you're saying to your reader, "Look out, there—I'm going to use something you might not catch unless I warn you."

Another quotation-mark misdemeanor is putting words that are not parts of the spoken passage inside the quotes. This sin occurs when a reporter decides he has to help the quotation along with instant clarification. Examples show the wrong way to do it:

"We'll take a vote on Thursday (Feb. 23)," the chairman said.

"We have no doubt we can lick the Crimson and White (Parker High)" said the coach.

And a longer example that did it up brown:

"There are many (students) who are likely to say, 'Well, I can't see the difference (between my educational facilities last year and those this year)'" Snoke said.

"If we demonstrate (through the pursuit of excellence) that we are going to make this place a great place, I think it (increased tuition) will be worth it to the students."

The passages in parentheses are not part of the quoted material—they are the reporters' attempts to fill gaps. Filling gaps is important, but not at the expense of structure or ease of reading. A little editing would remove the difficulties.

Quotation usages are discussed further in Chapter 17.

CREDIT-LINE USAGE

A credit line or attribution is a phrase that explains who said what—"He said" or "Ms. Winslow added." Skillful use of the credit is a mark of the professional. Here are some guidelines to competent practice:

1. Every sentence of indirect quotation ordinarily requires a credit line. Without either attribution or quotation marks, such a sentence does not tell the reader whether the speaker or the reporter is doing the talking. This rule obviously poses the problem that a long passage of indirect quotation may be monotonously spotted with "he said." When you write two or three sentences of indirect quotation, it's wise to try to move to a passage of direct quotation (see the next guideline).

There are exceptions to the one-credit-per-sentence rule. Suppose a first sentence is properly tied to the speaker; a second with obvious coupling may be able to get along on its own if it's followed by another with a credit line. But clarity is always to be preferred to misunderstanding despite the minor annoyance of repetition.

2. One credit line does the job for any continuous direct quotation within quotation marks, no matter whether its length is one phrase or twenty paragraphs. In the second paragraph of the Nixon story (page 258) one "Nixon said" works for two sentences; in a paragraph near the end of the story one works for three. One attribution, properly placed, could carry a dozen or more paragraphs of continuous direct quotation.

In a continuous quotation of several paragraphs, however, you may find the meaning clearer or the flow of your prose smoother if you insert additional credit lines: "the speaker went on" or "he concluded."

3. In direct quotations the credit line should always be attached to the first sentence of the quoted matter, usually at its close or in its body. You confuse a reader when you ask him to read two or more sentences before you tell him who is speaking. (Every sentence of indirect quotation in the Nixon speech is directly credited.)

Opening a quoted passage with the credit line is often clumsy. Because of the prominence of the speaker, however, this device occurs one way or another in twelve paragraphs of the Nixon speech. The credit line is part of the mechanics of a speech story, however, not of its gist, and it should be kept unobtrusive. Inserting it at the middle or the end of the sentence is one way to play it down.

4. Few words of attribution are as effective and as invisible as "said." Some composition teachers urge their pupils to seek elegance by substituting *stated, declared, averred,* and the like, but good writers think such expedients pretentious and distracting. On occasion an *added* or *went on* may fit a passage's rhythm as well as its sense. But such phony substitutes as *revealed* ("the mayor revealed that he will have turkey for Thanksgiving dinner") or *announced* ("the chairman announced that the regular meeting will be held next week") shouldn't be used unless a real revelation or a real announcement takes place. Misused, these words are at best pretentious and at worst a form of sensationalism. Communication researchers have produced evidence of higher consumer confidence in *said* than in other attributive verbs.

SPEECH STORY EXAMPLES

There are strengths and weaknesses in the story that follows. It has a brief, clear lead; several convenient exits for the reader who has had enough; excellent attribution; an adequate statement of the circumstances of the talk; and orderly arrangement of its subsections. But note the potential confusion in its sixth paragraph (is $15,300,000 needed for salaries or for all costs?) and the fact that there is no enlargement on the speaker's second demand—the element that opens the story. (Perhaps a careless copyreader, cutting the story, took out the essential supporting material.)

Personnel improvement and adequate financing are the major problems confronting the local schools, Dr. W. L. Printess, new superintendent, said Wednesday night.

Addressing a dinner given in his honor by the Chamber of Commerce, the Citizens' Committee on Public Education, and the Council of Civic Clubs, the superintendent outlined school problems as he has found them since his arrival here and gave his forecast of the future.

"There are two chief problems from the administrative point of view," Dr. Printess said.

"One is providing on a high level opportunities for self-improvement. We want to make it possible for each person in the school system to gain still clearer insights into the education of our children and to enrich himself with understandings and techniques for reaching the highest educational levels.

"Problem No. 2 is finding sufficient money to maintain our present excellent teaching staff and to employ 900 or 1,000 new teachers needed in the next five years."

The superintendent said the city has $36,000,000 invested in 93 school plants. It employs 3,500 persons in the school system, and pays them $12,000,000 a year. Its needs for the next year have been set at $15,300,000. Of this amount only $11,825,500 is in sight from present revenues, Dr. Printess said.

Three major possibilities for assistance on school financing were enumerated by the superintendent: increased aid from the state legislature, a new school charter amendment, and deficit financing.

The legislature, he pointed out, could give assistance in three different ways: by creating an independent school district; by granting more basic aid for all schools, including those in this city; and by granting local schools a greater proportion of available educational monies.

The superintendent said he is aware of the great differences of opinion in the city on all three possibilities.

"It may be that I am just naive, or that I am enjoying the honeymoon stage so intensely that I don't see the realities," Dr. Printess said, "but I have the abiding conviction that when the public is sufficiently and accurately informed in regard to the real needs of our school system, it will vote the necessary funds. Therefore I feel that the most crucial requirement for the success of the school program is the expansion of our hard-working Citizens' Committee on Public Education."

Now and again a reporter covers a speech that denies the conventions, one that can be told best in a pattern that would fit no other. Here is one, written shortly before Gertrude Stein's death, that took its cue from the fact that Miss Stein was so widely known as the "rose is a rose is a rose" poet. One newspaper had this kind of fun—not derisive, but good natured—with a Stein appearance at Princeton University:

PRINCETON, N.J.—Gertrude Stein, author and poet, delivered a lecture here tonight to an audience of 500 professors and students of Princeton at McCosh Hall. At the close of her address she asked, "Are there any questions?" There were none.

A hit and miss consensus taken unofficially after the lecture disclosed that few if any came even close to assimilating Miss Stein's literary theories. The audience was amused but otherwise unaffected by the obscurities which Miss Stein considers axiomatic.

She spoke, as far as could be ascertained, on the subject "The Making of the Making of Americans." It seemed to be, according to vague reports, a trilogy of excerpts from three of her books in an attempt to show the transition from the relatively harsh language of the first book to the softer combination of words in the last.

Several of the students took notes on the lecture hoping to be able to explain it later to their friends who were refused admittance because of Miss Stein's mandatory limit of 500 persons at her lectures. The notes were destroyed promptly at their first reading after the lecture.

When the doors of the hall were closed after the audience assembled, a detachment of police was necessary to keep in order those who had been barred.

Several hundred persons crowded about the entrance.

Miss Stein, garbed in a tan jacket, fawn-colored tweed skirt, and square-toed tan shoes, walked out on the platform and began her lecture without introduction or any of the preliminary functions ordinarily in evidence.

She thanked the audience "for controlling yourselves to 500" and said she was sorry to set that limit but felt that she could not interest more people than that at one time.

After the lecture, which was under the auspices of the Spencer Trask Fund, Miss Stein left the platform and her listeners left the hall apparently with the realization that their education had been sadly neglected, neglected.

When novelist Norman Mailer appeared before another university audience, most reporters wrote routine stories with substance but no flavor. One reporter decided that Mailer really didn't say much, but that the event was an entertainment. That's the way he wrote the story (closing it with a co-ordinated account of the news conference that followed the speech):

Norman Mailer, bad boy of American letters, street-fighter, masculine image, 45 years old now, wearing a blue, pin-stripe suit with a vest, for heaven's sake. Conservative red and blue striped tie. His hair is noticeably gray. Is he really that short or is he hunched over? Random observations.

Norman Mailer, author of "The Naked and the Dead," "Deer Park," "The American Dream," and "Why We Are in Vietnam," had just finished a speech and question-answer session in front of an overflow house in the Student Center on the St. Paul campus of the University of Minnesota. He evaluated his performance as fair. He remains uneasy in front of Midwest audiences.

A little earlier he had told the audience he'd come to St. Paul too fast. Fifty years ago it would have taken several days and he could have met people between New York and St. Paul and "been prepared for St. Paul."

Tuesday he'd simply been thrown from a plane to a podium and hadn't adjusted.

It was a completely sympathetic audience, and Mailer had enthralled it. Mailer's eyes were shining with victory as he left the speech.

But now he had to enter a press conference, and between the door to the ballroom and the room set aside for the confrontation he changed.

It showed on his face as he walked in, a subtle blending of arrogance and distrust.

The first question was something about exploiting the Vietnam war to sell books. "Speaking in public doesn't sell books. It usually hurts," he said, throwing off the answer with no anger. "That's why you never see John O'Hara, Bill Styron, or Louis Auchincloss in public." Next question.

You say you're not a protester and not a Gandhian nonviolent resister. What are you?

"I do things that make sense to me as they come up," he answered, distant, not enjoying himself or even bothering to be clever, but not hostile. "I don't worry about consistency, only the internal consistency of myself. People who are anti-Communist all the time or pro-civil disobedience all the time are in danger of becoming totalitarian."

He was asked where he gets his facts, and for the first time there was some anger. "You show ignorance of what a fact is," he told a reporter.

Then he talked about being in an Army platoon sent to find out if enemy soldiers were in certain towns. He said they'd stand on a hillside and look at the town through field glasses and report back that there weren't. "The Army moves on masses of misinformation," he said.

Sincere answers, but not eloquent.

He speaks again today at Northrop Auditorium, 2:15 p.m.[2]

[2] Copyright © 1973 by the Minneapolis *Tribune*. Reprinted by permission.

How to misuse an advance script Formal speeches are often composed in language that is routine, stuffy, or bombastic. When a reporter is working from an advance copy of such a speech, he needs to keep up his guard against letting the stuffiness debilitate his story. The writer of the story below fell into this trap; his managing editor provided pungent comments:

The Story as Published	*The M.E.'s Comments*
Wilmer Dodge, state budget administrator, told the state education commission today that the state has "ample financial resources for an orderly and effective attack on its many serious problems."	*Here is the type of news copy this paper can do without.*
Because of this, he said, "Our educators have a clear and challenging mandate to expand and improve the system at all levels."	*Note the pattern of linking high-sounding phrases into a chain.*
The committee held its first fall meeting today at the state capitol. High on its agenda was a report from a subcommittee assigned to evaluate the objectives and structure of the full group.	*Note how removed those quoted phrases, and some of the others, are from common language.*
Dodge praised the governor for what he called "courageous" insistence on refusing to be deterred by financial problems in improving the standards and services of the state's schools.	*You may conclude that the only hard news is in the last graf. (And even that news is not fresh news.)*
He said "it would have been easy for the governor to turn away from the full reality of the educational problem because the scope of the need obviously meant that appropriations would have to be greatly increased."	*What can we do with such stories?*
Dodge pointed out that the program approved by the legislature provided 59 million dollars more for the current biennium than was appropriated for the preceding two years, an increase of 32 percent.	*A copy editor can point out to the copy chief that a story is all wind.*
	A copy chief can ask the news desk whether the story should be spiked.
	The news editor may consult with the city desk regarding the importance of the story. (They may decide to run the story despite its faults.)
	The city desk may discuss the story with the reporter who prepared it.
	If the story came from the wire services, the city editor may address his remarks to the wire services.

Sidelights shouldn't become spotlights An unwary reporter may be deluded by a striking secondary issue. For example, a candidate for mayor talked soberly on campaign themes for forty-five minutes before a luncheon club; then he asked for questions. "What about those chiselers on relief?" somebody demanded. The speaker warned his listeners that he had not studied the relief problem and was not well informed; he added that "reports that hundreds of families in the city are getting relief money fraudulently" should be examined carefully, and that he would do so if he were elected.

A reporter made his lead say, "Hundreds of chiseling families in the city getting relief illegally will be cracked down on" by the candidate, should he be elected. Here are some of the errors he made in that lead:

1. He gave readers the false impression that most of the talk had been largely devoted to the lead theme.
2. He represented the speaker as claiming knowledge he disclaimed.
3. He presented the relief situation in what may not have been a fair light.
4. He made his skill as a reporter suspect, since only 200 families in the area were at that time on relief rolls. The speaker's disclaimer should have alerted him to do further checking.

A United States Senator who had been a competent political reporter commented on a fault of this kind in a story about a talk he had made:

> I spoke for a half hour on my political philosophy, and that was followed by an hour of Q-and-A, during which almost every current issue in domestic and foreign policy came up. Yet the whole story was built around my answer as to why I opposed retroactive terminal leave for enlisted men. A serious distortion . . .

Sometimes the minor element virtually commands elevation to first position. When a man speaking on "The Future of American Industry" tells his audience that "the largest atomic reactor in the world will be producing this community's heat, light, and power within five years," the reporter can hardly be blamed for seizing on the statement as his lead. But he is not a competent reporter if he does not make it clear that the remark was a throwaway, offered casually against a broader talk. (And he may remain a reporter for a very short time if he doesn't persuade the speaker, once the talk is ended, to develop the casual news tip.)

MEETING STORIES

Recall the statement at the opening of this chapter that more than half of all news stories are directly or indirectly derived from spoken words.

A large proportion of such stories come from formal or informal meetings of committees, clubs, PTAs, Women's Lib, and other groups. Most such meetings go uncovered in a metropolitan area; there are hundreds of them, and they carry interest for only a smattering of a big medium's audience.

In the small community, however, in which any meeting touches a larger proportion of the audience, the local media give them faithful attention. Many are dull, and reporters look on them with boredom; the result may be boring stories. It's hard to write a sprightly account of an event you feel you've covered a dozen times before. But almost every newsworthy event has some element of novelty or peak of interest, and the reporter's challenge is to unearth it.

Meetings provide one or both of two kinds of news material: business or group action; formal or informal talks. The reporter's problem thus becomes one of emphasis. Is the business—the election of officers, the decision to stage a fund drive, the resolution damning the park board for what it didn't do—the lead of the story? Or is it the outraged shaft leveled at the chamber of commerce by the director of the state grange?

If the decision is to leave out one element or the other, construction of the story is simple. If it is to include both, a two-element lead may be the answer:

> Local business interests are giving the farmer the run-around, Grange Director Wilfred Olstein told the Kiwanis Club last night.
>
> His talk followed the re-election of all current officers for another year's service.
>
> "We can't have farm prosperity without help from you bankers and retailers," Olstein said ...

> Decision to stage a drive for funds next fall followed re-election of all its officers at last night's Kiwanis Club meeting.
>
> The two actions came after Grange Director Wilfred Olstein had told the club that....

Either approach, with essential elements in a two-paragraph lead, makes for orderly development as the story continues.

The meeting story that follows is one in which the reporter seems to have found no formal business to report. His concentration is on the response to the speech that was its principal planned element (but which the reporter leaves virtually untouched). Analysis of the story shows its unorthodox but imaginative and easy-to-follow structural pattern:

A shouting match ended last night's Mayor's Human Relations Commission meeting after a black woman member said that most whites don't know what integration means.

"It does not mean one group 'rising up' to the other group," said Mrs. Hannah Empster, 2417 Index avenue.

"It means two groups coming together into something new."

Until human rights bodies learn this, "we are going to keep on talking at each other, instead of to each other," said Mrs. Empster, a social service worker at Neighborhood House.

Mrs. Empster had been set off by three assertions:

That by the evening's speaker, Alexander F. Milles, an official of the Anti-defamation League of B'nai Brith, that blacks were left without a culture by slavery.

That of Stephen Korsov, president of the Council for Civil and Human Rights, that minority groups need special treatment in employment but that it is offensive to the white community to say so.

That of Walter Meyer, executive director of the Jewish Community Relations Council, that newspapers should run news of successful blacks to "improve the black image."

To Milles, Mrs. Empster said: blacks have put together a culture combining their African heritage and "our European ancestors," the slave-masters.

"It's not a white man's culture," she said. "Not even the integrationists have taken the time to understand that."

To Korsov she said: "We don't need special treatment like you give your children. I don't want your help. Just get out of my way."

She said Meyer exhibited a patronizing attitude about black culture in claiming he wanted a "better life" for minority groups.

"YOU want it," she snapped. "What about what THEY want?"

The discussion flared after the lunch meeting at the Protestant Center as Meyer and Korsov attempted to explain their positions to Mrs. Empster.

To a comment about law and order, Mrs. Empster cried, "Whose law and order? Your law and order." Discrimination hides in Northern law and order, she said.

"I'm out of Alabama, and if I had the choice, I'd go back. I can see it there. I can fight it."

"Did you lose 6 million Jews in concentration camps?" Meyer demanded.

"Comparatively I lost that many hanging down there," Mrs. Empster snapped.

Later Mrs. Empster said she had seen six blacks hanged, among them her 14-year-old cousin, when she was 12. He had looked at a white woman in a bathing suit in Prichard, Ala., she said. "And they hung him then. Not later—then."

The reporter supplemented the meeting story with an interview in which Mrs. Empster explained her position more fully—and more calmly.

Projects

1. Make a study of the credit lines in five or more speeches, interviews, or meeting stories in your local papers. Check them against the guides to credit-line usage in this chapter.

2 Analyze the treatment of a speech in two media, print and air. Compare leads, content, structure, length, manner, credit-line usage, and anything else you think relevant.

3. Attend a business-plus-formal-talk meeting. Write two newspaper stories, one of seventy-five to 100 words, the other of 500 words. What are the differences?

4. Write a radio news story about the same event. What are the differences?

5. Attend a local meeting. Write the story for an appropriate paper *before* you see or hear it elsewhere. Be prepared for class discussion.

CHAPTER SEVENTEEN

Interviews

Newsworkers make an arbitrary distinction between interview stories and those that are merely based on interviewing. Though the terms are look-alikes, they don't mean the same thing.

Stories based on interviewing are those whose facts are gathered by the interview process—a reporter asks, a news or information source answers. The identity of the interviewee is secondary; the reader is not interested in him, only in the news he relates. Often the materials might have come from another source with no change in meaning or effect.

An interview story is, in contrast, one that grows from statements by an individual news source (or a number of them) whose authority, special knowledge, or personal circumstance gives the statements significance.

To illustrate: Your assignment is to get a story on the nonpolluting sewage disposal plant for which the county commissioners have just signed a contract. You go to the chairman of the commission and get his answers to a score of factual questions: Where will the plant be built? When will it be ready? Cost? Employment plans? Management personnel? Types of equipment? Differences in operation from the old system? You come up with an orderly statement of fact. It is a story you might have elicited from the county engineer, the chairman of the planning committee, or the contractor who is to install the plant, with no essential differences except those inherent in the truth that no two individuals say just the same things about any one set of facts.

You have a story based on interviewing.

Two days after this story is published, you are told to go to the president of the local Citizens Against Pollution group (called, of course, CAP) and get his views. How effective does he expect the plan to be in reducing water pollution? Does he think it will produce results as good as would the plan advocated by CAP? Will CAP support the commission's plans?

This is an interview story. Inevitably it will have elements like those in the first story—facts drawn from interviewing. But the emphasis will be on the judgments and validity of the source, his expertise. (Combination of the two approaches will get further attention in Chapter 21, Interpretive Reporting.)

Though interview stories take many shapes, three types common in modern journalism are:

1. The *news interview*, a form that gives the consumer competent illumination on a subject current in the news.
2. The *personality interview*, whose purpose is to let the interviewee reveal his individuality through his own words.
3. The *symposium interview*, in which the views or attitudes of a number of respondents, sometimes a large number, are reported.

WHENCE THE INTERVIEW?

Journalists of the twentieth century look on the interview as an essential tool. Yet it had to be invented, and not so long ago. James Gordon Bennett is generally given credit for its first use when, in 1836, he wrote a series of reports drawn from talks with the madam of a notorious New York "fancy house" (see page 13).

The interview at first met more scorn than applause. A London paper sneered that "this American interview is degrading to the interviewer, disgusting to the interviewee, and tiresome to the public." Edwin Godkin's liberal intellectual magazine, the Nation, said that "the interview is generally the joint production of some humbug of a hack politician and another humbug of a newspaper reporter." But at the same period Henry W. Grady of the Atlanta Constitution was building a national reputation for brilliant, perceptive interviewing. And half a century later Edward Price Bell, Chicago Daily News foreign correspondent in the great days of the News's international news service, called the interview a tool of major journalistic value, "bridging the gulf between genius and the common understanding."

NEWS INTERVIEWS

The CAP interview story suggested above is an example of the news interview. The genre has three dominant characteristics:

1. Its subject derives from a topic currently in the news.

2. Its source, the interviewee, is qualified to explain, amplify, or throw light that the facts alone don't shed. He is usually—by expertise, training, position, or status—a source in whom the audience will have confidence.
3. It adds significantly to public knowledge or understanding of the subject. It illuminates, expands, debunks, views with alarm or optimism. It offers depth that a simple factual story rarely possesses.

The importance of this kind of news is clear. No man in the complex twentieth century, as Chapter 1 pointed out, can bring to all the facts laid before him enough knowledge to evaluate, explain, or even digest most of them. More and more it has become the news media's responsibility to help the public by providing the background for understanding.

When war breaks out between Arabs and Israelis, the reporter goes to a recognized authority on Middle East affairs for a competent interpretation. When the home-town baseball franchise is sold down the river, the leading sports promoters, perhaps along with local bankers, retailers, motelkeepers, and others, are asked for comment. When a fire kills a score of elderly residents in a rest home in the next county, views and facts about comparable dangers locally are sought from county, city, arson, welfare, and health authorities.

These are the reportorial efforts that develop news interviews. Note again the three characteristics: a topic in the current news; interviewees whose competence will be generally accepted; enlightenment that throws clouded facts into understandable relief.

Case history of a news interview   A reporter finds this instruction on his (or her) assignment sheet:

```
    Dr. Ivan Meyer, the urban sociologist from U of
California, is visiting here next week. See whether he'll
talk about the effect of moving 300 new paper mill families
into our town. Will it dislocate our business patterns?
Our social balance? Since there isn't decent housing in
sight, what would Meyer advocate—suburban subdivision,
condominiums, scattered apartments? Let nature take
its course?
```

Preparation for an interview is much like that for covering a speech. But more important than in speech-reporting is knowing the subject. A certain amount of *ex post facto* cover-up is possible in speech reporting—you can sometimes go to the library or to an authority if you haven't understood the talk or some of its references. But in the interview you're on your own. You have to steer the interview, and you have to do it with questions that will neither make you look feebleminded nor turn off your interviewee.

The reporter in this case knows something about urban housing from college sociology; he may supplement it at a library. He knows from advance stories what plans the incoming industry has for housing its workers. The newspaper's morgue (see Appendix B, "The Jargon of Journalists") yields information about the city's housing shortages in recent years. Calls to real estate dealers and contractors provide current information (and perhaps tips for other stories). Recent periodical and book references to suburbia and the problems of cities may help. The reporter ends with knowledge of the problem both in broad terms and in local implications.

The interview situation is sharply personal, face to face; the success of the encounter may depend on establishment of rapport. Rapport can be built best when a reporter knows what kind of individual he is to meet.

The reporter uses the morgue, the library, telephone chats with Meyer's host, and other local contacts to provide a thorough "obit." Meyer, it develops, is forty-seven years old; born in Poland, educated at MIT. He has traveled widely, has several honorary degrees, has written half a dozen books (the reporter runs quickly through one called *The Doom of the City*). He's now on leave from his teaching post to act as consultant on housing projects; he has sometimes shown annoyance at reporters who, he asserts, "never quote me accurately." He was New England golf champion for two years in college. He has exacted from his host a promise that there will be "no cocktail brawls with more than six guests."

OBIT

Obit is journalistic argot for an obituary notice. In newsrooms it means not only the published story about a death but also any detailed account of a career, prepared in advance to be ready for instant use.

The reporter finds his questions taking shape. How does the hypothesis of *The Doom of the City* fit this community and its recent population growth? Can such growth be absorbed by normal school, trade, and social facilities? How have similar cities met similar problems? What about the Realtors Association proposal that the new families be scattered throughout the city and suburbs rather than concentrated in a new subdivision? Are there transportation problems? How long does it take a community to assimilate such a group?

These and like questions ought to lead to a meaty story or suggest other approaches. But there remains the problem of persuading Meyer, known to be less than cordial to reporters, to grant the interview.

The reporter decides on the direct approach. He telephones Meyer's prospective host:

This is Anderson of the *Herald*. I'd like to talk with Dr. Meyer about what the new paper mill families will do to the city. . . . Yes, a real problem. We think Dr. Meyer may have some of the answers. . . . Yes, I know it's a social visit. But if he could give us about an hour. . . . I've heard that. What I'm hoping is that I'll be one of the reporters he thinks is reliable. . . . Perhaps an hour before he goes to the golf club?

Thus the groundwork is laid.

A matter to which every reporter has to give thought is the setting of the interview. Where should it be staged? Experience has set up some general rules:

1. It's usually best to make the interview a twosome. If others are present, there may be disturbances, and the interviewee may not be as relaxed and responsive as he would be without observers. He also might not be as honest, if he feels the need to protect his "image."

THE SMALLER THE HARDER

A paradox well known to reporters is that it's often the little man rather than the big one who makes things hard. Public figures of stature are accustomed to reporters; they usually have an understanding of public relations and confidence that the more they help a reporter, the better will be the results. The man who has never been asked for an interview, the one just kicked upstairs (whether to a shag-carpeted office or as principal dogcatcher), is often likely to be overcautious or self-important.

---

2. In certain delicate instances it's a good thing to have witnesses (perhaps the photographer who goes with you on the assignment). Sometimes people don't like what they've said when they see it in print; sometimes they deny they said it. A tape recorder may come in handy.
3. Interviews over a cup of coffee or a stein of beer, in a restaurant or café, have advantages but also perils. It's usually easy to get into relaxed conversation in such a setting. On the other hand, you're subject to interruptions: the waiter, friends, Muzak, noisy kids in the next booth.
4. A home or a hotel room may be best. Something like the golf club is relaxed, but the interviewee isn't there to be interviewed—he's there to play golf. He may cut you short to get to the tee.

Thinking like this leads the reporter to try for a meeting at the home of the host. Normally he would telephone for an appointment soon after Meyer's arrival. This time he decides on a note as an icebreaker:

```
Dear Dr. Meyer:
     We're going to have 300 new families in our city next
year, and the Herald would like to let its readers know
what this will mean—to new families and to present
residents. The Doom of the City suggests that we may be in
for a hard time if we don't plan things right.
     I'm doing a story for the Herald on this, and I'd like
very much to include your views. I'll telephone Tuesday.
```

This approach, the reporter hopes, will indicate that he knows something about the subject. His little stratagem works. On the phone, Meyer says: "Come over at half past nine tomorrow morning—we'll have an hour to ourselves. . . . "

"I SAID IT – BUT . . ."

Some news sources don't know (or pretend not to know) when they're talking for publication. Even when a reporter identifies himself carefully—especially in a telephone interview—an interviewee may not realize what is happening. "Certainly I said it," such a source may complain. "But I didn't know he'd print it."

The remedy is easy. Sharp and clear identification to start; repetition if there's doubt. And then direct request for consent to use quotations. Open diplomacy is a prime reportorial tool.

At 9:30 the reporter is seated in a comfortable living room, facing a tanned man in slacks. The initial lead comes from the costume: "You've kept up your golf, I see."

Meyer responds heartily: "Yes, indeed—heart attack insurance, my doctor calls it."

The reporter lets the theme hold for a minute. The easy mood confirmed, he shifts to indirect attack.

"Dr. Meyer, I've noticed that you're retained by a number of cities as a consultant on housing and city planning. We were wondering at the paper whether you might be here on such an assignment."

Strictly a personal visit, Meyer says. "Fact is, I don't know much about the local problem."

This is the cue for the reporter. He talks for three minutes, answering occasional queries; he pulls a city map from his pocket and refers to it, to Meyer's evident satisfaction. Finally:

"I see some problems," Meyer says. "But they don't look insuperable to me, if the city council . . . "

The interview is launched, and the reporter may already have the theme for his story: *problems not too tough.* Exploratory questions confirm the theme; Meyer develops it, under the reporter's lead, so as to tie it to local circumstances. The reporter's task now is to sustain the flow of information and comment, to hold it on course should it tend to stray, to design questions that will draw understandable and quotable answers. He doesn't refer to the list of prepared questions in his pocket—to do so might dam the stream.

The interview well under way, the reporter starts to jot down notes. He watches closely to find whether his moving pencil is a distraction. As Meyer is giving statistical data, the reporter notices, he slows up to watch the note-taking. The reporter employs a time-tested device: handing his pad to Meyer, he says, "Would you check the figures?" Meyer glances over them, hands them back; now he ignores the pencil.

The reporter keeps an eye on his watch. When his hour is ending, he prepares to close the interview. Would Meyer say that such-and-such points are the ones to emphasize? Are there significant angles they haven't touched? Would Meyer be willing to check the story by telephone if the reporter finds himself in doubt?

Promptly at 10:30 he leaves. "Thanks again," he says. "I hope you mangle par."

Characteristics of interview stories   This case history presented no unusual problems, either in conduct of the interview or in writing the story. Thanks to preparation and to consulting the interviewee about appropriate emphases, the reporter can guide the elements of the story smoothly into place. The form of an interview story is substantially that of the speech story: summary lead, usually in indirect quotation; development of individual subtopics, in order of decreasing importance; alternation of direct and indirect discourse, the direct for elaboration of points of emphasis or for forceful or colorful language, the indirect for summarizing passages. (In her small book *Some Observations on the Art of Narrative* the British writer Phyllis Bentley describes the use of similar alternation. She calls it "scene and summary" as applied to fiction writing. A half-hour with this book would profit any writer.)

Even more than in the speech story, the personal mannerisms and appearance of the interviewee deserve attention. In the case study the reporter had to decide whether to describe Meyer's athletic appearance, his easy manner, his holding a golf club as he talked, his thump on the arm of his chair to underline a point. Would such details add meaning or readability to the story?

The gain in readability is likely to be considerable (and in the personality

---

WRONG QUESTIONS

A story told by Grantland Rice, for a generation the model of the American sportswriter, presented a truth even though it may have been only half truth. An undergraduate reporter came to him by appointment one day, Rice said, to carry out a journalism class assignment. Among the questions he asked: "What is your opinion of football? What do you think about tennis? Would you now discuss sailing and swimming?" The questions were not only infantile, Rice said, but unanswerable.

---

interview the gain is doubled). Most reporters writing major interview stories think such detail worth the space it costs. In routine interviews, and especially in stories based on interviewing as defined earlier, it is rare.

If a reporter were to record what he has learned about the interview story, his notes might run something like this:

- Don't generalize. Always make questions specific. A general question gets a general answer. It's better to say, "Can a city the size of this one provide housing for 300 new families?" than "Will a sudden influx of population hurt a city?"

- You're not the interviewee. Your job is to lead the conversation, to keep it on the beam—not to monopolize it.
- But don't let the interviewee wander or talk too long about the time he bid seven spades. Hold him on track. Be persistent.
- Remember that nobody has to give you an interview. You are in a real sense indebted to your interviewee. Don't impose on his time any more than you have to. Usually, if he's somebody who has anything to say, he's also one with plenty of other demands.
- But don't let him shove you around. You're entitled to treatment as good as you give.
- Be suspicious of the fellow who's begging to be interviewed. He may have a horse to trade. Look carefully at his interests and prejudices; find out what he has to gain from the interview. It's fair to give your reader this insight, whether it's to the interviewee's advantage or not.

Sources of interview error The most serious source of nonfactual errors in news stories is the reporter's lack of background information, according to a study conducted several years ago by Dr. David L. Grey of Stanford University. Both the news sources and the reporters involved in the stories agreed on this factor. Parts of the report (in American Newspaper Publishers Association Research Bulletin No. 21–1968) elaborate the findings:

> After lack of background information, reporters and sources again agreed, come news desk and editing practices as a significant cause of error.
> The news sources cited "sensationalism, overdramatization, and overemphasis in phrasing" and lack of personal contact with reporters; the reporters added the lack of time to report and write the stories and, surprisingly, a certain amount of reportorial "laziness and incompetence."

Dr. Grey comments:

> ... it is significant that news sources cite "sensationalism" and lack of contact, and that reporters emphasize lack of time. ... Emphasis on lack of personal contact indicates that it is a likely source of error, though news sources put more stress on it than do reporters. Reporters might well give the factor more attention, if for no other reason than that news sources consider it important.

The study suggests three further remedies: that reporters always seek news source advice as to appropriate emphases (whether they accept the judgments or not); that they be given time to prepare for interviews; and that they work more closely with editors, especially to guard against headline inaccuracy.

A helpful study of the techniques and products of interviews is reported in "The Interview, or The Only Wheel in Town" (No. 2 in the Journalism Monographs series, published by the Association for Education in Journalism). Here are not only suggestions for reportorial behavior in an interview but also tips on question formation, the values and dangers of leading questions, the influence of "interviewer expectation" on the interviewee's responses, and even the salutary effect of a few well-placed "mm-hmms" as the interviewee talks. The reprint of Allen Barton's tongue-in-cheek analysis of the different ways to ask the question "Did you kill your wife?" is both entertaining and instructive.

Another approach to successful interviewing comes from studies by psychologists and sociologists. Though it is "old" (1942) and designed to aid social workers in interviews, Annette Garrett's slim volume called *Interviewing: Its Principles and Practices* applies directly to journalistic practice. From these and other sources comes this small compendium of potential sources of error:

Intentional falsehood   Hundreds of impulses, usually impelled by some form of self-interest, may lead an interviewee to lie. For example:

- A woman charged with luring a man into an alley where accomplices slug and rob him tells a false story to cover herself.
- A man is ashamed to admit that he has been on relief.
- He fears the truth will make him look bad to family, friends, or employer.
- He wants to look wealthier, more traveled, or better educated than he is.
- He may be a publicity hound, for any of many reasons.
- He may distrust the reporter or the use to which the story is to be put.
- He may try to tell the reporter only what he thinks the reporter wants to hear.

Faulty memory   Passage of time may have dimmed the interviewee's recollections. He may have taken little interest in the event or topic. He may have been so deeply involved that he has fallen into wishful thinking.

Lack of information   A respondent may have less information than he thinks he has. He may not take the trouble to dredge up distant facts.

Misunderstanding   The interviewee may not grasp the questions he is asked; he may not put the questions into the right context. Here the responsibility is the reporter's.

Interviewer's errors   The reporter may use jargon or terminology that confuses his respondent. He may permit personal bias to misdirect or misinterpret answers. He may not be persistent enough; he may fail to put the interviewee at ease; he may close the interview before it is finished.

The experienced reporter knows that people sometimes find it distasteful or difficult to talk in some areas but easy and congenial in others. Few men and women like to tell how much money they earn; they often conceal what they consider shameful facts in family or personal history. They are often loose in stating dates: was it in 1968 that the family went to Mesa Verde, or 1967?

On the other hand, most people respond accurately to questions about their ages, education, nationality, and professional or business careers. They can tell you the names of their children, if not always the ages. They know the make (but not always the model or the horsepower) of the cars they drive. They are likely to be accurate and dependable when giving information that is of constant and personal interest to them.

Checking back   Many reporters let a news source review a story that is based on information the source has provided. Should this be common practice?

The answer is affirmative whenever the reporter has doubt about accuracy of fact or meaning or whenever, in response to an interviewee's request, he has promised to check back. (But make no promise to *change* the story.)

Checking back raises some problems. On occasion the news source makes suggestions or demands that the reporter can't accept. The source may dislike the wording of the story (note the criticism of "phrasing" that turned up in the Grey study); he may ask that this element be emphasized, that one played down. He may, if he is a scientist or some other variety of specialist, object to the use of lay instead of technical vocabulary.

The newsman's obligation is to assure the accuracy of fact, and the likelihood that his story will carry a fair impression to its recipients. Beyond this there is no compulsion to accept a news source's suggestions. If reportorial or news desk judgment differs from that of the interviewee, the question is whether the source's opinion or the qualified journalistic judgment should prevail. The reporter and his editors are representatives of the public, not the news source; they are specialists in how to reach their audi-

---

A BACK-CHECK THAT WORKED

Gail Sheehy, a contributing editor of New York *magazine, wanted to interview Dorothy Schiff, the strong-minded publisher of the New York Post. Ms. Schiff granted the interview on the agreement that she be permitted to "correct for facts and debate conclusions." [MORE], the news-analysis magazine, reports what happened:*

> *After reading the completed article, Ms. Schiff provided some additional facts and, according to Ms. Sheehy, made only one request: couldn't the number of references to the lady's age (she is 70) be reduced from three to two? (Granted.) If there had been any attempt to veto material, Ms. Sheehy declares, she would have "scrubbed the entire story."*

---

ence. Their concern is to inform and explain, whereas the source may be driven by interests that are self-centered.

In this kind of dispute there are a thousand shadings, and decisions are rarely easy. Often a news source views a story not as an instrument to inform a broad audience but rather as a kind of self-mirror; he may be more concerned with the opinion of his fellow professionals than in communication. Or he may have less admirable impulses, such as self-promotion.

There is also the matter of tactics. When reporter and source cannot agree, the reporter may have to risk his source's annoyance or anger, even though this may blockade an information channel he'd like to use again. Factors in the decision are the importance of the story to the public and the degree to which the source's suggestions will weaken it.

In most cases the advantages of checking back outweigh the perils of disagreement.

EXAMPLES OF NEWS INTERVIEWS

The stories that follow, though all are above average in competence, are chosen not for their excellence but for the way they illustrate effective construction of news interviews. Some are routine, others show how to break from the standard pattern.

The first is a typical news interview. Its topic was current (the occupancy of the Attorney General's post in the Nixon Cabinet had been a national concern for months; the new man was to be sworn in five days after the interview appeared). The interviewee was the best possible source on the subject: the appointee himself. And the story threw light on many questions the public was asking. The writer was a Los Angeles *Times* reporter who went to Ohio for the interview.

MECHANICSBURG, Ohio —Sen. William B. Saxbe (R–Ohio), fourth attorney general named by President Nixon, believes he has the best chance of any to pull the fragmented Justice Department together.

Lead states a major theme of the story and presents the interviewee.

Relaxing in his colonial-style home in this central Ohio farming community before taking the oath Friday, Saxbe said he senses "a tendency for the Justice Department to fly apart."

The setting is established; the direction of Saxbe's comments is indicated.

He said he believed this had resulted primarily from placing a multiplicity of federal bureaus and functions under department jurisdiction over the years. The integrated drug enforcement program is the latest example, he said.

Continuation of comment. (A present tense "believes" is to be preferred—Saxbe's belief presumably is not in the past.)

"There's a tendency for people in each bureau to feel that they should not necessarily be tied into the Justice Department—that they ought to make their own decisions, that they should have their own PR (public relations) people and pretty much run their own show," Saxbe said.

Further development of theme. (Note the faulty use of parenthetical material inside the quotation.)

Saying he would like to "tighten up" the burgeoning department, he added: "With the problems of law enforcement so pressing and big, we ought to really concentrate on working together. There's enough glory and recognition to go around.

Continuation of topic. (Burgeoning here is journalese. It means "budding" or "sprouting," not "expanding"; it relates to the beginning of growth, not to its continuation.)

"Because I'm not a candidate for anything and don't expect to be," Saxbe said, "maybe I can do it better than those in the past who have had ambitions.
"More than John Mitchell, Richard Kleindienst, or Elliot Richardson, I have a clear track to do some of these things," he said.

Introduction of a new angle.

Saxbe was critical of the "revolution by committee" now under way in the department—Richardson had committees weighing far-reaching proposals for modernizing the institution.

Another new angle. The reporter throws in his own clause (Richardson's committees) to explain a Saxbe phrase.

While he has not decided to terminate the committees' inquiries, he said, "I certainly want to calm things down. I would like to get the house in order and working smoothly.
"Some of Richardson's ideas are excellent, but many are long-range and have to be executed carefully and slowly."

Continuation of subtopic.

Saxbe rejected Richardson's proposal to push for election reform legislation to close the gaps covering "dirty tricks" in campaigns.
"Elliot was more ambi-

Another subtopic. The reporter lets a figurative remark into the quotation, to show the flavor of the interview and of the interviewee.

tious on these things than I am," Saxbe said. "I got more hay down than I can get in the barn now. To undertake congressional jobs, when I know how frustrating they are, is time I don't think I can spend now."

Pausing to eat a stand-up lunch—his back was aching from feeding his cattle earlier in the day—Saxbe seemed during an interview more knowledgeable on department activities than when he appeared Dec. 12 before his congressional colleagues on the Senate Judiciary Committee.

While stressing his need to "button my lip" in moving from the Senate to the Cabinet, Saxbe spoke far more candidly about sensitive subjects—his own appointment, the late FBI director J. Edgar Hoover—than others in the Administration. He often made conversational points with country expressions, telling, for example, of a fellow "who was such a liar he had to get a friend to call his hogs." [1]

More personality development. (But an illogical sentence, appearing to suggest a shadowy connection between eating lunch and the "new" knowledgeability.)

Less than half the story is quoted. More than a column of Saxbe comments on many topics follow: criticism of the FBI, appointments to his staff, his "tendency to speak expansively" (which is illustrated by a brief passage in Q-and-A form, apparently taken from a tape of the interview), and finally some comments on his lack of further political ambition. The story shows readers what kind of man the new Attorney General appears to be, in a combination of substantive comments on significant subjects with insight into his personal mannerisms.

The following Associated Press story was published when the United States and the world were deep in anxiety over the gasoline shortage. The first nine paragraphs are a news interview that presents authoritative comment on a newsy subject. Then the story departs from pattern to bring together information from many sources—facts and opinion related to the principal lead topic but not presented by the interviewee:

[1] Copyright © 1973 by the Los Angeles *Times*. Reprinted by permission.

WASHINGTON, Dec. 31 (AP)—Motorists soon will face longer lines for less gasoline at service stations than they experienced over the Christmas–New Year's holiday, an Administration source said today. He said the gasoline shortage would really make itself felt by the last part of January.

"It's going to get a lot worse because we're going to make less gasoline. We're getting down to where we're talking about 8 to 10 gallons of gasoline per week per driver.

"We're still riding off Arab oil, and we've been drawing on our stocks, but we can't continue it," the source continued. "No more ships are coming and we can't draw down on our stocks any further."

His comments were made as motorists experienced their second consecutive holiday weekend of long lines and empty pumps. Fewer automobiles than usual for a New Year's weekend took to the highways and there were reports in Washington that turnpike traffic was down sharply.

An investigation was started by the Federal Energy Office and four East Coast states. It concerned reports that oil tankers were waiting offshore for oil prices to rise before unloading their cargoes.

New York, New Jersey, Pennsylvania and Connecticut had begun or were preparing to begin investigations. However, the Administration spokesman and spokesmen for the ports of Boston, New York, Philadelphia and New Haven said they did not think there was much to the reports.

The Administration source put current gasoline stocks at about 200,000,000 barrels, enough for about 30 days at the current rate of consumption, 6,700,000 barrels a day.

He said that if stocks drop below 180,000,000 barrels the result would be shortages more severe than those that have occurred— "spot shortages, city shortages, where a city is out of gasoline," he said.

"People still don't believe there's a shortage. They feel it's a conspiracy, a way to raise prices and so forth. We're trying to tell them that come January or February it's going to be rough and that's all there is to it unless driving is cut back."

Demand for gasoline this weekend resulted in the closings of numerous stations that had planned to be open today.

Before the weekend began, service station associations and motor clubs had predicted that 75 per cent or more of the stations would be open today and closed tomorrow, New Year's Day. High demand emptied pumps on Saturday at many stations, and new supplies will not arrive before Wednesday.

Reports of price gouging kept local and federal officials on the lookout. The extent of illegal prices was not determined, although dozens of complaints were found to be valid.

In Philadelphia, Internal Revenue Service agents said they had found 23 stations overcharging and that all agreed to roll back prices.

Distributors gave service stations in Arizona and Oregon their January fuel allocations only to ease shortages.

Twenty-three business and industry trade associations announced the formation of an Energy Users Council. Its purpose is to keep business and industry informed on energy policies and to bring business problems to the attention of Government officials. . . .[2]

The story continues for half a column, detailing developments through the nation. Note, in the segment above, these characteristics:

- The interviewee is unnamed—"an Administration source." Lack of name and title weakens the story's effect.
- Most of the story after the interview ends is presented without attribution, since it is factual rather than subjective. Introduction of this material is justified by the lead which suggests a general rather than a localized story (the fourth, fifth, and sixth paragraphs develop the suggestion).

Question-and-answer interviews The direct Q-and-A interview has begun to appear more frequently, in part because of the tape recorder. The tempta-

[2] Copyright © 1974 by the Associated Press. Reprinted by permission.

tion is often to let such a story run long, since the material is ready to hand. However, a tape has to be edited to cut out verbosity, take out "ums" and "y'knows," and delete entire passages that do not support the story pattern or theme. But literal fidelity can be guaranteed.

Patterns for Q-and-A interviews do not follow any one set of rules. The story below opens with eight paragraphs to establish the interviewee's expertise, then goes into two columns of verbatim questions and answers. Made with the aid of a tape recorder, it is distinguished by its faithful reproduction of conversational mannerisms—repetitions, terse sentences, sentence fragments, even the loose "like" of popular speech. Here are the opening quotations:

Q. What do you think bothers adolescent girls the most?

A. What I hear over and over is that people do not listen to them. I do not say that it is only the girls. But I have heard a lot of this from the girls. They say people do not listen to them, especially the adults. It is not just listening, but also understanding.

Q. Is it the parents who are not listening or just adults in general?

A. It is a general complaint against the adult world. Most adults don't take them seriously. There is rarely a serious discussion. I was working with some people in youth organizations one time and I said, why don't you just sit down with the young people and ask them some serious questions? Like, if you were going to change the world, what would you do to change it? These people said later it was an absolute revelation to them. The young people were so delighted that someone asked.

This interview was the result of three hours' conversation, in two sittings. The interviewee called it "a totally accurate and understanding story."

In the following excerpt the questions and answers were drycleaned before publication, partly by use of ellipses (...) and partly by clearing away the conversational mannerisms to leave only formed sentences:

John Gilbert Graham flatly denies planting a bomb on an airliner which killed 44 persons, including his mother. He hints his mother herself might have planted the explosive.

My questions were direct and straightforward. Graham looked straight at me with his penetrating gray-green eyes when answering many of the questions.

But when it came to such questions as to whether he had experience handling ex-plosives, Graham would turn away or look down in his lap, his heavy lips pursing in annoyance.

Graham, dressed in the gray denim coveralls of the jail, sat with his hands folded in his lap in the office of Warden Gorden Dolliver.

Q. Jack, I understand the FBI obtained a signed statement from you, admitting you placed a bomb on that plane ...

A. Yes, I signed a state-ment. But it's not true. They told me they were going to put my wife in jail, and I'd better get it straightened out, myself.

Q. You mean, they used duress—they kept questioning you until you confessed?

A. Well, they started about noon that Sunday and didn't stop until I signed a confession about 4 a.m., the next morning. Oh, they took me out for dinner once and gave me

drinks of water and such ...
Q. They say you forged the insurance policies on your mother that night when the plane crashed. Can you straighten that out?
A. I didn't. My mother signed them. I made out three—one for myself, one for my sister and one for my aunt.
Q. How much were they for?
A. I don't remember.

There was a foul-up on the machine ...
Q. Did you put a present —or a bundle of dynamite —in your mother's luggage?
A. I didn't put anything in her luggage. I only bought some straps to put around the luggage ... I don't want to discuss the present.
Q. Did you have a premonition of your mother's death before you had been formally notified of it?
A. I didn't—she had. She

called everybody she could think of before she left ...
Q. Do you mean your mother might have planted the dynamite in her own suitcase to take her own life? Has your mother ever mentioned taking her life?
A. I won't answer that ...
Q. What is your opinion as to how that dynamite got on the plane—in your mother's suitcase?
A. I don't remember.

A different device for presenting questions, without the intrusion of Qs and As and without forcing the reporter into the reader's awareness, is this one:

The man stood looking at a rubble-filled hole in the ground. He stooped to pick up a crumpled mailbox. As he turned to his visitor, he spoke.
"That was on the road— 100 rods away," he said. "How it got here ..." You could make out a name on the box: George B. Linsson, Route 7.
Did the tornado leave you anything else, Mr. Linsson?
"Just what you see. We weren't at home. When we got back, we didn't have any house ... didn't have anything."
How about your neighbors?
"We were right in the path. Seems as if we got it harder than almost anybody ..."
Ever have any previous experience with tornadoes?
"Not in this part of the country. But we used to live in Kansas, and ..."

The disadvantages of the question-and-answer process are that it has a tendency to run a story long, and it sometimes makes organization and emphasis difficult.

Reporting with an "I"   A reporter is usually most successful when he is invisible. As representative of the news consumer, he tries not to get between the consumer and the news. When he writes "the reporter asked" or that the news source "told this writer," unnecessary attention is drawn to the mechanics of news gathering and away from the story's substance. A trademark of the tenth grader in his first journalism class is to write about himself: "I was so excited I could hardly stand it when I got the assignment to interview Jane Fonda!"

Putting the reporter in the story is justified in two circumstances:

1. *When he becomes a part of the event.* He pulls the child from the lake, he delivers the ransom money to the kidnapper. Even then, he is an intruder if he focuses more attention on himself than is needed to clarify the event.

   In some news situations he can't tell the whole story without describing what his senses told him. The *Twin Cities Journalism Review* was sharply critical of a newspaper whose keep-yourself-out-of-the-story policy prohibited one of its writers from revealing that he had sat in on "hostage negotiations" with jail-breakers who had captured a farm family. The paper "had the inside track on the story," said the *Review*, but it "let its own rules get in the way of coverage." The reporter's colorful and suspenseful account of the deal-making and of the hostages' fears, showing that he had been on the scene, was jettisoned in favor of an "objective" story that was less revealing. Such a newsroom rule is made to be broken when ocasion demands.

2. *When he is a personality of audience interest.* Feature and human-interest columnists are often privileged to write in the first person. Bob Krauss of the Honolulu *Star-Bulletin*, both as a reporter on assignment and as a daily columnist, tells a devoted audience what he does, sees, thinks, hears. He didn't do it, however, when he was a new reporter on the paper. His perceptive skills, his wit, and his unique point of view had to be established first.

Some journalists believe that third-person journalism is sterile. Dan Wakefield, an accomplished magazine journalist, devotes most of the first chapter of his book *Between the Lines* to a defense of his decision to "break out of the formulas of the trade." His justification is that he is bored with writing "in lofty omniscience" that leaves him a shadow behind the scenes. But Dan Wakefield is a writer who, like Krauss, has proved that he has something to say. That makes a difference.

Wakefield states another attitude that every reporter should adopt: impatience with the disguises for the first-person pronoun that are "silly at best and pompously misleading at worst." He refers to the self-conscious "we," "this paper," or "this reporter," the labored circumlocutions "this scribe," "the author," and—worst of all—"yours truly." A moderately successful device is to write "a reporter." Usually no such reference is called for.

Interview hazards   One interview story opened this way:

> "In Israel everyone starves equally. In Iran, 99 percent of the people starve while the rest drive Cadillacs."

The day after the story was published, a letter from the interviewee explained that the opening paragraph "conveyed a false emphasis." It added that "in Israel no one lacks the food essentials" and that in Iran "no one is really starving." The reporter offered this comment:

> I had a rough time getting an angle for this story because I thought the interviewee had nothing new to offer—his stuff was largely familiar. But he did use the precise words I wrote (I have them in my notes, in quotes, which means that they are verbatim). The story would have protected him if it had said, in a second paragraph, "That was the figurative impression..."
>
> I think his complaint legitimate, for he did not intend his words to be taken literally.

A story contrasting and comparing the tasks facing the national chairmen of the Democratic and Republican parties just after the 1972 presidential elections talked convincingly about the chairmen's views of their responsibilities...until you became aware that at no point did the story show direct interview contact between the men and the reporter. The story uses such phrases as "his immediate worry is," "his political judgment is," and "he readily admits that"—but how does the reporter know? An interview? From other sources? What sources? The reporter's background knowledge? How reliable was that?

The same story says several times that "he said" or "he added." But it does not say when the statements were made, or to whom, or under what circumstances. Confusion of present- and past-tense attributions leads quickly to reader confusion.

A college daily quoted a number of students at a basketball game as they criticized the quality of the officiating. Nothing in the story indicated whether they were qualified to evaluate whether a referee does his work well or badly.

"An authoritative source"   Reporters learn to put up their guards when news sources ask for anonymity. Such meaningless and occasionally dishonest attributions as "informed sources," "a spokesman high in the State Department," "authoritative circles" and other disguises have come into deserved disrepute—some media refuse to use them.

Reasons for avoiding them are easy to see:

1. They are vague and uninformative, even when they are accurate.
2. They can be misused by news sources. A "Defense Department spokes-

man" who asks that a reporter conceal his identity may be floating a trial balloon—suggesting a policy move only to test public reaction (if it's negative, he can say he didn't say it). One "reliable source" much used by careless reporters in Washington confessed (in [MORE] in 1973) that he had "spilled secrets on a scale that would have qualified a man for the firing squad" to gratify his ego. "I'll give reporters almost anything they want to keep them interested in me," he said.

3. They can be misused by reporters. Though examples are rare, there have been instances of fiction masquerading as fact under nonexistent "unnamed sources." The writers of such stories may be eager to get to the beach; they may want to protect their own self-interest or somebody else's; they may have missed their vocational calling.

4. Often they fool only the unsophisticated. As executive editor of the Washington *Post*, Benjamin C. Bradlee complained that "everyone in Washington," including the Soviet ambassador and Red Chinese spies, "knew that a certain reporter"—Bradlee named him—"was quoting Dean Rusk. Everyone, that is, but the readers. Who is conning whom?"

5. They diminish the credibility of the press itself.

Columnist Art Buchwald satirized the unnamed source syndrome at the time the Agnew vice-presidency was under attack. Buchwald wrote:

> A highly placed source close to an unidentified attorney general who formerly was secretary of HEW and defense denied that any leaks came from the Justice Department. "We are not the only people in Washington who have unnamed sources."

Sometimes the source "who prefers to remain anonymous" may be protected with reason—for his safety or to save him unnecessary humiliation or embarrassment. But the device debases coverage of the news.

THE SYMPOSIUM INTERVIEW

Associate membership in the news interview family is held by the symposium, or group interview. For this story the reporter gets information not from one or two sources, but from a dozen, a score, or a hundred. Normally the topic is one of current interest, one so dominant in the news that interviewees to comment on it can be found literally on any corner. Typically, the topic has broad (not often profound) impact; it affects everybody's pocketbook, personal comfort, general security, or funny bone. Such topics are the new state retail sales tax: do people like it or don't they? On the hottest week in the last thirty years: how do you keep cool? Or the end of a threat of a general strike: would you have struck if it had been called?

Interviewees for a symposium story are not chosen as authorities but as people who have "typical" views; their opinions taken together show how a news situation is affecting their community or group. The opinion of one of them, taken alone, wouldn't be worth reporting; cumulative weight makes the story. The story may be fluff: the purpose of the "how do you keep cool?" question is not to develop studied generalizations about lowering body heat but rather to laugh a little at summer discomfort.

Some symposiums may bring out opinions that, taken together, have weight. The New York *Times* once assigned its correspondents throughout the United States to ask union members their opinions of charges of misconduct by key officers of the Teamsters union; the reporters talked with truckers in New York, Denver, Jersey City, Minneapolis, Chicago, and a dozen other cities. The comments justified a lead saying that "sentiment for the ouster of key officers ... is growing among the rank and file of the giant truck union." Sometimes responses from a representative group of average citizens tell more than many pages of speeches in the *Congressional Record*.

The distinction between competent response and average response is the one that differentiates news and symposium interviews. Though most news interviews present the contributions of only one interviewee, some may draw material from several sources. In a campus newspaper detailing the liquor consumption in the stands at a football game (drinking at a game violated several laws), the comments came from three student drinkers, a ticket taker, the ticket manager, and the chief of campus police. All were authorities on one phase or another of the subject.

Several observations on developing symposium interviews are in order:

1. Finding interviewees is rarely a problem, though you don't identify any in advance. If you're working on the how-to-keep-cool story or the sales tax story, you station yourself at a busy street corner and query the first twenty-five passersby you can buttonhole. The general strike story calls for a different approach—attending a labor mass meeting, visiting a big industry, or finding some other locale where you won't waste time querying men and women whose responses are irrelevant.

2. There's no fixed rule about number of responses. If your purpose is only to report what a few people say, without drawing a conclusion (as in the familiar "inquiring reporter" features), you can stop with half a dozen. But if you propose to develop a story that will reflect a public attitude, you may need to question fifty or a hundred. If your purpose is to entertain, you keep asking questions until you have enough good answers to make an enjoyable yarn.

   Whatever the number, it's always necessary to let your reader know how big it is, and of what composition. If you conclude that "four-fifths of the city's taxpayers believe property assessments are too high" on the basis of interviewing ten citizens, you're writing nonsense. But if you've interviewed a hundred passersby at a streetcorner, and find eighty holding one opinion, you have basis for writing that "most of a random sample of local citizens said today that ..." or "many local citizens say that ..."

3. In order to arrive at a justifiable generalization, you must ask all respondents substantially the same question in substantially the same words and manner; only thus do you get classifiable and comparable answers. If you approach interviewees in different ways, you'll get responses to different concepts, and you'll end up with an amorphous mass of comments from which you won't dare generalize.

   You'll learn not only to ask the same questions, but to make them simple. You don't say, "If the authorized agents of your horizontally organized fellow workers, by the legal rights they possess, issue an ultimatum directing all members of affiliated associations to absent themselves from their places of employment, would you have the probable inclination to conform?" You ask, "Would you strike if the union orders it?"

   You design questions that avoid suggesting answers. The question above may be answered either yes or no. But if you say, "When you became a union member, you swore to obey a properly issued strike call. If such a call were issued, would you strike?" it might be hard for some respondents to answer negatively.

4. A simple summary lead is often the best choice for a symposium story. When interviewees show substantial agreement, the summary is easy and obvious. It's not much more difficult when they disagree, for it's as newsy to report disagreement as consensus.

   When the story is a light one, an entertainer, the lead usually reflects it:

> A week of sizzling sun has driven local citizens to drink (usually lemonade) or to six baths a day.

Near the lead, if not in it, should appear the news peg that occasions the story (this rule also applies to news interviews):

> And there's no letup in sight. Yesterday's 98-degree peak will be repeated today and tomorrow.

Some place in the story should appear a brief explanation of the circumstances of the fact gathering:

> What people are doing to moderate the heat was described by 20 local residents asked this morning by a Herald reporter, "How do you keep cool?"

5. One of the virtues of the symposium interview is its high specificity. It reports what men and women think or feel or do, and you make them real to readers by telling who they are. This means that you:

a. Identify them precisely whenever you can. Names and addresses are often used—certainly of those you quote exactly. If it's inappropriate to give name-address identification, you can bring respondents to life by writing that "a redheaded workman who had shed his shirt said . . . "

b. Use direct quotations freely.

c. Support your generalizations with specific evidence.

6. Try to follow one pattern throughout a story. If you start with a name, continue to do it:

> Joe Antonio, 2179 Robisdaile Ave.—I wouldn't strike if they gave me the plant.
> Sandy Tripp, 433 S. Pittern St.—I'm ready to strike at the drop of a beer can.

But if you decide on a different pattern, stick to it:

> "I wouldn't strike if they gave me the plant," said Joe Antonio, 2179 Robisdaile Ave.
> But Sandy Tripp, 433 S. Pittern St., said she was "ready to strike at the drop of a beer can."

The symposium interview that follows illustrates some of these suggestions. It comes from a high school paper more enterprising than most:

Students in the three local high schools appear to have no doubts as to whom to blame for teen-age "delinquency."

"Blame the teen-agers themselves," they say.

At least that's the opinion of 72 out of 100 of them queried this week by the Schoolmate.

But they don't think it's a black-and-white matter. Here are some of the differing views they offer:

¶Most teen-agers are "all right." They shouldn't all be held responsible for the misbehavior of a few.

¶Parents have to share some of the burden of their children's misconduct.

¶"More understanding policemen" could help to cut down on violence.

¶There isn't nearly as much drinking or pot-smoking among teen-agers "as people seem to think."

The "blame-the-teen-agers" theme, expressed in one way or another by nearly three fourth of the students interviewed by Schoolmate reporters, was well summarized by a senior girl at Foster High:

"You can't tell me that the kids who get themselves into trouble don't know better," said Caryl Pitson, senior, president of her school's Student Council.

"Most of us come from good homes, and our parents have told us the score," she went on. "I've never seen a teen-ager who was misbehaving—maybe drinking, maybe driving too fast—who didn't know he was acting foolish."

Why do they "act foolish"? Junior Fritz Apfchen of Worthington High has some answers.

"They like to look big," said Fritz. "They think it makes an impression on the girls."

Tony Karnak, junior, also of Worthington, qualified this. "Girls like to make impressions on boys, too," he said. "I don't think we're much different from older people, as a matter of fact. Don't adults ever do things they're sorry for?"

From Fannie Fergus, senior, of our own Horace Mann High came this angle: "Our speech class had a debate on this last week, and we all thought the affirmative won. It supported the question, 'Resolved, that juvenile delinquency must be controlled by juveniles rather than by school, church, or city.'"

But Fannie expressed the second most common theme:

"I think the kids who have the best home life—the ones who get along best with their parents—are the ones who get into the fewest jams."

About a third of the students interviewed supported variants of this view. Another third asked that the city's policemen "try to help high school kids keep out of trouble, rather than just show how tough they can get when we make mistakes."

Drinking, it seemed generally agreed, is not a major problem.

"Sure some of the students do it at times," said one Horace Mann sophomore boy. "I've done it my-self a couple of times—not that I'm very proud of it. But I don't think I'm going to do it again for a long time. And neither is the gang I go with. We've talked it over, and we know it gets us no place."

Another Horace Mann senior pointed out that there have been no local charges of marijuana possession or use by minors in the last year.

The questions were asked of a random sample of students at the three schools —33 each at Foster and Worthington, 34 at Horace Mann. Three Schoolmate reporters conducted the survey, with the approval of the three principals.

STATEMENTS AS QUESTIONS

An ingenious departure from the direct-question pattern was used by a reporter trying to find out, as the Vietnam war was winding down, what the job market held for returning veterans. His questions were statements on which he asked comment. A few examples:

Job fairs and job marts have been tried across the country. They generally have been failures.

The manpower expert in the governor's office: *"The results generally are not at all good. . . . It's one thing to get pledges, another to get actual jobs."*

Many veterans come back dead set against assembly-line work, even when it pays well.

A veteran: *"Those jobs are for robots . . . you know, where it's up, down, right, left . . . just punching a button. . . . I'm not going to start that because I'd be doing it for the rest of my life"*

They are bitter about their treatment compared to their fathers and brothers in other wars.

A veteran: *"You see these stories about World War II and Korea. The veteran comes home and there are plenty of jobs. . . . Today they don't give a damn about what you've been doing because they see it all the time on TV. They see it on TV and they don't want you to bring it home to them. . . . And you look for work . . . I was hired and then kicked off the job the same morning. . . ."*

PERSONALITY INTERVIEWS

There is no more discriminating a tool for revealing who and what people are than the personality interview, the story in which a reporter helps a subject to show what manner of man he is through what manner of thing he says.

The reason the pattern is effective is easy to see. To let a news figure or an individual who is merely interesting discuss his likes and dislikes, his attitudes about diet and dictatorship and doodling, his hopes and enthusiasms and frustrations, and to let him do it in his own words, is to place the news consumer squarely where the reporter sits.

This virtue underlines the distinction between the personality interview and the biographical sketch. The sketch, written at a respectful distance from its subject, tells you *about* him: where and when he was born, number of children, date on which he became an ambassador, and so on. It has its uses, one of them being that it serves as the structural pattern for many obituaries. It is a readable substitute for *Who's Who*. But it rarely achieves the warmth or intimacy of the interview, where a skillful reporter can let a man's words and manners bring him vibrantly to life.

The personality interview may be used with any subject with whom a reporter can communicate. Not every subject, however, is worth much time. There are two principal clues that help to decide whether a subject is likely to offer broad interest:

First clue: that a man or woman is a news personality, one who for one reason or another has gained a place in the current stream of events. He has been elected mayor; he has made his fifth hole in one; he has refused to accept a million-dollar bequest from an uncle he detested. She is managing the Christmas Seal campaign for the eleventh year; she has been awarded the blue ribbon for her cherry pie at the state fair; she is the district's new representative in Congress. That is to say, public attention is already centered on the news figure; the reporter thinks of it as natural progression that he should have a chance to show the public, in his own way, what kind of human he is writing about.

Second clue: that a person entirely outside the news orbits is made newsworthy by a trait of personality, a hobby, or an oddity of habit or work or play; something has set him apart from his fellows. Such an individual would be the teen-ager whose collection of samples of tree barks now contains 409 specimens; the professional foster mother who has given homes to a battalion of children; the old man who has read every book about the sea in the local library and is now starting over. None of these is involved in a newsworthy event, but an out-of-the-ordinary habit or practice gives him special audience interest.

Interviewees identified by the first clue are likely to be not only interesting but also to some degree important. Those in the second classification get attention largely because of their human interest.

Development of the personality interview differs little in technique from that of the news interview. Advance preparation is necessary, especially when the subject, as a figure in the news, is aware of his eminence (it's amazingly easy to offend newly newsworthy men and women by not knowing they were born in Flagstaff or Terre Haute or Kennebunkport). Moreover, a news figure is likely to be busy, and anything that will conserve his time is an advantage.

The suggestions about techniques of interviewing earlier in this chapter can be applied to personality interviewing almost intact. But here are some additional pointers:

1. It is good tactics to steer the interviewee to the subject that has led to his selection: the fact that he has been made chairman of the board (what does he think about it, and how did he win the position?) or that she has never seen a movie (does she consider this a plus or a deprivation?).

2. More here than in the news interview, the verbal and physical mannerisms of the interviewee are worth space. The news interview's emphasis is on *what* a man says; that in the personality story is on the *how* as well. That a medical researcher constantly repeats the phrase "Know what I mean?" is of no significance if the story is intended to clarify his new theory of cancer identification. Properly used, however, it may aid the reader to find out what kind of man he is.

3. The reporter writing a personality story ought to help the reader see the subject as well as hear him. Artfully interpolated lines of description belong in personality interviews. When they are injected with a heavy hand, however, they are liabilities. But it is helpful to the reader trying to understand what a man is like to know that there are overcareful creases in his trousers, that he has a middle-age bulge, that he scratches the bridge of his nose when he's thinking. Details accent individuality.

   Similarly, details of the environment of the interview—particularly if they relate to the interviewee's habitual surroundings—may help to establish personality and to give vitality to a story. But observe these cautions: don't load the story with excess detail; use color not for color's sake alone, but rather for the sake of what it adds to the effect you're seeking; don't always put all the detail either of setting or personal appearance in a separate paragraph, but sneak small touches of it in through the story; don't overwork the descriptive bromides (*pretty coed, sparkling blue eyes, beaming smile, pearly teeth, mane of snowy hair, vine-covered cottage*).

4. Remember that, though your purpose is to reveal personality, you are rarely justified in causing personal annoyance or injured feelings. For example, to reproduce the language mannerisms of the interviewee exactly, down to the last "he don't," is honest reporting and likely to be revealing of personality. But if the interviewee is a high school teacher, this kind of reporting would be embarrassing and might bring him incommensurate penalties (presidents of the United States make syntactical errors in public). The reporter has to ask himself: "Is the gain from literal reporting sufficient to offset the possible injury? When public obligation and personal values collide, which one do I protect?" Sometimes, indeed,

he has to ask a more drastic question: "If I cut out the bad grammar and the bad manners, I'll make the story misleading. Is it worth printing if I leave out these things?"

5. "Newspaper reporters have a lot to learn from magazine writers," one magazine journalist has said. "Some metropolitan reporters and feature writers understand that interviewing the subject of a personality piece is not the beginning and the end of this kind of research. But lots of reporters—especially those whose bosses don't give them enough time to be thorough—don't seem to know that they ought to carry their interviews beyond the subject. No competent magazine writer would let himself become the prisoner of everything his subject says. Some interviewees need to be checked and double-checked."

The man makes sense. Magazine writers may spend weeks or months gathering material for personality articles—profiles, *The New Yorker* calls its thorough personality pieces. When Nathaniel Benchley was unable to persuade the reclusive Greta Garbo to talk to him, he went to more than thirty interviewees for material and turned out a revealing article.

Examples of personality interviews emphasize some of these observations and suggest others.

The story about the young socialist, a Sunday feature, reproduced here in part and with name and locale disguised, successfully acquaints its reader with a figure modestly in the news. It uses standard devices—direct and indirect quotation, descriptive phrases, background information. Its theme is stated in the second paragraph—Ms. Nordstrom is dissatisfied with the world around her—and this is the key to the personality the young woman reveals through her words. The story, though an exacting copy pencil would improve it, achieves its purpose.

Helen Nordstrom is an inquisitive girl, an inquisitive slip of a socialist with wide eyes who is president of the controversial W. E. B. DuBois Club at Wilford University.

Looking at the world from round, Little-Orphan-Annie blue eyes, Ms. Nordstrom, at 20, is dissatisfied with it.

"I am committed to taking part in things," she explained one day last week. "The civil rights movement, for example. I believe that socialism has much to offer us in solving our country's problems.

"But the DuBois Club is very broad. There are many in it who are not socialists."

If Ms. Nordstrom were to vote (she hasn't yet had the opportunity under the new law that makes her eligible), she would vote Democratic. She considers herself an independent spirit, however; 50 years ago, she "might have been a suffragette."

"I suppose you've read Betty Friedan's 'The Feminine Mystique,'" she said. "Some of the things the suffragettes did were very interesting to me. The facts that they weren't masculin-ized women and that their cause got women into politics are very important.

"Women had unique qualities and there is no need for us to emulate men."

And then, with a beguiling smile, Ms. Nordstrom added, "But I'm not a man-hater."

Ms. Nordstrom is aware that men don't often listen to the political views of pretty women.

"I have to really fight sometimes to talk politics to people," she said. "Today, if a man sees a girl with a dress on, he assumes she's not political.' "You don't have to wear sneakers and slacks and be unwashed to think."

Ms. Nordstrom knows she's oversensitive about her looks and her age. "I just don't look as though I care about impeachment and the energy crisis," she said.

[*The flow of the story is broken by three paragraphs describing the DuBois Club —its purpose "to encourage the development of the United States as a socialist society"—and identifying the man for whom it is named as a Communist.*]

"DuBois is important to us," Ms. Nordstrom said, "because he symbolizes the growth of thinking throughout life. He was a socialist in the 1930s.

"Even my thinking has changed in only two years at the university." Ms. Nordstrom is a farm girl who grew up near Jackson. Her parents, Mr. and Mrs. Carl Nordstrom still live there.

"I didn't know what it meant to get people in a community to work for something, for example, until I came here.

"I think of the DuBois Club as an action group. It is interested in student problems at the U—student housing, for example. I'd like to see students have a say on housing rules and on the courses offered them.

"And that's why we participated in the sit-in against the rise in tuition fee. We were faced with higher tuition without consultation."

Ms. Nordstrom, a theater arts major, is a representative-at-large in the student government association of the university. "The university is a little United States," she said, "and there there are many students who don't take part. Only the involved students participate and work on these problems."

Looking at the world beyond the campus, however, Ms. Nordstrom, a former 4-H girl and high school cheerleader, said, "The reason I'm involved is that I don't feel I can do what I really want to do without changing things first."

What Ms. Nordstrom really wants to do is become a modern dancer, with her own dancing company. This summer she will study modern dance at Colorado College.

DIFFERENT INTERVIEWING PURPOSES

A number of professions use the interview to gain information primarily for the advantage of the person interviewed: social workers, probation officers, physicians, lawyers, clergymen. From this fact grows the accepted social principle that such interviews are confidential.

The newswriter, however, uses the interview not for the interviewee's benefit (though such may be the result), nor for his own, but to discharge his obligation to the public. His responsibility is to provide useful information to his clients, in more or less same pattern the clients would have received it had they had the opportunity and the skill. This is not only his justification for seeking the interview but also his guide to the kind of questions he asks and to the manner of presentation he selects.

The woodsman's story that follows is a personality interview. It is also a color story (see Chapter 18). You should look on it as a story above the routine level but one that nevertheless has faults. Cataloging its mostly minor shortcomings would be a useful exercise.

A few days ago a young bull moose chased Benny Ambrose while he was highstepping through the snow on frozen Ottertrack Lake.

"When it happens in the woods, you can always duck behind a tree," said Ambrose, "but out there in the open you just have to move."

At age 77 Ambrose moves pretty well. It comes in handy in this remote corner of Minnesota's North Woods, where the only contact with the outside world is the passerby and getting through the gnawing winter can depend on planning and hard work.

Ambrose lives alone in a one-room cabin perched on a ridge near the Canadian border, 40-some miles northeast of Ely, with a view of the woods and lake country that seems designed for a travel poster.

In the summer, canoe parties come by.

In the winter, when the snow settles up to two feet or more in the woods and temperatures get to 50 degrees below zero, outsiders dwindle to those few snowmobiling woodsmen who have some reason to roam far into the backwoods.

For a lot of people it would be too lonely. For Ambrose sometimes it isn't lonely enough. He complains that folks keep interrupting his work.

Strolling through the snowy woods at 15 below, his woolen shirt undone a couple of notches and a cap cocked over his eyes, the old woodsman observed:

"I always was sort of a loner."

In fact, he is one of the last full-time residents of this isolated corner of Minnesota's north country—an example of a way of life which is on the way out.

Sitting in his cabin among the smells of wood smoke and coffee, Ambrose rubs his beard stubble and declares that he's feeling pretty good. Of course, a touch of arthritis has slowed his hands some, but he is treating that with a mixture of lemon and vinegar and by wearing a copper bracelet, which he says is an old Indian cure.

Then there was a heart attack a few years back while he was waist-deep in Canadian water. He rode a tractor out of the woods on that occasion and spent 19 days in the hospital. "It was my own fault," he says.

Ambrose is a well-known figure in the North Woods, where he's called simply "Benny." He does some prospecting and he guides fishing parties occasionally. He has a reputation for sizing up visitors fast. If he feels like talking he'll spin yarns for hours, say the local residents. If not, you get the message quickly.

On this occasion he feels like chatting.

"I was raised in Amana, Iowa. It was nearly all woods then, but they cleared all that out and now it's corn. My mother died when I was young and my father married the devil's own grandmother. We all cleared out."

World War I came and Ambrose enlisted.

"I couldn't believe they would pay you $30 a month and give you shells, too," he remembers.

After the war he went north to prospect for gold, intending to stay in the woods only a year. The year stretched into a lifetime.

Much of the time he has been alone and that doesn't bother him. "I never got tired of my own company," he grinned.

At one point Ambrose pauses and says, "But a lot of this has already been in the paper."

When?

"1934," he says.

It isn't a world where time makes a lot of difference.

Animals are a big part of living in the woods, and Ambrose likes some better than others. He brings in feed over the long portages for flocks of ducks and partridges that stay near him. He has trained some of the small ground creatures to eat out of his hand, and the chickadees and whiskey jacks peck for the seeds he throws under trees next to his cabin.

Timber wolves he treats as a sort of wilderness fact of life to be respected if not cherished. In the raging northland controversy over whether wolves should be protected completely, Ambrose is not a staunch defender of the wolf.

He blames the ban on wolf-trapping for what he sees as a reduction in the deer population. It is an argument that can stretch a long way when the two sides get going.

"You might think I'm prejudiced against the wolf," says the keen-eyed woodsman.

"I'm not. You've got to have the wolf. But the wolf is ruining things for himself. He's eating himself out of food."

With his knowledge of the backwoods waterways, Ambrose is considered a connoisseur of fishing spots. He says there's a place he knows where you can still catch lake trout on a fly rod in the summer.

"But it's 12 portages and the portages are long."

Between 1940 and 1954 Ambrose was married. His two daughters still come to stay occasionally, although they now live in Maryland and Hawaii.

Of his marriage, Ambrose says:

"She wanted me to leave the woods. But that's out."

Ambrose is hand-building a new cabin complete with indoor plumbing (a backwoods luxury) and a stone fireplace. Folks in the area says he's been at it for 20 years. The work shows the touch of a craftsman. Some of the wood was hewn with a broad ax.

The new cabin has a

question mark over it. Residents of the Boundary Waters Canoe Area are supposed to be out by 1975. Ambrose keeps hoping he can work something out with the U.S. Forestry Service so he can stay in his corner of the wilderness.

But there is the possibility he'll have to leave. He doesn't like to think about that.

"The mistake I made years ago was that I should have gone farther up in the woods," he says. "Maybe to the Yukon." [3]

Pluses: The interviewee tells you about himself. Unpretentious style fits the homespun character of the man and his life. The story knits environment as intimately to characterization as the woods, lakes, and wildlife encircle the man. Without halting the ongoing story for a biographical history, it weaves details of Benny Ambrose's half-century in the woods among those of his current life and thoughts without jolt or halt. And the reporter keeps himself out of sight.

Minuses: The story is without a precise time element—you are told that an event occurred "a few days ago," but you find it hard to place the interview in so loose a reference. There is no clear distinction between present- and past-tense credit lines, "says" and "said," and a degree of confusion results. The story does not give you a word picture of the man (though four large photographs accompany it).

Whatever the criticisms, the story invites its reader to call the old woodsman "Benny," as do his neighbors.

Projects

1. From current newscasts and newspapers, pick out five or more local news topics to which the news interview process would lend understanding or illumination. Select an appropriate interviewee and write a series of leading questions for each one. Carry out one of the interviews and write the story.

2. Choose a man or woman newly placed in a position of influence in your community—preferably one not well known. Carry out the necessary background study, then interview the person so as to bring out personality characteristics. Write the story.

3. Choose a second individual on the basis of a distinctive personal characteristic—he collects eighteenth-century books, he walks nine miles to work every day, he has a better record than the Weather Bureau's for forecasting weather a month ahead. Interview him and write the personality story.

4. Dream up a topic for a symposium interview, one whose topic is of current concern to your community: Do we need a new local transit system? Has the integration program in our schools worked to your satisfaction? What name do you suggest for the new bear cub at the zoo? What do you think of the four-day work week? Station yourself at a strategic spot—bus station, airport, PTA meeting, sports event. Ask the question of twenty or more people; with their answers, write the story.

[3] Copyright © 1974 by the Minneapolis *Tribune.* Reprinted by permission.

Related Reading

William M. Ringle and others, *Get the Interview as Reader's Surrogate*, 1974. — This feature section of the Gannett Group Newspapers offers "practical" current comment on news interviewing.

Eugene J. Webb and Jerry R. Salancik, *The Interview, or The Only Wheel in Town*, Association for Education in Journalism, 1967. — Helpful and readable tips on the newspaper interview. Excellent bibliography.

CHAPTER EIGHTEEN

Feature and human-interest stories

WHAT IS A "FEATURE"?

The term *feature*, which is on every newsworker's lips a dozen times a day, has many different meanings. It is a newsroom catchall. In contests for news story excellence, categories labeled *feature, news feature, spot feature, short* or *long feature,* or *something-else feature* are sure to be included. Rarely is there a definition of the term, and the wide range of the entries shows no consensus.

Because he was so often asked to judge "feature" contests, the long-time publisher of the Denver *Post*, Palmer Hoyt, asked for help from Alexis Mc-Kinney, a veteran of thirty years in the newsroom. McKinney came up with a definition that said in part:

> A feature finds its impact outside or beyond the realm of the straight news story's basic and unvarnished who-what-when-where-why and how.
> The justification, strength, and very identity of the feature lie in its penetration of the imagination—not in departing from or stretching truth but in piercing the peculiar and particular truths that strike people's curiosity, sympathy, skepticism, humor, consternation, or amazement.

Writing a feature story is not just recitation of facts ... but rather adroit presentation of facts and ideas so as to spotlight those that may not be apparent to the casual observer.

The McKinney definition is a sound start, but it stops too soon. The term *feature* also includes many kinds of material of nonimaginative, nonemotive content. In its broadest meaning it is safer to say that it is material *selected for presentation primarily because of some element other than the timeliness of its materials.* This approach eliminates neither the McKinney emphasis on emotional values—indeed, it emphasizes it—nor the element of timeliness. It says instead that recentness is not the dominant characteristic, either for the medium or the consumer. Its interest peaks in one or more other elements.

Specifically, newsrooms refer to all the following types of materials— some newsworthy, some not—as features.

Simple human-interest stories

- The man who ate fifteen pies on a bet and ended in the hospital
- The girl who forgot to attend her own wedding because she was having her hair set
- The ambulance attendant who discovered that the boy in the auto accident was his son

These stories fit the McKinney definition: They get into the news because of their oddity, their pathos, their entertainment value, rather than because they contribute significantly to knowledge of ongoing community life. Some would be reported because they are also spot news; others wouldn't get a nod were it not for the human-interest elements. In any of them the recency factor would be included, though it would not be the point of emphasis or the reason for selection.

Sidebars or second-day stories

- The fact that nobody in town could get water pressure to sprinkle his lawn during the big fire downtown
- The resentment of the young man because his fiancée, just chosen Miss Jaycee, can give him only one date a week
- The pitcher's glumness—or his laughing it off—when the third batter in the ninth spoils his no-hitter
- The factual listing of all this year's heavy rains that made yesterday's downpour doubly disastrous

Stories like these combine a sense of timeliness with their function of adding something to the reader's understanding of an event reported elsewhere. Often they are strong in human interest, but they may serve only to illuminate or supplement the major facts of current news events.

News features   These stories might be called "featurized news." They are like sidebars in their dependence on timely news events; the distinction is that they treat news—often significant news—with emphasis on human-interest or secondary elements. Sidebars and "pure" human-interest stories are usually brief; news features are often long. For example:

- The report about the pistol-packin' Secretary of State (page 175)
- The horrors and fears of a pair of elderly women who, finding themselves locked in a burning house, feared they couldn't escape—and how they did
- The experiences of a ski-equipped search party trying to find climbers lost in a mountain snowslide

Background or interpretive stories

- A story showing that old-timers are more common offenders in traffic court than first-timers
- An analysis and explanation of the use and misuse of personality tests
- A evaluation of local housing problems in view of an influx of new families
- A physicist's explanation of why he thinks the public should (or shouldn't) be concerned about the possibilities of nuclear radiation

These stories would not be developed if the newspaper or broadcaster were interested only in reporting the news as it occurs. They add meaning to public understanding of current news.

Color stories

- The reaction of the crowd at an auto race when a fatal smashup occurred
- The behavior of the girls who didn't get crowned when the beauty queen was named
- The atmosphere of a college campus at 2 a.m. when nobody is around but watchmen, night-owl students, and researchers in a few offices

The color story attempts to put the reader or listener squarely into the setting it is describing. It is essentially descriptive of a scene or of the circumstances surrounding an activity of current interest. It tries to make the scene audible, visible, smellable.

Non-news   Household hints, child-care columns, horoscope columns, hygiene columns, how-to-win-at-bridge, etiquette, gardening, movie gossip, comic strips, do-it-yourself material . . . the list is endless. Such materials usually have no time element. They are often syndicated, prepared by a distant agency, and provided on contract to many media.

All of these are features. Many are, as news jargon has it, time copy. This chapter is devoted to features of the types that reporters face often: human-interest stories, news features, and color stories.

HUMAN-INTEREST STORIES

A story strong in human interest is one that has emotional impact through eye or ear. It makes you say "for gosh sakes," "what a shame;" "wish I'd been there," "sure glad I wasn't." Hard news often has human-interest elements—the shooting of President Kennedy, national tragedy though it was, also had some of the elements exhibited in the satirical example on page 49. But the "pure" human-interest story depends not at all on the element of significance. It establishes emotional contact quickly, and it remains an emotive rather than an intellectual experience. When a story horrifies a reader or makes him laugh, saddens or angers him, appeals to his self-interest, he becomes a vicarious participant. Such a story, with a grip on his emotions, requires less concentration and effort than hard news demands.

Should this description seem familiar, it is because it is lifted from Chapter 4. Human interest is one of the factors that newsworkers look for in deciding what news situations are worth space and time. It is the factor that most strongly draws and holds readers or listeners; it is commonly the element that gives them "immediate reward"—the element that one of Hearst's talented editors was talking about when he said, "We want papers that make the reader say, 'Gee whiz!' "

THE KATHY FISCUS STORY

A generation ago America was stirred to its bones by the tragedy of a little girl in California, Kathy Fiscus, who fell into a well shaft and died there. "For two days the great affairs of a nation took second place in the minds and hearts of the people," commented an editorial. Its concluding paragraph helps to define the place of emotion in the lives of men and women:

> The tragedy of a little girl in the shaft of a well is one that the human heart comprehends at once, and to which it responds with all the nobility that distinguishes it from the base and the brutal. But the tragedy of a million people in China or India in the grip of a famine, or of a city wiped out at a flash of a bomb, or of an army being cut to pieces on the steppes of Russia—this kind of mass calamity becomes as something read about abstractly in a book. The fate of the individuals is swallowed up in the vastness of the event. It is only when human suffering is broken down into the terms of one particular human being that it can be directly felt by the heart and comprehended by the mind.

Recognition, understanding, and evaluation of human interest as a constituent in news appeal must run through any thinking about news. You take it into account when you examine the composition of news audiences, when you talk about effective news style, when you consider functional patterns by which you package news, when you plan and execute a news-gathering assignment. Appreciation of emotional and sensuous values is basic to every phase of the work of a newsman.

Developing human-interest news   A city editor does not assign a reporter to a human-interest beat as he does to the city hall or the police station.

Human-interest news is not found only in circumscribed areas. Much police news, it is true, is strong in human interest. But the police reporter learns to think of such qualities as a kind of bonus—something always to be looked for but not always present. The city editor does not ask his reporters to "go out and get human interest stories"; he talks in specific terms: "See whether you can get a good yarn about how the family feels about their son's becoming an auto racing driver"; "Find out how people are acting, and what they have to say, when they're flooded out of their homes"; "Don't report just what firms have floats in the parade—get me the comments people are making about them." These examples illustrate the principle that human interest is likely to show itself in human situations—in situations involving people.

The development of the human-interest story, to put it differently, is likely to result from news imagination reacting to a set of news facts. The reporter observing an event or a situation thinks, "If I ask such-and-such questions, I can build a human-interest story out of it." Sometimes there is no other way to get a publishable story from it. Sometimes a sidebar or second-day story may develop. Sometimes a news situation can be shown in true light only by building the emotive values integrally into the major story (as, for instance, in the story of the Dakota blizzard, page 220).

One of the news services reported the development of such a story by Alvin L. Krieg, its reporter covering the Ohio Department of Education. Krieg learned that a little girl had written plaintively to ask whether her school was to be shut down. Krieg recognized in the occasion "a swell news story in itself . . . it had human appeal." He suggested to the department a sympathetic reply and got it—but in terms of three-mill levies and tax rates. Krieg redrafted the letter for the department "so that a 12-year-old could understand it" (he confessed his debt to the New York *Sun*'s famous "Yes, Virginia, there is a Santa Claus" letter). The story he wrote not only had meaning for the whole state, but was told in terms everybody would read. Its opening paragraphs:

The State of Ohio today gave its word that "the schools will stay open."

The promise was given in a letter . . . sent by Joseph W. Fichter, assistant Ohio director of education, to a little Alliance girl, 12-year-old Mary Eileen Kelly.

But it is more than a letter to one little girl—for it is the state's "word of honor" to every last one of the million and a quarter boys and girls in the public schools of the state. Fich-

> ter's letter contained this message:
>
> "Yes, Mary, your school will stay open. I cannot tell you at this moment just how long it will be done, but your questions will help us to find the answer."
>
> [*The story goes on at length to recite details of the girl's question and official action to answer it.*]

This kind of story depends not only on its facts but also on the reporter's recognition of its values. Without the personal contribution the newsman adds—not often in direct participation, but in perceptiveness and sensitive writing—human-interest news would be rarer and less meaningful than today's journalism has made it. (How much space would the appendectomy-under-enemy-waters story have earned, for example, if it had been written straight, without George Weller's sensitive perception?)

The suspended-interest form   Human-interest stories are often presented in the suspended-interest form, a rhetorical package that takes advantage of the nature of the component.

This form, like that of the straight-news story, is "contrived"—it is consciously structured to gain an effect. The straight-news form gets the consumer to the heart of the matter quickly. The suspended-interest form moves in the opposite direction. It compels the reader to continue the story if he is to learn its major facts. It intentionally holds back one or more of the story's principal points so as to inveigle him into staying with it. It is a self-conscious device, kin to the narrative pattern of the short story; its purpose is to keep its audience in doubt throughout some, or all, of the story.

Were it not for the effectiveness of this pattern, many trivial events that now find space in crowded news columns of air time would go unrecorded. The straight-news pattern is useless with most news of this kind. A straight face would make ludicrous the publication of much of it, as in the following familiar example—the ambulatory fire that goes looking for the firemen.

Take these facts: Two policemen in Denver stopped auto driver John Marselle on a crowded viaduct, their siren halting traffic. Marselle, puzzled, asked, "Why?" Police explained that his car was on fire. They radioed the police dispatcher, who told them to take the car to a fire station two blocks away. The dispatcher notified the fire station. When the car arrived, firemen put the fire out.

Were this story to be written as straight news, it would probably be told something like this:

> Firemen at Northeast Station extinguished a flame this morning in a car owned

> and driven by John Mar-
> selle, 689 Elm Street. Mar-
> selle had been halted on
> Midtown Viaduct, informed
> that his car was on fire, and
> sent to the fire station.

In straight form the story has little interest for anybody but Marselle and his friends. It is certainly not worth putting on press service trunk wires. But the Associated Press sent it, in suspended-interest treatment, to every member:

> DENVER, March 25 (AP)
> —"What in blazes are you
> stopping me for?" asked
> John Marselle when two
> policemen sirened his car
> to a stop on a crowded vi-
> aduct today. "You're car's
> on fire," they replied, radio-
> ing the police dispatcher
> for instructions. They were
> told to take the car to a
> fire station two blocks
> away. Firemen waiting
> there quickly extinguished
> the blaze.

The principal characteristics of the suspended-interest form appear in this brief story. Its facts are marked by one of the common human-interest characteristics—amusing oddity. Its lead is of the holdback type, which gets the story going and arouses reader curiosity, but it avoids giving away the heart

---

QUESTION OF TACTICS

In the AP story Marselle is credited with asking, "What in blazes are you stopping me for?" You wonder whether this is not a reportorial invention—gratuitous embroidery by a reporter who thinks the play on words adds to his story. It can be argued that this kind of "bright" writing sharpens a story, and that its false tone is unimportant since it misleads nobody about the major facts.

But any astute reader is likely to spot the play on words as a reporter's fiction; and he can hardly be blamed if, seeing one piece of fiction, he asks what others the reporter (and perhaps the paper for which the reporter writes, and perhaps all news media) may have indulged in. It is one thing to hang an invention on a participant in an event, as apparently has been done here. It is another, a defensible variation, to write it so that it is indisputably clear that it's invention, not reporting. Art Buchwald writes as though he's reporting facts; but his manner quickly tells you he isn't.

---

of the event. Finally, the reader must go to the end of the story to learn its dénouement, the dousing of the fire, which the straight story put first.

Look back at the statement of facts for the story and you'll see that it makes a pretty good suspended-interest story as it stands. That's because it's a narrative—beginning at the beginning, ending at the end (the chronological form). The following story, along with several examples later in this chapter, illustrate this pattern. The story is also notable for its economy of style: by short sentences, lack of adornment, and exclusion of unnecessary detail, its writer has made it move as fast as the event itself.

"My sister's in the hole... my sister's in the hole..."

This alarm, sounded quick and loud by 5-year-old Judy Johnston, 8308 Fouquet Av. S., Renton, produced a chain reaction about 8 p.m. Monday.

Tony Case, 45, 8313 Fouquet Av. S., who was fixing his fence, saw the girl running across the street from a storm sewer excavation.

Case understood. He dropped his hammer and ran toward the excavation, shouting for help.

Raymond C. Manders, 8301 Fouquet Av. S., dropped his newspaper and raced through his front door. Bruce O'Brien, 8337 Fouquet Av. S., was talking to Marvin Hanick, 580 Holly Av., a contractor's man keeping an eye on a pump.

The two men broke into a sprint. By the time they and Manders reached the spot, Case had discovered a speck of Jeanmarie Louise Johnston, 8, almost completely buried by an earth cave-in.

"First, I saw a hand, then I could see her eyes," Case said.

The four men got down on their knees and dug with their hands "like gophers," releasing the girl before emergency equipment arrived.

Jeanmarie, flustered and frightened, ran home unhurt.

A modified suspended-interest pattern holds back the significant fact only partly through the story. The Marselle story, for example, could have gone this way:

John Marselle took a fire to the firemen today.

Stopped by policemen on Midtown Viaduct with warning that his car was on fire, Marselle drove to the Northeast fire station, two blocks away. There the fire was put out.

Firemen at Northeast station had been alerted by the police dispatcher, whom the police had radioed.

In this version the key fact is revealed at the end of the second paragraph; the third paragraph, secondary material, could be omitted without much loss. This kind of compromise between the straight-news form and the form that holds back until the end illustrates what may be the most common usage in suspended-interest stories.

3 TICKETS TO L.A., THE MAN SAID . . .

That was the headline over a story that most newswriters would have opened with the name of the principal actor. The opening paragraphs:

> The man from Washington, making a holiday trip with his wife and daughter, bought three tickets to Los Angeles on a jumbo jet for $652.92 and finished the trip at a sedate 55 miles per hour, thus saving the nation about 40,000 gallons of fuel.
>
> President Nixon figured "he ought to set an example," an aide said.
>
> So Nixon made a surprise trip to the Western White House by commercial airliner yesterday. It was one of the few such trips by a president in office. . . .*

* Copyright © 1973 by the Minneapolis Star. Reprinted by permission.

It does not follow that, because the suspended-interest form is used so generally for news of emotional impact, human-interest news is always presented in this form. Some news exceedingly strong in human interest—a riot in New Delhi, an earthquake in Santiago, the release of a kidnapped hostage, the crushing of a rebellion—is so evidently important that sober, straight treatment is mandatory. The human-interest elements in the rebellion story—the savagery of conflict, the death of humans and their hopes, open and secret passions—shine through the structure of the conventional story without structural emphasis. If you open a story "angry peasants swinging machetes and ax handles today swarmed over the chancellery," you don't have either to tell the reader there's human interest in it or tease him into reading it.

Imagination and a seeing eye may turn routine material into something novel. A court reporter found himself with notes about a woman juror whose stocking had been torn on a jury chair. The lady wrote a piece of doggerel to the judge, asking damages. The reporter opened his story thus:

> A letter terse but rythmic, and framed in phrases gay arrived upon Judge Leary's bench in court the other day. The judge saw no one bring it and can't remember, now, the incident described therein, nor when, nor why, nor how.
>
> But ever since the letter came the judge has tried to find a way to solve the issue and get it off his mind. He's thumbed his tomes, he's scratched his head, he's racked his aching brain to reach a just decision the high court might sustain . . .

Examples later in this chapter further demonstrate adaptation of pattern to material.

Human-interest news on the air   Human-interest news on radio follows print patterns. Radio uses less human-interest news than most newspapers do, in sum and in ratio, largely because of its lack of time (though the more folksy newscasters like to close their programs with human-interest "kickers"). Informality and personalization, however, often give radio news an intimacy that is less common in print.

News on television, in contrast, thrives on human interest. TV's need to take advantage of its distinctive tool, the picture, leads it to use news that can be illustrated—parades, dramatic accidents, sports, fires, policemen's clambakes—people doing interesting things rather than announcers discussing ideas or sober governmental procedure. Features like the human-interest broadcasts of CBS's Charles Kuralt (imitated by a number of individual stations) and documentaries add variety and sometimes comic relief to television.

Shorter stories   The stories that follow illustrate strengths and weaknesses in the genre. Two short ones exemplify punch line placements (punch lines italicized):

> The city editor's telephone rang. "When is Robert Penn Warren scheduled to lecture?" the caller asked.
> The city editor got somebody to look it up and reported.
> "Thank you," said the caller. "Where's it to be? And what subject?"
> The city editor told him. Then he got curious.
> "Who is calling?" he asked.
> *"Robert Penn Warren,"* *was the answer.*

> CLARKSBURG, W. Va.— Kendall H. Keeney received a letter this week that made it through the mail with only a two-cent stamp.
> *And only 36 years late.*
> Postal officials said the letter was mailed from the Clarksburg Community Chest Nov. 29, 1938, was found during the renovation of the post office here.

Stories like these, sometimes called "briefs," are not always brief enough. The shorter such a story, the sharper its point. Note the story that follows, and the rewrite next to it:

Rewrite

BRIGHTON, England—A 22-year-old student brought a touch of Elizabethan England to the 20th century Friday.

As Queen Elizabeth II walked among the puddles on a visit to the new University of Sussex near Brighton the student, Peter Horne, threw down his black plastic raincoat for her to step on.

The queen smiled at the gallant gesture, as her namesake, Elizabeth I, had done four centuries earlier when Sir Walter Raleigh, so legend has it, threw down his cloak for her.

The queen walked across one corner of the raincoat and turned a handsome royal smile on Horne.

Crowds had waited in continuous rain for a glimpse of the queen as she drove from Brighton to the University, Britain's newest.

It was as she walked from her car to open a new 400,000-pound ($1.1 million) library that the modern-day Raleigh act took place.

As she picked her way among the puddles, student Horne dashed forward and threw down his plastic coat —price, when new: 30 shillings ($3.50). Horne is a postgraduate student of politics. [176 words]

The day of Queen Elizabeth I and Sir Walter Raleigh was relived here Friday, 400 years late.

As Elizabeth II picked her way among puddles, on her way to open the University of Sussex's new library, 22-year-old Peter Horne, a student, dashed out to throw down his raincoat before her.

The queen stepped on a corner of the coat, and Horne got a royal smile for his trouble. [69 words]

The first story tells its tale twice. The second, less than half as long, calls on the reader's knowledge of history and his imagination to fill in gaps.

Good humor and understated writing can make a neighborhood incident appealing. Note the chronological pattern, following the indirect opening:

Most little boys have dreamed at one time or another of building a real fort —complete with stockade and lookout towers.

Bruce Nauth, 8, and Bruce Barker, 9, did their dreaming one stormy day last month. And they wrote this letter to Mayor Frank North:

"Dear, Mr. Mayor North:

"We would like to build a fort on a swamp across from E. 58th St. in the woods.

"May we please cut down trees for our fort. well you please take this up at one of the meetings. Thankyou

"My friend and I are 8 an a half. We will build it in the next summer.

"signed
      sincerely your
   Major Bruce Nauth
   Colonel Bruce Barker"

Today, by official directive of the mayor, the boys will stand inspection by Col. Joseph M. McCarthy, chief of the state military district.

City Engineer Hugo Schindler will join a party of city and military officials who will survey the site.

North directed the party to be present at a "southern exploratory outpost at the corner of Fifty-eighth Street and Sixteenth Avenue S. at 1600 hours in accordance with the urgent request of Col. Barker and Maj. Nauth."

North said a decision on construction of the outpost probably will be made after the survey and inspection.

What do the boys think about the official reaction to their letter? Col. Baker summed it up in one word: "Gee!"

He's the son of . . .

The trivial story below sounds like a publicity handout ("wood," such filler material is called in some composing rooms). It's made publishable by its oddity, good humor, and a closing fillip.

If you are flying with Northwest Orient Airlines and the man in the next seat starts riffling a fresh deck of playing cards, don't jump to the conclusion that he's a gambler planning to relieve you of your money.

He may be preparing for his arrival in the Orient by selecting a card that says "where can I get a taxi?" in English at the top and in Japanese, Korean, and Chinese underneath. That card, incidentally, is the queen of diamonds. "May I see the manager?" is the jack of diamonds; "where is the nearest doctor?" the seven of spades; and "please bring the check" the jack of clubs.

Northwest Orient, which serves 38 domestic and seven Oriental cities, offers a pack to each of its customers. The cards, of course, are as useful to Japanese, Korean, and Chinese traveling in this country as to Americans visiting the Far East.

The trick for the traveler who needs the right phrase in a hurry is to memorize which phrase goes with which card. In some circumstances the time spent trying to find "where is the rest room?" might seem awfully long. It is the nine of hearts.[1]

The artificial holdback until the end of the story can be applied to a longer as well as a shorter story. More a sociohistorical commentary than a news story, the following example understandably comes from a weekly news review, *The National Observer.*

By tradition, the Mississippi Delta begins in the lobby of the Peabody Hotel here in Memphis and runs south to Catfish Row in Vicksburg.

Not too many years ago, candidates for governor of Mississippi announced their availability in the Peabody lobby, and more than one Mississippi campaign was charted in a smoky upstairs room.

Memphis is 70 miles north of Oxford, Miss., home of the University of Mississippi, one of the nation's great football powers. Over the years, Ole Miss has played many of its home games here in Memphis.

On such weekends, the Peabody has served as alumni house and fraternity row. The story is still told —but not quite vouched for —about the night an old grad, a wealthy Mississippi planter, broke his flask of bourbon on a lobby pillar after Ole Miss had dropped a close one.

"You can't do that, sir," the manager told him.

---

[1] Copyright © 1974 by The New York Times Company. Reprinted by permission.

Without a word, the old grad pulled a $100 bill from his pocket and dispatched a bellhop to buy a case of bourbon.

When the boy returned with the bourbon, the planter smashed all the bottles, slowly, one at a time. Or so the story goes, in a Delta land that changes slowly.

But if the Delta remains pretty much unchanged, the Peabody hasn't.

With no announcement, the Peabody a few days ago quietly registered its first black guest.

The following slice-of-life narrative is told with extraordinary restraint— pared to barest detail, without adornment. Its lack of sentimentality is one of its strengths; another is that it ends as do so many minor miseries ... in limbo.

The man was about 45 years old and drunk. He'd arrived at the State Capitol with some friends Monday afternoon, looking for a warm place to stand for a while.

But somehow, he was overlooked when his friends moved on, and he was left standing on the Capitol steps waiting for help.

Inside the Capitol, a senate subcomimttee was holding a hearing on drug abuse and the need for treating the state's 75,000 alcoholics.

Then a couple who had just testified on alcoholic rehabilitation at the hearing emerged from the building. "Look at that poor man," said the woman. "He could freeze in this cold. A lot of them do, you know. I wonder if they'd have room for him in a half-way house."

"The least somebody could do," said the man with her, "is call the police."

Then they got into their car and drove away.

The drunk stopped a visitor and asked for a ride to the West Side. The visitor asked the man to wait in the lobby while he tried to get him a bus.

While he was inside, the visitor asked building attendants if there wasn't a first-aid station or some department that might be able to handle the man's problem.

The attendants said they could call the police, but didn't want to because the man appeared to belong to a minority group, and involving the police might embarrass the governor.

Meanwhile, the drunk wandered down the Capitol steps, his hands shielding his ears from the cold. He turned down Falton St. toward downtown. He mumbled off and on, stopped and threw a few imaginary punches, once threw up his hands in a gesture of despair.

The police were called, and the operator said they'd try to reach the man right away.

But before they could find him, he stopped in front of a church, then turned in a side door. He asked a secretary for a meal ticket or money for food.

"We no longer have this service," the secretary said. "We would rather you be on your way now."

He stumbled as he left, not noticing a sign proclaiming, "Have a Great Day!"

He walked on, asking not for a handout, but for help. But passersby didn't seem to know what to do. People he talked to turned their heads away.

Finally he turned down Temperance St. at the edge of the loop. Then he turned off and was lost.[2]

COLOR IN NEWS STORIES

A wire service memo is instructive on color in news stories:

Color is part of the news. But news must never be colored.

[2] Copyright © 1974 by the St. Paul *Pioneer Press*. Reprinted by permission.

The distinction is sharp and clear, and artificial
coloring is usually easy to detect.
        One way to avoid false color is to omit human interest
and confine each story to a dull, bald recitation of the
barest facts minus all atmosphere. That would be safe but it
would be neither adequate nor complete coverage of the news.
The reader often needs to see, feel, sense the complete
picture. He should be able to capture the atmosphere as well
as the basic facts.

Color in the news, to put it another way, is its seasoning if not its meat—
its hues, its sounds, its flavors, its looks. It is the *mood* of the crowd that
attends the political convention . . . the *setting* of the regatta on Lake Cay-
uga's waters . . . the *atmosphere* of the smoke-filled room, rather than what
the politicos do there. It is often secondary news, not the heart of the event
—not the essential Ws but the surrounding human, emotive, or physical
background that throws major facts into relief.

Color is not discoloration. Color is fact; color is reporting, just as genuinely as the statement of what the speaker said. The wire service memo
quoted above continued thus:

To draw color from the imagination rather than from
accurate, unbiased observation is an unforgivable sin. It
departs from the field of reporting into the realm of
fiction, and fiction has no place in news.

To call the audience "enthusiastic" when half of it went to sleep, to write
of an "exciting" game when it was listless, is discolor, not color. These are
lies to reader or listener and destroy the integrity of the reporter; to the
consumer who knows the facts it is evidence of untrustworthiness.

Not every news story has to contain color. In practice, most news is reported flat, without the extra dimensions that color gives it; much news,
especially minor news, is not worth the extra space that color requires. But
some news is less than fully revealing without it.

Color is description   Writing a color story is a venture in description, just
as clearly as is the "descriptive theme" in an English composition class or
the fiction writer's painting of background for action he is going to develop.
The purpose of color in news is to take the reader to the scene, to provide
him the sensory stimulants he would have felt had he been in the reporter's
place. Its tool is putting into words what would have struck him had he
been present—what he would have heard, seen, smelled, touched, tasted,
and perhaps sensed.

The color story presents both similarities to and differences from descriptive themes and fictions. Like them, it depends on careful selection rather

than on photographic detail. It grows out of the writer's decision on basic theme—gaiety, confusion, noise, banality, anguish,—and his choice of supporting specifics. It must not include distracting nonessentials.

But since it differs in purpose from essay or fiction, it differs also in approach and, to a degree, in method. The essay or theme reports from a single, single-minded consciousness: that of its writer. Its purpose is to tell somebody else what the writer sensed and felt about a scene or an event—how it struck him personally, and what it meant to him alone. The fiction writer composes a picture, describes an Alpine slope, a Victorian drawing room, a bar or a bawdy house, as a background contrived to throw into relief a contrived life situation. The novelist or short story writer is bound by the limits of his imagination and knowledge and his artistic integrity, the essayist by the necessity to be honestly subjective.

The reporter, on the other hand, must seek something loosely called a universal point of view—universal, at least, for whatever universe his audience comprises. He has to see things as he thinks his universe would see them; like the fiction writer, he has to provide the backdrop against which the event occurs, one that will develop the "net impression" he thinks the event ought to leave.

And—it cannot be said too often—he is rigidly bound by the necessity to observe the facts.

"COLOR" OR "WITH COLOR"

Make this distinction: a color story is one whose purpose is color; a story with color is one whose purpose is reporting a substantive event against enough of its background that the consumer may get an added emotional message from it. This book, in its discussion of speech stories and elsewhere, has pointed out that straight news stories are often strengthened by the judicious injection of color.

Objectivity and color   A legitimate and often-asked question is, can the writer of a color story maintain objectivity? Can he keep himself out of such a story?

Rarely. It is fairly easy for the reporter covering a political speech to report impersonally what the man said, who sat on the platform, and how many attended. But when he attempts to capture the flavor of the event, there is no such thing as complete detachment. His obligation to see the scene as most of his audience would be likely to see it is governed by his experience, his wisdom, and his devotion to the exclusion of his own emotions and ideas. This he cannot fully achieve: some shading of personality or of individual attitude, held within control, is necessary to selection of materials for either a color story or a story with color. The shading may become deep-hued when the writer is a "trained seal," a star performer, who is of interest to the audience as a personality. Since most reporters are anonymous, however, the obligation to maintain a high level of objectivity remains paramount.

What makes a color story? Most color stories deal primarily with people. The horror-stricken crowd on a Dallas street as a murderer shoots a President—that is a source of a color story, as are the fans lining up in the rain at a Super Bowl ticket window twenty-four hours before it opens . . . spectators peering through sidewalk-superintendent knotholes at a Main Street building project . . . hymn-singing sit-in demonstrators demanding support for or impeachment of a President . . . women storming a department store anniversary sale. The circus, the annual parade of ancient gas buggies, the Christmas party for homeless youngsters—the list reaches from here to 1984. Such events are magnets for crowds, and crowds are charged with many kinds of emotional manifestations.

There are other color settings. The *Saturday Evening Post* once published a color story about a night on the University of Chicago campus, a story that took much of its savor from the very lack of people. A solitary exploration through the maze of heating tunnels under a great industrial installation yields such a story . . . a reportorial vigil at an isolated forest ranger's station, watching for sign of forest fire . . . a visit to Coney Island in midwinter . . .

BRUSH OR SPRAY?

More words of wisdom from Theodore Bernstein: "Some writers brush words onto their canvases with gentle precision and the utmost feeling for color; others spray them on and leave them to drip." Understatement and restraint mark effective color writing.

Nevertheless, most color stories grow out of circumstances rich in human interplay—crowd situations. Illustrative stories, in this chapter and elsewhere, demonstrate this principle.

Color reporting Three sentences hold the key to gathering material for a color story. *See what you see. Hear what you hear. Smell what you smell.*

This means not only keen perception of the facts, but also the ability to winnow, to select, to discard, to pick details that tint the event's description in honest strokes. Suppose the subject is the crowd at the homecoming football game. A sudden downpour in the second quarter soaks forty thousand fans. You decide that the rain and its effects give you your theme, your point of emphasis, your springboard, and you concentrate on the sodden hats, the newspaper-sheltered coiffures, the rush for the exits. You find out what the rain did to the sale of coffee and hot dogs, you report the instant mud on the gridiron. You keep your ear open for pungent remarks. You note across the field the bare spots in the stands that five minutes ago were jammed.

Not only that. You also decide what not to use. The bit about the sharp new band uniform goes out (or should you keep it to contrast with the soggy bass drum player?). Throw out the notes you took during the flag raising because the story has taken its new tack. As for the welcome speech by the president of the alumni association—well, it was dull anyway.

All of this points up several characteristics of color stories: they must have central points or themes; they depend for vividness and credibility on skillful choice of detail; and that the reporter must depend on specifics, on facts clear and clean enough to convince the reader or listener of their reality. Fact-gathering is rarely too careful or too thorough. A reporter on a color story becomes both spy and eavesdropper. He notes the adoration on the face of the little girl cuddled under her father's plastic raincoat. He listens to the good-natured complaints of a plump matron that she's wet to the skin. He makes quick notes of her exact words, asking himself whether he should use the simile that flashed into his mind: "She looks like a drowned rag doll." As he thinks, he gets her name and address.

Of one unfailing aid the experienced reporter is always aware: audience imagination. The news consumer does not have to be told that there are 9,247 soaked topcoats in the crowd, for description of one of them suggests the scene. He can generalize readily from the specific; when the reporter gives him a sharp detail, he places it in a context created out of his own knowledge and experience.

The color story has no characteristic pattern. Because it is an appeal to the senses, it will more likely follow the suspended-interest model than the conventional; however, it may use a thousand forms. Often it is what might be called episodic, stating the theme in a lead section and supporting it with evidence in one specific after another. The simple color story is less difficult to compose, in one way, than the story with color, for the story with color emphasizes a news event against color background. The interweaving that combines the two elements in proper proportion and order is anything but easy.

FALSEHOOD WILL OUT

Fabrication of detail in color stories is hard to conceal. One of America's most competent reporters, Damon Runyon, also a fiction writer, covered the funeral procession of Franklin D. Roosevelt in Washington. His story was widely praised for its warmth and color. But in one respect it came a cropper. Runyon reported a man and his small son as spectators at the Pennsylvania Avenue curb, and quoted them five times in a long story. Each time they speak they become less real. The reason: Runyon gave them no clear personality or physical reality, and he let them speak dialog that sounded as if it came out of a book. Correctly or not, a reader is inclined to think that Runyon put words into fictional mouths because they were typical words. They may in fact have been real, but they carry no truth to the reader who doubts their reality.

The long story that follows is pure color. Its purpose is to paint a sordid scene, to let the reader experience what the reporter experienced. It may also have a social purpose—to arouse public concern. (Reporting facts may stir citizen opinion more quickly and deeply than a sheaf of editorials.) This story is one of detailed description; it opens with a specific scene and goes on to a series of sharp vignettes. (Note that its reporter, Sam Newlund, refers to himself only in the third person.)

The black snub-nosed police van, manned by three shirt-sleeved civilians, stopped quietly in a warehouse section near downtown at 10:30 one night last week.

Crouching through the darkness, the three searched quickly by flashlight beneath parked semi-trailers to find what they were looking for.

Moments earlier, the police radio had crackled the word: A man has passed out beneath one of the semis.

The man turned out to be Arnold Pope, 62, craggy-faced and grayhaired, his body wedged against a pair of the trailer's wheels.

"Arnold, what are we gonna do with you?" one of the men half-joked as they gently guided the wobbly man toward the black van.

Pope eased himself through the van's side door and maneuvered his grease-stained body onto the dusty, carpeted floor. "I guess I gave up," he said.

Several minutes later the van delivered Pope to the County Alcoholism Receiving Center, commonly called "Detox," and another night in a month-old experiment was over.

The experiment involves the use of a pickup van manned by civilians. No police are on board, although police squads can and do pick up drunks.

Before July 1 the van duties were shared experimentally by police and civilians. Long before that, picking up drunks and drug addicts was exclusively a police chore. Many of the "victims" landed in the local jail's "drunk tank," and many were then sentenced to the workhouse.

But the 1971 Legislature declared drunkenness no longer a crime, and detoxification centers were established to dry out the nuisance inebriate and treat his behavior as an illness.

Since March, 1973, the main Detox Center has been housed in the River Villa Medicenter Building, a nursing home, at 22 27th Av. SE. From 900 to 1,000 inebriates are brought there each month.

The men in the van are two experienced Detox staff members—health aides or nursing assistants. They usually are joined by a civilian volunteer, frequently a Jaycee. They tour the city's central area nightly from 4 p.m. to midnight.

The unspoken assumption is that inebriates will get more humane treatment from paramedical personnel, whose goal is rehabilitation, than from policemen, who are used to dealing with criminals. The experiment also frees police time from pickup chores. But there is no expectation, according to Leonard Boche, director of the county's Alcoholism and Inebriety Program, that police squads ever will be entirely free of such duties.

The night that Arnold Pope was led from underneath the semi, the van crew consisted of John Wehrman, 24, a health aide; John Kehoe, 25, a nursing assistant; and a reporter acting as a volunteer.

During the night the crew made 10 contacts with drunks, eight of whom were taken to Detox. One man, found huddled in the vestibule of St. Olaf's Catholic Church, was allowed to go on his way. Another was taken to a neighborhood shelter for Indians.

When Pope climbed into the rear of the van, the volunteer stepped in with him for a bumpy, circuitous ride that included a swing around Loring Park, a common collapsing place for the over-drunk.

The van's "passenger section" is barren except for wooden benches on opposite walls. There are two small windows, but they don't open. The air quickly becomes stale, stifling, and hot. Nobody complained but the volunteer.

The back door is securely bolted—a fact tested by one of the evening's passengers. This passenger lay on his back and gave the door all he had with the heels of his shoes. Other passengers ignored him.

The volunteer wanted to know how Pope ended up with a pair of big truck wheels jammed against his body.

The van lurched forward and the man swayed. "I don't know how I got there," he said. "I don't know where I come from, and I don't know where I'm going."

Food? "I ain't had nothing to eat in three days," he said.

This was not Pope's first

visit to Detox. Wehrman and Kehoe knew him well, and the old man himself admitted to being in Detox, jail and the workhouse on many occasions.

There was no question about his preference. Detox, to him, was a place to "meet friends." Jail he described only in expletives.

In an expansive moment, bouncing along on the wooden bench, he said he was so glad to be going to Detox that "I hope to stay there the rest of my life."

But that isn't likely. Warren Jann, Detox administrator, explains that the average stay is just over three days. The law, in fact, allows the center to hold a patient for 72 hours without a criminal charge.

Whenever possible, Jann said, the policy not only is to dry patients out, but also to refer them to Alcoholics Anonymous or other treatment programs.

A "shelter care" section of the center, however, is set aside for drying out chronic repeaters for whom there seems little hope of rehabilitation.

At least some of those encountered by Wehrman and Kehoe the other night appeared to fall into that category. Nearly all the men—there were no women —were known to them as former Detox patients.

John, for example. He was found lying face down in a toilet stall in the basement of the Employment Service building.

And Ray, picked up on Hennepin Avenue after a wobbly bit of joshing with two policemen.

In the van, Ray said he has been picked for drunkenness "a hundred times," makes his living by panhandling, sleeps "under the post office," and lays claim to being "one of the best bums there is."

Ray said he is 60 years old, and he laughed heartily before he said it. He has never been married, he said, nor has he ever gone hungry. He guessed that he makes $15 a day panhandling.

The van door opened and an aging man with dark glasses entered. Ray knew him at once as "One-Eye." They shared a bottle of wine which one of them had concealed in his clothing.

Arnold Pope was the last man checked into Detox that night. Like the rest, he was given a rudimentary physical examination and issued clean pajamas. The center, clean and modern, looks like a hospital ward.

Kehoe, who shared the driving with Wehrman, seemed pensive before quitting time.

"What's the problem?" he was asked.

"Oh, I don't know," Kehoe said. "I was just thinking about the other guys out there who will be sleeping under semis tonight."

Whether such civilian concern is an argument for keeping the pickup chores out of police hands is a matter of opinion. The all-civilian setup is not totally without problems.

The presence of a police uniform, for example, may be a protection in the search of warehouse areas for men like Pope. After that search was over, the volunteer confided to Wehrman that he was envisioning a nightwatchman taking a shot at what might appear to be three burglars.

"I thought about that while we were doing it," Wehrman replied.

The following day at Detox, the new arrivals shuffled about the halls in pajamas and paper slippers with sobriety bordering on depression. Ray, the garrulous panhandler of the night before, was too sick to talk.

But Pope was all right. "I'm a little shaky, but not bad," he said, sitting on his white bedsheet.

He recalled nothing of the night before and had no idea how he had landed under the truck trailer.

"Trouble with me," he said, "I get to drinkin' and I'll lay down anywhere and go to sleep."

Sober now, Pope said he was born in Menomonie, Wis., worked as a railroad section foreman for more than 10 years, "never had time" to marry, and now lives in a Hennepin Av. hotel.

He said he lives on a railroad pension of "$62 or $64" a month, much of which goes for wine. He used to belong to Alcoholics Anonymous, he said, but it didn't take. "It's pretty hard," he observed, "to change the spots on a tiger."

Several floors below, food carts were being loaded onto elevators for distribution to the approximately 110 temporary Detox residents. Some stared at television sets in corner lounges; others milled about trying to light cigarets with trembling fingers.

Pope was asked what he would want from Detox if he could have anything at all that would help him. There was no hesitation.

"To stay sober," he said.[3]

[3] Copyright © 1974 by the Minneapolis *Tribune*. Reprinted by permission.

Political stories do not often become color stories (perhaps news of politics would be better read if they did). The following story is a mild satire on the smoke-filled room cliché, told with enough bite to give an edge to what could have been routine news. Note again the details, the dialog, and the short, simple, clear sentences.

SAN FRANCISCO, Calif. (Special)—The scene was a smoke-filled bathroom on the 15th floor of the Mark Hopkins Hotel, battle headquarters of Sen. Barry Goldwater, newly nominated Republican candidate for the presidency of the United States.

It was 1:45 a.m. Thursday.

Jammed into the room were seven of Minnesota's top Republican leaders, two of Goldwater's closest advisers, and three reporters.

They were there to discuss a matter of high political significance—the selection of Goldwater's vice presidential running mate.

The bathroom provided privacy from the champagne celebration outside.

An unidentified man, apparently intent on using the room for other purposes, opened the door, recoiled in surprise at the imposing assemblage, and decided to come back later.

The man the Minnesotans had come to see, Richard Kleindienst, Goldwater's co-director of field activities and a candidate for governor of Arizona, stepped into the bathtub to relieve the congestion.

Arrayed before him were Robert Forsythe, Minnesota Republican chairman; George Etzell, national committeeman ... [the paragraph names other members of the delegation].

In the back, against the wall, stood F. Clifton White, Goldwater's other field director.

Forsythe flicked the ashes off his cigar, put his foot up on one of the major appurtenances, leaned over, and started to talk.

"We are here on behalf of the Minnesota delegation, which has expressed interest in doing something on behalf of Dr. Walter Judd for the vice presidential nomination if there is reason to do anything.

"But the first thing we would have to know, of course, would be whether the choice of a candidate would be left to an open convention or whether Goldwater himself will be picking someone."

Kleindienst, dapper, composed, a drink in his hand and his face creased by the smile of the victor, replied as if speaking from a pulpit.

"It will not be open," he said curtly.

"All right," said Forsythe, "that answers one question. The other thing, of course, is whether as long as Goldwater will make the choice, the matter is already foreclosed or whether Dr. Judd might still be under consideration."

"It is foreclosed," said Kleindienst.

The Minnesotans blinked. Etzell was the first to speak.

"Thank you," he said. "We appreciate your candor and your brevity."

Kleindienst, starting to unwind slightly now that the pressures of securing the nomination for Goldwater were over, made a little gesture with the glass in his hand.

"I do not," he said, "mean to be abrupt. We all know the high regard in which the senator holds Dr. Judd ... "

[After reporting Kleindienst's three-minute response, the story reports the breakup of the bathroom huddle. It closes:]

Their mission concluded, the delegation went down the elevator, skirted a crowd cheering and singing "Dixie" in the hotel lobby, and walked out into the chill early morning air.

"That," said one, "didn't take long."

The political story, told straight, could have been compressed into a sentence: *Sen. Goldwater's decision to select his running mate himself has ruled out Dr. Walter Judd as a vice-presidential candidate.*

The graphic portrayal of a briefly dramatic moment at shipside, the story that follows, would never have been published had it been offered as straight news. Its color is what makes it. Two characteristics are worth observing:

first, it is constructed in straight-news form, with a one-paragraph summary lead, a second paragraph of secondary facts, and a third paragraph introducing the chronological recounting of the incident; second, it uses color words and phrases as well as color facts (*calloused mitts, pretty even when drenched, swaying gently, big man with a voice to match*).

NEW YORK, N.Y.—One hundred thirty steel-muscled longshoremen flattened their calloused mitts against the side of a 10,000-ton ship Wednesday, pushed it away from a Brooklyn pier, and held it back to save a 4-year-old girl from being crushed to death between the vessel and the pilings.

The feat was performed with a slight assist from three small loading machines and a large assist from a daring stevedore who was lowered by the heels into the narrow space between the ship and dock to help bring the child to safety.

The girl is Diana Svet, a blue-eyed blond, pretty even when drenched. The villain of the piece was the Yugoslav ship Srbija, hitting 10,000 tons with her cargo.

The Srbija docked Wednesday morning. In the afternoon the stevedores began unloading her. In mid-afternoon, Diana came to the pier with her mother, Anna, 25, to visit one of the vessel's officers, a cousin of Mrs. Svet.

They went aboard, learned that the cousin wasn't there, then began descending the stairway leading down the ship's side.

The lowest step of the stairway was one foot above the pier. Mrs. Svet, holding onto Diana's left hand, made it, but Diana, who jumped, didn't.

The jump carried her out of her mother's grasp, and into the 10-inch space between ship and dock outerstructure.

Screaming, she plunged 15 feet into the water, where she managed to grab a slippery piling.

The Srbija was swaying gently. But even the slightest sway, with 10,000 tons behind it, could be fatal.

Pier superintendent Ignatio Scibilia, a big man with a voice to match, bellowed an order, and 130 stevedores scrambled off the ship. The two lines holding the ship to the dock were cut.

Then the men and the three little machines pitted themselves against the ship. Inch by inch, it gave way. John Balzano, 45, Giuseppe Gambino, 49, and Joseph Zapulla, 25, went into action.

Balzano and Gambino lowered Zapulla, head down. Diana's strength was waning as Zapulla dropped a noosed rope and pulled it taut. Then he and the girl were pulled up to the pier.

Outside of a scare and a thorough wetting, Diana was all right. Mama took her home.

Zapulla, who had taken a banging around against the piling, went home, too.

Projects

1. Rewrite the little-girl-in-the-water story in the suspended-interest manner, condensing it to no more than two-thirds of its original length.

2. From a newspaper, select a color sidebar accompanying a parent story—for example, a color story about the shivering crowd at a football game (the "parent" is of course the game story)—and see whether you can combine the two in a condensed story. Evaluate the effectiveness of the new story in contrast to the two that it replaces.

3. Attend and cover a major address, the dedication of a new public building, or any occurrence that draws public interest and public attendance. Write two stories: one the major story reporting the important facts, the second a color sidebar.

4. Examine a week's issues of a metropolitan newspaper to discover the extent to

which it uses feature material (use the descriptions of a feature at the beginning of this chapter as a guide). Write a commentary of 500 words or more on what you find—whether the paper uses features well or badly, widely or sparingly, and so on.

5. Develop several topics on which you think you could write human-interest stories (see suggestions on page 302). Write the stories.

CHAPTER NINETEEN

Filling in the gaps

Warnings against the emptiness of surface news come from every side. Editors at their conventions talk soberly about reporting in depth. Lay critics of the media ask—naively, it would seem—that every newspaper report the news as abundantly as does the New York *Times* or as thoughtfully as the *Christian Science Monitor*. This book has more than once condemned photographic reproduction of the veneer of events without digging to find what lies below. The reporter's notes in Chapter 8 told you that a news worker "has to live beneath the surface."

ASK ENOUGH QUESTIONS

One face of this problem is what one critic of newsworkers has called the "hit and run reporter," who "partly through production pressures and partly because of personal inadequacy . . . appears content to grab a few facts, bang them out on paper, and turn to something new." Stories that report adequately the who, what, when, and where may be barren if they ignore the how and the why. Elmer Davis said that reporting that is merely objective isn't good enough. Examples of stories whose reporters stopped too soon:

- A story says that a legendary San Francisco store is to close its doors, but doesn't tell why.
- A story reports that postal inspectors "swooped down" on the Boston post office to check for suspected fraud, but doesn't identify the fraud or the reason for thinking it exists.
- A story announces that "militant women will storm the City Hall tomorrow," without letting you know what they hope to gain by it.
- A sportswriter says that a favorite local high school coach won't be around next year, but doesn't reveal why, or how he knows.

The critic just cited investigated scores of such stories and got his own answers to questions that reporters had failed to ask.

Reporting that pierces the crust grows from news imagination, energy, perception, and a passion to find causes and explanations. It is, in a sense, a luxury—expensive in dollars, time, manpower, and gray matter. Harry Ashmore, who as Arkansas *Gazette* editor took a Pulitzer Prize for his stubborn war on a segregationist governor, said in 1973 that "we can't expect a local teakettle radio station to do much in costly reporting in depth if the great newspapers, the networks, and especially the wire services do so little of it." But without it the public, like a passenger in a 747 at 42,000 feet, sees a sweep of land from such a distance that no meaningful details come through. Mount Shasta looks flat from 42,000 feet.

Some actual cases, sometimes disguised, offer suggestions to show where reporters go awry:

- Congress passes an appropriation bill that provides $100 million for damming a local river. The dam will create a flood-control reservoir; it may also provide cheaper power. Routine coverage, by local media and the wire services, reports what can be seen by the naked eye: how much, where, when, who voted aye and nay. This coverage is essential; without it there can be no follow-up. It's the kind that wire services, serving hundreds of customers who don't need to know the implication of every event, can afford to provide. The local reporter who let it stop there was either very dull or very tired. Had he been energetic and imaginative he would have started at this point to ask himself questions. *When will construction begin? When will it end? How much money will flow into the home town? How many farmers and villagers above the dam will be dispossessed? Is there a chance that power rates will go down? What about tax rates? How will it affect the area's cattle ranches?*

From questions like these grow stories that give future meaning to present news. They tell the citizen what effects events will have on him, his family, his neighbors. They reject reporting that merely tells, as one shallow definition of news has it, "what God lets happen." For newsmen to whom making news meaningful is a religion, this kind of reporting is the blood and marrow, the guts of journalism. It is the most exciting as well as the most significant part of the day-by-day job. Additional examples show why:

- The Supreme Court redefines obscenity in motion pictures and other public spectacles in terms of local mores and attitudes—one law for San Francisco, another for Bangor, Maine. *How are local standards to be determined? Will the definition lead to scores of cases in the lower courts? How will it affect your city's regulation of movies? How many youngsters will get into movies currently barred to them?*
- Two local grade schools burn down within four days. *Do police and the fire marshal think arson is involved? What will be done for children these schools normally serve? What insurance coverage was in effect? When can new or replacement buildings be ready? Will new facilities be improvements?*
- The high school basketball team walks out in protest against the coach's dismissal of a tall center for "insubordination." *Any chance they'll come back? Might the coach retract? What about next Friday's game . . . and the rest of the schedule? What avenues of appeal are open to the center?*
- The biggest home-owned manufacturing concern announces the election of an unknown nonlocal man as president. *Does this mean a change in the ownership pattern? Who is the man, and what are his qualifications? Any local noses out of joint?*

News enterprise that asks questions is a reasonable minimum expectation of reporters. The string of question marks is elementary in reporting a routine PTA meeting, an airplane catastrophe, a Sunday school picnic as well as an outbreak of diphtheria, a ten-million-dollar plan for a new city center, or a club-swinging, skull-splitting riot. It's basic to the business.

It is also basic in, but in an important way different from, the kind of reporting to which the rest of this chapter is devoted, enterprise reporting.

ENTERPRISERS

In some newsrooms, newspaper or broadcasting, you hear the term *enterpriser* or its equivalent, *made news*, misapplied to reporting of the kind just described. The terms mean something else. While color reporting generally bears an immediate relation to spot news, enterprisers and made news generally grow from a reporter's or an editor's observation and news imagination, from the realization that a certain set of questions asked in the right places, or a certain effort of observation or digging in a library, will yield a story worth publishing. Such a story—note the lack of spot-news peg—might be produced by any of the following efforts:

- An investigation of city council records to develop a story showing how each councilman had voted on tax issues since the last election.

- Interviews with real estate dealers, supplemented by material from public records, to show the trends of real estate transfers in the last one, two, five, or ten years.
- Explorations at the public library to discover how reading habits and book demands have altered in recent years.
- Collection of facts about the turnover of small business ownerships, vacancies of commercial property, and number of tax delinquencies in a rundown or blighted area of the city.
- Interviews with citizens who make their living in out-of-the-ordinary fashion: the woman who runs a yarn-import shop in her living room, the Ph.D. candidate who pays tuition and college expenses by writing other students' term papers, the man who sells genealogies to local residents of Scandinavian descent.
- Talks with the big local family that moves into the north woods every April to live off the land for six months.

Such stories go beyond the coverage of the flow of events and add depth and meaning to the news consumer's understanding or appreciation of the life of which he is a part or give him a view of how some of the other half live. Competently used, they can offer audience illumination and reporter *joie de vivre.*

Nothing need be said about the journalistic forms of such stories for the clear reason that they may take any form. When you develop a story beyond the minimum call of duty, it is news imagination and energy that you add, not new rhetorical pattern. Though enterprisers by nature are what were described in Chapter 18 as features—stories in which the spot news or time element is secondary to other components—they can take any form the news craft has developed. They are often treated effectively in the suspended interest form.

A prime example of the news story that grows from deep digging is the Washington *Post's* Watergate achievement. The Watergate burglary in June of 1972 was a shocking enough news event in itself, spotted as it was by White House and CIA thumbprints. But it could have died as a bungled but not very important crime had not two *Post* reporters, Woodward and Bernstein, started asking questions. With extraordinary support from their newspaper's owners and executives, they continued until the story of the century evolved. A spot news event was expanded through persistent, imaginative reporting to reveal a national scandal.

Every day's news presents more modest examples of this kind of reporting. There are not as many cases as there could be, for no news medium is able to free reporters for the time and effort really thorough reporting demands (newsworkers are often more aware of this fact than their employers; they hold with good reason that most newsroom purse strings are drawn more tightly than they have to be). Nevertheless, careful reading of your daily paper, however many missed opportunities it reveals, will also

"CREATIVE WRITING"

Is journalistic writing creative writing?

The question arises because of the unthinking distinction often suggested between the writing demanded in English composition classes and that in newspaper-magazine-advertising-broadcasting writing. The first is creative, so it is implied, because it is the stuff of the imagination or the intellect; the second is—well, something else because it grows out of actualities.

This is nonsense.

Creative writing is not merely putting words on paper so that they have impact, though that is part of it.

It is not limited to belles lettres—to fiction, poetry, and the essay—though they are sterile without creativity.

It is the kind of writing that grows from creative imagination . . . writing that evokes lucid, living images, that breathes vitality into concepts and realities, and that is supported on a substantive and emotive base that only lively and perceptive vision can provide. It involves the innovative generation of attitudes toward both the routine and the arcane, of ideas for plays or news interviews, novels or newspaper color stories, poems or personality portraits, as well as the rhetorical or literary sensitivity to language that is evocative.

For the journalist, creative imagination starts with the idea, the base on which he composes his story. It continues with the curiosity and inventiveness with which he envisions and collects the materials he will need, and the skill with which he selects among the superficial and the covert. And it depends for effectiveness on the art and the craft, knit into subtle alliance, with which he writes.

"The truly creative writer or artist," wrote Norman Cousins in Saturday Review/ World (August 10, 1974), "never has to choose between the ivory tower and the arena. He moves freely from one to the other according to his needs and his concerns. Nothing is more vital for the creative artist than his access to the arena. . . ."

Creative writing is a totality. It is the goal of any worker with words, not of one or another genus of writer.

---

show that the meaningful stories, the ones you remember, are those whose reporting has been imaginative and thorough.

The examples below are of the enterpriser type, stories that grew without immediate spot news impulse. The story on safety in the parks (its lead sentence unfortunately clumsy), taking its cue from a national magazine article, has no local immediacy.

Local parks are safe "but I would not advise using these areas after midnight," according to park police Capt. Elmer Bednagl, head of the department.

Bednagl was responding yesterday to questions about a recent article in *McCall's* magazine, which cited the parks of this city as among the safest in the country.

"I would hesitate to walk through our parks at night," Bednagl said, "but I would especially recommend against their use in the early morning hours."

The parks close officially at midnight.

"Some of these parks

have dark, wooded areas," Bednagl explained. "People shouldn't use such areas at night—and our experience shows that most people don't."

Park police statistical records show that there have been only three molestings and five robberies reported in city parks during the first eight months of this year.

There are 152 parks in the police jurisdiction of the county. Twenty-four patrolmen work the 600,110 acres of park property lying within and outside the city.

"Lighting is a deterrent to crime," Bednagl said, "The lighting is good now, especially at Franklin, North Side, Wilbur, and Pleasant Parks."

Since the lighting was improved at Franklin early last year, Bednagl said, there have been only three reports of crime. During the same period of the preceding four years there were 30.

The story about motels, below, was born in the perceptive curiosity of a reporter making a cross-country motor trip. Though it is based largely on what occurred on "one recent day" at a specific motel in New Mexico, its writer bolstered on-the-spot material with facts from Holiday Inn central-office statistics and other outside sources. It is a story that would not have been written without an initial impulse to find out "how it works." Notable in the story (by Andrew H. Malcolm of the New York Times Service) is the conviction it gains from specific names and incidents:

ALBUQUERQUE, N.M.— "Do you have a room for tonight?" the rumpled father asks wearily.

"For how many?" the desk clerk responds.

Out in the car a rumpled mother, three rumpled children, and a rumpled dog watch intently. When the father reaches for a pen to fill out a form, a soft cheer seeps from the air-conditioned station wagon.

Everyone begins gathering up coloring books, dolls, handbags, toy pistols and swim suits. And another motel room is rented.

It is a ritual as old as the automobile itself: Americans on the road in search of a night's lodging.

And across the land on these warm summer evenings during the peak vacation period, it is a ritual that is performed perhaps two million times a day, about once for every one of the 2,551,007 rooms in the 52,000 motels in the United States.

Here in New Mexico at the intersection of two major interstate highways 140 and 125, the cars begin streaming down the cement exit ramps soon after 2 p.m.

For many travelers, a computer has already made their reservations and promised to bill them, even if they do not appear. In fact, the computer based in Omaha, Neb., or Memphis, Tenn., or Phoenix, Ariz., has determined, in effect, how far each family will drive each day.

The average vacationing family will drive a lot farther this summer than before the high-speed interstates stretched a day's travel from an exhausting 300 to a fairly easy 500 miles.

It does not matter to these travelers in search of some vacation Valhalla that seven years ago the land around here was a sandy waste beyond the city limits.

Few people except the scouts for Holiday Inns knew that this property was destined to become, in effect, a new "transient town" dedicated to the needs of those thousands who pass through daily.

On Sept. 2, 1966, the interstates opened here. On Jan. 11, 1967, they began construction of a motel. The motel opened on Oct. 1, 1968. It was followed by several other motels, truck stops, and restaurants. And now just about anyone driving through this city passes by what the Holidex computer calls H. I. No. 126AB.

The result is an average annual occupancy rate of 98 to 99 percent, compared with the national average of 70 percent and the break-even average of 60 percent.

"And summertime," a motel official said here, "is family time when you really make your money."

Long before the sun came up one recent day, the innkeeper, Murphy Jenkins, and his assistant, Jim Sanders, knew very well that they would have no vacancies for the coming night, and, for that matter, the next night and the next night.

Frank Cortese, the bellboy, knew he would make close to $30 in tips. And Joe Roloson, the bartender, knew he would sell a case of beer and a quart of vodka every hour. Bennie Davis, the housekeeper, knew she would lose about 75 ashtrays and 50 towels and two families would forget luggage. And Sanders knew the morning mail would bring 10 keys that yesterday's guests had carried off. But Mrs. Margaret Parker could not know that there would be no $12-to-$22 room at the inn for her.

The day began at 4 a.m. when Steve Dillon, the night clerk, started the wake-up calls for travelers anxious to get on the road. At 6:30 a.m. Agnes Martinez arrived to handle the remaining guests checking out and, with colored paper slips in numbered slots, to begin plotting which guests, some of them still asleep hundreds of miles away, would stay in which room.

By 8 a.m. almost every guest had hefted his bags into gaping car trunks or tied them on rooftop luggage racks. The long hallways were empty, but silently they began to look like narrow, carpeted battle zones.

The maids, 18 of the inn's 96 employees, were attack-

ing each of the inn's 192 rooms, tossing the soiled linens and towels out the doors, emptying the trash, vacuuming the shag rugs and setting the partly used soap bars aside for charity.

The washing machines began to chew on the day's 550 sheets and 970 towels. The swimming pool, out where the construction crews were working on an additional 108 rooms, was little used. Jenkins, the innkeeper, was in Phoenix for an emergency regional meeting to update menu prices for this month's inflation. And Gordon Winfield had just left the Holiday Inn in Dallas, heading west.

Slowly the seven ice machines recovered from the onslaught of tourists surreptitiously swiping scoopfuls for their portable coolers. Then, at 2:30 p.m., Connie Brown and Loretta O'Brien, the two receptionists who would handle the brunt of the day's tourist barrage, went on duty.

Minutes later, like clockwork, they began arriving. Mrs. Rosalie Simon checks into Room 333. George Tarleton checks in with his wife and child. Mrs. Simon returns. Her room faces the highway.

"I need my sleep," she says. She gets Room 305. The Tarletons march by in their swim suits.

"You have to be very patient with people," says Mrs. Brown, who, like many out here, fled from the East.

"Families are the messiest guests of all," says Mrs. Davis, the housekeeper. "Businessmen use one towel, one bed, one ashtray and that's it. Not families. And families seem to steal more, too."

At 5 p.m. Ramsay Conyer of Morristown, N.J., arrives

with a reservation. The motel does not have his name, but he gets one of the few remaining rooms and never learns of the error.

Shortly before 6 p.m., Winfield, a Braniff Airlines pilot being transferred from Florida to San Francisco, drives the 652nd mile from Dallas. Next stop: a California Holiday Inn.

A young man drives in. He wants a good stationery store. Miss O'Brien directs him. Mrs. Parker, who is driving from Nashville, Tenn., to Los Angeles at 50 miles per hour, arrives. All the rooms are full or reserved. She is sent to another motel. One-half hour later she could have had one of the unused 6 p.m. reservations.

And so it goes into the evening, each traveler another face and another room number. Stretching their arms, rubbing their eyes and sucking their sunglass earpieces, they fill out forms, submit credit cards, get directions and become new numbers on the board.

At 7 p.m., Room 157 calls for more towels. Room 407 has toilet trouble. A young couple shuffles to the desk. Mr. and Mrs. Russell Barnes from Emporia, Kan. They are ill at ease and smile often.

Mrs. Brown looks at them briefly. "You're honeymooners, aren't you?" she says. The newlyweds look stunned.

"In that case," Mrs. Brown continues, "let's give you a room with a king-sized bed." The couple blushes. "Aren't they cute?" says Mrs. Brown.

Room 435, Eric Dickman, checks out. He prefers to sleep by day and drive by night.

At 9 p.m., 19 guaranteed reservations are unclaimed.

Mrs. Brown rents out a couple to a lucky few travelers. For the others there is no room.

At 10:30 p.m. Robert Keats, 13 hours out of Omaha, drags himself to the desk and pleads, "I can't go any farther. Please give me a room." He gets a couch in a meeting room.

At midnight there are 13 unclaimed guaranteed reservations. Dillon, the night man, starts renting them to "walk-ins," travelers without reservations.

At 4 a.m., Katherine Golden checks in and becomes Room 249. As it has been for 10 weeks, the inn is full. There are 343 paying guests in the building. Moments later Dillon begins the wake-up calls.[1]

The story about the night patrol in a small village is of a different nature. Read it, then ask yourself the questions that follow it:

Eleven-year-old Jeff Bouma is the only salaried employee of the "night patrol," a security force of more than 130 men who have patrolled this village from midnight to dawn for the past three years.

He makes about $4 every two months for distributing the nightly schedule to patrol members.

Despite the low budget for the patrol, the residents of Edgerton (population 1,100) take pride in their law-and-order record. The only night-time theft in the village in the last couple of years was solved with the arrest of the culprits 90 minutes after the County Sheriff's Office found out about the crime.

Here is how Edgerton's patrol works:

At about midnight, every night of the week, a team of two men starts checking the downtown stores. They rattle the Main St. doors of Jolink Pharmacy, Pete's Shoe Shop, Curt's Barber Shop, Willard's service station and the other businesses, making sure all the doors are locked.

Then they can get into the car and drive around to make sure that everything is quiet at the churches and the schools, at the DeKam Hatchery, Vanderstoep Furniture, the rendering works, the Hillside Cemetery.

For the rest of the shift they drive up and down alleys, along the side streets and down Main St., keeping the town tucked in for the night and noting suspicious cars—any car out after 1:30 a.m. is suspicious.

Since there are more than 130 men who contribute their time to the Civic Club project, a team of two sees duty less than one night every two months—after Jeff distributes the new schedule.

The nature of their work is made easier because in Edgerton:

¶No liquor is sold; the lone tavern sells only 3.2 beer and generally closes by 8 p.m.

¶The entire regular police force is Marion Pool, who operates the department out of his home and has an enviable collection of arrowheads and artifacts and more than a passing interest in Indian history.

¶Village morale is such that, after a few break-ins three years ago, Irvin Wolfswinkel suggested the idea of a night patrol at the Civic Club and it has been a success ever since.

Driving around Edgerton for six hours—even just once every two months—does get boring, said Paul Ward, the community services director, "but each time you read about a theft in another village and you haven't had one, you feel a sense of accomplishment."

Or take the early morning of May 12 when Harold Ten Cate and Oscar Van Essen jotted down the license number of a suspicious car. Later that morning some thefts were reported in Edgerton. Sure enough, within 90 minutes the sheriff's office caught the thieves with the stolen goods still in the car that Ten Cate and Van Essen had spotted.

"I'd like to know just how many cars we've chased out of town by tailing them in the morning," said Dean Gruys, who usually patrols with Jeff's father, Fred Bouma.

The vigilance has other dividends.

"You'll never know when you'll find a door open," commented Jerry Kreun, manager of the Central Telephone office in Edgerton. A 2 a.m. phone call to an errant merchant helps assure the door will be locked the next night.

The night patrol members have no formal connection with Pool or the sheriff's office. The members say they do not even think of

[1] Copyright © 1973 by The New York Times Company. Reprinted by permission.

making arrests. They just drive around, and if they see something they phone Pool or the sheriff.

Members of the night patrol drive their own cars and are not reimbursed for the miles they roll up in five or six hours of driving each night. The Civic Club pays Jeff, and no one ever thought of asking the state or federal government for funds to help support the crime-fighting program.

"Our policing is much different than in the city," said Pool.

Edgerton's effort is a clear exception among outstate communities that generally lack 24-hour police service. A 1970 study for the Governor's Commission on Crime Prevention and Control reported that a police department would need more than four men to provide a minimal level of 24-hour service. The study noted that nearly 80 percent of all police organizations in the state cannot provide that level of service.

Robert Crew, the commission's director, said in an interview that smaller communities "do not have the police protection that is desirable. They can't fund it."

Crew said that federal guidelines prohibit using federal funds to provide local police service and that "even if we could, we probably wouldn't." The reason, he said, is that "we would use up all our funds and more."

The state encourages small towns to contact with county sheriffs to provide a basic level of service, often at a cost lower than that at which the community could provide itself, Crew said.

Some communities have done that and others have cooperated in joint-powers agreements to help each other. But he said there are others that still follow the "strong American tradition" of local police, even when better service is available elsewhere.[2]

Some questions:

Does the story justify the use of "eleven-year-old Jeff Bouma" as its opening element? Do you expect to hear more about Jeff?

Is there a basic time element in the story?

Do you approve the variation between present-tense and past-tense credit lines?

Can you deduce exactly when and where the quotations were collected?

What comment do you offer on the last five paragraphs, in which Edgerton talks in statewide terms?

Do you agree that, whatever your answers to the questions above, it's "a pretty good story"?

There are scores of examples of made stories every day in the papers or on the air—short and long, solemn and light, color, personality, historical . . . every variety you can think of. Watching for them, and asking yourself questions like those above, will be rewarding.

A remarkable example of this kind of reporting is in Chapter 21, the story of the life and death of Linda Fitzpatrick (pages 355–360). It is not an unusual genre—the attempt to find out and report what led to tragic or bizarre human behavior has become one of the strengths of modern journalism. But its restraint and compassion in a situation laden with human agony put it on the highest plane of reportorial accomplishment.

Made stories can be short, like the one that follows. Sometimes, it is true,

2 Copyright © 1973 by the Minneapolis *Tribune*. Reprinted by permission.

the brief story seems to be no more than a synopsis that deserves more space and detail. This story could be almost endlessly expanded:

Nonfiction books, especially on sports, child care and personal and family adjustment, continued last year as the most popular on the library's shelves.

"The demand for fiction was probably no more than 50 per cent of that for nonfiction," Ms. Amanda Winthrop, librarian, said last week. "It's a trend we've experienced ever since the Korean War."

Watergate appears to have stimulated great interest in books on politics, Ms. Winthrop said. She cited the new David Wise book, "The Politics of Lying"—an account of governmental efforts to deceive the public—as an example of books "we can't have enough copies of."

Books on football, mental hygiene for school children, and "how to stay married, or how not to," she said, also had wide circulation.

A factual countdown on circulation of all types of materials will be issued next July in the library's annual report.

Radio and television have in recent years made extensive use of their own varieties of enterprisers, more commonly in documentaries than in direct news broadcast treatment. Among TV broadcasts, local and national, in the first month of 1974 were "Nixon on Nixon," a collection of excerpts from many Nixon speeches; an examination of businessmen sipping noon-time martinis and watching lingerie exhibitions; a recounting of the controversial trial of Julius and Ethel Rosenberg; analysis of the fear of change among patients in homes for the aged; a documentary reliving events just before President Lincoln's assassination ... to give only a small assortment. Similar in nature was an earlier radio broadcast, from a Great Lakes port, of a series about shabby reception facilities for visitors reaching the city by ship.

OTHER USES OF MADE STORIES

The campaign or "crusade" Newspapers often, and radio and TV with increasing frequency (critics say that none do it often enough), develop stories to reveal corruption, to present community needs, or to promote causes of various types.

The series An Albany newspaper assigned a reporter to write a series of stories about the city's amusement and recreation facilities. Many newspapers and broadcasters, in the face of inflation and "consumer protection" demands, developed stories in the early 1970s about comparative prices, reasons for rising food costs, and the like. The New York *Times* put twenty experienced reporters to work doing twenty stories on contemporary changes in New York City and its suburbs. The themes that have appeared are countless: teen-age drinking and the eighteen-year-old vote; governmental and private incursions into citizen privacy; the effects of equal-rights laws; the need for better mental health care; women's liberation; censorship; why Johnny can't read (when Nancy can).

Historical features are made stories. So are scores of features in science, medicine, industry, sports, finance, education. The front page of the business section of one Sunday paper exhibited these enterprisers:

- The increasingly sober and businesslike conduct of conventioneers
- The prospects for a profitable shipping season in the local port
- The development of a "professional approach" among secretaries in local offices
- The need for good weather as retailers approached the Easter season
- The probability of new agriculture-control laws from the current legislature
- The rousing success of a new local pizza emporium

Most such stories are built around cores that would yield similar features any place. City and assignment editors and reporters who are on the alert read papers from other communities regularly.

Stories for special occasions   Newsmen mutter "Here it comes again" when they are asked to do special-occasion stories, the usually brief pieces that have become routine in coverage of recurring nonevents. These are the yarns that tell you how Labor Day came about, what really happened to Washington's father's cherry tree, and the way April Fool's Day is celebrated in Scotland. The mutters arise from the suspicion that every approach known to man for such stories has been exploited (how many times, on February 1 or 2, have you seen a whimsical interview with a groundhog?). The stories continue to appear, despite all the muttering, and from time to time fresh approaches show up.

The genuine special-occasion story is not spot news. It is timely general information—timely in the sense that it must be published within a given period or not at all. But it is often timeless, for it would be as apt in 1980 as 1960. It is the story that gives the reader something new or entertaining to add to the flavor of a familiar holiday or season. Boredom comes more from the fact that it is trite than from any inherent dullness. Imagination and enterprise can always produce new angles.

Essentially a sidebar, such a story is distinguished from the spot news holiday story. On July 4 there are routine stories about community celebrations, speeches, fireworks; at Christmas there are stories about church services, the upturn in retail sales, the family that couldn't afford turkey and fixin's. These are spot news stories. The special-occasion story is related to the occasion as an institution, not to the current events it elicits.

Materials for special-occasion stories often derive from reference books: histories, encyclopedias, almanacs. A Lincoln's birthday story telling the world that Lincoln was the first President to wear a beard came from an old biography; one about the origin of Memorial Day came from the almanac; one on Veterans Day came from 1918 newspapers. A long feature reporting that only two men actually signed the Declaration of Independence on July 4, 1776, came from histories.

When Drew Middleton was Paris correspondent of the New York *Times*, he used historical material buttressed by personal experience to develop a story for an anniversary of V-E Day. Here is his explanation of the story's origins:

> A good deal of the story originated in my memory; it was not easily forgotten. The description of the school room and its surroundings on the day was reporting on the spot. I spent the day in Rheims talking to people in the city. By luck, I had come through the city earlier in the month and had met five couples, two American and three British, who had stopped to see the place "where it ended." These provided me the material about the middle-aged men from Oklahoma and Yorkshire.
>
> I also looked through the *Times* files in Paris to check some of the facts about the surrender and to get some of the atmosphere of the time.
>
> The genesis of the story was this: I thought we should have a piece from Rheims rather than Paris, told the foreign desk in New York, and went up to Rheims to write it.

The story that grew out of these efforts combined Middleton's background material with spot news. In this sense it is not the conventional special-occasion story.

RHEIMS, France, May 7—Up the street the boys were waiting for the girls to come out of school. When they walked off arm in arm in the soft May air, none gave a thought to the dusty room in the school where it all ended.

The room nowadays has that unreal air that haunts all shrines. The battle maps still hang on the walls. But the armies marked on it, and even the place names, seem irrelevant to the busy life that flows around the school.

A long plain table stands at one end of the room. There are seven chairs on one side, three on the other. On that other May 7 the three were occupied by Adm. Hans Georg von Friedeburg, Col. Gen. Al-fred Jodl, and Major Wilhelm Oxenius.

At 2:41 in the morning Jodl and Friedeburg signed the instrument that signified the unconditional surrender of the Third Reich. It was over, in Europe at least.

History chooses strange sites for her great acts of surrender.

Someone knew that the McLean house at Appomattox was undamaged and Lee rode up in his best uniform. There was a convenient railroad siding at Compiègne and to it came the Germans of 1918 and the French of 1940.

In May, 1945, Rheims was the advance command post of the Supreme Headquarters Allied Expeditionary Force Europe. Millions of men over half a continent answered the orders that came from the big red brick school.

Great men came and went: Eisenhower, Montgomery, Bradley, Tedder, Spaatz. Here were planned the last blows that felled Hitler's Germany.

But today the people of Rheims couldn't care less. The schoolroom, once General Eisenhower's "war room," is closed to the public until Sunday because it is being used by a television company for a program.

No one is going to miss it. The kids waiting outside the school know there was a war but they are a little vague about what actually happened there. And in the good cafés in the arcades of Rheims the surrender is good for perhaps two minutes of personal reminiscence, and then on to today's business: the next trip to the Riviera.

They may be callous to the touch of Clio, the Muse of History. Or perhaps Rheims knows the lady too well. What is the date May 7, 1945, to such a city?

Not far from the school, the great Mars Gate built by the Romans in the third century still stands. The archbishops of Rheims consecrated kings of France from the time of Philip Augustus to that of Charles X. Outside the medieval walls Joan of Arc dispersed an English army.

So, a generation after, this is a shrine for that one generation among many. They come, of course. Middle-aged men from Oklahoma or Yorkshire with rather impatient wives who can't understand why their husbands are interested.

The men, however, won't be hurried.

They look at the maps and point. "There's where we were, Edna," or "The map must have been bloody well out of date. We were well east of Hamburg."

The room, the school, the city amount to a punctuation point for a whole generation. This was the end of the belly-tightening, desperate years.

It is not dramatic now and it was not dramatic then. A friend once asked Lieut.-Gen. Walter Bedell Smith, General Eisenhower's chief of staff, who signed the document for the Allies, what he had thought of when it was all over.

"To tell you the truth," he said, "I thought of all the damned paper work this was going to mean in the morning."

The only touch of drama was provided by Jodl, the schoolbook soldier with the face from a medieval painting and the mind of a computer.

When he had signed, he stood at attention and said to General Smith:

"General! With this signature the German people and the German armed forces are, for better or worse, delivered into the victor's hands. In this war, which has lasted more than five years, both have achieved and suffered more than perhaps any other people in the world. In this hour I can only express the hope that the victor will treat them generously."

Outside the street is almost deserted. The few passersby don't even glance at the door with its brass plaque. After all, it was a long time ago.[3]

Sources range all the way from learned interviewees to unadulterated fantasy. A Friday the 13th story offers mock-serious interviews with community leaders about how to avoid bad luck. Few April firsts have passed without stories that open with some such lead as "federal income taxes have been abolished" or "importing green cheese from the moon would wreck the Wisconsin dairy industry, according to . . ." The Lockport, N.Y., *Union-Sun & Journal* one year published a doctored photograph showing an ocean liner entering Lockport's little harbor. Oslo newspapers urged readers to pour boiling water down their drains to set up a warm current to melt ice masses in Oslo Fjord. The Galveston *News* is still wondering why so many of its readers spent hours looking for the nonexistent grocery named in the story it thought was so clearly labeled a spoof:

The Monument Food Store at 25th and Broadway is doing something about the price of coffee. For one day only, L. Irpaloof, proprietor, is offering assorted brands at 33 cents per pound. "I won't make any money on this deal," says Irpaloof, "but I expect to have a lot of fun and I can't think of any better way to throw away money."

Incidentally, the sale has been set for April Fool's Day, if that means anything to you—and it should!

[3] Copyright © 1965 by The New York Times Company. Reprinted by permission.

Projects

1. Suppose that in your city or town the police announce that the number of juvenile arrests in the last three months has been only half that of the preceding three. Suggest five enterprisers—showing both the nature of each story and the sources of its material—that might be developed from this news peg.

2. Watch the wire news in your local paper until you find a story originating elsewhere that suggests a local angle. Follow up the angle and write a local story.

3. Write for your local paper a time-copy, special-occasion story to be published on the next holiday on your calendar.

CHAPTER TWENTY

Investigative reporting

When Joseph Pulitzer died in 1911, he left behind not only two distinguished newspapers, the New York *World* and the St. Louis *Post-Dispatch*, but also two significant bequests to perpetuate his devotion to public service through enlightened, tough-minded reporting. One was a fund to establish the Columbia University School of Journalism. The other was endowment of the Pulitzer Prizes, awards for "distinguished and meritorious public service" in reporting and related fields. These awards have been made annually since World War I; the two that have come to be thought of as *the* Pulitzer Prizes, the ones newsworkers cherish most, are those for outstanding reporting and for extraordinary service to communities.

This is what Pulitzer hoped. His *World* and his *Post-Dispatch* stood for the sturdiest kind of reportorial zeal, courage, and imagination. "Never be satisfied with merely printing the news," he commanded. He might well have said "merely printing the news you can see," for he believed in burrowing deep and aggressively—dangerously, when necessary—for hidden facts. He urged especially the search for hidden corruption, for private misbehavior. Though he insisted on a vigorous editorial page, he believed that searching, aggressive reporting was the heart of newspaper service. It had to be reporting that was unafraid, that dared probe the deeds of a President as readily as those of a town constable (Theodore Roosevelt brought about a criminal libel indictment against the *World* in 1908).

Though few newspapers have excelled the *World* and the *Post-Dispatch* in devotion to crusading or investigative journalism, high achievement in this field neither began with Pulitzer nor ended with him. James Franklin is given credit for America's first newspaper crusade in his New England *Courant* fight of 1771 against smallpox inoculation. Thomas Nast, the cartoonist who invented the GOP elephant and the Democratic donkey, was offered a bribe by the corrupt Tweed Ring in New York in 1871 (he didn't take it, and his satires plus New York *Times* documentation drove Tweed out). The turn-of-the-century period in which Pulitzer flourished is looked on as a heyday of journalistic crusading—the day of the muck-rakers, of the exposure of crime and antisocial behavior in government and business. Such magazines as *Collier's* and *McClure's* and such journalist-reformers as Ida M. Tarbell, Lincoln Steffens, and *World* editorial writer David Graham Phillips flourished in this period. Pulitzer's greatest crusade, that against the towering life insurance companies and their misuse of policyholders' investments, started in 1905.

The pattern has continued. A campaign by the Canton (Ohio) *Daily News* in 1926 cost its editor, Don Mellett, his life and won the paper a Pulitzer. The Sacramento *Bee* fought another Pulitzer campaign for public electric power in California and against corruption in Nevada. Two Portland *Oregonian* reporters won a string of awards for their dogged and often dangerous revelation of scandalous mismanagement of the teamsters' union on the West Coast. KAKE–TV in Wichita, Kansas, revealed in 1973 and 1974 that private interests were working to alter plans for a $3.5 million art museum—apparently to private benefit rather than the public's.

More recently three Detroit *Free Press* reporters—Barbara Stanton, Gene Goltz, and William Serrin—took six weeks and 300 interviews to reveal facts about police and National Guard shootings following a bloody Detroit riot. Emerson Moran and Graham Cox of the Rochester *Times-Union* disclosed lax enforcement of building codes and kickbacks in granting town contracts in a Rochester suburb. WNET, a public TV station in New York City, showed up city financial irregularities and questionable voting solicitations in Brooklyn, a monopoly of the bus market on Manhattan, and the improper rape conviction of a young black. The Santa Ana (California) *Register* broke much of the concealed story about the financing of President Nixon's San Clemente real estate holdings.

Reporting in depth to unearth significant information about matters of public policy has always been a favorite tool of responsible news media. But all too many newsrooms limit themselves to the comfort of safe recording of routine news. Some critics, among them the acid-tongued H. L. Mencken, protest what they consider the apathy of twentieth-century journalism. But Silas Bent, a zealous critic of the press whose book *Newspaper Crusades* recounts many notable campaigns, finds the charge poorly founded. One of

CREDIT WHERE IT'S DUE...

Americans applauded the news media when they brought word of the political and personal corruption in Washington—Watergate, a bribed Vice President, scattergun electronic spying, cynical lying. But, as David Halberstam and others have noted, it wasn't so much "the media" as a handful of reporters or publications that earned the credit. It wasn't "the media" that broke Watergate open—it was two reporters and the backing of their paper, the Washington Post. It wasn't "the media" but two or three loners that defied Washington to publish the Pentagon Papers. Once the breaks were made, "the media" went along. But only a few reporters, almost all from print media, put forth the effort or the daring to achieve what has properly been called "great journalism."

The kudos gained by the Post, the New York Times, the Los Angeles Times, and Time and Newsweek gratifies journalists and encourages more of the same enterprise. (It was one of the causes of swollen enrollment in journalism schools.) But the principal credit could be carried in a handbasket.

the judges of an annual Heywood Broun competition, Dr. Ralph D. Casey, then director of the Minnesota School of Journalism, commented that reading the nearly 100 entries gave him "renewed confidence in the performance of the working journalist ... "

This kind of news enterprise is not limited to the giants of the news industry or to the printed press, as evidenced by the awards of the Broun, Clapper, Pulitzer, Sigma Delta Chi (now the Society of Professional Journalists), Radio-TV News Directors, and many other state and regional associations. The Case of the Wooden Doors, described later in this chapter, is the accomplishment of a small-city daily committed to aggressive attack on attempts to throttle voices the public ought to hear.

In the early 1970s there was hardly a meeting of newsworkers that did not give time to investigative reporting. It was as much the fad as news interpretation had been a generation earlier. Like interpretation, it is sure to hold high news media priority.

Reporting is not the only journalistic weapon to serve public purpose. The editorial pages, which bring interpretation and sometimes moral reflection to the support of the news columns, often give the final thrust to the crusading lance. Some editorial-page staffs have investigative reporters assigned directly to them, a result of the knowledge that editorials without the undergirding of thorough fact-gathering have not won many battles.

Two kinds of investigative reporting   A California editor, speaking before a news conference at Stanford University, distinguished between two species of investigative reporting:

> The cases of exposure of corruption in public office. These are the more dramatic cases.
> The cases of solid community-interest investigative reporting that lead to

progressive action. These justify the existence of the news medium and its championing of the public's right to know so that it can act informedly.

Not all "meritorious public service" by newspapers or broadcasters is linked to crime and corruption. Many media have waged campaigns to persuade their publics to new points of view, to support improved community sanitation or protection of minority rights, to bolster public economy, morale, or social well-being. A Pulitzer Prize went to the Bismarck (North Dakota) *Tribune* for a sober series of reportorial and editorial articles that aided a drought-stricken community to pull itself up by its own bootstraps.

LOOK-AHEAD REPORTING

A common criticism of the press is that most of its reporting is ex post facto— reporting that tells about events after they become history. "Why not," say the critics, "dig out the causes of disaster in time to prevent it?" Pinpointing social, economic, or political trends before they crystallize into bonanza or catastrophe takes time, money, and often manpower. But that's what investigative reporting is all about.

Two reporters for the Philadelphia Inquirer, *Donald L. Bartlett and James B. Steele, saw the 1973 oil-and-energy crisis coming and warned the public about it. Both experienced investigative reporters, they noted in early 1973 that "the five American oil giants" were "pumping their capital abroad and slackening their productive efforts in the U. S." Their editor, Gene Roberts, gave them the green light. Their series of stories began, in July, to report that: oil firms were forecasting shortages at home and building up supplies abroad; similar "crises" had occurred before, each time disappearing to the profit of the oil industry; stockpiles in America were the biggest in history; enough foreign oil was coming in to meet current demands; tanker sailings from Arab countries (which had embargoed oil to the U. S.) increased in the final months of 1973.*

The Inquirer's *revelations did not reverse panic or price rise in U. S. Perhaps if more American media had paid attention to them, the oil crisis of 1974 might have been another story.*

How is investigative reporting different?   No new techniques of reporting had to be invented for this arm of news practice. It differs from day-by-day legwork not in methods but rather in the circumstances that surround it: the story tip or news concept may be obscure rather than easy to see; the reporting itself demands more patience, perseverance, and often imagination than everyday fact-gathering; the reporter is likely to meet roadblocks and somtimes personal peril. And the deadline may be not tomorrow but months in the future.

The reportorial techniques of the investigative reporter, however, must be sharpened not alone by experience but also by the polish that comes from thoughtful analysis of experience. One of America's most successful investigative reporters, Clark Mollenhoff of the Cowles newspapers, developed a checklist for use by reporters digging into local governmental practices. The list shows, first, "some common evils found in local government"—payroll padding, false billing, misuse of expense accounts, nepotism, and the like; then the principal city and county agencies to be checked, with the kinds of questions to be asked of each; then sources for personal information about news figures. Few reporters systematize their procedures so carefully, but Mollenhoff's orderly methods are similar to guides prepared by other newsmen. Here are the principal suggestions derived from a survey among large-city newspapers (reported in the *A.S.N.E. Bulletin*, No. 506, March 1, 1967):

1. *Evaluate tips carefully.* Make sure there is "something worth going after"; don't be misled by tipsters with axes to grind; do enough preliminary investigation to avoid waste of time and money in a fruitless cause.

2. *Pick the right reporter.* Often the veteran "who can ask a direct question without flinching" or the specialist with expertise is the right choice. But one newspaper selected two young reporters with almost no experience to do a series on radical left- and right-wing organizations. Sometimes a black reporter can get into places nobody else can go; sometimes a woman can do what a man can't (or vice versa). The Kansas City *Star* plan is to "turn loose one reporter each month" to work on special projects. The St. Louis *Post-Dispatch* holds that "virtually everyone on the staff is an investigative reporter." Good reporting is good reporting.

3. *Investigative reporting needs full support.* It is costly and slowmoving. Months may pass without a line of publishable copy. The St. Petersburg *Times* sent a man to Brazil as part of an investigation; the *Post-Dispatch* sent one to Turkey on what turned out to be a false lead. The same paper offered $20,000 to an informer (thought most papers' policies stop short of paying informers).

Investigative reporting is heavily directed toward revelation of bribery, graft, error, deceit, or mere incompetence in public places. The seed from which such reporting grows is hard to identify, since one of its prime characteristics is that it is hidden. The initial hunch may turn out to be sugar and cream on the surface; it becomes significant only when a discriminating eye perceives that its true color is mud or a murky purple. It is not news that a city councilman has bought a car, but when three county commissioners who voted in favor of the glossy new stadium appear with glossy new Cadillacs, it bears looking into.

Clifton Daniel, as managing editor of the New York *Times*, pointed out that the increased investigative reporting of the *Times* in recent years has been concerned largely with social, economic, or political trends and developments. Often a reporter, or a team of reporters, is released from other duties to give maximum attention to an investigation. It is common, however, for the reporter to carry his search for hidden answers along with regular work. "You just have to keep everlastingly at it," explains the reporter in the Wooden Doors case (page 343). "You do a little now, and a little tomorrow. Sometimes you think you're getting nowhere. But you keep plugging, working plenty of nights and weekends that don't show on your overtime card, and eventually, if you juggle the pieces often enough, you find that they start fitting together."

HOW INVESTIGATIVE REPORTING WORKS

Team investigation   Investigative reporting by two or more newsworkers has become fairly common in the 1970s. It is true that teams for years have been assigned to specific news problems. The New York *Times* used teams often for in-depth reporting in the 1950s on such subjects as segregation in eighteen southern states, the extent of Eisenhower support in 1956, Middle East tensions and danger spots. Usually such assignments were opportunistic: problem areas presented themselves and reporters dug into them. The new attack is the organization of teams whose permanent assignment is investigative reporting. Only a few newspapers and broadcasters have gone beyond the identification of one or two reporters solely for such tasks. But the Long Island newspaper *Newsday*, under the guidance of Pulitzer Prize-winner Robert W. Greene, established in the early 1970s a "projects department" with a sociological investigative team to "probe the root causes of suburban concerns, such as justice, housing, and drug use." *Newsday's* earlier success in revealing political graft and corruption on Long Island served as a model. *Quill* magazine (February, 1974) described the team's assignment:

> In theory, the team could function in a variety of ways. Employing *Newsday* experts in the fields of medicine, religion, minority affairs, media, consumer affairs, education, environment, politics, courts, and police, as well as general assignment reporters, it could take a look at a group—for example, Puerto Ricans on Long Island—and assess their problems, needs, and accomplishments. It could use those same specialists to dissect a community and put it under a journalistic microscope.

Other journalistic investigations by reporter-groups have made press history. A joint team from the Chicago *Daily News* and the St. Louis *Post-Dispatch* exposed corruption involving newsmen who were getting illicit income direct from the Illinois capital. The work of a three-reporter team in Detroit, two reporters in Philadelphia, and others is cited in this chapter. Two-name bylines appear often in the Washington *Post*; three top reporters spent three months on "juvenile justice" for the Minneapolis *Tribune*. But investigative reporting has largely been individual response to an unplanned news impulse.

Broken nose   Before Gene Goltz went to the Detroit *Free Press*, he was a suburban reporter for the Houston *Post*. In addition to being an experienced newsman, he was also an accountant. His knowledge of financial procedures helped him to scent irregularities in the municipal finances of one of the suburbs on his beat. After six months he started investigation of rumors that six million dollars from a bond issue had been spent in curious ways. For half a year he ran into refusals to let him see records that were legally public, denials of irregularities, secret meetings of officials, and finally threats. But at length he collected enough information to assure him and his city editor that misbehavior existed.

His first stories told of no illegality, but they triggered responses from many sources—midnight telephone calls, anonymous voices—that opened new avenues of investigation. One led to a major investment firm which, Goltz was able to prove, had received a 2 percent commission for handling city bond sales (four times the usual rate) and had kicked half of it back to city officials. Others developed information that mayor, councilmen, and others had paid themselves illegal fees.

And one avenue led Goltz to an encounter with the suburban police commissioner, whose furious punch broke his nose.

Eventually, though Goltz was warned that he better stay away, though his wife's safety was repeatedly threatened, though the citizens of the suburb were reluctant to believe the stories the *Post* printed, the campaign won out A grand jury indicted city officials. The voters, finally convinced, cleaned house. Other communities in the area reexamined their financial procedures and their public records laws.

And the *Post* and Goltz got an armful of prizes—the Broun, a Pulitzer, a National Headliner.

These prizes were won through the use of the classic tools of investigative reporting: keen observation; patient, tireless digging; persistence over weeks and months (grand jury indictments came a full year after the first story appeared); courage (and, Goltz says, a wife who can take punishment). One of the truisms the campaign reiterated was that many sources knew the facts that Goltz worked so hard to find, but that to open mouths it took the public knowledge that a reporter and his paper were providing.

The Case of the Wooden Doors   Aggressive investigative reporting by the East St. Louis (Illinois) *Journal*, a small-city daily, is described by Bruce Kipp, who carried most of the load. His account:

I was fresh on the school beat, knew no one, and found school officials close-mouthed and distrustful. The district was building a new senior high school under contracts adding up to nearly 4 million dollars. Suspicious of a number of "change orders" on the job, my editor, Thomas Duffy, asked me to work up a complete tabulation of the costs. We found that these change orders altered original specifications so as to boost the cost to the school district by more than $150,000. Among them was an order calling for substitution of hollow wooden doors for the steel doors originally specified, at an added cost of $68,455. This looked odd to me. I called the structural engineer to ask about it. He defended the change and the added cost mightily (and 10 minutes later appeared in the newsroom for no apparent reason other than to see what I looked like).

We printed our compilation of construction costs and sat tight, but there was no immediate reaction other than that in the breast of the structural engineer.

About six months passed. We thought of using our own money to get an outside audit of the school district's construction program, but the plan fell through. I kept those doors in mind, however, and checked their costs with a lumber dealer, an outside architect, and others. This information was enough for Duffy to give me the go-ahead.

It took two weeks of cost checking to make sure we were not wasting time. The powers-that-be always have enemies. Of these one who was most helpful was an architect hired on the job and later replaced. We located him by long-distance telephone in Lincoln, Nebraska.

When we felt we were well grounded about the costs and quality of wooden, steel, and aluminum doors, as well as door frames and hardware, it was time to approach the principals.

The first approach was made to the prime architect. I considered him evasive, but truthful. He said the general contractor was the man to see.

The general contractor furnished explanations, but no concrete figures. He did supply the name of a kind of middle man who had dealt in one capacity or another with all the change-order items.

After checking into facts about this middle man, I went to the general contractor again, this time with a witness. He repeated essentially the information he had supplied before.

Then I went to the middle man, his former employer, and the head of the local lumber company which supplied the change-order items to the contractor; from them I obtained the names of several distributors. Included among those I approached was a school board member whose name came up repeatedly.

We now wrote our story, letting all the conflicting statements about door costs and the change orders speak for themselves, without attempting to evaluate them. We wrote a separate story about the middle man, who was dealing in the wooden doors shortly after giving up an attempt to sell competitive steel doors to the high school.

We roughed out a cost sheet to show that the taxpayer was paying $240 for each of the replacement doors, installed. The manufacturer of the doors regarded a price anything like that as "crazy."

We didn't stop with the initial stories. Duffy, who was more than cooperative all along and contributed a great deal of the thinking, worked up a separate door cost story from a supplier's catalog. Later, to add strength to the investigation and show we weren't the only ones interested, we induced the St. Clair County Taxpayers Association, an independent private agency, to come up with something approaching an exact cost analysis.

Two investigations were launched by official agencies, one by the state superintendent of public instruction and the other by the school board. Both resulted in whitewashes.

We kept after statements from the contractor, the school board, and others mixed up in it. We twice published mug shots of the board and other figures in the case with lines to the effect that "these men refuse to tell the public the public's business."

Finally the state's attorney, who had meanwhile received an anonymous letter about alleged fee-splitting, put the door issue before a grand jury. We were instrumental in getting a key witness to the state's attorney. Through our assortment of school administration "enemies," we were able to locate this witness, who lived beyond Illinois subpoena power in Missouri, when he came to Illinois one Sunday.

The grand jury handed down two indictments, one for perjury against the general contractor and one for malfeasance against a school board member.

Other examples   WNEW-TV in New York City filmed scenes at a Bronx subway yard of employees drinking beer, playing cards, reading, sleeping, fixing their automobiles—all on company time, for much of which they collected overtime pay.

Mike Wallace and the CBS-TV magazine-format show called "60 Minutes," thanks to a lot of tough reporting, revealed a phony "most decorated Korean War soldier" and his phony charges against superior officers—after the man had for two years fooled the New York *Times*, the Dick Cavett television show, a lot of other news media, and apparently the United States Army.

Two Philadelphia *Inquirer* reporters used computer research (and 9,618 punched cards from court records) to disclose inequities in the city's criminal justice system.

Jean Heller of the Associated Press disclosed that the U. S. Public Health Service had used Black syphilis victims as guinea pigs.

The Omaha *Sun* newspapers, through exploration of federal records and persistent on-the-scene reporting, revealed that the Boys Town Home for youngsters had a net worth of more than $200 million dollars and an enormous income from its annual solicitations.

These examples testify that investigative reporting can be carried on in the smallest orbit. Curiosity is worth more than a bank account, and energy and patience more than a platoon of assistants.

Consumer reporting   Protection of the consumer has become a newspaper and broadcasting phenomenon in response to the work of Ralph Nader, local and state consumer service agencies, ombudsmen, and the consumers themselves. Critics say the media should have seen the need coming and anticipated it; few did.

An elaborate effort in consumer reporting was initiated by the Minneapolis *Star* in 1971. The *Star*, an afternoon paper with heavy home delivery (which means a retail-buying audience and copious retail advertising), put a team of three seasoned reporters to work on the project. One of the results was a twenty-six-week series called "Your Dollar's Worth," feature stories and charts that often took more than a full page of space to show comparative prices of everything from toothbrushes to ice cream, gasoline, and liquor by drink or bottle. The series proved both informative and un-expectedly magnetic as a circulation and advertising attraction. An article comparing prices and quality of hamburger in some twenty groceries and meat markets—one-room neighborhood stores to supermarkets—brought the heaviest reader-response the *Star* had ever experienced.

The reporting team commented:

> Minneapolis is a pretty clean city in politics and government . . . but the consumer rip-offs are as great as anywhere else.
>
> Management made a major commitment to the project. It took a lot of time and money. But we were never told, "You can't print that." In one piece we reported that the city's biggest department store had the most expensive eye-glasses in town, and the lousiest.
>
> We worked hard to be totally fair. We weren't editorializing, just reporting. No consumer has the time to go to 20 drug stores to make a good buy of a bottle of aspirin. We told him where he'd buy best.
>
> Since Watergate, investigative reporting has a better public image than it used to have. It's become respectable.

Infiltration reporting   An investigative reporting assignment that developed unexpected overtones was carried out by two staff members of the Washington *News*. A reporter, Clare Crawford, attended a meeting of a Maryland White Citizens Council chapter. Her identity unsuspected, she was elected recording secretary; her lawyer husband was made the Council's legal ad-viser. Another *News* reporter joined; soon other friends came along. Their group gained control. They persuaded national headquarters to bar the gen-uine segregationists from the chapter and ended up by affiliating it with CORE, the Congress of Racial Equality.

This comedy ended as a comedy. But it didn't face up to the ethical quan-dary posed by this reportorial method. Two Philadelphia *Bulletin* reporters employed such infiltration tactics as reporters rather than as social activists. They joined a far-left and a far-right organization, concealing their newspaper identification. Unrecognized after a series of meetings, they wrote a de-scriptive series called "The Left and the Right—the View from Within." The series was described by two of the leftist group's members as "pretty in-nocuous" but "quite fair and accurate." But they also offered critical views. "Was it absolutely necessary for you to infiltrate secretly?" asked one. "We wouldn't have let them in if we had known," said the other.

The reporters, in a thoughtful commentary later, concluded that their results justified their tactics. They quoted "Areopagitica," John Milton's historic 1644 plea for press freedom; they pointed out that the reporter whose identity is not known is the uninhibited reporter, that he has no worry about offending news sources, that he has the clandestine privilege to see and hear news figures when they are off guard. But they also said:

The moral issue posed by infiltration journalism is not unlike the free press–fair trial controversy, and it is just as difficult to resolve. In abstract terms, the public's right (or need) to know is pitted against the person's right to privacy.... The two groups were political in nature and vociferous in tactics.... [Their] internal operations were unknown ... to the general public they were trying to influence. By maintaining a shield of privacy while seeking publicity, they had been in a sense deceiving the public....

They went on, however, to show their uneasiness with infiltration tactics:

To say there are circumstances in which infiltration journalism can be morally justified, however, is not to say it can't be abused. When it is, the quality of the finished product is likely to be small.

The disagreement on this difficult question is a constant. In 1973 a Houston *Chronicle* reporter posed falsely as a former friend of a murdered man and was admitted to a postfuneral family gathering. He interviewed the dead man's mother but the *Chronicle* did not use the story. "I just couldn't print that—it's not honest," said the paper's news editor (he called the reporter "inexperienced").

The next year a New York *Daily News* reporter received an award for an investigation that exposed abuses in the Medicaid program he had uncovered while pretending to be a Medicaid recipient. The cases are not comparable, for one was invasion of privacy and the other investigative reporting into public malfeasance. But the contrast is worth noting.

Most reporters appear to believe that the necessity of revealing significant information the public can't get otherwise overbalances any question of impropriety. The end justifies the means, that is, if the end is itself justifiable.

It is not a totally satisfying conclusion.

Projects

1. This chapter says that "no new techniques of reporting have to be invented for this arm of news practice." Write a 500-word definition of investigative reporting, showing what its distinctive features are if they are not "new techniques."

2. Undertake a "consumers' investigation" in your community, one in which you gather enough information about the costs or the quality of a group of consumer products to write a revealing news story. Write the story for a local paper or broadcast station. Remember that your facts may show that there is no cause for consumer concern—not all such stories must uncover misbehavior.

3. Make a list of five or more local areas in which you believe investigative reporting would yield useful results. Develop one or more of the stories.

Related Reading

Columbia Journalism Review:

Laurence I. Barrett, "The Dark Side of Competition," July–August, 1974.

Nat Hentoff, "Lingering Questions," July–August, 1974.

Eugene L. Meyer and Charles Doe, "Infiltration Reporting," Fall, 1966.

"Watergate and the Press," November–December, 1973.

Houston Journalism Review:

Randy Covington and Carole Kneeland, "Newspapers: Chronicle Skunks Post," September, 1973.

CHAPTER TWENTY-ONE

Interpretive reporting

Reporters count how many times an audience applauds a speaker.
Analysts study what gets applause and try to figure out why.

INTERPRETATION, ANALYSIS, BACKGROUND

The aphorism above defines one distinction between news reporting and news interpretation. Though it oversimplifies, the heart of the matter is in it.

Interpretation of the news—clarification of what the news means—is older than investigative reporting. In earliest American journalism the news was reported to mean just what each editor wanted it to mean—he interpreted it to his own taste. Objective reporting changed all that. By the 1930s and the Depression that drove a President out of office, news that was only objective was not good enough. Thoughtful news consumers were asking, "Why didn't we see this coming? What caused it? What will it do to us? Will there be another?"

The first attempts to answer these questions came on the editorial pages. Columnists in print and then commentators on the air became fixtures: Marquis Childs, Raymond Clapper, Walter Lippmann in print; Raymond Gram Swing, Boake Carter, Dorothy Thompson on radio. Day after day such men and women tried to tell a puzzled world why things were happening. Some of them made sense, some only pious nonsense.

However wise they were, news explanation became established. And quickly the personal, subjective kind of opinion-explanation was supplemented by a new kind of commentator who reported the news in context. Men like Elmer Davis and Edward R. Murrow in broadcasting and Erwin D. Canham and James B. Reston in the newspapers developed the technique of news analysis. Murrow explained his view of the distinction between interpretation, or commentary, and analysis:

> News periods should be devoted to giving facts emanating from an established newsgathering source, to giving color in the proper sense of the word, without intruding the views of the analyst.
> The news analyst can very often give light on the meaning of events. The news analyst should not say that they're good or bad, but should analyze their significance in the light of known facts, the results of similar occurrences, and so on.
> He should always be fair. He should give the opinions of various persons, groups, or political parties when these are known, leaving the listener to draw his own conclusions.

Whether analysis could remain objective has been vigorously debated. Some journalists have denied both the possibility and the desirability. "What's important," they have said, "is the opinion about the news that expert knowledge can supply." Eric Sevareid, Murrow's CBS colleague, accepted the Murrow thesis but did not believe complete objectivity is possible.

The continuing dispute led eventually to acceptance of a distinction in somewhat different terms: the distinction between commentary and "background." The first was taken to mean what the word denotes: comment, criticism, and illumination of the news in the light of whatever knowledge and opinion the commentator could bring to it. Thus a departure from full objectivity was reintroduced to news presentation. It was recognized that responsible journalism called for responsible subjective analysis, always clearly identified for what it is and from whom it comes.

Background, in contrast, is the factual material underlying or surrounding or affecting a news event, presented on its own merits and solely with the purpose of helping the news consumer to place the event in appropriate context. This is no more a novelty than the presentation of comment editorials. But it has received recognition as being essential to comprehension of the news. The broadcast listener, if he were to understand the process called impeachment, had to know what impeachment is. The reader learning from a newspaper column that air pollution in his city has doubled in the last ten years must be informed why it happened and what exactly air pollution is, if he is to decide about moving to another state. Relevant background does not evaluate meaning for the consumer, but it frees him to provide the evaluation himself.

Awareness of the need for materials of these kinds has led to development of many devices, beyond those clearly labeled commentary or opinion, to illuminate complexity and obscurity in the news. Among them:

- The insertion of background paragraphs to provide information against which a news development may be laid. The background precede, an explanatory paragraph at the head of a story, is one form. Similar paragraphs may be inserted into a story's body, often in parenthesis or in contrasting type.
- The regular use, on the editorial page or elsewhere, of material in a background column. An Ohio paper developed a staff-written column called "Reviewing the News." The London *News Chronicle* provided explanatory material in a column titled "The World This Morning."
- Use of sidebars, often with captions such as "What the News Means," to elaborate complex news developments.
- The use of news interviews in which competent interviewees provide background fact or personal insight.
- The development of weekly "news review" departments. The New York *Times*' "The Week in Review" was one of the first such efforts; scores of papers, and some broadcasters, offer similar material.

REPORTING THAT EXPLAINS

What may be the most fruitful approach of any, however, has been the emphasis on background and explanatory reporting. The phenomenon is not American-owned: the staid *Times* of London, in desperately bad health in the early 1960s, underwent a reshaping that included spending millions of pounds for development of explanatory news. The *Times* set up an eight-reporter research team for no other purpose than to "give the fullest explanation of a news event as soon as they can" (sometimes "soon" meant several weeks).

Background and interpretive reporting in America means reporting in context, either in spot news or in sidebars and folo stories. The term *background* is generally taken to mean additional facts, presented without comment; interpretive reporting generally means presentation of news facts with the writer's evaluations and explanations. It is accepted practice that the interpretive story must appear under a by-line, so that the consumer knows whom to credit (and, sometimes, whether to credit him). It is what a professor at the Wisconsin School of Journalism, Harold L. Nelson, calls "the journalism of cause-and-effect relationship." Nelson suggests that this kind of reporting says "the causes that led to this news event were such-and-such..." or "the results are likely to be thus-and-so."

Thoughtful newsworkers do not delude themselves into thinking the tool is used enough. Warnings to newspapers come from the faithful audiences of *Time, Newsweek, U. S. News & World Report,* and the *National Observer,* from the penetrating current-events analyses of *Harper's,* the *Atlantic, Sat-*

INTERPRETATION VS. OPINION

"What," asks the perplexed journalism student, "is the difference between news interpretation and editorializing?"

A fair question, and one not easy to answer because sometimes there is no difference. The purpose of either may be only to clarify complexity. But some distinctions can be discerned:

1. The purpose of interpretive reporting, honestly used, is just what the term implies—adding to understanding. If it is used to lead or shape opinion or to state conclusions, it departs from its defined purpose. Editorials may serve many purposes: clarification, illumination, opinion-shaping, incitement to action, entertainment.

2. The editorial is usually institutional—the voice of the newspaper or broadcasting station as an institution. The interpretive news story represents only its writer.

3. Editorials are anonymous. The interpretive reporter is usually identified; if his story presents opinion, its source ought to be known.

Lester Markel, for years an associate editor of the New York Times, once said it more briefly when he was asked the question above. The question, he said, was a fact. Saying why the question was asked would be interpretation. Saying whether the interpretation was correct would be opinion.

---

urday *Review/World,* and such limited-circulation publications as the *Center Magazine* and *Society.* News backgrounding, from the national networks (including the public, noncommercial networks) and in slowly increasing volume from local stations, is building audiences.

Background stories   The classic backgrounder is the story that presents facts to explain facts. It takes off from a current news event and uses either straight fact or relevant opinions to give its consumer a setting into which to fit the event. You have seen, in this book, one such story: the combination of news interview and spot reporting about the gasoline shortage in Chapter 16. That story is a backgrounder all the way, though in form it fits other categories; it first reports competent opinion to help the troubled motorist understand what's happening, then it goes (in paragraph 10) into spot reporting that helps him to see the total issue and how it may affect him.

The backgrounder below is unusual because it paints a broad-scale picture in intimate personal terms: what is happening to one family represents what is happening to thousands. A more conventional story would have talked in gross terms—cubic feet of gas, watt hours of electricity. Here the reporter speaks in the householder's terms: how much electricity one home's TV sets used, how much gas it took to keep a house at 70 degrees for a day.

The alarm clock (3 watts) went off at 6:30 a.m. Tuesday at the Dowell home in Apple Valley.

Michael Dowell, 33, stumbled out of bed, made his way to the dresser where he turned on a lamp (60 watts), and then, still half asleep, headed for the bathroom where he switched on two more lights (60 watts each). He reached for his electric toothbrush (350 watts).

By the time the Dowells shut off the lights that night, they had consumed about 29,000 watt hours of electrical energy, a Minneapolis *Star* survey found.

That meant that about 29 pounds of coal were burned Tuesday by Northern States Power Co. (NSP) to keep the Dowells' seven-room suburban home supplied with electricity. Coal is the fuel NSP uses most to produce electricity. Other NSP sources include nuclear and hydroelectric power plants.

Although the Dowells were above NSP average Tuesday for residential use —19,000 watt hours is about the daily norm—Judy Dowell said she is a vigilant housewife. She has gone so far as to cut her sons' allowances whenever she finds that they've left light bulbs on unnecessarily.

Mrs. Dowell said she thought President Nixon's speech on the energy crisis "was the best he ever made—and that's not saying much."

Since the Nixon talk, Mrs. Dowell has put on a sweater and lowered the house temperature 2 degrees to 70.

But despite what Mrs. Dowell describes as her systematic effort to cut down electrical use, the kilowatts added up rapidly in Tuesday's survey. A kilowatt, 1,000 watts, takes about a pound of Illinois coal to produce, according to NSP.

A kilowatt costs the homeowner about 3 cents, NSP says.

The Dowells—Mike and Judy and sons, Kevin, 8, and Kenny, 11—turned on 32 light bulbs Tuesday; they used 43 hours and 34 minutes of electric light. The light fixtures that had more than one bulb pushed the number of watt hours up quickly.

But the Dowells' basic appliances consumed the largest chunk of electricity.

The electric stove was used three times Tuesday: a small burner for coffee at breakfast, two burners at lunch, and one burner and the oven at dinnertime.

It added up to about 7,000 watt hours, or about seven pounds of coal.

Dowell, an advertising manager at Fuller Laboratories in Eden Prairie, needed a shirt ironed after he showered Tuesday morning. The iron used up about 13 watt hours, or about two-tenths of an ounce of coal.

But the electrical washer and dryer were used twice Tuesday, running for about two hours, and requiring more than 5,000 watt hours —five pounds of coal.

The Dowells are not wanting for luxury electrical devices. They have an electric can opener, knife, broom, rotisserie and broiler, fondue, frying pan and water pic. But Mrs. Dowell turned none of them on Tuesday, and said she rarely uses them.

The luxury, predictably, that got the most wear Tuesday was the 23-inch color television set. TV was on for about 11 hours.

It was turned on at 7:25 a.m. for kiddie cartoons, and at midday was switched on again by Mrs. Dowell, who likes to watch soap operas.

Later in the afternoon the TV droned in the background and then on into the evening until Mike and Judy retired to their bedroom about 10:30 p.m. They turned on the black-and-white 11-inch model, turned it off at 1 a.m.

The color TV gobbled up about 3,330 watt hours Tuesday, and the black and white used 294 more—about three and a half pounds of coal.

Meanwhile, the Dowells were consuming gas, too. Mrs. Dowell reduced the temperature 4 degrees to 68 immediately after the President's speech, but pushed it back up to 70 because she said it was too cold. The Dowells' home Tuesday used approximately 700 cubic feet of natural gas, according to an NSP estimate.

And Mike Dowell burned more than two gallons of gasoline Tuesday driving his Volkswagen to and from work.

As she sat in her living room Tuesday talking about the energy crisis, Mrs. Dowell admitted that she is skeptical.

"When I see the skyscrapers at night with lights on in every single floor, I just can't take the crisis seriously," Mrs. Dowell said.[1]

The readers of this story finished it with a much better understanding of just what they do with the energy they buy. Readers of this book might have the same experience.

A background story of a different sort was one "from our wire services"

[1] Copyright © 1973 by the Minneapolis *Star*. Reprinted by permission.

compiled by a Midwest paper at the time of the Patricia Hearst kidnapping in early 1974. By pulling together information from many sources, the copydesk gave answers to some of the readers' questions. The story sought to answer the question in its lead, "What is the Symbionese Liberation Army?" and to throw light on other facets of the bizarre crime: how the "army" grew out of radical-ideologist meetings at a California prison: the identity of Cinque, then apparently the leader of the kidnappers; how the group changed from intellectual leftism to terrorism; what others were connected with the group; how Cinque was identified and where the nickname came from.

As you were told in Chapter 19, there is no end to the number of backgrounders or explanatory stories that can be developed in complex news situations. This fact was emphasized soon after the revelation of the sexual abuse and murder of more than twenty Texas teen-agers in 1973, when the *Houston Journalism Review*—the forthright critical journal then published by Houston newsworkers—listed some of the questions that local broadcasters and newspapers had *not* answered:

Why have so many teenagers left home for a lifestyle amply supplied with sex and drugs? Why have conventional social services failed to help these youths? What could be done to help them? What do the state and national proposals aimed at helping runaways mean? Would they work? What causes families to break down? What effects do such breakdowns have on children? and what can be done to alleviate these effects?

You might come to two conclusions about such suggestions: first, they are obvious and sometimes oversimplified, but nevertheless worth thought and in some cases follow-up; second, almost every one of the techniques for story development described in the preceding chapters—but especially interviews of various kinds—could grow out of them. There were many background or interpretive stories following a Nixon "Watergate explanation" speech (see Chapter 16): for example, a Chicago *Tribune* news analysis expressed the writer's opinion that "Nixon offered little to those who hoped for the President's version," calling the speech "imprecise" and "a delicate balance of self-defense and attrition": the New York *Times* collected opinions about the speech from several cabinet members, Ralph Nader, a labor leader, a left-wing commentator, some political leaders, and the President's former director of communications; a *Christian Science Monitor* story combined the *Tribune* and the *Times* methods; an Associated Press "Background of the News" dispatch chose a single theme—"President Nixon's survival strategy is built in belief that Americans ... are willing to forgive" and supported it with quotations from the speech; and the London *Times* interpretation had as its closing point the writer's opinion that Americans would not accept Nixon's wish that "Watergate be forgotten."

Portrait of a life-style   "The Two Worlds of Linda Fitzpatrick," which appeared in the New York *Times* in 1967, is a *tour de force* that fits no single category. It is a news interview, bringing together comments and observations from family and friends on the life and savage death of a teenage girl. It is a backgrounder, with telling detail of facts that underlay the tragic event. It is a human-interest story that needs no embellishment. It is a made story, developed by high reporting skill and extraordinary news imagination. And insofar as it describes a life-style about which most *Times* readers knew little, and makes some of the counterculture impulses and circumstances clear, it is interpretive reporting.

Above all, it is a story whose writing is disciplined when its opportunities for extravagance must have been hard to resist; its accents are those of restraint and implication rather than of visible underscoring. Its structural pattern, not unique but often effective, gives it rhythm and suspense. J. Anthony Lukas, its writer—like George Weller in the story of the undersea appendectomy—makes it all seem easy. That may be the hardest writing task of all.

The windows of Dr. Irving Sklar's reception room at 2 Fifth Avenue looked out across Washington Square. A patient waiting uneasily for the dentist's drill can watch the pigeons circling Stanford White's dignified Washington Arch, the children playing hopscotch on the square's wide walkways and the students walking hand in hand beneath the American elms.

"Certainly we knew the Village; our family dentist is at 2 Fifth Avenue," said Irving Fitzpatrick, the wealthy Greenwich, Conn., spice importer whose daughter, Linda, was found murdered with a hippie friend in an East Village boiler room a week ago yesterday.

Mr. Fitzpatrick spoke during a three-hour interview with his family around the fireplace in the library of their 30-room home a mile from the Greenwich Country Club.

For the Fitzpatricks, "the Village" was the Henry James scene they saw out Dr. Sklar's windows and "those dear little shops" that Mrs. Fitzpatrick and her daughters occasionally visited. ("I didn't even know there was an East Village," Mr. Fitzpatrick said. "I've heard of the Lower East Side, but the East Village?")

But for 18-year-old Linda —at least in the last 10 weeks of her life—the Village was a different scene whose ingredients included crash pads, acid trips, freaking out, psychedelic art, witches, and warlocks.

If the Fitzpatricks' knowledge of the Village stopped at Washington Square, their knowledge of their daughter stopped at the familiar image of a young, talented girl overly impatient to taste the joys of life.

Reality in both cases went far beyond the Fitzpatricks' wildest fears—so far, in fact, that they are still unable to believe what their daughter was going through in her last weeks.

It is perhaps futile to ask which was "the real Linda" —the Linda of Greenwich, Conn., or the Linda of Greenwich Village. For, as The New York Times investigated the two Lindas last week through interviews with her family and with her friends and acquaintances in the Village, it found her a strange mixture of these two worlds, a mixture so tangled that Linda probably did not know in which she belonged.

The last weeks of Linda's life are a source of profound anguish for her parents. The forces at work on young people like Linda are the source of puzzlement for many other parents and of studies by social workers and psychologists, as they seek to understand the thousands of youths who are leaving middle-class homes throughout the country for the "mind expanding drug" scene in places like Greenwich Village.

Until a few months ago, Linda—or "Fitzpoo," as she was known to her family and friends—seemed to be a happy, well-adjusted product of wealthy American suburbia.

"Linda is a well-rounded, fine, healthy girl," her mother, a well-groomed blonde in a high-collared chocolate brown dress, said during the interview in

Greenwich. Throughout the interview Mrs. Fitzpatrick used the present tense in talking of her daughter.

Attended Good Schools

Born in Greenwich, Linda attended the Greenwich Country Day School, where she excelled in athletics. She won a place as center forward on the "Stuyvesant Team," the all-Fairfield County field hockey team, and also gained swimming and riding awards. She went on to the Oldfields School, a four-year college preparatory school in Glencoe, Md.

A blonde tending to pudginess, she never quite matched the striking good looks of her mother, who as Dorothy Ann Rush was a leading model and cover girl in the thirties, or of her elder sister, Cindy.

At country club dances, Linda often sat in the corner and talked with one of her half-brothers; but, apparently more interested in sports and painting than dancing, she never seemed to mind very much.

According to her family, Linda's last summer began normally. In mid-June she returned from Oldfields after an active year during which she was elected art editor of the yearbook. She spent several weeks in Greenwich, then left with the family for a month in Bermuda.

Vacations With Family

"The family always takes its summer vacations together; we always do things as a family," said Mr. Fitzpatrick, a tall, athletic-looking man in a well-tailored gray suit, blue tie, and gold tie-clip. "Sometimes we went to Florida, sometimes to the Antibes, but for the past few summers we've rented a house in Bermuda. This time it was at Paget."

The famiy included seven children—Linda and 9-year-old Melissa ("Missy") from this marriage; Perry, 32; Robert, 30; Cindy, 27, and David, 25, from Mr. Fitzpatrick's first marriage, which ended in divorce, and Cindy from Mrs. Fitzpatrick's first marriage, which also ended in divorce. But this time only Linda and Missy accompanied their parents to Bermuda, while Cindy and her husband joined them later for 10 days.

As the Fitzpatricks remember it, Linda spent "a typical Bermuda vacation" —swimming in the crystal ocean; beach parties on the white sands; hours of painting; occasional shopping expeditions to town.

'The Girl We Knew'

On July 31 the family returned to Greenwich, where Linda spent most of August. The family insists she was "the girl we knew and loved."

They say she spent most of her time painting in the studio in the back of the house. But she found plenty of time for swimming with friends in the large robin's-egg blue pool, playing the piano, and sitting with Missy.

"Linda and Missy were terribly close," their mother said, biting her lip. "Just as close as Cindy and Linda were when they were younger."

If Linda went to New York during August, the family said, it was "just a quick trip in and out—just for the day."

The 'Village' Version

Friends in the Village have a different version of Linda's summer.

"Linda told me she took LSD and smoked grass [marijuana] many times during her stay in Bermuda," recalls Susan Robinson, a small, shy hippie who ran away last May from her home on Cape Code. "She talked a lot about a fellow who gave her a capsule of acid [LSD] down there and how she was going to send him one."

Susan and her husband, David, who live with two cats and posters of Bob Dylan, Timothy Leary, Allen Ginsberg and D. H. Lawrence in a two-room apartment, at 537 East 13th Street, first met Linda when she showed up there some time early in August.

The Robinson apartment served this summer as a "crash pad"—a place where homeless hippies could spent the night or part of the night. Scrawled in pencil on the tin door to the apartment is a sign that reads: "No visitors after midnight unless by appointment please." It is signed with a flower.

"Linda just showed up one evening with a guy named Pigeon," Susan recalls. "She'd just bought Pigeon some acid. We were fooling around and everything. She stayed maybe a couple of hours and then took off.

Flying on Acid

"But we liked each other, and she came back a few nights later with a kid from Boston. She turned him on, too [gave him some LSD]. She was always doing that. She'd come into the city on weekends with $30 or $40 and would buy acid for people who needed some."

David Robinson, a gentle young man with a black D. H. Lawrence beard who works in a brassiere factory, recalls how Linda turned him on on Aug. 22. "We went to this guy who sold us three capsules for $10 apiece," he said. "She put one away to send to the guy in Bermuda, gave me one and took one herself. She was always getting burned [purchasing fake LSD] and that night she kept saying, 'God, I just hope this is good.' We were out in the Square [Tompkins Park] and we dropped it [swallowed it] right there. Forty-five minutes later—around midnight—we were off.

"We walked over to a pad on 11th Street just feeling the surge, then over to Tompkins Park, then to Cooper Union Square, where we had a very good discussion with a drunk. By then we were really flying. She was very, very groovy. At 8 a.m. I came back to the pad to sleep, and Linda took the subway up to Grand Central and got on the train to Greenwich. She must still have been flying when she got home."

That weekend in Greenwich, Mrs. Fitzpatrick was getting Linda ready for school. "We bought her almost an entire new wardrobe," she recalled, "and Linda even agreed to get her hair cut."

For months Mr. Fitzpatrick had complained about Linda's hair, which flowed down over her shoulders, but Linda didn't want to change it. Then at the end of August she agreed. "We went to Saks Fifth Avenue and the hairdresser gave her a kind of Sassoon blunt cut, short and full. She looked so cute and smart. Hardly a hippie thing to do," Mrs. Fitzpatrick said.

The first day of school was only 11 days off when Linda went to New York on Sept. 1. When she returned to Greenwich the next day, she told her mother she didn't want to go back to Oldfields. She wanted to live and paint in the Village.

A Surprise for Family

"We couldn't have been more surprised," Mrs. Fitzpatrick said, fingering her eyeglasses, which hung from a gold pin on her left shoulder.

"Linda said her favorite teacher, who taught English, and his wife, who taught art, weren't coming back. She just adored them— when they went to Europe she just had to send champagne and fruit to the boat —and she couldn't face going back to school if they weren't there.

"What's more, she said there wasn't anything else she could learn about art at Oldfields. They'd already offered to set up a special course for her, but she didn't want more courses. She thought she'd be wasting her time at school."

Mother and daughter talked for nearly two hours that Saturday morning of the Labor Day weekend. Then Mrs. Fitzpatrick told her husband, who at first was determined that Linda should finish school.

Reluctant Consent Given

"But we talked about it with all the family and with friends all through the weekend," Mrs. Fitzpatrick recalls. "Finally, on Sunday night, we gave Linda our reluctant permission, though not our approval." Linda left for New York the next morning and the family never saw her alive again.

"After all," her mother put in, "Linda's whole life was art. She had a burning desire to be something in the art world. I knew how she felt. I wanted to be a dancer or an artist when I was young, too.'

The Fitzpatricks' minds were eased when Linda assured them she had already made respectable living arrangements. "She told us that she was going to live at the Village Plaza Hotel, a very nice hotel on Washington Place, near the university, you know," her mother said.

" 'I'll be perfectly safe, mother,' she kept saying. 'It's a perfectly nice place with a doorman and television.' She said she'd be rooming with a girl named Paula Bush, a 22-year-old receptionist from a good family. That made us feel a lot better."

A Room at 'The Plaza'

The Village Plaza, 79 Washington Place, has no doorman. A flaking sign by the tiny reception desk announces "Television for Rental" amidst a forest of other signs. "No Refunds," "All Rents Must Be Paid in Advance," "No Checks Cashed," "No Outgoing Calls for Transients."

"Sure I remember Linda," said the stooped desk clerk. "But Paula Bush? There wasn't no Paula Bush. It was Paul Bush."

Ruffling through a pile of stained and thumb-marked cards, he came up with one that had Linda Fitzpatrick's name inked at the top in neat Greenwich Country Day School penmanship. Below it in pencil was written: "Paul Bush. Bob Brumberger."

"Yeh," the clerk said. "She moved in here on Sept. 4, Labor Day, with these two hippie guys, Bush and Brumberger. They had room 504. She paid the full month's rent—$120—in advance. Of course, she had lots of other men up there all the time. Anybody off the street—the dirtiest, bearded hippies she could find.

'She Was Different'

"I kept telling her she hadn't ought to act like that. She didn't pay me any attention. But you know she never answered back real snappy like some of the other girls. She was different. She had something —I don't know, class. The day she checked out—oh, it was about Sept. 20—I was out on the steps, and as she left she said, 'I guess I caused you a lot of trouble,' and I said, 'Oh, it wasn't any trouble, really.'"

"You want to see the room? Well, there are some people up there now, but I think it'll be O.K."

The elevator was out of order. The stairs were dark and narrow, heavy with the sweet reek of marijuana. A knock, and the door to 504 swung open. A bearded young man took his place again on the sway-backed double bed that filled half the room. The young man and three girls were plucking chocolates out of a box.

Against one of the light green walls was a peeling gray dresser, with the upper left drawer missing. Scrawled on the mirror above the dresser in what looked like eyebrow pencil was "Tea Heads Forever" (a tea head is a marijuana smoker) and in lighter pencil, "War Is Hell." Red plastic flowers hung from an overhead light fixture. The bathroom, directly across the hall, was shared with four other rooms.

"Would you like to see Linda's room?" her mother asked, leading the way up the thickly carpeted stair-

way. "That used to be her room," she said, pointing into an airy bedroom with a white, canopied bed, "until she began playing all those records teen-agers play these days and she asked to move upstairs so she could make all the noise she wanted."

On the third floor Mrs. Fitzpatrick opened the red curtains in the large room. "Red and white are Linda's favorite colors; she thinks they're gay," Mrs. Fitzpatrick said, taking in the red and white striped wallpaper, the twin beds with red bedspreads, the red pillow with white lettering: "Decisions, Decisions, Decisions."

Orange flashed here and there—in the orange and black tiger on the bed ("that's for her father's college, Princeton; we're a Princeton family") and in the orange "Gs" framed on the wall, athletic awards from Greenwich Country Day School.

On the shelves, between a ceramic collie and a glass Bambi, were Edith Hamilton's "The Greek Way" and Agatha Christie's "Murder at Hazelmoor." Nearby was a stack of records, among them Eddie Fisher's "Tonight" and Joey Dee's "Peppermint Twist." In the bright bathroom hung blue and red ribbons from the Oldfields Horse Show and the Greenwich Riding Association Show.

"As you can see, she was such a nice, outgoing, happy girl," her mother said. "If anything's changed, it's changed awfully fast."

Downstairs again, over ginger ale and brownies that Cindy brought in from the kitchen, the Fitzpatricks said they had been reassured about Linda's life in the Village because she said

she had a job making posters for "Poster Bazaar" at $80 a week.

"Later she called and said she'd switched to a place called Imports, Ltd., for $85 a week and was making posters on weekends. She sounded so excited and happy," Mrs. Fitzpatrick recalled.

Nobody The Times interviewed had heard of a store called Poster Bazaar. At 177 Macdougal Street is a shop called Fred Leighton's Mexican Imports, Ltd., where, the records show, Linda worked for $2 an hour selling dresses for three days —Sept. 11, 12 and 13. On the third day she was discharged.

"She was aways coming in late, and they just got fed up with her," a salesgirl said. Although Linda was given a week's notice, she left on Sept. 14 for a "doctor's appointment" and never came back.

A Try at Panhandling

Before she left, she asked the manager not to tell her parents she had been discharged, if they called. The manager said the parents did not call after Linda left, although there had been one call while she was working there.

David Robinson said Linda supported herself from then on by "panhanding" on Washington Square. "She was pretty good at it," he said. "She always got enough to eat."

Linda may have had some money left over from what her mother gave her before she left ("I gave her something," Mrs. Fitzpatrick said. "I thought she was going to be a career girl"), although she never had very much those last weeks.

Yet, David recalls, Linda frequently talked about

making big money. "She had a thing about money. Once she told me she wanted to get a job with Hallmark cards drawing those little cartoons. She said she'd make $40,000 a year, rent a big apartment on the Upper East Side and then invite all her hippie friends up there."

Experimenting With Art

"We're a great card-exchanging family," Cindy said. "Whenever the occasion arose—birthdays, holidays, illnesses—Linda would make up her own cards and illustrate them with cute little pictures of people and animals."

From a pile on the hall table, Cindy picked out a card with a picture of a girl and an inked inscription, "Please get well 'cause I miss ya, love Linda XOX." In the same pile was a Paris street scene in pastels, two forest scenes made with oils rolled with a Coke bottle, several other gentle landscapes. "Linda was experimenting with all sorts of paints and techniques," Cindy said.

"You want to see some of the paintings she did down here?" asked Susan Robinson, as she went to a pile of papers in the corner and came back with five ink drawings on big white sheets from a sketching pad.

The drawings were in the surrealistic style of modern psychedelic art: distorted women's faces, particularly heavily lidded eyes, dragons, devils, all hidden in a thick jungle of flowers; leaves and vines, interspersed with phrases in psychedelic script like "Forever the Mind," "Flyin High," "Tomorrow Will Come."

"Linda was never terribly

boy crazy," her mother said. "She was very shy. When a boy got interested in her, she'd almost always lose interest in him. She got a proposal in August from a very nice boy from Arizona. She told me, 'He's very nice and I like him, but he's just too anxious.' The boy sent flowers for the funeral. That was thoughtful."

The Robinsons and her other friends in the Village said there were always men in Linda's life there: first Pigeon, then the boy from Boston, then Paul Bush.

Bush, the 19-year-old son of a Holly, Mich., television repairman, is described by those who knew him here as "a real drifter, a way-out hippie." He carried a live lizard named Lyndon on a string around his neck. Bush, who says he left New York on Oct. 4, was interviewed by telephone in San Francisco yesterday.

The Nonexistent 'Paula'

"I met Linda at the Robinsons about Aug. 18—a few days after I got to town," he recalls. "We wandered around together. She said her parents bugged her, always hollered at her ... So I said I'd get a pad with her and Brumberger, this kid from New Jersey.

"She said she'd tell her parents she was living with a girl named Paula Bush, because she didn't want them to know she was living with a man. That was O.K. with me. I only stayed about a week anyway, and Brumberger even less. Then she brought in some other guy. I don't know who he was, except he was tall with long hair and a beard."

This may have been Ed, a tall hippie, whom the Robinsons saw with Linda several times in mid-Sep-

tember. Later came James L. (Groovy) Hutchinson, the man with whom she was killed last week.

Toward the end of September, Susan Robinson says, Linda told her she feared she was pregnant. "She was very worried about the effect of LSD on the baby, and since I was pregnant, too, we talked about it for quite a while."

Father Inclined to Doubt

"I don't believe Linda really had anything to do with the hippies," her father said. "I remember during August we were in this room watching a C.B.S. special about the San Francisco hippies. I expressed my abhorrence for the whole thing, and her comments were much like mine. I don't believe she was attracted to them."

However, Linda's half-brother, Perry, recalls that during August Mr. Fitzpatrick also read a story about Galahad, a New York hippie leader, and expressed his "disdain" for him. Linda mentioned casually that she had met Galahad and that she understood he was "helping people," but her father let the remark pass, apparently considering it of no significance.

Her friends say Linda was fascinated by the scene in the Haight-Ashbury section of San Francisco. In late September she apparently visited there.

Susan Robinson recalls that she did not see Linda for some time in late September and that suddenly, on Oct. 1, Linda turned up at her pad and said she had been to Haight-Ashbury. "She said she stayed out there only two days and was very disappointed; that it was a really bad scene; that everybody was on speed [a powerful drug called methadrine]. She said she got out and drove back."

In the first week of October, the Fitzpatricks got a postcard postmarked Knightstown, Ind., a small town 30 miles east of Indianapolis. Mrs. Fitzpatrick did not want to show the card to a visitor because "it was the last thing I've got which Linda touched." But she said it read roughly: "I'm on my way to see Bob [her brother, who is a Los Angeles lawyer]. Offered a good job painting posters in Berkeley. I love you. I will send you a poster. Love, Linda."

Also in the first week of October a girl who identified herself as Linda telephoned her brother's office in Los Angeles but was told he was in San Francisco. She never called back.

When Linda saw Susan on Oct. 1 she told her she had met two warlocks, or male witches, in California and had driven back with them.

"This didn't surprise me," Susan said. "Linda told me several times she was a witch. She said she had discovered this one day when she was sitting on a beach and wished she had some money. Three dollar bills floated down from heaven.

"Then she looked down the beach and thought how empty it was and wished there was someone there. She said a man suddenly appeared. She was always talking about her supernatural powers. Once she was walking on a street in the Village with this girl Judy, and she stumbled over a broom. 'Oh,' she told Judy, 'this is my lucky day. Now I can fly away.'"

"Linda told me she met these two warlocks out there and that they could snap their fingers and make light bulbs pop. She said one of the warlocks took her mind apart and scattered it all over the room and then put it together again. Ever since, she said, she felt the warlock owned her."

'That's Not True'

"One of the newspapers said Linda was interested in Buddhism and Hinduism and all that supernatural stuff," Cindy said. "That's not true at all. I don't think she ever even knew what it was."

Last Friday a self-styled warlock who said he was one of the two who drove Linda back to New York was interviewed in the Village. The warlock, who called himself "Pepsi," is in his late 20's, with long, sandy hair, a scruffy beard, heavily tattooed forearms, wire-rim glasses, and long suede Indian boots.

"My buddy and I ran into Linda in a club in Indianapolis called the Glory Hole," Pepsi said. "We took Linda along. You could see right away she was a real meth monster—that's my name for a speed freak, somebody hooked on speed.

"We were two days driving back. We got in on Oct. 1, and she put up with me and my buddy in this pad on Avenue B. She was supposed to keep it clean, but all she ever did all day was sit around. She had this real weird imagination, but she was like talking in smaller and smaller circles. She was supposed to be this great artist, but it wasn't much good. It was just teeny bopper stuff— drawing one curving line, then embellishing it.

'A Lot of Potential'

"It sounds like I'm knocking her. I'm not. She was a good kid, if she hadn't been so freaked out on meth. She had a lot of, what do you call it—potential. Sometimes she was a lot of fun to be with. We took her on a couple of spiritual seances, and we went out on the Staten Island Ferry one day at dawn and surfing once on Long Island."

Pepsi saw Linda at 10 p.m. Saturday, Oct. 8, standing in front of the Cave on Avenue A with Groovy. She said she'd taken a grain and a half of speed and was "high." Three hours later she and Groovy were dead—their nude bodies stretched out on the boiler room floor, their heads shattered by bricks. The police have charged two men with the murders and are continuing their investigation.

"It's too late for the whole thing to do us much good," her brother Perry said on Saturday after he had been told of her life in the Village. "But maybe somebody else can learn something from it."[2]

Projects

1. Write an essay defining the similarities and differences among follow-up reporting, enterprise reporting, investigative reporting, background reporting and interpretive reporting.

[2] Copyright © 1967 by The New York Times Company. Reprinted by permission.

2. Select a current event of major interest in your community (or, if you think yourself well versed in it, an event in state or national politics or social policy) and write a background story for a local medium—a story with the purpose of telling its audience strictly what it needs to know to place the topic in its significant relationships.

3. On the same topic, write an interpretive story with comments by experts. If you are not competent to provide opinion on the event yourself, use the news-interview technique to gain and present others' opinions.

4. Write a combination story—one that reports what's new in a current situation and at the same time presents qualified opinion about it. Make sure that the distinction between the one and the other will always be clear to your reader.

CHAPTER TWENTY-TWO

The reporter as specialist

When I hire a sportswriter, I hire a reporter. He doesn't have to be a sports expert. First of all he must have mastered the craft of reporting—preferably in a city room, on the police beat, covering schools and Rotary Clubs and the suburbs. Second, he has to like sports.

I first heard that principle from the sports editor of the Detroit *News,* back when Babe Ruth was hitting home runs. I heard it next from the sports editor of one of the Minneapolis papers, a generation later. And I heard it less than a year ago (the subject field this time was medicine) from the managing editor of one of the best small-city dailies in the Midwest.

Readers of this book live in an age of specialists. Newspapers, newsmagazines, and to some extent broadcasters are peopling their editorial rooms with men and women who can report with authority in particular

---

ARE SPECIALISTS NEEDED?

Oil reporters and oil industry PR men have agreed that news coverage of the 1973– 1974 "energy crisis" was "shallow, conventional, and cliché-ridden"; and that a prime reason was the lack of reporters knowledgeable about the financial, production, and delivery problems of the petroleum industry.

The media, said the PR men, overdramatized and oversimplified the problems of getting gasoline into automobile tanks. The oil reporters concurred with terms like "hurried" and "superficial." The absence of expertise, they said, often meant that the right questions were not asked. (They also said that the industry frequently tried not to answer any questions.)

---

fields. To report education—high, low, or medium—you have to understand the structures, the governance, the teaching methods, the social problems that embroil teachers, school boards, and PTAs. If you're hired to write sports, chances are that before long you'll be spending most of your time on football, golf, or some other one sport. But before you get to that point you are pretty sure to have covered every kind of sport your community supports. First of all, then, you're a reporter.

This surprises nobody. Before a medical student gets the M.D. after his name, he has to learn a lot of anatomy, chemistry, and physiology. If he is to specialize, he then learns a lot more about children's diseases, or the intracacies of ear, nose, and throat, or the curious things that can happen to the human skeleton. Whatever his area, it is a superstructure built on the bedrock of fundamentals.

The axiom that a newsworker needs to know a little about practically everything does not deny this principle. Reporting profiicency explores a thousand byways, and the need for specialists does not mean the end of the generalists. A newsroom staffed only by experts would be in trouble when the unclassifiable comes along. And no special-field reporter is ever sure he won't be asked to work outside his own area. Every now and then the women's editor (who may be either male or female) is asked to write the color story on the county fair, and the church editor to leave his desk and cover an airplane disaster in the next county.

Learning the fundamentals first, then, not only prepares a journalist to undertake any kind of assignment that comes this way, but also lays the foundation for specialization.

Toward specialization How does a reporter move from the broad to the particular?

There is no unique path. Reporters in special fields have got there by many routes:

- Ruth Ellen Church, for many years foods editor of the Chicago *Tribune*, graduated from college with a home economics-and-journalism major, learned her trade on a small daily in Iowa, and went on to the *Tribune's* foods department.
- Victor Cohn, the Washington *Post's* distinguished science editor, followed journalism school and a stint on the copydesk of a metropolitan paper by becoming its atomic science writer (the paper gave him six months' detached service to learn what atomic science is), then moved into medical and other scientific fields.
- Emil Schneider, a J-school graduate, was a general reporter for several papers before he developed enough interest and expertise to become one of the Milwaukee *Journal's* business writers.
- Cathy Watson's journalism major led her to a general reporting job. After she was put on the public schools beat, she took a year off to get a master's degree in education, then continued as a school reporter.

- Frank Wright worked as a general reporter, interrupted his journalistic career to take graduate work in political science, decided he could prepare himself adequately for political reporting on his own, and wound up as head of a major newspaper's Washington bureau.
- Dwayne Netland, with a journalism B.A., spent a year as a small-city general reporter. He then followed his sports interest (he had been sports editor of his university's paper) to a metropolitan sports page; there he wrote football, golf, baseball, and most of the other sports. And that led to an editorial post on a sports magazine.
- Porter Hedge took a degree in agricultural journalism, went into the U. S. Department of Agriculture information service, and then established an agricultural newsletter and magazine service of his own.
- David Skoloda, after leaving college with a political science B.A., gained reporting experience on a small paper, joined the Milwaukee *Journal* as a general reporter, then followed personal interest into agricultural writing with emphasis on "agribusiness." The *Journal* supported him for a long leave to amplify his specialized knowledge through university work.

These examples emphasize a number of common factors:

- Each of the reporters had college background in liberal arts or journalism (most journalism degrees put emphasis on general education).
- Most gained general reporting experience, often on small papers, before settling into their specializations.
- Most followed personal interests that directed them toward special fields.

It does not always work this way. Some men and women with recognized expertise have been brought into journalism in the belief that they can acquire the journalist's skills on the job. Sometimes they can. But it's not surprising that most scientists write like scientists, most lawyers like lawyers ... and that scientists' writings are designed for other scientists, not for lay readers. Which is the chicken and which the egg? The argument is as old as journalism. Most newspaper and magazine employers appear to prefer to start with journalistic craftsmen. (*Better Homes & Gardens,* a magazine that has fairly specialized contents, for years met the problem by having in each of its subject areas not one but two top editors, a specialist and a journalist.)

When does a journalist decide on his specialization? There is no pat answer. A good many know in college and design curricula that give them a start toward mastery of chosen fields. But many don't know until after they become professional journalists. This is one of the reasons (not the principal one) that advanced college work for established young journalists—those between twenty-five and thirty-five, say—has become an American fixture. The distinguished Nieman Fellowships at Harvard recognize that journalists need continually to deepen their knowledge and broaden their horizons; under this program some fifteen midcareer men and women a year spend nine months studying what they think will help them do their jobs better. Programs of this kind are too numerous to list. The number of young reporters who earn advanced degrees through part-time and evening study while they are on their jobs is in the thousands.

One school of thought urges journalists just out of college not to enter graduate study at once. The contention that they will be able to guide their advanced work with more certainty and better results if they let it follow firing-line experience is hard to refute.

The time is not here—it may never be here—when every reporter has to channel interests and hopes into one field. But the need for specialists is greater today than it was yesterday, and it will grow tomorrow. Specialist or not, every newsworker needs expanding knowledge, not only to deal with the grand opera story on Tuesday and the energy-and-oil crisis on Wednesday, but also to arrive at sound judgments about interrelationships of news events across the sweep of a precarious world. To do his job well a reporter must be truly educated; and a good education relates not only to what a classroom offers but also to what the communicator is able to do with it.

To repeat: A specialist a reporter *may* be; a generalist he *must* be.

Preparation of copy

A page of news copy for the biggest newspaper and one for the smallest look a lot alike. The newsrooms of the nation have developed a set of standardized practices that justify themselves because they are simple, they make it possible to write and edit copy fast, and they say the same things to everybody. They are not absolute, but their wide acceptance is the test of their practicality. Every newsworker has to know and use them.

The suggestions—not quite "rules"—that follow are those on which there is wide consensus.

NEWSPAPER COPY

1. Always typewrite copy, double- or triple-spaced (*never* single-spaced). Make sure your typewriter ribbon is good and your keys clean.

2. Type on one side only of soft-finish copy paper. This paper is often newsprint cut to the standard 8½ x 11″ size (some newsrooms use half-sheets, 5½ x 8½″; some copy paper is tinted). Never use onionskin; avoid hard-finish paper.

3. Keep your copy clean. Though it need not be stenographer-perfect, it must always be legible and unmistakable. If typing errors or editing make it hard to read or follow, retype it.

4. Always put your name and a short slugline at the upper left corner of page 1. Thus:

```
Cooper—Valley basketball                Cooper
                               or       Valley basketball
```

If you need to give other information to the city or copydesk, type it under the name and slugline or opposite them in the right corner: "For release March 16" or "Hold for name check" or "Basketball page."

5. Leave the upper third of page 1 blank, except for slug and name. This provides space for headlines, a new slugline, typographical instructions. Leave margins of 1 or 1¼" on each side.

6. Indent paragraphs five to ten spaces from the left margin.

7. Write your name or the slugline and the page number at the upper left of pages following page 1. Thus:

```
Cooper–2                       or       Valley basketball–2
```

Some newsrooms prefer to number the second page "Add 1" or "1st add," and succeeding pages to correspond. This would make the third page "Add 2."

8. It's best to avoid splitting words at the ends of typewritten lines, and to avoid breaking sentences or paragraphs from one page to another. Some newsrooms put the word "MORE" at the bottom of each page of a story that continues to another page.

9. Write an endmark, either typewritten or in pencil, at the end of the story; circle it in pencil to make it unmistakable. Two endmarks are in common use, placed below the last line of copy (don't use both):

– 30 –

###

Some newswriters use their own initials, lower case—a practice borrowed from the wire services, whose writers "sign" their copy in this fashion.

10. Edit all copy completely with a soft black copy pencil. Use the copyreading symbols accepted in your office (the traditional and near-universal symbols are shown on page 370). Do not use proofreading symbols—and don't refer to copy editing as proofreading. Mark all paragraph openings. Make final fact checks. Clarify anything that might puzzle or be questioned.

11. If your office asks it, paste sheets of a story together to make one continuous piece of copy. Never put more than one story on a page.

COPY EDITING AND PROOFREADING

On page 370 is an example of a reporter's copy marked for the printer, with the editing symbols explained at the left. On the facing page is the galley proof of the story as it comes from the composing room. It presents, as you'll note, a most unlikely collection of errors—"typos"—all properly marked by the proofreader for correction. Alongside it is the corrected story, all errors eliminated. This is the way it would look in print.

COPY FOR BROADCASTING

Some newspaper copy editing practices are used for broadcasting copy; some differ widely. The differences stem principally from two facts: first, copy for print can be read only as fast as a linotype operator's fingers can trip keys, but copy for the air must be read at the speed of speech; second, errors made in transcribing copy into type can be corrected at any of several later stages, but errors in reading copy into a microphone are instantly and sometimes embarrassingly transmitted to the audience. Copy for radio and TV, therefore, has to be totally legible, accurate, and understandable. When it isn't, its mistakes or its muddiness may become parts of a broadcast that can't be called back.

In editing copy for broadcast, fewer standard symbols are used than in newspaper or magazine editing. The purpose is to express every change or correction in unmistakably clear form. For this reason editors tend to write corrections in full rather than to use symbols, and often to retype copy that might be made unclear by what a black pencil has done to it.

Another difference between the two is that unusual words in print don't have to be pronounced; on the air they do. And they ought to be right. So phonetic spellings appear in radio or television news copy where they're needed. Example: "...the Yugoslav sculptor Mestrovics (MESH'-TRA-VEETS)..."

Radio and TV copy are written and edited in similar manners (TV copy has two columns to a page, one for video). Few broadcast newsrooms use, or need, formalized style sheets as do newspapers (you would miss capital letters or periods in print, but on the air you can't hear them and you don't miss them). But usual practices may be summarized:

1. Copy must be typewritten with black ribbon and clean keys. It is more commonly double- than triple-spaced, though triple spacing is required in some newsrooms and demanded by some newscasters. Because wire service copy comes from the teleprinters in capital letters, some newsrooms type local copy in caps. (Some of the ease-of-reading experts say that copy in caps is harder to read than cap-and-lower-case copy.)

2. Copy is written only on one side of the paper. The paper must be soft-finish so that it won't crackle into the microphone as it is handled.

Italics Center in column	Other basketball news on Page 11
Paragraph Insert letter	Mitford remain*e* the only undefeated team
Insert word or phrase Overline longhand o, m, n	*conference high* in the Valley school basketball race Thursday
Substitute phrase Delete word and letter, draw together	*when it beat* ~~by beating~~ Perkins on the ~~big~~ Perkins floor
New paragraph	~~in a tight game.~~ 59 to 54. The victory, fourth
Delete fault Clarify bad typing	straight ~~fro~~ for the *P*onies, kept them
Spell out figure Spell out abbreviated word	①game ahead of ⓅPt. Arthur, which has won
Use figure instead of word Abbreviate word	⟨fourteen⟩games since⟨December⟩1.
Insert comma Remove space	Perkins‸always troub̷lesome for Mitford
Insert space Capitalize	at͜home, carried the ponies right down to
Use small letter	the wire, ₿ut the closest game of the night
Transpose words Transpose letters	Alhambra found easing Littledale 52 to 51.
Continue without paragraph break No new paragraph	*No ¶* Dave Larson scored 15 points in the
Period (or ⊙)	last period, when Alhambra rallied to win⊗
Overline longhand o, m, n, underline a, w, u Insert quotation mark	*one* "We felt lucky to win that ~~woa~~, Peter
Ignore change; "let it stand"	*stet* Edmond, Alhambra ~~coach~~, said.
Boldface	Other results last night:
Correct spelling—do not change	Port Arthur 62, Shantietown (CORRECT) 41
Correct spelling—do not change	*FOLO COPY* Washburn 70, Retreet 67
Endmark (or ###)	⟨-30-⟩

ital
A/d/tr
≥ l.c.
conference
I
A
O
s/
l/
No A/l.c.
O
⊙ A
A

Other basketball news on Page 11

Mitford remained the only undefeated team in The Valley high school basketball race thursday when it beat Perkins on the Perkins floor 59 to 54. The victory fourth straight for the Ponies, kept them one game ahead of Port Arthur, which have won 14 games since Dec. 1.

Perkins, always troublesome for Mitford at home, carried the Ponies right down to the wire. But the closest game of the night found Alhambra edging Littledale 25 to 51. Dave Larson scored fifteen points in the last period when Alhambra rallied to win. "We felt lucky to win that one, Peter Edmond, Alhambra coach, said.

Other results last night/
Port Arthur 62, Shantietown 41
Washburn 70, Retreet 67

Proof from the composing room, with the proofreader's marks

l.c.
e
#
⊙
⌒
∧
⌒
↑
⊂tr
↑
∾
⊙

Other basketball news on page 11

Mitford remained the only undefeated team in the Valley conference high school basketball race Thursday when it beat Perkins on the Perkins floor 59 to 54.

The victory, fourth straight for the Ponies, kept them one game ahead of Port Arthur, which has won 14 games since Dec. 1.

Perkins, always troublesome for Mitford at home, carried the Ponies right down to the wire, but the closest game of the night found Alhambra edging Littledale 52 to 51. Dave Larson scored 15 points in the last period, when Alhambra rallied to win.

"We felt lucky to win that one," Peter Edmond, Alhambra coach, said.

Other results last night:
Port Arthur 62, Shantietown 41
Washburn 70, Retreet 67

The story as it appears on the printed page

3. Paragraph indentations are ten to fifteen spaces, so that they are unmistakable.

4. Each page of copy carries a slugline and page number at the upper left.

5. Splitting words at the ends of lines or sentences from one page to the next is a cardinal crime. Paragraphs ought not to carry over from one page to the next. An endmark (usually the typewritten or longhand symbol ####) or a "continued" line (usually a penciled MORE) should end every page.

6. Copy must be scrupulously edited and corrected, with editing marks that cannot be misunderstood. Copy made confusing by poor typing or involved editing must be retyped.

Advice about radio and TV news style, as distinguished from that for print media, has been offered in Chapter 5, Chapter 13, and elsewhere. There are editing distinctions, too. Among the practices of broadcast newswriters and editors are the following:

1. Never merely strike over a typing error. Black it out, with pencil or the typewriter's xxxxxxx, and write it again. This is vital when you make errors in initials, other capital letters, and numerals.

2. Provide phonetic spellings whenever they're needed. For instance, almost nobody pronounces *clandestine* right (the accent is on the second syl-

lable); if you're not sure of your announcer, give him a crutch: CLAN-DES'-TIN.

3. Use periods, commas, and dashes generously, to indicate voice or meaning pauses or inflections. Use capital initial letters freely—they identify important words. Underline words that ought to get special notice from the announcer—names, difficult words, points of emphasis.

4. Use few abbreviations, or none at all. Write out such titles as Mister, Doctor, President. Write figures and numerals precisely as they should be spoken: *sixteen hundred*, not *1600:* Use round numbers when precise figures aren't necessary: *ten thousand families* rather than 10,149 families.

5. Write on the copy paper *only* what is to be read (excepting such necessities as sluglines, page numbers, and sharply identified instructions).

6. Avoid most copyreading symbols. In copy for print a circled numeral tells the compositor to spell it out; in copy for broadcast it may throw the announcer for a fall.

The sample of broadcast news copy on this page, as edited, is fairly typical.

When the next ~~Presidential~~ Presidential election rolls around
you may not find out so quickly who the winner ~~will be~~ is.

The Senate voted today to make it a crime to broadcast
any returns BEFORE midnight, ~~Eastern Standard~~ Eastern Standard Time. That means that
if you live in ~~Saint~~ Saint Louis you'll get no returns until ~~10~~ 11
in the evening; in Denver, 10; and in Seattle 9.

This would ~~mean~~ BE a change from the recent practice of broadcasting predictions figured out by computers soon after 9 o'clock,
New York time.

The Senate vote ~~was the result of~~ followed an argument
by Senator Henry Bellmon, an Oklahoma Republican, that voters on the
West Coast may be influenced by hearing Eastern returns before they
cast their ballots.

A Democrat, Senator Humphrey of Minnesota, agreed. Humphrey
lost the ~~1968~~ 1968 election to Nixon, and he said, ~~that~~ "I believe those
announcements made a difference."

The vote was 43 to 39. The bill as passed provides federal
funds for campaigns ~~for~~ FOR federal offices, as well as limitations on
~~campaign~~ campaign spending.

(#######)

Related Reading

Blanche G. Prejean and Wayne A. Danielson, *Programed Newspaper Style,* American Continental Publishing Company, 1972. — Vastly simplified "review of the mechanics of newspaper style," presented in programed-learning pattern. Excellent for beginners in writing and editing.

The jargon of journalists

Reporters, like specialists in any field, have developed a private language—a jargon made largely of common words and terms with special meanings. It is not a difficult language, for it is simple, informal, and practical. Every newsworker must know it.

This glossary is limited to terms and usages you are likely to hear in a newsroom. The technical language of printing and broadcasting is excluded, except the terms in common newsroom use.

ad   Short for *advertisement*

add   Addition to a story already written, or in process of being written

advance   Story announcing a coming news event. Similar to **prelim**

angle   The approach or perspective from which a news fact or event is viewed, or the emphasis chosen for a story. *See* **slant**

AP   The Associated Press

art   Pictures or other graphic illustration for print media

assignment   An assigned news task, whether a single story or a continuing responsibility such as a beat

audio   The aural, or sound, portion of a telecast

background   Informative factual material related to current news, presented to aid audience understanding

backgrounder   A background news or feature story

bank   A section of a newspaper headline. Same as **deck**

banner   A headline across, or near the top of, all or most of a newspaper page. Same as **line, ribbon, streamer**

beat   **1.** A combination of news sources or areas assigned to a reporter for continued coverage. Same as **run.**   **2.** A story published by a medium ahead of its competition. Same as **exclusive, scoop**

bf   Boldface, blackface—heavy black type

body type   The small type in which a news story (excluding heads and display lines) is printed. Usually 8 point (9 lines to an inch) or 9 point (8 to an inch)

boil, boil down   Shorten or condense copy

boldface   *See* **bf**

break   **1.** The specific moment at which a newsworthy development becomes known and available′ for publication.   **2.** The point at which a printed story "breaks" from one page to another. Noun and verb in both meanings.

bridge   The transition from one element or story in a newscast to another. Noun and verb

bulldog   An early—usually the first—of a day's editions of a newspaper

bulletin   Brief announcement of a late-breaking news event. In broadcasting bulletins usually break into other programs; in print, they get prominent position and boldface type

by-line   The writer's name at the head of a story

cap   Capital letter. Same as **upper case**

caption   Title or head above a printed picture; often used loosely to refer to any descriptive text with a picture

CRT   Cathode-ray tube terminal

clc or **c&lc**   Capital initials followed by lower-case letters

clip   A clipping. Usually denotes a story clipped from a newspaper

clip sheet   A sheet of printed stories, usually publicity stories, from which an editor may clip for reference or reprint

cold type   The typesetting process that uses direct imaging of type faces onto paper without metal type; among the methods are typewriter composition and photocomposition. Cold type must be printed by offset (q.v.). *See* **hot type**

copy   The written or graphic form in which a news story or other matter is presented to the printer or the newscaster

correspondent   A reporter who delivers his copy to his editor by wire, radio, or mail

credit or **credit line**   **1.** The printed or spoken acknowledgment of the source or ownership of a picture or other journalistic matter.   **2.** The phrase showing the source of quoted matter ("he said," etc.)

cut   **1.** The metal or plastic plate from which an illustration is printed.   **2.** The printed illustration.   **3.** To shorten or condense copy

cutline   Descriptive text accompanying a picture

dateline   Words opening the first paragraph of a news story to identify its place and date of origin

deadline   Stated hour by which copy for an edition or a newscast must be ready, or an assigned task completed

deck   *See* **bank**

delete   Take out, remove from copy. Primarily a proofreading term

dog watch   Latest shift on a morning paper or (sometimes) earliest on an afternoon. Same as **lobster trick**

dope story   A story of speculation, prediction, comment, or background. Most used in sports and political reporting

down style   An editing pattern calling for a minimum of capital letters

dummy   A chart or pattern showing how a page is to be composed. *See* **makeup**

dupe or **duplicate**   A carbon copy

ear   The upper corners of a news page (usually page 1)

edition   One version of a newspaper. Some papers have one edition per day or per week; some have many. Not to be confused with **issue,** which usually refers to all editions under a single date

effects   Sound or music to back or support voices in a broadcast

em   Unit of typographical measurement (one-sixth of an inch, or 12 points)

exclusive   *See* **beat**

feature   **1.** A news story or other matter differentiated from straight news (*see* Chapter 18).   **2.** Emphasize or play up

file   To send a story to the home office, usually by wire; to put stories on news service wires

filler   Material used to fill space or time

flag   The printed title of a newspaper on page 1. *See* **logo**

flash   Brief news bulletin of great urgency (more emphatic than **bulletin**), taking precedence over all other matter

fluff   An announcer's error on the air, analogous to **typo** in print. Similar terms are *beard* and *boo-boo*

folio   Page number

folo   Short for *follow*—a story about an event after its occurrence

format   The pattern or structural outline of a newscast

galley   A metal tray for storing or carrying type

graf or **graph**   Paragraph

guide or **guideline**   Identification at top of page of copy to facilitate editing and handling. Similar to **slugline**

halftone   Metal or plastic plate from which a photograph is printed

handout   Prepared news matter offered by news sources or special interests to aid reporters or to gain publicity

head, headline   Display type above a printed news story, or the concise summary of news stories in some news broadcasts

hold   Do not release without permission

hot type   1. A line of type cast from molten metal by a line-casting machine. 2. The method of typesetting characterized by use of hot type

HTK   "Hed to kum," shorthand used by copyreaders on copy to indicate that the headline will follow the copy to the printer

insert   Words, phrases, sentences, paragraphs inserted in previously prepared copy

issue   The editions of a newspaper or other periodical under one date. *See* **edition**

italics   Type designed to slope to the right (thus: *italics*)

jump   To continue a story from one page to another; as a noun, the continued matter. *See* **break 2**

kicker   1. A short story, usually humorous, used to close a newscast.   2. A subordinated phrase preceding or following the main deck of a headline

kill   To destroy type matter or to eliminate portions or all of a story

lc   Lower case—small letters in contrast to capitals

lead   (pronounced lede) Opening section of a news story; often spelled "lede"

lead   (pronounced led) A thin extra space between lines of type

lean against   To be contiguous to. A local newscast *leans against* a network newscast if it immediately precedes or follows

legman   A reporter—particularly one who does not write his own stories, but telephones them to a rewrite desk

letterpress   Printing direct from type or from plates cast from type. *See* **offset, stereotype 2**

line   *See* **banner**

live   Broadcasting from actuality rather than from recorded talent or sound

lobster trick   *See* **dog watch**

lower case   *See* **lc**

logo   Short for *logotype*. The established title design of a periodical

make over   To change the design of and re-form a newspaper page already in type

makeup   The arrangement of body matter, headlines, and illustrations on a page (spelled *make up* as a verb)

masthead   The formal statement of a paper's title, officers, point of publication, and other descriptive information. Usually on the editorial page

morgue   The newspaper or broadcasting station library (the term is becoming passé)

move   To send a story by wire. *See* **file**

must   A story whose publication or broadcast is imperative

net   Short for *network*

newshole   The space in a newspaper reserved for editorial (nonadvertising) matter

obit   Short for *obituary*

offset   A lithographic method of printing from photomechanical plates. *See* **letterpress**

off the record   Information given to reporters that is not for publication

one-shot   A single broadcast or news story, not part of a series or continuing pattern

overhead   A story filed by commercial telegraph rather than on leased wire or news service

overset   Matter in type and ready for print but held back for later use or discard

pad   To fill out, extend, stretch a story, usually with unneeded matter

paste-up   **1.** A newscast made up of wire service copy pasted or arranged in the desired order.   **2.** A composition of type matter, illustrations, etc., pasted in page form to be photographed for offset printing

pix   Short for *picture* or *pictures*

plate   *See* **stereotype**

play   Degree of emphasis on a piece of news. A story may be played up or down.

play story   The story that receives highest emphasis in a newspaper or broadcast

point   Smallest unit of type measurement (about 1/72 of an inch)

precede   A descriptive or explanatory passage preceding the lead of a story

prelim   Story announcing a coming event. *See* **advance, folo**

printer   A teletypewriter or teleprinter used in wire service transmission

proof   A print-off of newly set type matter on which errors are marked for correction

publicity   Promotional matter presented as news

punch   To emphasize a word, a story, or an idea in a newscast

put to bed   To take final steps necessary to start the presses

query   A correspondent's inquiry as to whether he should cover a particular story

release   A story provided to news media for use at a stated time

replate   To make over a page and restereotype it

retrieval   Recovery of materials from a computer or other information storage facility

revise (pronounced *REE-vise*)   A revised or rewritten version of a story

rewrite (pronounced *REE-write*)   **1.** Same as **revise.**   **2.** The newsroom operation in which writers take stories by telephone from legmen and write them for publication

ribbon   *See* **banner**

rim   The outer edge of the horseshoe desk around which copyreaders work. Becoming outdated as CRTs and individual desks take over

roman   Vertical (in contrast to *italic*) type

roundup   A newscast summarizing principal late news

run   *See* **beat 1**

running story   A news development continuing over two or more days

runover   Same as **jump**

scanner   An electronic or optical device for transforming news copy or other graphic images to the form necessary for printing

scoop   *See* **beat 2**

screen   The glass surface in a cathode-ray tube (CRT) terminal on which is projected the "copy" of a news story under preparation

script   Copy written for broadcast

shoot   To take photographs

show   A radio or TV program. A news show is a newscast

sidebar   A secondary news story, amplifying or supporting another story

slant   **1.** Same as **angle.**   **2.** To shape a story so as to lead the reader's thinking; to editorialize in news; to color or misrepresent

slot   The inside rim of a U-shaped copydesk

slot man   The head of the copydesk

slug or **slugline**   Brief identification of a story, written at top of pages of copy. *See* **guide**

sob sister   A reporter whose specialty is writing tearjerkers

spike   To hold back a story—to place it on a spindle for possible future use

spot news   News printed or broadcast as soon as possible after it becomes available

stereotype   **1.** A bromide, cliché, hackneyed expression or news concept.   **2.** A metal printing plate cast from a matrix molded from type or other raised surface

stet   Copyreader's or proofreader's term meaning "let it stand"—ignore editing changes or corrections, print as originally written or set

still   A single-exposure photograph, as distinguished from moving pictures

storage   Placing news or other information in a facility such as a computer or a library for possible later use. *See* **retrieval**

story   The report of a set of facts, prepared for presentation to an audience through a news medium

straight news   News written straightforwardly for informative purposes, as distinguished from human-interest or feature news

streamer   *See* **banner**

stringer   A correspondent paid on a piecework basis—by the number of stories he provides or their length

tack-up   A newscast formed by assembling wire stories and pasting or stapling them in order, with little editing. *See* **paste-up**

take   A section of a story taken from the typewriter or CRT before the story is completed (usually one or two paragraphs), to hasten its movement to the copydesk

terminal   *See* **CRT**

text   The verbatim report of a speech or public statement

30   Symbol widely used in news copy to indicate "the end"

time copy   Copy with small or no element of immediacy

top head   A major headline at or near the top of a page

transition   *See* **bridge**

trim   To cut or condense copy. *See* **boil, cut 3**
typo   A typographical error
underlines   Descriptive matter used with illustrations. *See* **cutline**
UPI   United Press International
upper case   Capital letters. *See* **cap**
up style   Editing pattern calling for liberal use of capital letters
video   The visual portion of a telecast
video typewriter   A machine with typewriter keyboard that produces its "copy" electronically on a glass surface

APPENDIX C

Code of ethics

Approved by the Society of Professional Journalists, Sigma Delta Chi, 1973

The Society of Profesional Journalists, Sigma Delta Chi, believes the duty of journalists is to serve the truth.

We believe the agencies of mass communication are carriers of public discussion and information, acting on their Constitutional mandates and freedom to learn and report the facts.

We believe in public enlightenment as the forerunner of justice, and in our Constitutional role to seek the truth as part of the public's right to know the truth.

We believe these responsibilities require journalists to perform with intelligence, objectivity, accuracy, and fairness.

To these ends, we accept the standards of practice here set forth:

RESPONSIBILITY: The public's right to know of events of public importance and interest is the overriding mission of the mass media. The purpose of distributing news and enlightened opinion is to serve the general welfare. Journalists who use their professional status for selfish or other unworthy motives violate a high trust.

The code is presented here in slightly abridged form.

FREEDOM OF THE PRESS: Freedom of the press is to be guarded as an inalienable right of people in a free society. It carries with it the freedom and the responsibility to discuss, question, and challenge actions and utterances of government and of public and private institutions. Journalists uphold the right to speak unpopular opinions and the privilege to agree with the majority.

ETHICS: Journalists must be free of obligation to any interest other than the public's right to know the truth:

1. Gifts, favors, free travel, special treatment or privileges can compromise the integrity of journalists and their employers.

2. Secondary employment, political involvement, holding public office, or service in community organizations should be avoided if it compromises the integrity of journalists and their employers. Journalists and their employers should conduct their personal lives in a manner that protects them from conflict of interest, real or apparent. Their responsibilities to the public are paramount.

3. Communications from private sources should not be published or broadcast without substantiation of their claims to news value.

4. Journalists will try constantly to assure that public business is conducted in public and that public records are open to public inspection.

5. Journalists acknowledge the ethic of protecting confidential sources of information.

ACCURACY AND OBJECTIVITY: Good faith with the public is the foundation of all worthy journalism.

1. Truth is our ultimate goal.

2. Objectivity in reporting the news is the mark of an experienced professional. It is a standard of performance toward which journalists strive.

3. There is no excuse for inaccuracies or lack of thoroughness.

4. Newspaper headlines should be fully warranted by the contents of the articles they accompany. Photographs and telecasts should give accurate pictures of events.

5. Sound practice makes clear distinction between news reports and expressions of opinion.

6. Partisanship in editorial comment that knowingly departs from the truth violates the spirit of American journalism.

7. Journalists recognize their responsibility for offering informed analysis, comment, and editorial opinion on public events and issues. They accept the obligation to present such material by individuals whose competence, experience, and judgment qualify them for doing so.

8. Special articles or presentations devoted to advocacy or the writer's conclusions and interpretations should be labeled as such.

FAIR PLAY: Journalists at all times show respect for the dignity, privacy, rights, and well-being of people encountered in the course of gathering and presenting the news.

1. The news media should not communicate unofficial charges affecting

reputation or moral character without giving those accused a chance to reply.

2. The news media must guard against invading the rights to privacy.

3. The media should not pander to morbid curiosity.

4. The news media should make prompt and complete correction of their errors.

5. Journalists should be accountable to the public, and the public should be encouraged to voice its grievances against the media. Open dialog with readers, viewers, and listeners should be fostered.

Index

Hentoff, Nat, 38, 348
history, news as, 24
hoaxes, 30
Houston *Chronicle,* 347
Houston *Journalism Review,* 348, 354
Houston *Post,* 54, 342
"how," 193–194
human interest news, 23–24, 301–321; audience response, 49–52, 304; in broadcasting, 310; definition, 304; exploitation, 157–158; materials, 304–306; reporting, 304–306; writing, 306–313

identification, of juveniles, 151–152; by race or nationality, 152–153; of reporter, 286–287
imagination, 114–115
infiltration reporting, 346–347
information, freedom of, 10
interest, as a news element, 49–59
interpretive reporting, 19, 349–361; in broadcasting, 349–350; characteristics of, 351–354; definition, 349–351; development, 349–351; and editorials, 352; and news magazines, 351–352
interviewing and interviews, 13, 271–299; checking back, 280–281; magazine, 296; news interviews, 272–284; note-taking, 276; personality interviews, 293–299; preparation for, 273–275; question-and-answer, 284–286; sources of error, 278–281; symposium interviews, 289–293
inverted pyramid, 164, 167
investigative reporting, 337–347; kinds, 339–340; methods, 342–347; obstacles, 340–345; by teams, 342
Ivins, Molly, 34, 115

jargon, 242–243
Jefferson, Thomas, 12, 13
Johnson, Lyndon B., 20, 261
journalese, 41, 239
Journalism Monograph Series, 278

Kansas City *Star,* 341
Kennedy, John F., 20, 77, 123
Kilpatrick, James J., 30
Kipp, Bruce, 343
Knievel, Evel, 4, 18

Krauss, Bob, 287
Krieg, Alvin L., 305
Kuralt, Charles, 310

laws of journalism, 144–149
leads, 185–211; AP lead, 186; article lead, 208; brevity, 188; cartridge lead, 201; clothes-line lead, 188; credit-line lead, 207; dependent clause lead, 205; design and content, 185–186; elements, 186–194; folo lead, 200; guides, 185–186; length, 188; longer leads, 202; "modern" lead 185 ff.; multiple-sentence lead, 209–210; name lead, 199; one-idea lead, 197; participle lead, 205; preposition lead, 204; question lead, 201; quotation lead, 200; radio and TV, 187, 202–203; and story organization, 203–204; straight-news lead, 186–188; strong leads, 198; summary lead, 185–186; suspended interest lead, 210; time element in, 191; variations, 210; weak leads, 206–207; writing, 194–196; use of "you," 201–202
leaks, 120
Le Monde, 16, 66
libel, 10, 23, 146–148; avoidance of, 147–148; New York *Times* decision, 147, 159
Liebling, A. J., 61
Liebling III counterconvention, 37, 53, 61
Lippmann, Walter, 35, 39, 138, 349
Loble law, 151–152
London *Times,* 351
"look-ahead" reporting, 340
Los Angeles *Free Press,* 65
Los Angeles *Times,* 35, 97, 136, 281, 339
Louisville *Courier-Journal,* 21, 22, 133, 138
Lukas, J. Anthony, 170, 355
Lyons, Louis M., 72

"made" news, 325–336
Mailer, Norman, 55, 266
Malcolm, Andrew H., 328
management of news, 120–121
Markel, Lester, 352
"mass" communication, definition, 7
McCormick, Robert R., 34

W9-BLI-999

Instructor's Manual to Accompany

RESPONDING TO LITERATURE

Judith A. Stanford
Rivier College

Mayfield Publishing Company
Mountain View, California
London • Toronto

Copyright © 1992 by Mayfield Publishing Company

All rights reserved. No portion of this book may be reproduced in any
form or by any means without written permission of the publisher.

International Standard Book Number:1-55934-167-X

Manufactured in the United States of America

Mayfield Publishing Company
1240 Villa Street
Mountain View, California 94041

PREFACE

Writing an instructor's guide presents one especially daunting problem: audience. Some instructors using this text may be teaching an introductory literature course for the first time; others may have taught the course for many years. Some may teach in small, two-year colleges; others, in large universities. Some may teach mainly traditional-age students from small rural communities; others may teach students of diverse ages from diverse backgrounds.

Never forgetting the complexity of this audience, yet trying to make writing this guide easier for myself, I tried to imagine a common ground. As I wrote, I envisioned teachers of great variety but with a common commitment: exploring various ways of teaching a course that introduces literature and also stresses the development of reading and writing skills. Keeping this audience in mind, I've written suggestions for those who are beginning to teach, discussed approaches for developing an interactive classroom, considered the development of goals and methods of evaluation, provided sample syllabi, and discussed approaches for the first week of class. In addition, I've made specific teaching suggestions for the first three chapters as well as for the thematic and genre anthology sections. Please realize that I wrote each section of this guide to offer options. Intending to open possibilities—not to prescribe the only correct way, or the only useful way, or the only humane way to teach this course—I suggest processes and approaches that have worked for me and for my colleagues

I would like very much to hear your responses—and your students' responses—both to the suggestions in this guide and to the text. Any teaching ideas you send will be considered for inclusion in the guide for the next edition of *Responding to Literature*.

CONTENTS

FOR BEGINNING TEACHERS:
PREPARING TO TEACH INTRODUCTORY
LITERATURE/WRITING COURSES

What assumptions can be made about instructors who are teaching this course for the first time? Many will be graduate students; others will have just completed a graduate degree. Some instructors will have taken courses or participated in training seminars designed to help them as they begin teaching; others will have no such formal background. I'm going to take an enormous leap of faith and assume that all instructors—new or experienced— have one thing in common: love of literature. The question, then, becomes how to put this love to work in the classroom.

After talking to people whom I consider outstanding teachers of introductory literature and writing courses, and after constantly examining and evaluating my own teaching, I've concluded that the teaching process is both incredibly fascinating and incredibly fluid. I don't believe it's possible to ever come to a point where one says, "Well, this it it. Now I know how to teach this class in the most effective way. This is how I'll teach it for the rest of my life." The options that I suggest in this manual are those that work right now for me or for instructors I know and respect. I offer these possibilities, knowing that within the next year—even within the next few months—I'll reread what I've written and see that I've changed my way of looking at a process or that I've discovered a new idea I wish I'd included.

To keep working on my own approaches to teaching, I've found the following processes essential:

LISTENING

I do a great deal of informal listening both to colleagues and to students. If you're lucky enough to teach at a school where instructors readily share ideas and are not afraid to discuss classroom disasters as well as successes, then you know what I mean. I listen carefully to what other instructors say about their teaching. Learning what texts they are using, what writing assignments they are giving, how they are inspiring discussions, and how they view their students helps me to think about what I want to do—and not do—in my own courses.

I listen, also, to what my students tell me. Most colleges and universities provide end-of-term evaluations, and students' suggestions have often provided me with easy ways to make the course more effective. The problem with end-of-term evaluations, of course, is that the students who make the suggestions fail to benefit from them. I've found it helpful to give questionnaires after four or five weeks of class, asking students to respond anonymously and return their completed evaluations in the campus mail. This process allows me to use a class-specific format (for instance, one class might need changes to facilitate discussion, whereas another might have problems with group work). I don't jump to make a change in response to every student's criticism, but I've found many of their observations astute and helpful.

Another kind of listening that encourages, inspires, and sometimes infuriates me is the listening I do at conferences. Consider attending local and national conferences held by organizations such as National Council of Teachers of English (NCTE) and Modern Languages Association (MLA). Keynote speakers as well as presenters in smaller sessions provide so much to think about that you need the long plane or car ride home to mull over what you've heard.

TALKING

The twin of listening is talking. I am forever grateful to the many friends, relatives, colleagues, and students who have allowed me to talk out my ideas about teaching. By putting thoughts into words, watching the expressions of others as they listen, and hearing their responses, I come to understand how I am changing—and how I need to change—as a teacher. (Spontaneous conversations are great, but we are all incredibly busy. I find it essential to plan time—early breakfasts often work well—to talk with the people whose willingness to listen gives me a chance to grow.)

In addition to informal talking, consider speaking at local or national conferences. Putting thoughts together for a workshop or panel presentation forces me to rethink my ideas and to consider them in light of a broader audience than my own students and colleagues.

OBSERVING

I'm fortunate to have colleagues who welcome visitors to their classes. Watching different people with different teaching styles helps me to see classroom interaction from a new perspective. In addition to visiting classes taught by others, I pay close attention whenever I find myself in the role of student. For instance, when I attend a conference, I stay alert not only to the content of workshops, panel discussions, and addresses but also to the approaches the presenters use to reach their audience. As I monitor my own responses, as well as the responses of others attending the session, I can easily identify which approaches gain intrigued attention and which elicit yawns, restless squirming, and impatient gazes at the clock.

Besides observing other teachers and their students, I also observe my own students. Their expressions and gestures often let me know who is bored, puzzled, irritated, amused, or amazed. Understanding their responses helps me to know when our work is going smoothly and when to anticipate and to try to correct problems.

READING

Of course I read the authors whose works I will be teaching as well as biographies and critical books and articles about these authors and their works. Although it's impossible to do thorough research about each author in an anthology I'm using as a text, I pick two or three every semester and every summer as a focus for pleasure reading. Usually I choose at least one author who is new to me: someone a colleague may have mentioned or I may have read about in a review. I also read familiar authors, rereading one or two favorites poems or stories and then seeking out works of theirs that I have not read before. I've found that reading new selections is absolutely essential to keep in tune with what my students feel as they approach a complex work for the first time.

In addition to reading literature, biography, and criticism, I read works explaining the theory and practice of people I consider master teachers. As I read what these teachers have to say, I never agree with everything they think and do. I usually find myself involved in a hot debate, resisting this idea or that observation. Later, when I read the notes I've scribbled in the margins and on the end papers, I'm often astonished at how intensely I originally disagreed with a point that no longer troubles me. Observing these changes, I've come to realize that sometimes what at first strikes me as unworkable or wrongheaded later "fits" with something I see in my own classroom and provides me with a new way to approach a problem or difficulty I've never been able to solve.

Most college and department libraries subscribe to journals about the teaching of literature and writing. Periodicals such as *College English, College Composition and Communication, Teaching English in the Two-Year College, College Teaching,* and *Reader: Essays in Reader-Oriented Theory, Criticism, and Pedagogy* provide a broad range of possibilities.

Although there are dozens of fine books related to the teaching literature and writing, these five have been most important to me:

Nancie Atwell, *In the Middle* (Boynton/Cook/Heinemann, 1987).

> I list Atwell's book with a bit of trepidation because she describes teaching literature and writing to eighth-grade students rather than to college freshmen and sophomores. However, her philosophy of teaching, her practical approaches to classroom management, and most of all, her engagement both with the reading/writing process and with her students make what she has to say useful and inspiring to teachers at all levels.

Mike Rose, *Lives on the Boundary* (Penguin, 1989).

> Rose's account of his own struggles to be admitted to the "literary conversation" and his description of his students' struggles suggest new ways of looking not only at students but also at each instructor's progress through the academic world. Rose's refusal to write students off as culturally illiterate or as ignorant beings who are nearly impossible to educate provides new hope and encouragement for those teaching introductory courses.

Louise Rosenblatt, *Literature as Exploration,* 4th edition (MLA, 1976) and *The Reader, the Text, the Poem* (Southern Illinois University Press, 1978).

> In these books, Rosenblatt sees reader and literary work as equally important. She provides a compelling, lucid, and sensible description of the literary experience (of both neophyte and experienced readers). In addition, she proposes a classroom where the instructor is not expected to provide an accepted interpretation (or even several accepted interpretations) of a given work. Instead, instructor and students work together to explore the possibilities their reading opens. Rosenblatt has the admirable ability to combine theoretical explanation with practical examples from her own reading process as well as from classroom experiences and observations.

Robert Scholes, *Textual Power: Literary Theory and the Teaching of English* (Yale University Press, 1985).

> Scholes convincingly demonstrates that literary theory cannot be separated from the teaching of literature. My favorite parts of the book are Chapters 2, 3, and 4, where Scholes invites the reader to explore a text—Hemingway's *In Our Time* —with

him. I found myself digging out my dusty copy of these interconnected short stories, stopping to read the sections Scholes suggested, and then reading his discussion. The experience provides a glimpse of what it must be like to study texts in a classroom with Scholes. His approaches left my mind racing with possibilities for my own teaching.

WRITING

I have always written with my students. Although I don't do every assignment, I try to complete at least one for each class I teach, and I often write outlines for others. Sometimes I use these as sample pieces to suggest possibilities to students. Sometimes the writing simply alerts me to the strengths and weaknesses of that assignment. When students write in class, I write along with them. I still feel a clutch of anxiety before I read what I have written aloud, and that reminds me how much more difficult it must be for many of the students when their turn comes.

In addition to writing with students, it seems to me a good thing for those of us who teach English to write something, every year or two, that we intend to submit for publication. (Of course, I realize many colleges and universities require faculty to publish far more.) It's been important for me to write about the works I teach and about my teaching process because, true to what we tell our students, writing is a way of thinking. When I write, I discover questions, possibilities, and ideas I never knew I had. In addition, waiting for responses from editors and reviewers—and then reading those responses—keeps me in touch with the hopes and anxieties of my students as they submit papers for me to judge. I find myself far less irritated with students who worry about grades when I stop to consider my own responses to the acceptance, rejection, criticism, or praise of something I have written.

DEVELOPING AN INTERACTIVE CLASSROOM

For teaching and for learning in the introductory literature and writing course, I believe an interactive structure works more effectively than does a traditional, lecture-dominated structure. In the interactive classroom, students and instructor work together. The instructor does much more than simply prepare a lecture and deliver information to students. Students do much more than read assignments, listen to lectures, and write exams and papers that merely give unprocessed information back to the instructor.

In the interactive classroom students take responsibility for their own learning while the instructor provides whatever help and encouragement they need to accomplish this task. Here are some strategies that encourage interactive learning:

1. Build a sense of community and trust in the classroom.

2. Use warm-up writing sessions to initiate discussion.

3. Breakup a large class into small groups for discussion or for work on writing projects. Often students who are uncomfortable speaking or asking questions in a large class situation are more at ease working in groups of three to five. In addition to the possible approaches to group work, consider the following issues.

   - *Should students choose their own groups or should the instructor assign groups?* I like to vary my approach. Sometimes I ask students to form their own groups; at other times I assign groups to ensure a variety of voices in each group.

   - *Should instructors participate with groups or stay away?* Opinion varies greatly among the proponents of group work. Most believe that instructors should interfere very little. Some believe that the instructor should leave the room entirely while groups meet. I usually sit by myself, reading or writing and not looking at students for the first few minutes. Then I move around from group to group, mostly listening, but occasionally responding to a question or making a comment.

   - *Should groups always or nearly always work toward or reach consensus?* I think it's important to stress that the point of much group work is to discover multiple possibilities. Certainly students should be encouraged to think critically about others' ideas, but it's not always necessary or desirable that a group arrive at a single, neatly planned response.

4. Be aware of the dynamics of full class discussions.

- *Recognize that the arrangement of chairs can foster or hinder the free exchange of ideas.*

- *Understand that students often choose to sit in the same seats at each class and that "silent ghettos"—areas of the classroom from which no voices are heard—can develop.* I find that I can sometimes break the silence barrier by sitting in that area of the classroom and speaking directly to the students sitting there. If anyone makes eye contact with me, I direct my next query or "long pause" toward him or her.

- *Recognize that some students may dominate discussion.* I sometimes take this approach to allow students who may be shy, or who may think more cautiously than others, the time to speak. I watch the clock and halfway through class announce that I appreciate the hard work and thoughtful observations of those who have already commented. Then I encourage them to sit back and enjoy listening for the rest of the class period (or for the next ten or twenty minutes or whatever seems right) while those who have not yet spoken offer their ideas. Sometimes I have to wait many seconds before one of the quieter students volunteers, but once one has spoken, the floodgates open. (This strategy works best if the discussion has started with a warm-up writing. Then everyone has some thoughts committed to paper. Reluctant speakers may be willing to read what they have written as a way to begin their participation.)

- *Understand that gender issues can affect classroom participation.* Research suggests that, contrary to popular belief, men tend to dominate discussions and to interrupt more often than women do. In addition, discussion often follows "gender runs." If a man speaks first, then other men are likely to follow. When a woman does break into the conversation, others usually follow her. If I notice a gender run going on too long, I'll sometimes interrupt and direct the discussion to someone of the opposite sex. I watch students carefully and choose someone who looks as if he or she is waiting for the opportunity to speak.

- *Understand that cultural differences may affect willingness to participate in class discussion.* For instance, some silent students may come from cultures where teachers do all the talking in the classroom. In some cultures, it is considered extremely rude to challenge or question the statements of an authority figure. In addition, students whose first language is not English may fear that others will ridicule them for speaking hesitantly or making mistakes in grammar.

5.   Require at least one office conference for each student. Seeing students on a one-to-one basis, as early in the semester as possible, gives them an opportunity to discuss their concerns about the class. In addition, the early visit shows them the way to my office, lets them know that I am available, and encourages them to return with any questions or observations they may have about the assigned reading and writing.

ESTABLISHING GOALS
AND MAKING EVALUATIONS

Establishing goals and making evaluations go together. I have to know what I (and my department) expect students to gain from the course before I can judge to what degree they have succeeded.

PLANNING GOALS

As I plan course goals, I keep in mind both short-term and long-term objectives. For example, a short-term objective might be for students to learn how to integrate quotations into their own writing, a skill commonly required in academic settings. Another short-term goal might be learning how to write a well-planned, clearly organized response to a literary work. A long-term goal might be for students to develop pleasure in their own responses to literature and confidence in their own ability to evaluate what they read. Ideally, achieving this goal would lead them to regard reading as an integral, enjoyable part of their lives and not as a tedious chore to be dreaded. I usually state goals on the syllabus in rather general terms to allow flexibility during the term. In addition, I encourage students to establish their own goals within the framework of the course requirements.

Establishing goals requires thinking about the direction the course will take. Will it emphasize reading literature or writing about literature? Or will both processes be equally valued? Will literary genres be stressed? Or will literary themes be emphasized? Or will students spend equal time studying genres and themes? How much will students be expected to write? What kinds of writing will they do? Primarily response? Primarily evaluative or analytical? Or a combination of both?

Establishing goals and considering the direction of the course also lead to thinking about ways of teaching. If I want students to learn to evaluate literature, how am I going to help them do that? If I expect them to be able to integrate quotations usefully and sensibly into their writing, how will I demonstrate that process?

For an example of the goals I set for "Writing and Literature," the introductory course I teach, see the syllabi in the next section.

EVALUATING

While I'm setting goals, thinking about the direction of the course, and planning ways to teach, I consider how I will evaluate students as they work toward those goals. Short-term goals—goals that students can be expected to achieve before the course ends—are the only goals I can evaluate. The students themselves must evaluate the long-term goals. For example, I can assess students' ability to use evidence from a text to support an explanation of their response to that text (a short-term goal) but I cannot evaluate whether they have come to regard reading literature as an important and enjoyable part of their lives. While discussing the syllabus during the first week of classes, I discuss the distinction between short-term and long-term goals so that students will understand clearly the objectives I'll consider as I evaluate their progress and determine their grades.

To establish the evaluation process, I decide how many papers I will assign and how much weight I will give to each paper as well as to the midterm and final exams. In addition, I decide how much weight I will give to journals and to class discussion. For a sixteen-week course, I usually assign a journal, three papers, one in-class essay that serves as a midterm exam, and a final exam. I've found that students do best in my classes and develop the most positive responses toward literature and writing when I use an evaluation process that stresses growth and improvement. For instance, I encourage students to revise their papers, and I consider both the original paper and the revision when writing my final comments and determining the grade. Here is one evaluation system that has worked well for me:

Three short papers (3–5 pages)   *each paper, 20%*

For each paper, I read and provide global comments for the *first draft,* but I do not grade it. I read and comment carefully on the *next submitted draft* and grade it.

Students may choose to submit a further *revision,* for which I also provide comments and a grade. I arrive at the final grade for the paper by averaging the two grades. If students choose not to submit a revision, the original grade counts the full 20%.

Assignments for the papers vary. I want each student to write one response, one comparison, and one analytic or evaluative paper during the semester.

In-Class Essay (Midterm Exam)   *10%*

Journals (two entries per week totaling at least 250 words)   *10%*

> I read and comment on journals, but I do not grade them. If
> students complete the requirement, they receive full credit.

Class participation   *5%*

> I'm very lenient on this one. If a student attends class regularly
> (missing no more than three to five class hours) and makes a
> serious effort to participate at least in small groups, I give full
> credit even if he or she has spoken very little in the large class
> setting.

Final Exam   *15%*

SAMPLE SYLLABI

FIFTEEN-WEEK SEMESTER:
EMPHASIS ON LITERARY THEMES

LITERATURE AND WRITING EN 220–E

Judith Stanford   Office Location: Writing Center
Fall 199x

                                         Office Telephone: x581
                                         Office Hours:
                                               Tues. 5:00–6 :00 P.M.
                                               Thurs. 7:30–9:30 A. M.

Required Text: *Responding to Literature*, Stanford, 1992, Mayfield

Goals:

- To develop the following abilities by reading and responding to
  literature:

    Reading thoughtfully, critically, and creatively

    Understanding and practicing the writing process more fully

    Expanding vocabulary

    Developing oral communications skills

- To consider the connections among literature and other parts of life
  by exploring literary themes related to the human experience

- To enjoy reading literature, to trust your responses to what you read,
  and to develop confidence in your ability to evaluate what you read

Evaluation Criteria:

    Three papers, 3–5 pages, each worth 20%; journals, 10%; midterm
    (in-class essay), 10%; class participation, 5%; final exam 15%.

Attendance Policy:

I will make every effort to attend each class and to be well prepared; I expect you to do the same. If you must miss more than three class hours, please make an appointment with me. Excessive absence may prevent your successful completion of the course.

Week 1:   Introductions

Reading assignment: Chapter 1

Writing assignment: Make notes on poem of choice leading to an oral response.

Week 2:   Reading assignment: Chapter 2

Writing assignment: Write four paragraphs; each should respond to one of the four works at the beginning of Chapter 2. For inspiration, see the suggestions for responding that follow each selection.

Week 3:   Reading assignment: Chapter 3

Writing assignment: Assign first paper, "Writing to Respond."

Week 4:   Innocence and Experience

Reading assignment: 2–4 short stories
1–3 poems
1 essay

Writing assignment: Submit first draft of paper.

Week 5:   Innocence and Experience

Reading assignment: 1 short story
1 play
1–3 poems

Writing assignment: Draft of response paper returned with comments; group work on revision.

Week 6:   Work

Reading assignment: 2–4 short stories
1–3 poems
1 essay

Writing assignment: Submit response paper.

Week 7:   Work

Reading assignment: 1 short story
1 play
1–3 poems

Writing assignment: Midterm In-class essay (1 hour)

First paper returned with comments and grade.

Comparison paper assigned. (Reread and discuss comparison section in Chapter 3.)

Week 8:   Men and Women

Reading assignment: 2–4 short stories
3–5 poems
1 play
1 essay

Writing assignment: Draft of comparison paper due.

Week 9:   Parents and Children

Reading assignment: 3–5 short stories
3–5 poems
1 essay

Writing assignment: Draft of comparison paper returned with comments; group work on revision.

Final revision of response paper due; all drafts to be submitted with revision.

Week 10:   Parents and Children

Reading assignment: 1–2 short stories
1 play
1–2 poems or 1 essay

Writing assignment: Submit comparison paper.

Week 11:   War

Reading assignment: 2–4 short stories
(or 1 play and 1 short story)
1–3 poems
1 essay

Writing assignment: Comparison papers returned with comments and grades.

Analysis or evaluation paper assigned. (Reread analysis and evaluation sections from Chapter 3.)

Week 12: Learning and Teaching

Reading assignment: 3–5 short stories
3–5 poems
1 essay

Writing assignment: Draft of analysis or evaluation paper due.

Week 13: Learning and Teaching

Reading assignment: 1–2 short stories
1 play
1–2 poems or 1 essay

Writing assignment: Draft of analysis or evaluation paper returned with comments; group work on revision.

Final revision of comparison paper due; all drafts to be submitted with revision.

Week 14: Death

Reading assignment: 2–4 short stories
1–3 poems
1 essay

Writing assignment: Submit analysis or evaluation paper.

Week 15: Death

Reading assignment: 1 short story
1 play
1–3 poems or 1 essay

Writing assignment: Analysis or evaluation paper returned; revisions to be submitted at least two days before final exam.

FIFTEEN-WEEK SEMESTER:
EMPHASIS ON LITERARY GENRES AND LITERARY THEMES

LITERATURE AND WRITING EN 220–E

Judith Stanford   Office Location: Writing Center
Fall 199x

                                        Office Telephone: x581
                                        Office Hours:
                                                Tues. 5:00–6 :00 P.M.
                                                Thurs. 7:30–9:30 A. M.

Required Text: *Responding to Literature,* Stanford, 1992, Mayfield

Goals:

- To develop the following abilities by reading and responding to literature:

    Reading thoughtfully, critically, and creatively
    Understanding and practicing the writing process more fully
    Expanding vocabulary
    Developing oral communications skills

- To consider the connections among literature and other parts of life by exploring literary themes related to the human experience

- To enjoy reading literature, to trust your responses to what you read, and to develop confidence in your ability to evaluate what you read

- To understand and appreciate literary genres, including fiction, poetry, drama, and nonfiction

Evaluation Criteria:

Three papers, 3–5 pages, each worth 20%; journals, 10%; midterm (in-class essay), 10%; class participation, 5%; final exam 15%.

Attendance Policy:

I will make every effort to attend each class and to be well prepared; I expect you to do the same. If you must miss more than three class hours, please make an appointment with me. Excessive absence may prevent your successful completion of the course.

Week 1:   Introductions

Reading assignment: Chapter 1

Writing assignment: Make notes on poem of choice leading to an oral response.

Week 2:   Reading assignment: Chapter 2

Writing assignment: Write four paragraphs; each should respond to one of the four works at the beginning of Chapter 2. For inspiration, see the suggestions for responding that follow each selection.

Week 3:   Reading assignment: Chapter 3

Writing assignment: Assign first paper, "Writing to Respond."

Week 4:   Reading assignment: Introduction to Short Fiction

3–5 short stories

Writing assignment: Submit draft of first paper.

Week 5:   Reading assignment: Introduction to Poetry

8–10 poems

Writing assignment: Draft of response paper returned with comments; group work on revision.

Weeks 6 and 7:   Reading assignment: Introduction to Drama

2–3 plays

Writing assignments:

Week 6: Submit response paper.

Week 7: Midterm in-class essay (1 hour)
First paper returned with comments and grade.

> Comparison paper assigned. (Reread and discuss
> comparison section in Chapter 3.)

Week 8:   Reading assignment: Introduction to Nonfiction

> 3–5 nonfiction selections

Writing assignment: Draft of comparison paper due.

Weeks 9–15:   *(For the remaining seven weeks, consider these possiblities.)*

Reading assignments: Exploring literary themes

1. Assign seven themes, one per week, reading and discussing 2–3 stories, 4–6 poems, and 1 essay OR 1 story, 3–4 poems, 1 play, and 1 essay.

2. Assign four themes, spending two weeks on each of three themes and one week on the fourth theme. *(See assignment sequences in thematic syllabus for suggestions.)*

Writing assignments: Same as weeks 9–15 on thematic syllabus.

EIGHT-WEEK QUARTER:
EMPHASIS ON LITERARY THEMES

LITERATURE AND WRITING EN 220–E

Judith Stanford   Office Location: Writing Center
Fall 199x

> Office Telephone: x581
> Office Hours:
> > Tues. 5:00–6 :00 P.M.
> > Thurs. 7:30–9:30 A. M.

Required Text: *Responding to Literature*, Stanford, 1992, Mayfield

Goals:

- To develop the following abilities by reading and responding to literature:

  > Reading thoughtfully, critically, and creatively
  > Understanding and practicing the writing process more fully

Expanding vocabulary

Developing oral communications skills

- To consider the connections among literature and other parts of life by exploring literary themes related to the human experience

- To enjoy reading literature, to trust your responses to what you read, and to develop confidence in your ability to evaluate what you read

- To understand and appreciate literary genres, including fiction, poetry, drama, and nonfiction

Evaluation Criteria:

Two papers, 3–5 pages, 25% each; journals, 10%; midterm (in-class essay), 15%; class participation, 5%; final exam, 20%.

Attendance Policy:

I will make every effort to attend each class and to be well prepared; I expect you to do the same. If you must miss more than three class hours, please make an appointment with me. Excessive absence may prevent your successful completion of the course.

Week 1:   Introductions
Reading assignments: Chapter 1 and Chapter 3, Introduction and "Writing to Respond"

Writing assignment: Assign response paper.

Week 2:   Reading assignments: Chapter 2 and Complete Chapter 3

Writing assignment: Write four paragraphs; each should respond to one of the four works at the beginning of Chapter 2. For inspiration, see the suggestions for responding that follow each selection.

Submit draft of response paper.

Week 3:   Innocence and Experience

Reading assignment: 2–4 short stories (or 1 story; 1 play)
1–3 poems
1 essay

Writing assignment: Draft of response papers returned; in-class group work on revision.

Weeks 4–8:   Reading assignments: 3–5 literary themes

(One to two weeks on each theme; follow assignment structure suggested in week 3.)

Writing assignments:

Week 4: Response paper submitted; analytic or evaluative paper assigned.

Midterm in-class writing (comparison): one class hour.

Week 5: Draft of analytic or evaluative paper due; response paper returned.

Week 6: Draft of analytic or evaluative paper returned; group work on revision.

Week 7: Analytic or evaluative paper due.

Week 8: Revision of response paper due; analytic or evaluative paper returned.

EIGHT-WEEK QUARTER
EMPHASIS ON LITERARY GENRES AND LITERARY THEMES

LITERATURE AND WRITING EN 220–E

Judith Stanford   **Office Location: Writing Center**
Fall 199x

Office Telephone: x581
Office Hours:
Tues. 5:00–6 :00 P.M.
Thurs. 7:30–9:30 A. M.

Required Text: *Responding to Literature*, Stanford, 1992, Mayfield

Goals:

• To develop the following abilities by reading and responding to literature:

Reading thoughtfully, critically, and creatively
Understanding and practicing the writing process more fully
Expanding vocabulary
Developing oral communications skills

- To consider the connections among literature and other parts of life by exploring literary themes related to the human experience

- To enjoy reading literature, to trust your responses to what you read, and to develop confidence in your ability to evaluate what you read

- To understand and appreciate literary genres, including fiction, poetry, drama, and nonfiction

Evaluation Criteria:

Two papers, 3–5 pages, 25% each; journals, 10%; midterm in-class essay, 15%; class participation, 5%; final exam, 20%.

Attendance Policy:

I will make every effort to attend each class and to be well prepared; I expect you to do the same. If you must miss more than three class hours, please make an appointment with me. Excessive absence may prevent your successful completion of the course.

Weeks 1–3:   Reading and writing assignments: Same as for eight-week course, emphasis on literary themes.

Weeks 4–8:   Writing assignments: Same as for eight-week course, emphasis on literary themes.

Week 4:   Reading assignment:

Introduction to Short Fiction
3 stories
Introduction to Poetry

Week 5:   Reading assignment:

5–8 poems
Introduction to Drama
1 one-act play

Week 6:   Reading assignment:

                        1 longer play
                        Introduction to Nonfiction
                        2 nonfiction selections

Weeks 7–8:   One or two literary themes

INTRODUCTIONS: THE FIRST WEEK

Planning the first class meeting often requires ingenuity. Many students have not yet purchased their books. In addition, at most colleges and universities, instructors can expect several students not present at the first meeting to show up at the second.

Some instructors keep the first class short by simply calling the roll, distributing the syllabus, and dismissing students with an assignment for the next class. But with the few hours each semester provides for class time, early dismissal seems to me a terrible waste. Other instructors prepare a lecture that introduces the study of literature and explains the syllabus and then spend time in their office going over the information with students who join the class late. My own favorite way of getting started conveys essential, practical information; begins to develop a community of readers and writers; and introduces the study of literature.

ADDRESSING PRACTICAL CONCERNS

I accomplish the first goal in the time-honored way of distributing the syllabus and mentioning practical items that are generally of great importance to students: for example, required texts, methods of evaluation, attendance policy, office hours, and, of course, the assignment for the next class. I then ask students to read the syllabus carefully and to bring any questions they have to the next class meeting. At the first class meeting, I try to limit time spent distributing and commenting on the syllabus to five minutes.

The strategy of delaying detailed discussion of the syllabus and course requirements and asking students to read the syllabus has several benefits. Students often discover questions they might not have raised following a cursory skimming during the first class. This process also encourages students to spend time getting an overview of the course and to seek information actively rather than listening passively to my paraphrase of the syllabus. In addition, at the second class meeting, late arrivals get a chance to hear their fellow students' questions, as well as my responses, and then to ask their own questions. (If the class meets only once a week, I pass out the syllabus during the first part of class, ask students to read it during the break, and then discuss their questions during the second part of the class.)

BUILDING A COMMUNITY OF READERS AND WRITERS

Trust among students as well as between students and instructor is essential in a course based on sharing both written and oral responses to literature. Obviously, I don't march into class the first day and announce, "This class will have trust!" But I do begin each new course by helping students to get to know me and to know each other.

If the chairs in the room are movable, I arrive early and arrange them into a circle or, if the class is large, into several nested semicircles. The point is to have a configuration that encourages students to talk to each other and not to address every comment or observation primarily to the instructor (a practice that is hard to avoid when chairs are arranged in rows). At the end of the first class meeting, I ask students to help return chairs to their original location; I also ask those who arrive early for the next class, and subsequent class meetings, to arrange the chairs into circles.

On the day of the first class meeting, I arrive at least twenty minutes early to move the chairs and greet early arrivals. By asking their names as they arrive and writing them down along with a quick description ("George Porter: dark-rimmed glasses"), I usually learn several names before the class even begins.

At the start of class, following the five-minute distribution of syllabus, I introduce myself and then ask students to introduce themselves. The easiest way to do this is simply to begin at any point in the circle and have each person, in turn, give his or her name plus one or two introductory statements. I encourage students to tell something that suggests their special interests or abilities because we are all developing a sense of audience. (And I point out that when I say "we," I really mean "we." I need to know my audience just as much as they need to know theirs.) We are all getting to know the people we will be writing for and talking with during the weeks to follow. I also suggest that students try to learn the names of at least five other students during the introductions. I believe that, by calling each other by name, students often begin to see each other as individuals and not just as "that kid in the back" or "that older guy" or "the one who wears black all the time."

Taking this approach provides a fine opportunity for reviewing (or introducing) the concept of audience: of writing with readers in mind and speaking with listeners in mind. Consider asking students to suggest some categories of information they would like to know about the people who will be listening to what they say and reading what they write. Have them jot down a few questions they would like to ask potential readers/listeners and then ask them to volunteer responses that you can write on the board.

Even when students have prepared a list, you can expect some reticence when you ask them to suggest questions they might want to ask. Try to wait out the silence if you don't get an immediate response. Research suggests that teachers typically wait less than three-tenths of a second before answering their own questions. Try waiting at least ten seconds (which seems like a very long time when there's utter silence) before prompting students further. This strategy is especially important at the first meeting because that class often sets patterns that students come to expect for the rest of the semester.

These are typical questions students say they would like to ask each other:

- What kind of paid work do you do or have you done?

- Do you do any kind of volunteer work?

- What activities do you enjoy?

- Where do you come from?

- What other states or countries have you visited? What was your reaction to those places?

- What made you decide to come to this school?

- What goals do you have for after you graduate?

- What kind of films do you like? Why?

- What was the most important decision you ever made?

- What were the results of that decision?

After students have suggested their questions, I usually give examples of the questions I'd like to have answered. Because we will be reading together, I'd like to know what kind of reading they most enjoy. I'm curious to know whether they read a daily newspaper. What section do they turn to first? And why? Do they subscribe to or read certain magazines? Which ones? And, of course, what books do they read purely for pleasure? For information?

I ask students to keep the questions they have generated in mind, as well as questions I have suggested. To make the introductory exercise more varied and lively, give them a few minutes to jot down some observations about themselves and provide them with examples of previous students' comments .

Here are some examples of introductory comments:

I've changed my major three times because every time I take a new subject I get convinced that that's what I want to do.

I work at a hospital as a nurse's aide and I don't know what I want to do when I grow up, but I do know I don't want to do anything that has to do with the medical profession.

I made a decision not to go to college when I got out of high school. Now, ten years later, I feel like a different person, and that decision doesn't fit anymore. So I changed my mind and came back.

> My family has lived in England for the past five years. The
> thing that has surprised me most is how much most people
> there know about American history and American politics.

Although comments such as these are not directly related to the study of literature, they help both the instructor and the students to connect with each other's lives. I believe such connection is essential for developing a classroom atmosphere that promotes the risk taking necessary for honest writing and open discussion.

For a 55-minute class, I allot 20–30 minutes for these introductions. If your class meets for longer than 55 minutes, you may want to use a more elaborate version of this exercise. For example, after using the process described above to discover possible questions, you might ask pairs of students to interview each other for five to ten minutes. Students then introduce each other rather than themselves. When I use this scheme, I usually invite the person who is being introduced to add any comments he or she would like to make.

INTRODUCING LITERATURE

After distributing the syllabus and leading the introductory exercise (about 30 minutes), I ask students to sit back and relax, put down pens and pencils, and close notebooks. I tell them that I'm going to read them a story (or a poem or an essay) that I like. I talk about literature as having a strong oral tradition, explaining that long before most people could read or write, and even before written language existed, men, women, and children told stories and sang or recited poetry.

In modern times, once children can read to themselves, they are seldom read to, but in the not-so-distant past, before the advent of radio and television, families and friends gathered to hear the latest installment of a serialized novel or to listen to the familiar rhythm of a well-known poem. I read aloud often in class, and I frequently ask students to read aloud because I believe that language becomes far more moving and powerful—and is often understood in more varied ways—when it is heard as well as read.

I tell students that, when I finish reading, I'll be interested in hearing their responses but that they will not be quizzed or tested on what I read. I also tell them that they will not be asked to come up with a "correct meaning"; I'm simply interested in the thoughts and feelings the selection evokes.

In choosing a selection, I look for something quite short and highly accessible. I also read the selection several times before class so that, while I am reading, I can look up at students most of the time, using eye contact to keep them engaged in what they are hearing. Here are some selections in this text that work well for this purpose:

Fiction

The Use of Force	William Carlos Williams	page 241
The War Prayer	Mark Twain	page 559
War	Luigi Pirandello	page 562

Poems

We Real Cool	Gwendolyn Brooks	page 170
Aunt Jennifer's Tigers	Adrienne Rich	page 401
My Papa's Waltz	Theodore Roethke	page 467
Making the Jam without You	Maxine W. Kumin	page 468
The School Children	Louise Glück	page 715
Ethics	Linda Pastan	page 717
Those Winter Sundays	Robert Hayden	page 1164
Unlearning to Not Speak	Marge Piercy	page 1179

Nonfiction

Salvation	Langston Hughes	page 225
Ain't I a Woman?	Sojourner Truth	page 1494
Football and Snowballs	Annie Dillard	page 1539

After I finish reading, I ask students simply to sit and think about what they have heard for a minute or two. Then I ask them to write for five minutes, describing their response. Usually, I do not collect these responses. I tell the students that I will not be reading them but that they will be sharing what they have written during class discussion.

I provide the following examples of responses, assuring them that their own responses need not conform to these patterns; they are offered only as possibilities.

- A description of the emotions (anger, amusement, indignation, pleasure) the selection evoked and an explanation of what specifically caused this response

- A comment on an idea, character, description, and so forth, that seemed particularly intriguing, irritating, strange, powerful, and so on

- A comparison between some event, conflict, idea, character, or place in the selection and a similar event, conflict, idea, character, or place from the student's own experience

- A question about something that was puzzling, strange, complex, or hard to understand

- An explanation of why the reader agreed or disagreed with the opinions, choices, or values suggested by the selection

After students have written for five minutes, I ask them to stop. If the class meets for 55 or 75 minutes, I ask them to save their responses to bring to the next class, thank them for their hard work and attention, repeat the assignment for the next class, and say good-bye.

If the class meets for two to three hours at a time, I usually have students take a break at this point. When they return, I respond to their questions about the syllabus (which they have read during the break). Then I ask them to work in small groups of three or four, sharing with each other their responses to the story, poem, or essay I read during the first part of the class. (For classes that meet for 55 or 75 minutes, I do this same exercise at the second class meeting, following the extended discussion of the syllabus. I usually reread the selection to refresh students' memory and to introduce it to those students who have just joined the course.)

I ask students to use the following structure for the small group discussion:

1. State their names and try to use names as they talk with each other.

2. Choose one person to take notes during the discussion and to act as speaker for the group when the class reconvenes.

3. Have *each* person read his or her response *before* any discussion of the responses.

4. Discuss reactions to the responses.

While the small groups are working, I move from group to group. Sometimes, I sit down and listen for a short while. I try not to comment, although I do answer, briefly, questions that are addressed to me.

I usually allow 10–15 minutes for the discussion, depending on the length of the class period and the engagement of students with the discussion. For instance, if after 5 minutes they've all read their responses and are sitting silently or have moved onto topics unrelated to the task at hand, I reconvene the class and ask the speakers to describe what their group had to say. I ask speakers to address their comments to the whole class, and not just to me, and I invite students to take notes so that they can remember their responses to what they hear. They can use these notes during the discussion following the speakers' reports.

As each speaker talks, I take brief notes and work hard to refrain from commenting aloud. After all speakers have given their reports, I invite discussion. Usually, after a warm-up like this, several students volunteer observations or questions. When a lull comes, I ask whether their responses changed at all after they heard what others had to say. After discussing this possibility, I like to reread the selection—or parts of the selection—sometimes stopping at crucial points to comment on observations that have come from the previous discussion.

To bring this class meeting to a close, I repeat the assignment for the next class. Then, using the notes I made as the speakers talked, I comment on the responses that came from the group discussions. Because I think is it essential to establish a positive tone at the beginning of a course, I work hard to acknowledge the strengths I saw. I might mention a particularly intriguing connection that had not previously occurred to me, a question that I'll think about when I next read the selection, or an observation that seemed especially aptly phrased. I praise at least one comment from each group. Although I believe any class meeting is improved by gentle humor, I try my best not to say anything that students could interpret as ridicule or sarcasm.

Because I usually have a good time during this first class, I state my pleasure, thank students for their energy and effort, and tell them that I look forward to hearing more of their responses throughout the term.

TEACHING CHAPTER 1: WHY READ LITERATURE?

This text will be used most frequently in required courses that are often taken somewhat reluctantly by students who have diverse backgrounds, varying interests, and dissimilar career goals. During the past fifteen years, fewer and fewer of the students in introductory classes have been English or humanities majors. Many start their required literature and writing classes with a combination of resignation, resentment, and a desire to "get it over with." In addition, students come from high school English classes that range from superb to absolutely dreadful—with far too many in the middle ground of dull mediocrity. Many students view literature as difficult, puzzling, and boring; they see no reason why they should have to read literature, and many have vowed in their hearts never to read another literary selection after they complete their college requirements.

Through the years, my students have repeatedly voiced fears and complaints similar to these:

- I like to have clear answers and to be able to see what answer is right. In literature classes that never happens.

- Literature has hidden meanings, and I can't ever seem to see them.

- Literature is so hard to read. Why can't they just say it in simple terms?

- Most literature is sad and depressing. I have enough troubles of my own; I don't want to read about other people's problems.

- Most literature is boring. I just can't get interested.

- I like to read literature, but I can't remember all the little details so I never get good grades on quizzes.

- I never have the same view as the teacher so I can't get a good grade.

- I don't see what reading literature has to do with being a nurse (or a computer analyst, business executive, technical writer, lawyer, and so on).

Recognizing such complexities, instructors have every right to feel discouraged. Yet, I believe we can convince many of these reluctant students that reading literature does add an important and rewarding dimension to their lives. Because I've come to anticipate concerns such as those listed above,

I try to make sure to address these issues (although not always directly) during the first week or two of class.

To prepare students for discussion, assign Chapter 1 as homework, and ask students to come to class with brief written responses to each of the exercises. You may want to collect these written responses at the end of the class period to get an idea of your students' literary sophistication and writing ability. If you do plan to collect and read these paragraphs, consider these options:

- Ask students not to put their names on the papers. Explain that you will be reading them to get to know the class as a whole, not to judge the abilities of individuals.

- Ask students to sign their papers. Explain that you will not be grading or returning the papers; you are simply reading them to get to know them better.

- Ask students to sign their papers. Explain that you will not be grading them but that you will return them with a brief comment.

- Ask students to sign their papers. Explain that you will grade and return them. (My own preference is to grade nothing so early in the term.)

Begin the discussion by asking students to read or explain their response to the ideas expressed by the sample paragraphs in the chapter. You might mention that many students see a sharp distinction between what they read for pleasure and what they read for school assignments. This is a great time to get them talking about what they read for relaxation. The discussion sometimes moves faster if you discuss your own pleasure reading, particularly if—like most of us—you sometimes enjoy a mystery, a science fiction novel, a spy thriller, or even those thick tomes that trade publishers call "family sagas." Students seem to think that professors spend all their leisure time reading obscure epics in the original Greek. Letting them know that you, too, sometimes read strictly for entertainment helps to establish common ground.

Sometimes students are reluctant to describe what they read, but those who are self-confident enough to be honest often express variations of these responses:

Stephen King! I could relate to the guy who reads King because I've read every novel he's written. To me he's great.

I read Danielle Steele. Her stories have happy endings, and they make me forget my own problems.

The guy who writes about places and how they got started . . . yeah . . . Michener. The first hundred pages you really have to struggle, but then the story gets good.

The *Clan of the Cave Bear* and her other stuff. I couldn't
believe all the research, and she made ancient history seem
real.

Certainly these are not reading choices to gladden the heart of the
literature instructor, yet they open the door of possibility. After listening to
some examples of students' relaxation reading and after mentioning some of my
own, I explain that in my own mind I see two distinct kinds of reading that I do
for pleasure. The first kind of book I read strictly for entertainment. The
example I usually use is the mystery novel with an academic setting, for
instance, Amanda Cross's books. I tell students that I probably enjoy these
mysteries so much because, in some ways, I can identify with their hero,
English professor Kate Fansler. Yet, in many ways, Fansler's adventures—and
Fansler, herself—also provide me with experiences that I will never have. She
eats what she wants, yet remains thin and elegant as she solves one hair-
raising murder case after another. As much as I enjoy reading these adventures,
however, I have to admit that I don't remember much about them after I've
finished reading. These books hold my interest, they are very easy to read, and
they require almost nothing from me—perfect for evenings when I am exhausted
or when I want to take my mind off my latest project. I read them without
apology and regard them as one of the few pleasures in life that are reasonably
inexpensive, nonfattening, and (as far as I know) noncarcinogenic.

Yet precisely because these books require little from me they also give me
very little to keep permanently as part of my life's experience. And that's
where the other kind of reading comes in. The other kind of reading is, for me,
quite often difficult. I may have to read and reread several lines or even a
whole passage before I can make sense of it (or decide that "making sense of it"
is not important). When I read a book, poem, play, or nonfiction selection of this
kind, I gain more from the experience when I can share my responses and
thoughts with someone else. Selections such as these invite questions,
expressions of strong feelings, and quite often friendly (or not-so-friendly)
arguments. Sometimes I think I decided to become an English professor so that I
would have readily available groups of people with whom I could read works
that require such energy and effort. Selections of this kind do not provide easy
answers and often have unhappy or even indefinite conclusions. But what I love
about reading books, stories, poems, or plays such as these is that they stay
with me. Years after I've finished an initial reading, I'll be moved to return to
a familiar piece, wondering if I'll see it in the same way or if this older me will
have a different reading.

For me, a complex, difficult work is often not entirely pleasurable—and
almost never relaxing—the first time I read it. I can compare the experience to
visiting a new country, or even a new city, for the first time. I have to spend a
great deal of time and energy getting to know my way around. Each hour brings
new challenges and surprises: some breathtakingly beautiful, some exciting,

some infuriating or frustrating. I am watchful, somewhat on guard, hoping not to miss anything. Only after I know where I'm going, perhaps when I return for another visit, do I begin to feel relaxed and able to be more fully open to what the city or country has to offer. And, of course, when I'm home again, I replay the experiences of the visit in my head. Those images and memories become a permanent part of me. I think that they make my life larger and fuller, just as I believe that reading challenging works of literature makes my life larger and fuller.

These are my own ways of thinking about why I read literature. You may have an entirely different way of looking at the demands and pleasures of reading literature. Whatever your beliefs, I am convinced that explaining to students how you read helps them to see that learning to read literature is a complex process that gives much, yet demands much. No one is born loving Shakespeare or Dickens or Dickinson or Baldwin. And very few readers fall in love with these writers at "first read." Yet those of us who have chosen this profession surely believe that giving challenging literature a fair chance is well worth the effort.

After discussing my own way of looking at reading (and of course admitting that many works do not fall clearly into either the category of pleasure reading or challenging reading), I ask students about their own experiences with reading that they considered difficult when they first encountered it. I ask them to take a few minutes to make a list of such works and then to note what they remember about reading them. Some students' examples will show that they have gained something they value from challenging reading; others will claim to remember little or nothing of reading that has been difficult for them in the past. I try to listen carefully to their experiences and to understand what they are telling me both about their frustrations and their positive experiences.

At some point in the discussion, I address any concerns students may have raised. These usually are similar to those listed at the beginning of this section. Because one of the main fears students express is not having the "right" answer, it's helpful to ask for volunteers to read their responses to Frost's "The Road Not Taken." This poem is quite accessible, and many students will have read it before. By comparing your students' comments with the student comments in the text, you should be able to point out that there are many different ways of looking at this poem and that the details of the poem support or back up many different readings.

For example, you might call attention to the section called "Commentary." The idea that a sigh may be interpreted in different ways might not have occurred to all students, but seeing these various possibilities opens new ways of looking at the poem. You may want to point out that these differences in interpretation don't necessarily mean that one person is right and the other wrong; they simply suggest new possibilities.

ORAL RESPONSE

This chapter provides a transcript of a planned oral response to "The Road Not Taken." As part of the assignment for the next several classes, you may want to ask students to read a poem and to plan a response that they will give orally. I ask that the response take no longer than three minutes, and I allow students to write out what they are going to say, although I encourage them to talk from notes rather than to read. I tell them I'm looking for responses that in some way relate the poem to something they have experienced or observed in their own lives. Like the model in the text, the response should refer to the poem, but it does not have to "explain what the poem means." I like to have no more than ten students give an oral response per class. Five per class is ideal. Keeping the number of responses low provides time for you or the student to read the poem aloud before giving the response and also permits discussion of the poems and the responses. I provide a list of suggested poems and then ask students working on the same poem to give their responses on the same day. The following poems work well for this assignment:

Incident	Countee Cullen	page 158
Fifteen	William Stafford	page 171
My Mother	Robert Mezey	page 471
Patterns	Amy Lowell	page 596
Dulce et Decorum Est	Wilfred Owen	page 599
"Out, Out—"	Robert Frost	page 853
And She Did	Natalie Safir	page 1179
Unlearning to Not Speak	Marge Piercy	page 1179
Telephone Conversation	Wole Soyinka	page 1183

JOURNALS

If you plan to have students keep journals during the semester, review Chapter 1, which describes journals and provides an opportunity for you to explain what you expect. How many entries do you want students to write each week? Will you specify a length for each entry? Should the entries be carefully written, revised, and edited? Or are the journals to be a place where students can explore ideas, free from the restraints of formal writing?

For many years now, I've asked students to keep journals in all the courses I teach, from basic writing classes to graduate seminars. I find in journals the most important writing the students do during the semester, perhaps because I structure them to encourage and reward risk taking. I urge students to think of the journals as a place to try out ideas and to explore responses both to the literature we read and to class discussions. At least one entry per week must concern the works assigned for reading and discussion during that week. In the other entry, they may express new thoughts about works we've read earlier or comment on issues raised during class discussion. Each week, students write at least two entries, which, together, must total approximately 250 words. As long as students fulfill these requirements, they earn full credit (I make the journals 10% of their grade).

Sometimes I use the journals to get discussion started, either by inviting volunteers to read entries they have written on a specific work or by asking students to work in small groups, reading to each other what they have written. (As always, one member of the group acts as recorder and later as speaker for the group.)

Journals are a great place for students to explore possibilities for oral responses or for formal papers. In Chapter 2, samples of student journal entries introduce each section, and in Chapter 3 several sample entries show how journals help students discover and work through ideas for further development in formal papers.

Usually I encourage students to find their own journal topics, although I do provide a list of suggestions (see the guidelines at the end of Chapter 1). I assure students that I will not be correcting or editing what they write in their journals. Instead, I will read carefully what they have to say and respond with my own comments and questions. As I read students' journals, I jot observations in the margins and usually write a sentence or two at the end of each entry. I try to keep these comments as positive as possible. Obviously, I do not agree with or admire everything I read in the journals, and I often ask questions or suggest possibilities that I think might interest or encourage the student. For the most part, however, I try to praise an intriguing insight, a perceptive observation, or a moving personal connection.

The journals also provide a private and safe setting for communicating with students each week. For instance, if I notice that a student seems uncomfortable during group work or during discussion, I make a note in the journal, asking if I can be of help and suggesting that the student visit me during office hours or talk with me after class. Just as I can communicate with students through the journals, so, too, have I found that they use the journals to tell me about some troublesome or rewarding aspect of the course.

I collect journals once a week and return them no later than a week after the day they were submitted. To facilitate handling journals, I ask students to write on loose-leaf paper and to submit just one week's entries to me in a pocket folder. When I return the journals, students remove the entries with my comments and store them in a three-ring notebook. Then they place their new entries in the folders and hand them back to me. In this way, I carry home slim folders rather than heavy notebooks of varying sizes and shapes.

Some instructors do not collect journals but do ask students to bring them to class to use as a basis for discussion. Some instructors collect journals and return them with only a checkmark to indicate "accepted" or a minus sign to indicate "needs improvement before I can accept it." Some instructors collect and grade journals, evaluating them much as they would an essay or research paper. My preference, as I suggest above, is to make the journal count for 10% of the course grade. As long as students submit the required number of entries and write 250 words per week, they receive full credit. If a student misses entries and does not make them up, I deduct credit, 1% for each missing journal entry. Usually students work hard on the journals because they are writing in a grade-free context that allows them a great deal of freedom. If, however, I feel that a student is putting in very little effort, I'll ask for an office conference to discuss the way the student sees the journal assignments and the way I see the journal assignments. We usually come up with a satisfactory solution.

The journal work has many helpful side-effects. For example, because students have to make journal entries about the assigned readings, they come to class prepared, having thought about what they've read. Since I've been assigning journals, I've found quizzes neither necessary nor useful. Also, journal writing helps to put students at ease with the process. Journals convince them that writing *is* a way of thinking, and many of them begin to be more comfortable with formal writing as well. Finally, journals provide a window into thoughts, hopes, and feelings that students might not readily express aloud in class. You have a chance to know what they really think and feel as they read the assigned selections, and often these insights can help to shape future class plans.

TEACHING CHAPTER 2:
JOINING THE CONVERSATION

As I suggested in my discussion of teaching Chapter 1, students often show some hostility or anxiety as they begin their required literature and writing courses. A frequently voiced concern relates to literary vocabulary. Students often believe that they cannot join the conversation because they don't know how to express and explore their responses. They know that a short story infuriates, bores, or confuses them; they read a poem that they like well enough to read a second time; they find a scene in a play puzzling, but intriguing. Yet when they try to explain or evaluate these responses, they feel shy and defensive.

This text differs from many in approaching the language of literature as a cohesive whole rather than as separate lists of terms that apply only to fiction, or to poetry, or to drama, or to nonfiction. Of course, each genre does have unique aspects, which are addressed in the brief introductory sections to the genre anthologies. Chapter 2 contains four readings, Patricia Grace's short story, "Butterflies"; Langston Hughes's poem, "Theme for English B"; Wendy Wasserstein's play, *The Man in a Case*; and E. B. White's essay, "Education." Because all of these selections are short, I assign them for one class. In addition, I ask students to come to class with a short written response (perhaps a journal entry) for at least one of the selections. Suggestions for responding follow each of the works. These exercises and the explanations that accompany them introduce literary language in a natural, informal way.

At the beginning of the class, students might work in groups, with each group focusing on a different selection. If there are more than twenty-five students in the class, more than one group may work on a selection, since groups of more than five or six become unmanageable. After students share their responses, reconvene the class and have the recorders from each group summarize their discussion.

After the discussion, you might point out to students that many of the comments addressed certain aspects of the selections:

Actions and events

People

Times and places

Sounds and images, words and patterns

Ideas

You might write these aspects on the board and then ask students to see whether their own written responses addressed any of these points. Note, also, that many times a comment addresses more than one aspect. After students think about what they've written, ask for volunteers to read comments and to explain whether the comment addresses one of these categories, several of these categories, or, perhaps, none (which, of course, is fine).

This exercise leads to reading and discussing the rest of Chapter 2, which introduces students to ways of thinking, reading, and writing about literature. I recommend that you spend one class hour on "Actions and events," "People," and "Times and places," and another on "Sounds and images, words and patterns" and "Ideas." In addition, you'll probably want students to read some selections from the anthology section of the text to use as part of class discussion.

Each section includes observations, evaluations, or questions written by students who read and responded to the selections that appear at the beginning of the chapter. Obviously, students are not expected to write responses exactly like these; they are included to suggest possibilities. In addition, these sample writings can serve as inspiration for journal entries.

Following the students' responses in Chapter 2, a commentary showing how these responses reflect the language of literature introduces literary terms. Each section ends with a list of terms related to the aspect of literature just discussed and with exercises designed to help students explore new ways of thinking, reading, and writing about literature. Frequently, an exercise asks students to apply the new terms to television programs or films. Because many students will have seen the same television programs and films, these examples provide common ground for exploring and thinking about literary terms. In addition, most students are comfortable with their knowledge of television and film and feel confident in expressing their ideas about these media.

Examples of comments relating to the television/film exercises include the following:

Events and Actions:

On an episode of "L.A. Law," one of the lawyers had a brother who was seriously injured in a car accident and was brain-dead. The family had to decide whether or not to remove him from life-support systems. There were conflicts among family members and between the family members and the medical professionals. You could see that it was not an easy decision, and everybody seemed to have their good reasons for what they wanted to do.

People:

When I was watching "China Beach," I was amazed at the changes in Colleen McMurphy. At first, she was really idealistic, and then she got more and more cynical. After the war, she became an alcoholic. But it was easy to believe these changes because the program showed all the things these people went through. She was a nurse who saw people die all the time in horrible ways. Then, after the Vietnam vets and nurses came home, nobody cared. I think that's why she became so depressed. Nobody wanted to think or talk about what had happened there.

Times and Places:

If you take a program like "Star Trek," it absolutely has to be happening in the future. Also, because it has the idea of going "where no one has gone before," it really has to take place either in a spaceship or on a space station—something like that. So I would say that setting is very important. Even some of the characters, like complex androids or the blind person who has glasses to make him see, could exist only in the future. And every conflict I've seen on the program is related to a space-travel or future-related situation.

Ideas:

The film *Do the Right Thing* really made me think a lot because it seemed like no one was really a hero. No one was all right or all wrong. But the idea that seemed to come to me was that unless people start looking at each other as humans and as individuals, instead of "black" or "Italian" or "Korean" or whatever, this country is going to be completely torn apart.

Writing and discussing observations like these helps students to see that they already understand varied ways of looking closely at literature.

The exercises at the end of each section in Chapter 2 relate the language of literature not only to films and television but also to familiar aspects of students' lives. Consider using one or more of these exercises as the basis for a brief in-class writing assignment. Ask students to think about the topic before they come to class, and then ask them to write for five or ten minutes when they first get to class. In this way, everyone will have something to offer in a discussion.

After an introductory warm-up writing assignment like this, I often ask one student to volunteer to read his or her comment and then continue around the circle, asking each person to read or summarize what he or she has written. Before they begin to write, I tell students I plan to ask each person to respond. I want to let them know that they are writing for the whole class and not just for me or for themselves.

I don't usually collect the brief in-class writings that have been read and discussed in class. Sometimes, however, I do use one or more of the exercise topics as the basis for a longer, more formal in-class essay, which I do collect and grade. Of course, if I am going to collect and grade anything the students write, I always tell them ahead of time. I also find that I get much stronger, more interesting formal in-class essays if I announce the topic (at least in a general way) at the class meeting before students are scheduled to write. I encourage them to think about topics ahead of time and to feel free to bring in a 3 x 5 card with an outline (to be signed and attached to the essay with a paper clip).

TEACHING CHAPTER 3:
WRITING ABOUT LITERATURE

This is a long chapter that covers a great deal of information. Students are asked to consider different ways of thinking and writing about literature and in addition are encouraged to review aspects of the writing process.

As I suggested earlier, students with varying interests, career goals, and academic preparation enroll in introductory literature courses. Nowhere are their diverse backgrounds more obvious than in their writing skills. When you begin discussing Chapter 3, consider asking students to jot down any memories they have of writing about literature in their previous English courses. For example, did they write papers? In or out of class? Essay exams? Did they write about their own responses? Did they write research papers? If so, what kind of research were they asked to do? What other kinds of writing did they do? Did they keep journals? What, if anything, seemed difficult about writing about literature? What, if anything, seemed rewarding?

By opening with this discussion, you give students a chance to express their concerns, and you have a chance to discover issues you may want to address during the term. As you listen to what students have to say, you'll be able to predict accurately that some will be fine writers who will further develop their abilities in this course. For example, some students, fresh from innovative classrooms with dedicated, energetic teachers, will have written response papers, including creative as well as evaluative and interpretive essays. Some students will have learned how to integrate details and examples from what they have read into the essays they write. Some will have learned how to use secondary sources in thoughtful, original ways. Many more will not.

For instance, at least half the students in every literature class I teach describe high school English courses where little or no writing about literature was required or encouraged. The short-answer or objective exam was, for many, their only experience in writing about literature. Other students wrote responses to the questions at the end of the chapter in the text book and then read them aloud in class while the teacher praised or corrected them. One student described a course where the teacher stopped frequently to consult the instructor's guide to see whether the "answers" were "right or wrong."

In addition to lacking the special skills required for writing about literature, many students still need instruction in the process of writing. Consider, for instance, the students whose first language is not English or those who took their freshman writing course ten or more years ago and have not have used formal writing skills since that time. The introductory literature and writing course presents special problems for these students. In addition, although your college or university may have a fine introductory writing program, some students may have fulfilled their freshman writing requirement at a college or university that takes a less rigorous approach to the course. Still other students may have barely earned a passing grade in their freshman writing course. Whatever the circumstances, most students need to review the writing process and, in addition, learn specific ways to write about literature. This chapter provides that opportunity.

Although the chapter is far too long to cover in detail during one class meeting, you might ask students to skim the whole chapter and to read carefully the introduction as well as the section "Writing to Respond." You might mention that each section of the chapter provides a model of a student's process, demonstrating possible approaches to writing about literature in different ways.

During class discussion, you might point out the different parts of the student's process demonstrated in "Writing to Respond" and remind students that each section contains the same (or similar) parts:

Discovering Ideas

Considering Audience

Narrowing the Topic

Devising a Preliminary Thesis Statement

Planning Organization

Drafting

Revising Focus

Editing Focus

Proofreading Focus

Of course, each section provides different possibilities for these aspects of the writing process. Following this class discussion, encourage students to read through the chapter to be sure they are aware of the many options open to them. In addition, as you assign papers during the course, you may want to ask students to read carefully and to discuss in class an appropriate section from Chapter 3.

ON BEING HUMAN: LITERARY THEMES

Each of the seven parts of this section of the book contains five fiction selections, ten to fifteen poems, one play, and two nonfiction selections relating to a single theme. Each theme reflects some aspect of the human experience:

Innocence and Experience

Work

Men and Women

Parents and Children

War

Learning and Teaching

Death

Each section begins with a photograph, chosen to provide inspiration for writing and to stimulate discussion of that section's theme. To get students thinking about the theme they'll be considering as they read the selections that follow, ask students to respond to the photograph.

Following most of the selections are "Considerations": suggestions for thinking, talking, and writing about the section's theme. At the end of each section are "Connections": suggestions for seeing relationships among the selections.

In this guide, the introduction to each part suggests possibilities for teaching that theme. Following the introduction is a list of additional selections related to the theme but appearing elsewhere in the text. Using this supplementary list makes it possible to choose only two or three themes for a term's work. You might also ask students to explore works in this supplementary list and write about them on their own. At the end of each supplementary list, I suggest possibilities for thinking, discussing, and writing about these selections.

Although many instructors using this text will choose to teach the first three chapters and then several thematic units, my own approach is to follow the first three chapters with a week or two on each of the genre anthology sections. After giving students a brief introduction to fiction, poetry, drama, and nonfiction, I then work with three or four thematic units for the rest of the term, spending approximately two weeks on each theme.

PART I
INNOCENCE AND EXPERIENCE

Most people can remember specific moments when a cherished idea was suddenly challenged or a much-admired friend or relative showed a particularly disillusioning weakness. You might begin this thematic section by asking students to write a brief reflection on such a moment in their lives. Consider suggesting that they focus on an event that is no longer deeply distressing for them. Even so, some students may not be comfortable discussing such sharp and often intimate disappointments, but others will provide examples that demonstrate clearly the move from innocence to experience. Some may even have gained enough emotional distance to see humor in what was originally upsetting or even shocking.

Nearly all the selections in this section focus on the changes of young people: children or adolescents. You might initiate discussion, however, about the nature of the move from innocence to experience. Does this passage occur primarily in childhood, adolescence, or young adulthood? Or does it keep happening throughout one's life? Even if all class members are adolescents or young adults, students should be able to generalize from their observations of older friends and relatives or of older characters they have encountered in books and films.

"Bad Characters" and "The Bass, The River, and Sheila Mant," combine humor and pathos to suggest both the beauty and the pain of innocence. You might generate lively controversy and discussion by asking students to consider what the main characters gain—and what they lose—from the insights they attain. "By the Sea," "The Circling Hand," and *The Glass Menagerie* take a more somber look at the clash of illusion and reality. All three of these works focus on the dynamics of family relationships, exploring how those relationships affect the way children and young people develop their hopes, fears, and visions of the future.

To introduce the poems, ask students to consider the many parts of our lives that are touched by the move from innocence to experience. The poems offer a wide range of possibilities: the effects of racial bigotry in "Incident"; the betrayal of love in "When I was one-and-twenty" and "In the Orchard"; the conflict of desire and responsibility in "Fifteen"; encounters with sexual stereotyping in "The Centaur," "In the Counselor's Waiting Room," and "Snow White and the Seven Dwarfs"; and the contrast of life and early death in "First Death in Nova Scotia" and "We Real Cool."

ADDITIONAL SELECTIONS FOR CONSIDERATION: INNOCENCE AND EXPERIENCE

Title and Author		Text Page
Journey of the Magi	T. S. Eliot	1151
In the Waiting Room	Elizabeth Bishop	1162
Those Winter Sundays	Robert Hayden	1164

Drama

All My Sons	Arthur Miller	478
The Lesson	Eugène Ionesco	722
An Enemy of the People	Henrik Ibsen	1341
A Raisin in the Sun	Lorraine Hansberry	1414

Nonfiction

I Remember Papa	Harry Dolan	551
Purpose, Blame, and Fire	Donald Hall	644
Learning to Read and Write	Frederick Douglass	757
Shooting an Elephant	George Orwell	1528
Arrival at Manzanar	Jeanne Wakatsuki Houston and James D. Houston	1534

SUGGESTIONS FOR TEACHING ADDITIONAL SELECTIONS

1. Consider the connection between family relationships and the journey from innocence to experience. How do the parents in these works affect their children's development? What do you see as positive about the relationships? Negative?

	Text Page
The Man Who Was Almost a Man	264
My Oedipus Complex	435
Through the Tunnel	445
Today	477
My Papa's Waltz	467
Those Winter Sundays	1164

All My Sons	478
A Raisin in the Sun	1414
I Remember Papa	551

2.   In the following works, the journey from innocence to experience is
     described with varying degrees of humor. After reading these works,
     compare the way these authors use humor to describe their character's
     passage. Consider also episodes in your own life that moved you from
     innocence to experience. Did you consider any of them funny at the time
     they happened? Do you consider any of them funny now?

	Text Page
My Oedipus Complex	435
Why I Like Country Music	657
To Hell with Dying	816
A Temple of the Holy Ghost	1022
Purpose, Blame, and Fire	644

3.   In the following works, characters are affected because someone else
     sees them as different and, therefore, as inferior. Consider how
     individuals are moved from innocence to experience by the way others
     view them.

	Text Page
The Man Who Was Almost a Man	264
Battle Royal	683
A Teacher Taught Me	716
A Raisin in the Sun	1414
Learning to Read and Write	757
Arrival at Manzanar	1534

4.   Consider how an encounter with death, or contemplation of death,
     relates to the passage from innocence to experience.

	Text Page
Guests of the Nation	566
The Garden Party	966

THEMATIC PHOTOGRAPH (page 109)

Considerations

1. Describe the people in the picture. What do they look like? What are they doing? Do their expressions suggest particular emotions?

2. Describe the relationship between the woman and the boy.

3. Write a dialogue suggesting the conversation between the woman and boy that has been interrupted by the picture taking.

4. Does one person in the picture suggest experience and the other innocence? Explain. As you respond, consider your definition of innocence and of experience.

READINGS

James Joyce, Araby (page 110)

Readers who describe themselves as "enjoying a good plot" or "liking stories with lots of action" often have a hard time with "Araby." Many of my students have described their initial response to the story in two words: "Nothing happens." They are particularly disappointed with the ending which either makes no sense to them or seems vastly exaggerated. In addition, many first-time readers do not see that the person telling the story is much older than the person experiencing the throes of adolescent love.

To address these issues, I usually read several passages aloud. I start with the opening description, asking students to picture the world in which the narrator lives. Then I read a paragraph or two describing his reveries as he thinks of Mangan's sister. Students relate especially well to the fantasies he creates as he sits listening to the boring drone of his teacher. One student suggested that the external scenes seem like old sepia-print photographs whereas the day dreams are like paintings done with a full-range of colors. The young narrator moves from the dreariness of his day-to-day life into dramatic, chivalric scenes with his own vision of Mangan's sister serving as the means of transportation: "Her image accompanied me even in places the most hostile to romance."

Students often initially think nothing happens in the story because most of the action takes place inside the narrator's head and heart. Addressing this point often leads to a lively discussion of whether they see their own journeys of the mind and spirit as equally significant to journeys of the body. Even those who are reluctant to offer personal experiences can usually relate to the idea of events, changes, and insights that have been extremely important to them, yet have seemed trivial to others who have not understood the emotional impact of these events, changes, and insights.

Another problem, especially with younger readers, is the lack of background knowledge to understand the details of the religious quest for the Grail. The narrator knows the story of King Arthur and his knights. He can relate both to the concept of courtly love and to the search for the chalice of faith. It's useful to recount briefly the details of this legend—and perhaps to ask students to see how this legend has become part of many of the films they watch. Also, discuss the implications of the name "Araby." Currently, many students have negative responses to things middle eastern and you'll need to remind them of the different responses young boys in early twentieth-century Ireland would have had.

After students discuss the issues just mentioned, I close the class by reading the final passage and asking them to consider moments in their own lives when they may have felt themselves to be "creature[s] driven and derided by vanity." Most have no trouble doing so, and I've read many moving and powerful journal entries written in response to this request.

Jean Stafford, Bad Characters (page 115)

Nearly all students appreciate the combination of humor and pathos in Emily's story, but they usually disagree strongly in their responses to her. Many see Emily as thoroughly disagreeable at the beginning of the story. She acts cruelly to her friends and apparently terrorizes her younger sister, Tess. According to this reading, Emily allows herself to be taken in by the sly Lottie Jump because, having alienated everyone else, Emily is desperate for companionship. Even with Lottie, Emily cannot control herself and has one of her "attacks" of meanness during the shoplifting episode. Because Lottie pays her back in kind, Emily becomes a more compassionate and tactful person. She is rewarded by having "two or three friends at a time."

Other students see Emily as a lively, impetuous girl who finds herself out of step with her staid family and well-behaved but boring friends. Like her cat, Muff, she has an untamed quality that scares and shocks her proper community. In Lottie Jump, Emily almost certainly sees something of herself. Like Emily, Lottie can "swear vilely," and like Emily, she is bored by ordinary pursuits. Lottie, however, comes from a world very different from Emily's. And perhaps when Emily is faced, finally, with acting not just outrageously but also illegally, she says no to Lottie as well as to her own wild self. In this view, Emily stops herself; Lottie is simply a means to an end. At the conclusion of the story, Emily claims not to have "root[ed] out every bit of badness," but it seems clear that she is headed toward a life of outward conformity. She may long to knife her brother or swear at her sister, but she restrains herself. Like Muff— who calms down, grows up, and starts "having literally millions of kittens"— Emily recognizes that she is destined, at least on the surface, to follow the conventions of her community.

A. E. Housman, When I was one-and-twenty (page 157)

In just one year the speaker, originally filled with optimism, moves to a pessimistic view of romantic love. In the first stanza, the wise man advises the speaker not to take emotional risks. He seems to urge the speaker to avoid commitment to any one woman ("Keep your fancy free"). In the second stanza, the advice is retrospective. The wise man comments on what has already occurred, noting that the result of giving oneself fully is "sighs a plenty" and "endless rue." Students readily debate whether or not the advice given is truly wise. Many argue that the speaker's misery simply reflects his recent experiences with romantic love and that he may well change, depending on what happens in the future. The "wise man," however, maintains his view from one year to the next. He is apparently a confirmed cynic who will go through life avoiding connection with others because of the pain he may encounter.

Anne Sexton, Snow White and the Seven Dwarfs (page 163)

Admired primarily for her virginity and her doll-like appearance, Snow White may well find herself in later life following the path of her stepmother and dancing in red-hot shoes (note in the final two lines the ominous reference to Snow White's "referring to her mirror/as women do.") This poem suggests that age cannot be equated with wisdom. For women like Snow White and the Wicked Queen, trapped in the myth of beauty, the passage from innocence to experience brings disillusionment rather than enlightenment.

William Blake, London (page 167)

As the speaker walks through London, he sees images that appall and disgust. Even babies, symbols of innocence, are blighted by the circumstances of their tawdry, impoverished lives. Young boys work at the dangerous, filthy job of chimney sweeping; young girls become prostitutes. Nothing is untouched by the corruption of the city.

Gerard Manley Hopkins, Spring and Fall: To a Young Child (page 168)

The older narrator speaks to a child, Margaret, as she mourns the passing of the seasons. His tone suggests sympathy and consolation as he gently leads Margaret to see that she regrets more than the falling leaves: she also senses her own passage from innocent childhood to the responsibilities and knowledge of adult life. She sees that like the Goldengrove, she, too, is mortal.

Robert Frost, Birches (page 168)

At the end of the poem, the speaker imagines himself riding the birches. Earlier he has admitted that a storm may well have bent the trees. Yet he favors another possibility: perhaps a country boy, innocent of the games known by children in town, has climbed up and swung down, causing the trunks to bow under his weight. The boy, and vicariously the speaker, take on power through the experience of swinging on the birches. Note especially line 28, where the boy symbolically subdues authority as he bends "one by one . . . his father's trees."

John Crowe Ransom, Blue Girls (page 170)

Compare this poem to "Spring and Fall" (page 168). In both poems, an older (probably male) speaker gives advice to young girls. The speaker in Ransom's poem is less gentle, more despairing, about the plight of the young students he sees walking toward their school. Unlike the speaker in "Spring and Fall," he urges the girls to resist their coming maturity and loss of innocence, instructing them to "listen to your teachers old and contrary/Without believing a word."

Also, compare the final stanza, and the image of tarnished female innocence and youth, to the final stanza of "Snow White and the Seven Dwarfs" (page 163).

Gwendolyn Brooks, We Real Cool (page 170)

As the pool players at the Golden Shovel brag about their activities, they sound anything but innocent. How should the final line be read? Is it the voice of an outside speaker, commenting ironically? Or do the players themselves see where their choices almost inevitably lead?

William Stafford, Fifteen (page 171)

Why does the speaker keep repeating his age? Perhaps this incident marked the moment when he really understood the nature of moral choices. As much as he desires the motorcycle—or, at the very least, the chance to take a joy ride—he stops to think, and realizes the rider of the cycle might be nearby. He acts responsibly, loses the chance to live out his fantasy, yet becomes in the eyes of the injured rider (and perhaps in his own eyes) a "good man."

Muriel Stuart, In the Orchard (page 171)

If two students will volunteer to prepare a reading, the story of desire and betrayal told by this narrative poem will come alive. Identifying the two voices—where one speaker stops and the next begins—leads to asking why Stuart set the poem up as she did. Why not, for example, start a new line each time the speaker changes? Here is one possibility: The intertwining of the voices suggest the pace of the speakers. They are nearly interrupting each other as each rushes to tell his or her side of the story.

Tennessee Williams, The Glass Menagerie (page 173)

Because this play experiments with so many staging devices, students are usually intrigued by imagining how these devices might work at an actual performance and thinking about what they contribute to the play's meaning. Consider asking students to work in groups, with one group addressing the screen device, one the music, and one the lighting. To prepare for class discussion, ask each group to pay special attention to that device as they read the play.

As students discuss their proposed stagings of the play, ask them to base their choices on their own responses to the play and on their evaluations of the characters, setting, action, conflicts and so on. Each group may elect a recorder to explain to the class the group's staging decisions and the reasons behind them.

Williams stated in his own production notes that the Broadway production of the play omitted the screen device (slides projected on a screen at the side of the stage). He decided, however, to retain them in the published manuscript because he believed that these devices emphasized the episodic structure of the play. Each scene, he said, "contains a particular point (or several) which is structurally the most important." He believed that the images and legends on the screen would "strengthen the effect of what is merely allusion in the writing and allow the primary point to be made more simply and lightly than if the entire responsibility were on the spoken lines."

Although it's always dangerous to insist too strongly on autobigraphical connections in fictional works, students are usually interested in the relationship between this play and parts of Williams's life. Like the absent father in The Glass Menagerie, Williams's father was something of an advernturer who held fast to his memories of the years he served as a lieutenant in the Spanish-American War. In addition, he apparently had a serious drinking problem. Unlike Tom and Laura's father, however, Mr. Williams did not desert the family, although his job as a traveling shoe salesman kept him away from the family for long periods of time. The playwright's mother, like Amanda Wingfield, was raised in a genteel Southern household where her mother and father—an Episcopal clergyman— upheld the values of the antebellum South. WhenThomas (later Tennessee) was born, his mother left the small, crowded apartment where she was frequently left alone by her salesman husband and returned to the comfort and shelter of the Episcopal rectory where she grew up. Williams delighted in the attention of his grandfather, a great storyteller, and was heartbroken when, at age seven, he was forced to move to St. Louis where his father had retained a shabby apartment much like the one described in *The Glass Menagerie*. The play, to some extent, reflects Williams's family life during his adolescent years. Like Tom, Tennessee disliked the work he was able to find and often sought to escape through marathon movie-watching sessions, writing poetry, and, eventually, through travel. Like Laura, Williams's sister Rose was painfully shy, although she was not physically disabled nor did she collect glass animals. When she was committed to an insane asylum in 1939, he was devastated because he had been unable to help her and because her institutionalizaton cut him off from the family member with whom he felt the closest connection.

The music, again according to Williams's stage notes, is to be a "single, recurring tune, 'The Glass Menagerie.' " The music is intended to be associated primarily with Laura and to suggest the connection between the narrator in the present and the narrator as he remembers the past episodes that make up the play. The music, then, would be "like circus music, not when you are on the grounds or in the immediate vicinity of the parade, but when you are at some distance and very likely thinking of someone else." Students may want to speculate about the role music plays in connecting their own present selves with remembered people, places, and events.

According to Williams, the lighting is not realistic. Instead, the stage is kept dim. Often spotlights focus on selected actors or areas of the stage that are not, apparently, the center of the action. For example, during the supper scene, while conversation continues at the table, Laura sits silently on the sofa. Williams notes that her figure is lighted and that the light used "should be distinct from the others, having a peculiar pristine clarity such as light used in early religious portraits of female saints or madonnas."

As a logical continuation of the discussion of staging, have students consider the role of the narrator. If there were no narrator, the play would be very different. The luminous quality of filtered memory would be lost; there would be no sense of retrospection. As an older, more experienced man, Tom as narrator can look back on his younger self—and on his family—with a full and varied vision not possible if the play were presented simply as present action. In addition, the older Tom provides a historical context for the play. For instance, he lets us see that the battles in the Wingfield household are being fought at precisely the time that the innocent, music-filled world outside is marching unaware to the cataclysm of World War II.

Students respond vigorously to the relationships between Amanda and her children and between Laura and Tom. Although Amanda comes in for her share of criticism, she also has her defenders. Some readers see her as the victim of a society that trained women to be social ornaments for men and then stigmatized them when they no longer filled that role. Not many years ago, students were almost unanimous in their defense of Tom, claiming that he was driven to escapist behavior by his mother's need to control and his sister's fragile dependence. Now, however, the changes in attitude toward drinking and drunkenness lead to an ambivalent response; students often see Tom's drinking not only as an act of defiance, but also as an intricate part of the family's dysfunction. The absent Mr. Wingfield—who never appears on stage, but whose portrait dominates the action in several scenes—seems to hover over Tom like a spirit who symbolizes past losses and portends future decisions. Like Mr. Wingfield, Tom will leave the family rather than stay to face both the dangers and the strange beauty of Amanda's and Laura's fantasy worlds.

In connection with this section's theme, you might ask students which characters in the play are innocent and which are experienced. Do some, or all, of the characters move from innocence to experience? I would say that each of the four characters has a degree of innocence during his or her initial scenes in the play. Tom believes that drinking and going to the movies will keep alive a private world where he can escape his tawdry surroundings. He also believes that better times are possible if he could just get away from his present circumstances. Laura is the most innocent character in the play, and, although she suffers a cruel disillusionment, she does not seem to move from that innocence. Amanda holds firmly to her romantic dreams of an idealized girlhood, refusing to accept or recognize fully the nature of the troubles in her household. She believes there are easy, one-step solutions. Laura must find a husband or a job. Tom must work hard. Then all would be well. Jim is the most practical character in the play, yet, in his own way, he is also innocent. He believes in the American dream—have interests, work hard, and you'll get ahead. He also shows himself to be innocent—or at least naive—about male-female relationships. In spite of Amanda's broad hints, he doesn't seem to realize that he has been invited as a prospective beau for Laura. When he realizes that he has hurt her, he learns that his simple approach to life may not work for everyone. He sees complexities he had not considered before.

Laura, on the other hand, fails to change. During her dance with Jim, it seems that she might come to realize that she no longer has to think of herself as a glass unicorn—different and separated from the rest of the world. Yet her moment of warmth and acceptance is too short; Jim almost immediately reveals that he is engaged and Laura returns to her simple, fantasy world.

Amanda and Tom are the most complex innocents. At the end of Scene VI, Amanda accuses Tom of being a "selfish dreamer," and, as she turns to comfort her daughter while Tom walks out the door, it seems possible that she realizes her own dreams for her daughter must be abandoned. But the question remains whether she is emotionally strong enough to fully face the world of experience and to step firmly from the romanticized past to the complex, difficult present.

The narrator's final words suggest that Tom does not, and cannot, move fully from the world of innocence to the world of experience until he tells his family's story. If this play were not told retrospectively, by an older Tom who looks back on this significant time in his life, it would not be clear that Tom does grow and learn. Leaving his mother and sister is one step, but, to lay to rest the ghosts of the past, he must look honestly at what happened. He honors his sister by telling her story, yet he must urge her to blow out the candles that illuminate the disturbing images that have continued to haunt him.

PART II
WORK

In "The Virtues of Ambition" Joseph Epstein explores the definition of "ambition" and considers the connection between ambition and work. Consider assigning this essay as the initial reading for this thematic section. (This selection is short enough to be read in class, especially if the class periods are longer than one hour.) After students read Epstein's essay, ask them to write their own definitions of ambition and to discuss the connection between ambition and work in their own lives.

As students consider Epstein's essay, some will also note his interest in the relationships among ambition, work, and the family. Exploring these relationships leads logically to considering how work was traditionally divided into "men's work" and "women's work." Younger students are often amazed to hear that newspaper "Help Wanted" advertisements used to be divided into "Help Wanted-Male" and "Help Wanted-Female." Discussing whether or not these distinctions still exist in any way provides entry into the followings works: "Tom's Husband," "A Letter to Her Husband," "The River-Merchant's Wife," *Trifles*, and "Professions for Women."

"The Use of Force," "The Catbird Seat," "The Man Who Was Almost a Man," "Bartleby, the Scrivener," and *Trifles* look at values and at moral choices related to the world of work. Ask students to list moral choices that might arise in the work they are currently doing or hope to do when they complete school. Writing some of these choices on the board facilitates discussion of this aspect of work.

Most students have held jobs and are eager to recount their own experiences with worker-management or worker-customer relations. These student anecdotes encourage deeper appreciation of works that explore relationships between workers and those who have authority over them or those whom they must serve. Consider, for example, "The Man Who Was Almost a Man," "Bartleby, the Scrivener," "Waiting Table," "The Unknown Citizen," and "The Death of the Hired Hand."

ADDITIONAL SELECTIONS FOR CONSIDERATION: WORK

Title and Author		Text Page
An Enemy of the People	Henrik Ibsen	1341
A Raisin in the Sun	Lorraine Hansberry	1414

Nonfiction

Being a Man	Paul Theroux	422
I Remember Papa	Harry Dolan	551
Learning to Read and Write	Frederick Douglass	757
Ain't I a Woman?	Sojourner Truth	1494
Shooting an Elephant	George Orwell	1528
In Search of Our Mothers' Gardens	Alice Walker	1542

SUGGESTIONS FOR TEACHING ADDITIONAL SELECTIONS

1.   What is the relationship between work and the creative arts? Can creating be considered work only when there is a visible product? Must the artist gain fame, acclaim, or monetary reward for his or her effort to be considered work? Do you consider activities like making jam, building models, or embroidering as art, work, recreation?

	Text Page
Shiloh	361
A Hunger Artist	959
Sonny's Blues	997
Aunt Jennifer's Tigers	401
Making the Jam without You	468
Digging	473
Being a Man	422
In Search of Our Mothers' Gardens	1542

2.   How are workers affected by their employees or others on whom their continued employment depends (for instance, the guests a waitress

serves or the audience for whom an actor performs)? When do workers have power over their own lives? When do they lack power? How do they respond to having or lacking power?

	Text Page
By the Sea	130
A Dirty Story	378
The Fly	576
The Revolt of "Mother"	923
A Hunger Artist	959
All My Sons	478
An Enemy of the People	1341
Ain't I a Woman?	1494
Shooting an Elephant	1528

3. The following works suggest the relationship between work and family. How do parents' attitudes toward work affect the way their sons and daughters approach their work? How do family tensions and pressures affect the work people choose and their attitude toward that work? To what extent do — or should— people consider the values, aspirations, and hopes of family members when they choose or reject their own work?

	Text Page
By the Sea	130
The Revolt of "Mother"	923
Sonny's Blues	997
Digging	473
The Glass Menagerie	173
All My Sons	478
An Enemy of the People	1341
A Raisin in the Sun	1414
I Remember Papa	551
In Search of Our Mothers' Gardens	1542

4. In the following works, black writers explore issues related to work. Use these works as a starting point for further research on questions and

concerns unique to members of minority groups in their quest to find
meaningful work.

	Text Page
Sonny's Blues	997
A Raisin in the Sun	1414
I Remember Papa	551
Learning to Read and Write	757
Ain't I a Woman?	1494
In Search of Our Mothers' Gardens	1542

THEMATIC PHOTOGRAPH (page 240)

Considerations

1. Describe the person visible through the window of the restaurant.
   What does he look like? Speculate on his feelings about his job, his
   dreams, his hopes for the future.

2. Imagine this restaurant in the morning. Describe the people who work
   there as well as those who come to eat. Write a dialogue between
   someone who works there and a customer or group of customers.

3. Write a detailed description of the restaurant as you see it through the
   window. What items seem especially significant to you? Explain.

4. If you have ever worked at a job that seems in some way similar to the
   one held by the man in the picture, describe one hour of that work that
   you consider typical or that you recall as particularly memorable (for
   either negative or positive reasons).

READINGS

William Carlos Williams, The Use of Force (page 241)

Students are intrigued to learn that, in addition to writing prolifically,
Williams worked full time as a pediatrician. You might also point out that in
1938, when the story was first published, diphtheria was a terrifying threat to
children's lives. There was no vaccine against it and no antibiotics to fight it.
To the parents of yesterday, diphtheria and a host of other diseases struck the
same note of fear as leukemia does to today's parents.

Readers' responses usually shift back and forth as they read this story. Mathilda, a sick child, certainly evokes instant sympathy, yet her stubborn refusal to let the doctor examine her, including her physical attack on him, helps us to understand his growing impatience. Because the story is told from the doctor's point of view, his fears and concerns are clear and immediate in readers' minds. Nevertheless, by the end of the episode, the doctor is, as he admits, out of control. Blinded by fury, he experiences "a feeling of adult shame" and calls his final actions an "unreasoning assault."

Class discussion of the story usually raises more questions than it answers. For example, is the doctor's use of force in any way justified? Would Mathilda's life have been seriously threatened by his failure to get the culture specimen at that particular moment? Or might he have left and come back later when she had calmed down? Is force ever justifiable between a professional and a client? And what about the parents? What role do they play? What role should they play?

For an intriguing look at gender issues in the story, see R. F. Dietrich's "The Use of Force" in *Studies in Short Fiction* 3 1966: 446–450. Dietrich suggests that the doctor's behavior would have been different had the child been a boy. Indeed, some of the doctor's comments suggest that he looks at her not only with the eyes of a physician but also with those of a man: He says, for instance, that she is "an unusually attractive little thing" and admits that he "had already fallen in love with the savage brat. . . ."

James Thurber, The Catbird Seat (page 245)

Almost anyone who has ever experienced the tyranny of a supervisor at work will identify with Mr. Martin's outrageous fantasy. When the fantasy is replaced by an equally satisfying, real-life revenge, it's easy to admire the ironically perfect triumph scored by the head of the F & S filing department.

We are given absolutely no reason to sympathize with Mrs. Barrows. By naming her "Ulgine," Thurber suggests both her moral and physical ugliness. Mrs. Barrows terrorizes everyone at S & L, male and female alike. She has gained the upper hand over Mr. Fitweiler by appealing to his vanity at a party, and, in addition to her attempt to take control of S & L, she has an amazing repertoire of irritating personal habits.

Students are usually divided on the issue of whether or not Mr. Martin goes to Mrs. Barrows's house truly prepared to commit murder. Certainly he shows that he is desperate, yet it seems unlikely that anyone as methodical and careful as he would set out to kill someone with no weapon in hand—or even in mind. Having never seen the inside of Mrs. Barrows's house, he could not know whether or not a suitable death-dealing object would be handy. Although he may have convinced himself that he was going to kill Mrs. Barrows, it seems clear that he actually is driven by the desperation to do something— anything—to relieve the anxiety he feels.

In addition to these details of plot and character, the tone of the story is clearly comic. If we believe that Mr. Martin is truly a failed murderer, the delightful irony of the final revenge is tarnished.

Sarah Orne Jewett, Tom's Husband (page 253)

This story was published in 1884, long before most women worked outside the home, and certainly long before nearly any man worked at keeping house. Mary's and Tom's plight suggests the complexities of the issue of finding meaningful work. You might begin discussion by asking who—Mary or Tom—has more options within the framework of the story. Although Tom certainly has the power to grant Mary her wish to manage the factory—and in the end to convince her to leave her work—he does not have the power to find a vocation that will bring him peace and satisfaction.

Unlike Mary, Tom seems unable to escape from the burden of public opinion. When the old woman who lives nearby innocently asks to borrow some yeast, Tom is driven into a rage. Later, his stepmother's praise of his housekeeping, made "without any intentional slight to his feelings," leads him to insist that Mary take time off from the factory so that they can spend the winter in Europe.

Although early in the story Tom tells Mary that he "always rather liked" housekeeping, Tom is unable to cope with the departure of the female servants who have long kept the household running. He is not a person who truly longs to do work that has traditionally been done by the other sex; instead he longs to work at hobbies—collecting coins and stamps. In other words, he wants to lead a housewife's life, as men have traditionally imagined it: a life of leisure and few responsibilities. When he recognizes the reality of women's lives—particularly when he realizes how little the outside world or family members value the work of housekeeping—he wants out. Unlike most women of his day who had few options, Tom has options: he can step back into the dominant male role and insist that his wife resume a more conventional family life. Perhaps the most interesting questions raised by the story are why Mary goes along with Tom's demand and what this decision bodes for their future life.

Richard Wright, The Man Who Was Almost a Man (page 264)

Some critics see Dave at the end of the story as becoming "truly a man" and as locating "his ultimate target" when he contemplates shooting Mr. Hawkins. (Brooks, Purser, Warren, An Approach to Literature, 5th ed., Englewood Cliffs: Prentice, 1975. 164.) You may want to begin discussion by stating this view and asking students for their responses.

Most will agree that Dave is justifiably angry about the work he is forced to do and his paltry wages. Yet many will also see that Wright's story does not focus entirely on racial issues. Dave is angry at nearly everybody: his mother, his father, even the other field workers. Most of all, he seems angry at himself.

Unable to recognize his anger or to put it to productive use, Dave fantasizes that buying a gun will give him the power he lacks. He sees no middle ground between working as a day laborer and living a life outside the law. He rejects his mother's hope for him to go to school and instead chooses to set out on his own with his gun as the sole evidence of his manhood.

The episode with Jenny, the mule, suggests the shaky ground on which Dave bases his manhood. When Dave first shoots the gun and is hurt by the kickback, he throws the weapon to the ground, kicks it, and hurls accusations at it as though it were alive, rather than an inanimate object. After he shoots Jenny, he panics and tries to hide what he has done. Later, even though he is "glad that he had gotten out of killing the mule so easily," he cannot accept responsibility for what he has done and expresses anger that "all he did was work."

Herman Melville, Bartleby, the Scrivener (page 274)

Having taught this story many times over the past twenty-five years, I've noticed an intriguing shift in students' responses. The first time I taught "Bartleby" was at the University of California at Santa Barbara in 1970. I was under the age of 30 (barely) and, therefore, according to the definition of the times, "trustable." The campus, of course, was torn with protests against the war in Vietnam and against police actions toward the protesters. The students who read the story with me at that time saw him as heroic, passively resisting the corrupt values of a materialistic society.

Somewhere during the 1980s, I found students' sympathies shifting from Bartleby to the narrator. Although they found the Wall Street lawyer a bit stuffy and pretentious at first, they sympathized with his dilemma, most students could not understand why he puts up with even the first stages of Bartleby's resistance. Now, at the beginning of the 1990s, only a few isolated voices defend, or even offer possible reasons for, Bartleby's insistence that he "would prefer not to" work, or indeed to participate in the world in any way.

In one classic reading of this story, Bartleby is seen as representing the artist or philosopher in conflict with the demands of society. Some critics see Bartleby as a thinly disguised version of Melville himself, yet Leo Marx (*Sewanee Review* 41 1953: 602–627) points out that Bartleby's fate suggests that Melville himself challenged the scrivener's preoccupation and withdrawal.

Is the story Bartleby's, or is it the narrator's? Certainly, as William B. Dillingham, points out, the narrator's compulsion to help Bartleby is related to his fear of self-revelation (*Melville's Short Fiction 1853–1856*. 1977. 23–25). Bartleby's rejection of the work of the law, on which the lawyer has based his life, challenges the lawyer's very identity. Still, the lawyer's persistence cannot be explained so simply. Although the lawyer clearly retains many of his original values, Bartleby touches him in an important way. He continues to care for the scrivener long after most people would have turned their backs. The scene at the Tombs shows the lawyer facing his worst fears and seeing in Bartleby not simply an isolated misfit but rather a fellow man who, like the lawyer, plays an intricate role in society.

At the end of the story, the lawyer learns that Bartleby once worked in the dead letter office. Students enjoy speculating on the significance of this discovery. My own belief is that the work at the dead letter office does not explain why Bartleby behaves as he does but rather serves as a symbol of the broken lines of communication, the failed messages, in all our lives.

Marge Piercy, To Be of Use (page 302)

The speaker admires Greek amphoras as well as Hopi vases because, although they are now viewed as museum pieces, they originally had a practical use. Just as she admires art that has a function, she also values workers who put their full energy into what they are doing and who are not afraid to strain muscles or perform repetitive tasks to "do what has to be done." Although the images are all of physical labor, it's possible to read the poem as a hymn to unpretentious, committed work of all kinds. The speaker holds in contempt the "parlor generals and field deserters" of all occupations and professions.

P. K. Page, Typists (page 303)

The typists in this poem are "without message." They type other people's words but have no time or energy to record their own thoughts. As they perform their rote task, ideas and questions form in their brains but never reach fruition. The final stanza suggests that typists working in a room together feel a sense of connection and recognize their own despair in their coworkers' plights. Page's tone is sympathetic, yet also condescending. Students who have worked as typists may challenge her view of the job as mindless and boring.

Richard Wilbur, The Writer (page 304)

The speaker—perhaps the poet himself—hears his daughter pause as she types a story. He listens to her efforts with the same astonishment and pain he felt when he watched a bird, trapped in a bedroom, as it tried to escape. He realizes that he can't help his daughter because he might "affright" her (perhaps intimidate her or scare her out of her own ideas). Yet just as he felt joy when the bird found its way out of the room, he rejoices when his daughter resumes typing, indicating that she has found her own way further into her story. Why does he call that moment a matter of life and death? Perhaps because he values writing, sees it as important work, and does not trivialize his daughter's struggles to create meaning.

Judy Grahn, Ella, in a square apron, along Highway 80 (page 305)

Ella, the copperheaded waitress, may be an auburn-haired woman, but she also takes on the guise of a fierce rattlesnake who knows how to protect herself against a hostile world. She values herself and refuses to let those who do not respect her or her work treat her with contempt. She "flicks her ass/out of habit, to fend off the pass/ that passes for affection" and "turns away the smaller tips, out of pride."

Kraft Rompf, Waiting Table (page 306)

The key lines, 19–22, underline the speaker's attitude toward his work, his customers, and himself:

> . . . But for a
> tip—for a tip, or a tip—
>
> I would work so very, very
> hard, . . .

The repetition stresses his concern with making money and his willingness to serve people he obviously holds in contempt. (Compare his attitude with Ella's).

Anne Bradstreet, A Letter to Her Husband, Absent upon Public Employment (page 308)

According to some students, this poem, written in the seventeenth century, strikes a surprisingly modern note. The wife is left behind while the husband travels as part of his work. Her consolation is her children: "those fruits which through thy heat I bore." Other students see the speaker's attitude as hopelessly outdated, claiming that no woman today would mope about the "tedious day so long" that she must face during her husband's absence.

Robert Frost, The Death of the Hired Man (page 308)

Contrast Mary's view of Silas with Warren's. Warren cannot forgive Silas's wanderings, whereas Mary feels sorrow and compassion for the old man. Warren can think only of his own troubles. Mary has empathy for Silas, recognizing why he reruns old arguments with young Wilson in his head. She knows "just how it feels/To think of the right thing to say too late," and she understands why Silas was frustrated by young Wilson's stubborn refusal to appreciate either his talent to find water or his ability to build a load of hay.

Mary recognizes why the farm feels like home to Silas: he has returned to work there so many times. Warren, by contrast, mocks with the famous definition, "Home is the place where, when you have to go there,/They have to take you in." Mary's response, less well known, reflects her deeper understanding, "I should have called it/Something you somehow haven't to deserve."

Ezra Pound, The River-Merchant's Wife: a Letter (page 313)

Compare this poem to "A Letter to Her Husband, Absent upon Public Employment" (page 308). Here is another poem that shows the wife at home waiting while the husband goes off to earn a living. As she waits, the focus of her life is the love relationship between her and her husband.

W. H. Auden, The Unknown Citizen (page 314)

Some students, noting the discrepancy between the speaker's voice and the impression of the citizen conveyed by the poem's images, see the poem as ironic. Others read the poem as praise of an ordinary person who led an ordinary life. Some students may point out that the capitalization of certain phrases, such as "Greater Community," "Producers Research," and "High-Grade Living," suggests a satiric tone. Certainly the comic name of the Citizen's employers, Fudge Motors, Inc., demonstrates that we cannot take the speaker's words entirely at face value. In relation to the work theme, consider especially the Citizen's attitude toward his work, toward his union, and toward those with whom he worked.

Elizabeth Bishop, Filling Station (page 315)

The speaker carefully observes the details of a family-run filling station. Have students list some of these details and elicit their thoughts on what the details suggest about the father's and sons' views of their work. Consider particularly the final six lines, which describe the neatly arranged Esso cans and offer the rather surprising pronouncement: "Somebody loves us all." (You may want to tell students that "Esso" was a precursor to "Exxon.")

John Ashbery, The Instruction Manual (page 316)

The opening lines of the poem explain the task the writer faces: meeting the deadline for writing an instruction manual. Faced with this mundane assignment, he daydreams, imagining a wonderfully varied fantasy scene before he returns to the manual. The tension between the world of the instruction manual and the world of Guadalajara suggests the connection between creativity and satisfaction in work. One of my students said that he saw the opening and closing sections, which focus on the manual, in black and white, but he saw the Guadalajara scenes in vivid color.

Susan Glaspell, Trifles (page 319)

This play considers the significance of the traditional division of labor between men and women. The men work at farming (Lewis Hale) and at professions related to the law (George Henderson and Henry Peters). The women—Mrs. Peters, Mrs. Hale, and the absent Mrs. Wright—work at keeping house. The list of characters gives the full names of the men, along with the work they do. The women are identified only by their husbands' surnames, preceded by "Mrs." Throughout the play, two of the men—the sheriff and the county attorney—are identified primarily by their professional titles.

The women, at first, defer to the men and pay respect to the work they are doing; the men, by contrast, sneer at what they consider the "trifles" of women's work. They have no sense of how hard it is to keep clean towels available or to provide food for winter by canning on hot summer days. You might remind students that at the time the play was first published, 1916, farm women had no modern conveniences. Running hot water, air conditioning, and freezers were not yet available.

As the action of the play unfolds, we see the women putting together the details (the men would call them the "trifles") of Minnie Wright's life. When they discover the dead bird, they see her motive for the desperate murder. They not only find the evidence but also act as a "jury of her peers," seeing beyond the violent act and considering the circumstances. We might venture a guess that they allow Minnie to go free either by reason of temporary insanity or by reason of justifiable homicide. (You might mention to students that in 1916 women, who did not yet have the vote, could not serve as jurors.)

The grandly ironic final line of the play is a pun on the word "knot," suggesting that the men's view both the murder and women's work in general is "not it" at all. In addition, Mrs. Hale's reply to the county attorney's condescending question—"We call it—knot it, Mr. Henderson"—brings to mind Minnie Wright's desperate knotting of the rope that would kill her husband and free her from her isolated, empty life.

Virginia Woolf, Professions for Women (page 331)

Woolf builds her essay through a series of complex analogies that students sometimes find difficult to understand. First, Woolf personifies her impulse to behave in what she understands as traditionally female patterns. She names this impulse "the Angel in the House," a phrase from the poem by the same name by Victorian poet Coventry Patmore. Patmore's Angel epitomized the ideal of late nineteenth-century, upper-class womanhood. This Angel aimed to please others—particularly men—no matter what the cost to her own sense of self. For young women of Woolf's generation, the Angel was cast as a model to emulate. No wonder, then, that as she went about writing reviews of books written by men, Woolf found it very difficult to be honest. Some students may not understand the extended metaphor of the struggle with the Angel, and you may need to explain that the murder was only symbolic.

In the second analogy (paragraph 5), Woolf compares her experiences as a novelist with a girl who is fishing. She casts the line of her imagination, and suddenly the bait is taken by a huge, unmanageable fish, who represents images of sexuality. As the fish leaps and struggles, it stirs up "foam and confusion." No longer does the fisher control the fish; instead she, and her imagination, are "dashed . . . against something hard." She faces the dilemma of avoiding any mention of sexuality in her novels or of earning public disapproval by writing about subjects thought unsuitable for women.

In the final paragraph of the essay, which was first delivered as a speech to an organization of professional women, Woolf asks her audience to consider her experiences as a writer and to think about similar issues related to their own work. She suggests that women envision the professional world as a house previously occupied only by men. Now, however, women have earned access to some of the rooms in that house. Woolf challenges women to consider carefully what they will do now that they have "won rooms of [their] own in the house hitherto exclusively owned by men." Her questions can lead to thoughtful writing and discussion related to the changes (or lack of change) students discover in professions dominated by men in 1931, when Woolf wrote the essay, but now accessible to women.

Joseph Epstein, The Virtues of Ambition (page 336)

Some students may challenge Epstein's contention that most people define ambition as somewhat negative. In fact, his own response to the *Webster's* definition makes an intriguing subject of the Rorschach test mentioned in the first sentence. For example, Epstein claims that " 'ardent' immediately assumes a heat incommensurate with good sense, and stability." Yet my edition of *Webster's* offers "intensely enthusiastic or devoted" as possible definitions of "ardent." Neither enthusiasm nor devotion seems negative to me. In addition, Epstein's protest that "rank, fame, and power have come under fairly heavy attack for at least a century" is not supported by any specific examples or other evidence.

In developing his argument, Epstein raises intriguing questions but he also puts simplistic reasoning into the mouths of those he considers his opponents. For instance, in paragraph 6, he suggests that those who see ambition as negative believe that because *all* (emphasis mine) politicians in high places must be ambitious, they must therefore be without moral scruples. First, as I suggest above, Epstein is not necessarily convincing when he claims that ambition is no longer admired. Second, given that some people do question the effects of ambition, would they necessarily believe either that *all* politicians are ambitious or that *all* ambitious people are "without moral scruples." Epstein claims simply to be listing the negative things that can be said about ambition, but, in fact, he cleverly makes those who disagree with his views look like shoddy thinkers who are capable only of knee-jerk responses to those interested in careers, power, and money.

In paragraph 8, Epstein introduces examples of ambition gone astray that I find far more intriguing and thought-provoking than his earlier generalizations. He describes specific instances of individuals who enjoy the rewards of ambition (or of their ancestor's ambition) yet now proclaim their opposition to behavior that (to them) suggests ambition. This point brings to mind the recent spate of articles in the popular press featuring middle-aged lawyers, doctors, and bankers who have left their six-figure salaries behind and moved to Vermont where they apparently live on the interest from their investments and give interviews about the importance of "getting back to basics."

Epstein suggests that if all of us had the money to eschew ambition, society would fall apart and, in addition, we would lead lives that are "unrelievedly boring." Students should have a good time discussing these two propositions. The first assumes that people work primarily to gain personal fame, to attain power, and to amass money. Without these goals, Epstein suggests, no one would bother to put energy and effort into their jobs, yet surely many people choose work that fulfils none of these three goals. As for the second proposition, would a world without competition, conflicts, demands, and abrasions really be boring? Students might describe in writing their vision of such a world. And why would such a world make the family unit superfluous? Why does Epstein regard the power of the family to "[bring] about neurosis" as positive?

PART III
MEN AND WOMEN

Many selections in Part III look at love relationships between men and women. All selections focus on gender issues in our own, as well as earlier, times; in our own society as well as others.

Consider assigning Paul Theroux's "Being a Man" as the first selection. Theroux's definition of manhood and masculinity is certain to be controversial and should lead easily to discussion of womanhood and femininity. I'd ask students what they think it means to "be a man" or to "be a woman." Do males in the class define themselves as men or as boys? Do females call themselves girls or women? Pursuing and defining these terms focuses students' attention on the gender-related questions this section raises.

Kate Chopin's "The Storm" and D. H. Lawrence's "The Horse Dealer's Daughter" begin this part by considering both the physical and emotional connections between men and women. Bobbie Ann Mason's "Shiloh," on the other hand, shows a couple who are growing apart, while Moravia's "The Chase" and Kemal's "A Dirty Story," look at men who believe women to be their possessions.

Strindberg's play *The Stronger* shows two women struggling with the role they play in the life of the same man.

"To His Coy Mistress," "The Willing Mistress," "The Passionate Shepherd to His Love," "The Nymph's Reply to the Shepherd," and "To the Virgins, to Make Much of Time," all offer playful voices debating whether and when to make love. "For My Lover, Returning to His Wife," and "The Gesture" both show the end of a love affair while "Aunt Jennifer's Tigers" and "My Last Duchess" offer portraits of women whose lives have been controlled by their husbands. "To me he seems like a god" and "How Do I Love Thee" are tributes paid by women to the men they love. Both May Swenson in "Women" and Kristine Batey in "Lot's Wife" examine and challenge the subservient roles women have often filled.

Paula Gunn Allen provides a view of male-female relationships in a culture quite different from ours in the United States. The most intriguing points in this essay, however, may be not how men and women in other cultures are different from us but how they are the same.

ADDITIONAL SELECTIONS FOR CONSIDERATION: *MEN AND WOMEN*

SUGGESTIONS FOR TEACHING ADDITIONAL SELECTIONS

1. How would you define a "good" marriage or a "bad" marriage? Consider the marriages depicted in the following works as you develop your definition.

	Text Page
Tom's Husband	253
Lullaby	460
Patriotism	822
The Revolt of "Mother"	923
Death in the Woods	949
A Letter to Her Husband, Absent upon Public Employment	308
The River-Merchant's Wife: a Letter	313
Let me not to the marriage of true minds	1096
The Canonization	1099
Trifles	319
On Tidy Endings	857
Othello	1226
A Raisin in the Sun	1414

2. Suppose you were an anthropologist from another time—or even another world—and had only the following literary selections to assist with your assignment: to define typical images of women and the roles they played or were assigned by nineteenth- and twentieth-century society.

	Text Page
Tom's Husband	253
The Jilting of Granny Weatherall	764
The Wives of the Dead	898
The Lady with the Pet Dog (Chekhov)	910
Moonlight	936
Death in the Woods	949
The Lady with the Pet Dog (Oates)	1042
Snow White and the Seven Dwarfs	163
In the Orchard	171

	Text Page
Patterns	596
La Belle Dame sans Merci	1117
The Lady of Shalott	1123
Trifles	319
A Raisin in the Sun	1414
Professions for Women	331
Ain't I a Woman?	1494

3.   Suppose you were an anthropologist from another time—or even another world—and had only the following literary selections to assist with your assignment: to define typical images of men and the roles they played or were assigned by nineteenth- and twentieth-century society.

	Text Page
Tom's Husband	253
The Things They Carried	581
Patriotism	822
The Lady with the Pet Dog (Chekhov)	910
Moonlight	936
The Bride Comes to Yellow Sky	940
Hills Like White Elephants	986
The Lady with the Pet Dog (Oates)	1042
In the Orchard	171
To Lucasta, Going to the Wars	605
The Flea	1098
The Man in a Case	16
On Tidy Endings	857
A Raisin in the Sun	1414

4.   Recent research suggests that men and women sometimes speak a different "language." Consider the communication between men and women in any of the following works. How do they send messages to each other? With spoken words? Written words? Gestures? Actions? Do

the men and women understand these words, gestures, and actions to mean the same things? How do their responses suggest their values?

THEMATIC PHOTOGRAPH (page 341)

Considerations

1. What differences or similarities can you imagine between the couple in the car and the couple on the screen?

2. Describe relationships between men and women as depicted in films and on television. Cite specific examples to support the observations you make.

3. Consider relationships between men and women as depicted in films made before 1960 (for example, *Gone with the Wind, Casablanca, The African Queen*) and films made in the past ten years. Describe the differences and explain your response to these changes.

READINGS

Kate Chopin, The Storm (page 342)

Most students are surprised that "The Storm" was written in 1898. They are not surprised to hear that Chopin did not try to publish the story at that time or to learn about the scathing reviews of her novel *The Awakening*, which was published in 1899 and, like "The Storm," presented a frank view of human sexuality (specifically, of female sexuality).

Perhaps the most shocking aspect of the story to many readers even in the 1990s is the lighthearted treatment of adultery. Alcée and Calixta meet accidentally, make love joyfully and apparently without guilt, and return to their daily lives where "everyone [is] happy."

This story is a sequel to another, "The 'Cadian Ball," in which Alcée urges Calixta to run away with him. However, he becomes entranced with Clarisse and leaves Calixta behind. The speech of the characters hints at the reason. Alcée's language—and Clarisse's language as reported from her letter—suggest upperclass, educated patterns. Both Calixta and Bobinôt, on the other hand, speak a patois, combining nonstandard English with French expressions. Quite possibly, Calixta and Alcée both chose mates who were deemed appropriate by their society but for whom they failed to feel the intense, intimate connection they sensed with each other.

Many students will condemn Alcée and Calixta. Calixta, especially, is often regarded as unsympathetic because in the opening and closing scenes both her husband and son are shown as loving and caring. Nevertheless, Chopin's description of the interlude in the storm creates a tone of tolerance. The lovers' passion is as brief, intense, and frighteningly beautiful as is the weather that allows them their isolated moment together.

D. H. Lawrence, The Horse Dealer's Daughter (page 347)

You might begin discussion of this story by asking students to respond to Edwin Muir's observation of Lawrence: "His spirit is exalted only when it takes fire from his senses. . . . [He] is on the side of instincts, and against all the forms, emasculated or deformed, in which they can be manifested in a civilized society."

Certainly the language in the first five paragraphs of the story reflects Lawrence's view of the way emotion can be deformed into hopelessness, despair, and paralysis. A list of some of the words and phrases describing Mabel and her brother might look like this:

foolish	confused
desultory	dark
dreary	hot, flushed
sullen-looking	shallow
impassive	sensual

The list suggests the web of depression and inaction in which Mabel Pervin and her brothers are trapped. Looking at the words that describe Joe (particularly in the fifth paragraph), students will note an aura of sensuality. The contrast between despair and sexual energy reflected by the images of the introduction establishes the central tension of the story: the juxtaposition of hopelessness and passion.

Although the title refers to Mabel, the story belongs equally to Jack Fergusson. Mabel can't bear to leave the place where she has spent all of her life yet sees no acceptable way to live in her brothers' coarse world without the cushion provided by money. Jack Fergusson rescues himself as well as Mabel when he acknowledges his strong attraction to her. Before the rescue, he has become numbed by the experiences of being a country doctor and has found only transient relief by frequenting the local taverns and seeking the company of Mabel's "rough" yet "strongly-feeling" brothers.

Although the story's final scene does have a love-at-first-sight, fairy-tale quality, a careful rereading suggests that Jack's feelings for Mabel have been gradually building. For instance, early in the story we learn that he has found Mabel's eyes "dangerous" and "unsettling," and later at the cemetery, "some mystical element" touches him as he watches her. Jack may tell himself that he doesn't want to love Mabel, but his emotions don't listen to his rationalizations, and he plunges, finally, not only into the pond but into a life that promises sense and sensation—a release from the numbing routine that has marked his existence.

Bobbie Ann Mason, Shiloh (page 361)

At the battle of Shiloh, Southern soldiers attacked the Union forces who were led by Ulysses S. Grant. Although the Southern troops were ultimately defeated in this battle, they were regarded by their compatriots as daring heroes and lauded for their astonishing first-strike raid against a much larger and more powerful enemy.

In Bobbie Ann Mason's story, Leroy, Norma Jean, and Mabel Beasley all seem to be fighting battles against enormous odds. Leroy, from whose point of view we see all the conflicts, struggles against the pain and disablement caused by his injured leg. Most importantly, he tries desperately to understand where his life is going and what he can do to get it under control. During this soul-searching, of course, he examines closely his relationship with Norma Jean in a way he never has before, working to address their old conflicts and to look squarely at the problems they have never faced before.

Norma Jean does physical exercises to develop her body, starts taking an English course, and begins to stand up to her domineering mother. Like the Southern soldiers at Shiloh, Norma Jean makes these daring raids against the boredom, inertia, and powerlessness of her life. As Norma Jean struggles to become independent, she moves in exactly the opposite direction of Leroy, who yearns for more connection and intimacy.

Mrs. Beasley, Norma's mother, battles against the changes of time. She would like to keep her daughter dependent and to see Norma and Leroy behave like her version of a nice, normal couple. Like Norma and Leroy, Mrs. Beasley seems never to have come to terms with the death of her infant grandson, Randy. She refuses to confront that loss in a constructive way yet continually reminds Norma Jean of the tragedy by her unthinking comments.

Some students have read the final paragraph as ominous, suggesting that Norma Jean jumps off the cliff and kills herself. Although I can find no textual evidence absolutely in contradiction of that view, my own feeling is that, of the three characters, Norma Jean has the most promising future. While Leroy becomes more introspective and dependent on a relationship that has never seemed to work, she strives to move away from her old life and toward emotional and intellectual growth.

Alberto Moravia, The Chase (page 373)

The analogy established in the first few paragraphs of the story suggests the narrator's view of his relationship with his wife. In the hunting story, he is impressed by the bird, who, he says, "is autonomous and unpredictable and does not depend on us." When his father presents him with the body of the dead bird, he grieves, apparently because that sense of freedom has been lost. Yet when he makes the comparison between the bird and his wife, it's easy to see that this freedom is only an illusion. Of course the bird *was* dependent on the hunters—dependent on them to decide whether it lived or died. Before the narrator was married, his future wife, like the bird, gave the illusion of wildness and vitality. Because of this illusion, the narrator pursued her. After the first years of their marriage, she became tamer, losing her "air of charming unpredictability, of independence in her way of living," and the narrator no longer found her fascinating.

The central incident in the story shows the narrator unexpectedly noticing his wife as she walks toward a bus stop. He sees in her once again the wildness he admired. When he discovers that her sense of energy and freedom quite probably comes from the fact that she is meeting a lover, he faces a conflict. Should he confront her and thus assert his power over her, or should he let her continue with her assignation and thus retain the autonomy he so admires?

Remembering the hunting incident and the dead bird, he decides not to interfere. He wants his wife to retain her wildness, although he acknowledges that "this wildness was directed against" him. He has come to believe that "wildness, always and everywhere, is directed against everything and everybody."

Students may differ in their evaluation of the narrator. Does he truly value his wife's independence for its own sake? Or is he motivated primarily by the desire to continue seeing his wife in a way that fascinates and excites him? Is his decision to leave his wife alone with her lover based on respect for her innate qualities or on his need to see her in a particular way? Does he himself become wild and free through his choice? Or does the choice simply confirm his sense of control over the situation?

Yashar Kemal, A Dirty Story (page 378)

Students may be interested to learn that Kemal, born in 1922, is a highly respected Turkish writer who was nominated for the Nobel Prize in literature. Kemal has been active in the Turkish Workers' Party, and many of his fictional works reflect his liberal political views. In "A Dirty Story," he shows the problems faced by many Turkish people who still live in dire circumstances resulting from corrupt government and a subsistence-level agrarian economy. "A Dirty Story" was translated from Turkish by Thilda Kemal, the author's wife.

This story reveals the ugliness and horror caused by individuals who look at others as less than human. At the beginning of the story, the men who try to convince Osman to find a wife see women as equivalent to animals: "A good woman's worth more than a team of oxen." Later in the story, the women who gossip about Fadik compare her to a dog and a donkey. Huru, who worries always about her financial circumstances, thinks nothing of buying Fadik as though she were just another domestic beast of burden.

A particularly painful aspect of the story is its failure to acknowledge Fadik's humanity and pain fully. Only at the very end does Fadik speak directly and express her feelings. And even then, her ordeal seems to be presented mainly as an inconvenient circumstance that troubles the men because Huru may call in the local tax collector as revenge against their actions.

Osman always follows the instructions of others, and at the end of the story he simply has to choose between obeying the Agha or remaining loyal to Huru. He decides to obey the Agha, and his flight with Fadik seems merely a desperate gesture rather than a move that indicates any real connection with or compassion for his wife.

Andrew Marvell, To His Coy Mistress (page 395)

Although images of time dominate the poem, the speaker's exaggerations ("I would love you ten years before the flood"; "An hundred years should go to praise/Thine eyes") all lead to his central argument. He tries to convince his mistress to give up her virginity because both he and she are mortal. They will not have long to enjoy physical passion.

Students have a good time evaluating the argument, with many agreeing that this same reasoning could be used to satisfy any desire. Why not steal a great car? After all, if you had enough time, you could work and earn the money to buy one. But, because all of us are mortal, you might die before accumulating the funds you need. So why not just take the easier, more convenient, and direct route: take what you want with no real thought of consequences or moral implications?

Aphra Behn, The Willing Mistress (page 396)

Aphra Behn, who lived during the seventeenth-century and made her living writing plays, shows a view of women quite different from Marvel's in "To His Coy Mistress." Whereas Marvel depicts his mistress as a shy virgin, reluctant to make love, Behn's speaker returns her lover's kisses eagerly. Just as the boughs in the opening stanza yield to "the winds that gently rise," so, too, does the speaker make it easy for her Amyntas "to prevail."

Alan Dugan, Love Song: I and Thou (page 397)

The speaker apparently loves his wife, but the extended metaphor of the house, which seems to represent their relationship, suggests great complexity. During the early stages, nothing was ideal. The speaker "spat rage's nails/into the frame-up of [his] work." Then, for one, brief moment everything seemed to be perfect: "It settled plumb,/level, solid, square and true." Now, however, the house is once more askew, and presumably the relationship, too, has its problems. The final image (lines 27–31) suggests that the house (and thus the relationship) has become like a cross on which the speaker will be martyred. He accepts the sacrifice and calls on his wife to help him remain nailed to the "cross-piece" of their marriage.

Anne Sexton, For My Lover, Returning to His Wife (page 398)

The first thirty lines contain these images of the wife and the mistress:

Wife	Mistress
melted carefully down for you	a luxury
cast up from your childhood	a bright red sloop in the harbor
Fireworks in February	littleneck clams out of season
real as a cast-iron pot	
all harmony	
the potter who produced his children	

These are some images of the wife and mistress in lines 31–48:

Wife	Mistress
a bomb with "a fuse inside her"	a watercolor
a drunken sailor	
the sum of [himself]	
like a monument . . . She is solid	

The early images of the wife show her as beautiful, familiar, and down-to-earth. She is the girl of the man's youth and the mother of his children. She is necessary to his existence. The mistress is strikingly exotic. She adds excitement to the man's life, but she is, in the end, not someone who will remain permanent. The wife is like a statue carved in lasting stone. The mistress appears, for a moment, beautifully evocative yet, like a watercolor, easily faded and forgotten.

Elizabeth Libbey, The Gesture (page 400)

The final stanza suggests that this couple has already grown apart and that for each the moment has arrived when "the beloved is already no longer with us." Each goes through a ritual of pleasing and accommodating the other, yet neither feels truly connected with the other. This man and woman seem to stay together out of habit rather than from any real need or feeling.

Adrienne Rich, Aunt Jennifer's Tigers (page 401)

Aunt Jennifer's "terrified hands" and "fingers fluttering" suggest that she is everything her tigers are not. She is chronically anxious, whereas they march across the tapestry "proud and unafraid." As she sits weighted by Uncle's wedding ring and "mastered" by "ordeals," the tigers "prance" freely, undaunted by "the men beneath the tree." The tigers are, of course, Aunt Jennifer's creations and thus may represent aspects of herself hidden beneath the surface of her life and the façade of her marriage to Uncle.

Sappho, To me he seems like a god (page 402)

The speaker uses extremely painful images to describe her reaction to the man who "seems like a god." She loses the ability to speak or to see light, and her skin burns as if cracked by fire. The speaker's response seems to stem from her sense of powerlessness. As a woman lacking in material wealth, she feels unable to meet the godlike man on his own terms.

Christopher Marlowe, The Passionate Shepherd to His Love (page 403)
Sir Walter Raleigh, The Nymph's Reply to the Shepherd (page 403)

Ask two students to read this pair of poems aloud and then ask the class to evaluate the speakers in each poem, explaining which offers the more convincing argument. Responses vary, but my students usually favor the nymph. Although the shepherd's pleas seem similar to those of hopeful suitors everywhere (and from every age), the nymph's answer shows that she is thoughtful and perceptive; she does not rely on clichés. Unconvinced by the promise of material gifts, the nymph thinks about philosophical concerns. Although she does not deny the pleasure of passionate love relationships, she declines involvement in a fleeting moment of physical joy that is unrelated to more significant connection.

John Donne, A Valediction: Forbidding Mourning (page 404)

According to Donne's biographer, Izaak Walton, Donne left this poem as a memento for his wife while he journeyed from England to France for several months.

Students who are not familiar with the conceits of seventeenth-century poetry will need time and encouragement to work on the following sections of the poem:

Lines 1–8: Just as people who have lived virtuously pass to the next world trusting in their reward, the speaker and his wife can part temporarily because each trusts the other's love.

Lines 9–12: People fear dramatic physical movements of the earth, such as earthquakes, but they are calmed by the majestic orbiting stars and planets. The husband and wife, then, are compared to heavenly bodies, and their parting is not permanent but rather an orderly, predictable motion, comparable to orbiting.

Lines 25–36: The compass (like those used in geometry) is compared to the lovers. The leg of the compass that remains fixed is like the wife who remains at home. The husband is like the leg that can stretch in many directions and yet remains always joined to the fixed point at home.

Robert Herrick, To the Virgins, to Make Much of Time (page 405)

Austin Warren tells a wonderful story confirming the joys and insights brought by rereading familiar texts (see "Herrick Revisited," *Michigan Quarterly Review* 15. Summer 1976: 245–267). As a young student, Warren read the first lines as "Gather ye *roses* while ye may." He reread and taught the poem many times, yet only after fifty years did he realize that Herrick had actually written "Gather ye *rosebuds* while ye may." When he realized that difference, the poem became entirely new for him.

Telling Warren's story leads students to look carefully at that first line as they read the poem and to speculate why Warren believed that one small change in diction so profoundly affected his response to the work.

Elizabeth Barrett Browning, How Do I Love Thee? (page 406)

Many students know the story of Elizabeth Barrett Browning's daring escape from her overbearing father, who insisted that she stay shut away from the world because of her delicate health. He reluctantly allowed her to write and publish poems. When Robert Browning read some of her work, he insisted on seeing her in spite of her father's protests. Eventually Robert convinced Elizabeth to listen to her own desires rather than to her father's commands. They married and fled to Italy, where they lived and wrote until her death fifteen years later. "How do I Love Thee" is her tribute to the relationship she saw as having given her back her life.

Robert Browning, My Last Duchess (page 406)

This poem works well as an example of the distinction between speaker and poet. Browning was a generous nineteenth-century British man of letters while the mean-spirited Duke, his creation, imperiously demands respect and blind obedience in Renaissance Italy.

Most students see the Duke as both egotistical and dangerous, although a few have suggested that he had a right to insist that his wife, the "last Duchess," pay attention only to him. Although nothing in the text absolutely states that the Duke ordered the Duchess killed, I think it is reasonable to assume that the smiles stopped because of his intervention. It is also highly unlikely that the Duke has simply locked the Duchess away or banished her. The Count, whose daughter the Duke hopes to marry, would certainly be extremely distressed to find out that a former Duchess was still lurking in the wings somewhere.

May Swenson, Women (page 408)

When I first taught this poem in 1985 I was astonished at how many students read it as a "guide for girls." Some were outraged by the advice given, and others claimed that the role was one many women enjoyed. Very few students saw the irony I believe is there. As I considered my own reading, I realized that I read the poem as ironic at least partly because I had read many other works by Swenson as well as biographical and autobiographical essays describing her ideals and values. I knew she would not really think that women should move "to the motions of men." Also, however, phrases such as "chafed feelingly/and then unfeelingly" and "until the restored egos dismount" have, for me, a distinctly negative connotation. When I mention these phrases in class discussion, I find that many students do not know the meaning of "chafed" and read the dictionary definition, "rubbed," as neutral. I now prepare students to discuss this poem by asking them to watch for lines that suggest an ironic commentary rather than a sexist directive.

Kristine Batey, Lot's Wife (page 409)

The Bible depicts Lot's wife as a disobedient, worldly woman who, against God's orders, turns to look at her native city of Sodom, burning as punishment for the sins of the people who live there. In retribution, she is turned into a pillar of salt. Students may want to compare the biblical account of this story, Genesis 19:1–26, with Batey's version.

August Strindberg, The Stronger (page 410)

Because we hear only the ranting diatribe of Mrs. X, a clearly unreliable narrator, it's difficult to know what Mr. X (Bob) is really like. If, however, we can accept some of what she says as true, it seems likely that he is a thoroughly reprehensible man. Apparently he sees himself as lord and master of his household, demonstrating his superiority over the servants by insulting them when they are out of hearing range. In addition, Mrs. X. suggests that he has had a series of affairs with hopeful young actresses whom he has led to believe he will help with their careers (even though he does not have the power to get them the roles he promises). If this is true, Miss Y may be simply another conquest in a long line of relationships that meant little to Bob.

On the other hand, Mrs. X's extreme anger with her husband and with Miss Y suggests that Mrs. X may not be capable of telling any of her story in an honest way. She clearly wants Miss Y to suffer. Consider, for example, that she chooses Christmas Eve—traditionally the loneliest night of the year for the "other woman"—for the confrontation. In addition, she silences any response Miss Y tries to make; perhaps she fears that even the mildest defense would destroy the picture she has created to protect herself.

Most students see Miss Y as "the stronger" referred to in the title. As Mrs. X raves on, she sits listening. Although she cannot interrupt Mrs. X, she does convey her disbelief and her surprise through her gestures, actions, and ironic laughter. Mrs. X. may have a career, a husband, and children, but these trappings she sees as indicative of a successful life have not brought her happiness. She is reduced to rationalizing her relationship with her husband and to projecting the blame for her circumstances onto the silent Miss Y, who sits quietly refusing to engage in argument or to defend herself.

Paula Gunn Allen, Where I Come from Is Like This (page 415)

A Laguna Pueblo/Sioux, Paula Gunn Allen teaches at the University of California, Berkeley, where she is a professor of Native American and Ethnic Studies. She has published several books of poetry and a novel, *The Woman Who Owned the Shadows* (1983).

The opening paragraphs of Gunn Allen's essay suggest the importance of cultural definitions. People's views of themselves relate directly to the expectations of the community in which they live. In the second paragraph, Gunn Allen emphasizes the diversity of roles Native Americans may play within their tribal structures, yet she also notes the differences between those tribal definitions and the definitions of "women in western industrial and post industrial cultures."

Gunn Allen describes the men and women in her culture as living in a balanced way; the women have as much power as the men. Some students may question Gunn Allen's interpretation of the scenarios she describes. For example, what does the banishment of menstruating women, in the belief that their power will interfere with male power, imply about the balance she claims exists?

Gunn Allen's description of the double-bind that Native American women face also raises controversial questions. She describes, for instance, feeling powerless only when she seeks approval outside the Native American culture. Most people feel less comfortable and less powerful when they are away from their own culture, and perhaps the approval she gets within her tribal structure is due to her willingness to accept, rather than resist, their definitions of women's roles.

Paul Theroux, Being a Man (page 422)

Theroux's opening paragraph shocks many readers. Both the definition of the shoe fetishist and Theroux's statement, "I cannot read that sentence without thinking that it is just one more awful thing about being a man" are disturbing. Yet the discussion of fetishism also seems absurd and Theroux's reaction exaggerated, putting me immediately on the alert for irony.

As I read on, the details, examples, and diction continue to be hyperbolic and even downright unfair. Consider, for example, Theroux's statement that "there is no book hater like a Little League coach." Surely he realizes that many Little League coaches enjoy books as well as baseball. It seems that he intentionally sets out to insult many of his readers, perhaps to stir up their emotions and to engage them with his argument.

While most students will strongly disagree with Theroux's evaluation of high school sports, many will agree with his premise (paragraph 3) that boys and girls are raised to see members of the opposite sex as adversarial or, at best, as the objects of sexual or matrimonial conquests. This essay lends itself very nicely to setting up debates, using small groups to prepare arguments for and against Theroux 's assumptions and the conclusions he bases on these assumptions.

I find astonishing Theroux's contention that Americans expect male writers to be dismissive or apologetic about their profession. Since nearly all writers who have been accepted as part of the traditional canon are male, I find his complaint difficult to understand. Theroux bases this claim partly on his belief that male writers are only taken seriously when they demonstrate their masculinity. I think most men—whether they are business executives, doctors, plumbers, or bus drivers—are constantly under societal pressure to prove their male attributes. Is there really much evidence to suggest that male writers are particularly bedeviled by this expectation?

Comparing Theroux's view of gender issues as related to the profession of writing to Virginia Woolf's view in "Professions for Women" suggests that women who choose to be writers have had—and continue to have—more gender-related obstacles to face than do men. In addition, Woolf concentrates on issues related to her own writing process while Theroux seems concerned not so much with how being male affects how he writes but rather with how being a male writer affects the way people perceive him.

PART IV
PARENTS AND CHILDREN

The frustrations, rewards, pains, and pleasures of family life both drain and renew of energy in almost everyone's life. The works in this section examine parent-child relationships from nearly every vantage point. "Idiots First" provides the father's view of his responsibilities for and relationship to his child. In "My Oedipus Complex," "My Papa's Waltz," "Digging," and "I Remember Papa," adult sons look at their connections with their fathers, focusing on remembered scenes from childhood, whereas "My Father in the Navy" shows a daughter's memories of her father. "Idiots First" gives a father's view of his responsibilities for and relationship to his child. Mothers contemplate their roles in their children's lives in "I Stand Here Ironing," "Lullaby," "Making the Jam without You," "Today," and "On Being Raised by a Daughter." "Amniocentesis," "Metaphors," and "The Mother" suggest connections between mothers and unborn children.

Arthur Miller's play *All My Sons* shows parents and adult children struggling with questions of public morality versus family loyalty. In a different way, Harry Dolan's essay "I Remember Papa" raises the same question: Is a parent's first loyalty to the welfare of the family or to the laws of the greater community?

Characters in "My Oedipus Complex," "Through the Tunnel," "I Stand Here Ironing," "Making the Jam without You," "Today," and "On Being Raised by a Daughter" face issues of growth and independence as the child develops a life apart from the parent. In "Idiots First," "Lord Randal," "The Mother," *All My Sons,* and "I Remember Papa," children and parents face or have endured separation caused by death.

"I Stand Here Ironing," "Lullaby," *All My Sons,* and "I Remember Papa" provide rich opportunities for looking at the impact of economic circumstances and societal pressures on family relationships.

ADDITIONAL SELECTIONS FOR CONSIDERATION:
PARENTS AND CHILDREN

Title and Author   **Text Page**

Nonfiction

SUGGESTIONS FOR TEACHING ADDITIONAL SELECTIONS

1. Can one generation understand another? Consider the following works
    to identify patterns of conflict between parents and children. In
    addition, note patterns of empathy and understanding. What aspects of
    life are most likely to evoke parental anger? Parental support? The
    anger of children? The support of children?

2. Read any of the following works and consider how family traditions
    and rituals affect the lives of parents and children. Compare your
    observations about these works with observations about the role played

by traditions and rituals in your own family or in other families you
know well.

	Text Page
The Circling Hand	147
The Loudest Voice	677
The Garden Party	966
A Worn Path	990
Everyday Use	1068
Mother and Poet	601
The School Children	715
Those Winter Sundays	1164
The Glass Menagerie	173
A Raisin in the Sun	1414
Salvation	225
Arrival at Manzanar	1534
In Search of Our Mothers' Gardens	1542

3. The following selections focus on themes related to the lives of families
who are not members of the dominant culture in their society. Use these
selections as sources to discover complications, joys, and problems you
consider unique to those families belonging to minority groups.
Investigate your discoveries through further reading and research. As
you work, consider both fictional and nonfictional sources as well as
interviews and conversations.

	Text Page
The Man Who Was Almost a Man	264
The Loudest Voice	677
A Worn Path	990
Everyday Use	1068
A Raisin in the Sun	1414
Arrival at Manzanar	1534
In Search of Our Mothers' Gardens	1542

4. Read the following works to identify the roles played by mothers and fathers in their children's lives. How are they similar? Different? How do these fictional mothers and fathers, and the roles they play in their children's lives, compare to the parents you know? Do you think the roles played by mothers and fathers are changing? For the better? For the worse? Explain.

	Text Page
By the Sea	130
The Circling Hand	147
The Man Who Was Almost A Man	264
War	562
The Fly	576
Everyday Use	1068
Spelling	1075
Mother and Poet	601
For My Father	1180
Those Winter Sundays	1164
The Glass Menagerie	173
A Raisin in the Sun	1414
Arrival at Manzanar	1534

THEMATIC PHOTOGRAPH (page 426)

Considerations

1. List the details you notice in this picture. Consider the three people as well as their surroundings. What inferences can you make based on your observations?

2. Notice the expression on the woman's face. What emotions does the expression suggest? What might her relationship be to the man? To the baby? Explain all the possibilities you see.

3. Write the dialogue that has taken place just before this picture was snapped. As you create this scene, consider such points as what the three people are doing, what time of day the scene takes place, where

the people are, and where they might be going (both literally and figuratively).

READINGS

Bernard Malamud, Idiots First (page 427)

Throughout the story, references to time are significant because Mendel has bargained with Death (represented by Ginzburg, whom we learn early on "doesn't bother young people so much") to gain him a little more time on earth. Mendel works frantically to get money for Isaac's train ticket to Los Angeles, where family will care for the retarded Isaac.

The scene with Fishbein demonstrates the truth of Mendel's implication that the wealthy have the power of life and death over the poor. Yet even though he comes to Fishbein as a supplicant, Mendel demands respect from the millionaire. For instance, when Fishbein refers to Isaac as a "half-wit," Mendel retorts, "Please, without names." Fishbein shows himself to be uncaring, crude, and miserly, whereas Mendel exhibits both his devotion to his son and his quiet dignity.

Like Fishbein, the rabbi initially is irritated by Mendel's request and has little inclination to help him. Finally, he does offer Mendel a fur coat to sell, but it's clear that his main intention is to rid himself of the troublesome dilemma Mendel and Isaac present.

At the train station, the stranger who rises from the bench is almost certainly Ginzburg. Mendel confronts Death (Ginzburg) full of strength and determination. In spite of his terminal illness, Mendel is able to defeat Death temporarily because of his love for his son and his need to take care of his earthly duties. In the struggle, Mendel forces Ginzburg to acknowledge Mendel's humanity and to fall back briefly while he shepherds Isaac on the train to the sanctuary of family.

Frank O'Connor, My Oedipus Complex (page 435)

This story derives its comic vision from the dual point of view. We see the events through the eyes of five-year-old Larry, yet those events are described by, and filtered through the consciousness of, the adult Larry. You might point out, for example, that few young children would compare waking up elated to "feeling like a bottle of champagne." In addition, only an older, more sophisticated mind could recognize the humor and irony in the father's seeking refuge with Larry. The father who had replaced the older son in his mother's bed is now in turn replaced by the upstart Sonny.

During the first part of the story, Larry sees himself and his mother as enjoying a perfect relationship. His view, of course, must be somewhat different from his mother's because, unlike Larry, she recognizes the dangers her husband faces and no doubt also worries about the increased burdens and responsibilities she must assume at home. The second section of the story shows the father's triumphant return and Larry's loss of his mother's undivided attention. Again, the juxtaposition of the child's view and the view of the adults creates irony and humor. Certainly Larry's father, and quite probably his mother, prefer the new sleeping arrangements. In this section, Larry and his father are pitted against each other, yet we are prepared for the final section because we see the father as having many childlike qualities. For instance, he growls at his son for touching his war souvenirs, causing the mother to warn, "You mustn't play with Daddy's toys unless he lets you." In the final scenes of the story, Larry and his father turn from adversaries into allies. As they unite against Sonny, the common enemy, Larry takes on the role of the comforting adult as he hugs his cold, bereft father and murmurs soothing words.

Doris Lessing, Through the Tunnel (page 445)

Lessing offers a moving view of a boy striving to gain independence from his mother and to develop a sense of self. The opening paragraphs show that the mother and son care deeply for one another. The mother is not a stereotyped overprotective parent. Nonetheless, her recognition that her son is old enough to go off on his own doesn't stop her from worrying about him. She acknowledges her anxiety yet courageously encourages him to explore the rocks he has pointed out to her. Jerry, sensitive to his mother's emotions, feels somewhat guilty about going off without her. But his ambivalence does not paralyze him, and he is able to let her walk down the beach in one direction while he goes in the other.

As the story progresses, Jerry continues to be torn between growing up and remaining a child. He admires the older boys yet tries to attract their attention by showing off. After watching the boys swim through the tunnel, he longs to do the same, yet he begs his mother for the necessary swim goggles by nagging and pestering her just as a young child would do. As he works on his plan for swimming the tunnel, Jerry grows increasingly autonomous, getting to the point where he does not ask her permission to go the beach. He also works persistently to develop his ability to hold his breath, demonstrating a "most unchildlike persistence, a controlled impatience."

In the scene where Jerry finally swims through the tunnel, the details build suspense, yet the outcome seems clear. He will not drown but will make it through the metaphorical birth canal to be reborn as a fledgling adult—someone who can give in to his mother's request not to "swim any more today" because he now knows that he can face dangerous and difficult tasks on his own. He no longer needs to resist his mother's simple request or to challenge her because he has successfully met his challenge to himself.

Tillie Olsen, I Stand Here Ironing (page 453)

Someone from Emily's school, a teacher or counselor, has called her mother. The meditation at the ironing board represents the mother's imagined response both to that call and to the voices of authorities who, over the years, have tried to tell her how to rear her children and have then criticized her for the result of following their advice. Consider, for instance, her description of Emily's feeding patterns. When her first daughter was an infant, child-care authorities strongly urged parents to feed babies on a strict schedule. The mother followed their advice, although Emily often cried from hunger during the four-hour stretch between feedings. Now the mother fears (and modern child-care authorities would agree) that following their advice may not have benefited her child. She also recalls the time when Emily was sick with red measles. Disdainful social workers urged the mother to put Emily in a convalescent home because they believed she would receive better care there than at home. The mother's description of the convalescent home suggests that, instead, Emily was virtually imprisoned in a cold, rigid, draconian institution.

In both cases, the mother regrets having acquiesced to the experts. Certainly she was free not to follow their advice, and, because she made the wrong choices, some students will see the mother as responsible for Emily's problems.

One of the most intriguing questions posed by the mother's meditation is the degree to which parents are responsible for the way their children turn out. Students differ widely in their views of the mother. Usually, older students are at least somewhat sympathetic toward the mother, whereas younger students tend to condemn her for not overcoming her early economic problems. (You may want to call students' attention to paragraphs 8 and 9, which note that Emily's father deserted the family during the Great Depression of the early 1930s, a "pre-relief, pre-WPA world" without the welfare services of today.)

Leslie Marmon Silko, Lullaby (page 460)

Leslie Marmon Silko grew up listening to the stories of her great-grandmother, A'mooh, who lived next door to Silko's family on the Laguna Pueblo Reservation. Silko completed the first eight grades at Bureau of Indian Affairs schools. After finishing high school in Albuquerque, she graduated magna cum laude from the University of New Mexico. After three semesters of law school, she decided to devote her time to writing and to graduate studies in English.

Ayah's memories show the importance of her family—her children, her mother, and her grandmother. Her memories of her family intermingle with images of nature that relate directly to Ayah's life. The same snow that makes her cold also causes her to take up Jimmy's blanket and reminds her of how her babies reached out to touch the fluffy whiteness. She sees the snow as "thick tufts like new wool—washed before the weaver spins it."

The story describes a series of losses in Ayah's life. She loses Jimmy, her oldest son, in a war (probably Vietnam, since he died in a helicopter crash), loses at least two children in infancy, and loses two other children to tuberculosis. This latter loss is the most bitter, because Ayah feels she was tricked into signing the papers that allowed government officials to take the children from her. An old woman at the time of the story, Ayah also describes the losses in her husband's life, particularly his treatment by the rancher to whom he had devoted a lifetime of work.

The final section of the story shows Ayah's dignity and power as she goes into the bar to find Chato. She no longer worries about those who in the past have looked at her with hostility. She sees that they now regard her with respect, and even fear, as she sets out with determination to find her husband. Although she has been angry with Chato in the past for participating in the white culture (for instance, by learning to speak, read, and write English), she now recognizes him as a partner in her misery and loss. When she finds Chato and they walk together, she reviews in her mind the changes old age has brought. The final lullaby Ayah sings is for herself as well as Chato; both have struggled through the cycle of mortal life and will now return, like children, to their mother, the earth.

Theodore Roethke, My Papa's Waltz (page 467)

For years I viewed this poem as a loving but unsentimental picture of a bedtime romp shared by father and son. Recently students began pointing out to me how dark the images really are. Of course, I had always noted the frowning mother, but she had seemed to me perhaps only mildly disapproving. Possibly she didn't want the boy excited when he should be getting ready for sleep or maybe she resented being left out of the celebration, or perhaps she frowned because her pans are falling from the shelf.

How could I have ignored phrases such as "I hung on like death" and "At every step you missed/My right ear scraped a buckle"? At the very least, these images suggest that the boy finds the waltz frightening and painful in some ways. Many of my students go further, believing that the poem shows the terror of a family trapped by the father's alcoholism.

Maxine W. Kumin, Making the Jam without You (page 468)

I read this poem as a gift from a middle-aged mother to her nineteen-year-old daughter. The mother remembers the sensual pleasures she shared with her daughter as they went through the summer ritual of making blackberry jam. But rather than longing for the return of days when the daughter was with her, this mother fantasizes a delightful encounter between her daughter and a wonderful young man. She sees the two picking berries together and making jam while their "two heads/touch over the kettle." At the end of the poem, the wise, generous mother slips out of the fantasy, leaving us with the final image of the daughter and the young man with their "two mouths open/for the sweet stain of purple." I find this image sexual, but many students disagree, arguing instead that the encounter is innocent and childlike, as suggested by the fairy-tale imagery of the castle and the thicket of brambles. (Suggesting the sexual nature of fairy tales has, so far, earned me only groans and exasperated sighs.)

Judith Ortiz Cofer, My Father in the Navy: A Childhood Memory (page 470)

The images in this poem distance the father from the world of his family. Some images show the father as a holy figure, revered by the speaker, her mother, and her brother, who keep a "vigil" until he arrives. His navy cap sits on his head "like a halo"; his uniform is a "flash of white . . . like an angel." But the father is also an "apparition on leave from a shadow-world"; he works beneath the sea in the "bellies of iron whales." These images suggest that the father inspires fear as well as reverence. The speaker also sees the family as sirens, luring the father back from the sea and his ship, where he feels most at home.

Robert Mezey, My Mother (page 471)

Almost every reader will agree that this mother is downright irritating. She tries to run her son's life first by manipulation (lines 4–13), then by example, (lines 13–25), and then, in the final twenty lines of the poem, through appeal to authority (the "great writer" Sholem Aleichem) and direct pleas ("try to put some money away").

Still, although every line reveals the mother's intrusiveness, the son seems to view her with good-natured humor rather than with anger and resentment. The fourth line may be read ironically, yet the mother's breathless appeal to her son also seems to reflect genuine concern and love.

Ellen Wolfe, Amniocentesis (page 472)

Amniocentesis, a prenatal test for birth defects, seems to be performed more and more frequently in this age of older mothers and technology-conscious doctors. The speaker in this poem addresses her unborn child as she thinks about the medical professionals who will look for problems as they perform the test. The final line of the poem is her prayer for the child and for herself.

Seamus Heaney, Digging (page 473)

As he describes the hard physical labor his father and grandfather performed, the speaker discovers connections between them and himself. He shows pride in his father's and grandfather's ability to "handle a spade," the first while harvesting potatoes, the second while digging fuel from peat bogs. Although the speaker will not carry on the tradition of physical labor, like them he will bring energy and effort to his work. Rather than using a spade to dig for potatoes or peat, he will use a pen to unearth words, images, and ideas.

Anonymous, Lord Randal (page 474)

The relationship between the mother and son in this poem is puzzling. She knows almost as soon as the son returns that he has been poisoned (stanzas 3–7). Yet instead of mourning or placing blame, she immediately asks him what he has left to her and to the rest of the family. The final stanza suggests that Lord Randal has finally lost his patience. He will not leave anything to the woman whom he and his mother both know has poisoned him. The repeated final line of each stanza, traditional ballad form, reinforces Lord Randal's growing distress as his mother relentlessly questions him rather than leading him to the rest for which he longs.

Gwendolyn Brooks, The Mother (page 475)

Expect strong reactions to this poem. Some students will read this poem as an admission of guilt and regret; others will read the poem as an acknowledgment of loss, an acceptance of the decision to abort, and a tribute to lives that never came to be.

Sylvia Plath, Metaphors (page 476)

I'm always surprised that so few students solve the riddle easily. Perhaps because I had already given birth when I first read the poem, the melon strolling about on vinelike legs was, for me, an unmistakable picture of pregnancy. And, of course, the opening line—"I'm a riddle in nine syllables"—instantly brought to mind the nine long months of pregnancy. The image of the red fruit and ivory timber is not as immediately accessible; I think it refers to the body and bones of the fetus. (A future engineer in one of my classes pointed out to me that the poem has nine lines, each with nine syllables, reinforcing the metaphor in the first line.)

Margaret Atwood, Today (page 477)

The innocent young daughter (probably two or three years old) is led to the bluegreen water of a pond or lake by the soft, white allure of the ducks. The sun shines on the water, making it look like gold. The mother sees the danger (the daughter may drown) and knows she must pull her daughter back. But she also recognizes the loss that comes with experience. From now on, her daughter will begin to view her world with wary questioning, always looking for the possibility of danger, never simply plunging forward and joining with beauty for its own sake and with no conscious thought of consequences.

Arthur Miller, All My Sons (page 478)

The most significant decision in the play is made three years before its current action. Joe Keller chooses to value family above all else by fulfilling his defense contract with defective cylinder heads, destined to be used on fighter planes. To ensure the success of his business and thus the financial welfare of his family, Joe sends the heads and sets his partner up to take the blame.

Joe's action raises the central moral question of the play: To whom do we owe our greatest loyalty? To ourselves? To our families? Or to the larger communities to which we all belong? In her single-minded determination to deny the death of her older son and to protect her husband, Kate Keller reflects Joe's values. In addition, minor characters Jim and Sue Bayliss act as foils for the main characters. Like Chris, the Kellers' son, Jim is an idealist, whereas his wife, like Joe and Kate, holds the family sacred above all. Jim longs to become a researcher, following his own ideals, and perhaps make discoveries that will help others. Sue, by contrast, believes that his first and greatest concern should be providing a comfortable living for his family.

Unlike his father, Chris Keller is above all an idealist. He genuinely believes that he has fought in a war that will herald the beginning of world peace. His idealism, however, makes him rigid. For instance, even though he loves Ann Deever, he can see no circumstances extenuating her father's actions. Bitterly, he urges Joe to "kick [Deever] in the teeth." And when he learns of Joe's complicity in shipping the defective cylinders, Chris turns against his father completely, refusing to consider either his father's absolute devotion to his sons or his mother's pleas to temper justice with mercy. If Joe Keller represents the person who willingly compromises the greater good for personal gain, Chris represents the opposite extreme. He is the individual who loses all sense of human compassion in a rigid adherence to his own idealistic standards.

Nancy Mairs, On Being Raised by a Daughter (page 539)

Nancy Mairs expresses the frustrations of many modern parents reacting to the discrepancy between their own actions and responses as they bring up their children and the actions and responses that various experts consider appropriate. In paragraph 7, she expresses her concern about the pronouncements of these authorities: "The real danger these voices pose lies not so much in what they say as in what they leave out about motherhood, whether through ignorance or incapacity."

To describe her life with her daughter, and to define how Anne's existence has changed her life, Mairs envisions herself as being "raised" by Anne rather than vice versa. Each step in Anne's growth brings about a concurrent step in Mairs's growth. Rather than focusing entirely on the child, Mairs pictures herself and her own development as equally significant and important. She also offers an unusual perspective by casting her daughter, from infancy to adulthood, as faced with a task for which little help or support is offered: "raising a mother." In addition, however, she notes that most writers commenting on mother-daughter relationships fail to acknowledge the power of the daughter. Most experts see the mother as entirely in charge of the relationship; Mairs, instead, describes the control Anne exerts over her mother's life.

As she explains various experiences she and Anne have shared, one theme becomes apparent: the difficult, yet necessary, path both mother and daughter must walk toward separation and independence. Students usually enjoy discussing their responses to Anne's choices, Mairs's choices, and the mother's and daughter's reactions to each other's choices.

Harry Dolan, I Remember Papa (page 551)

Dolan's father advises him that "the pitfall sometimes seems to be the easiest way out" and urges him to "beware of the future" because he must be the one to fulfill his father's dreams and ambitions. The episodes in the rest of the story show Dolan believes he, too, may be faced with choices as desperate as those that finally closed the door on his father's hopes and aspirations, even though circumstances of those choices may be different. As the opening narrative suggests, Dolan's choices will concern not how to make a living for his family but rather how to defend his own honor as a black man faced with racist actions and attitudes.

Dolan takes an admiring view of his mother. Although she is sick (apparently with tuberculosis), she tries hard to keep the family together and to comfort her husband through every difficulty he faces. The essay shows the mother mainly in relation to Dolan's father rather than as a separate individual. His view of his father, by contrast, is far more complex. After his father's imprisonment for stealing five loaves of bread and twelve dollars, Dolan does not see his father for many years. When he finally visits his father in prison, Dolan at first feels resentment. However, he reevaluates his bitter feelings toward his father as he thinks about the wasted energy and ability now locked behind bars. The episodes in the rest of the essay show how difficult life was for Dolan's father and certainly demonstrate that he does not fit the stereotype of the lazy black man given in the essay's introduction.

By explaining his father's life, and particularly by ending with the stunning episode of the kitten, Dolan urges readers to examine, and perhaps reconsider, their own views of families like his own and, particularly, of the choices made by the men who are the fathers of those families.

PART V
WAR

At a recent conference I attended, the keynote speaker asked, "Why is it that every city and every small town has memorials to men who died in war, yet none have monuments for the women who died in childbirth?" The speaker's question made me stop and think about war and ask whether it was, as she implied, primarily a male concern. You may want to introduce this theme by asking students to respond to this speaker's question with five minutes' worth of writing; then ask volunteers to read their comments as a way to initiate discussion.

Nearly all wars have been fought mainly by men. Even in the recent conflict in the Persian Gulf, where female troops became visible, they were not allowed in combat. Yet whether or not women have actually fought in wars, their lives have been profoundly changed in ways that may be less obvious than the changes wrought in the lives of men suffering from combat wounds or post-traumatic stress. Consider, for example, the speakers in "Patterns" and in "Mother and Poet." And Aristophanes' comedy *Lysistrata* suggests a comic, bawdy view of women as protestors; as supporters of love rather than war.

Most of the selections in this section ask questions about war and about traditional assumptions concerning war and duty to one's country. To introduce those traditional assumptions, you might ask students to read "To Lucasta, Going to the Wars," "Mother and Poet," "Dulce et Decorum Est," "War Prayer," or "War." Each of these works suggests conventional views of war and patriotism. Thinking about these views leads to considering the following questions.

- How are those left behind affected by war? ("War," "The Fly," "Patterns," "Mother and Poet," "To Lucasta, Going to the Wars")

- How do young people form their assumptions about war? ("Mother and Poet," "Dulce et Decorum Est," and "Purpose, Blame, and Fire")

- How do we know "the enemy"? ("The War Prayer," "Guests of the Nation," "The Man He Killed," "The Conscientious Objector," "What Were They Like," and *Lysistrata*)

- What is the relationship between private and public duty? ("War," "Guests of the Nation," "The Things They Carried," "The Conscientious Objector")

100

- What role do religious values play in war? ("The War Prayer" and "The Fury of Aerial Bombardment")

ADDITIONAL SELECTIONS FOR CONSIDERATION: *WAR*

Title and Author		Text Page

Fiction

Patriotism	Yukio Mishima	822
My Oedipus Complex	Frank O'Connor	435

Poetry

My Father in the Navy: A Childhood Memory	Judith Ortiz Cofer	470
Naming of Parts	Henry Reed	710
plato told	e. e. cummings	719

Drama

All My Sons	Arthur Miller	478

Nonfiction

My People	Chief Seattle	1495
Arrival at Manzanar	Jeanne Wakatsuki Houston and James D. Houston	1534

SUGGESTIONS FOR TEACHING ADDITIONAL SELECTIONS

1. How do the families of those who serve in the military respond to their close relatives' war experiences? To consider this question, read the following works that show families affected by war and military service.

	Text Page
Patriotism	822
My Oedipus Complex	435
My Father in the Navy: A Childhood Memory	470
All My Sons	478

After reading these selections, do additional research to address the question that opens this topic. In addition to reading more fiction and nonfiction, consider interviewing people whose family members served in the military during wartime.

2.   Create a dialogue on the topic of honor, duty, and responsibility during wartime between the following individuals. (You may imagine these people as they are at any point in the selection or as they might speak from beyond the grave, looking back at their experiences.)

	Text Page
The wife in "Patriotism"	822
The speaker in "plato told"	719
The father in *All My Sons*	478
Chief Seattle in "My People"	1495

THEMATIC PHOTOGRAPH (page 558)

Considerations

1.   Describe the details of this picture that you noticed first. Then look carefully for other details. Do the new details you discovered change your response to the picture? Explain.

2.   Explain how this picture relates to the theme of war. What aspect or aspects of war does it represent? Is this a picture you would have chosen to represent war? Explain.

READINGS

Mark Twain, The War Prayer (page 559)

Twain chooses these phrases to describe the times:

"great and exalting excitement"

"the bands playing"

"toy pistols popping"

"a fluttering wilderness of flags flashed in the sun"

"a glad and gracious time"

Twain is equally expansive in his description of the people:

"in every breast burned the holy fire of patriotism"

"young volunteers marched down the wide avenue gay and fine in their new uniforms"

"proud fathers and mothers and sisters and sweethearts cheering them with voices choked with happy emotion"

"packed masses listened, panting, to patriot oratory"

"half-dozen rash spirits . . . ventured to disapprove of the war"

"young faces alight with martial dreams"

"glowing eyes and beating hearts"

Ask students to compile this list, and perhaps ask them to read phrases aloud as you write them on the board. This exercise should make them aware of Twain's outrageous use of hyperbole. Twain's exaggeration and, particularly, his description of the fate of those few who questioned the war, should lead students to recognize Twain's scathingly ironic and satiric tone.

The man who claims to be a messenger from God asks the blindly patriotic churchgoers to consider carefully the implications of their prayers. If their prayers are answered, what might be the cost, both to others and to their own souls? The people who listen to the messenger must reject his version of the prayer as madness. To do otherwise would require them to think deeply, seriously, and critically about the jingoistic slogans and shallow emotions that lead them to support the war.

Luigi Pirandello, War (page 562)

When I first taught this story, I began by asking students to discuss the title, which seemed to me narrow and unclearly focused. Although I didn't voice my opinion until after students had offered theirs, perhaps I communicated a negative response because I found my view reinforced. Typical comments: "The story's not really about the war"; "It's about people left behind by war"; "Pirandello actually seems to avoid talking about the war. It's more about the parents' feelings." Following one discussion that moved along these lines, a quiet student who had not spoken in class wrote a journal entry that went something like this:

> It seems to me that the story is about a war, but not a war on a battlefield. It's about the war that is going on inside the train car between the different people with their different views. But most importantly, I'd say it's a war that is going on inside the parents—it's about whether the children have a duty to their parents, their country, or themselves.

With the student's permission, I started the next class by reading this journal entry. The lively exchange of ideas that followed showed me how narrowly I had originally viewed my question about the title. It's often difficult to come to class with entirely open-ended questions in mind since it's nearly impossible not to start thinking about responses even as you frame a question. This experience reinforced for me the importance of keeping open various ways of responding to a question.

"War" offers an intriguing use of point of view. During most of the story, we see the thoughts of the woman whose only son has just left for the front. At the end, we see the thoughts and feelings of the man whose son has died. He has seemed to accept the necessity of sending his son off to war and claims to be entirely resigned to his son's death. The woman, in contrast, appears hysterical and selfish as she mourns her son even while he is still alive. At the end, however, she moves beyond her self-centered actions and recognizes the man's pain with her question, "Then . . . is your son really dead?" When she looks at this painful reality ("almost as if waking up from a dream"), the old man suddenly understands fully his loss. Now it is his turn to concentrate on himself and to mourn publicly his dead son. The platitudes about "decent boys" who "die inflamed and happy" are forgotten. Just as the woman begins to think she is wrong in her sorrow and fear, the man who has been lecturing her shows that he, too, feels deeply the death of his son.

Frank O'Connor, Guests of the Nation (page 566)

Although the setting of the story may seem obvious, I've found that many students do not recognize where this story is taking place. Since understanding setting is essential, I begin teaching this story by asking for evidence suggesting the story's locale. Details include the following:

> Irish place names such as Claregalway
>
> Irish dances such as "The Seige of Ennis"
>
> Irish names such as Mary Brigid O'Connell

References to the English as "the enemy"

Irish dialect such as "Ah, you divil, you . . ."

Students may also need to be reminded that although Ireland was officially granted home rule by the British in 1914, hostilities continued, leading to the creation of Sinn Fein, the political group which, following the Easter Rebellion in 1916, formed a military wing called the Irish Republican Army (IRA).

Some students may find it difficult to believe that prisoners could become so friendly with their guards, so you may want to mention that there are groups of German POWs from World War II who have held reunions—and invited their American guards to attend. The psychology of how and why such friendships occur may prove an intriguing discussion topic.

Nobel and Hawkins both enjoy a good argument; Buonaparte and Belcher are quieter. The prisoners seem more experienced and knowledgeable than do the guards, yet all four clearly grapple with the concept of loyalty. Buonaparte, the narrator, reflects the way each character struggles with the sense of individual loyalty in conflict with loyalty to a government or to a cause. Jeremiah Donovan's cold-hearted excitement at the thought of the execution provides a foil for the anguish that Buonaparte and Belcher experience. The old woman, a magnificent minor character, is a seer who recognizes the prisoners' humanity as well as their failings and, in the end, forces both Buonaparte and Nobel to face what has happened.

The details of the execution insist that the reader recognize the terror, agony, and ugliness of death in war. These are not stereotyped executions of brave prisoners smoking a final cigarette and refusing a blindfold. Instead we see the botched shooting, the pleas of the condemned, and the moral dilemma faced by the executioners.

Katherine Mansfield, The Fly (page 576)

The first scene introduces and contrasts old Woodifield and the boss. One is employer, one employee. Although very different in manner and in status, they share the common fate of having lost sons in the war. In the second scene, the boss sits alone thinking about his dead son. Woodifield's comments have forced the boss to contemplate how his response to his loss has changed. Only a short time ago he wept hysterically about his son's death; now he is unable to feel that pain.

The third scene seems at first unrelated. The boss tortures a fly, wishing that it would die while admiring its bravery. What does this action represent? Some students have suggested that the boss is a shallow individual who has more response to the fly's death than to his son's. Others believe that by killing the fly, the boss tries to force himself to feel something. He is terrified by the loss of feeling and seeks any substitute. Another possibility might be that the boss himself tries to control the destiny of the fly as he was unable to control the fate of his son. This reading brings to mind King Lear's comparison of humans to flies, where humans are killed randomly by "the gods" simply for "sport."

Tim O'Brien, The Things They Carried (page 581)

To begin discussion, you might read aloud the first two paragraphs of the story, asking students to listen for details they find particularly memorable. Follow the reading by requesting a list of the "things" these troops brought with them into the jungle. As students mention items, list on the board the names of the troops and the items they carried. Then ask students to focus on one soldier and to quickly skim the story looking for other items carried by that man. Next ask for a brief written response speculating on what that soldier's choices suggest about his hopes, fears, and values. Begin discussion with several students reading aloud what they have written.

The story focuses on the letter Lt. Cross carries with him. When Ted Lavendar is killed, Cross blames himself for the incident, believing that his daydreams of home and of girls like Martha caused him to relax discipline in a way that was dangerous to his men. Yet even before Lavendar's death, Cross questions the pebble Martha sends him. He carries it, perhaps, as a desperate attempt to believe that magically he, and his troops, will be safe from the traps, buried bombs, and snipers' bullets that surround them. Cross's response when Lavendar dies shows grief not only for the young soldier but also for the lieutenant's own youth and past. After this he can never again be the same; he can never return in the same way to the world he once knew.

Thomas Hardy, The Man He Killed (page 595)

The speaker in the poem is almost certainly a manual laborer; perhaps, judging by the reference in line 15 to "traps," he hunts for a living. He enjoys having a drink at a local bar and has the imagination to speculate that a man he has killed in battle might also enjoy such a pursuit. The repeated word "because" in lines 9 and 10 suggest the speaker's struggle to understand why he killed the other soldier. At first he comes up with the obvious, standard answer—perhaps the one he heard from his superiors—"I shot him dead because/Because he was my foe." Yet when he thinks further and tries to discover just why this man was his enemy, he simply comes up with more examples suggesting parallels between the dead soldier and himself.

Amy Lowell, Patterns (page 596)

The formal garden provides a pattern as does the speaker's dress. She describes herself as "Just a plate of current fashion." As she weeps, the drops from the fountain provide a counterpoint pattern to her tears. She sees herself as caught in the patterns of manners and social graces that stifle members of her class in society (particularly women). She had dreamt that her fiancé, Lord

Hartwell, would have provided an escape from those patterns, that with him she would have felt free enough even to make love in the garden sunlight (suggested by lines 87–89). Now Lord Hartwell himself has been destroyed by yet another "pattern called a war."

Wilfred Owen, Dulce et Decorum Est (page 599)

Because of the publicity concerning the use of chemical weapons in the Gulf War, some students may think the setting of this poem is recent. In fact, Wilfred Owen was a British soldier who fought in World War I and was killed just a few weeks before the armistice was signed. The "old beggars under sacks" are his compatriots, sick and weakened from trench warfare. Owen's diction (*lame, blind, drunk, deaf, blood-shod*) suggests the exhaustion and disaffection of the men—a very different picture from those offered by recruiting posters. The graphic details of the gas attack insist that the reader see and think about the ugliness and horror of war rather than the glory and honor suggested by patriotic slogans.

Karl Shapiro, The Conscientious Objector (page 600)

The final stanza suggests that the speaker is not one of the conscientious objectors but rather an observer. Because he says, "Your conscience is/What we come back to in the armistice," he may be a soldier. Yet he also discusses how "the soldier kissing the hot beach" will feel, so I think it more likely that the speaker is instead a somewhat detached voice—perhaps a member of the press?—who comments on what he sees.

Students may not know the story of Noah, so you may want to explain the significance of the dove, the bird Noah released at the end of the flood. When the dove returned with an olive branch in its mouth, Noah knew that somewhere it had found dry land, signaling (along with the attendant rainbow) that God was now at peace with humankind. Since then, the dove remains a symbol of peace.

Students also may not fully understand what the term *conscientious objector* signifies. This poem was first published in 1947, so Shapiro was almost certainly describing C.O.'s from World War II, but there have been resisters to every war since then.

Elizabeth Barrett Browning, Mother and Poet (page 601)

This poem works well in emphasizing the difference between poet and speaker. Although Barrett Browning may have shared the views attributed to Laura Savio, the poet is distinct from the woman she creates. It's also intriguing to speculate on the relationship between history and literature. Barrett Browning wrote the poem in 1861, immediately after the battle in which the second son is killed. Does she entirely invent Savio's response? Is this poem based on something Savio wrote? Was Barrett Browning in communication with Savio? Here's a topic for research.

Richard Lovelace, To Lucasta, Going to the Wars (page 605)

Lovelace, who fought on the side of Charles I during England's Puritan Revolution (1642–1645), probably shared the sentiments expressed by the speaker. This is a useful poem to use as an example of the patriotic stance against which poems like "The Man He Killed," "Dulce et Decorum Est," and "Mother and Poet" react.

Carolyn Forché, The Colonel (page 606)

First question: Is this a poem? Certainly it does not follow any of the traditional poetic forms, yet I would call it a prose poem (rather than simply a prose paragraph). Both the staccato, insistent rhythm of the short sentences and the powerful figurative language ("The moon swung bare on its black cord over the house"), place this work in the realm of poetry.

Why did Forché choose to arrange her images as a paragraph rather than in stanzas? I think a clue may come in the third-to-last sentence: "Something for your poetry, no? he said." Perhaps she chooses not to oblige in any way the unspeakably cruel and arrogant colonel. These images will not be recorded in what he would call poetry but will be set out starkly, almost in the form of a report.

Randall Jarrell, Gunner (page 606)

Speaking of another poem, Jarrell said that he wrote it "acting as next friend." His view of the Gunner's description of his life and death suggest the same persona in this poem.

The speaker uses ordinary, mundane images to describe his life before the war and, rather surprisingly, also uses homely images ("like rabbits"; "like a scab") to envision what happens to him in war. In the final stanza, he imagines his medals being sent home to his cat and his pension being like "so many mice" with which his wife is rewarded. War, then, becomes like a horrifying game of cat and mouse. This speaker refuses to glorify war or death in war.

Walt Whitman, Cavalry Crossing a Ford (page 607)

Whitman volunteered for nursing duty during the Civil War, and many of his poems reflect his thoughts and experiences during this time. I am struck with this particular poem because it seems like a color photograph that comes to life before our eyes. The visual images are vivid, almost sprightly. Without the final images of the regimental flags (or the title), we could imagine this parade of men heading off for a pleasurable outing of some kind. The juxtaposition of these bright images with their unstated, yet implied destination (war) creates a fragile, bitter irony.

Richard Eberhart, The Fury of Aerial Bombardment (page 607)

As a naval officer in World War II, Richard Eberhart worked as an instructor in a gunner school. This may be where he came by the images in the final stanza, which serve as a powerful, realistic counter to the unanswerable questions posed in the first three stanzas.

Perhaps Van Wettering and Averill represent the names of students to whom he taught or tried to teach the names of machine gun parts. Following the mundane routine of the classroom, did these young men imagine where their knowledge would take them? If they did imagine, did they also question? And what is their relationship to God? Why, the speaker asks, does God continue to permit humans to wage war? If we can learn to distinguish "the belt feed lever from the belt holding pawl," why can't we learn the lessons of "the fury of aerial bombardment"?

Denise Levertov, What Were They Like? (page 607)

Levertov, who was an active participant in protests against the Viet Nam war, published this poem in a volume called *Poems 1960–1967*. These dates show that she felt deep concern for the people and culture of Viet Nam even before the war escalated in 1969–1971. Knowing that the poem was written early in the war helps to explain the setting: far in the future where nothing is left of the Vietnamese culture because of the war's destruction. Whatever might have been beautiful, joyful, or treasured has been lost.

Who are the two speakers in this poem? The first may be an archaeologist, a historian, or possibly a military officer now thinking back over his time in Viet Nam. Whoever he is, the second speaker acknowledges him as an authority figure, twice addressing the first speaker as "Sir."

Aristophanes, Lysistrata (page 609)

Born in 450 B.C.E., Aristophanes celebrated his twenty-first birthday in 431 B.C.E., the year the Peloponnesian Wars began. He was deeply affected by living during these wars; three of his eleven surviving comedies—*Acharnians*, *Peace*, and *Lysistrata*—have antiwar themes. By the time *Lysistrata* was produced in 411 B.C.E., the war had gone on for more than twenty years, so it is not surprising that this play provides a powerful blow against the absurdities of war. What is surprising is the vehicle Artistophanes chooses to carry his theme. Fifth-century B.C.E. Greek women held no direct political power and were regarded by men as unfit for such concerns. Thus Arisotophanes' conception that women could stop a war was radical in way we can hardly imagine. It is a tribute to the playwright's genius that the comedy was accepted by his audience. It also became a frequently repeated drama, and since many Greek plays were performed only once, this repetition emphasizes the play's popularity.

Aristophanes' plays are the only examples of fifth-century B.C.E. Greek comedy that survive. Judging from these plays, the form combined satire with fantasy. Each play revolves around one fantastic situation with repeated variations that suggest an outlandish, comic approach to solving a current political or social crisis. Even in translation, it's clear that Aristophanes used puns and witty language as one of the main devices of humor. In addition, the play abounds with visual jokes provided by absurd props and exaggerated costumes. And, of course, such scenes as the ballyhoo between the chorus of old men and the chorus of old women suggests the roots of modern slapstick comic action. Although the leader of the men and the leader of the women may seem equally violent, it's intriguing to note that the men bring fire to fight with while the women bring water to put out the fire. Thus even in this fantastic scene, the action suggests that the men want to keep hostilities going while the women wish to quell them.

One of the qualities that made Aristophanes' comedies so popular was his refusal to ignore any likely target of satire. Although he aimed at one main problem—the prolonged war—he held nothing sacred. Notice, for instance, that the women gather in the Acropolis where their actions and words poke fun at inept political action and at falsely pious religious rituals. In addition, *Lysistrata* is an equal-opportunity play. Yes, the men and their war are the main focus of the satire, but the women also come in for their share of criticism. For instance, the opening scene suggests that several women do, indeed, live up to the stereotype of being late. And several scenes indicate that at least some of the women would be quite willing to give up their cause simply to satisfy their own sexual desires.

Although the play provides scene after scene of comic variations on the same theme (the women withholding sex until the men stop fighting), there are moments that suggest the antiwar theme was meant to be taken seriously. For example, at one point the chorus of women directly addresses the citizens of Athens, begging them "to hear useful words for the state." Certainly the play makes the point that wars often begin for reasons that are unclear to many of those who are fighting and that hostilities continue long after the original rationale for the war has been obscured. The play also suggests—in a way representative of the slogan popular during the Vietnam era, "Make love, not war"—that activities other than war may provide more productive and pleasurable ways of expending time and energy

Donald Hall, Purpose, Blame, and Fire (page 644)

Hall's introduction (paragraphs 1–4) suggests a fine way to begin discussion of this essay. Ask students to list the names of any films about war that they can remember seeing. Then ask them to choose one film and to write a brief response statement. (If students cannot think of a film, they might write about a television program—perhaps a series like" China Beach.") Asking several students to read their response statements leads to discussing "Purpose, Blame, and Fire" and to considering Hall's response to *The Last Train from Madrid*.

This essay appears in an anthology of Hall's work, *The Movie That Changed My Life*, (Viking, 1991). Students should have plenty to say about how, why, and whether this film did, in fact, change Hall's life. Some may question whether an eight-year-old could actually be so deeply moved; others may recall memories from their early lives that confirm the kind of profound insight and change that Hall describes.

Reading Frost's "Design" (page 1146) aloud could lead to a discussion of one of the essay's central issues: the terrifying randomness of death, typified by the arbitrary executions in *The Last Train from Madrid*. Both Frost's poem and Hall's essay might be compared with Amy Lowell's "Patterns" (text page 596) to pursue this theme further.

Ernest Hemingway, A New Kind of War (page 651)

Hemingway calls the Spanish Civil War "a new kind of war." From the earlier descriptions, perhaps he uses that title because this war's vicious battles are fought while civilian lives continue nearby in some semblance of normalcy. The civilians he encounters see the reality of the war yet seem concerned mainly with their own lives rather than with the outcome of the military encounters.

Hemingway begins this essay using second person, which has at least two significant effects. First, although he is clearly talking about himself, Hemingway invites the reader to share the experience in an intimate way. Second, by saying "you" rather than "I" he establishes distance, creating himself as a character who is on the scene being observed by the writer who describes him. He becomes, then, both actor and observer, and I think this dichotomy reflects the milieu he describes. This "new kind of war" seems unreal at times because instead of fighting in it, Hemingway and the people with whom he lives are watching it.

The war becomes real, however, when the American Friends of Spanish Democracy (Americans who have volunteered to fight against the fascists) call Hemingway to the bedside of the badly wounded Raven. At that point, the narrative switches from second person to first person as Hemingway feels personal connection with the fighting that has previously existed only as distant gun fire.

The conversation between Raven and Hemingway shows Raven's idealism and bravery. One of the first questions he asks Hemingway concerns not his own wounds but American public opinion about the war. Hemingway is sympathetic to Raven, yet he finds his quiet courage difficult to believe. When Raven describes how he was wounded, Hemingway assumes that he is exaggerating.

Later, Hemingway discovers from another man who fought with Raven that Raven has told the truth. Hemingway implies that this is a war where soldiers are not fighting for medals and personal glory. Unlike soldiers

Hemingway knew from other wars, these "new warriors" do not stretch the truth about their encounters with the enemy. In this war, he sees "Jay Raven, the social worker from Pittsburg with no military training," fighting heroically and motivated strictly by idealism.

PART VI
LEARNING AND TEACHING

Loren Eiseley's "The Hidden Teacher" works well as an initial assignment. If you choose to introduce this theme with Eiseley's essay, consider reading aloud the first few paragraphs or perhaps parts of the final section where he describes his own classroom experiences. After reading these excerpts, ask students to list predictions and questions they'll keep in mind as they read the essay. You might ask several students to read their lists while you write their observations on the board. Then, at the next class meeting, consider asking students to work in groups, sharing the predictions and questions they developed as well as their responses to those predictions and questions. When the class reconvenes, discussion can move easily from Eiseley's essay to general issues related to learning and teaching.

Eiseley describes lessons he has learned both from traditional teachers and from unorthodox instructors: "I once learned a lesson from a spider," he tells readers. His perception that we learn from many different sources and that instructors in school may teach us in unexpected ways leads students to consider and discuss their most profound and important learning experiences. Also, while Eiseley does not discuss the idea directly, you might have students talk about their own teaching experiences or teaching experiences they anticipate in the future. At first, some may say they have never been teachers, but almost everyone has shown a fellow worker how to begin a new task; led a younger sibling through the rules of a new games; or introduced a friend to a new way of thinking.

"The Lesson," "Battle Royal," "The Loudest Voice," "A Teacher Taught Me," "Learning to Read" and "Learning to Read and Write" all look at aspects of education related to students who are not part of the white, Christian majority. Harper's poem and Douglass's essay suggest the power of learning as a means of gaining freedom and show the historic background that often denied education to oppressed people. Both "Battle Royal" and "A Teacher Taught Me" show that even when schooling is mandated for all, educational institutions can be co-opted to maintain oppression rather than to fight it. "The Loudest Voice" addresses the question of assimilation, asking what is lost and what is gained when children are educated by teachers and institutions (however well meaning) that do not share their culture and values.

Some selections criticize formal education: "Battle Royal" shows a corrupt school superintendent; "The Scholars" suggests that professors have their heads and hearts buried in dusty research tasks; the teacher in Anna Lee Walters' poem patronizes and condescends to her Native American student; and the professor in Ionesco's *The Lesson* is brutal and absurd. Other selections, however, offer a contrasting view. In James Alan McPherson's "Why I Like Country Music," Mrs. Esther Clay Boswell chides her students about clock-watching, but she also clearly cares for them and teachers them lessons about academic subjects and about life. Sugar and Sylvia in Toni Cade Bambara's "The Lesson" challenge Miss Moore's every word and action, but this persistent teacher, remaining calm and determined, pursues the neighborhood children beyond the classroom to make certain they learn for themselves the lesson of economic inequality. Edna O'Brien's Sister Imelda takes the risk of caring deeply about her students and of reaching out particularly far to one special student. Finally, Loren Eiseley's essay provides a look at two men who are admirable instructors in and out of the classroom.

Many of the selections in this section invite a look at the power structures in the teaching-learning relationship. I begin with Ionesco's *The Lesson* and follow with "Battle Royal," "Sister Imelda," "The School Children," "A Teacher Taught Me," and "Ethics."

ADDITIONAL SELECTIONS FOR CONSIDERATION: *LEARNING AND TEACHING*

Title and Author		Text Page
	Fiction	
Butterflies	Patricia Grace	12
A Temple of the Holy Ghost	Flannery O'Connor	1022
Cathedral	Raymond Carver	1056
	Poetry	
Theme for English B	Langston Hughes	14
When I was one-and-twenty	A. E. Housman	157
Spring and Fall	Gerard Manley Hopkins	168
What Were They Like?	Denise Levertov	607
Elegy for Jane	Theodore Roethke	854
The Mind Is an Enchanting Thing	Marianne Moore	1148
Unlearning to Not Speak	Marge Piercy	1179
Geometry	Rita Dove	1184

SUGGESTIONS FOR TEACHING ADDITIONAL SELECTIONS

1. Read the following selections to see how a speaker tells a story or uses anecdotes as a way of teaching or convincing others, either directly or indirectly. Then compose a story or anecdote of your own that you believe will teach your audience something new (perhaps showing a new way of looking at a familiar idea, belief, person, or place). Your story may be as fanciful as you like; remember that the lesson you teach may be subtle and indirect.

	Text Page
A Temple of the Holy Ghost	1022
Cathedral	1056
Theme for English B	14
What Were They Like?	607

2. Consider the relationship between power and education. What power do teachers hold? What power do learners hold? How can the balance of power affect what one learns or teaches? Consider the following works as inspiration for further research on this topic.

	Text Page
Butterflies	12
Cathedral	1056
Theme for English B	14
Unlearning to Not Speak	1179

	Text Page
Lysistrata	609
Graduation in Stamps	228

3. What role do parents, grandparents, or other relatives play in the education of young people? What role—or roles—should they play? Consider the following works as inspiration for further research on this topic.

	Text Page
Butterflies	12
A Temple of the Holy Ghost	1022
Education	22
Graduation in Stamps	228

THEMATIC PHOTOGRAPH (page 558)

Considerations

1. What has the woman in the picture learned? Think beyond the easy literal response as you answer.

2. How does the instructor respond to his student's success? What might he have learned from teaching this particular student?

3. Write a journal entry assuming the persona of either the student or the teacher. Describe a significant event that led up to moment captured by the picture.

READINGS

James Alan McPherson, Why I Like Country Music (page 657)

As he tells his story, the narrator thinks about Gloria, a sophisticated black woman who makes a witty comparison between the New York Stock Exchange and country music. Born and raised in the north, she views all Southern white customs and culture with suspicion. The narrator recalls the incident of the Maypole celebration partly to imagine how he would try to convince Gloria that his memories are personal and individual and should not be judged by generalizations. He also tells the story to retrace, and to understand, the paths he traveled from his Southern childhood to uptown Manhattan, where he still appreciates the square dance but where he has also "learned to dance to many other kinds of music."

Looking back on his younger self, the narrator describes a boy who was not a dancer in a society that valued dancing for itself and as "a form of storytelling." Being unable to dance, he felt, was a kind of illiteracy. His pain increased along with his admiration for Gweneth Lawson—whose name suggests a romantic heroine straight from days of knights and ladies—and his dislike for the slick, city-wise Leon Pugh.

When Mrs. Esther Clay Boswell first appears on the scene, she seems like a strange teacher, indeed. She insults her students, encourages fourth-grade boys and girls to think about love relationships, and often reduces "the more emotional among us" to tears. Yet under her harsh methods and her dictatorial approach to classroom discipline lie a sharp wit and a sense that these children had best grow up as fast as they can and learn to rely on themselves— what she calls recognizing "the footpaths through the *sticky* parts of the rosebed."

Why does Mrs. Boswell give the narrator the chance to dance with Gweneth? Perhaps because even though Leon Pugh gives all the "right" answers about sticking up for yourself and blowing your own horn, she is bored by Leon and recognizes his self-centered attitude as destructive rather than constructive. Perhaps she rather admires the desperate measures the narrator has taken to get a place by Gweneth for the Maypole plaiting. Or perhaps she, too, has learned a lesson and sees that the race need not always go to the loud and the bold. Sometimes, perhaps, those who speak "quietly and mostly to [themselves]" should come out ahead. And so, playing her benevolent dictator role, Mrs. Boswell banishes the frustrated and furious Leon, giving the narrator his chance at happiness. Coming out a winner on this one occasion gives the narrator confidence and hope. He can square dance now and he will learn to dance other dances. And forever after, the sound of country music reminds him that he can remain a thinker and dreamer, not afraid to argue a point but "as always, quietly, and mostly to myself."

Toni Cade Bambara, The Lesson (page 670)

In her dedication to her anthology *The Black Woman,* Bambara writes: "To the uptown mammas who nudged me to just set it down in print . . . so maybe that way we don't keep treadmilling the same old ground." This dedication suggests the reason for Miss Moore's summer lessons and field trips. Although Sylvia has a grand time describing Miss Moore in terms often reserved for the stereotyped elementary school teacher—prim, proper, and always looking "like she was going to church"—it is clear that her teaching goes way beyond ordinary classroom exercises.

When I teach this story, I continue to be amazed by many students' initial response. Over and over I hear some version of this statement as Miss Moore's purpose for bringing the children to F. A. O. Schwartz: "She wants them to see what they can have if they work hard and get into better circumstances." Usually someone else will point to details like the shame even the ebullient, self-confident Sylvia feels as she enters F. A. O. Schwartz, or Sugar's comment that she doesn't think "all of us here put together eat in a year what that sailboat costs." Surely we are meant to be sympathetic with Sylvia and Sugar—we are not to feel that Sylvia should be ashamed or that Sugar is simply envious. Finally, consider Miss Moore's comment, "Imagine for a minute what kind of society it is in which some people can spend on a toy what it would cost to feed a family of six or seven." She asks the children to think about the *society* in which they live. She knows that no matter how hard most people work—and this certainly includes middle class as well as poor people—their salaries will not buy them "their share of the pie."

Sylvia and Sugar are deeply affected by their trip to F. A. O. Schwartz. Sugar voices her view of the lesson, but Sylvia does not want to give Miss Moore the satisfaction of hearing her acknowledge the deeply troubling inequities she is beginning to recognize. Sugar responds to the lesson by racing swiftly away, thinking of the ice cream Sylvia has proposed. Sylvia, confident that she can run even faster, stays behind "to think this day through"; to consider the endless complications and complexities of growing up in a democracy that often seems to foster inequality.

Grace Paley, The Loudest Voice (page 677)

I've found that students respond more fully to this story when they understand certain basic tenets of Judaism. For instance, many Christian students do not know that Jews do not believe in the divinity of Jesus. They need to recognize that Chanukah is not "Jewish Christmas" and to understand the relentless persecution Jews have experienced throughout their history.

Certainly Shirley's father is developed as the more sympathetic parent. He argues that being exposed to Christmas is not the worst thing that could happen to a Jewish child. He points out that "history teaches everyone. We learn from reading this is a holiday from pagan times also, candles, lights, even Chanukah. So we learn it's not altogether Christian. . . . What belongs to history, belongs to all. . . ." He sees his daughter's participation in the holiday religious pageant as "introducing us to the beliefs of a different culture." The mother, however, fears that her daughter will gradually be pulled away from Judaism if she participates in ceremonies relating to the Christian religion. It's easy to see the father as broadminded and sensible and to stereotype the mother as narrow and whining. Still, near the end of the story, the mother offers an insight into her objections when she defends Mr. Hilton's failure to give major roles in the pageant to several Christian children: "They got very small voices; after all, why should they holler? The English language they know from the beginning by heart . . . the whole piece of goods . . . they own it."

With this speech, she grudgingly acknowledges the wisdom of Mr. Hilton's choosing Jewish children to play major roles, but she also demonstrates her understanding of who holds the power in the school her child attends and in the new country where they now live. Shirley's father may see the play as simply being introduced "to the beliefs of a different culture," but Shirley's mother understands that, in fact, they have been introduced to the beliefs of the dominant culture. Certainly the Christians in the story show no interest in or understanding of Judaism; otherwise how could they end the play with Shirley's describing the crucifixion of Jesus by proclaiming "as everyone in this room, in this city—in this world—now knows, I shall have eternal life." The father is apparently willing to to look on this appalling ignorance as something benign; the mother is less comfortable with what she hears and sees.

Shirley herself seems entirely at ease with her experience. From her participation in the pageant, she has learned that she may be "foolish," but she is not "a fool." I take this to mean that, like her father, she takes a lighthearted, humorous approach to the troubles of the world, but like her mother she recognizes the need to face those troubles squarely. Her prayer at the end suggests that has she retained her own religious beliefs and also feels sorry for the "lonesome Christians," who, in her eyes, lack the warmth and connection of community in which she lives. The final two lines suggest that while she obviously feels the deepest sympathy with her father, she also understands her mother's views. She plans to keep speaking out loudly so that her voice may be heard over the "very small voices" of her fellow classmates who are "blond like angels."

Ralph Ellison, Battle Royal (page 683)

The action of "Battle Royal," which appears as the first chapter of Ellison's novel *The Invisible Man,* divides into six sections:

Section I:	Main characters introduced and hear grandfather's mysterious deathbed charge
Section II:	Narrator arrives at the hotel, along with the other fighters
Section III:	Blonde stripper dances
Section IV:	Narrator and others fight battle royal
Section V:	Narrator gives graduation speech
Section VI:	Conclusion: narrator dreams of his grandfather reacting reacting to the award of the college scholarship

Through these scenes, the narrator traces his education about the racist world in which he lives. The grandfather's startling instructions suggest that a man who has appeared to be gentle and subservient all his life has, in fact, been inwardly angry and resistant to the injuries, slights, and condescensions of white people. The narrator arrives at the hotel full of hope, but as the blonde stripper dances, he becomes increasingly uncomfortable with the way the white men watch the young black men for any signs of sexual arousal and with the parallel he sees between the woman and himself. Both are there for the entertainment of the whites; both are regarded as objects or possessions.

The power of the battle royal scene is enhanced by the narrator's being blindfolded. He is literally "in the dark" yet he "sees the light" with all of his other senses and, particularly, with his mind. His physical pain and emotional confusion are expressed in language often achingly beautiful (see his description of the blood he has shed as "shaping itself into a butterfly"). In this section, the narrator recognizes that he has not been brought here because of the quality of his graduation speech but rather as an amusement to be displayed.

His growing understanding leads him to substitute, perhaps subconsciously, the phrase "social equality" for "social responsibility." Although he later recants, this dramatic moment marks a significant point in the narrator's life. He sees how truly "invisible" he is unless he is doing something to upset what white culture sees as the natural order. The scholarship to "the state college for Negroes" seems designed, as the ending dream indicates, to keep him running on the same treadmill for which his high school has trained him.

Edna O'Brien, Sister Imelda (page 695)

Born in the village of Tuamgraney, County Clare, Ireland, Edna O'Brien was educated at the National School in Scarrif, the Convent of Mercy at Longrea, and the Pharmaceutical College in Dublin. From all accounts, the Convent of Mercy was much like the school depicted in "Sister Imelda." This school provided O'Brien with her first experience away from home where her brutal, alcoholic father dominated the family.

Baba and the narrator take a breezy view of their education, but Baba is more aggressive and more willing to question authority. She thinks Sister Imelda must have "something wrong" in the "upstairs department" to have returned to the convent after her years at university. The narrator, on the other hand, mildly notes that Sister Imelda must "have a vocation." Following the incident when Sister Imelda throws a chalkboard eraser at the narrator, Baba proposes, "We could get her defrocked." The narrator sees that the action "was as much to do with liking as it was with dislike." Perhaps most indicative of Baba's rebellious nature is when she tries to cut the window on the confectioner's shop and nonchalantly sasses the prefect (senior student monitor) who stops her.

Sister Imelda is a wonderful, rich character. Clearly intelligent and wise, she has returned from taking an honors degree to teach teenage girls geometry and cookery. In geometry class, she approaches the work with deep seriousness.

When the students do not understand she becomes frustrated, yet she continues to work with them, seeing their triumphs as her own. In the cookery class, on the other hand, she is warmer and more relaxed. There she encourages a sense of camaraderie and good fellowship. When the narrator describes the cookery class, she notes that she does not want Sister Imelda to be like a mother. The narrator is searching for another kind of relationship, but she doesn't clearly understand what it is.

Sister Imelda's response to the narrator's Christmas performance suggests that she holds deep, quite possibly sexual, feelings for the narrator; the shower of kisses she bestows on the narrator are the only strong physical indication (other than brief touches and chaste hugs) of her feelings. The narrator recognizes that Sister Imelda sees her as a special favorite, but her naïveté prevents her from seeing anything more than that. Still, she longs to join with Sister Imelda in the only way she can imagine—becoming a nun. Her profound sense of sorrow and guilt in the final scene suggests that she has at least a subconscious understanding of her betrayal. By rejecting the convent, she has turned away from the love Sister Imelda held for her, but what she regrets is her lack of courage in failing to write to her beloved nun to let her know of the change of heart.

Henry Reed, Naming of Parts (page 710)

This poem shows in a poignantly ironic way a breakdown in communication between student and teacher. The instructor, whose voice is heard in the first four lines of the first three stanzas, explains the parts of a rifle. He is almost certainly a military instructor. The young trooper who hears him translates his dry lecture into a sensual reverie. As the instructor explains an instrument of death, the student imagines the life-giving flowers and bees. The "spring" of the rifle becomes in his mind the season of "Spring." In the final stanza, the student's vision integrates his own images with those of the instructor, showing that the "naming of parts" can mean much more than the instructor realizes.

William Butler Yeats, The Scholars (page 711)

The bald heads probably represent aging scholars who have forgotten their sins and the bodies that committed those sins. They are now identified only by the part of them that holds their brains; presumably the only part of themselves that still functions. They are contrasted with the young men, who seem to be writers, probably poets. The poets write the works that the elderly scholars "edit and annotate," yet the contrast here is not simple. The poets, after all, write lines "to flatter beauty's ignorant ear," suggesting that they also lack a clear vision of the world.

Still, it is the scholars who come in for the heaviest criticism. Pacing back and forth, they echo ideas deemed acceptable by others in their profession. The speaker's regard for their work is brilliantly summed up by his observation that they "cough in ink."

These scholars might admire the Roman lyric poet Catullus, but as they write their dry commentaries they can never hope to fill his shoes.

Walt Whitman, There Was a Child Went Forth (page 712)

This poem suggests that education comes not just from school but also from the events, objects, people, and places that we observe each day. The child will become a combination of these images, some of them positive, some negative.

Students will disagree about the effects of the parents on this child. Some see the father as entirely negative, yet he is described as "strong, self-sufficient, and manly." Without the details that follow, he almost certainly would be seen as a positive role model. The mother, at first, seems positive, yet on second reading, her "mild words" and clean cap seem to suggest a passive person without much to distinguish her or make her an individual personality.

Marianne Moore, The Student (page 713)

The speaker suggests that the true student must learn voluntarily. Unlike sheep that can be forcibly shorn of their wool, students cannot be forced to give forth what they truly have learned. Students are like wolves—their coats (what they have come to know) are magnificent—but they must give them over voluntarily. The true student may also seem sometimes to be unmoved by significant things; but the apparent lack of response may, in fact, indicate that the student is so overwhelmed by what he or she has comprehended that no reaction is possible.

Louise Glück, The School Children (page 715)

As these children go to school, it is as if they are crossing a great ocean. Teachers "on the other shore" wait behind great desks. The children are like apples offered up by the mothers to the teachers who will teach these children to be orderly and to learn in silence. The mothers, left behind, try to imagine how to escape from their homes, which are now like orchards barren of fruit.

Anna Lee Walters, A Teacher Taught Me (page 716)

The short lines and recurring refrain give this poem a chant-like rhythm. Students will probably find the narrator's response to the boy with "transparent skin" readily understandable, but opinion may be divided over her reaction to the teacher. Why does she resent what seem to be sincere expressions? Students who have been in this situation themselves will see the condescension in the teacher's choice of words and in the way she makes the narrator stand apart from the other students.

Linda Pastan, Ethics (page 717)

The first section of the poem sets up a typical classroom situation where the teacher poses a hypothetical question which the students find tedious and distant. When the speaker, Linda, suggests an alternative possibility to the teacher's either/or dilemma, she is ridiculed. Years later, when the speaker's own visit to a museum makes the ethics teacher's query truly meaningful, she finds that none of the classroom possibilities fit. She sees that human life and fine art are intertwined; one cannot be valued above the other. And certainly very young people cannot be expected to fully understand the depth of this truth. Ethics, she suggests, cannot be learned at school, but only by living life in a full and thoughtful way.

Gary Gildner, First Practice (page 718)

The speaker looks back with the eyes of childhood on Clifford Hill, who coached the football team. The reference to the grade school basement (where students went for atomic attack drills) suggests that the players are quite young. In addition, the speaker takes literally, as would a young child, Hill's contention that this is a dog-eat-dog world. Some students may be surprised by Hill's request that any girls leave, but others will know that this cigar-chomping coach regards the word "girl" as equivalent to coward or weakling.

Hill's approach to sports teaches team members that winning is the most important goal and that learning to hate is an essential part of becoming a successful athlete. I take his command "but I don't want to see/any marks when you're dressed" to mean that he is also calculating and sneaking, showing his players how to injure without making any bruises that parents or other authorities are apt to notice and question.

Some students contend that even coaches like Clifford Hill have something valuable to teach. Others claim that few coaches share his views. Still others see Hill as typical and use his attitude as evidence that young people—particularly young men—are often harmed by what they learn when they play organized sports. (For a similar view of sports, see Paul Theroux's "Being a Man," page 422.)

e. e. cummings, plato told (page 719)

The speaker suggests that no matter how well known or well respected the authority who delivers advice, most people learn most readily through experience. The lesson here is particularly grim: apparently the person who could not or would not learn from philosophers; from religious, political, or military leaders; or even from friends and acquaintances has been killed in war. What lesson, then, does the speaker imply? Perhaps that those who refuse to learn from history are doomed to repeat it? Yet how much choice does the individual have to act on historical lessons that he or she may have learned?

Perhaps, instead, what the "he" of the poem has learned is that we all are mortal; that all soldiers are vulnerable in battle.

Frances E. W. Harper, Learning to Read (page 720)

Frances Watkins was born to free, black parents in Baltimore more than forty years before the Civil War began. Orphaned at age three, she was raised by her uncle who ran a school for free black children. Through her schooling and later work as a teacher, she became passionately devoted to the abolitionist movement. Before and after marrying Fenton Harper, who was also committed to the abolitionist cause, she lectured widely for antislavery organizations. Like "Learning to Read," many of her poems suggest the importance of education as a means of liberation. A theme worth pursuing is the subversive nature of true learning. Every oppressed group has been to one degree or another denied the opportunity to study in the same way as those who hold power in their society.

Eugène Ionesco, The Lesson (page 722)

An intriguing way to begin discussion of this play is to note what might be called its "non-setting." Whereas most works of literature have some clear social or political context, this play belongs to no specific place or time. The apartment could be almost anywhere; all we know is that it overlooks a small town with red-roofed houses. Neither the stage directions nor the dialogue suggests any particular country, culture, or era, although the reference to the Nazi armband at the end indicates that it is post–World War II.

Just as unusual as the drama's setting are the characters. Their personalities and motives do not develop and reveal themselves as we have come to expect. Instead, the maid, the professor, and his pupil deliver lines that apparently have little to do with the action of the play. Just as the setting of the play does not meet common expectations, the words and actions of the professor and his student defy standard logic.

The play stands as a splendid example of Theater of the Absurd (see text page 1191). You might point out that the word "absurd" in this context does not mean "silly" but, in the words of drama critic and absurdist scholar Martin Esslin, "out of harmony" (*The Theater of the Absurd*, New York: Doubleday, 1969. 5–7).

At first the professor seems kindly, though a bit eccentric. As the play progresses, however, he becomes a tyrant who terrifies and finally kills his student. Commenting on Ionesco's choice of the student-teacher relationship to examine the dynamics of power, Esslin says:

> What Ionesco is saying is that even behind so apparently harmless an exercise of authority as the teacher-pupil relationship, all the

violence and domination, all the aggressiveness, the cruelty and lust are present that make up any manifestation of power.

(*The Theater of the Absurd*, 96)

Although the play certainly contains elements of terror, it also provides grimly ironic comic moments. From the beginning, the play makes fun of rote learning as the student strives to please by recalling that Paris is the capital of France and, soon after, reciting—with some hesitancy—the names of the seasons. When the professor claims that he can successfully instruct his student in the principles of "linguistic and comparative philology" in fifteen minutes, we laugh at his arrogance in assuming that so complex a subject can be successfully condensed and summarized. The fast verbal shuffle is demonstrated when he insists that the Italian word for "France" is "Italy" because when Italians say, "My country is Italy," they mean the same thing that French citizens mean when they say, "My country is France." He's obviously wrong, yet the convoluted logic sounds disturbingly familiar.

Ionesco suggests that although language can be used to dominate, control, and intimidate, it does not serve as an easy or straightforward means of communication. Words can be used in too many different ways, and the maid's warning that "philology leads to calamity" is certainly borne out. She seems to stand apart from the central action of the play as an observer who both comments and criticizes. Aware of the professor's strange ways, she cleverly avoids his attempt to kill her and scolds him as if he were a small boy who has misbehaved. That he has just killed his fortieth student does not faze her and the final scene simply shows the two of them cleaning up what is regarded as merely a messy complication.

Students will not miss the parallels between rape and murder in the death scene. This scene powerfully suggests that physical, sexual, and emotional domination and abuse are interrelated. When the professor violates the student's mind, he violates her body and her life as well.

Loren Eiseley, The Hidden Teacher (page 747)

Eiseley begins this essay with the story of Job. After Job challenges what he believes to be the injustice of God, Elihu, who stands watching, suggests that although Job believes God has deserted him, perhaps He may speak in ways other than those that humans expect. Eiseley moves from this biblical story to his thesis. "Sometimes what we learn depends upon our own powers of insight. Moreover, our teachers may be hidden, even the greatest teacher."

To illustrate this idea, Eiseley describes his encounter with the spider. To discuss this example, you might read paragraph 3 aloud. The detailed description of the spider's web shows us the spider's world in a way most of us have not previously considered. The intrusion of the pencil point (paragraph 4) dramatically sets the spider in action; she vibrates the web, anticipating that she will catch the intruder. Because she expects to trap her usual prey, she looks for the results of her web vibrations and—Eiseley implies—is puzzled or surprised to find no dinner waiting.

Because no precedent existed for such an extraordinary event as a pencil entering the web, the spider had no way to deal with the experience and could not possibly conceive of the being who controlled the pencil. Eiseley recognizes that to the spider, he does not exist, and he goes on to think about the white blood cells in his body. He is dependent on them and they on him, yet, like the spider, they do not know he exists.

He sums up his insights from the encounter with the spider in paragraph 6: "I began to see that, among the many universes in which the world of living creatures existed, some were large, some small, but that all, including man's, were in some way limited or finite." Eiseley implies that just as the spider and the phagocytes could not conceive of him and his world, so, too, may we be unaware of dimensions of existence which may profoundly affect us.

What is intriguing about Eiseley's defining the spider as a teacher is the way the supporting anecdote leads clearly to one of his main points: "Sometimes what we learn depends upon our own powers of insight." Many people could have seen a spider in a web and perhaps even poked the web with a pencil, yet they would not have discovered the insight Eiseley found (or any insight) unless they moved from action, observation, and response to analysis and evaluation.

In the second part of the essay, Eiseley moves from discussing teachers in nature to discussing a more traditional setting for learning and teaching. But even as he describes the exchange between the professor of linguistics and the young student, he explores realms that go beyond the common classroom experience. Several extraordinary things happen. First, the student thinks comparatively. As the professor discusses "some linguistic peculiarities of Hebrew words," the student is not simply taking dutiful notes. Instead, he makes a connection with something in his own experience: the Mohegan language. Next, the student makes the effort—takes the risk—to communicate this connection to the professor. Then, although the professor is quite brusque in his reply, the student has the courage to value his own knowledge and to persist. Finally, the professor shows the good sense to recognize that he might possibly be wrong and to invite the student to discuss his ideas further.

The young student later becomes Eiseley's teacher. Perhaps he is able to be such an "excellent canoeman" over the rapids of higher education because during his own undergraduate years (and almost certainly before that) he received the encouragement and affirmation necessary to value his own thoughts and to take control of his own learning. In describing what he learned from this teacher, Eiseley says, "To this day, fragments of his unused wisdom remain stuffed in some back attic of my mind. Much of it I have never found the opportunity to employ, yet it has somehow colored my whole adult existence." Such marvelous observation leads to a discussion of how we are often deeply affected by things we learn even though we may never "use" them in our daily lives.

The final section of this selection describes Eiseley's friend who gains an important insight from a dream. As Eiseley describes his friend's experience with the dream, it becomes clear that, like the spider and the two professors, the dream acts as teacher primarily by being a stimulus. It is the friend's response, evaluation, and analysis that bring him to recognize his intricate, complex, ambiguous connection with his long-dead parents.

The final sentence may refer to the Bible or perhaps to a broad principle of ancient wisdom. The capitalization of "Teacher" suggests that the teacher within us may represent a higher being, a higher plane of existence than that we now call reality.

Frederick Douglass, Learning to Read and Write (page 757)

As Frederick Douglass describes his process of becoming literate, he focuses on the people who helped him and people who tried to deter him from his determination to learn. Master Hugh's wife plays both roles. At first she treats Douglass as she would any other child and instructs him in the rudiments of the alphabet. Her husband soon puts a stop to this by making clear "that education and slavery [are] incompatible with each other." Once she has been warned, she becomes almost fanatical in her attempt to keep Douglass away from books. Douglass attributes her change in heart to her husband's training, although he says, "She was not satisfied with simply doing as well as he had commended; she seemed anxious to do better."

Perhaps, as Douglass suggests, Master Hugh's wife has simply been corrupted by the institution of slavery, but his earlier description of her as "a pious, warm, and tenderhearted woman" who "had bread for the hungry, clothes for the naked, and comfort for every mourner that came within her reach" makes her striking change hard to understand as self-motivation. Being completely dependent on her husband, her changes might well reflect her fear of him and her recognition that her own survival rests on fulfilling his wishes.

Douglass describes several white people who help him learn to read. The poor children who teach him in return for the bread Douglass gives them are presented as particularly sympathetic. Douglass notes that he must withhold their names to protect them from reprisals for their kindly acts. Through telling this episode, Douglass helps gain support for his cause among the predominantly white audiences to which he often spoke.

He also establishes common ground by describing Richard Sheridan's defense of Catholics (predominantly Irish) in England. Until 1829, Catholics were not allowed to vote in England. Douglass further suggests his sympathy for and connection with the Irish by describing his encounter with the two "good Irishmen." After helping them unload a scow, he engages them in a discussion of slavery and they encourage him to seek freedom. He implies, then, that there are many people—women, poor white children, Irish Catholics—who can understand the plight of the slave and who have themselves experienced oppression.

Throughout the essay, the primary theme is Douglass's incredible drive to become literate. He shows the painstaking means he had to follow to learn to read and write, and he describes how his anger against slavery increased as he became able to read the works of those who fought against all kinds of enslavement. The connection between education and freedom becomes clear. Those who remain ignorant or who, like Master Hugh's wife, turn their backs on what they know to be true, can never be fully free.

PART VII
DEATH

Although death and dying are currently popular topics, I find the beginning discussion of this theme difficult. Many students are far too familiar with death. In any given class, several people will have lost close family members or friends. Especially when the death is recent, any reading and discussion may be extremely painful for such students. Keeping these students in mind, I introduce this theme by assigning Elizabeth Kübler-Ross's essay comparing modern attitudes toward death and dying with traditional views. Kübler-Ross suggests problems these modern attitudes raise for those who are dying and for their survivors. Her essay "On the Fear of Death" provides the opportunity for students who may not have experienced the death of someone close to them to understand, to some degree, the feelings of those who have. In addition, discussing Kübler-Ross's essay allows those students who have had close experiences with death to express their own beliefs and responses. When I teach this theme, I usually begin by saying that, for most people in our society, death is a painful and difficult topic. I tell students that, as always, their observations and comments are welcome, but I remind them that they will not be forced to share any feelings or opinions they wish to keep to themselves.

"The Jilting of Granny Weatherall," "The Death of Iván Ilych," "Patriotism," "The Bishop Orders His Tomb," and "I heard a fly buzz—when I died" take the point of view of people who know they are dying or about to die. "Patriotism" also shows this point of view, but because this story details the thoughts of two people planning ritual suicide, because these people come from an Eastern rather than Western culture, and because they are relatively young, this story does not fit exactly with the other selections just listed. To look inside the mind of those who are dying or who contemplate death, you might assign "Patriotism" either first or last as a contrast to the other selections which show people who are dying but not by choice.

"To Hell with Dying," "The Bustle in a House," "To an Athlete Dying Young," "Richard Cory," "Elegy for Jane," "Mid-Term Break," and *On Tidy Endings* all focus on those who have survived the death of someone they loved, knew well, or admired. Assigning these pieces together provides the opportunity for discussing what, if anything, the survivors have gained from their loss. Do they have new insight concerning their relationship with the dead person, with others, or with themselves? What future can students project for these survivors? In connection with survivors, consider, also, Mitford's "The American Way of Death," which calls for a critical look at American funeral practices.

Most of the selections—such as "To Hell with Dying" and "Death, be not proud"—look on death as an enemy to be fought. Yet other attitudes are also suggested. For example, throughout "The Death of Iván Ilych" the title character fights his sickness, yet at the end he seems able to accept death. The same is apparently true for Collin whose final hours are described in detail in *On Tidy Endings*. And, in a much different way, the young husband and wife in "Patriotism" consider death a friend. These complex, controversial attitudes should provoke thoughtful writing and discussion.

ADDITIONAL SELECTIONS FOR CONSIDERATION: *DEATH*

Title and Author		Text Page
Fiction		
Idiots First	Bernard Malamud	427
The Fly	Katherine Mansfield	576
The Wives of the Dead	Nathaniel Hawthorne	898
Death in the Woods	Sherwood Anderson	949
A Rose for Emily	William Faulkner	978
The Handsomest Drowned Man in the World	Gabriel García Márquez	1032
Poetry		
Do Not Go Gentle into That Good Night	Dylan Thomas	54
First Death in Nova Scotia	Elizabeth Bishop	158
The Death of the Hired Man	Robert Frost	308
Mother and Poet	Elizabeth Barrett Browning	601
Gunner	Randall Jarrell	606
Drama		
All My Sons	Arthur Miller	478

Title and Author		Text Page
	Nonfiction	
I Remember Papa	Harry Dolan	551
Shooting an Elephant	George Orwell	1528

SUGGESTIONS FOR TEACHING ADDITIONAL SELECTIONS

1.   Consider violent, premature death as compared to death in old age. Think of how you might personify death in each case. How would Death look, talk, and act? Read the following selections as you think about this comparison.

Violent, Premature Death

	Text Page
The Fly	576
Death in the Woods	949
A Rose for Emily (Homer)	978
Mother and Poet	601
All My Sons	478
Shooting an Elephant	1528

Death due to Aging and Illness

	Text Page
Idiots First	427
A Rose for Emily (Emily's father)	978
Do Not Go Gentle into That Good Night	54
The Death of the Hired Man	308

2.   Consider the impact of death on those who witness it or on those who survive the deaths of others. Use the following works to raise possibilities for further research on this topic.

	Text Page
The Fly	576
The Wives of the Dead	898
Death in the Woods	949
The Handsomest Drowned Man in the World	1032
First Death in Nova Scotia	158
Mother and Poet	601
All My Sons	478
Shooting an Elephant	1528

3. Consider how the perception of death changes with point of view. For instance, choose an incident directly relating to death from three or four of the following works and describe it from a point of view different from the one provided. For example, describe the opening scene in "The Fly" from Mr. Woodifield's point of view. Is he as casual about "poor Reggie's" death as he seems? Does he understand his boss's grief or speculate about the boss's reasons for not visiting his son's grave?

	Text Page
Death in the Woods (from the point of view of the old woman)	949
A Rose for Emily (from the point of view of the old servant, Tobe)	978
First Death in Nova Scotia (from the point of view of the speaker's mother or uncle)	158
Shooting an Elephant (from the point of view of a person in the crowd)	1528

THEMATIC PHOTOGRAPH (page 763)

Considerations

1. What is your overall impression when you first look at this picture? What one word or phrase (other than "death") would you use to describe it? Explain.

2. Contrast the photographer's view of the cemetery to the view the person driving the truck might have.

3.   Describe and comment on the trees that grow among the gravestones and
      their significance in the photograph.

READINGS

Katherine Anne Porter, The Jilting of Granny Weatherall (page 764)

Certainly the concept of jilting is central to this story. As Granny lapses in
and out of consciousness during her final hours, her mind wanders through the
past and she fixes especially strongly on the day she was left at the altar by
her fiancé, George. Of all the experiences of her life, including—apparently—
the death of her daughter, Hapsy, the aborted wedding was the most
profoundly disturbing and disappointing. And, at the end of the story, as
Granny approaches death she once again feels jilted. She has no sense that
Christ, the bridegroom, awaits her. This moment of emptiness, of spiritual
void, far outlives any other sorrow in her life.

How are we to read the story of this jilting? Some students see Granny as a
strong, independent woman, a person who has, as her name suggests, weathered
all that life has brought. She deserves admiration and sympathy as her
children, the doctor, and the priest hover around her, disturbing her last hours
with their own concerns. For those who see her this way, the concluding image
seems a cruel irony. Others, however, consider Granny self-centered and filled
with unreasonable pride. No one can suit her or please her, and most of her
memories involve recalling her accomplishments and the days when her
children were dependent on her. Although she does say a brief prayer
acknowledging that she could not have done all she did without the help of
God, in the end she turns to human comfort rather than religion. The rosary
beads slip from her fingers as she grasps her son's hand. Some students see this
as evidence that Granny fails to end her life with peace because she is unable to
give herself over to faith.

I favor some version of the first reading. Granny seems to me a remarkable,
feisty woman who banishes young doctor Harry with sharp words even as she
feels the physical and emotional evidence of death: "Her bones felt loose, and
floated around in her skin, and Doctor Harry floated like a balloon around the
foot of the bed." She has always been able to overcome adversity, looking with
scorn on the fiancé who deserted her and managing to raise her children alone
after her husband's death. Now she wants to control death by denying its
power, and when she cannot, she finds herself once again on her own—deserted
in time of need.

Leo Tolstoy, The Death of Iván Ilych (page 722)

I like to assign this short novel in two segments—Part I, followed by the remaining sections. After students read Part I, I ask them to speculate about the rest of the story, listing who they expect the important characters to be and noting what they can about Iván Ilych from what they have read. Because of the reverse chronological order of the first section, many are surprised to learn that Iván Ilych will be the main character and that most of the other characters will play either minor or entirely peripheral roles. Often they have a difficult time telling very much about Iván Ilych himself because the characters in the first section are so busy focusing on themselves. With the exception of his young son, no one mourns. The widow concerns herself with financial issues, and Iván Ilych's friends worry more about their bridge game than they do about his death. Rather than eliciting grief, Iván Ilych's absence stimulates conjectures about positions that will now be open. By beginning the story this way, Tolstoy provides a grim setting against which to play the scenes of Iván Ilych's life. Every mediocre action, every crass decision, every shallow thought takes on a deeper significance because we cannot forget that disturbing funeral where almost no one feels that any loss has been suffered.

In the flashback section, Iván Ilych appears as a young man, content to follow a conventional path, never failing but never really excelling. He gets a job through political patronage and marries as a response to social conventions. As a judge, he takes casual, sadistic pleasure in the power he holds over those who come before his bench. He loses interest in his wife as soon as she becomes "troublesome," and he expects his family to stay out of his way and not intrude as he seeks the perfect house with the perfect interior decoration.

Once he becomes ill, Iván Ilych sees with terrible clarity the cost of his empty life and shallow values. Just as he has wanted no trouble from his family, now they want no inconvenience from him. Just as he has exercised power unfeelingly, so too do the doctors treat him. He resents their half-answers and condescending attitudes and finally comes to realize how those who stood before him in court must have felt. Only the peasant servant, Gerasim, brings Iván Ilych some modicum of comfort. Gerasim sees death as a natural part of life and so he is neither fearful, nor impatient, nor horrified with his master's physical or emotional suffering.

The final scene, I believe, represents triumph. Iván Ilych finally accepts death and also honestly admits the failings and omissions of his life. When he is able to accept death, in a sense he defeats it. Although he found no lasting comfort when the priest came to offer communion, he seems able at the end to make the leap of faith, believing that "Death is finished . . . it is no more."

Students will almost certainly notice the similarity between Tolstoy's description of dying and the descriptions given by people who have had near-death experiences. Of course, the research on near-death experiences, done primarily after 1968, could not have been known to Tolstoy. It is interesting to note that prior to writing this story, Tolstoy experienced a serious illness from which he had not been expected to recover.

Alice Walker, To Hell with Dying (page 816)

Some students consider Mr. Sweet Little an inappropriate companion for young children. They cite his alcoholism, his lack of ambition, and what they regard as his manipulative, phoney, deathbed scenes as evidence that he provides an extremely negative role model for the narrator and her siblings. Other students note his kindness toward the children and his ability to be the perfect playmate because he regards them as his equals. The narrator also provides an explanation for Mr. Sweet's lack of enthusiasm for work, telling us that he "had been ambitious as a boy, wanted to be a doctor or lawyer or sailor, only to find that black men fare better if they are not." Some students find this reason a rationalization, but others sympathize with Mr. Sweet's response; when he discovered he could not follow the careers he favored, "he turned to fishing as his only earnest career and playing the guitar as his only claim to doing anything extraordinarily well."

Although the story focuses on Mr. Sweet, the narrator is an equally important character. As she tells the story, she unfolds the discovery of Mr. Sweet's importance in her life. Just as Mr. Sweet gave unquestioning acceptance to the narrator and her family, so, too, did they give unquestioning support to him. Never challenging his choices or giving him lectures, they troop dutifully to his bedside each time he announces a crisis. The narrator comes to believe in the strength and importance of love, and, by the time, Mr. Sweet really does die, she has become a strong, caring adult capable of understanding that a literal resurrection need not take place. Mr. Sweet may not be revived in body, but he has passed his gift of love to her.

This story raises the intriguing question of the connection between fact and fiction. In the Georgia countryside where Walker grew up, her grandparents had a neighbor named Mr. Sweet Little. Like the character in the story, Mr. Sweet was a talented guitar player who drank to excess, loved to gamble, and who, in Walker's words, "went 'crazy' several times a year." She and her brothers and sister grew to love and respect Mr. Sweet, whose music and attitude toward life made them "feel empathy for anyone in trouble." Walker says nothing about any deathbed scenes during her childhood, but when she was a student at Sarah Lawrence College, she received word that Mr. Sweet had died. Feeling isolated and depressed on a campus where "there were only three or four other black people, and no poor people at all as far as the eye could see," she had contemplated suicide. When she thought about Mr. Sweet's life and death, she wrote "To Hell with Dying" to honor his memory. She describes the experience like this:

> I was too poor even to consider making the trip home, a distance
> of about a thousand miles, and on the day of Mr. Sweet's burial

I wrote "To Hell With Dying." If in my poverty I had no other
freedom—not even to say goodbye to him in death—I still had
the freedom to love him and the means to express it, if only to
myself. I wrote the story with tears pouring down my cheeks. I
was fighting for my own life. I was twenty-one.

> from "The Old Artist: Notes on Mr. Sweet" in
> *Living by the Word, Selected Writings 1973–
> 1978*; New York: Harcourt, 1988.

Walker later showed the story to one of her professors, who, in turn, sent it
to poet Langston Hughes. Two years later, Hughes published "To Hell with
Dying." It was Walker's first publication.

Yukio Mishima, Patriotism (page 822)

This story requires some political and historical background. The action
takes place in pre–World War II Japan. On February 26, 1936, following a long
period of political unrest, a group of young Imperial Forces officers led a coup
attempt. Rebel units seized and controlled Tokyo for several days during which
time their leaders assassinated several high-ranking government officials.
Finally, officers and troops loyal to the government crushed the mutiny and
ordered the execution of those responsible.

The story takes place on February 28, 1936, when Lt. Shinji Takeyama
learns that several of his closest comrades took part in the rebellion. He knows
he will soon be required by the Imperial troops who put down the mutiny to
assist in executing the rebels. Outraged at the thought of the mutiny yet
equally appalled by the idea of "Imperial troops attacking Imperial troops,"
he decides to commit ritual suicide (*seppuku*). Reiko his wife determines to
follow him in death, suggesting a parallel between the devotion of wife to
husband and the devotion of Lt. Takeyama to traditional ideals of Japanese
imperialism.

Traditional Western views consider love and familial relationships as
private, standing apart from public, political life. The title of Mishima's story
suggests a different view, one which sees all relationships, no matter how
personal, as intimately connected with the political views one holds.

Students respond strongly to this story. Most see Reiko's suicide as
particularly tragic because she seems to die mainly to follow the pattern set by
her husband. Even as she prepares for the ritual, she thinks of the small, day-
to-day tasks—shall she get dinner? shall she unlock the door? Unlike her
husband's thoughts, hers lie with this world.

A question to consider: Is her choice made primarily from love for her
husband or, as he wants to think, from the obedience to the state he believes he
has trained her to accept? My reading is that for Reiko, the marriage is her

whole existence; for Lt. Takeyama, the marriage to Reiko is merely a microcosm reflecting his symbolic marriage and loyalty to the imperial state.

Miguel de Unamuno, Juan Manso: A Dead Man's Tale (page 841)

Unamuno's tale takes an irreverent look at a question nearly everyone has pondered: What happens after death? The story suggests that the roles we assume on earth are played out eternally after death. While Juan Manso may gain readers' sympathy as he perpetually yields his place in line, a rereading of the scenes describing his time on earth suggests that he is not entirely worthy of pity. His motto during life came from a Chinese saying: "Never commit yourself, and stick to the person who can help you the most." He may be described as "harmless" and as a person who "during his whole life had never hurt a fly," yet that description is ironic. A person who is unwilling to make any kind of commitment may not act in a harmful way, but he does harm because of what he fails to do. In addition, someone who remains loyal "to the person who can help [him] most" certainly does not sound very moral.

Those who take advantage of Juan in the line to paradise are not admirable either; they, too, follow their earthly patterns. They are ambitious and take what they can get. The parable suggests that such people are eventually rewarded. When Juan returns to earth, he is much more aggressive and eventually succeeds in pushing his way into paradise where he substitutes his policy of passivity and hypocrisy (hoping that others will help) for a policy of greedy self-serving. Unamuno's darkly ironic tale suggests a disturbing picture. Death becomes not a momentous passage but an insignificant transition to continued petty struggles.

John Donne, Death, be not proud (page 844)

The speaker sees death as a powerful enemy, yet in line 4 this frightening force is addressed as "poor Death." The pity implied by this phrase foreshadows the paradox in the final lines. When the speaker asks death in line 12 "why swell'st thou then" (i.e., why are you filled with pride?), he is preparing to deliver the *coup de grâce*. Death will "die" because it cannot keep the faithful from passing into eternal life.

Emily Dickinson, Apparently with no surprise (page 845)

Dickinson's poem might be compared with Donne's "Death, be not proud." Here Frost, the agent of death, is personified. But unlike Donne's Death, Dickinson's Frost acts without intent, "in accidental power." After the death of the flower, Frost ("the blonde assassin") leaves, replaced by Sun. Note the play on the word "unmoved," meaning, I think, that the sun continues in its usual path and that it is unaffected by the drama that has taken place. Frost and Sun are part of the natural cycle that is approved by God. Flower's happiness is of no concern to Frost.

Questions to ponder: Does the phrase "an Approving God" suggest a pagan rather than Christian deity? Does the first line describe the flower or the frost? Does the poem suggest the way death may creep up on all of us?

e. e. cummings, [Buffalo Bill's] (page 845)

Like Donne in "Death, be not proud," cummings directly addresses Death, giving him the honorary title "Mister." The word choices, as well as the rhythmic patterns, establish the poem's ironic tone. The speaker describes Buffalo Bill as "defunct" which makes him sound like a species that has become extinct rather than a human being who has died. Bill's handsome appearance, his blue eyes, and his amazing feats—riding a "watersmooth-silver stallion" and shooting clay pigeons—are destroyed by death. The final question, addressed to "Mister Death," seems to ask the meaning of death and to ponder what we become after death. The capitalized "Jesus" in line 7 may suggest a possibility of salvation or may make an ironic comment on the traditional hope for salvation.

This poem provides a fine example of the visual impact poets achieve through line and word arrangement. As an experiment, ask students to write the poem in sentence form, using standard capitalization, punctuation, and the spacing between words. How does their response to the poem change with these alterations?

Ruth Whitman, Castoff Skin (page 846)

The speaker regards the elderly woman with affection yet without mawkish sentiment. Recalling the woman's pride and sense of humor when she described herself as having a "pretty good figure/for an old lady," the speaker explains her view of the woman's death.

When the woman's spirit leaves her body, it is like a snake leaving its old skin. The body, "a tiny stretched transparence," has been outgrown and the soul now moves on to its next stage of existence.

Jane Cooper, In the House of the Dying (page 847)

I believe that the speaker in the poem is the daughter of the woman who lies dying in an upstairs bedroom. The "tired aunts," her mother's sisters, have come to help during the final illness. The speaker sees a significant division between the way she thinks about death and the way the aunts—and by extension—the dying mother think about death. To the speaker, death seems a constant, daily presence (has she lost many people she loved? is she contemplating suicide? does she think about death as it comes to those she does not know but hears and reads about?).

To the aunts, death is a solemn and momentous event, like the visit of a priest to the terminally ill. The speaker questions her feelings because, although she is able to accept death, she is uncomfortable with love and cannot make the commitment to marriage. Her mother, on the other hand, has been "washed through by the two miracles." What are these miracles? Perhaps love for husband and love for children? Or the miracle of birth and the miracle of death? (And the ability to be touched and moved by each of these miracles.)

Robert Browning, The Bishop Orders His Tomb at Saint Praxed's Church (page 848)

The speaker in this poem, a character created by Browning, is a bishop who lived in Renaissance Italy. This poem works well when compared with "The Jilting of Granny Weatherall." Like Ellen Weatherall, the bishop lies dying and, like her, he is surrounded by his family. In addition, his final thoughts and words often relate to incidents in the past and to those he thinks have wronged him. He particularly focuses on Gandolf, his rival, wishing to have a tomb that will be far grander than that of his old enemy.

Although the speaker is a religious dignitary, pledged to celibacy, the men who surround his bedside—whom he at first calls nephews—are, in fact, his sons. His dying reverie includes memories of his mistress, and his description of his imagined tomb readily mixes sensual, pagan images with Christian symbols: "Pans and Nymphs" join "The Saviour at his sermon on the mount."

Unlike Granny Weatherall, the bishop fails to recall moments when he worked effectively or helped others. His last thoughts are entirely selfish, and the blessing he gives his sons (line 119) seems cursory, automatic, and certainly ironic after the long description of the elegant tomb.

Emily Dickinson, I heard a fly buzz—when I died (page 851)

In Jane Cooper's "In the House of the Dying" (text page 847), the aunts who have come to keep the death watch "buzz on like flies around a bulb." In Dickinson's poem, the dying person hears a fly. Why might flies be associated with death? Of course, flies are attracted to carrion, and yet in Cooper's poem the image suggests they are also attracted to light. And for Dickinson's speaker, the fly seems to be the final symbol of this world; the last thing the speaker hears as she passes from this world into the next. In line 15, the "Windows" are probably the speaker's eyes (the "windows of the soul"). As the speaker's life ebbs, the light fades and she cannot "see to see": she is unable physically to see her current world or to comprehend emotionally and spiritually the next world.

Emily Dickinson, The Bustle in a House (page 851)

"I heard a fly buzz" focuses on the experience of dying; "The Bustle in a House" offers images that capture the essence of grieving. In the nineteenth century, most people died at home rather than in hospitals or nursing facilities. So, as the family prepared for the funeral, there would have been literal cleaning to be done. Dickinson makes that cleaning image a metaphor, showing those who are left "Sweeping up the Heart/And putting Love away." The survivors don't stop loving the person who has died; instead they store the love in their memories, that they will be able to display that love fully only after they, too, have become part of "Eternity."

A. E. Houseman, To an Athlete Dying Young (page 852)

This poem uses classical allusions to foot races, laurels, and the dead hero who visits the underworld to suggest a theme common to all times: Those who die young do not have to endure aging and the gradual loss of their physical and mental powers. For those who do live, the victor's chair can become like a coffin that buries them in images of their past glory.

To begin discussion of this poem, ask students to write briefly for or against the following proposition: It is better to die during the height of one's triumph and success than to outlive fame and become forgotten.

Edwin Arlington Robinson, Richard Cory (page 853)

Why does Richard Cory commit suicide? It's far too easy to say simply that he committed suicide because "money can't buy happiness," but the poem does not indicate that being poor is necessarily better than being wealthy. The final stanza does, however, suggest that the speaker (and the people he represents) made the assumption that those who are handsome and wealthy would not have problems and difficulties as do the poor. They assumed that Cory was satisfied, since he seemed to have all that they longed for, and were ironically surprised to find they were wrong.

As an initial writing leading to discussion, consider asking students to respond to the following criticism of "Richard Cory":

> The poem builds up deliberately to a very cheap surprise
> ending; but all surprise endings are cheap in poetry . . . for
> poetry is written to be read not once but many times.
>
> Yvor Winters, *Edwin Arlington Robinson*,
> Norfolk: New Direction, 1946. 52.

Robert Frost, "Out, Out—" (page 853)

The boy in this poem, already expected to do "a man's work," seems a child who has been made to accept adult responsibility before his time. The speaker (perhaps a neighbor or family friend) telling the story comments that he wishes "they" (presumably the adults involved) might have said "Call it a day. . ./To please the boy by giving him the half hour/That a boy counts so much when saved from work." Yet the blame is not placed too heavily on the parents, probably farmers who have to work hard to grub a living out of the New England soil. The boy's death is a random event, with no clear cause or purpose.

Although the poem is highly accessible, you may want to read to students the passage from *Macbeth* from which the title is taken, asking them if (and how) their response changes when they recognize the allusion.

> She should have died hereafter;
> There would have been a time for such a word.
> To-morrow, and to-morrow, and to-morrow
> Creeps in this petty pace from day to day
> To the last syllable of recorded time;
> And all our yesterdays have lighted fools
> The way to dusty death. Out, out, brief candle!
> Life's but a walking shadow, a poor player,
> That struts and frets his hour upon the stage
> And then is heard no more. It is a tale
> Told by an idiot, full of sound and fury,
> Signifying nothing.
>
>   (Macbeth, on learning of Lady Macbeth's death)
>   Act V, Scene 5

Theodore Roethke, Elegy for Jane (page 854)

A list of images from this poem suggests the qualities the poet admired in his lost student:

pickerel smile

startled into talk

A wren, happy, tail into the wind

My sparrow

my skittery pigeon

Jane, who "balanced in the delight of her thought," was a young woman whose every move suggested life, energy, and quickness. The "pickerel smile" flashed across her face like a slim fish darting through a stream. Her words, thoughts, and actions took her quickly in many directions as though she were a bird startled from brief repose. Death has silenced her forever, and the poet takes no comfort from what is left, "the sides of wet stones" (her grave marker? or simply representative elements of nature?). These stones and the moss that surrounds them stand still and rooted, dark contrasts to the vital student he remembers.

William Stafford, Traveling through the dark (page 855)

The speaker travels through the dark literally and figuratively. He drives through the night, and, when he encounters the body of the pregnant doe with the still-living fetus, he must travel through the dark of his conscience and imagination to reach a decision.

The line "I thought hard for us all" suggests that the speaker weighs all the possibilities and probabilities. He knows he has to push the carcass into the canyon because cars coming across the body in the night might get into an accident. Yet he also has the sensitivity to acknowledge that to serve human lives, he must cut off an animal life.

I think the speaker has no other choice, but students frequently argue that he could have dragged the deer to his car and taken her to a veterinarian to see if the fawn could be delivered. Alternately, they suggest that he could have at least tried to deliver the baby himself. I have to acknowledge these as possibilities, but I think very few people would even have the decency to stop after seeing an animal's body in the road. Even fewer would hesitate while thinking about the fawn "alive, still, never to be born."

Several students have suggested a correlation between the speaker's decision and the decision to have an abortion. To me, this is a farfetched connection. Certainly the speaker does do some soul-searching, but the dilemma seems much different from that faced by a pregnant woman. (For example, the speaker could simply drive away, leaving the danger and the decision by someone else.)

Seamus Heaney, Mid-Term Break (page 855)

The title to this poem proves a real shocker. Expecting a poem related to a vacation from the rigors of college study, the reader instead finds a wrenching description of a young man called home for his four-year-old brother's funeral. The break, of course, is the loss and separation the speaker feels from his brother. In addition, the title suggests the traditional metaphor for grief—heartbreak.

Harvey Fierstein, On Tidy Endings (page 857)

This play is certain to raise heated discussion since it deals with several controversial issues related to gay relationships and to AIDS.

When Collin died from an AIDS-related illness, Marion, Jim, and Arthur suffered a wrenching loss. Marion loses an ex-husband whom she still loves; Jim, a father; and Collin, a lover. The play focuses on the complex dynamics among these three people, particularly Marion and Arthur.

The circumstances and the setting (the apartment Collin and Arthur shared, now neatly packed as Arthur prepares to move out) are grim. Yet the tone of the play, much of the time, is light and wryly humorous. Marion and Jim argue, each using the standard clichés of mother-son disagreements. If Jim asks,

"Why" too many times, Marion responds with "Because I said so." When Marion invites Jim to look around the apartment one last time, Jim tells her to "get a real life." And after Jim has left the apartment supposedly bound for his friend's apartment, he delays and hangs around in the elevator and the lobby.

When Marion's lawyer, June, arrives, they discuss the papers that delineate the division of Collin's property between Marion and Arthur in very much the same tone they use to discuss June's being double parked. June even makes jokes about using her commission from a life insurance policy to pay the bill if her illegally parked car is towed. However, the conversation between Marion and June also has serious moments, all of which indicate that Marion is a thoroughly decent person. She resists June's suggestion that they contest Collin's will and points out that Arthur deserves to have what Collin has left him as witness to their three-year relationship. And when June callously notes that "no one wants to buy an apartment when they know the person died of AIDS," Marion quickly silences her and June apologizes.

Still, Marion is not perfect. She rationalizes taking several items from the apartment by saying that then Arthur will have "one less thing to pack." In addition, she presents him with a list of friends and relatives and suggestions of items which belonged to Collin that Arthur might give them. The tension between Arthur and Marion becomes increasingly clear as Marion awkwardly tries to assure him that Jimmy doesn't blame him for Collin's death. Arthur confronts Marion with Jimmy's pain and with his own pain, demanding that she see complications he believes she has ignored. Marion, in turn, spills out her anger at having lost both a man she loved and, also, the dream she had for a happy family life.

From this intense scene, the play moves for a moment to sadly ironic humor as Arthur describes his weight gain following Collin's death: "I called the ambulance at 5 A.M., he was gone at nine, and by nine-thirty, I was on a first-name basis with Sara Lee." But, refusing the easy path of continuing with the tension-breaking humor, Arthur further expresses his anger and resentment, insisting that Marion acknowledge his place in Collin's life and the sorrow he feels at being forced to leave the apartment they shared. In the play's most powerful speech he orders Marion to let go of Collin and to admit that Collin belongs to him: "This death does not belong to you, it's mine! Bought and paid for outright. I suffered, I bled for it . . . I paid in full for my place in his life and I will *not* share it with you."

While Marion does defend her decision to sell the apartment, she also recognizes that Arthur has been mistreated: ignored by many of Collin's friends at the funeral and omitted from the obituary notice. Yet she explains her actions and words by describing in detail Collin's decision to leave and her discovery that he had AIDS. She also admits that she was jealous of Arthur and Collin's relationship, yet she assures Arthur that he made Collin happy, as she could not, and she praises Arthur's incredible loyalty during Collin's sickness.

Arthur thinks back over the past few months, concluding by asking that he be left "an intangible place in [Collin's] history." Marion's reply, "I understand," suggests that she now sees Arthur's situation more clearly and, in the bargain, has gained more knowledge of herself. As a gesture to confirm this new understanding, for herself and for Arthur, she insists that Jimmy come to the apartment to say good-bye. Just before he arrives, Marion acknowledges that she has AIDS antibodies in her blood. The announcement suggests that she and Arthur will, in fact, continue to share Collin no matter what either of them thinks. Looking at the legal papers, Arthur says, "You know, we'll never get these done today," and Marion replies, "So, tomorrow," suggesting that they will not say "Good-bye" and neatly "tidy things up" as June, the lawyer, insisted. The pain of this problem goes beyond any one relationship or any one death.

Jessica Mitford, The American Way of Death (page 877)

To deal with her highly emotional subject, Mitford chooses to take a breezy, ironic approach. She begins by creating the corpse, Mr. Jones, as a character who takes on an existence quite apart from the person who once occupied the body. She provides a list of the processes to which the corpse is subjected that is at once horrifying and humorous. By piling detail on detail she suggests the excesses of the American funeral industry and the absurdity of a society that tolerates such excesses.

According to Mitford, the practice of embalming, required neither by civil nor religious law, is not necessary because of "considerations of health, sanitation, or even of personal daintiness." She believes that the desire to make the dead person "presentable for . . . public display" motivates the family. And she strongly implies that the funeral director is motivated by greed. Rather than simply performing a necessary service, the director—according the Mitford—goes through a series of rather grotesque procedures that are costly to the survivors and serve only to render the deceased cosmetically acceptable to a death-denying public.

By quoting from the professional journals and textbooks used by funeral directors, Mitford suggests that the excesses of the funeral industry are organized and intentional. She strengthens her argument by showing that her examples are neither isolated instances nor far-fetched projections; instead they represent the norm.

Discussing this essay leads, as Mitford's title suggests, to considering the American way of death. Students vary greatly in their response to her challenges. Some believe that anything that provides comfort to the bereaved is well worth the money spent. Some believe that an elaborate funeral procedure represents the final gesture of love toward someone who has died. Others agree with Mitford and see the entire process as barbaric and as increasing, rather than alleviating, suffering.

Elizabeth Kübler-Ross, On the Fear of Death (page 883)

Like the poem Kübler-Ross chooses as an introduction, this essay suggests that death and dying are meaningful subjects worthy of concern. But, with the rising cost of medical care and the increasing tendency to hospitalize or in other ways institutionalize the seriously ill and dying among us, we have come to ignore—and fear unduly—the final stage of life.

Although the essay relates to all humans, Kübler-Ross writes with counselors (such as chaplains and social workers) in mind. She believes that our society increasingly turns its back on the elderly and on those who suffer life-threatening illnesses. Doctors often look on terminal patients as failures; because the physician is pledged to protect life, death becomes the enemy who must always be fought. Friends and relatives may fear the dying person because his or her struggle reminds them of their own mortality, which they want to ignore or deny.

In addition, Kübler-Ross notes the complex relationship between fear and guilt. Because every era and culture has regarded death as negative, death has come to be "associated with a bad act, a frightening happening, something that in itself calls for retribution and punishment." People close to someone who dies may feel that somehow (perhaps through a wish, subconscious or expressed) they have caused the person's death. Children are particularly prone to these feelings, and Kübler-Ross warns that pretending death has not happened, by using euphemisms such as "he's just asleep" or "she's gone on a long journey," may magnify their convictions that they are somehow guilty and that death is too terrible to even talk about.

Through the example of the farmer, Kübler-Ross suggests what she considers a more healthy approach to death—for the person who is dying and for those who care about that person. She argues that professionals should support the person who wants to die at home, claiming that following such "old-fashioned customs" shows that the counselor can accept "a fatal outcome." In addition, death in familiar surroundings "requires less adjustment" for the patient and helps the "family to accept the loss."

The sections describing children's reactions to death, and particularly the incident of the old farmer, might be compared with Alice Walker's "To Hell with Dying" (page 816). Kübler-Ross also mentions aspects of modern funeral customs (see especially paragraphs 15–22) that might be compared with Jessica Mitford's "The American Way of Death" (page 877).

CONNECTIONS: ART AND LITERATURE

As students consider these works, you might ask them first to look at the art that inspired (or was inspired by) the accompanying poem. Ask them to list the details they notice and to make inferences based on what they see. Then ask them to read the poems, noticing new details or different inferences that come to mind.

Knight, Death, and the Devil, Albrecht Dürer (1471–1528)
The Knight, Death, and the Devil, Randall Jarrell (1914–1965)

Jarrell provides a twentieth-century look at Dürer's medieval engraving. Dürer (1471–1528) shows Death taunting the knight who rides stolidly along, refusing to acknowledge either his own mortality or the ever-present evil that lurks in the form of the Devil.

Jarrell sees Dürer's Death as a "teetotum" (a child's toy) who seems far less menacing than his companion, the Devil. Students may see more threat in death and may also be less apt than Jarrell to interpret the knight's expression as "folds of smiling." Does the knight's persistence in the face of the inevitable represent the strength and conscious resolution suggested by Jarrell's poem? Or does it indicate the human resistance to acknowledge danger and the potential for threat and change? The knight may be intent on reaching the safe harbor of his castle; perhaps he does not even see the strange figures or perhaps he refuses to admit they are there.

Two Girls, Henri Matisse (1869–1954)
Matisse: Two Girls, Molly Peacock (1947–   )

Peacock's speaker suggests the connection between art and the viewer when she describes the trees as "the tops of old maples," but then quickly adds that in Matisse's painting "They are not maples . . . they are green clouds slashed with brown stripes." Then she asks this significant question: "but don't you like to look/at the places and faces in pictures to find out/where and which you are?"

The speaker at first identifies herself as "the frightened one in blue" and the figure in the yellow dress as the person to whom she addresses the poem. Yet later, as she notices the lack of wine and cigarettes, she says, "it is not us." Continuing her speculations, the speaker ponders her mother's role in the scene she imagines. Perhaps the single place set on the table is for the mother who has not yet had breakfast. She does not hesitate, then, to introduce figures, events, and objects that exist outside the painting to which she is responding.

Details such as the exact match between the colors in the window scene and the colors of the dress and the hair of the woman in blue become the basis for inferences: "Her hair . . ./is the color of the antlered branches/behind her, and her dress matches the sky. What a burden she has to distinguish herself!" Perhaps most memorable in Peacock's poem is the way the speaker moves through various interpretations and possibilities. She does not seek a single correct way of seeing Matisse's work but rather immerses herself in its infinite possibilities. In addition, she sees the painting in personal terms. She does not wonder who Matisse had in mind as he worked but instead considers what she can learn about herself as she responds to his "Two Girls, Red and Green Background."

The Starry Night, Vincent van Gogh (1853–1890)
The Starry Night, Anne Sexton (1928–1975)

Sexton chooses as an epigraph for her poem a line from one of van Gogh's letters. In it, he suggests that, for him, going out into the night to paint the stars is comparable to a religious experience. Sexton's poem reflects the sense of spiritual exaltation suggested by van Gogh's painting. She sees the night sky as overwhelming, awesome, and yet also offering deliverance. Her poem is filled with female images (a tree looks like a "drowned woman" and the moon seems about to give birth). Sexton sees the magnificent swirling star masses as a serpent or a "great dragon" which she may regard with fear but which she also sees as a glorious means to leave her earthly life.

Mourning Picture, Edwin Romanzo Elmer (1850–1923)
Mourning Picture, Adrienne Rich (1929–   )

The poet assumes the persona of the child in the foreground of the painting and describes her responses to the grief of the two people who sit in chairs on the lawn and whom she identifies as her parents. What other possibilities do students see for the relationship between these people? The speaker's observation that her parents "will move from the house,/give the toys and pets away" suggests that the man and woman may be mourning the death of another child. The speaker's terrible recognition of her own separation from her parents reflects Elmer's vision of her, standing apart and gazing into the distance.

The Lady of Shallott, William Holman Hunt (1886–1905)
The Lady of Shalott, Alfred, Lord Tennyson (1809–1892)

Painting in response to Tennyson's poem (full poem, text page 1123), Hunt envisions the lady turning from her mirror and struggling to free herself from the threads of her weaving. While the poem does not show her physically caught by the weaving, certainly Tennyson's images suggest that she is mystically held back by her lonely occupation. Hunt also suggests the forces that may pull at the lady. On one side is an image of the virgin, kneeling in devoted prayer while on the other a male figure, probably Sir Lancelot, stands waiting. The lady, then, hears the call of the contemplative, spiritual life but also longs for the world of humans and, perhaps, for romantic connection with the brave and handsome Lancelot.

The Kermess, Pieter Bruegel, the Elder (1520?–1569)
The Dance, William Carlos Williams (1883–1963)

Bruegel's painting captures a group of lively, lusty peasants dancing the Kermess at a country fair. Participants in this dance join hands and form an ever-increasing circle as they weave in and out, welcoming new participants. Students will be quick to notice the marvelous rhythm of the poem which captures the energy and joy conveyed in Bruegel's painting. The enjambed lines and, particularly, the repetition in the final line suggest the movement of the dancers as they "go round and/around."

This poem must be read aloud!

Walking Man, Alberto Giacometti (1901–1966)
Giacometti, Richard Wilbur (1921–   )

You may need to help students see the way this poem falls into two sections: lines 1–29, which describe the speaker's discomfort with statues of humans that are sculpted from rock; and lines 30–60, which contrast the speaker's response to Giacometti's bronze sculpture, *Walking Man*. The speaker sees the tall, thin figure as capturing perfectly the sense he has of being "unspeakably alone." Particularly powerful is the speaker's description of Giacometti's man as an anonymous figure who can hide nothing; his "fullness is escaped/Like a burst balloon's: no nakedness so bare/As flesh gone in inquiring of the bone."

I Saw the Figure 5 in Gold, Charles Demuth (1883–1935)
The Great Figure, William Carlos Williams (1883–1963)

Williams's poem inspired "I Saw the Figure 5 in Gold" which Demuth completed in 1928 as a symbolic portrait of the poet. Students enjoy finding the clues Demuth provided, including the initials "W.C.W," and the names "Carlos," and "Bill." Demuth uses lettering reminiscent of advertising billboards to create this painting which is one of his "poster portraits." The figure five dominates the painting as well as the poem; Demuth's repetition of the figure 5 echoes Williams's "gong clangs" and "siren howls" and, in addition, suggests the staccato rhythm of the poem. The squared-off red forms in the painting bring to mind the fire truck, and the white circles remind the viewer of the lights (perhaps street lights?) of the poem's second line.

TEACHING AN INTRODUCTION TO SHORT FICTION

To begin the study of short fiction, I ask students to read the introduction and bring to class a one- or two-paragraph response suggesting the ways they see early forms of fiction incorporated into modern films and television programs. For instance, one of my students pointed out that the *Star Wars* movies borrow heavily from allegory with a hero named Skywalker and a villain called Darth Vader (suggesting both death and invader). Other students argued that these films weren't truly allegorical because not all of the characters had names that matched their personal qualities.

Someone always mentions the now-cancelled series "Beauty and the Beast" and there's usually some discussion as to whether this program was fairy tale or fable. Students are also quick to see the fairy-tale qualities of films like *Ghost*, with Whoopi Goldberg playing a hip fairy godmother who ultimately works magic and banishes the forces of evil.

After ten minutes or so of such discussion, I move to consider the relationship between fiction and truth, asking students to jot down—and then discuss—any instances they can remember when they read a fictional work that seemed particularly true to them. This exercise leads to exploring the complexities encountered in developing a definition of truth and in deciding what can be learned and valued as truth from the reading of fiction.

If time permits—or as an alternate exercise to introduce the pleasures and puzzles of short fiction—I ask students to meet in groups and read aloud to each other from a story I select. Each person reads for a few minutes, stopping at any point he or she chooses. The next person continues the reading, again stopping where he or she chooses to allow the next person to begin. The reading continues until everyone in the group has read, and then the first person begins the reading chain again until the instructor signals time to stop. (Five to eight minutes works well.) After the reading, students write their questions and responses, predicting possible outcomes as well as pondering issues that the reading raises.

I then ask students to read that story for the next class (or, in a two-and-a-half hour class, I'll have them read silently in class; those who finish before others are asked to reread). When they are ready for further discussion, I ask them to jot down brief responses to these questions:

1. What differences, if any, did you notice in hearing the story read aloud, in reading aloud yourself, and in reading silently?

2.   As you reread the story to yourself and as you finished the parts you
     had not heard read aloud, did you change your initial impressions?
     Were your predictions accurate? Did you find answers to your questions?
     Explain.

Stories that work well for this exercise include:

		Text Page
The Wives of the Dead	Nathaniel Hawthorne	898
The Black Cat	Edgar Allan Poe	903
The Revolt of "Mother"	Mary E. Wilkens Freeman	923
The Garden Party	Katherine Mansfield	966
Hills Like White Elephants	Ernest Hemingway	986

To complete the introduction to short fiction, I call students' attention to
the list of "Considerations," noting that these suggestions offer possible ways of
reading, thinking, and writing about short stories.

READINGS

Nathaniel Hawthorne, The Wives of the Dead (page 898)

Considerations for Writing and Discussion

1.   How would the story be changed if the introductory sentence were
     omitted and the events were reported as happening in the present
     rather than in the past?

2.   What are the similarities and differences you see between Mary and
     Margaret's responses to the events reported in the story? Which seem
     more significant to you, similarities or differences? Explain.

3.   What do you make of the good news Mary and Margaret apparently
     receive? Are they both dreaming? One of them? Neither of them?

The opening sentence provides a frame setting the story in the past. It's
interesting to note that the storyteller sets the scene "a hundred years ago," a
number that evokes the atmosphere of the fairy tale (for example, Sleeping
Beauty slept for a hundred years before being awakened by the prince). The
frame story also makes me wonder why the teller is recounting these events.
Are they significant enough or intriguing enough to continue being passed down
from generation to generation?

I'm also fascinated by the sensitive, intimate look at death and grief provided by the narrator. Hawthorne first published this tale in 1832, yet the responses of the two sisters seem to follow the most recent research on the reactions of those who have lost a close relative. Mary weeps, yet she struggles to accept her loss and return to "her regular course of duties" in order to help her sister; Margaret acts in anger and despair.

The events of the night suggest that both sisters, in spite of their efforts to be brave, still have to suffer through the pain of denial. As the narrator notes, "It is difficult to be convinced of the death of one whom we have deemed another self." I believe that each sister dreams what she wishes most to be true: Her husband is alive. The knocking they hear suggests an outside stimulus that each incorporates into her own dream as a means to create a messenger who will bring good news. While there are many possible readings to this sequence, I believe that Mary and Margaret hear the sound at the same time and that they dream simultaneously rather than in tandem. At first Margaret's dream seems believable, but Mary's messenger—a sailor who appears dripping wet, as though he had been at the bottom of the sea—is almost certainly an apparition created by her longing and distress. After reading Mary's dream, I returned to Margaret's account of her messenger and found this passage which suggests that she, also, is dreaming:

> So saying, the honest man departed; and his lantern gleamed along the street, bringing to view indistinct shapes of things, and the fragments of a world, like order glimmering through the chaos, or memory roaming over the past.

In the final sentence, Hawthorne uses deliberately ambiguous pronouns to suggest that Mary and Margaret are entwined in each other's dreams; both will awake to tears and sorrow.

Edgar Allan Poe, The Black Cat (page 903)

Considerations for Writing and Discussion

1. Who is to blame for the events in the story? The narrator blames the cat, and early in the story the wife suggests that "all black cats [are] witches in disguise." Is the cat a supernatural being that causes the narrator to go mad? What other motivations can you suggest for his actions?

2. How reliable do you find the narrator's descriptions and explanations? For example, he contends that he is bothered "but little" by his wife's murder and also says that he feels no concern when the police arrive at his house. Do you find these claims believable? Explain.

3. What is your response to the narrator's question, "Who has not a hundred times found himself committing a vile or stupid action, for no

other reason than because he know he should *not?*" Do you agree?
Explain

This narrator is a study in amoral madness and corruption. He describes the black cat, whom he has named Pluto for the Greek god of the underworld, as a faithful pet who grows old "and consequently somewhat peevish." It's intriguing to note that the narrator himself is growing older and somewhat worse than peevish. As he becomes increasingly dependent on alcohol, he becomes less and less able to distinguish real from imagined ills. He projects onto the cat his own feelings of anger and helplessness, punishing and torturing the cat for no reason the sane reader can imagine.

It would be oversimplifying, I think, to read this tale as a horror story showing a rational man who simply drinks a little too much and becomes possessed by a supernatural spirit. Instead, the evidence far more strongly suggests that the narrator's disintegrating mind grasps at an external object on which to expend his wrath. When he kills his wife as she tries to defend the cat he believes to be the reincarnated Pluto, he shows that he has become incapable of either distinguishing right from wrong or of caring what is right and wrong. The one thing that suggests to me any small remaining portion of human caring or concern is the narrator's behavior when the police arrive. Why should he invite them to search the house? Perhaps he is trying to convince himself that no abomination lies rotting behind the cellar walls. Or perhaps he recognizes, but cannot admit, his need to be caught and stopped. Whatever his motives, he continues to the end his obsession with the black cat and never consciously wavers from the conviction that the cat has brought him to his doom.

Anton Chekhov, The Lady with the Pet Dog (page 910)

Considerations for Writing and Discussion

1. Trace the relationship of Anna Sergeyevna and Gurov, describing any changes you see in either of them.

2. Compare Chekhov's treatment of the extramarital affair with Kate Chopin's treatment of the same subject in "The Storm" (page 342). Are you more sympathetic with Chekhov's characters or with Chopin's? Explain.

3. Referring to details from the story, write a short scene predicting the future relationship between Anna Sergeyevna and Gurov. Include dialogue in the scene.

At the beginning of the story, Gurov looks anxiously for another love affair to fill the blank he feels in his life. He sees Anna Sergeyevna but dismisses her as "pathetic." Part II shows Anna and Gurov coming together and beginning their affair. Gurov looks on Anna as a pleasing plaything. He is delighted with her at times, but mostly he continues to display the insensitivity suggested by his earlier observation that women comprise the "lower race." For example, while Anna sits weeping and distressed after the two have first made love, Gurov remains silent for more than half an hour as he cuts slices of watermelon and eats them. Finally, he makes a half-hearted attempt to reassure Anna, but he soon decides it's time to end the affair. He seems unmoved by Anna's return to her husband. In part III, Gurov shows the beginning of a striking change. A particularly telling moment occurs when he dines out with his friends and tries to tell them about his relationships with Anna. Just as he once sat eating a watermelon while she struggled to express the depths of her emotions, Gurov's companions now ignore his pain and, instead, comment on fish they have eaten. Feeling that no one but Anna can help him, Gurov decides he must go to the city where she lives. He even takes the extraordinary step of meeting her in public. In the final section, Gurov finally faces the change in himself when he catches a glimpse of his face in the mirror just as he is about to murmur something conventionally comforting to the distressed Anna. He sees that he is growing old and understands that what he longs for is real love and connection; not a series of surface relationships from which he can easily disengage.

Mary E. Wilkens Freeman, The Revolt of "Mother" (page 923)

Considerations for Writing and Discussion

1. Characterize the relationship between Sarah Penn and her husband, Adoniram, at the beginning of the story. Pay attention not only to their conversations but also to their actions. How do these two people differ in the way they see their family, each other, and themselves?

2. Describe the changes that take place in the two main characters and also in their children. Do you think the changes suggested by the resolution of the conflict over the house and barn will be permanent? Explain.

3. Choose any incident in the story and describe it from Adoniram's point of view. Try using the nineteenth-century New England dialect as you record his thoughts.

Some readers object to Freeman's sympathetic portrait of Mrs. Penn, seeing her as a wife who acts in a devious way to assert power over her husband. Sarah Penn's defenders, however, point out the opening scene as evidence that she had exhausted all other means to achieve a reasonable standard of living for herself and her children. As the story begins, Sarah asks her husband, "What are them men diggin' over there in the field for?" Adoniram avoids her question and finally, when she persists, orders her back into the house. As he roughly saddles and bridles his horse, while keeping his back to Sarah,

Adoniram shows that he understands very well what the battle is all about. He wants a new barn; Sarah wants better living conditions. Unwilling to face these differences or to discuss them with his wife, he rides off.

It's important to note that Sarah is not initially depicted as a particularly assertive woman. She has always meekly accepted her husband's will and is generally content to make do with what she has, taking care of her family as best she can. Now, however, she is faced with a dilemma. She wants a place where her daughter, Nanny, can meet her fiancé and, eventually, get married. After trying her best to convince Adoniram to build a new house, she gathers her courage and, for apparently the first time in her life, forces the issue.

While Sarah's move to the barn has its comic aspects, most modern readers sympathize with her and rejoice in her husband's ability to accept what she has done with humility and sorrow rather than anger and destruction. In the end, no one wins and no one loses. Adoniram recognizes the strength and justice of Sarah's feelings; and she sees that, far from being the tyrant she had envisioned all these years, he "was like a fortress whose walls had no active resistance, and went down the instant the right besieging tools were used."

Guy de Maupassant, Moonlight (page 936)

Considerations for Writing and Discussion

1. Describe the abbé's attitude toward women and explain his reasons for this attitude. Consider the reasons he admits to himself as well as those he may keep hidden.

2. How and why does the abbé change? Consider how the language used by the narrator suggests the abbé's move to enlightenment.

3. Adopting the persona of the abbé, write a journal entry describing your responses to your niece's request to perform the wedding ceremony for her and the young man she met in the moonlight. As you write the journal entry consider the abbé's feelings before and after seeing his niece with her lover.

The abbé has always hated women, seeing them as tempters and simpering fools who defy the "absolute and admirable logic" he claims to see in the rest of God's creations. It's useful to note that the abbé's rage against women is intriguingly complex. While he rants against what he sees as their "weakness," he also finds them "curiously disturbing." And what seems to disturb him most is not woman's "devilish body, " but rather "her loving soul." In addition, like so many bigots, he fails to see the contradiction in loving and caring for his niece while condemning the group of humans to which she belongs. He finds her an exception, although her concept of God as existing in the beauty of nature around her—rather than in the prescriptive rules and texts he follows—leads him to declare her view of religion "tainted with sex."

During the first part of the story, the imagery reflects the abbé's rigid theological views and his anger when he learns of his niece's secret meetings. He storms through his house, smiling at the walking stick which he uses as a cudgel to demolish a chair blocking his way. Once he leaves the house, however, the violent images suddenly stop. As he walks out into "a splendor of moonlight such as he had rarely seen," his thoughts are described in lyrical, intuitive language that contrasts sharply with the earlier images that alternated between anger and reason. The change in diction foreshadows the stunning change in the abbé himself. He is forced to recognize the beauty of feeling as well as thought and to see love between man and woman as holy. Although he had started out as the avenging scourge of God, he gazes with amazement on the beauty of the night that shelters and blesses his niece and her lover. Then, turning away, he recognizes himself as the one who is out of place and leaves "distraught, almost ashamed, as if he had entered a temple where he had no right to be."

Stephen Crane, The Bride Comes to Yellow Sky (page 940)

Considerations for Writing and Discussion:

1. List the phrases used to describe the clothes and gestures of the two main characters. Considering these details, list several words or phrases to define each man's character. Do you see the two as similar in any way? What significance do you see in their similarities and differences?

2. How appropriate is the story's title? Of what importance is the bride to the story's conflict and to the resolution of that conflict?

3. What elements of the story seem like stereotypical characters and actions from old Western movies, comic books, and television programs? What aspects are not stereotypical? Explain your response to the stereotypes and to the departures from the patterns these stereotypes may have led you to expect.

Most students easily identify the saloon and the people who drink there as Western stereotypes—dry-witted Texans, silent Mexicans, the fast-talking Eastern tenderfoot, and the raging, "likkered-up" cowhand. Scratchy Wilson's menacing challenge to the town is also expected, as is the response of the people who believe that a shootout between their stalwart town marshall and the troublesome villain is inevitable.

The final section of the story, however, reverses the stereotypes and suggests something significant not only about Yellow Sky but also about the Western frontier that the town represents. Rather than engaging in a gunfight, the newly married Jack Potter appears on the scene unarmed, like a diplomat ready to negotiate a treaty. Disappointed and demoralized, Scratchy backs down, admitting that "it's all off now."

The conclusion may seem at first like an anticlimax, yet, in fact, it suggests a profound change in the American character. The motion of the rushing train in the initial scene gives passengers the sense that the "plains of Texas were pouring Eastward." This powerful bit of description suggests the intermingling of Eastern and Western culture inevitably brought about by the improved means of transportation and communication between the two regions. Both Scratchy and Jack Potter seem somewhat comic in their Eastern clothes. Jack in his suit is uncomfortable as he rides in the pullman car; Scratchy may long for the good old days of six-guns and brawls, but he wears a shirt made by Jewish immigrants on the East Side of New York and boots that are similar to those worn by New England children to protect their feet when sledding.

It is not the bride alone who causes changes in the town. Note that the saloon already has a name, The Weary Gentleman, that sounds more like an English pub than Western barroom. Yet the bride's arrival does suggest the domestication of the West. Both cowboys and ruffians will be forced to give up their games of "good guys and bad guys," forced into a more civilized and, some might say, more mature and balanced way of approaching their world.

What has been gained or lost? Where do Crane's sympathies lie? And what about the sympathies of modern readers? Do we laugh at Jack and Scratchy or with them? Do we regret the passing of a rougher, simpler time, or do we see that time as a model of boasting, posing, and violence disguised as bravery (or even as fun)?

Sherwood Anderson, Death in the Woods (page 949)

Considerations for Writing and Discussion

1. The narrator says that he has been "impelled to try to tell the simple story over again." How does he put the story of the old woman together? How does he relate the old woman's story to his own life? After telling the story he says that he will not "try to emphasize the point." What is the point? Why has this story been so significant to him?

2. What relationships exist between the old woman and the dogs? How are the dogs significant to the story of her life and to the narrator's story of his own life?

3. How would you characterize the old woman? Do you admire her? Feel sorry for her? Do you see any particular significance in her life and death?

In the powerful and mystic scene in the woods, Mrs. Grimes for the first time in the story is shown as being at one with a living creature. My guess would be that most people reading the story for the first time expect the dogs to eat Mrs. Grimes's body. The fact that they do not takes on enormous significance. Their actions can be explained away by their hauling away the food-filled sack, yet why would they stop at that point? The narrator's earlier description of the dogs suggests a possibility:

> There were four Grimes dogs that had followed Mrs. Grimes
> into town, all tall gaunt fellows. Such men as Jake Grimes and
> his son always keep just such dogs. They kick and abuse them,
> but they stay. The Grimes dogs, in order to stay alive had to do
> a lot of foraging for themselves . . . .

As the dogs circle Mrs. Grimes, and as the narrator describes them, it is clear that their story is her story. Men like Jake Grimes and his son always have women like Mrs. Grimes to serve them—women who often have, in their earlier lives, been brutalized in one way or another. As adults, these women accept as inevitable whatever abuse is handed out. Like the dogs, Mrs. Grimes stays, foraging for herself and for other creatures whom she keeps alive more from a sense of routine and obligation than from any feelings of love and connection. The dogs do not eat Mrs. Grimes because she is one of them.

Later, when the narrator describes the discovery of the body, the men and boys from the town circle around just as did the dogs. They see Mrs. Grimes as a beautiful young woman, not a worn-out, abused wife. Perhaps they see what might have been or perhaps they see her beauty because at that one moment, like the dogs, they too feel a connection to Mrs. Grimes and to her fate. Certainly the narrator makes his own sense of this connection explicit when he describes living through many of the same situations Mrs. Grimes endured. The cycle of his life is entwined with hers, yet the outcomes have been different. Because he was young, he lived through the night of the circling dogs. Because he was male, he was able to leave the employ of a harsh German farmer without being trapped into a life of servitude with another brutal man. Yet he cannot forget the old woman and he cannot deny the uncanny circumstances that make him, in some ways, her double.

Franz Kafka, A Hunger Artist (page 959)

Considerations for Writing and Discussion

1. What details make this story seem realistic? What details make it seem more like a parable or allegory? If you read it as symbolic, what possibilities exist for the identities of the artist, his manager, the crowds, and the panther?

2. What is your response to the artist? Do you find his actions, goals, or explanations of his fasting in any way admirable? Or do you see them

as selfish? Do you find his motives understandable or puzzling and strange?

The title, as well as scores of published interpretations, suggests that this story depicts the role of the artist in the modern world. His art is not traditional. He does not create something tangible that can be framed or mounted and exhibited in a museum. His art, perhaps, comes close to post-modern performance art; yet he is not really performing, he chooses not to act. The public, at first, is fascinated by the oddity of the fasting but soon tires of its constancy. Yearning for variety and ever-changing amusement, they turn to the sleek, lively panther who represents everything the artist is not. Several students have pointed out to me, however, that the artist and the panther share one thing: they are both locked up and at the mercy of those who make money from their special qualities. They lack even the freedom of the crowds, who, although trapped by their banal view of art, can move around in the world at will.

The artist is apparently trapped by his need to practice his art. He says that he would have eaten if he could have found anything that would have satisfied him. He makes the point, then, that true art is practiced for its own sake, not to satisfy managers or viewers.

Many students see the story as more than a parable about art and artists in the modern world. I agree with their suggestions that the artist seems like the free, creative, dissident thinker from all time and all cultures. These individuals seem driven by an inner vision that often fascinates others for a time but soon is dismissed as fad or fashion; the real free thinker lives on the periphery of society, ignored and often imprisoned by poverty and lack of acceptance as the crowd, unable or unwilling to pursue the thinker's vision in depth, moves on to the next attraction.

Katherine Mansfield, The Garden Party (page 966)

Considerations for Writing and Discussion

1. Early in the story Laura denies that she feels any "absurd class distinctions." To what extent do you believe her claim to be true? Does she care less about class distinctions than do the other members of her family?

2. Should Laura's family have cancelled the garden party? What would have been gained or lost through the cancellation?

3. What future do you predict for Laura? Will her visit to the dead workman's cottage make any lasting change in her?

Most students find Laura somewhat more admirable than her parents or siblings because she at least questions the implications of class distinctions rather than blindly accepting them or, like her sister Jose, exulting over her power to order servants around. Nevertheless, Laura's view of the world is incredibly naive and as false in its own way as are the more obvious prejudices expressed by her family. The opening scene provides several fine examples. Laura romanticizes the workmen simply because one smiles at her and another smells a sprig of lavender. She imagines that all workmen (not just a particular workman) are "extraordinarily nice." Then in a spirit of self-congratulation, she allows herself to eat while she oversees the assembling of the marquee. Laura tells herself that she is "just like a work-girl," believing that eating in front of the "extraordinarily nice" workmen" is a bold statement of democratic principles.

When the family receives news of the carter's death, Laura has what seems a genuine and honest response, although her desire to cancel the garden party may stem from the same romantic impulses that made her wish she could be friends with workmen rather than with the shallow boys from her own class. Yet her perception seems to move beyond that. She puts herself in the place of the carter's family and imagines what it would be like for those mourning a father and husband while a lavish party, complete with band music, went on in the elegant home overlooking their cottage.

Nevertheless, Laura is easily distracted from her concern when she glimpses herself decked out in the new hat her mother has given her. She enjoys the party fully and only at the end does her attention once more return to the misery nearby. Her visit to the cottage apparently produces moments of insight, yet once again she falls into her romantic dream as she gazes at the dead carter and imagines him "sleeping so soundly" and "happy" and "content." Shortly after leaving the carter's house, she describes the visit to her protective older brother as "simply marvelous." As she searches for words to describe the revelation she believes she has experienced, Laura once again makes herself and her world view central. "Isn't life . . . isn't life. . . " she stammers to Laurie. She is unable to find any clear meaning in what has happened, and Laurie, who has the final word in the story, trivializes the experience with his patronizing, "*Isn't* it, darling?"

William Faulkner, A Rose for Emily (page 978)

Considerations for Writing and Discussion

1. Who is the narrator? What is his attitude toward Miss Emily? What values are reflected by his observations about Miss Emily and about the town and its citizens?

2. Reread the story, making note of details that mean more to you or something different from your first reading. In addition, make a list of the events of the story in chronological order. How would the story be different if it were told according to the chronology you have outlined?

3. What is your response to the title? How does it relate to the story's action and themes?

Although some of my students say they were not surprised by the ending of the story, I have to admit that the first time I read it, I was astonished by the final scene. The iron-grey hair on the pillow burned itself into my mind as I raced to reread what I had believed to be a rather simple character sketch of a Southern lady during her declining years.

Faulkner's chronology lulls many first-time readers into complacency and then jars them awake to confront the concluding images of Emily's bloated body, Homer's rotted skeleton, and—most of all—the indentation on the pillow next to Homer. In *William Faulkner: Toward Yoknapatawpha and Beyond* (pp. 382–384) Cleanth Brooks suggests the following chronology. Although dates are not actually given in the story, Brooks bases his reading on internal clues as well as on several of Faulkner's other works set in Yoknapatawpha County.

1852: Emily Grierson born

1884: Emily's father dies

1884–1885: Homer Baron arrives

1885–1886: Townspeople note smell

1901 or 1904/1905: Emily stops china painting lessons

1906 or 1907: Colonel Sartoris dies

1916: Aldermen talk to Emily about taxes

1926: Emily dies

Students are quick to notice, on a second reading, that reconstructing the chronology makes Miss Emily's story clear in a way the original chronology does not. They also see that Faulkner's decision to play fast and loose with the time frame leads readers to be as shocked as the townspeople themselves and to rethink the events of the story, trying to make sense of what has happened. In addition, one student pointed out that the narrator provides certain details while withholding others so that the unsuspecting reader leaps to fallacious conclusions. For example, the narrator describes the delegation of men who surreptitiously slink to Emily's house at night and spread lime near the foundation, hoping to speed up the decay of whatever is causing the smell. After a week or two the smell goes away, and the townspeople—like most readers—fall into *post hoc* thinking and assume that the lime has done its work.

After recovering from the shock of acknowledging Miss Emily's necrophilia, students usually wonder about Faulkner's theme. Certainly the story has to do with the consequences of denying change. From the beginning, Emily refuses to admit the passage of time. She hides her father's body for days, she lives in a house surrounded by a decaying neighborhood, she refuses to allow the post office to give her a mail box. The townspeople both resent and admire Emily's position as a member of one of the old, antebellum grand families. She represents to them a monument to the fallen South which they regard with a mixture of shame and nostalgia. In addition, they pity Emily as a woman who was first repressed by her father and then (they think) deserted by her lover. Both the ambivalent attitude of the townspeople and the story's evocative title reflect Faulkner's themes. Certainly, to deny the passage of time and the need for change is dangerous. On the other hand, the past is not all bad; its strengths should be recognized. Suggesting the first theme, Homer may be Emily's rose: preserved, yet dead and decayed. Suggesting the second theme, the rose may be the townspeople's regard (or the story itself) offered as gift to the person who most clearly represented the town's own conflicted feelings about the passing of the old South.

Ernest Hemingway, Hills Like White Elephants (page 986)

Considerations for Writing and Discussion

1. What is the issue the man and woman are discussing? How do they differ in the way they see this issue? How do you think the conflict will be resolved?

2. How does the title relate to the story's action and characters?

3. Write two dialogues. In one, show the man describing this incident to a male friend. In the other, show the woman describing this incident to a female friend.

Each time I teach this story, I am surprised by how many students do not at first understand exactly what Jig and the man who accompanies her are discussing. There may be other possibilities, but for me the "perfectly simple" procedure that the man claims is "not really an operation at all" is clearly an abortion. For those who are still unconvinced, pointing out the man's explanation that "[i]t's just to let the air in" usually dispels doubts. Some students may not know that abortion was illegal in the United States and in many other countries at the time this story was written. The illegality may be one reason the man and woman never use the word "abortion," but their reluctance to speak directly also reflects their eroding relationship and their inability to see the world in the same way.

The title of the story also suggests this breakdown in communication. Jig admires the hills and makes a clever comparison, hoping that the man will praise her. He resists her comments because he is desperately trying to convince her not only to have the abortion but also to believe that after she has it everything will "be fine" and they will be "[j]ust like we were before." Throughout the story, he becomes increasingly insistent that the operation will change nothing and that if Jig would only be reasonable they could "have the whole world." Jig's increasingly bitter comments indicate that she sees his selfishness and resents his unwillingness to acknowledge that for her the decision is much more complex than it is for him.

Reflecting on the man's denial of the inevitable changes they face and of Jig's that those changes will, in fact, occur, one student asked a perceptive question: Why does the narrator call Jig a "girl" and her companion a "man" rather than calling him a "boy" and Jig a "woman"?

Eudora Welty, A Worn Path (page 990)

Considerations for Writing and Discussion

1. Describe Phoenix's responses to the white people she encounters on her journey. What do these brief meetings suggest about her? About the people she meets?

2. Describe Phoenix from the point of view of the hunter or the nurse at the clinic.

3. Research Phoenix's name and discuss the relationship between the legend of the Phoenix and the journey described in the story.

In her discussion of "A Worn Path" in her book *The Eye of the Storm*, Welty says:

> A story writer is more than happy to be read by students; the fact that these serious readers think and feel something in response to his work he finds life-giving. At the same time, he may not always be able to reply to their specific questions in kind.

Welty goes on to explain that the question she most often receives from students and their instructors who write to her after lively classroom discussion is this: Is Phoenix Jackson's grandson really *dead*? While assuring readers that they do not have to have the same responses to the story as does the writer, she explains that in writing the story she identified as fully as possible with Phoenix and in this capacity she, like Phoenix, believes the grandson to be alive.

The important focus in the story is the journey itself. Whether or not the grandchild is alive may be intriguing, but it is not essential. What makes a difference is Phoenix's belief in her own power to keep going year after year on this essential errand. Like the bird whose name she bears, she cannot be destroyed either by her own infirmities, by grinding poverty, or by the condescending observations of others. When, at the end of her visit to the doctor's office, we learn that "Phoenix rose carefully" we are reminded of her endurance, of her commitment to life, and of how the Phoenix rises from the ashes.

James Baldwin, Sonny's Blues (page 997)

Considerations for Writing and Discussion

1. How does the story's chronology affect your response? Consider, for example, how the story would change for you if the events were recounted as they occurred rather than retrospectively.

2. Describe the relationship between Sonny and his brother. Explain the changes they go through in the course of the story and speculate on the reason for those changes.

3. How do the song lyrics that sound as grace notes throughout the story relate to the conflict, action, and characters?

The story begins with the narrator's distress over Sonny's arrest for selling and using drugs. Because the narrator's description is pain filled, yet also concerned, most reader's feel strong sympathy for him. Yet the story is titled "Sonny's Blues" and, in fact, concerns Sonny as much as it does his brother, the narrator. Sonny's story comes to us in fragments with recurring motifs, somewhat like jazz improvisation.

From their early years, Sonny and his brother have heard their parents disagree. Sonny follows his father's view, leading a life that suggests the father's pronouncement that there "[a]in't no place safe for kids, nor nobody." The narrator has adopted their mother's belief that they can escape the prisons of poverty and racial injustice. He has become a teacher and a committed husband and father.

No one in the family can understand Sonny's need to become a musician or the desperation he feels in trying to face down the dangers of the old neighborhood. The brothers grow apart, and yet when the narrator's young daughter dies from a painful illness, Sonny responds with sensitivity and kindness. Recognizing Sonny's willingness to put the past behind him, the narrator—perhaps because of the pain he has experienced in his own life—becomes less judgmental and more forgiving.

In the final scene, the narrator listens to the notes of "Am I Blue" while Creole urges Sonny to create his own song. The narrator knows the attraction heroin still holds for Sonny, yet he is able to see also the powerful attraction music holds. Sonny has managed to survive long enough to play his own song, and the narrator can now see the beauty as well as the danger in his brother's world.

Flannery O'Connor, A Temple of the Holy Ghost (page 1022)

Considerations for Writing and Discussion

1. Describe a moral or spiritual question you can remember from your own childhood. Explain how you tried to find answers, then discuss your response to answers either given by others or suggested by your own observations.

2. Describe the narrator's personality. What is your response to her? Are you entirely sympathetic to her and to the judgments she makes, or do you find some aspects of her traits and characteristics less than admirable? Explain.

3. How does the title relate to the story's theme and characters? How does the title suggest the conflict the narrator faces?

Although this story deals with serious, complex questions, the narrator's sharp perceptions and sharper tongue make it one of the funniest short stories I know. Asking students to identify passages that made them laugh (or at least smile) and to read those passages aloud encourages engagement with the text and usually leads to lively discussion. After appreciating the narrator's wicked wit, students often express widely differing views about her. She is clever and filled with energy; she is also extremely judgmental and manipulative. She is not above telling lies and making rude comments to adults who, although they may be tedious, seem harmless and pose no threat to her.

At age twelve, the narrator is becoming increasingly aware of herself—both her spiritual and physical self. Although her fourteen-year-old cousins make fun of the nuns' reminders that they should consider their bodies "temple(s) of the holy ghost," the narrator finds pleasure and comfort in this description. However, when the cousins return from the freak show and describe the hermaphrodite, she is haunted by his plaintive defense: "This is the way He wanted me to be and I ain't disputing his way." The narrator wonders how this strange and misshapen body can—like her own and her mother's and her cousins' and the nuns' at the convent—manifest the perfection of its creator.

No easy answers come to her as she sits at the convent mass. Nor do any of the nuns say anything that might help her with her unspoken struggle. Still, as she sits beside her mother on the drive home, the landscape itself comes to life with fire and energy, suggesting an all-powerful, all-knowing creator. The girl does not arrive at any firm conclusions; instead, she has progressed from the comforting harbor of childhood where spiritual questions receive simplistic answers to the open seas of adult life where spiritual questions become more troubling. Writing in a Christian context, O'Connor suggests, with the final view of the sun sitting above the horizon like the host "drenched in blood," that even for the most thoughtful among us, the leap of faith is possible.

Gabriel García Márquez, The Handsomest Drowned Man in the World (page 1032)

Considerations for Writing and Discussion

1. García Márquez subtitles this story "A Tale for Children." What elements remind you of the traditional folk or fairy tale? In what ways is the story also a tale for adults?

2. List several descriptive phrases that you find particularly striking and explain what they add to the story's setting, characterization, or action.

3. Try your hand at writing your own "Tale for Children," using "The Handsomest Drowned Man in the World" as a model.

You might begin class with a discussion of descriptive phrases students have listed. Examples that have intrigued my students include:

> [H]e would have had so much authority that he could have drawn fish out of the sea simply by calling their names . . . .

> . . . his soft, pink, sea lion hands

> [H]e would sink easily into the deepest waves, where fish are blind and divers die of nostalgia.

The story abounds with elements of fairy tales. A mysterious stranger arrives in the village. His size and personal appearance make him different from and more than the villagers. For instance, we learn that "[t]he tallest men's holiday pants would not fit him, nor the fattest ones' Sunday shirts, nor the shoes of the one with the biggest feet." Although the stranger is dead, he seems larger than life, and the story's conclusion, like so many fairy tales, suggests that some essence of this astonishing figure still remains to remind the villagers of Esteban.

The women who discover him compare him to their husbands and find their own men lacking. Yet they also see that Esteban's unique and marvelous qualities must have caused him trouble during his lifetime. This complexity suggests that Esteban might be looked on as a savior figure. Although I think it would be a mistake to insist too strongly on a strictly Christian interpretation, several students have pointed out that Esteban is both human and superhuman and that, through his death, he enables the villagers to see their shared humanity.

Chinua Achebe, Marriage Is a Private Affair (page 1037)

Considerations for Writing and Discussion

1. Identify ironic aspects of the story and consider how irony underlies the story's themes.

2. How does each of the following—Nnaemeka and Nene; Nnaemeka's father; the Ibo tribe—see marriage as a "private affair"?

3. Do you believe that marriage is a "private affair"? What is your definition of "private"? Should family, community, government, or religious institutions have some say (or any say) in deciding whether two people can marry?

Irony abounds in this story. The father, who will seem hopelessly old fashioned to many students, is a practicing Christian who is believed to be "obstinately ahead of his more superstitious neighbors." In addition, he has rejected traditional African beliefs and customs, turning instead to patterns he considers more progressive and enlightened. Unfortunately, his self-described enlightenment does not extend to acceptance of his son's desire to marry outside the tribe. The comic contrast between his view of Ugoye Nweke, the bride he has chosen to be his son's wife, and Nnaemeka's memories of her as "a girl who used to beat up all the boys" ironically emphasizes the generation gap.

The conflict becomes more serious, however, when the father refuses to accept as grandsons the two boys who are born to Nnaemeka and Nene, the bride of his choice. In the final, powerful scene, the father turns to his adopted religion, believing he will find solace and affirmation in humming "a favourite hymn." As he struggles to maintain his distance from his son and grandsons, however, he hears the steady beat of the jungle rain which drowns out the Christian music. Perhaps he feels a primal connection with the world around him, and from this revelation comes to see the undeniable relationship that ties him forever to his kin. He rejects the customs of the Ibo tribe as well as the rules he believes Christianity imposes; instead of looking to external authority, he finds the answer to his dilemma within himself.

Joyce Carol Oates, The Lady with the Pet Dog (page 1042)

Considerations for Writing and Discussion

1. Oates begins the story by describing Anna's reaction to her lover's unexpected appearance at the concert. Later, this incident is retold. How does the retelling differ from the original account? What effect is created by the retelling of other significant details in the story?

2. At the end of the story, Anna's lover asks her why she is so happy and says, "Is it because . . . ?" Anna replies, "Yes." What might those

unspoken words have been? How has Anna's view of herself and of her relationship changed?

3. Read Chekhov's "The Lady with the Pet Dog." What relationships do you see between the two stories? Does Oates' story reinforce or challenge Chekhov's themes? Explain.

The telling and retelling of incidents suggests the cyclical nature Anna sees in her life: "Everything is repeating itself. Everything is stuck." In fact, however, everything is not stuck. Each time an incident replays in Anna's consciousness, it changes slightly. Gradually she comes to see that neither her husband nor her lover can define her. Her husband may make certain claims and her lover may draw pictures of her, but neither man can create her as a living, breathing individual. Anna's lover may say to her, "You have defined my soul for me," but he comes to see that he and Anna lead separate lives. He chooses to stay with his wife and family; she chooses to stay with her husband. When her lover confronts her with the choice she has made, she first contemplates suicide but then realizes that she can, in fact, live as a woman who is a separate individual and not a creation of or part of a man. Realizing her ability to truly live on her own terms, she is able to contemplate more meetings with her lover. She will be as independent as he, controlling her own life rather than depending on others.

Oates' story, which provides a full picture of Anna and her lover, can be read and enjoyed on its own, yet it picks up on key scenes from Chekhov's narrative. The two stories are richer if read together because the similarities suggests the universality of the characters' circumstances and emotions. There are several obvious differences, however, the most prominent of which are the setting and the point of view, Chekhov provides the man's view of the affair; Oates' offers the woman's perspective. Chekhov sees the man as coming to seek more connection; Oates sees the woman as progressively freeing herself from dependence on relationships.

Raymond Carver, Cathedral (page 1056)

Considerations for Writing and Discussion

1. Read the first part of the story (stopping when Robert arrives at the narrator's house), then write a brief description of the narrator and of your response to him.

2. In an article in *Studies in Short Fiction* (Summer 1986), Mark A. R. Facknitz suggests that what motivates one to continue reading this story, in spite of its unattractive narrator, is "a fear of the harm he may do to his wife and her blind friend" (p. 293). Do you agree with this observation? Explain.

3.   What happens in the final scene? Why does Carver choose to have Robert and the narrator watch a television program about cathedrals rather than, for example, old schoolhouses or national monuments?

If students read aloud their descriptions of and responses to the narrator, the discussion will start with energy and humor. Not since Archie Bunker has there been a bigot who makes such easy pickin's yet who also demands such careful attention. The narrator's view of blind people is incredibly prejudiced. He claims that his "idea of blindness came from the movies," yet his narrowness seems to move even beyond screen stereotypes. He is amazed that Robert wears a beard and cannot imagine that a blind man would drink alcohol or smoke.

His initial negative response to Robert's visit is compounded by jealousy of his wife's former relationships. When she describes to him her final day at work with Robert, the narrator clearly interprets Robert's desire to "see" her face with his fingertips as a move that is primarily sexually motivated.

As the story progresses, however, Robert leads the unwitting narrator to grow and learn in spite of himself. As he sits drawing the cathedral, he thinks of Robert's question "[A]re you in any way religious?" The narrator begins to see that he has been spiritually blind and that Robert is the one who sees the world in its fullness and beauty. As the narrator sits with his eyes closed tracing the final lines of the cathedral, he feels truly free for the first time in his life. "I was in my house, " he says. "But I didn't feel like I was inside anything."

Alice Walker, Everyday Use (page 1068)

Considerations for Writing and Discussion

1.   Give a brief summary of the first four sections of the story and discuss how they relate to the longer final section.

2.   Discuss the significance of Dee's name change. How does her adoption of a new name relate to her desire to protect the quilt from "everyday use"?

3.   Why does Walker subtitle her story "for your grandmama"? Whose grandmama is she talking about?

When you assign this story, you may want to talk with students about the Black Muslim movement and its influence, particularly in the 1960s, so that students will understand why Dee and Hakim-a-barber have taken new names and why they don't eat pork.

Walker's subtitle refers specifically to the older generation of black people, and especially black women, who found the rush to adopt African culture bewildering and, in some cases, insulting. In a larger context, the subtitle may refer to all grandmamas who look at the younger generation and see a repudiation of their own way of life.

Walker's story shows the narrator's and Maggie's side of the story. Certainly the first four sections demonstrate the contrast between what Mama, Maggie, and the home place are and the way Dee/Wangero would like to romanticize them. For example, the first section shows Mama admiring her beautiful, carefully swept yard. Later in the story, Dee ignores the yard and instead takes pictures of the dilapidated house, intending no doubt to regale her friends with stories of her backward mother and sister who still live in quaint rural poverty.

While Dee definitely comes off as the villain of the piece, several students have pointed out that she is not entirely wrong. She sees her heritage from one narrow perspective, but Mama and Maggie are equally adamant in refusing to see the possibilities Dee's new awareness might bring them.

Alice Munro, Spelling (page 1075)

Considerations for Writing and Discussion

1. Describe your response to Flo. Do you see her as admirable in any way? Explain.

2. What are the major contrasts between Rose's lifestyle and Brian and Phoebe's? Whose lifestyle seems more similar to Flo's? Why does Rose feel so committed to making sure her stepmother has proper care?

3. Why is the story called "Spelling"? How does the episode of the old lady who communicates only through spelling words she hears relate to Rose and Flo?

This story provides a fine opportunity to discuss responses to aging and to the aged. Most students agree that Flo is irritating and exasperating, yet at least some admire the enormous effort she makes at keeping herself "on track" and at preventing others from noticing when she is "off track." Consider, for example, her telephone discussions of the weather. She may have no idea what the weather is, but she has not forgotten the familiar pattern. Long-distance discussions with her daughter-in-law, Phoebe, have always, no doubt, begun with the standard questions, "How are you?" and "What's the weather like there?"

The old woman in the nursing home seems pathetic and yet somehow powerful as she manages to demonstrate that one part of her brain is still in working order. Rose connects the old woman's experience to Flo. In Rose's dream, the night before she takes Flo to the county home, she sees her stepmother sitting in an ornate, beautiful cage. Flo is trapped in one sense, yet she's being fed magnificently, and she's spelling words "in a clear authoritative voice." She looks pleased because she is "showing powers she had kept secret till now." Rose certainly sees the misery, weakness, and sorrow of old age, but she also sees that the mind is its own place and that those who are aging may in some unexplained way reach places—both terrible and beautiful—that the young can only imagine.

Donald Barthelme, The Balloon (page 1086)

Considerations for Writing and Discussion

1. After reading the first paragraph, what were your predictions for the rest of the story? What details confirmed or challenged your predictions as you continued to read?

2. Describe the responses different people—and groups of people—have as they watch the balloon. What do these responses suggest about the story's theme? Or do you share the view of some critics that the story has no theme? Explain.

3. Did you find the conclusion surprising? Satisfying? Strange? How does the narrator's explanation relate to the responses the balloon's observer's have expressed.

Most students see the playful quality in Barthelme's postmodern love story. They are able to accept the paradox of a balloon that is both "there" and "not there." The final paragraph suggests that the balloon is a work of the imagination, dedicated to the narrator's absent lover and symbolizing the enormity of his loneliness and—as he puts it—"sexual deprivation." As he creates this work of art, it draws an audience whose members borrow it and make it their own. Each person, or group of people, ascribes his or her own meaning. Adventurous children see the balloon as a delightful plaything; their more timid comrades are cautious and wary. Public officials want to analyze the balloon but—as they find they cannot discover how it works and as they watch their constituents' primarily positive responses—they take the politic *laissez-faire* approach.

I've enjoyed closing discussion of this piece by asking each student to write a paragraph describing his or her projected response (or explanation) if the balloon suddenly appeared over campus as they left this class. I ask them to hand me the responses as they leave, and I read several of the most innovative or humorous as a warm-up for the next class.

TEACHING:
AN INTRODUCTION TO POETRY

Students often tell me that they dread studying poetry. More than any other genre, poetry seems to them a form of literature that contains hidden meaning to which only the initiates (read: teachers) hold the key. Few students have had the luxury of listening to poetry read aloud, immersing themselves in the sound before even beginning to think about the sense.

To begin addressing this lack, my favorite way to begin teaching poetry is to read aloud several favorite poems. I try to choose poems that are short, that are particularly appealing to the ear, and that offer reasonably accessible feelings, ideas, and images. Students have been particularly surprised when I bring in a poem I've just discovered in *The New Yorker, The Atlantic Monthly,* or one of the small press magazines. They know that poetry is still being written, yet they tend to think of poems as old, dusty relics of the past. I also believe in the importance of reading an old favorite poem, perhaps several times with changes of voice that imply multiple possibilities, not one definite "right answer."

Poems that have worked well for me include:

		Text Page
The world is too much with us	William Wordsworth	1110
Kubla Khan	Samuel Taylor Coleridge	1110
Ozymandias	Percy Bysshe Shelley	1112
La Belle Dame sans Merci (Long, but great sound and a great story—sometimes I just read parts and ask them to finish outside of class.)	John Keats	1117
Fire and Ice	Robert Frost	1145
And She Did	Natalie Safir	1179
Unlearning to Not Speak	Marge Piercy	1179
Telephone Conversation	Wole Soyinka	1183

I introduce students to writing about poetry by asking for a response paper, emphasizing that I am looking for their own views, not for a preordained answer. I try to be especially open-minded as I respond to what they have written. Another assignment that works well in a small class is asking each student to choose a short poem (perhaps from anthologies placed on reserve at

171

the library). Students bring a copy of the poem to class and read it aloud, later submitting both the poem and a short paper explaining why they chose it.

My goal with these assignments is not to train literary analysts but to encourage students to read poems with energy, hope, and wonder rather than with a sense of doom and failure. Depending on the population of the course, I may move from these assignments to work that requires more literary sophistication.

Anonymous, Western Wind (page 1095)

Considerations for Writing and Discussion

1. Try reading the poem with these revised lines as the conclusion:

    God, I'd sure like to be at home
    and in bed with my girl friend

2. How does the poem change for you when you read it this way?

An exercise like this works well to suggest the importance of word choice. The change from "Christ," with its ambiguous suggestion of both prayer and desperate blasphemy, to the more common, clichéd "God" is particularly noticeable.

Thomas Wyatt, They flee from me that sometime did me seek (page 1095)

Considerations for Writing and Discussion

1. Who are the "they" mentioned in the first stanza?
2. How do they relate to the "she" of the second and third stanzas?

Students enjoy knowing that Wyatt was deeply involved in various court intrigues. This bit of historical information suggests that "they" may be fickle friends who change their loyalties when it best suits their own cause. Like these friends, the mistress in stanzas 2 and 3 has also deserted the speaker, who berates her with gentle irony in the poem's final lines.

Queen Elizabeth I, On Monsieur's Departure (page 1096)

Consideration for Writing and Discussion

1. Read a description of Queen Elizabeth I in an encyclopedia, making a list of words and phrases used to describe her.
2. Then read this poem and make a list of adjectives you would use to describe the speaker.

3. How does the poem suggest a part of the Queen's personality not defined in the encyclopedia account?

Some words and phrases used by *Funk and Wagnall's* include:

potential menace (to her sister, Mary)

innate shrewdness

skill in diplomacy

colorful personality

toying constantly with the idea of marriage

intended to live and die a virgin

William Shakespeare, **Let me not to the marriage of true minds (page 1096)**
                       Shall I compare thee to a summer's day? (page 1097)
                       That time of year thou mayst in me behold (page 1097)

Considerations for Writing and Discussion

1. As you think about each sonnet, read the first sentence (which may be longer than the first line) to yourself. Then read it aloud. Next, jot down your predictions for the rest of the poem based on that line.

2. As you read the rest of the sonnet, note how each sentence (which, again, may be longer than a line) relates to the opening sentence and to your predictions.

3. Read the final two lines (the closing couplet) several times. What does this pair of lines contribute to your response and to your understanding of the poem?

Before using these considerations, I like to read the whole poem aloud. Then, I ask students to work in groups, considering the poem in sentences—rather than in lines. When they find a place where meaning breaks down, I ask them to see whether the problem is vocabulary or word order. Often other students can suggest possibilities; if not, I usually offer several readings that make sense to me. After looking carefully at the poems, members of the groups reconvene as a class; we discuss responses and possibilities and close with an oral reading (preferably by a student volunteer) to leave the whole poem as the final impression.

John Donne,   The Flea (page 1098)
Batter my heart, three-personed God (page 1098)
The Canonization (page 1099)

Consideration for Writing and Discussion

1.   In each of these poems, identify the central *conceit* (extended
metaphor, linking two apparently different subjects to suggest new
possibilities and connections).

Although students may not catch on immediately, nearly all of them
respond strongly to "The Flea" and its witty comparison between a flea bite and
the loss of virginity. They enjoy knowing that in the seventeenth century, when
Donne was writing, pregnancy was believed to result from an exchange of blood
which they thought occurred between men and women during sexual intercourse.
Understanding this bit of historical/medical trivia makes the flea-bite
analogy clearer.

In the first eight lines of "Batter my heart, three-personed God," the
speaker compares the sinners to a town ensnared by the forces of evil. God, then,
becomes a defending warrior who must use violence to reclaim the besieged soul.
The final six lines compare the sinner to a beloved woman, who, like the town,
has been held captive by Satan.

The lovers in "The Canonization" are compared to Christian martyrs. Like
the early Christians, they are not deterred by their critics but are willing to
die to defend the right to their devotion. (The first line of this poem *must* be
read aloud—few students fail to be moved by the speaker's passionate
exhortation.)

John Milton, When I consider how my light is spent (page 1100)

Consideration for Writing and Discussion

1.   This poem is sometimes subtitled "On His Blindness." Milton was
indeed blind when he wrote the sonnet. The subtitle was the invention
of a printer who typeset the poem nearly a century after it was written.
What possibilities other than blindness can you see for the central focus
of this poem?

The poem certainly suggests the loss of symbolic light as well as physical
light: Milton had fallen from favor with the government. In addition, the
Puritan beliefs to which he adhered were being widely questioned and he may
have felt he was losing his audience. Certainly the final lines apply to spheres
beyond Milton's own, since he did not "stand and wait." Although blind and no
longer favored by many of those in power, he continued to write and composed
some of his most admired works after his sight was completely gone.

George Herbert, Easter Wings (page 1101)

Consideration for Writing and Discussion

1. How does the intricately and carefully planned structure of this poem relate to the poet's subject?

The wings formed by the poem's lines, as well the wings of the title, suggest butterflies rather than angels. The butterfly seems a particularly apt symbol to suggest the resurrection of Easter, since it is the final, beautiful form that arises triumphant from the earthly prison of the chrysalis.

Jonathan Swift, A Description of the Morning (page 1101)

Considerations for Writing and Discussion

1. After considering the details of Swift's morning, what adjectives would you use to describe it?

2. What does the speaker's description suggest about his state of mind?

Swift's speaker takes a cynical, ironic view of morning. Normally the time of new hope and possibility, the speaker's morning instead suggests corruption, lust, greed, and the grindingly hard work of the poor. On a lighter note, it's hard for the boys who dally on their way to school, clearly dreading the lessons awaiting them, to have much hope of escape.

Alexander Pope, from Part II of *An Essay on Criticism* (page 1102)

Consideration for Writing and Discussion

1. The subtitle of Part II is "Causes That Hinder a True Judgment." Using outline format, summarize this section of the poem, noting what causes Pope believed would interfere with logical thinking. Here is one possibility—a paraphrase of Pope's own summary of this section of the *Essay*:

    I. (ll. 85–183) Do not judge something by its parts; instead look at the whole.

        A. (ll. 89–104) Do not judge by considering only clever comparisons and witty figures of speech.

        B. (ll. 105–136) Do not judge by looking at language apart from context .

        C. (ll. 137–183) Do not judge only by the sound, rhythm, and structure of a work.

II.   (ll. 184–193) Do not make a false judgment because you are either too hard or too easy to please.

III.   (ll. 194–207) Do not make a false judgement because you favor only one type or one group of writers.

IV.   (ll. 208–223) Do not make a false judgment because you want to agree with the generally accepted opinion.

V.   (ll. 224–251) On the other hand, don't go too far in the opposite direction and make a false judgment simply because you want to oppose the currently popular opinion.

VI.   (ll. 252–273) Do not base your judgment solely on whether or not you can identify with the writer or the situation the writer describes.

VII.   (ll. 274–293) Do not make a false judgment because you are too impatient to wait and see what will endure.

VIII.   (ll. 294–307) Do not allow envy to lead you to make a false judgment.

A.   (ll. 308–325) Do not judge harshly just because the writer is praised by others.

B.   (ll. 326–359) On the other hand, be confident that there are times when harsh judgement is called for.

William Blake,   The Lamb (page 1108)
                   The Tyger (page 1109)

Consideration for Writing and Discussion

1.   "The Lamb" is part of Blake's collection entitled "Songs of Innocence"; "The Tyger" appears in the group of poems called "Songs of Experience." Do the contrasts in the poems justify their classification into these categories? Explain.

Although both poems ask questions related to creation, "The Lamb" offers a fairly direct and commonly expected response that suggests an innocent world view. "The Tyger" never provides an answer but continues to open up new questions. Whereas the lamb is depicted as a simple, easily understood creature, the tiger is mysterious, strange, and complex—a worthy symbol of experience.

William Wordsworth,   My heart leaps up (page 1110)
**   The world is too much with us (page 1110)**

Considerations for Writing and Discussion

1. Describe the contrasting responses to nature suggested by the images and by the speakers' tone in these poems.

2. Which response seems closest to your own? Explain.

"My heart leaps up" suggests the pleasure and hope the speaker feels when he sees a rainbow. He indicates that he has felt this connection with nature since he was a child and suggests, with the oft-quoted line "The Child is father of the Man," that we develop in our earliest years the attitudes that will stay with us throughout our lives. In contrast, the speaker in "The world is too much with us" expresses his sorrow and concern that the modern world (this poem was written in 1807) has fallen out of touch with natural elements like the sea and earth. Rather than suggesting a literal return to the worship of gods and goddesses, the final lines indicate his yearning for a time when he believes human spirits were more connected with the elements of nature.

Samuel Taylor Coleridge, Kubla Khan (page 1110)

Considerations for Writing and Discussion

1. If you had the opportunity to travel to Xanadu, would you accept the offer?

2. Explain by discussing your response to the description provided by the poem.

While discussing the mysteries of Xanadu, I recommend Douglas Adams's 1987 satiric time-travel novel, *Dirk Gently's Holistic Detective Agency*, which expects readers to have read "Kubla Khan" and to understand the circumstances of its composition. (Coleridge is supposed to have imagined the poem during an opium-induced dream. He claimed that on awaking, he began to write down what he had dreamt but was interrupted by a visitor who caused the concluding stanzas to vanish from his memory.)

George Gordon, Lord Byron, She walks in beauty (page 1112)

Consideration for Writing and Discussion

1. Create a dialogue between the speaker in the poem and the woman he describes. The topic of the conversation is up to you, but be sure to reflect both the speaker's description of the woman and his attitude toward her.

Although the beauty of this poem cannot be denied, my students have often enjoyed writing satirical dialogues suggesting, for instance, that the woman does not enjoy being compared to elements of the night and would, instead, like to shine more brightly, like the sun.

Percy Bysshe Shelley, Ozymandias (page 1112)
Ode to the West Wind (page 1113)

Considerations for Writing and Discussion

1.   Ozymandias is depicted as a long-dead ruler. List his qualities as suggested by the poem's images. Can you compare him in any way to modern rulers or was he entirely different? Explain.

2.   Explain the speaker's response to the west wind. What strengths does he see in the wind? What relationship does he see between himself and the wind?

The images in stanza five suggest that the speaker wishes he could become like a musical instrument played by the wind (perhaps a reference to an eolian lyre which hangs in a window and, like modern day wind chimes, produces musical notes in response to breezes that move it). The speaker (closely identified with the poet) sees the wind as paradoxically powerful, having the means to destroy and to preserve. He would like his words to speak as strongly as does the wind and believes that if he can become the wind's instrument he will be able to communicate mysterious and awe-inspiring truths to those who hear him.

John Keats, Ode on a Grecian Urn (page 1115)
La Belle Dame sans Merci (page 1117)

Considerations for Writing and Discussion

1.   The "Ode on a Grecian Urn" raises more questions than it answers. List several questions from the poem and, in addition, list several lines that are not questions followed by the questions those lines raise in your mind.

2.   The title of "La Belle Dame sans Merci" translates to mean " The Beautiful Lady without Mercy." Does she deserve this title? Develop an argument either exonerating her or confirming her guilt in the fate of the "Knight at arms" who is found "[a]lone and palely loitering."

Questions found in "Ode on a Grecian Urn" include:

> What leaf-fring'd legend haunts about thy shape/Of
> deities or mortal, or of both,/In Tempe or the dales of
> Arcady? (lines 5–7)

> What men or gods are these? What maidens loath?/What
> mad pursuit? What struggle to escape?/What pipes and
> timbrels? What wild ecstasy? (lines 8–10)

Lines inspiring questions from my students include:

> Sylvan historian, who canst thus express/A
> flowery tale more sweetly than our rhyme (lines 3–4)

Why is the urn called "sylvan"? Why is the urn a historian?

> Bold Lover, never, never canst thou kiss,/Though winning
> near the goal—yet do not grieve (lines 17–18)

*Why should anyone or anything be happy to be constantly in the state
of not achieving a desired goal?*

> "Beauty is truth, truth beauty,"—that is all/Ye know on
> earth, and all ye need to know. (lines 49–50)

*Who says the words after the quoted sentence? The speaker or the urn?
Is the speaker getting a message from the urn or giving a message to the
readers?*

In most classes, opinion divides sharply on the lady in "La Belle Dame sans
Merci." Often the men in the class are willing to accept the explanation of the
knight's dreadful condition as the result of his love for the mysterious lady.
Women point out that although the lady may be supernatural, her behavior
does not seem particularly threatening or dangerous: She sings to him, brings
him food, and admits her love for him. She seems as deeply wounded by the
relationship as does the knight. For instance, in stanza 8, she weeps and sighs,
possibly deeply distressed by knowing that she cannot have a continued
relationship with a mortal.

Edgar Allan Poe, The Raven (page 1118)

Considerations for Writing and Discussion

1. Choose several stanzas to read aloud, experimenting with different
reading styles (tone of voice, pace, emphasis, and so on).

2. Write a response describing the different possibilities you discovered
from planning and carrying out these readings.

This exercise works best if done in class. You might ask students to work in groups and then have one representative from each group deliver the reading the members have prepared.

Alfred, Lord Tennyson, Ulysses (page 1121)
The Lady of Shalott (page 1123)

Considerations for Writing and Discussion

1. What do the details of "Ulyses" suggest about the differences between Ulysses and his son Telemachus? Write the letter Ulysses might leave behind for his son as he sets off on his journey. Then write the reply Telemachus sends by messenger several months later, hoping the letter will reach his aging father.

2. Summarize the action in each section of "The Lady of Shalott" and then describe the conflict the Lady of Shalott faces. Evaluate her response to that conflict as well as to the outcome of her action.

Some students see Ulysses as contemptuous of his son, but most read the second stanza of the poem as a loving father's acknowledgement that his son is different from himself yet not necessarily less. The final line of that stanza, "He works his work, I mine" provides convincing evidence that Ulysses believes Telemachus's choices to be worthy and important, although nearly the opposite of his own.

"The Lady of Shalott"

Part I: The scene is set: common people working in the fields stop from time to time to gaze at the island of Shallot where the Lady is reputed to live in her towered refuge. Camelot is mentioned in each stanza, yet the Lady is clearly separated from this ideal place.

Part II: The next stanza takes readers inside the Lady's refuge, where she sits weaving a magic web that depicts the scenes of the world she sees played out in her mirror. She is not supposed to look out toward Camelot. If she does, some unspecified curse will strike. Yet, at the end of the stanza, she declares "I am half sick of shadows," indicating that she longs for more than the second-hand experiences reflected in her mirror.

Part III: The bold and glittering Sir Lancelot appears in the Lady's mirror as he heads toward Camelot. She is entranced and defying all warnings, looks out the window toward Camelot. At that moment, the mirror cracks and she cries out, "The curse is come upon me."

Part IV: Leaving her fortress, the Lady discovers a boat. She lies down in it and floats to Camelot through a night of storm and strange noises. She sings an eerie, mournful chant and dies before she reaches the first house in Camelot. The residents of Camelot are awe-stricken and fearful when they discover the mysterious woman in her boat with "The Lady of Shalott" written around the prow. Yet as Sir Lancelot looks at her, he recognizes her beauty and asks that "God in his mercy lend her grace."

What is the temptation here? To leave the protection of an innocent world and to move into the real world? To leave an autonomous existence and seek connection with a handsome knight? What exactly was the curse? Why must the Lady die? How will the residents of Camelot be affected by her decision not to remain alone on the island?

Walt Whitman, Beat! beat! drums! (page 1127)
A noiseless patient spider (page 1128)

Considerations for Writing and Discussion

1.   "Beat! beat! drums!" is included in a group of fifty-three poems that Whitman called "Drum-Taps." Inspiration for many of these poems came from the time he spent nursing injured soldiers at the front lines during the Civil War. Later, when Whitman assembled his long collection of poems called "Leaves of Grass," he included "Beat! beat! drums!," as well as other poems from "Drum Taps," because he was convinced that they reflected an essential and representative democratic experience. Considering the details included in "Beat! beat! drums!," do you agree with him? To what extent does his view of war reflect your view?

2.   List the qualities of the spider that the speaker stresses in "A noiseless patient spider." How does the speaker see these qualities as related to his soul? What is your response to this comparison?

In "Beat! beat! drums!," the speaker sees war as a relentless force that must be given attention. Some of the images seem strictly descriptive, but others (especially those in the final stanza) suggest that the speaker believes the call of war must not be denied for any reason.

In "A noiseless patient spider," the speaker compares his soul to a spider, seeking to make connection by casting its webs. Does the speaker long to unite his soul with the soul of another human? Or is he searching for a bridge that may lead to union with a higher power? Or do other possibilities exist?

Matthew Arnold, Dover Beach (page 1128)

Considerations for Writing and Discussion

1. As an alternative to the traditional male voice most readers hear, try reading this poem with a female voice as the speaker. Describe the response of the person to whom the final stanza is addressed. Then read the poem again imagining the traditional male voice as the speaker.

2. Describe the response of the person to whom the final stanza is addressed. Does the poem change for you as you try these different voices?

This is an interesting exercise to do in groups. Ask half the groups to work on the female voice and response and half to work on the male voice and response. When I have asked students to read in this way, the differences between the voices responding to the male speaker and those responding to the female speaker have sparked intriguing discussion. The exercise is particularly lively if you give each group's speaker a photocopy of the assignment. Groups receive different assignments, but they work under the assumption they are all using the same point of view.

Emily Dickinson, Selected Poems

Considerations for Writing and Discussion

1. This collection of Dickinson's poetry provides an opportunity for students to look closely at several selections by the same writer and suggest aspects of subject and style that exemplify her work. You might ask them to read eight to ten of these selections and then to work in groups compiling lists that suggest typical aspects of her poetry.

2. After the groups reconvene, consider reading several selections aloud while students follow in their books. Ask for comments on how they responded to aspects (visual as well as aural) that they have identified. Do they find Dickinson's poetry puzzling, intriguing, musical, stark, maddening, enlightening, or . . . ?

Possibilities include:

1. Unusual use of syntax (for example, sentences where words or even entire phrases are omitted).

2. Unusual use of punctuation, particularly dashes.

3. Unusual use of capitalization.

4. Exploration of the inner self as typical subject.

5.   Comparisons of aspects of inner self with aspects of natural, physical world.

6.   Use of a single extended metaphor or symbol to explore a theme.

7.   Emphasis on themes of death, love, faith, and doubt.

8.   Exploration of ideas in ways that tend to raise questions rather than provide answers.

Thomas Hardy, The Darkling Thrush (page 1136)

Considerations for Writing and Discussion

1.   In the second stanza, the speaker depicts the closing century as a dying corpse. What do the images in the first and second stanza suggest about the speaker's view of circumstances as the century comes to an end?

2.   Compare this view, which refers to the close of the nineteenth century, to your own view of our civilization during the closing years of the twentieth century.

3.   Do you, like the speaker, see the possibility of hope as described in the final two stanzas? What might today's voice of hope be?

Responses vary widely, of course. Before closing discussion of this topic, I try to make sure that at least some possibilities for hope have been suggested. At the very least, students usually note some of the positive changes that have occurred since the turn of the last century (medical advances; more rights for women and minorities; and so on).

Gerard Manley Hopkins,   God's Grandeur (page 1137)
Pied Beauty (page 1138)

Considerations for Writing and Discussion

1.   What possibilities does the speaker suggest when he says that "[t]he world is charged with the grandeur of God"? How does this opening line relate to the final image of "the Holy Ghost" which broods "over the bent/World"?

2.   After reading "Pied Beauty," try writing a poem or a tightly planned paragraph, beginning with the line "Glory be to God for _____ things." Create your own list, which need not rhyme nor be as complex as Hopkins's.

Hopkins's poetry is wonderfully evocative, suggesting many possibilities. The opening line suggests a world that is filled with the grandeur of God just as a battery might be charged with electricity. This reading suggests that the world also gains its energy from the beauty that God has created. Another possibility would be to read the word "charged" as meaning "charged with responsibility." We who live in the world are given the task of caring for the glory of nature. In the final lines, the Holy Ghost (the spirit of God) broods (nurtures, or, alternatively, worries about) the bent world. Bent suggests the curve of the earth yet also might comment on the way humans have distorted the beauty with which they have been charged.

William Butler Yeats, The Lake Isle of Innisfree (page 1138)
Crazy Jane Talks with the Bishop (page 1139)

Considerations for Writing and Discussion

1.   List several images the speaker provides to describe his ideal refuge at Innisfree. What qualities of life do these images suggest? Describe your own ideal refuge, the one you can imagine as solace when you "stand on the roadway" or "on the pavements grey."

2.   Paraphrase the Bishop's message to Jane and her reply to him. What values does each message suggest?

Students choose different images of Yeats' Lake Isle retreat, but most agree that the qualities represented include simplicity, quiet, peace, solitude, self-sufficiency, and natural beauty.

The Bishop calls Jane's attention to her aging body and, following conventional morality, suggests that she change what he sees as her sinful way of living and look to the preservation of her immortal soul. Jane replies that although her way of getting and giving love may be looked on as dirty by the Bishop, she believes that no one can become spiritually whole until they have experienced the full range of earthly love, including love of the body.

James Weldon Johnson, O Black and Unknown Bards (page 1140)

Consideration for Writing and Discussion

1.   List several of the questions Johnson asks and then explain the responses to these questions suggested by the images in the final stanzas.

Johnson's praise for the music and poetry created by black slaves opens possibilities for students to do research leading to further questions and answers related to this topic.

Paul Laurence Dunbar, We wear the mask (page 1141)

Considerations for Writing and Discussion

1. The speaker suggests that we all wear masks and that these masks serve a purpose. Do you see this purpose as positive?

2. Do you agree that nearly everyone wears masks? If so, do you picture others and yourself as wearing the same mask throughout life or as changing them? Explain.

This poem provides a fine opportunity for students to respond visually to a poem. They might draw the masks they see confronting them in some situation in their lives or they might create one of their own masks.

Robert Frost, Selected Poems

Considerations for Writing and Discussion

This collection of Frost's poetry provides an opportunity for students to look closely at several selections by the same writer and suggest aspects of subject and style that exemplify his work. In addition to the selections in this section, the following poems by Frost are included in *Responding to Literature*: "The Road Not Taken" (page 5); "Birches" (page 168); "The Death of the Hired Man" (page 308); and "Out, Out—" (page 853).

1. You might ask students to read eight to ten of these selections and then work in groups compiling lists that suggest typical aspects of his poetry. After the groups reconvene, ask for comments on their responses to the various aspects that they have identified. After reading the selections in this text, would they choose to read more of Frost? Why or why not?

2. Frost had a gift for writing powerful lines that stay with readers even in this age that eschews memorization. Consider asking students to write in their journals several lines from Frost's poetry that they find worth remembering and to explain why they chose these lines.

Possible aspects of subject and style include the following:

1. Poems tend to fall into two groups: (1) short lyric poems like "Fire and Ice" or "Nothing Gold Can Stay" that often look at some aspect of nature as a path to a philosophical observation, stated or implied; (2) longer narratives like "Death of a Hired Hand" and "Out, Out—" that often suggest the harshness and sorrow of rural New England life

2. Use of rhyme and other sound devices that simultaneously create the rhythms of poetry and the rhythms of human speech

3. Use of unrhymed, yet rhythmic, lines (blank verse) in many of the longer narratives

4. Images and subjects related to nature (and to human nature)

5. Nature shown as beautiful, yet untamed, full of surprise, with the potential for evil and well as good

Ezra Pound, In a Station of the Metro (page 1147)

Considerations for Writing and Discussion

1. What is the relationship between the first and second lines of this short poem?

2. What extra dimension does the title add to the poem?

Using the haiku form, Pound first provides an image of faces in a crowd and then, in the second line, comments on his response to those faces. They are like petals, which suggests that they are delicate and beautiful. Because they are together on a wet, black bough they are also connected and related to each other.

Students may not know that the metro is the French subway system. Recognizing the mundane setting makes Pound's vision of the crowd all the more remarkable.

H. D. (Hilda Doolittle), Helen (page 1147)
Marianne Moore, The Mind Is an Enchanting Thing (page 1148)
The Fish (page 1149)

Considerations for Writing and Discussion

1. Read the story of Helen of Troy to discover why the speaker says that "[a]ll Greece hates" her.

2. How are the heart and the mind contrasted in "The Mind Is an Enchanting Thing"? What is your response to this comparison? Do you agree with Moore?

3. Describe, in your own words, the underwater landscape evoked by the images in "The Fish." What is the "it" referred to in the final stanza?

According to Greek mythology, Helen was the astonishingly beautiful daughter of Zeus (King of the Gods) and Leda (a mortal). Later, Helen married the Greek king Menelaus, but Paris, the Trojan Prince, kidnapped her from Sparta and took her to Troy. Her abduction led to the Trojan War.

In "The Mind Is an Enchanting Thing," the mind is highly praised as multifaceted and capable of reasoning, remembering, and creating. The mind seems to be the protector of the heart, making certain that the heart does not remain blinded by emotional responses that have not been tried in the crucible of the mind.

The underwater scene in "The Fish" combines beauty and destruction. The "black jade" of mussel shells look like ash heaps of burnt coal. In addition, the mussels look like "injured fan[s]" that open and shut themselves. "It" in the final stanza seems to refer to the cliff that holds and shelters the sea life described in the poem. The cliff is protected by the mussels and starfish it hosts, yet they cannot make it young again.

Robinson Jeffers, Hurt Hawks (page 1150)

Considerations for Writing and Discussion

1. What qualities does the speaker admire in the hawk?

2. Who are the "communal people" mentioned in line 15? Who is it they have forgotten, but the "hawks, and men that are dying" remember?

The injured hawk recognizes that he has lost the power to do what he must: he can no longer fly to scout out and capture game, yet he has not lost his arrogance and aggressive nature. He will not cry out to the "wild God" to hasten death and free him from his pain. It is this "wild God" that the "communal people" who live ordinary lives in ordinary towns have forgotten. But wild creatures—like hawks and men who still value independence over all else—understand this harsh God who grants mercy only to those who beg for it.

The poem ends with the speaker acting in place of the wild God; he frees the spirit of the hawk (and of the fast-dying breed of men he believes to be like hawks?) from its injured earthly body.

T. S. Eliot,   Journey of the Magi (page 1151)
The Love Song of J. Alfred Prufrock (page 1152)

Considerations for Writing and Discussion

1. Read the account of Jesus's birth and of the attendance of the Wise Men (the Magi) in the New Testament books of Matthew and Mark. How do those accounts compare with the view of that event suggested by "The Journey of the Magi"?

2. Write a character sketch of Prufrock. What kind of a man is he? Which of his qualities do you admire? Which do you find less than admirable?

The biblical gospels see the birth of Jesus in the Christian context. Every detail emphasizes the miraculous nature of the event. The speaker in Eliot's poem, however, does not understand the relation between Jesus' birth and his subsequent earthly death and so remains puzzled. The speaker was deeply moved by what he saw in Bethlehem and questioned the old faith he had previously followed. Yet he has not made the leap to enlightenment and so feels weighted with doubt and disillusionment.

Most younger students are very hard on Prufrock, a man who cannot decide whether to wear the bottoms of his trousers rolled and who ponders the wisdom of eating a peach. Older students, however, have more sympathy with Prufrock's anxiety, seeing him as approaching middle age without having discovered a true center to his life. The "you and I" of the opening line can be read as different parts of Prufrock's nature, suggesting the conflicts he lives with every day and night.

e. e. cummings, if everything happens that can't be done (page 1156)
in Just—(page 1157)
[l(a] (page 1158)

Considerations for Writing and Discussion

1.   Reread the final line of "if everything happens that can't be done." How does this mathematical image suggest the speaker's central idea?

2.   The "goat-footed/balloonMan" is probably a modern relative of the Greek god Pan. How does understanding this allusion affect your response to the poem?

3.   Sort out the literal statement in "[l(a]." What does the poem lose when it is written in conventional order?

The speaker in "if everything happens . . ." celebrates the dizzying excitement of falling in love. The final line is a wonderful paradox. Throughout the poem, the speaker eschews teachers and books, yet this simple bit of arithmetic perfectly symbolizes his feelings. One times one equals one. One lover times the other lover equals a new "one" (a united relationship).

In Greek mythology, Pan is the pastoral god of fertility. Often depicted as an ugly, merry man with goat's horn, ears, and legs, he is the central figure in myths that relate his amorous affairs. His appearance suggests that spring brings the innocent play of childhood even as it sounds the note of renewed sexual energy and desire.

The letters in "[l(a]" that appear outside the parentheses spell "loneliness"; those inside the parentheses spell "a leaf falls." The conventional arrangement fails to enclose the image of the leaf within the sense of loneliness. In addition, as written, the poem's letters suggest the pattern of a leaf falling. Finally the word "one," which underlines the sense of loneliness, appears as the single whole word in the groups of syllables that comprise the poem's lines.

Jorge Luis Borges, The Blind Man (page 1159)

Consideration for Writing and Discussion

1.   Compare the blind man depicted by Borges with the blind man depicted in Raymond Carver's story "Cathedral" (page 1056).

Borges's images emphasize the losses suffered by the blind man (both the "he" and the "I" of the poem seem to be the blind man). Carver's story shows a blind man who has discovered new dimensions in his life. Neither sentimentalizes being blind, but Borges's blind man lives in a world of deprivation and nightmare whereas Carver's lives in a world of new experiences and possibilities.

Langston Hughes, Harlem (page 1159)

Consideration for Writing and Discussion

1.   This poem is often titled "Dream Deferred," but Hughes' original title was "Harlem." Does your reading of the poem change in response to the two different titles? Explain.

With the title "Harlem" eliminated, the poem is no longer clearly rooted in the black American experience. Instead, the venue becomes much broader and could apply to any goal that is continually denied and delayed. For some readers, ignoring Hughes' original title defuses the energy and power of the poem's smoldering anger. For others, the poem gains broader meaning and possibility when it is not specifically tied to the Harlem experience.

Pablo Neruda, The Word (page 1160)

Consideration for Writing and Discussion

1.   Identify the biblical reference in the first stanza and suggest how that allusion relates to the images introduced in stanzas 5, 7, and 8.

The first stanza suggests the creation story in Genesis which begins, "In the beginning was the word." The entire poem explores the speaker's sense of language as being the connection between human and divine. References to the standard communion symbols—blood, wine, cup, and goblet—enforce this sense of the importance of language as a unifying, life-giving, affirming, mystical force.

Elizabeth Bishop, In the Waiting Room (page 1162)

Consideration for Writing and Discussion

1. Describe what happens to the nearly seven-year-old Elizabeth as she
    sits waiting for her aunt. Consider especially your response to her
    sudden realization:

> . . . you are an *I*,
>
> you are an *Elizabeth*,
>
> you are one of *them*.

As Elizabeth looks at the people in the pictures in *National Geographic,*
they initially seem far away and strange, even horrifying. She then hears, or
thinks she hears, a yelp of pain from her aunt, whom she quickly dismisses as
"a foolish, timid woman." Almost immediately, however, Elizabeth realizes
that these creatures she has seen as "other" are, in fact, human, just as she is
human. This realization probably brings with it the recognition that she is also
linked to her aunt and to her aunt's experiences and responses. This child now
sees that she cannot escape being part of the world with all its faults,
peculiarities, strangeness, and wonder.

Robert Hayden, Those Winter Sundays (page 1164)

Consideration for Writing and Discussion

1. List the qualities the speaker sees in his father as he looks back at his
    childhood. Do you see all the memories as positive? Explain.

Students generally see that the speaker looks back on the cold Sunday
mornings of his childhood and realizes that his father made a great effort to
keep his family comfortable. On the other hand, they may want to skip over
images like the "chronic angers of that house" which suggest that all was not
perfect. Did the anger belong only to the mother? Or to the children? Or was
the father, too, sometimes angry? Does keeping the fire going and polishing
shoes really constitute an act of love or are these merely routines belonging to a
role that many men accepted with a sense of resignation rather than love?

Robert Lowell, The Drinker (page 1165)

Consideration for Writing and Discussion

1. How do the man's actions and thoughts suggest the justification he gives himself for drinking? How reasonable do you find these justifications?

This man is clearly a heavy drinker who has already begun to destroy his body through alcohol abuse. The first part of the poem describes his physical deterioration; the second part, beginning with lines 17–18, suggest his rationalization for this particular binge. A woman has left him. He suggests that her appointments and meetings were more important to her than he was, but most readers will wonder whether the meetings and appointments were a response to the drinking rather than the cause of it.

Philip Larkin, The Whitsun Weddings (page 1165)

Consideration for Writing and Discussion

1. Whitsun, short for Whitsunday, is a legal holiday in England and part a three-day weekend that falls in May or June. Whitsun weddings are traditional in Britain just as June weddings are in the United States. What do the images in the poem suggest about the speaker's view of these weddings? Do you share this view?

The speaker takes a cynical view, seeing no beauty in these weddings but only an assembly line of stereotypes like the uncle who stands "shouting smut" and the "lot and fat" mothers. The speaker's view is neatly summed up by his describing the women at the wedding as sharing "the secret like a happy funeral."

Lawrence Ferlinghetti, I Am Waiting (page 1168)

Considerations for Writing and Discussion

1. What *is* the speaker waiting for?

2. The poem is full of references to other works of literature and allusions to historic events, religious symbols, and patriotic slogans. How do these references and allusions suggest what the speaker is searching for?

While not every student will know every reference, it's fun to ask them to identify what they can. Most will see that Ferlinghetti has loaded the poem with the hopeful clichés and catchwords of our civilization, juxtaposing them with each other and with his own observations to suggest his own disillusionment with easy answers and glib assurances.

James Dickey, The Heaven of Animals (page 1171)

Considerations for Writing and Discussion

1. What are the key elements the speaker sees as comprising a heaven for animals?

2. What values are suggested by the speaker's view of the animal heaven?

3. How might this same philosophy be expressed if he were describing a heaven for humans?

The speaker seems primarily concerned with allowing animals to follow their instincts. If this means killing, then they shall kill perfectly; but the victims will feel no fear or pain and will rise from the experience unharmed. Would a heaven for humans allow those who harbor strong aggressive instincts to express those feelings completely (with their victims, of course, not suffering)? Somehow the image of the animals who are victims is not completely comfortable for most students. How can "acceptance [and] compliance" be heaven for any living creature?

Mari Evans, I Am a Black Woman (page 1172)

Considerations for Writing and Discussion

1. What primary role does the speaker see herself playing?

2. How does this role make her "strong/beyond all definition . . ."

The speaker envisions the black woman always watching the men in her life suffer and die: by leaping overboard to escape the slave ship; by lynching; and by dying in wars (Anzio Beach, World War II; Pork Chop Hill, Korea; Da Nang, Vietnam). She also suggests that she, too, has fought (perhaps in civil rights conflicts where tear gas was used to control protesters). She has endured these horrors and still survives.

Although most students admire this prototype of the black woman, some find her description too strongly rooted in and dependent on male, rather than female, experience.

Denise Levertov, In Mind (page 1173)

Consideration for Writing and Discussion

1. Describe the women who fill the speaker's mind. What conflicts do the details suggest?

The first figure seems like a stereotyped "good woman." She seems perfect, yet she lacks imagination. The second figure may be a young girl or an old woman (or a combination). She seems like a figure who is both magical and menacing; she's intriguing, fascinating, but she lacks kindness. Perhaps the speaker feels that to have imagination—to have the gift necessary to be creative—a woman must give up all the qualities described in the first part of the poem. Can these two women exist together in the artist's mind? Or must one become dominant?

Allen Ginsberg, A Supermarket in California (page 1174)

Consideration for Writing and Discussion

1. The speaker's images suggest ironic disdain for the supermarkets and the people who shop there. He imagines encountering Walt Whitman "poking among the meats" and then walking with Whitman "dreaming of the lost America of love." Read the poems by Walt Whitman included in this anthology and explain whether the America he describes seems any more loving than the contemporary society described by Ginsberg.

Although Whitman certainly saw America and Americans as more noble, more filled with possibility than does Ginsberg, students often suggest that Whitman's "lost America of love" is not so idyllic as Ginsberg's poem suggests.

James Wright, A Blessing (page 1174)

Considerations for Writing and Discussion

1. What does the final line suggest about the speaker's experience?

2. Why does it seem so significant to him?

The incident seems quite ordinary to most readers. The speaker and his friend stop their car, and two ponies come over to greet them. The final image suggests that the speaker is so touched by this moment of connection that he feels himself a beautiful, joyous, and fruitful part of nature. To understand the impact of this moment, ask students to think of an apparently insignificant incident that they can still somehow remember vividly. Most people have moments like this; these out-of-time experiences are extremely difficult to describe, but, like the speaker, we cling to them as touchstones during the far more common days and nights that offer no such small miracles.

Adrienne Rich, Planetarium (page 1175)

Consideration for Writing and Discussion

1. Explain the comparison the speaker implies between herself and Caroline Herschel.

Caroline Herschel persisted in exploring unknown possibilities in the heavens in spite of the difficulties she faced as a woman working in a field traditionally considered the province of men. In the final stanza, the speaker sees herself as the recipient of impulses from unknown, strange, and unexplored territories. Like an astronomer creating maps of the heavens, she tries to translate (through her poems, perhaps) those extraterrestrial (therefore mystical) impulses into images "for the relief of the body and the reconstruction of the mind."

Robert Bly, Words Rising (page 1177)

Consideration for Writing and Discussion

1. How does the title relate to the experience the speaker describes in the poem?

The speaker suggests that until humans had language they could not fully express what they saw, felt, and did. Yet preliterate experiences are not diminished because they could not be fully celebrated in language. Instead, those experiences are stored up like honey which can now be fully savored by those willing to seek the cache of stored sweetness—primal images that liberate the spirit as they rise in words from the minds and pens of poets.

Gary Snyder, Riprap (page 1178)

Consideration for Writing and Discussion

1. A *riprap* is a dam or wall formed by pieces of stone that have been arranged together as a means of strengthening a weak or soft place in the bottom or bank of a stream. How does this definition relate to the subject of the poem?

Snyder's images themselves form a riprap for readers. The lines of poetry come together and provide strength; they become a foundation on which we can build our own responses.

Natalie Safir, And She Did (page 1179)

Consideration for Writing and Discussion

1. Point out and read examples of Safir's playful use of language to suggest her admiration of the Little Red Hen.

You may want to ask a student volunteer to summarize the events in the folk tale that tells the Little Red Hen's story. With that background, it's easy for students to appreciate Safir's wit as she puns on words related to eggs ("hard boiled"; "crackle"; "poachers") and poultry ("squawks"; "winging"; "cluck";

"chick"). The double meanings of these words suggest that the Red Hen represents the hard-working woman who not only makes literal bread but also earns "bread" in the slang sense of making a living—and does this all on her own.

Marge Piercy, Unlearning to Not Speak (page 1179)

Considerations for Writing and Discussion

1.   Who has taught the woman in this poem not to speak?

2.   Why would these people want her to be silent?

This poem usually leads to lively discussion. Many students—both men and women—believe that women talk more than men and find it difficult to believe that women have often been silenced by traditional authority figures. They are surprised to learn that studies have shown the opposite to be true. In this poem, the authority figures are male teachers who maintain their own sense of superiority by keeping women from describing either their "pleasure" or their "rage."

Margaret Atwood, you fit into me (page 1180)

Consideration for Writing and Discussion

1.   Explain the word play that hooks the reader's eye in "you fit into me."

Students usually respond strongly to "you fit into me." Some feel cheated and tricked because the first stanza seems to promise a romantic (and sexually suggestive) comparison with the female speaker as the eye of a fastening device and the male she is describing as the hook that fits into and completes the device. The second stanza, however, defines the simile more fully. Now the female speaker is like a human eye the male becomes like a fish hook. The ugliness and pain evoked by this comparison provide a stinging contrast to the coziness suggested by the first two lines.

Janice Mirikitani, For My Father (page 1180)

Consideration for Writing and Discussion:

1.   Tule Lake, located in a desert area of the Southwest, was the location of one of the camps where Japanese citizens were interned during World War II. Mount Fuji is a shortened form of Mount Fujiama, the sacred mountain of Japan. How does the speaker evoke these two places to suggest her father's character?

The father had Mount Fuji "on his back." He carried with him the memories and customs of his Japanese ancestry but came seeking new possibilities in the United States. Those dreams were destroyed by the internment at Tule Lake where the father was forced to eke out a living by farming the nearly barren desert soil. The speaker understands her father's deep disappointment but regrets his silence (perhaps part of his heritage). She sees him as physically strong and emotionally determined but as withered spiritually like the desert where they were forced to live.

Compare this poem with Jeanne Wakatsuki Houston and James D. Houston's "Arrival at Manzanar" (page 1534).

Wendy Rose, Loo-wit (page 1181)

Consideration for Writing and Discussion

1.   Wendy Rose, a Native American poet, creates a modern legend using the traditional figure Loo-wit, the name given to the "Lady of Fire," who inhabited Mount Saint Helens. What does Rose suggest as the reason for the eruption of Mount Saint Helens?

Rose shows Loo-wit as an old woman, disturbed from her sleep by the machinery that "growls,/snarls and ploughs/great patches of her skin." She hears the boots that scrape her blanket of earth (perhaps those who come to cut lumber or to develop the land), and she rises to strike back, singing with triumph as she does.

After reading this poem, some students have enjoyed trying their hand at creating their own modern legends to explain current-day phenomena.

Wole Soyinka, Telephone Conversation (page 1183)

Consideration for Writing and Discussion

1.   In this poem, the speaker, who is African, reports his telephone conversation with a prospective landlady who is disturbed to learn that she has been interviewing a black man. Write a dialogue (or monologue) showing this woman as she describes this telephone encounter to a friend. What are her fears? What are her concerns? How does she explain and justify her responses?

This exercise works well as a journal assignment.

Victor Hernandez Cruz, urban dream (page 1184)

Consideration for Writing and Discussion:

1.   What is your response to the striking contrast between the long, multi-image first and second stanzas and the two-word third stanza?

The first stanza shows urban chaos. The images depict rioting and looting, with police officers ordering people to stop, even though they don't really understand what is going on. The second stanza offers a surrealistic view of the aftermath, with politicians making a show of appearing on the scene. The final stanza suggests that nothing has changed, yet destruction is replaced by celebration. Who celebrates? I think the same people who rioted now return, in the wake of the ineffectual city and state officials, to take over; these triumphant demonstrators show that the streets belong to them.

Rita Dove, Geometry (page 1184)

Considerations for Writing and Discussion

1. How does the speaker feel about proving the theorem?
2. Why is her response so dramatic?

Perhaps proving the theorem has been extremely difficult. Solving the problem makes the speaker feel as though her house (her "self"? her mind?) has expanded. But as she exults in her pleasure, her imagination moves beyond the geometry problem. She imagines herself "in the open," drifting after windows that have metamophosed into butterflies that fly rapidly away from the world of angles and theorems to a place where truths may exist, untried and unproven.

Cathy Song, The Youngest Daughter (page 1185)

Consideration for Writing and Discussion:

1. The speaker says that her mother knows she is "not to be trusted" and that she is "planning [her] escape." Do you believe her? Explain.

I think the youngest daughter may plan an escape, but she will never be free even after her mother's death. The details of the poem suggest her close relationship with her mother and her ability to see her mother as a complex woman, not simply as an idealized parent or as a burden. Like the cranes that pattern the curtains by the window, the daughter cannot leave, but she can "fly up in a sudden breeze" and surprise both her mother and herself by thinking new thoughts and imagining myriad possibilities.

TEACHING:
AN INTRODUCTION TO DRAMA

I start discussion by asking students to jot down what comes into their minds when they hear the word "drama." In the last class I taught, several students said that they thought "drama" meant a film, television program, or play that was serious or sad. When I pursued the source of this impression, they cited the labels at video cassette rental stores ("Drama," "Comedy," "Adventure," and so on). I had never thought about this new definition of drama, and these comments led to a lively exchange of opinions and ideas when other students contributed quite different definitions. Several, for instance, had attended live performances of plays and contended that these plays (whether comic or tragic) were "drama," whereas those same plays performed on television would be "programs." I asked how they would classify a Shakespearean play performed on screen. Some said it would still be a drama, others said it changed and became a movie. One person preferred the word "film," which she said indicated a screen performance that was serious and profound. Still another student said that if the Shakespearean play was a film of an actual performance it would be a drama, but if it was adapted and changed it would be a movie or film.

All of this may sound like quibbling, but we worked hard at defining exactly what it was that qualified a work to be called a drama. After reading the introductory section, and thinking about their own experiences, my students decided that to qualify as "drama," a selection should have the potential for being performed on a stage. It didn't matter whether the work was tragic, comic, tragi-comic, satiric, or romantic, but an essential dimension should be the dynamic between actors and audience. Most of them agreed—after some discussion—that a drama could be read silently or viewed on television or screen. But they insisted that the "live audience" element had to be imagined and held in the reader's or viewer's head. One student compared the distinction to seeing a concert performed live and then hearing the same performance on tape or disk. The music might be the same, but the experience of the audience is very different.

Because the live performance aspect also seems important to me, I always have students volunteer to prepare and read selected scenes from several of the plays. And when possible, I arrange voluntary field trips to see plays being performed on campus or at nearby theaters.

Sophocles, Antigone (page 1195)

Considerations for Writing and Discussion

1. Summarize briefly the sections of the play, identifying significant action, conflict, or character development.

2. Explain the problem Antigone faces. How do her beliefs and values conflict with Kreon's? What arguments can you make for and against each characters' views?

3. Sophocles titled this drama "Antigone," yet much of the action focuses on Kreon and his conflicts with his advisors and with his son Haimon. How do these conflicts relate to his struggle with Antigonê?

4. From reading the opening dialogue between Ismene and Antigone, what inferences can you make about their relationship, about the character and values of each woman, and about the role of women in ancient Greece?

5. Choose a scene you find particularly significant and describe the way you would stage it if you were directing the play. As you plan the scene, consider the way the actors will move on the stage, where they will sit or stand, and what gestures and facial expressions you'll have them use. Do not feel limited by the description of traditional Greek theater in the introduction to this chapter. Feel free to use modern technology as you envision the lighting, scenery, props, and costumes.

When I assign *Antigone,* I spend a few minutes providing the background of the play which would have been familiar to Sophocles' audience. Ismene explains the story of her father and brothers in lines 36–42, but students often miss the significance of what has gone before unless the complexities of this family intrigue are discussed.

Born to the king and queen of Thebes, Oedipus is banished from birth because an oracle had predicted he would kill his father and marry his mother. He is raised by a shepherd and his wife who never tell their foster son about his origins. Later, after hearing the same prediction from another oracle, Oedipus leaves his foster parents, believing that he can thus prevent himself from killing the shepherd, whom he believes to be his father, and marrying the shepherd's wife, whom he believes to be his mother.

When he flees from his foster home, he heads for Thebes where he encounters the king on the road. After a quarrel, Oedipus, not realizing the king is his birth father, kills him and in a short while marries Queen Jocasta. Of course, neither mother nor son recognizes each other. They have four children, Eteocles, Polyneices, Antigone, and Ismene. When Oedipus discovers that he has killed his birth father and married incestuously, he blinds himself and flees Thebes, leaving his two sons to assume the throne. Originally, the sons agree to rule in alternate years, but when Eteocles' first year as king ends, he refuses to yield to his brother. Polyneices then convinces Adrastus, the king of Argus, to help him attack Thebes and overthrow Eteocles. During the ensuing battle, Polyneices and Eteocles fight a duel and both are killed. Kreon, the brother of Jocasta (Oedipus' mother and wife), then ascends the throne, ordering that Eteocles be buried with full honors. Kreon also decrees that Polyneices be left to die in the field where he fell because he had attacked his native city.

Since the Greeks believed that the soul of a person who had not been buried with proper rites could not be received into the world of the dead, Antigone's distress is understandable. She faces not only the loss of her brother but also the pain of believing that his soul cannot find rest. Kreon, on the other hand, insists on the primacy of civil law. He believes he cannot make an exception, even for his nephew, because to deviate at all could lead to the breakdown of order.

Most readers are far more sympathetic with Antigone than with Kreon, yet the play does not present simple stereotypes. Kreon endures enormous pain and loss and, in the end, comes to see that his rigid refusal to consider alternatives has led to a tragic outcome. Antigone, on the other hand, may be justified in her final action, but her insistence on the rights of the individual have caused enormous pain—to herself and to others.

To help students see the role of the chorus and Choragos and to understand the structure of the drama, you may want to use this guide:

Prologue: Antigone and Ismene discuss their brothers' deaths, and Antigone urges Ismene to help her bury Polyneices, defying Kreon's order and his threat to impose the death penalty on anyone who disobeys him. In this scene, Ismene serves as a foil to Antigone. Antigone is impetuous, strong-willed, and convinced that justice should follow the law of god not the law of man; Ismene is cautious, concerned with civil law, and fearfully convinced that women should assume a subservient role to men.

Párados: The chorus and Choragos describe the battle between Eteocles, whom they portray as a stalwart defender of Thebes, and Polyneices, who leads an alien army against his homeland and engages in a duel with his brother which leads to both their deaths.

Scene I: Kreon, who has assumed the throne of Thebes, proclaims his intent to uphold the laws of the state; he forbids the burial of Polyneices. At that moment, a soldier who had been guarding Polyneices body arrives and fearfully informs the king that someone has attempted to bury the body. Kreon is outraged; losing control of his temper, he questions the sentry furiously and then argues bitterly with the Choragos.

Ode I: The chorus provides philosophical observations about the wonders of the human race, noting that humans are more powerful than animals and have control over all forces except death. In addition, the chorus commends the human reason which leads to creating and observing civil law.

Scene II: A defiant Antigone is brought before Kreon. She admits burying her brother and says she is willing to die rather than follow what she believe to be an unjust law. Kreon and Antigone argue about customs, values, and laws related to honoring the dead. Ismene now wants to defend her sister, but Antigone refuses to allow it, claiming that Ismene lacked the courage to act and cannot, therefore, take credit for what has happened.

Ode II: The chorus reminds the audience of the tragedy of Oedipus and of the continuing curse that haunts his children. Kreon is denounced as arrogant and filled with pride, and the Ode ends with a warning that "man's little pleasure is the spring of sorrow."

Scene III: Although Haimon is betrothed to Antigone, he swears to support his father, Kreon. (Students are sometimes surprised that Haimon and Antigone could be engaged, since they are first cousins, but such relationships were expected among royalty in ancient Greece.) Kreon praises Haimon as a worthy son and says he will be better off without Antigone. When Haimon urges his father to take a more moderate view of the civil laws and to pay attention to his advisors, Kreon becomes angry. It is clear that he sees any act against the state as a personal affront. Although the Choragos urges against it, Kreon orders Antigone's execution.

Ode III: The chorus describes the power of love and the danger of love carried to an extreme.

Scene IV: The chorus and Choragos pay homage to Antigone and express sorrow for her death sentence. Antigone fears that people will not understand her actions and will ridicule her; the chorus again ponders the connection between Oedipus' tragedy and Antigone's fate. Kreon refuses to reconsider, and, as he orders Antigone taken away, she says she looks forward to dying.

Ode IV: The chorus recounts the tragic stories of those who have opposed the will of the gods.

Scene V: Teiresias, an ancient blind man with a reputation for wisdom, advises Kreon to look at recent strange occurrences in nature as a warning to reconsider his treatment of Antigone. Kreon stubbornly refuses until the Choragos reminds him that Teiresias has never been mistaken in his pronouncements. Kreon then leaves, determined to save Antigone.

Paean: The chorus and Choragos invoke Iacchos (Bacchus or Dionysius, the god of misrule and chaos as well as of wine and revelry).

Exodus: A messenger arrives and describes to the Choragos the dramatic change in Kreon, from "happy once" to "a walking dead man." Haimon and Antigone have both committed suicide. When Eurydice, Kreon's wife and Haimon's mother, learns the news from the messenger, she also commits suicide. Kreon ends the play a broken old man, finally realizing that pride kept him from seeing reasonable alternatives or from taking good advice. He has learned to be wise but only after he has lost all that he valued.

William Shakespeare, Othello (page 1226)

Considerations for Writing and Discussion

1. How important is Othello's racial identification? Would the tragedy have been played out in the same way if he were white rather than black? Explain.

2. Do you consider Othello a figure whose tragedy comes from problems created primarily by his own personal qualities and values or from externally imposed problems? Or do you see the tragic action as a combination of inner qualities and external circumstances? Provide reasons and examples from the play to support your view.

3. What motivates Iago to destroy Othello? How does he manipulate various characters to achieve his goal? Why do these characters fail to see—and to resist—his efforts to use them against Othello?

4. Choose one scene you find particularly important to the revelation of character. Explain what you learn from that scene and how you learn. For instance, consider the scene where Cassio talks to Bianca while Othello hides and watches (Act IV, Scene 1).

5. What is your response to the two cities where the play takes place? What values and ideas are suggested by Venice? By Cyprus? How do these two places suggest the conflicts faced by the play's characters?

At least three characters in the play, Roderigo, Brabantio, and Iago, demonstrate stereotypical racial prejudices not so different from those held by today's hatemongers. For example, Othello is seen as overly sensual (Act I, Scene 1) and is declaimed as an unfit husband for the white Desdemona (Act III, Scene 3). In addition to being black in a white society, Othello is also a Moor, an outsider in Venice. Because Othello is unfamiliar with the customs and mores of the Venetians, and because he belongs to a different race, Iago finds it easy to prey on Othello's own self-doubts.

Yet Othello cannot be written off as simply a jealous husband whose own weak image of himself leads to his downfall. Contributing equally to the tragic denouement is Iago's stunningly evil ability to manipulate nearly anyone he chooses to serve as a dupe in the diabolical plot he carefully works against Othello. As the play progresses, Iago shows himself a master of trickery and deceit. He knows everyone's weakness—Cassio's vulnerability to alcohol; Roderigo's desire for Desdemona; Brabantio's bigotry and love for his daughter; Emilia's penchant for flattery—and he exploits those weaknesses without shame or mercy.

In Act I, Othello appears confident, open, and full of energy. People respect him, and he accepts their admiration with grace, recognizing that their acclaim is based on the reputation he has built. Yet Othello's soliloquy in Act III, Scene 3 demonstrates that Iago has successfully begun the process of undermining him. In this speech, Othello shows the beginning of jealousy and suspicion, but later in Act III, in spite of his doubts, he still maintains hope, refusing to act unless he is given irrefutable proof of Desdemona's infidelity.

Iago works his treachery on Othello in at least three identifiable patterns. The first ploy he uses is to suggest a possibility to Othello, who later repeats this possibility to Iago. Iago then confirms what Othello now believes to be his own suspicion. The second device begins with Iago starting a sentence and waiting for Othello to complete it. When Othello provides the words Iago hopes for, he confirms them. Finally, Iago, a master of the *double entendre,* uses words that play to Othello's jealousy and lead him to false interpretations. By Act V, Iago's evil insinuations have completely undermined Othello's earlier confidence and faith. He kills Desdemona, convinced that he is justified in doing so and also that dying is the only way for her to expiate what he believes to be her betrayal.

Reflecting the play's contrast of the civilized and the barbaric, the dual setting—Venice and Cyprus—suggests how quickly the human heart can move from order and trust to violence and chaos. Venice is a city ruled by law and typified by peace, balance, and civil justice. Cyprus is a military outpost dominated by explosive passions, a setting that suggests barbaric action, uncontrolled revenge, and social disorder.

Molière, The Doctor in Spite of Himself (page 1315)

Considerations for Writing and Discussion

1. Evaluate the humor in this play. Which scenes might have evoked laughter from Molière's original seventeenth-century audience but indignation or anger from today's audience?

2. How does Molière satirize the medical profession? What attitudes and values does he criticize or ridicule? What is your response to his view

of physicians and their attitude toward their work and their patients? Have times changed or do some of the problems suggested still exist?

3. Do you feel sympathy for either Sganarelle or Martine? Cite specific scenes to explain your response to each of these characters.

4. Many things—and many people—are not what they seem in this play. How does the theme of illusion and reality expose truth and falsity in the world these characters inhabit?

5. Consider one of the play's minor characters; for example, Monsieur Robert or Jacqueline. How would the play be changed if these characters did not appear?

Many students are distressed by the play's opening scenes which show wife-beating as comic and which suggest that Martine herself believes her husband to be justified in hitting her with a stick. Today's audiences probably would not laugh at this scene as Molière's devotees almost certainly did. It's necessary to point out that Martine does not really believe she deserves to be beaten or that it is Sganarelle's right to chastise her. In fact, she smolders with anger and devises a revenge which gives the unwitting physician a taste of his own medicine.

Another, less crucial, scene that modern audiences will find troubling comes in Act III. When Sganarelle gives the peasants a false cure for a desperately sick woman, he goes beyond the comic bounds of the play. It's easy to laugh when he exposes feigned illnesses and the hypocrisies of society, but adding to the peasants' pain is not funny. As a parting shot, Sganarelle advises the worried husband and son to give their wife and mother "the best burial you can" if she should die. Recognizing the aversion most modern audiences would feel toward this scene, many directors now cut this scene.

Apart from those scenes—and from the deeply ingrained sexism of the romantic themes—students find the play amazingly current, filled with wit that undercuts posturing and deflates pompous egos. The reversals in the play make the reader laugh and think at the same time. Sganarelle begins as a beater but soon finds himself on the receiving end of blows. Forced by pain and fear to become a phoney doctor, he ironically does cure the illness he's been directed to treat. And everyone appreciates the irony when the concluding marriage takes place only after the prospective groom has fortuitously inherited the money that makes him acceptable to the bride's father.

Minor characters in this play generally serve primarily as additional comic figures who underline the theme of appearance versus reality. For example, Jacqueline, the wet nurse, speaks eloquently on the virtues of a loyal marriage yet is only too willing to dally behind her husband's back. M. Robert, however, plays a more significant role. If it were not for him, we would have an entirely sympathetic view of Martine, the abused wife married to a man who admits to being a lecher, drunkard, and gambler and who also acknowledges selling off the furniture to support his bad habits. However, when M. Robert intervenes on Martine's behalf, she turns on him in fury and slaps him for "interfering." We cannot help seeing that Martine, while certainly not deserving to be beaten, does have a mean-spirited way of looking at the world. Her response to M. Robert prepares us for the revenge she plots and carries out a few scenes later.

Students usually disagree about the jaundiced view Molière takes toward the medical profession. When the characters in the play believe that Sganarelle is a doctor, they do not question his pronouncements even when he jabbers in nonsense phrases, combining bits of Latin with meaningless symbols. Even when Sganarelle says something that they know to be untrue, these characters back down, humbled in the face of self-proclaimed authority. Some students see this behavior as completely absurd and fail to recognize any modern parallel. Others point out that far too many people still accept a physician's word as law and feel intimidated by the medical professionals who often have control over significant aspects of their lives.

Henrik Ibsen, An Enemy of the People (page 1341)

Considerations for Writing and Discussion

1. Explain the definition of "enemy of the people" as the phrase is interpreted (and applied) by various characters in the play. Then develop your own definition and explain what kind of individuals you see as current-day "enemies of the people."

2. Although Thomas and Peter Stockmann are brothers, they have strikingly different personalities and values. Compare these two characters and suggest the forces in society that might be represented by each.

3. What role in the drama is played by each of the following characters: Petra, Hovstad, Captain Horster, Aslaksen? How would the play be changed if any of these characters were eliminated?

4. The doctor makes several difficult decisions. Often he is forced to choose between his obligations to his family and his loyalty to higher ideals. Describe several of these choices and explain your response to the values his decisions represent.

5. In Act IV, Doctor Stockmann angrily lectures the town meeting. He claims that the intellectual minority is far better equipped than the "solid majority" to make wise decisions. What is your response to this claim?

As background to the play, students are usually interested to know that Ibsen wrote *An Enemy of the People* at least partially in response to events that actually happened.

> Ibsen had heard of a certain Dr. Meissner at Teplitz whose house was stoned in the thirties [1830s], because he reported an outbreak of cholera, and so ruined the spa's season. Also a certain Thaulow (1815–81), an apothecary in Christiania, who had a long feud with the Christiania Steam Kitchen . . . had been howled down at a public meeting . . . and died a fortnight later.

> (F. L. Lucas, *Ibsen and Stringberg*, Cassell, 1962)

In addition to being inspired by the controversial actions of individuals who spoke out against what they saw as the corrupt attitudes of the "solid majority," this play has also served to encourage those who follow the dictates of their conscience. For example, *Enemy* was performed at the Moscow Art Theater in 1905, on the day government troops slaughtered a group of revolutionaries. Following the performance, audience members sympathetic to the revolutionaries risked their own safety by leaping onto the stage, applauding energetically, and shaking the hand of the actor who portrayed Dr. Stockmann.

Thomas Stockmann and Peter Stockmann represent the polar extremes of private men and public men. Peter Stockmann, an elected official, thinks only of his own political welfare and, in order to preserve the economic status quo, willingly ignores the health of those who elected him and of those who visit his city. In his private life, he is petty and mean spirited, unable to enjoy sharing a meal with others or to resist the chance to criticize the values of those who do enjoy such pleasures. He is a realist, an opportunist, and a hypocrite. Thomas Stockmann, on the other hand, lives his public and private lives with expansive goodwill, cheer, and optimism. He believes that the people of his community share his values and will act honestly when he reveals his discovery of the polluted baths. The central irony in the play is that Thomas Stockmann is labeled an enemy of the people while Peter, who undermines public welfare in a truly profound moral sense, continues to win the support and praise of the electorate.

Some students point out that Thomas cannot be regarded as a model of perfection because like many idealists, he takes an absolutist view. He apparently spends no time thinking about those who will suffer economically if the baths close and, in addition, takes an elitist view of how the town should be governed. Using a complex metaphor, he compares humans and animals, seeing himself and those like him as comparable to thoroughbred dogs who are superior to mixed breeds (like the members of the "solid majority"). Needless to say, this analogy does not win the doctor friends at his town meeting, and many students find this speech insulting and insensitive. Most agree, however, that Dr. Stockmann is at the end of his wits when he delivers this speech and so reveals the human failing of losing his temper and speaking from anger and resentment rather than from reason and compassion.

In the final act, Thomas Stockmann gains back most readers' sympathy. Faced with the loss or destruction of nearly all his and his family's material possessions, he maintains a wry sense of humor, noting ruefully that a man should not wear his best trousers when setting out to fight for truth and freedom. The final act also underlines the hypocrisy and moral weakness rampant in Stockmann's community. Their landlord evicts the Stockmanns because he "doesn't dare not to." The directors at the school where Dr. Stockmann's daughter teaches dismiss her because they "don't dare not to." The ship owners who employ the Stockmanns' friend, Captain Horster, fire him because they "don't dare not to." And, finally, Peter Stockmann sends his brother a note dismissing him from his post because the politically savvy mayor "doesn't dare not to."

Students generally respond strongly to this play. They see many connections with current political and social issues, and they appreciate a play that addresses serious themes yet also offers marvelously comic episodes like the confrontation in the final scene when Dr. Stockmann shows his continued will to fight by grabbing an umbrella and driving the sniveling opportunists Hovstad and Aslaksen from his home.

Lorraine Hansberry, A Raisin in the Sun (page 1414)

Considerations for Writing and Discussion

1. The opening stage directions give the setting as "sometime between World War II and the present." Cite details from the drama suggesting a more accurate date for the play's time frame.

2. Contrast Beneatha's and Walter's dreams. How do Mama's responses to their dreams suggest her values? Do you find yourself more in sympathy with one of these three characters than with the other two? Explain.

3. Discuss your response to the view of the black experience in the United States as suggested by the conflict between the views of Joseph Asagai and George Murchison. How does this conflict relate to the dilemmas the Younger family faces?

4. Write a scene that takes place five years after the ending of the play. Consider where various members of the Younger family will be living and what they will be doing. Consider what conflicts in their lives may have been resolved and what new conflicts they may be facing.

5.   Hansberry uses a phrase from Langston Hughes's poem "Harlem" (text page 1159) as the title of this drama. Read the poem and then comment on the relationship between Hansberry's and Hughes's themes.

Lorraine Hansberry, the youngest of four children, lived with her family in a middle-class black Chicago neighborhood until she was eight years old. Then her father and mother decided to act against the laws that forbade blacks to live in certain areas and moved their family to an all-white, neighborhood. This courageous action precipitated a civil rights case that eventually culminated in Supreme Court decision, where the Hansberry's were granted the right to live in the house they had purchased. During the long years before this judgment was handed down, the Hansberry family were harassed and threatened daily. Acts of physical violence and warnings of worse to come finally moved Lorraine Hansberry's mother to keep a loaded gun in the house to protect her children.

As an adult, Hansberry was haunted by memories of her family's never-ending battle against injustice. These remembered childhood scenes moved her to write plays that dramatized the conflicts faced by black families as they struggled with domestic concerns and also with violent racial prejudice in their neighborhoods, their schools, their cities, and their nation.

Although the setting of the play is given as "sometime between World War II and the present," students should notice that the Civil Rights Movement of the 1960s has not yet taken place. In addition, the cost of the house and of medical school tuition should indicate that the setting is at least thirty years ago. The play probably takes place in the mid-to-late 1950s; it was first produced in 1959. You may want to mention to students that abortion was against the law in this country at the time the play takes place, so Ruth faces a complex emotional decision which could lead to a physically dangerous and illegal operation.

Most students see Mama as a strong, admirable, yet inflexible character. She admires Beneatha's desire to be a doctor, but her religious beliefs keep her from being supportive of Walter's wish to own a liquor store. She also fails to see that she has always tried to control Walter and her overly concerned attitude has become intrusive and, perhaps, contributed to his inability to think for himself and act as an adult. Beneatha shows herself willing to work for her goal, but Walter tends to blame others for his problems and to look for easy solutions. He is extremely self-centered and, thinking only of himself, risks (and loses) not only the money Mama has given him to invest in the liquor store but also the money intended for Beneatha's medical school tuition. In the end, however, Walter finds within himself the strength to think of the whole family rather than his own selfish concerns. Whether the change will be permanent or not remains to be seen, but the play ends on a note of hope and possibility: Walter refuses the offer from the white "Welcoming Committee," and Mama picks up her "raggedy-looking" plant that she has said "expresses me," determined not to reject her old identity but equally motivated to move physically and emotionally toward new possibilities for her family, herself, and her race.

Joseph Asagai and George Murchison reflect a theme closely related to the family's conflict over the move to the white neighborhood. Joseph Asagai represents new pride in African roots; Murchison symbolizes rejection of ethnic heritage in favor of total assimilation into white society. When the Younger family moves into the white neighborhood, they do so on their own terms. They refuse to compromise as George Murchison has, yet they also intend to remain in this country. They are not ashamed of their African heritage, but they demand the right to equal treatment in the country that has been home to their people for more than two hundred years.

TEACHING:
AN INTRODUCTION TO NONFICTION

As I suggest in the text, I believe the key issue related to teaching nonfiction in a literature class is the question of definition. Even after reading the discussion in the text, some students (and instructors) will not be convinced that the selections in this section can legitimately be called literature. This controversy can lead to fruitful discussions about the nature of literature and of the literary experience for the author and the reader. In addition, because this section provides nonfiction selections that fall into a number of subcategories (speeches, letters, documents, journals and diaries, and essays), discussion may focus on specific kinds of nonfiction as literature. (For example, some readers may be willing to define essays as literature yet believe that no documents or letters can be so classified.)

Sojourner Truth, Ain't I a Woman? (page 1494)

Considerations for Writing and Discussion

1. What is your response to the contrast Truth suggests between men's images of women and the reality she experiences in her life? Do such contrasts still exist?

2. Read paragraph 3 closely. What is Truth saying about intellect? Do you agree with her observations? Explain.

3. Explain the religious objections to equality that Truth refutes. How convincing do you find her arguments? How do you think her audience would have responded to her comments?

Sojourner Truth points out the double bind that women have traditionally faced. Upper- and middle-class women have been told that they cannot work in certain professions because they are too delicate or too weak, but poor women have always had to work at hard, dirty, physical labor. The contradiction suggests that the image of the helpless female has been constructed simply to keep the wives and daughters of powerful men away from activities that might have led to their independence. By ignoring the plight of poor women, these same men doom them to the same drudgery faced by poor men but deny them even the rights granted to those men.

Students may question the reasoning in paragraph three. Truth asks, "If my cup won't hold but a pint and yours holds a quart, wouldn't you be mean not to let me have my little half-measure full?" Her analogy seems to imply that blacks and women may not have the same intellectual capacities as men. Since she is addressing an audience where white men still hold all the power, she may deliberately suggest that giving white and black women and black men equals rights would not be much of a threat. Or—and I think this possibility is more likely—her comments may simply show how deeply stereotyped views can affect all of us (even those who try to resist).

Chief Seattle, My People (page 1495)

Considerations for Writing and Discussion

1. Notice the images and comparisons Chief Seattle chooses to express his ideas. What does his language suggest about his view of the world?

2. The tone of Seattle's message is complex. Identify and discuss specific passages that suggest his view of white people and of their offer to buy the lands where his tribe has lived.

3. This message was composed in 1853. To what extent has Seattle's prophecy proven true? Consider particularly the vision he projects in the last part of paragraph 8.

Images relating to the natural world are interwoven throughout Chief Seattle's speech. He sees nature as responsive to his people; for example, the sky becomes a compassionate guardian who "has wept tears upon my people for centuries untold." He expresses his observations about white people and their proposals by using metaphors from nature. He says that the country is now filled with white people who are so numerous that they are "like the grass that covers vast prairies."

His use of natural images suggests his conviction that his people and their lives are inextricably linked with the land on which they have lived. It's nearly impossible to read his words and fail to understand the pain that must have been experienced by the displacement of a people who believed that their essential selves—as well as the selves of tribal members who had died—were one with the fields, mountains, and prairies where they hunted, gathered food, and worshipped.

Seattle's speech is a masterpiece of diplomacy. Although he indicates his appreciation of the offer to buy his land and even notes philosophically that the passing of his own tribe may simply be part of the cycle of nature, he reminds the white men with whom he is dealing of their part in the demise of Native Americans. When he condemns the impetuous young men of his tribe, he also notes that "our paleface brothers" hastened the tribes "untimely decay." Then, he does not simply hand over the lands but instead shows keen understanding of what he and his people are losing. He makes the agreement primarily because the military strength now lies entirely with white people, and he reminds Governor Stevens that the treaty calls for the white military to protect Seattle's people against attacks from other tribes. Seattle ends his speech by insisting that his people be granted permission to visit their old lands whenever they want and by creating the powerful vision of those tribal members who have died as lingering spirits that will not go away. They will linger to remind white people where their lands came from and to act as a warning that no matter how great and powerful a people may seem, the time will come when they will be forced to give way to others who have become more powerful.

Martin Luther King, Jr., Letter From Birmingham Jail (page 1498)

Considerations for Writing and Discussion

1. King's salutation suggests that he is writing to men, who, like himself, are religious leaders. What aspects of the letter suggest that he keeps this audience clearly in mind? What aspects of the letter suggest that he has a broader audience in mind? How would you define that broader audience?

2. What writing strategies does King use to establish his voice as reasonable and believable?

3. Explain the arguments King uses to defend his actions. How convincing do you find his arguments? Do you believe that nonviolent civil disobedience is ever justified? Use specific examples to explain your point of view.

King uses many references to the Bible and to religious philosophers, which suggest that he does keep in mind the audience he addresses in his salutation. Nevertheless, his carefully detailed explanation of non-violent resistance and his view of himself as a citizen of the world rather than as an "outside agitator" indicate that he knows his letter will be read by many people other than his fellow clergymen. The statement these clergy members published in a Birmingham newspaper provided King with the opportunity to explain his concerns and to defend his actions not only to them but to the citizens of Birmingham and, later, of the United States and of foreign countries.

King demonstrates his keen understanding of rhetorical strategies when he begins by explaining that he is accustomed to criticism and that he seldom responds to it because he is too busy with "constructive work." This statement suggests that he is not writing simply to defend himself but to defend a far larger and more significant issue. Next, he describes the clergy, who have criticized him, as "men of genuine good will," thus establishing himself as fair-minded and generous. He will not stoop to *ad hominem* attacks.

He begins his argument by challenging the definition of "outsider," claiming that he is not an outsider because he sees all communities as interrelated. He responds to the objection to direct action and demonstrations by noting that these activities are not intended to incite injustice and violence but to oppose them, and he outlines the carefully planned process of such activities. Refuting the charge that the actions he led were untimely, he quotes Niebuhr, "Justice too long delayed is justice denied," and, addressing the accusation that he and other civil rights demonstrators are breaking laws, he cites St. Augustine's pronouncement that "an unjust law is no law at all."

He uses Christ, Amos, and St. Paul as examples of historical figures who, like him, have been accused of being extremists. He protests the lukewarm support of white liberals as ardently as he denounces the Birmingham police department's brutal behavior, which the clergymen to whom he is writing have ignored.

Throughout this detailed, carefully planned essay, King's tone is calm, reasonable, and courteous yet not subservient. While many of his observations may be read with an edge of irony (particularly his comments on Hitler as a follower of the law and on the behavior of the Birmingham police department), he never lashes out with anger, bitterness, or sarcasm. His references to biblical, historical, philosophical, and legal precedents demonstrate his deep understanding of his work and serve to convince many readers that his convictions are firmly rooted in the intellect as well as the spirit.

Elizabeth Cady Stanton, Declaration of Sentiments and Resolutions (page 1511)

Considerations for Writing and Discussion

1. Compare the Declaration of Sentiments and Resolutions with the Declaration of Independence. Why might Stanton have chosen to write her opening paragraphs to closely parallel the introduction of the Declaration of Independence?

2. What does Stanton mean when she argues for "the elective franchise"? How is this right connected to the others issues she addresses?

3. What is your response to paragraphs 20–35? Are these resolutions outdated now or do some of them address inequities that still exist between men and women? Explain.

Because most of Stanton's audience (U.S. citizens in 1848) believed wholeheartedly in the principles set forth by the Declaration of Independence, Stanton used the familiar opening words to suggest a parallel between the 1776 Declaration and the Seneca Falls Resolutions. Students find the parallels even more interesting if they read a copy of the Declaration of Independence, substituting "women" where Jefferson refers to the colonists or the colonies and "men" where he refers to King George or to England. This exercise dramatically underlines the relationship between men and women, showing women as the ruled and men as the rulers.

Some students may not realize that the "elective franchise" refers to the right to vote. This right is central to Stanton's argument because most of the other issues she raises can be addressed only by those who hold the power given by voting rights. If women are granted the vote, they will have legal recourse for making the changes suggested in the final paragraphs of the document. (Many students also do not know that women did not have the vote, nationwide, until the 19th amendment was ratified and enacted in 1919–20. You might point out that many women alive today—perhaps your students' own grandmothers—were born into a country where members of their sex had not yet been granted suffrage.)

I like to have students break into groups to discuss the resolutions in paragraphs 21–35, asking each group to work on three or four of the resolutions. Many students believe that these issues are astonishingly current.

Sei Shonagon, from *The Pillow Book* (page 1515)

Considerations for Writing and Discussion

1. What do Sei Shonagon's observations suggest about her personality and character?

2. Compare Shonagon's definition of the ideal lover with the image of the ideal romantic man conveyed by films, television programs, and advertising.

Sei Shonagon's pillow book is typical of the diaries kept by ladies of the Japanese court during the eighth and ninth centuries. The journal entries reprinted here suggest the emphasis the society in which these women lived placed on the customs and manners related to courtship. Shonagon's observations show her deeply sensual appreciation of the world around her. She notices small things like the "first cry of the birds" or the sudden noise of a crow that flies past the lovers' trysting place. She enjoys being with her lovers, but she also values her time alone and feels impatient when a man stays too long. She cherishes a romantic (and idealized) view of love and wishes not to see her lovers as ordinary humans who stumble in the dark or mutter to themselves while hunting for a lost item. While Sei Shonagon may seem to have a great deal of freedom, she is, of course, entirely dependent on her position at court. Nothing is definitely known about her after the empress she served died in childbirth in A.D. 1000; however, an ancient legend suggests that she fell out of favor and was dismissed from the court. According to this tale, she was forced to live in a decaying hovel and seek her living selling rags and bones.

Henry David Thoreau, from *Journals* (page 1517)

Considerations for Writing and Discussion

1.   What do these journal entries suggest about Thoreau's views of writing? Do you find that his practice follows his theories? Explain.

2.   What do these entries suggest about the way Thoreau sees his relationship with nature as well as his relationship with his fellow human?

3.   Choose one entry and explain the responses it inspires.

Thoreau suggests the wisdom of writing on many subjects and trying many themes, and certainly this small segment of the journal shows that he follows his own advice. He also urges the use of analogies as an avenue "to a perception of the truth." Again, he practices what he advises. For example, he compares the writer experimenting with themes to nature who "makes a thousand acorns to get one oak."

No matter what subject Thoreau addresses, he shows enormous respect for the world around him and for those who inhabit that world. His entries describe his work for the underground railroad (a group of abolitionists who defied the fugitive slave laws to aid those who had escaped from Southern masters); his wry reaction to the poor sale of his book *A Week on the Concord and Merrimack Rivers;* and his observations of the plants and flowers growing in his native town. As he describes these plants, he expresses his philosophy:

> What confirmation of our hopes is in the fragrance of the
> water-lily! I shall not soon despair of the world for it,
> notwithstanding slavery, and the cowardice and want of
> principle of the North. It suggests that the time may come
> when man's deeds will smell as sweet. Such, then, is the odor
> our planet emits . . . If Nature can compound this fragrance still
> annually, I shall believe her still full of vigor, and that there
> is virtue in man, too, who perceives and loves it.

Jonathan Swift, A Modest Proposal (page 1521)

Considerations for Writing and Discussion

1.   Describe the speaker in this essay. What details first lead you to suspect that the speaker and his views may differ considerable from Swift and his views?

2.   How does the speaker develop his argument? Does he make appeals that are aimed primarily at the heart or at the mind? (Remember to separate the speaker from the author as you respond.)

3. Write a "Modest Proposal" of your own, using ironic exaggeration to criticize the plans others have suggested to solve a current problem.

While the essay begins with a heart-wrenching picture of destitute mothers and children which seems sympathetic, the tone begins to change by paragraph 4 when the speaker identifies himself as one of the many projectors who is busily looking for a solution to the "Irish problem." In this same paragraph, the images alert readers to the speaker's callous view of the Irish poor. For example, when he refers to "a child just dropped from its dam," he shows that he sees the mother and newborn not as humans but as animals. In paragraph 7, he describes boys and girls over the age of twelve as "salable" goods, and if any reader still doubts that the essay is ironic, in paragraph 9, Swift has his proposer offer a list of tempting recipes to cook an Irish child into a tasty meal. Be aware, however, that some students will read the entire essay believing that Swift's views are represented throughout. You'll need to help them see the increasingly dreadful suggestions as evidence that Swift's intention is to attack outrageous proposals regarding the lot of the the Irish.

The proposer takes a pragmatic approach, determined to appeal to the minds of his audience. He quotes "authorities" such as the American who provided the directions for cooking surplus children and, in paragraphs 4–7, offers a dazzling array of statistics and analyses of the benefits of the proposal. To underline his argument, he offers more statistics in paragraphs 11, 12, 14, and 15.

While the proposer uses so-called rational appeals, Swift calls on readers to look into their hearts and find outrage at the exaggerated proposal offered by his invented proposer and also at the plans offered by actual projectors whose solutions Swift finds equally outrageous. For a suggestion of possibilities Swift would favor, see paragraph 29 where the projector notes several options that he summarily dismisses.

George Orwell, Shooting an Elephant (page 1528)

Considerations for Writing and Discussion

1. What is your response to the speaker's dilemma and to the decision he makes? Why do you think he decides to shoot the elephant?

2. The speaker uses several analogies to explain his actions. Choose any one of the analogies and discuss its implications.

3. Describe a situation where you or someone you know faced a dilemma in some way similar to the one the speaker describes.

In discussing this piece, I distinguish Orwell from the speaker because there is some doubt about whether the incident actually occurred. Orwell did serve as a police guard in Burma, but several biographers believe the elephant incident is apocryphal. I usually mention this point to students as a way of suggesting the thin line between fiction and nonfiction. This selection is nearly always viewed as an essay rather than a short story, but if the central episode never actually occurred—or never happened to the author—is it still nonfiction?

Students' initial response to the speaker's dilemma is often that he yielded to peer pressure. But, of course, he does not see as peers the people whom he describes as "evil-spirited little beasts who tried to make my job impossible" (paragraph 2). Nor do they see him as their equal. Although he was "secretly . . . all for the Burmese and all against their oppressors, the British" (paragraph 2), the Burmese people could not know that. To them he was simply another police officer who represented the hated forces who occupied their country. His response—shooting the elephant—comes from the pressure he feels from those over whom he supposedly has control. Lively discussions come from students' seeing that the speaker is motivated, at least in part, by fearing ridicule. He does not want to look foolish or to be seen as lacking in decisiveness and courage. Students usually have no trouble making connections between the speaker's decisions and decisions made by various authority figures they have encountered, read about, or watched on television.

To describe the speaker's dilemma, Orwell uses three particularly significant analogies. Two of these comparisons relate to the world of theater, suggesting the speaker's sense that he is merely playing a role rather than acting out of deep conviction. As the crowd watches him, he feels like "a conjurer about to perform a trick" and describes himself as "seemingly the lead actor of the piece; but in reality . . . only an absurd puppet pushed to and fro by the will of those yellow faces . . ." (paragraph 7). Later in the essay, Orwell suggests the sympathy the speaker feels for the elephant by comparing it to an elderly person. He says the elephant has a "preoccupied grandmotherly air" (paragraph 10), and, after he fires his gun, he describes the wounded animal as looking "suddenly stricken, shrunken, immensely old. . . . An enormous senility seemed to have settled upon him. One could have imagined him thousands of years old" (paragraph 11).

Jeanne Wakatsuki Huston and James D. Houston, Arrival at Manzanar (page 1534)

Considerations for Writing and Discussion

1. Describe Jeanne Wakatsuki's childhood view of other oriental people. Where did her views come from? What is your response to the way she reacts to the children she meets in school and at Terminal Island?

2. Cite details that indicate the values held by those people who were involved in some way in the involuntary internment of the Wakatsukis and other American families with Japanese ancestry.

3.   Do research to discover why only Japanese Americans were interned during World War II, whereas German Americans and Italian Americans were not (even though both Germany and Italy were fighting against the Allies).

This section of *Farewell to Manzanar* does a fine job of showing how prejudice develops in children. As a child, Jeanne Wakatsuki (whose father has kept her separated from other Japanese families and has threatened to "sell [her] to the Chinaman" if she doesn't behave) fears all Oriental faces that do not belong to her relatives. The people who decide to intern the Japanese seem guided by the same kind of unreasoning terror. Since Japanese nationals are fighting against the Allied forces, it is assumed that Japanese Americans will also be a threat. Like the young Wakatsuki, these people do not see individuals, they simply see ethnic characteristics like the "very slanted eyes" Wakatsuki mentions in paragraph 3.

As the Wakatsukis prepare to be evacuated, they encounter an antique dealer, who is clearly making a huge profit on their undeserved misfortunes, and a bus driver, who sternly performs his task, unable (or unwilling) even to return the smile of a small child. At the camp, conditions are primitive and, perhaps worse, humiliating: Those who provide food have not even tried to find out what the Japanese families would normally eat. Assuming that their own tastes and values are universal, these officials serve rice with sweetened fruit. The Japanese, who only eat rice with salty or savory food, have lost not only their homes and their means of making a living but even the right to eat what they please.

You might point out the racist implications in the fact that only Japanese Americans were interned. Americans of German or Italian ancestry were not, as a group, considered dangerous to national security.

Annie Dillard, Football and Snowballs (page 1539)

Considerations for Writing and Discussion

1.   What was your initial response to the final sentence of the second paragraph, "I got in trouble throwing snowballs, and have seldom been happier since"? Did your response change after reading the essay? Explain.

2.   This essay is called "Football and Snowballs," yet only the first paragraph is about football. How does this opening section relate to the much longer second section that details the snowballing and subsequent chase?

3.   Dillard reports that nothing in her life "has required so much of me since as being chased all over Pittsburgh in the middle of winter. . . ."

What has been required of her that makes this incident so memorable? Had you been in her place, do you think you would have felt the same?

The opening paragraph explains the "concentration and courage" Dillard sees as essential to playing football well. She describes the need to "[fling] yourself wholeheartedly at the back of [your opponent's] knees." This sense of bravery in the face of danger and the willingness to commit fully to an action with no fear or wavering also underlie the soaring surge of power she feels after the encounter with the "sainted, skinny, furious redheaded man."

Some students empathize and can recount their own dangerous (and often slightly illegal) activities that have provided a similar sense of exhilaration. Others note that Dillard's response could not happen today because children would be far more afraid of being chased by a stranger than she obviously was. She treats the idea of the man molesting or harming her and Mike Fahey as pure fantasy—a possibility as remote as being chased to the edge of the Panama Canal. Today's students often see the backyard race as far more ominous and as having much more potential danger than the essay suggests.

Students also note that Dillard glorifies activities generally deemed "masculine" and seems proud that she developed a "boy's arm" (even though she does find the designation "weird").

Alice Walker, In Search of Our Mothers' Gardens (page 1542)

Considerations for Writing and Discussion

1. Identify the main sections of this essay and suggest how the sections are related.

2. Consider carefully the epigraph by Jean Toomer that introduces the essay and the poems Walker quotes. Suggest the relationship between one of these quotations and the ideas Walker explores in her essay.

3. Compare the experience of black women as suggested by Sojourner Truth in "Ain't I a Woman?" (page 1494) with the view suggested in Walker's essay.

This memoir can be divided in two parts. The first considers the history of black women in the United States, focusing on colonial American poet Phyllis Wheatley as a central example. The second section moves the focus from Wheatley to Walker's mother. The heritage of today's black women who are writers and artists then, is two-fold: First, they gain inspiration from women like Wheatley, who, under extremely trying circumstances, persisted in their art; second, they are motivated by women who created beauty from whatever they found around them.

The quotation from Jean Toomer that introduces the memoir praises the strength that comes from a full-spirited life of the mind and heart, suggesting that this power allows those deprived of external freedom to thrive in spite of the repression they suffer. Toomer's quotation leads to Walker's opening paragraph where she describes his observations about the black women he met on his trip through the South. Commenting on their intense spirituality, Toomer said that "they were themselves unaware of the richness they held."

The rest of the memoir looks at the lives of black women and at the way they create beauty from what they see and find around them. Walker suggests the connection between the current generation of black women who are artists, writers, and poets and their mothers and grandmothers who "handed on the creative spark, the seed of the flower they themselves never hoped to see: or like a sealed letter they could not plainly read." At the beginning of the memoir, Walker challenges Toomer's definition of Southern black women as "saint," claiming that instead they should be called "artist." She explores this theme through historical examples as well as through the example of her mother who created beauty through the flowers she cultivated around "whatever shabby house" their family was forced to live in. Walker concludes with an analogy, showing the relationship between her forbears, who, under the most disheartening conditions, found a way to express their creativity, and the women of her own generation, who are now free to use whatever media they choose—words, paints, clay, and so on—to reflect their own inner visions.